ACCIDENTALLY, ON PURPOSE

ACCIDENTALLY, ON PURPOSE:

THE MAKING OF A PERSONAL INJURY UNDERWORLD IN AMERICA

Ken Dornstein

St. Martin's Press
New York

ISBN 0-312-12992-0

Library of Congress Cataloging-in-Publication Data

Dornstein, Ken.
    Accidentally, on purpose : the making of a personal injury
underworld in America / by Ken Dornstein.
        p. cm.
    ISBN 0-312-12992-0
    1. Insurance crimes—United States—History. 2. Personal
injuries—United States—History. 3. Fraud investigation—United
States—History. I. Title.
    HV6769.D67 1996
    364.1'63—DC20   96-6941
                                                                  CIP

Book design by Acme Art, Inc.

First Edition: December 1996
10 9 8 7 6 5 4 3 2 1

CONTENTS

PART THREE

UNDERWORLD: LOS ANGELES
(TO THE PRESENT)

ACKNOWLEDGMENTS

I began the research which became this book thinking that the book had already been written by someone else, somewhere, if only I looked hard enough for it. What I found instead was a lot of separate accounts from varied sources which, only after several years of work, began to fit together for me as the larger story I sought. Along the way, I have been helped in diverse and wonderful ways by many people, including:

Jim Applebaum, Henry Avina, Richard Baldwin, Jack Benjamin, Reed Boland, Mike Bush, Chris Calhoun, Robert Chambers, Michael Clarke, Mery-Grace Costello, Jerry Davis, Elizabeth Delgado, Esther Diaz, Jerry Dolan, Nancy Dyer, Shawn Ferris, Scott Finger, Peter Gravin, David Guthman, Sara Guzman, John Healy, Christine Hennessey, Gary Hernandez, Max Huntsman, Michael "Bud" Ingram, Andy Jackson, Joe Jaskolski, Elliott Kastner, Jeff Kauppi, Craig Kennaugh, Leslie Kim, Bill Kizorek, Scott Koppel, Kim Kosman, Jay Langford, Richard Litsinger, Albert Mackenzie, Gary Mizumoto, Tom Morningstar, Jason Multon, Sue Mustaffa, Loren Naiman, Danny Naranjo, Tom Norton, Frank Passerini, Lisa J. Polk, Gil Rosas, Myron Sanders, Tom Sarinana, Joyce Seltzer, Jim Sheehan, Larry Stanford, Richard Stenzel, Richard Suckle, Jerry Treadway, James Trovarello, Tom Valent, William Welch, Justine Zinkin.

I also owe special thanks to: Steve and Larry of the Venice office; the staff of the Harvard Law School Library; and all of the newspaper, magazine, and television reporters on whose work I have relied so heavily for many of the accounts in this book. Throughout, I tried to be true to those facts of individual stories that illuminated the broader history, general trends, or the themes of the book. Any errors of fact or interpretation are, of course, all mine.

At St. Martin's Press, I want to thank: Alan Bradshaw, Rick Delaney, Michael Flamini, Nancy Hirsch, Wendy Krauss, and Debbie Manette.

Most of all, I thank my family and Kathryn, who absorbed every bump along the way with patience, humor, and unwavering support; without her, it is no mere cliché to say, this book would never have been written.

ACCIDENTALLY, ON PURPOSE

WHO KILLED JOSÉ LUIS LOPEZ PEREZ?

AN UNSENTIMENTAL EDUCATION

"What's their set-up?" I asked.

"The ploy is called a 'swoop-and-squat' which requires the use of two cars. They pull this maneuver out on one of the surface roads, probably five or six times a week."

"I'm surprised they don't try the freeways," I remarked.

[The investigator] shook his head. "Too dangerous. These guys aren't interested in getting killed."

—Sue Grafton, *"H" Is for Homicide*, 1991

A T THE LOS ANGELES COUNTY CORONER'S OFFICE, they searched the dead man's pants pockets for clues. Earlier that Wednesday evening in June 1992, emergency workers had lifted the body from the backseat of a crushed 1978 Pontiac Firebird. The car was once sporty perhaps—a racy black body with glitter-paint flames licking up the sides. Now the Pontiac was a wreck, barely discernible as a car at all. It had been hit from behind by a big-rig tractor-trailer on the I-5 freeway fifteen miles north of downtown L.A. The truck, a car-carrier, had jackknifed attempting to stop short of a collision and had rolled onto its side, dumping new sedans onto the freeway. One of the cars—a new Mercedes—came to rest directly on top of the Firebird. The massive collision closed freeway traffic in both directions for several hours.[1]

When Highway Patrol members arrived at the scene, they found twenty-seven-year-old Rubidia Lopez struggling through one of the Firebird's windows. Emergency teams, using power tools and a wrecker, worked for an hour and a half to reach her. By 8:30 P.M. that night, rescue workers had succeeded in freeing Lopez and a fellow Salvadoran, Isiais Aguilar (who had been in the country for little more than a week), as well as the Pontiac's driver, Jorge Sanchez. All three were taken to local hospitals by ambulance and by rescue helicopter. Remarkably, each was released from care by the end of the night, having sustained only minor cuts and scrapes. The driver of the big-rig truck had also escaped serious injury, climbing to safety through the broken glass of his front windshield. José Luis Lopez Perez,[2] a twenty-nine-year-old day laborer from the same region of El Salvador as the others, was not so fortunate, however. He was found dead in the backseat of the Pontiac. His facial features, already round, were further bloated from asphyxiation. Perez was taken from the crash site in a van from the L.A. County Coroner's Office.

At the coroner's office, investigators from the California Highway Patrol (CHP) found a business card for a local personal injury law firm in Perez's pockets. The card was colored money-green with a red bulls-eye beneath the acronym A.I.M—Aid to Injured Motorists. At the center of the bulls-eye was a cartoonish rendering of a wrecked car with a body lying along side. Designed to look like a credit card, the solicitation came with a letter indicating that the cardholder had an "account" with a certain attorney whose name and toll-free 1-800 number were printed on the back. Also recovered from Perez's wallet was a business card from a different law firm listing the name of an office administrator who had been arrested a few months earlier on charges of trading in fake accident cases.

Even before they searched Perez's pants pockets, investigators suspected that the accident that left him dead had been staged in order to generate a personal injury claim: The driver of the big-rig truck told the Highway Patrol how the Pontiac had swerved in front of him several times over five or six miles of road, then halted suddenly in an apparent effort to cause a rear-end accident. "I was trying to go around this car," trucker Peter Liebich later told a grand jury. "I slowed down and I changed lanes, but if I changed lanes, he changed also." Twice the trucker slowed and swerved in order to avoid ramming the Pontiac from behind—a fact corroborated by other drivers who witnessed the Firebird's erratic moves. The third time was the charm: The horrible freeway accident was unavoidable, the Highway Patrol investigators concluded by the end of the night, because, incredibly, the accident was on purpose.

Dreaming of a better life in America, José Luis Lopez Perez left his two children with his parents in El Salvador and traveled north to Los Angeles with his wife, Martha, in 1990. Eighteen months later, what he found was a seat in an old car that would absorb a rear-end collision from a truck on a freeway. With hopes of gaining his share of fabled American prosperity, Perez risked his life for a payoff that probably would have worked out to less than a few hundred dollars, and might have been as low as twenty-five.

José Perez died in a type of faked accident known as a *swoop-and-squat*. The scheme involves two or three cars—one "squat" car stuffed with passengers and one or two "swoop" cars to assist. The drivers and passengers of the cars take to the roads looking to trap another car (or a truck) into rear-ending the squat car so that the passengers can make personal injury claims against that other driver's insurance company. The swoop cars are usually driven by more experienced ring members skilled in the art of creating believable accident scenarios. The squat cars are often stuffed with anyone who happens to be around at the time of the planning; squat passengers either do not mind or are not fully aware of the danger. Procuring the cars, filling them with the right people, and directing the collision (sometimes with the aid of cellular phone calls from one car to another) is the job of another fake accident specialist: the *capper*. In the fatal Perez staging, members of the CHP's Staged Collision Unit were able to find the capper by first finding the owner of the Pontiac, a man named Oscar Portillo, who had bought the car at a salvage auction a week or so earlier. Portillo had not been directly involved in this accident, but, he later admitted, he had driven the squat car in a different freeway crash with a truck a month earlier. Interviewed in a cell at the L.A. County jail, Portillo told investigators that, soon after buying the Pontiac, he had traded it to a man he met at a barbecue—Filemon Santiago—who wanted to use the car in a staged freeway accident. CHP investigators soon suspected that Santiago, a twenty-four-year-old whom everyone called "Phil," had been the capper in the fatal staging. Several witnesses told investigators how Phil often came to their apartment buildings looking for participants or cars to use in staged accidents. Phil seemed to have begun his capping career a few years earlier, scripting low-speed accidents on surface streets or in parking lots. In recent months, however, he had turned to freeway accidents with trucks because they paid more money (more quickly and more surely) than standard, less-dangerous staged accidents. A sampling of some of Phil's suspected stagings in the months prior to the fatal crash included: the rear-ending of a carload of Latino immigrants by a truck hauling salt on the I-5 in May 1992; two separate carloads of squat passengers rear-ended by tractor-trailers at the Burbank Boulevard exit of the I-5 in April; and a handful of similar crashes, all occurring on freeways and all targeting big-rig trucks.

Phil's crashes did not always go as planned. In the Perez staging alone, Phil's recruits had attempted three times to get the Pontiac rear-ended by a truck. On the first attempt, José Perez himself had been the driver of the Pontiac. On the second attempt, the targeted truck managed to skid to a stop before making contact. Ruben Garcia, a backseat passenger in that attempt, was so shaken by the experience that he swore off staged accidents for good. Angel Hernandez had also been a backseat passenger on the second attempt; he later claimed that he had no idea that the crash was going to involve trucks on the freeway until he actually got on the road. Juan Carlos Amaya, suspected of being a swoop-car driver for Santiago, had been responsible for picking out the truck, then for giving the squat car a reason to stop short by cutting it off and exiting the freeway before the police arrived. Amaya, in his lower-risk job, was apparently undeterred by the failures and went back out on the freeway each time to try again. José Perez was troubled by the previous failed staging attempts, however. Just after the cars entered the freeway, he pulled to the shoulder and asked one of his passengers, Jorge Sanchez, to take the wheel. Perez moved to the relative safety of the backseat, where, he thought, he was less likely to be impaled on the steering wheel or to fly through the windshield on impact. Rubidia Lopez sat next to Perez. Eyeing the car carrier through the back windshield minutes before the collision, the twenty-four-year-old woman asked nervously: "Can't someone get killed doing this?" José Perez did not respond, Lopez later recalled, except to indicate a half-hearted agreement with Phil's earlier assurances of safety.

When investigators finally interviewed Phil Santiago, the young Los Angeles transplant from El Salvador claimed to know nothing about accidents or lawyers, saying, instead, that he worked in "food service." At Santiago's apartment, however, investigators found a rental agreement on which he stated that he was an attorney's "field investigator," a common euphemism for accident cappers. Investigators also uncovered business cards and blank retainer forms for that same attorney—Gary P. Miller. Later searches of Miller's home in the San Fernando valley and his high-rise office near Beverly Hills turned up evidence that Phil Santiago capped cases for him: Check payments from Miller to Santiago were found, as was an apparent extortion note from Santiago to Miller written sometime in the weeks following Perez's death. Phil asked the attorney for $20,000 to "get myself and my family out

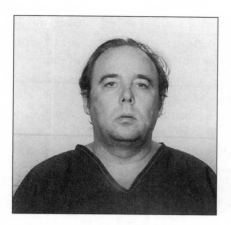 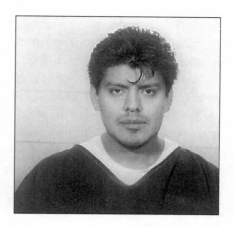

FIGURE P.1. Booking photographs of Filemon Santiago (right) and attorney Gary P. Miller. According to L.A. County Prosecutors, Santiago arranged the accident that led to the death of José Luis Lopez Perez. Attorney Miller was allegedly in line to pay Santiago for the rights to the resulting faked claims. (Photographs provided by the Los Angeles County Sheriff's Office.)

of here in order to start a new life," then closed with what seemed either a veiled threat or a desperate plea: "Please don't let me down," he wrote, "because I won't let you down if you work with me."[3] By the time the note was uncovered in mid-July 1992, Phil Santiago had been a fugitive for several weeks. He would not be heard from again until March 1994, when he was arrested in Houston, Texas, outside of a video store, following the national broadcast of the Perez story on TV's *Unsolved Mysteries*.[4] One year later, Juan Carlos Amaya, also initially a fugitive in the case, would be found in this same section of Houston.

    Santiago and Amaya were each brought back to L.A. to stand trial. In the years since the two men fled, the charges against them (and against Miller and the three surviving crash participants) had been augmented beyond simple insurance fraud to include second-degree murder: Santiago for scripting the accident; Miller for his role as the probable purchaser of the passenger's personal injury claims; and the Pontiac passengers for their accomplice roles.[5] Attorney Miller was the last of the three men to be officially named in the case, but the first to be arrested. Early one morning in October 1992, CHP investigators drove to his ranch house in Encino; they parked their unmarked cars next to the attorney's two Mercedes sedans—each, in a sadly ironic footnote, like the car that had landed on top of Perez's Pontiac. Within the hour, Miller, a paunchy, slightly dull-looking man, was led outside in his nightclothes, becoming the first lawyer in American history charged with murder in the death of a participant in an accident staged for insurance money.

In the years prior to this gray day, Gary Miller had come to see himself as a "truly lucky man."[6] He and his wife had been happily married since the early 1980s. They lived comfortably in their handsome home in the Valley with their daughter who was two and a half at the time of the Perez staging. Miller had also been doing well in his career. His law firm's gross income had quadrupled from 1989 to 1991—from $347,000 to $1.64 million—and he now had a corner office in a black glass-and-chrome building across from the L.A. County Art Museum. Miller's defenders claimed that his rapidly changing fortunes were the result of hard work and of the coincidental settling of several large cases at once. Prosecutors countered that Miller, who held a law degree from a school in the San Fernando Valley (which had since gone out of business) and who had often struggled in solo practice prior to his ascendance to his fourteenth floor office, had finally hit on a way to make money by trading in staged accidents brought to him by cappers. Miller's defense attorney maintained the legitimacy of his client's cases, but added that even Miller himself had privately acknowledged that his practice was growing too fast and "was out of control."[7]

Once charged in the case, Miller denied any knowledge of cappers in general and disavowed any acquaintance with Phil Santiago in particular. But the same search of his office that revealed the checks he signed to Santiago also turned up a number of files marked in some way as "Phil's," which Miller allegedly told his staff "to drop" in the days after the fatal staging. Among these cases were a number of freeway swoop-and-squats, all of which involved a carful of Latino immigrants stopping short—or, in one case stopping completely—in front of big-rig trucks on a ten mile stretch of the I-5 freeway north of downtown L.A.[8] As damning as this evidence seemed, Miller apparently believed that there was much more that had not been found: In a meeting with an insurance adjuster who Miller believed was his friend but who actually was working for the government, the attorney boasted that the CHP investigators "didn't get the good stuff."

The death of José Luis Lopez Perez was first reported on a back page of the L.A. Times in June 1992. In the weeks and months to follow, the story was picked up by the major wire services and TV news shows. In most accounts, the fatal staging attempt was important mainly as a tragic example of a larger trend—"a bizarre new scam that has carried the practice of staging accidents to collect insurance money to a new, high-risk extreme."[9]

Miller and Santiago were not the only attorney-and-capper team doing the new freeway swoop-and-squats with big-rig trucks. For more than a year before the fatal crash, in fact, investigators Marco Ruiz and Sue Mustaffa of the CHP Staged Collision Unit had been charting suspected staged big-rig accidents throughout L.A. County. By the summer of 1992, they believed that anywhere from five to ten different rings might have staged several hundred such crashes during the previous year and a half. They had uncovered wreck scripts detailing accident plans and had matched testimony from bewildered truckers to accident reports that were virtually identical in their description of cars stopping short in front of them—once, twice, and three times. ("This guy seemed almost disappointed I didn't hit him," one trucker later told others attending a seminar on how to avoid being targeted for a staged collision. "I missed him by an inch. I think he wanted it.")[10] The undercover officers heard cappers explain to prospective passengers which trucks to target and how to soften the collision impact by stuffing tires in their cars' trunks. "Every area in our division is experiencing the same phenomenon," Marco Ruiz stated a few weeks after the Perez staging. "It seems like it was something that just sprung up out of the last few months or else we were in the dark all these years and didn't know that this was happening right under our noses." Sue Mustaffa added that it seemed likely that other people had been injured, or maybe even killed, in the crashes but that it was just too hard to know for sure who or how many. At a press conference in a salvage yard, State Attorney General Dan Lungren stood in front of the wrecked Pontiac and stressed the danger of this new type of freeway staged accident. "We're talking about more than ripping off insurance companies, as bad as that seems . . . We're talking about recklessly endangering the lives of innocent Californians."[11]

Despite the concern for the truckers and the innocent drivers who might get hurt as a result of staged collisions, most of the interest and fascination with the staged big-rig accidents centered on the motivations of the crash participants themselves. "It is hard to imagine that anyone would drive in front of a big-rig truck for the express purpose of being rear-ended," one national news reporter remarked.[12] "It just doesn't make sense that this would become something popular because of the risk involved," said a lawyer who specializes in insurance fraud work. Ira Reiner, the L.A. County District Attorney agreed: "It is a mystery to me how they can get people to do this," he said before conjecturing that the cappers must understate the risks to the participants. "Who would be foolhardy enough to take part in such a dangerous con?" one newspaper writer asked rhetorically. "The answer is desperately poor Latino immigrants recruited to ride in the crash cars for as little as $100." This last explanation seemed to fit the information that the CHP had developed about the big-rig stagings. But it was an answer that did not sit well with José Perez's brother, Concepcion: "[My brother] had just started to live his life," Concepcion said of José's efforts to make money doing odd jobs to help support his kids back in El Salvador. "How could anyone put themselves in a position to die like that? Everyone I know says that's ridiculous."[13]

Ridiculous, mysterious, foolhardy, tragic—it was hard to know what to make of the staged big-rig accident phenomenon, this "bizarre new scam" as the *L.A. Times* termed it. Was targeting trucks for crashes on freeways truly "new"? Were Latino immigrants the first to take to the roads in a "bizarre" predatory way either to put bread on the table or to make some money, quick and easy and only slightly dirty?

In Los Angeles alone, records indicated, Anglo and Black swoop-and-squatters had been staging crashes on the freeways at least as far back as 1974, when the L.A. County Board of Supervisors conducted hearings into capping practices in the city.[14] Freeway swoop-and-squats had also been documented in other cities and at other times. A few years before Perez's death, two men in Cleveland were arrested for staging freeway swoop-and-squats, albeit at low speeds. "When it looked like the truck driver had looked away for a moment," a federal agent explained, "they would slam on their brakes and then let the truck hit them."[15] Even earlier, in Chicago, several gangs were suspected of conspiring with truck drivers to stage crashes on that city's Dan Ryan and Eisenhower expressways: "At first, the ringleaders would pick any truck," said an investigator involved in the case. "But now they have a [better] idea who's self-insured: moving companies, grocery lines."[16] Cases with a familiar ring were reported even earlier, in the 1950s and 1960s: A four-person "band of fakers" was shown to have staged $27,000 worth of highway crashes in Texas and Colorado. "Minutes before one of the accidents, the 'victims' had approached a trucker at a highway café and offered him $200 to ram them 'accidentally,'" one account stated. "The skill of the car's 'wheelman,' and the fact that its trunk was stuffed with sandbags and old tires, prevented the passengers from being more than shaken up. But their agonized acting worried the insurance company sufficiently to cause it to settle quickly."[17] In another early case, a man from Fort Hancock, Texas, loaded his wife and nephew into his black Ford then went out to U.S. Route 80, where he soon found a flatbed tractor-trailer to target for a rear-end collision.[18] The case was mentioned in a magazine article from 1961 beneath a heading that read: "Some fakers will take fantastic chances, even with the lives of their wives and children." The article included an illustration with a caption that seemed like a strange foretelling of the death of José Perez thirty years later: "The black car kept passing, then slowing down," it stated. "The truck driver had no way of knowing that he was being deliberately baited." In another hauntingly familiar passage, this same account discussed the ring's final staging on U.S. Route 67 in Missouri: "The crash was worse than intended. The truck jackknifed, skidded, tossed the Chevrolet into a ditch. The fakers were now playing close to murder."[19]

Who killed José Luis Lopez Perez? The answer would prove more elusive than it first seemed. The question itself was not at all one I could have imagined when I started down the blind alley of this subject some five years ago.

As a senior at Brown University in 1991, I signed up for an unlikely on-campus interview for a job at a small private investigation company in Los Angeles. My questions then were basic and, it now seems clear, naive: Did private investigators hire liberal arts graduates as trainees? Was this some kind of cloak-and-dagger way for the CIA to recruit on college campuses without inciting protest? Would I learn to trade irreverent remarks with jaded homicide detectives at 3:00 A.M.? Would I have contacts giving me the word on the street? Would I carry a gun? A video camera?

In time, I would come to understand about real-life private detectives what a steady stream of journalism on the subject has reported for decades: that today's Sam Spade carries a laptop computer as often as a gun or a camera; that the PI, reluctant protaganist of countless romantic fictions, often works dead-end cases and writes dull reports which no one reads carefully; and that one could often be wrong in presuming the sex of the modern private dick.[20] Before I fully understood any of this, however, or even knew the breadth of tasks packed into the generic term of private investigation (from shopping mall rent-a-cop to forensic super sleuth), the idea of being a PI struck me as something I would love to do and might even be good at.

On my first day on the job, I knew enough not to wear a suit. Not only had I flown out to see the office before accepting the job, but, once I arrived in California, I had been living there—sometimes sleeping on the floor in my corner of the large, open room where all of the investigators had their desks; sometimes setting up camp in one of the apartments attached to the office at the other end of the building. The atmosphere was informal, to say the least. Located on the second floor of an old bank building at the heart of the original Venice, the office was accessed mainly by a rickety wooden staircase leading up from an alley; the street entrance was an unmarked dirty glass door between a hamburger stand and a health food store.

The cast of characters in the Venice office was small enough to get to know right away. There were the two college recruits, Peter and I, along with a few investigators who worked in other parts of Los Angeles, and Jack, a surveillance man who tailed people by foot and by car, filmed them, took notes on bar napkins, wore Hawaiian shirts, and, for pathos, even had a dog with sad eyes named Cleo. Then there were the two partners with the investigation licenses, for whom everyone else was a sort of deputy, at least in the eyes of the law: Steve, who had recruited me, was one of them, and Larry, a slightly older and somewhat shorter man, was the other. Steve, I had gathered in my time with him, had fallen into private investigation work through a friend of a friend, having come out of a liberal arts background himself. He stayed, I later imagined, because he liked making his own schedule and having his own office; and I think he especially liked to consider himself in the Philip Marlowe tradition of detectives who traveled the city's mean streets without themselves being mean. Larry I knew less about: When I first visited him in his loft apartment down the hall from the main office, we did not talk much about work. He fixed us each a coffee and we drank them on bar stools in a makeshift kitchen that felt like it should have been in a trailer home. Just before getting his investigator's license, Larry later told me, he had been a repo man, bird-dogging cars for tow trucks to haul away.

The only person connected with the office who looked to me as if he could possibly shoot someone was Rick Smith, who founded the business, then sold it to Steve and Larry and went to Hawaii. Though I never met Rick, Steve showed me his picture in an oversize, coffee-table book of portraits of Venice personalities. Photographed in front of a wall map of Los Angeles, Smith had a full salt-and-pepper beard, a Panama hat, and a gun in the palm of his right hand. The caption said that Smith liked to kill cats as a young man just to watch them die. Rick Smith's image in that book quickly became a totem for me, an emblem of the world I now hoped to enter, just as the somber oil paintings of the university's gray-haired patriarchs had symbolized the world from which I had come. I had been aiming high for so many years, it seemed—the Ivy League, the study of philosophy and literature—and now I would aim low. How low I did not yet know; but, after months of waiting and trying to act like someone who doesn't miss a trick (such was my shorthand idea of being an investigator), I was eager to find out.

Much of what today's private investigators do, I was surprised to learn—and almost entirely what I did in Venice—is to investigate personal injury cases for insurance companies. This book began for me during these investigations, in places that I can now only half remember: in junk yards and driveways and curbsides, where I photographed cars wrecked in auto accidents, taking a rough measure of dents and dings and broken lights with a yardstick mounted on a block of wood, then snapped my pictures from prescribed angles for my reports; in medical clinics with bars on the windows, where I did my closest graphological inspection of patient signatures in log books (were they all signed at once? was the signature consistent?) then certified in my own informal way that therapeutic roller-beds, electrical muscle stimulation calipers and prods, and other physical therapy equipment functioned in the manner that it was supposed to; and in the waiting areas of personal injury law offices, where I came to interview claimants.

My most frequent investigative task was to obtain recorded statements from people. My first statement resulted from a call by a woman who said that her former boyfriend was faking his auto accident claim and she could prove it. At the woman's apartment, Steve let me do most of the questioning. During the next hour and a half, I strayed radically from the point at hand mainly because I did not really know the point. I spent most of the week transcribing the interview, then Larry refused to bill the client because it was of so little value. The first statement I took on my own was from a supermarket detective who witnessed an accident in the parking lot in front of his store. After the statement, the man showed me his rogues' gallery portraits of shoplifters he had caught, along with the items they had attempted to filch. Polaroid images of shamefaced men and women clutching sirloin tips, fifths of liquor, and alkaline batteries stuck with me more than anything I may have learned about the auto accident the man witnessed.

The people I interviewed most often as an investigator were those who claimed to have been injured in an accident and who had retained lawyers to ask for money from an insurance company. Claims adjusters would look through their files for "fraud indicators"—anything from the fact that the claimant's address was a P.O. box to the fact that the accident occurred the week the insurance coverage started—then they would send us their most suspicious cases. Larry would study the cases briefly at his desk, then would assign them to one of us depending on how heavy a load we carried already. At any given time, we each had around thirty cases in various stages of investigation. Some files could be turned around from start to finish in a week; others languished for months in my desk drawers. Perhaps the claimants' attorney was refusing to allow statements, or the claimants themselves had not yet finished their chiropractic treatments, or the teenagers who all but ran the law offices and medical clinics never answered my calls or letters. Some of my billing log sheets were nothing more than long lists of fruitless calls; sometimes my reports were simply summaries of this type of non-activity presented in my tersest, most professional prose. Few of my cases ended with any kind of finality; rather, the files just kind of atrophied in my desk, then were pronounced officially dead either by me or by the claims adjuster who sent the case.

Posted on our office bulletin board was a quote about accident insurance investigation work that I sometimes read before going to my desk. The quote was from a scene in the movie *Double Indemnity* in which the claims investigator, played by Edward G. Robinson, talks about his vocation with an insurance salesman, played by Fred MacMurray: "A desk job? Is that all you can see in it? Just a hard chair to park your pants on from nine to five? Just a pile of papers to shuffle around, and sharp pencils and a scratch pad to make figures on, with maybe a little doodling on the side?" Robinson asks MacMurray. "Well, that's not the way I see it," Robinson continues: "To me, a claims man is a surgeon, and that desk is an operating table, and those pencils are scalpels and bone chisels. And those papers are not just forms and statistics and claims for compensation. They're alive! They're packed with drama, with twisted hopes and crooked dreams. A claims man is a doctor and a bloodhound and a cop and a judge and a jury and a father confessor, all in one."

This was the romantic conception of insurance investigation; although I sometimes took refuge in it, my day-to-day work was so much at variance that the movie quote soon came to have no meaning for me. More accurate, I thought, was a description of the job printed in a *New York Times Magazine* article from 1960: "Most insurance investigation is rather routine work," the article stated, "and the life of the insurance detective is, for the most part, safe, dull, and distinctly unglamorous."[21]

Throughout much of my time in Venice, I had a hard time satisfying myself one way or another about the legitimacy of the personal injury claims I investigated.

In the typical case, I headed east from the beach to a law office usually located on Wilshire Boulevard somewhere between Beverly Hills and downtown L.A. The buildings I visited often had expensive underground parking, some even had valet service; most had lobbies with marble-look tiles and elevators with shiny metal and mirrors. This is where I would meet the claimants—four or five people, mostly Spanish-speaking men in their twenties or thirties dressed in jeans and t-shirts and dirty baseball caps emblazoned with the logo of some agribusiness or trucking company. When I first encountered the claimants, they would be loosely huddled around a piece of paper which I took to be a letter from their attorney, and they would be trying to find the office. I would help them, then would pass several uncomfortable minutes seated nearby while they figured out that I was to be the person interrogating them about their accident.

While waiting, I usually busied myself with files in my briefcase. The claimants would talk among themselves in Spanish and I would pretend to follow the details of their conversations, both to show that I was sympathetic with them, if their case were legitimate, and that I was on to them, if they were pulling a fraud. Then a "legal assistant" or an "office administrator" would send for the claimants. A few minutes later, they would send for me and my Spanish interpreter, Sara. All of us would be led to a conference room, and I would ask that all but one of the claimants leave the room so I could take their statements separately. After the first dozen or so of these meetings, I stopped worrying that I did not know enough about the law to be taking statements sworn under penalty of perjury; and I stopped being surprised that this whole statement process took place without the presence, or the apparent knowledge, of the attorney whose name was on the office door and on the letterhead stationery. Despite the trappings of the law, it soon became clear to me that I was working in a largely extralegal world where the real business of personal injury in America is conducted.

Initially I enjoyed taking statements, in and outside of law offices; they gave me a chance to understand the lives of people about whom I might otherwise know very little. Before living in Los Angeles, I had little awareness of Southern California's enormous shadow population of immigrants newly arrived from Mexico and Latin America or from Pacific Rim nations such as the Philippines, Vietnam, and Cambodia. In the Los Angeles that I had always heard about—the place where "everyone" was writing a script, doing lunch, or developing a project—these were the people I saw cutting the lawns, washing the dishes, and parking the cars. My job most often took me to the vast "other" Los Angeles, however, where the claimants from my cases often lived. There, in the endless flat regions located south, east, and north of downtown, I knocked on doors, photographed cars, and attempted to interview witnesses in neighborhoods where I may have been the only English speaker. Sometimes people looked at me suspiciously through their window shades or talked to me through screen doors. Other times they invited me inside their squat, single-family homes, where it was usually hotter than it was outside in the sun. They would sit me in a room with a baby playing in the corner and religious iconography on the walls; maybe they would offer me a Coke, and I would feel like a visitor from another country grateful for their hospitality. When I started questioning them about the make of their car, or which of two lanes of traffic they were driving in at the time of their accident, or whether their doctor had a mustache or not, I always felt a little stupid.

If I relied purely on my own experience of investigating personal injury claims for a little over a year in Los Angeles, I might have arrived at a few rough conclusions: There are many law offices and medical clinics that deal in high volumes of accident claims, and their presence is especially strong in poorer neighborhoods, where public buses carry placards asking people if they have had an accident, and billboards, looming high over rows of ramshackle houses, show toothy Anglo personal injury lawyers and their 1-800 numbers. There are also people who will exaggerate the extent of their injuries after an accident, or else will make-up an accident altogether, in order to get money from insurance companies.

That there might be a larger picture here, though—that intimate connections might exist between the claimants and the lawyers and the doctors— was not immediately clear to me: There was always a lot of talk around the office about accident "rings," organized groups of people who would stage crashes and make claims, aided by doctors and lawyers, or maybe even directed by them; but I did not at first believe that any of my cases were products of ring activity. I had watched L.A. district attorney Reiner on TV suggesting that attorneys who ran accident rings were like the "big boys" atop drug rings; but everything that I had seen of the accident business seemed too *dis*organized, banal, and out in the open to be organized crime. Besides, I asked myself, did crime bosses have billboards and 1-800 numbers and waiting rooms with *Architectural Digest?*

Still, I found it increasingly difficult to ignore the suggestions of a larger picture. During my brief time in Los Angeles, accident rings were frequently written about in the *Los Angeles Times.* One article described the "Casino" fraud ring which reportedly generated $50 million over two years by staging more than 3,000 accidents. (Steve, my boss at the Venice office, obtained a list of all of the locations searched in the Casino investigation and I kept a copy of it on my desk; occasionally I would check the list to see if any of my cases involved these offices, and, more than once, they did.) Stories that told of an equally large but unrelated case, in which state investigators had infiltrated an accident ring led by a middle-age woman who held seminars on how to stage a crash and how to fake injuries for insurance examiners, prompted new questions: Were the people I was interviewing graduates of these seminars? Had I sat in living rooms, drinking my can of Coke, feeling good about my cultural experience while blundering over some kind of fraud ring? And what about increased news reports of swoop-and-squat crashes? Steve had diagrammed this kind of crash back at the information session at Brown; and I had written down the words "swoop-and-squat" with a rush, feeling that I was learning the way things really worked in the world. But did any of the files on my desk involve swoop-and-squats orchestrated by organized fraud rings? It was hard to know.

The more that I learned about the fake accident trade in Los Angeles, the more I began to pick up on things that I might have missed at first. Among the claimants I would meet in the lobby of a law office, for example, there was often one person who directed the others but did not stay to give me his statement. This person was probably a capper like Phil Santiago in the José Perez case. On at least two occasions I lingered in the parking lot of law offices after taking my statements to glimpse cappers pay off claimants in cash, then leave in a separate car. Witnessing a few payoffs helped me believe in the office folklore and news reports about organized accident rings. I wanted to know more: Several times I rushed to my car after a statement so I could follow the claimants. To where I didn't know: To the Mr. Big discussed by the D.A.? To some kind of map room where fake accidents were planned for the L.A. metro area? Lacking the willingness to break the traffic laws necessary to do the job right, however, I usually gave up pursuit after a few blocks.

Toward the end of my time as an investigator, I managed to uncover a minor accident operation in which both the insured party and the claimants had been using the same post office box. I presented my findings to the attorney representing the claimants in these faked cases, and he promptly sent me letters saying that he was "discontinuing representation" of his clients. Around the office, we called these "drop" letters (just like the letters Miller's office reportedly sent out after the failed Perez staging), and getting one was as close as we came to the fabled notion of solving a case. Whenever I got drops, I celebrated them back at the office like everyone else. But I think it bothered us all at some level that our investigations ended so inconclusively. A dropped client could always reappear months later with a new attorney and then the process would begin again from scratch. Larry always said that we were just impartial finders of fact who wrote reports with no concern for the outcome of the case. "Just put it in the report," he would counsel; then put it out of your mind, go surfing, look at the freaks on the Venice Boardwalk. To count my billable hours and call it a day just didn't sit right with me, although this is what I did for many months.

Disillusioned with private investigation, and bored with the everyday outrageousness of Venice Beach, which seemed largely put on *for* tourists *by* tourists, I felt myself drifting out of the world of personal injury investigation. During the summer of 1992, however, I read a book that renewed my interest in the fake accident culture. It was about a private investigator from Southern California who, while working for an insurance company, stumbles into the inner circle of an accident ring operating in Los Angeles. She meets and befriends a capper, Raymond, who at one point brings her along for an afternoon's stagings. The investigator is alternately exhilarated and depressed by the accidents. "I'd been at the wheel for the first couple of accidents," she says, "then Raymond had taken over. . . . At four, much to my relief, he decided we'd done enough."[22] In the end, she helps a federal task force shut down the ring.

Although fiction, Sue Grafton's "H" is for Homicide was based on research she had done with state and local insurance investigators; and the details rang true to some of my experience. One reviewer called Grafton's work "a vivid, funny portrait of life in an ethnic underworld, viewed without judgment." The words helped me begin to rethink my trips to certain law offices and clinics and body shops as excursions into a bizarre criminal underworld: not an underworld like any I had ever heard of, centered on drugs or prostitution or loan-sharking or gambling, but an underworld built on the improbable foundation of faked accidents and injuries—an underworld, perhaps long unnoticed because cloaked in the legitimacy of this-worldly office suites and medical clinics and, sometimes, TV ads. I was excited that Grafton's book had been published just a year earlier and that she credited the experts with whom she had consulted. I resolved that I would meet with these people to find out what they knew—to what end I still was not sure.

With Grafton's book under my arm, I began to research a sort of nonfiction companion volume about L.A.'s personal injury underworld. Later in the summer of 1992 came the story which galvanized my thinking on the subject: the phenomenon of the big-rig freeway accidents and the death of José Perez. The connections among Miller, Santiago, and Perez were stark and tragic, and, unlike my feint investigations, very real. Some of the reporting on this story started me thinking of a national perspective on accident faking, and this led me to the only aspect of the story which was truly "new" or "bizarre": its history.

There is a personal injury underworld in America, I gradually came to see over several years—not one giant master organization, but a distinct and recognizable criminal culture of cappers and attorneys and doctors who use similar methods of faking accidents and claims, and whose very existence is unique in the world. How to know this underworld, though? How to map its dimensions, chart its history, or chronicle its rise and (frequent) falls? Most importantly, how to understand this underworld in the context of the larger culture?

At first, I contacted people known to have traveled to L.A's personal injury underworld. I met with officers from the Highway Patrol Staged Collision Unit who had gone undercover to gather evidence about accident rings just as Grafton's fictional Kinsey Milhone had done; I talked with the head of a newly formed staged accidents unit of the Los Angeles Police Department; I met with the chief investigators for the State Department of Insurance; and I talked with assistant district attorneys who prosecuted accident fraud rings. At the National Insurance Crime Bureau, I learned about a network of ex-FBI men who worked cases similar to mine in cities across the country. Early in my research, I was excited to read about an attorney in Orange County who specialized in insurance fraud and was said to have "a library" of significant cases at his office. Being only a year or so out of college, I pictured a wall of leather-bound volumes of accident frauds dating back many years or decades or even centuries. I met the attorney for lunch, and we talked about some of the cases he had been involved with personally. Later, when I asked him about his library of accident frauds, he pointed to a few manila folders on his desk and asked me if this is what I meant. Although the attorney was nice and encouraging, our meeting ended as my meetings with most of the others had. We both realized that I seemed to be looking for something that he just did not have, and he wished me the best of luck in finding it.

At the end of 1992, I left Venice. Setting off to make some kind of sense of my own experience as an insurance investigator and of the seemingly senseless death of a young Salvadoran immigrant, I soon found the first traces of a lengthy and revealing history of accident frauds. More than just the "latest new scam" which raises insurance rates, as the story is continually reinvented by reporters and the insurance industry, accident faking for money in the United States stretches all the way back to the late nineteenth century when men and women carved out a grifter's living by pretending to slip and fall on steam trains throughout the Midwest. In old court records, I found an accident underworld peopled by an earlier group of immigrants—the Jews and Italians from eastern and southern Europe—operating on the streets of New York in the early 1920s; later in the decade, bar associations around the country led a nationwide "war" against ambulance chasers. During the Great Depression, I found places where self-mutilation for money was one of the few profitable trades around. Along the way I encountered a long tradition of European "malingerers"—beggars, soldiers, and thieves whose centuries-old methods would later form the foundation of this American big business. As I've assembled my own library on the topic, it has become clear to me that staging accidents and making money through the nothingness of faked personal injuries has been one of the most persistent and most lucrative American dreams never to have been fully set down and interpreted.

Who killed José Luis Lopez Perez? With apologies to Larry, this book is the report of one investigation I just could not drop.

PRELUDE TO A FALL

> We are occasionally treated to a newspaper report
> of an isolated case, but nothing like a general history
> of frauds upon underwriters has ever been given to
> the public; and, indeed, such a publication should
> be oftentimes repeated, as the ingenious plans of the
> swindlers vary with the times.
>
> —*Hunt's Merchant's Magazine*, 1840

WILLIAM TURTLE WAS BORN IN ENGLAND IN 1829. For a time he worked as a dry goods salesman (and first grew his trademark muttonchop side-burns) before emigrating to Chicago and joining the municipal police force. Later, as the principal member of the Chicago Police and Insurance Bureau, Turtle would become perhaps the most famous insurance detective in the country. In his work, Turtle had nothing to do with fake accident cases, though. He made his living, and earned his nationwide renown, by uncovering life insurance plots in which husbands murdered wives, wives did in their husbands, and miscellaneous beneficiaries feigned bereavement to collect on policies, passing off, as their loved ones, anonymous corpses purchased from medical suppliers.[1]

Dr. John B. Lewis was a surgeon who served with the Army of the Potomac during the Civil War. A stern-looking man with a sharp Vandyke beard, Lewis rose in the ranks from field surgeon, piling up amputated limbs, to the directorship of a major Union hospital. After the war, Lewis found work in civilian life investigating suspicious insurance cases near Baltimore.[2] Lewis's

FIGURE I.1. William Turtle was one of the nation's first, and most well-known, insurance detectives. In 1866, Turtle founded "The Chicago Police and Insurance Bureau." Over the following decades, Turtle earned a national reputation for exposing several high-profile life insurance plots. (The likeness of Turtle was originally printed in Elias Colbert's *Colbert's Chicago*, a book of sketches of Chicago personalities published in 1868.)

work did not involve fake accidents, either. Like Turtle, he often worked at unraveling all of the "remarkable stratagems and conspiracies" that people devised to defraud life insurance companies; he also occasionally checked into dubious fire policy claims.

Alexander Colin Campbell did not investigate insurance cases at all, but he knew more and thought harder about insurance crimes than anyone alive at the turn of the century. In his definitive study, written in 1902, Campbell offered readers 400-plus pages on ship scuttling, life insurance murder, and arson for profit. He even dealt at some length with the matter of "wildcat" frauds by shady underwriters on policyholders—a separate but equally rich vein of historical inquiry for Campbell, who was looking to map the "whole systems and cycles of evil" brought about by the institution of insurance. In all those pages, though, Campbell dismissed accident fakers with just one sentence, writing "A man who practically makes a living by having minor 'accidents' happen to him—breaking his fingers, bruising himself by falls, even fracturing a leg or two when nothing less will serve his turn—would be regarded by most of us a rather strange development of this humdrum life of ours."[3] Just how strange a development faking accidents for money in America would become during the century since he wrote those words, Campbell could not have begun to imagine.

When they first stumbled onto the American scene in the late nineteenth century, accident fakers were like the punch line to a long, and largely unfunny, joke about the excesses to which people have gone throughout history in order to collect insurance money.

Accounts of the particular misdeeds of the earliest insurance criminals, the ship scuttlers, have mostly been lost to history, like the rotten boards of the scuttled vessels themselves. Only sparse evidence exists of an isolated scuttling in ancient Greece carried out by two shipowners, Hegastratus and Zenothemis. Some fifteen hundred years later, the appearance of anti-scuttling legislation in Spain implied significant scuttling activity, as did the coinage of the term "scuttling" itself in seventeenth century England. But few substantive records of the schemes survive. The story of one scuttler from the mid-eighteenth century, John Lancey, is buried in the dusty chronicles of a British book of notorious public characters: The young sea captain, we read in two unevenly typeset pages, was persuaded by his wealthy father-in-law to sink an old brig on its journey to the American colonies.[4] Later, betrayed by a crew member, Lancey was found out, tried, convicted, and sentenced to the full extent of the strict British ship scuttling statute of 1723: death by hanging. The sentence was carried out before a sizable crowd at Execution Dock on June 7, 1754.

During the half century or so following the hanging of Captain Lancey, scuttling became dramatically more profitable and more widely practiced. Owing to the advent and growth of modern marine insurance, at times scuttlers became as numerous as car thieves today. By 1810, scuttling had become so serious a problem for insurers that a select committee of the British House of Lords finally met to hear testimony on the subject. On the first day of the hearings, the question was put to a leading underwriter named John Fisher Throckmorton: "Are not frauds frequently practiced or attempted to be practiced upon Underwriters?" To which Throckmorton replied straightforwardly: "I have known a great many."[5] The underwriter went on to cite a number of instances of ship scuttling familiar to him during his long career. The ship *Hannah and Mary*, he said, had been "sunk by design after being insured at Lloyd's to a very considerable amount." The *Aurora*, bound to the Brazils from Lisbon, had been "burned by design" in the Madeira shipping lanes; and the ship *Merry Andrew* had been scuttled for insurance money near Bristol in 1803. ("The captain was hanged," Throckmorton added about this last case, "and the owner absconded.") One case involved a Captain William Codling, two shipowners, George Easterby and William MacFarlane, and the sinking of the brig *Adventure*. No doubt the case was familiar to most of the men assembled in the room at the time for, almost from the day the fraud occurred, Captain Codling became one of the best-known scuttlers in marine insurance history.

What earned Captain Codling's sinking of the *Adventure* its place in maritime legend was not the scheme itself. Shipowners Easterby and MacFarlane bought the old ship at a salvage auction (typical of ships to be scuttled), repaired it just enough to earn Lloyd's lowest passing grade of seaworthiness, and overinsured it. Then they loaded it with cargo—cutlery, linens, firkins of butter, hogsheads of tobacco—and paid Codling to surreptitiously sell off the cargo for a profit and scuttle the ship on its route into the Mediterranean, leaving no trace. Codling's method of scuttling was not particularly unique, either: One evening in early August 1802, he created a diversionary rum party on deck, then secretly gave an order to Thomas Cooper, an inexperienced first mate promoted to his post despite his ignorance of the rudiments of navigation. Cooper was told to go below deck and do something that even he recognized as odd. "I was in liquor at the time," Cooper later testified. "Codling told me to go down and I should find an auger lying on the cabin deck and I was to take the scuttle hatch up and bore a hole . . . as near the bottom as possible."[6] Cooper did as he was told. When the ship failed to founder fast enough, though, the captain ordered Cooper to enlarge the hole. Still unsatisfied, Codling himself went below deck, moved aside a locker, and, with the aid of a crowbar, ripped a plank from the ship's bottom. Later, the torn board, recovered by a salvage team, would literally become a plank in Codling's coffin when it was displayed by prosecutors at trial.

In the end, what made Codling a legendary (and borderline ridiculous) figure was that the sinking of the *Adventure* took place so near the beach at Brighton, England, that Codling was forced into the awkward position of vigorously warding off the assistance of the fishing vessel *Swallow* with "a barrage of salty oaths."[7] Even when the brig finally tipped, one sunny Sunday morning, both masts still showed, so shallow was the water. Dozens of baffled Brighton residents witnessed the scene from the beginning to its bizarre end. Seventy-five years later, a Lloyd's historian summarized the opinion of the beachgoers that morning: "All the fishermen and other watchers who had seen the proceedings of the brig and the crew before sinking, and the refusal of the captain to accept aid, freely and unanimously exchanged with each other their opinions of this being a gross case of scuttling."[8]

Under pursuit by Captain Robert Douglas, an investigator dispatched by underwriters from Lloyd's, Captain Codling returned to England briefly, then boarded a ship for Germany. Midjourney, investigator Douglas discovered Codling hiding beneath a pile of blankets in a ship's berth, with falsified travel papers identifying him as "Mr. Postato." Several months later, on November 27, Codling was hanged at Execution Dock. Testimony at Codling's trial, especially the details divulged by First Mate Thomas Cooper, provided underwriters with some of the most specific information ever obtained about the scuttling relationships among shipowners, captains, and crews. The trial, according to Lloyd's historian Frederick Martin, "brought to light a strange tale of corruption, showing that the wilful sinking of vessels had become a sort of business, carried on quite openly, like an ordinary mercantile transaction."[9] Later British trials further revealed the extent of the ship-scuttling business. In one of the more famous cases, prosecutors described Captain Edward Loose as maneuvering his ship, the *Dryad,* close to the shore near Haiti, "seeking an opportunity to effect his purpose"—the sinking of the ship for two shipowning brothers named Wallace.[10] In November 1839, weeks into his crossing of the Atlantic, the aging sea captain was just off the coast of Cuba when he finally mouthed the command to scuttle the *Dryad* on a reef. The order would later be immortalized in the cliché about loose lips (read Edward Loose's lips) sinking ships.

"The wrecking of vessels for insurance was an immense trade," A.C. Campbell observed of the early nineteenth-century British ship scuttlers, "and it was one pursued, so far as the owners were concerned, with absolute impunity."[11] Codling's case was typical in this sense. He was hanged, while the shipowners—one of whom upbraided Codling for "making a stupid job" of something he himself had done "hundreds of times and always succeeded"— were not even fined for their role in the scheme. The prosecutorial climate surrounding ship scuttling became slightly less friendly to shipowners by midcentury, however. Captain Loose was never caught, for instance, having fled to South America. But his employers, shipowners Patrick and Michael Stewart Wallace, were sentenced to life in exile.[12] Some years later, two other shipowners, Lionel Holdworth and Thomas Berwick, were found guilty of having contracted with a sailor named Charles Webb to sink the *Severn* en route to Shanghai, China. Each was sentenced to twenty years of penal servitude. Berwick alone was shown to have been involved in more than a dozen scuttlings dating from the sinking of the *Uncle Donald* in 1844.[13]

By the second half of the nineteenth century, ship scuttling in England had evolved from the earlier, more deliberate, more slapstick schemes of Captains Codling and Loose, to become more subtle, less transparently larcenous affairs. Shipowners would grossly overburden unseaworthy brigs with overinsured cargo, then would welcome a sinking somewhere at sea if it should happen or else collect the profits from an unusually successful haul should the ship arrive safely. "If the crew go with her, then 'dead men tell no tales,'" A.C. Campbell explained the new scuttling logic. "And, if they escape, their evidence as to 'rotten plates puttied up with tar,' or overloading, or deliberate scuttling is without the support it might have if the hull were left anywhere where representatives of the law might see it."[14]

In the early days, ship scuttling was dangerous only if the scuttlers were caught and convicted; and this rarely occurred. "There were islands and other places unwatched by police or by insurance inspectors, where vessels could be 'wrecked' in the gentlest manner," Campbell wrote. "But, as these points were brought under surveillance, the game became more dangerous, and more desperate grew the ruffians who staked their lives upon it." The newer marine insurance schemes would have to be played out in deeper waters, where lives were more likely to be lost in the process. In 1879, for instance, Captain William Tower told his crew that he had been paid by a shipowner to wreck the *Barque Brothers' Pride* off the coast of Cuba. Ships' mate Howard Thomas, a twenty-one-year-old who signed up with Captain Tower in Philadelphia on a promise that he would see Cuba—but who ultimately found himself buying a $4 auger and drilling several holes in the hull of the *Pride*, then setting it aflame—asked the captain, "What about our lives?" In response the captain offered only silence, followed by an expression of belief that they would all be picked up by an American coast guard schooner.[15] "Impossible as it may seem," A.C. Campbell wrote, "the abuse of insurance has, more than once in history, bred a class of men ready to risk their lives for a comparatively small share of the money they 'earned' by casting away ships they commanded . . . The power of the skipper to throw away his vessel and still escape with his life was the central point of centuries of evil."[16]

Some of the men who worked long and successful careers in ship scuttling were immortalized in poems like Rudyard Kipling's "Mary Gloster," where a millionaire shipowner on his deathbed looks back at his early days as a scuttling captain risking his life for a "big fat lump of insurance." (*"Lord what boats I've handled—rotten and leaky and old!/ Ran'em, or—opened the bilge-cock precisely as I was told"*). An earlier Kipling poem, "The Ballad of 'The Bolivar,'" told of a ship "leaking like a lobster-pot, steering like a dray . . . overloaded, undermanned, meant to founder" whose crew successfully gets her across the sea, thwarting the owner's scuttling intentions. Ship scuttlers also found their way into late-nineteenth century fiction: They were featured in two of Charles Reade's short novels, *The Scuttled Ship* and *Foul Play*, which ends with the captain, a lifelong wrecker for shipowners, going down at sea. In W. Clark Russell's *A Salt-Water Cure*, a minor tale of moral instruction, a shipowner is made to take one of his own doomed brigs to sea, an experience that forever cures him of the ills of ship scuttling.

Many without benefit of a saltwater cure paid with their lives for their education in the dangers of scuttling. By the last few decades of the nineteenth century, some writers suggested that hundreds, maybe thousands, of seamen were dying in these increasingly dangerous marine insurance plots. The grim, often doomed, character of many shipping ventures was widely known. In 1875, for instance, a cartoon appeared in the British magazine *Punch* under the heading "THE COFFIN SHIPS." The illustration depicted a seaman standing at the edge of a dock with a woman weeping on one of his shoulders; over the other shoulder is pictured a ship shrouded in darkness. The couple was rejoicing at the man's not having to serve as crew member aboard the old hulk, an assignment that both knew to be life-threateningly dangerous:

Polly: O, dear Jack! I can't help crying, but I'm so happy to think you're not going in one of those dreadful ships!

Jack: What, and be one of Davy Jones's Decoy ducks? No! no! Lass—never more!—thanks to our friend Master Plimsoll, God bless him![17]

The man to which this fictional "Jack" referred—Samuel Plimsoll—was a self-styled whistleblower and energetic man of the people who, as a member of the British House of Commons in the early 1870s, brought the matter of these new scuttling schemes to public attention. In 1871 Plimsoll published a book, *Our Seamen: An Appeal,* based on his years of personal investigation into the matter. In his own idiosyncratic way, he documented the practices of unscrupulous shipowners. "Do you want to know more about the [sailors] who thus are cut off in their full manhood?" Plimsoll asked. "Do you want to know how their loss is felt by their widows? Come with me a few minutes, and I'll show you."[18] He then detailed the systematic overvaluing, overinsuring, and overloading of merchant ships, which imperiled the lives of the poor seamen who were forced on board by a combination of their own penury and by a law that forbade them from abandoning ships once they had willingly contracted as crew members. Plimsoll put the blame for the existence of the coffin ships squarely on the shoulders of shipowners who were willing to risk the deaths of their crews for monetary gain. He wrote:

> Such is the evil reputation which some bad men acquire, so generally are they known for their habitual overloading, for their terribly frequent and disastrous losses, for their cynical disregard for human life, that after paying increasingly high rates of premium for insurance in the ports where they are known, the time sometimes comes when they can only insure in London, where they are as yet unknown, and even there, after still further experience, their names become so black with infamy, that nobody will insure their risks at any premium.[19]

To denounce these men further, Plimsoll coined the term "ship-knacker," adapting a word originally used for those who bought worn out or diseased horses to slaughter for hides, hoofs, and flesh, which was sold for dogmeat. Plimsoll refused to name specific ship-knackers, although he did reveal that several of them were influential members of Parliament—a fact that he believed partly explained why legislation had not been crafted to remedy the problem. Plimsoll claimed to have confronted one such ship-knacking member of Parliament—"a man whose name you will hear in any coffee-room or exchange . . . one notorious for excessive and habitual overloading, and a reckless disregard for human life, who has lost seven ocean-going steamers, and drowned more than a hundred men in less than two years." Plimsoll claimed to have threatened to expose the man on the floor of the House, which left the man stunned. ("I thought the man would have fainted," he later wrote.)[20] At other times, however, it was Plimsoll who felt the strain: "I felt utterly alone in my work, and so sick with excitement and fear, that I was compelling myself to think of the poor widows in order to keep up my courage."

In the summer of 1873, Plimsoll succeeded in empaneling a Royal Commission to look into scuttling practices, but the inquiry did not go the way he had hoped. Few people came forward to corroborate his findings, and many people flatly contradicted his contentions that thousands of seamen had been lost to insurance plots.[21] On July 22, a frustrated Samuel Plimsoll took to the floor of the Parliament and, in the words of one English historian, enacted "one of the most extraordinary scenes that ever took place in the House of Commons." Justin McCarthy, the author of *A History of Our Own Times*, later described the scene:

> Mr. Plimsoll, under the influence of disappointment and of anger, seemed to have lost all self-control. He denounced some of the shipowners of the House; he threatened to name and expose them; he called them villains who had sent brave men to death. When interrupted by the Speaker, and told that he must not apply the term villains to members of the house, he repeated again and again, and in the most vociferous tones, that they were villains, and that he would abide by his words . . . He shouted, shook his fist at the leading members of the Government, and rushed out of the House in a state of excitement that seemed little less than that of an actual maniac.[22]

In the end, most people agreed with McCarthy's assessment: Plimsoll had "surrounded a good cause with an unfortunate adornment of exaggeration, extravagance, and ill-temper"; nevertheless, he had been largely right about the evils of the system that made it profitable to operate coffin ships. In the years following these hearings, a Merchant Shipping Bill was passed that forbade shipowners from overloading their vessels. All merchant ships were to be marked with a line—henceforth the Plimsoll Line—above which cargo could not be stowed. When Plimsoll's Royal Commission on Unseaworthy Ships met again in 1887, it was widely agreed that "the most glaring and outrageous methods" of ship scuttling, if ever they had existed in any of the scale Plimsoll alleged, had come to an end.[23]

The literature on insurance-motivated murder dates back many centuries, like the record on ship scuttling, with deepest roots in European soil. For as long as there have been wives or husbands eyeing one another greedily, or townsfolk sizing up their old, feeble, or infirm for speculation, there have been interested readers trailing close behind. Thick compilations have long offered such titilating tales as: "A French Wife Destroyer," "An Austrian Triple Murder," and a "Sensational Poisoning Case in Prussia." Pretended death schemes, too, while not as intriguing as murder, have had their enthusiastic chroniclers in print: One book devotes an entire section to what is called "The Monotonous Repitition of the Drowning Trick," an exposition of the overused plot in which an insured feigns a fall from a boat or dock, then hides from company loss adjusters until the case is settled.

The earliest recorded life insurance fraud, a case of pretended death, comes from England in the 1730s, where a father and daughter staged a succession of scenes in which the daughter appeared to convulse with heart spasms, then go limp in apparent death, while the father stood by in equally convincing grief. "Physicians were sent for in haste," one such instance was described, "and satisfied that life had fled, they took their fees, shook solemnly their powdered wigs, and departed."[24] The pair's success was great—they were said to have lived high in every city they visited, their house becoming a "resort for the young and thoughtless" who came to drink and gamble. But the source of this success has long been a subject of curiosity for insurance historians. "Either the woman possessed that power of simulating death of which we read occasional cases in the remarkable records of various times," John Francis reasoned in his *Annals, Anecdotes, and Legends of Life Assurance.* Or else the physicians had been bribed. Twenty-five years later, the coauthors of another book on life frauds would not explicitly endorse the bribery thesis, but they did cast serious doubt on the ability of anyone to simulate death so completely. They wrote: "Counterfeiting death by means of the hypnotic or cataleptic state, whether induced by mesmeric agency, or by recourse to anaesthetics or somnifacients which suspend sensation and motion, is so extremely rare that it need not be seriously considered as a factor in the machinations of the assailants of insurance companies."[25]

More common than such baroque pretended death plots was the simple "life speculation" fraud. Betting on the lives of people who were known to be uniquely imperiled, deathly sick, in chronic bad health, or who were simply famous had become so popular a sport in England during the eighteenth century that a statute prohibiting it was signed into law by George III in 1774. George III himself was well aware of the kind of wagering that the statute aimed to prevent. When his father, George II, fought at Dettingen in the War of Austrian Secession in the early 1740s, several life insurance companies sold policies on the likelihood of the king's safe return; those who bought the policies stood to gain twenty-five percent profit only if the king were killed or taken prisoner. "Sometimes the news arrived that he was taken prisoner and the underwriters waxed grave," John Francis later recorded in his *Annals*. "Sometimes it was rumored he had escaped, and they grew gay again. Thousands were ventured on his whereabouts, and tens of thousands on his head."[26]

Likewise, in 1770, London's *Public Advertiser* printed a notice intended for all those who had wagered on the death of another one of the royals: "We have the pleasure to assure the public . . . that the repeated accounts of her Royal Highness the Princess Dowager of Wales being very ill and her life in great danger are entirely false, such reports being only calculated to promote the shameful spirit of the gambling by insurance on lives."[27] For those public personages who actually were in the throes of fatal disease, however, the *London Chronicle* noted a few years earlier, life speculations came like a shove over a precipice. "When such persons cast an eye over a newspaper for amusement and saw their lives had been insured in the Alley at 90 per cent, they despaired of all hopes, and thus their dissolution was hastened."[28]

It was only a matter of time before life insurance speculators exhausted the limited stock of aristocrats and public people and turned to regular folks. In 1765, for example, a boatload of German immigrants in search of work arrived in England, then were abandoned by the person who had transported them. More than 800 men, women, and children camped in Goodman's Fields outside of London with no food reserves. Within days, some of the Germans, weakened by exposure to cold, hunger, disappointment, and, increasingly, emotional desperation, died. In west London, it was later reported, "considerable feeling was exhibited for these unhappy creatures . . . but, indubitably the greatest interest was felt by those operators in the Alley and underwriters of Lloyd's Coffee-house, who had made contracts on their distresses, and speculated on their deaths."[29] A relief effort for the Germans ultimately ended this particular line of speculation, but others like it flourished.

Speculation on the lives of strangers continued well into the nineteenth century, despite statutes prohibiting it. In the 1840s, for example, weekly insurance auctions were held at London's Royal Exchange in which buyers bid for policies of old men who were unable to pay their premiums. It was thought to be a good deal all around. The old men would get some cash while they were still alive, and the highest bidder would come into the full benefits of their policies if they were cooperative enough to expire within the agreed-upon term of insurance. Uncooperative old folks, of course, often were helped to a more timely death by impatient policyholders looking for a quick return on their investments. "[The lure of] life insurance money . . . stands as a constant bribe to inhumanity," A.C. Campbell once observed, "and that bribe has been taken by varied villains to commit the very blackest of crimes. The cases cited, if they stood alone, would mean nothing. My contention is that these are but the mountain-peaks of crime which indicate a slowly rising continent of evil."[30]

In order to learn the extent of speculations on human life in England during the 1850s, Henry Mayhew, an English journalist and social commentator, visited the offices of the thirteen largest London life insurers. At the first office, no specific cases of speculation were mentioned. It was generally acknowledged, however, that beneficiaries often acted to help end the lives of insureds. "Insured persons were encouraged to dissipation, and the means of procuring drink were constantly placed within their reach," Mayhew was told, "and there had been cases of men whose lives were insured, who had then been *urged to ride steeple chases* by persons to whom their policies had been assigned."[31] Several of the insurance officers also tried to impress on Mayhew their belief in the importance of the race or nationality of the participants in these life insurance frauds. At the third office, they spoke of the "Irish cases"; at the fourth office, it was the "German cases"; and, at the eleventh, the manager told Mayhew that "the German Jews in Frankfort had now learned the trick of insuring failing lives." One magazine account of Mayhew's researches—reported under the provocative title "Does a Man Shorten His Life by Insuring It?"—closed with a call for information about the experience of American life insurers: "Can anyone give us the facts?" the editors of *Hunt's Merchant's* magazine asked. In 1878 two American insurance examiners, John C. Lewis, the former Civil War surgeon, and Charles Bombaugh, provided the beginnings of an answer. The sheer bulk of their book on "remarkable stratagems and conspiracies" to defraud life insurers surprised many who were unaware of the extent of such activity across the Atlantic. A few decades after its first publication, the book would have to be "revised and enlarged" to begin to document a story with which Europeans had no experience: the rise of the accident fakers.

The earliest modern insurance crimes were initially the sport of the wealthy. Only shipowners, not captains or crewmen, owned the marine insurance policies that could be abused through scuttling. And only the lives of the high born were deemed valuable enough to insure, making them, or those who pretended to be like them, the only ones with an opportunity to profit through fraud. The early crimes of these wealthy policyholders had a rarefied air about them. Scuttling schemes were often elaborately planned, with secret deals between shipowners and shipmasters culminating in high-seas intrigue. And many of the early life frauds were enacted dramatically with all of the plot twistings of a drawing-room mystery. With time, marine and life insurance schemes became more routine, more "business like" and "systematised," A.C. Campbell observed. Ornate scuttling conspiracies gave way to the everyday fact of the "coffin ships." In the realm of life frauds, opportunities for people of moderate income to make profitable insurance wagers began with organized betting on the royals, then, over time, devolved into speculation on the lives of folk like themselves.

In America, the democratization of insurance crimes from parlor sport to back-alley dealing was less a matter of centuries than decades. While Edward Loose's lips were sinking ships one at a time for shipowners, accounts of American ship scuttling described a "clique or fraternity of plunderers" based in New Orleans whose business was "bilging by boring."[32] American scuttling cliques—"wrecking crews"—were said to be doing essentially what the Europeans were doing, only on a mass scale from the start. Old ships were bought cheap, then repaired superficially to get insurance and loaded with dummy cargo. "The rest of the adventure is easily described," one account stated. "The vessel sails, is burnt, scuttled, or otherwise cast away." This same account spoke of wreckers who stalked busy ports in Louisiana and Cuba "with a supply of doubloons to make bargains with needy or gambling captains, to get them 'to stop' upon some reef. . . . At this rate of progression, it will not be long before these wreckers will have their agents in New York and elsewhere, with cash in hand, ready to make contracts at 'reasonable rates' for the greater perfection and advancement of their system."[33] In 1853 a half-dozen such American wreckers were found guilty of conspiring to burn and sink the steamboat *Martha Washington* on the Mississippi River. The case was a rare prosecution of the wrecking cliques, who were frustratingly elusive. Their sentence proved light by European standards, however: The men were ordered to serve ten years at hard labor.[34]

Early life speculation frauds in America did not concern the fate of royals or their colonial equivalents but seemed to be concentrated from the beginning on the lives of the low born. In one typical case, the owner of a variety theater in Philadelphia, a Mr. Robert Fox, insured the life of John Clark Lee, a doorkeeper and distributor of playbills. Lee was a good bet to die young. He had been a drunkard and a journeyman, tramping for fifteen years between New York, Washington, and Philadelphia. Investigators with the Penn Mutual Insurance Company later uncovered the full story: "Lee had been an habitual hard drinker; a man of notoriously dissipated habits; a man whose employments had been those of keeping bar and distributing theater bills."[35] To conceal years of Lee's hard living from the insurance examiners, Fox had taken the man to Turkish baths for steam treatments and facials, sobered him up, then bought him a suit of new clothes. After the insurance was effected, though, Fox reintroduced Clark to the bottle and made sure that he was not without a drink until death finally ensued. When confronted with this information by the president of Penn Mutual, Fox adamantly refused to allow the policy to be canceled retroactively or to admit guilt in Lee's death. After years of wrangling in the courts, Fox was finally forced to abandon his claim, but he was never prosecuted for causing Lee's death.

Over time, speculative life insurance frauds in the United States crept ever closer toward outright murder—first of the extraordinary variety, with famous isolated cases similar to those in early England, then, increasingly near the turn of the twentieth century, more businesslike and systematic frauds. Of the extraordinary type of cases, late nineteenth-century America had more than its share. The second part of Lewis and Bombaugh's *Stratagems and Conspiracies*—a section numbering some 300 pages entitled "Homicide, Poisoning, and More Violent Forms of Assassination"—is filled with the records of famous cases. The authors offer a sprinkling of sordid tales: "Angie Stewart, The Murdered Child," "Katharine Ging, the Dupe and Victim of Harry Hayward," and, "Meyer, With Many Aliases," a twisted tale of a repeat murderer from New York.

One story from 1873—"The Wichita Monsters, Winner and McNutt"—tells how A.N. Winner, a house contractor in his thirties, hatched a plan to make $5,000 by first insuring his friend J.W. McNutt, then staging a fire in which McNutt would be said to have perished. For the scheme to work, Winner and McNutt needed a body to use in the fraud, a stand-in for McNutt. At trial, McNutt, a thirty-one-year-old painter who had known Winner for just a few months at the time of the crime (and who had been urged by his wife to stay away from Winner), offered a full confession. McNutt told how he and Winner used the promise of a job to lure their victim, a man named Sevier, to Wichita from Kansas City; then he told how Sevier was murdered. One night Winner and McNutt got Sevier drunk on brandy. "When Sevier was so thoroughly unconscious that he could do nothing," McNutt explained, "we were prepared to do the bloody work which Winner's hands itched to perform." McNutt continued with the macabre details of the act:

> Winner poured down Sevier's throat about a pint of ether which he had
> brought from Kansas City. We then placed his head in an iron pot filled
> with benzene, and set fire to it. We watched him as his head began to

simmer and crackle like burning meat, but as he was unconscious, I do not think he felt any pain. When his features were burned and disfigured beyond recognition we laid him on the bed which was saturated and dripping with oil.[36]

After the murder, Winner and McNutt tried to arrange their carpentry shop in such a way as to make it look as if they had been violently attacked by robbers. They extracted blood from Sevier's body and smeared it over Winner. The story was to be that Winner had escaped the robbery attempt but that bandits had killed McNutt and burned the shop, the truth of which was to be vouchsafed with Sevier's body. Although McNutt ultimately stood trial for the murder of Sevier, Winner was never caught.

Just one year before Winner and McNutt's scheme in Wichita, a man in Delaware known as the "Professor" had attempted to stage a similar death in order to claim the insurance he had taken out on his own life. In carrying out his plan, Professor Isaac C. West Jr., tenured only in his own mind, left investigators a box containing the charred remains of a man's body that lacked a head, hands, or feet. Presumably the remains in the box were to be understood as those of the Professor himself following an accidental explosion in his laboratory. But closer inspection revealed that the limbs had been sawed off, not ripped by explosion. It was soon suspected that West, who had been experimenting with ways to remove pigment from the skin, had killed his assistant, a black man named Henry Turner, then prepared the body to look like his own in order to collect on his $25,000 life insurance policy.

After a failed escape by train, Professor West surrendered to police and confessed. Initially he claimed that Turner had tried to rob him and that, in defending himself, he had accidentally killed Turner and left him in his basement overnight. The next day the Professor tried to get rid of the body. "I thought I would cut Turner in pieces and bury him," West stated. "So I cut off his head, hands, and feet with my penknife. . . . I cut off his head and feet . . . and skinned the body. . . . I broke one of the blades cutting the bones."[37] West continued, for some reason, trying to remember how much of this he had done before eating dinner that night. In the process of sorting out the chronology, he recalled that, during the afternoon, he had borrowed a horse and carriage to take Turner's remains away for burial, but the horse spooked at the smell of Turner's skin, which the Professor carried in an old bucket. West allegedly spent the rest of that day early in December 1872 trying to bury parts of Turner around town, but his task was made more difficult by the unyielding, frozen ground.

At trial, West's claim to have accidentally murdered Turner was seriously called into question. In the months before the incident, it was shown, West had been sizing up someone else for the fraud—one Frederick Windolph, a tailor with a build similar to his own. Windolph told the court how he had resisted two attempts to be drawn into the Professor's "laboratory." After Windolph's testimony, West's defense lawyer tried to change his client's plea to one of insanity. Then, when this defense seemed to be failing, the attorney resorted to playing on popular racial prejudice, which might excuse the murder of a black by a white. The jury found Professor West not guilty of the murder of Henry Turner on the grounds of self-defense. West was convicted only of arson and was sentenced to two years in prison.

In a trial of a similar crime that took place around the same time, William Udderzook of nearby Baltimore would not get off so easily. More than half of Lewis and Bombaugh's section on insurance homicides is devoted to "The Goss-Udderzook Tragedy"—an affair that began with a newspaper notice announcing the death of Winfield Scott Goss on February 3, 1872.[38] In the months before his apparent death, Goss, an inventor like Professor West, had been experimenting with making a cheap substitute for India rubber, and had rented a house on the York Road outside of Baltimore in which to conduct experiments. It was here that Goss was said to have been burned to death by an exploding kerosene lamp. Suspecting fraud, however—was it just coincidence that Goss had closed his savings account and executed his will just days prior?—insurers resisted settlement.

In January 1873, almost a year after the alleged fire, lawyers for each of the three companies that together had written policies worth $25,000 on Goss's life called for an exhumation of the body. On the afternoon of February 10 the burned remains of a man taken to be W. S. Goss were dug out of five feet of soft clay in the Baltimore Cemetery; the next day an autopsy was performed. The coroner's report concentrated on the severely decayed and missing teeth of the exhumed body; they were not at all like the excellent teeth Goss was said to have flashed often in a broad, gleaming smile. Mrs. Goss herself had testified to insurers that her husband's teeth were "quite regular" and "not artificial"—certainly not as awful as the corpse's—although she was distinctly unwilling to provide details. The inconsistencies over the teeth were serious enough to force a trial.

As the trial began in May 1873, Eliza Goss's prospects for collecting on her husband's death did not look good. Not only did an endless stream of witnesses testify to the strikingly good quality of W. S. Goss's teeth, but other testimony was starting to reveal a different theory of "Goss's" death: It was not

Goss at all who was burned in the fire and exhumed a year later; rather, it was a corpse that had been obtained from a medical supplier, then was placed in the house before it was set aflame. Of the availability of corpses, one medical professor testified that "there is an almost unlimited supply of them." ("You can get them for $15 to $20 apiece, any quantity of them," the witness added.)[39] In further support of this theory, a coworker of Udderzook's later testified that a large, unmarked box measuring more than five feet in length had been delivered to Udderzook on the morning of the fire. None of these witnesses was seen by the jury, however—the evidence had been deemed inadmissible on legal grounds—and, on June 6, Eliza Goss was awarded the full $25,000 with interest. The insurers immediately filed for a new trial. More to the point, they let Udderzook know that they were going to begin an intensive search for the real W. S. Goss, whom they were certain was still alive. The insurers were right about Goss, of course, and, when they began to circulate photographs of Goss throughout the United States and Canada, Udderzook panicked. He realized that Goss, a lifelong drunk, might soon become careless in concealing his whereabouts. The original scheme would have to be changed: Goss would now have to be killed for real.

Late in June 1873, William Udderzook checked into a small hotel in Chester County, Pennsylvania, near where he was born and where his parents still lived. He was accompanied by an unnamed man. Udderzook ate supper that night and breakfast the next morning in the hotel's main dining room; his friend, whom he described as "an invalid," remained upstairs in the room. In the early evening of July 1, Udderzook left the hotel with his friend in a rented horse and buggy. When he returned at around midnight, he was alone. Ten days later a farmer passing through the Baer's Woods, a few miles from the hotel, noticed buzzards circling in a field; he then followed a foul stench to the place where body parts lay covered by a thin layer of earth, leaves, and tree branches. A representative of the local coroner's office was brought to the site. "The Deputy Coroner had the covering removed," according to court records, "and it was then seen that the legs and arms were off . . . that part of the abdomen was open . . . and the entrails had disappeared. In another part of the woods, about sixty-five feet distant, the arms and legs were found, also under a slight covering of earth and leaves."[40] An autopsy revealed that the man, soon identified as the real W. S. Goss, had been stabbed repeatedly with a knife or screwdriver.

For most of the year and a half since his feigned death, Goss had been hiding in Newark, New Jersey, under the name A. C. Wilson. By the summer of 1873, however, his brother, his wife, and his brother-in-law had found him to be a loose end in their life insurance scheme. Udderzook took Goss to the woods in Pennsylvania and killed him; he then began a leisurely return to Baltimore by way of his parents' home. In mid-July William Udderzook was arrested for the murder of W. S. Goss. The following year he was tried in a Pennsylvania court; on November 12, 1874, he was hanged. On the scaffold, Udderzook said nothing of his guilt or innocence, according to a later account by Lewis and Bombaugh, "nor did he appear disconcerted to any noticeable extent."

Herman Webster Mudgett, a trained doctor with a medical degree from the University of Michigan, surpassed all previous American insurance murderers in numbers of killings, gruesomeness of method, and total monetary gain. Mudgett, who operated under the name H. H. Holmes, began his career in insurance murder during the early 1880s with the well-established technique of palming-off a cadaver as an insured, then collecting the money. Some fifteen years later, Holmes confessed to having killed twenty-seven people, including men, women, and at least one young child, whom he had asphyxiated in a locked trunk. Some of Holmes's victims had been dismembered and buried in basements in rented houses around the Midwest and Canada. Some had been incinerated in Holmes' man-size kiln. Dr. Holmes "articulated" some victims' skeletons, then sold them to teaching hospitals. His most recent biographer labeled him "America's first serial killer."[41]

Not all of Holmes's murders were committed for insurance profit. Some victims were murdered to eliminate witnesses to earlier crimes; other murders seemed to have been motivated primarily by Holmes's peculiar psychopathology. (Holmes locked one of his victims in a specially constructed asphyxiation vault in his Chicago "Castle," for instance, then sat in a chair nearby listening to the woman's desperate pleas for help while masturbating into a shirt.) Holmes's career began and ended with life insurance schemes, however, and included many insurance plots along the way. Early in the 1880s, Holmes tried the well-established life fraud of palming-off a cadaver from a medical college as an insured, then collecting the money.[42] Although Holmes was reportedly unsuccessful in his first attempted fraud, his obsession with wealth and his facility with taking human life sustained him in his next attempts. In 1886 he killed Dr. Robert Leacock of Baltimore, whom he described as "a friend and former schoolmate" who Holmes insured for "a large sum."[43] During the following decade Holmes established himself as a pharmacist in Chicago. He hired several personal secretaries, made them mistresses, then had a number of them insured before killing them by asphyxiation, starvation, or poisoning. Holmes was finally caught attempting to defraud a Philadelphia insurer of $10,000 written on the life of one of his associates, Benjamin Pitezel.

Like Goss and Udderzook twenty years earlier, Holmes and Pitezel had conspired to insure Pitezel's life, stage his death, then split the money; but, as in the earlier case, the plan led to murder. Benjamin Pitezel, like W. S. Goss before him, had been a heavy drinker, and Holmes counted on this for the working of his scheme. After Pitezel had set himself up in Philadelphia as a patent clerk named Perry and insured his own life in the summer of 1894, Holmes journeyed north from St. Louis to meet him. "Then came the waiting from day to day until I should be sure of finding Pitezel in a drunken stupor at midday," Holmes later stated in a chillingly well-reasoned exposition of his crime. "After thus preparing, I went to Pitezel's house, quietly unlocked the door, and stole noiselessly within and to the second-story room, where I found him insensibly drunk, as I had expected." The murder plan was proceeding apace until "one difficulty" presented itself. Holmes explained:

> It was necessary for me to kill him in such a manner that no struggle or movement of his body should occur . . . I overcame this difficulty by first binding him hand and foot, and having done this I proceeded to burn him alive by saturating his clothing and his face with benzene and igniting it with a match. So horrible was this torture that in writing of it, I have been tempted to attribute his death to some more humane means—not with a wish to spare myself, but because I fear that it will not be believed that one could be so heartless and depraved.[44]

Holmes's capture in 1895 resulted from an extensive investigation which was initiated by insurance investigator William Gary, continued by Philadelphia detective Frank Geyer, and aided crucially by Marion Hedgepath, a famous train robber who had once shared a cell with Holmes in St. Louis. In October 1895, Holmes's trial began; it was, in a word, "sensational." Newspapers in Philadelphia, New York, and elsewhere around the country recorded everything that occurred in the courtroom, especially after Holmes dismissed his lawyers and set about representing himself. That year a replica of the "Holmes Castle" became the featured attraction at C. A. Bradenburgh's Dime Museum on Ninth and Arch streets in Philadelphia. Several books about Holmes were published, not the least popular of which was *Holmes' Own Story*, "penned by the fiend himself" while he awaited trial in the summer of 1895. In the end, only the evidence pertaining to the insurance plot on Pitezel's life was admissible in court; but this was more than enough to get a conviction. In November

1895 a Philadelphia jury found Holmes guilty. The jury reportedly reached a guilty verdict before the door to the deliberation room closed behind them, but decided to take their free dinners before announcing their decision.[45]

In May 1896, H. H. Holmes was hanged. He was said to have been "cool to the end," just as William Udderzook had been twenty years earlier.[46] Holmes's body was placed in a pine box and laid in a grave ten feet deep; then, according to his explicit instructions, his coffin was encased in a ton of cement. It was the last wish of a man who, as a teenager, had ransacked burial grounds and sold the corpses to medical schools: He wanted to be sure that his body would be safe from grave robbers for all time.

At the same time many viewed H. H. Holmes in horror, increasing numbers of Americans were easing their way into life insurance murder themselves, impelled less by bizarre psychopathology than by a combination of common avarice and economic depression. The progress from pretended death schemes to murder was perhaps no more common in the United States than in Europe; it was, however, often accomplished in the New World with more mob brutality than individual twisty-mustached panache.

Early in the 1880s, several counties near Philadelphia experienced what Lewis and Bombaugh termed "a graveyard epidemic" of insuring lives, then actively encouraging death.

> The disclosures of this scandalous roguery showed that in some cases paupers were insured to the amount of $60,000 or $80,000; that drunkards were insured for large sums, and then supplied with rum enough to kill them; that dying men and women were passed as good risks by collusive agents and examiners, and the policies were "put on the market" by desperate gamblers anxious to realize money before the call upon the undertaker; in brief, that the worst forms of wagering in the history of insurance were carried to an extent never before attempted. Whenever the doomed wretches lingered for an inconvenient length of time, they were in danger of assassination by the impatient vampires. As no insurable interest was required, no one's life was safe.[47]

One life made unsafe by life insurance speculators was that of Joseph Raber, a frail old man from rural Lebanon County, Pennsylvania. A half dozen of Raber's neighbors—men who had been lumberjacks and coal miners prior to the depression of the 1890s—sensed that the old man was on his way out and decided to effect $30,000 insurance on his life. "On completing their arrangements," according to Lewis and Bombaugh, "they decoyed old man Raber to a plank over a small and narrow stream not more than twenty inches deep, tripped him over into the water, and then jumped upon him and pressed him down until he was drowned."[48] Investigation into the incident revealed the conspiracy on Raber's life had been carried out by Henry Wise, Israel Brandt, Isaiah Hummel, Charles Drews, Frank Stechler, and George Zechman. At trial, Drews and Stechler broke down and confessed to the murder. In the end, all of the conspirators were found guilty of the murder of Joseph Raber and all but one was executed.

In Pottstown, Pennsylvania, a similar scheme was disclosed in the early 1890s; it reportedly grew out of a conversation that now reads like a neat, motivational sales talk on murder for profit: "Do you want to put yourself on your feet?" the ringleaders put the question to one individual. "I'd like to, if I only knew how," was the reply. "I'll tell you how," the ringleaders continued. "There's old man Richardson; he'll die soon; he can't last three months, anyhow. Now, if you want a $2,000 policy on him I'll let you have it. Make up your mind soon, for the old man is as likely to go off in a couple of days as in three months." These sales pitches were often followed by letters like this one, which Lewis and Bombaugh later reprinted:

> Dear—
> I have just got old Mr. and Mrs.— insured. He is 74, and she is 73. Will you join me in paying assessments? If you will, write me immediately . . . The old lady will never go out of doors again.[49]

In most of the Pennsylvania cases the ringleaders were agents working for insurance cooperative societies—"death rattle cooperatives," as they soon became known—which were supposed to be nonprofit life insurance bodies for moderate—and low-income people. Soon, however, these societies became nothing more than a way to pool the money of poor people in order to redistribute it among the boards of directors. Death rattle cooperatives were active not only in Pennsylvania, but also in Maryland, Ohio, Indiana, and Massachusetts. The cooperatives were largely run by thieves, not insurance men—"the professional confidence operators, bunco men, sawdust swindlers, and the fraternity of adventurers generally" who "appeared to have discovered that the assessment insurance game paid better than any other at the time." They would not have been successful, however, if their agents had not been able to entice ordinary townsfolk to take out policies on the heads of the aged, the dying, and the stupid. As Lewis and Bombaugh later phrased it: "The infection rendered the public dumb to the enormity and the baneful and corrupting influence of schemes in furtherance of which all classes—merchants, mechanics, farmers, professional men—held wagering policies; and frauds of the most outrageous character were conducted and encouraged as warrantable matter of speculation."[50]

By the end of the 1880s, the Pennsylvania attorney general's office alone had taken action against more than 200 death rattle cooperatives: According to one newspaper account of the prosecutions, the "ghouls" who had organized this "cold-blooded and disgraceful traffic in human life had been driven into "exile." But not for long. In October 1894 word of the reemergence of the cooperatives issued from the hills of Beaufort, North Carolina. A "desperado" named C. R. Hassell, along with a man named Levi Noe and two brothers with the last name Delamar, had started an insurance agency in Beaufort and promptly hired locals to get names of all of the oldest and sickest people in the area. Yet another Delamar brother was a local doctor. He not only provided the names of "the lame, the halt, the blind, and other first class risks," but he also provided the false medical documentation needed to secure insurance from real companies.[51]

The Delamar brothers' frauds constituted perhaps the greatest chapter in the history of the graveyard insurance cases, Lewis and Bombaugh concluded after reviewing the records of the case. They wrote: "It seems incredible that such a multitude of paupers could be insured for large sums, that so many negroes could be passed off as whites, and that intelligent invalids and cripples could be insured and used for speculative purposes without knowledge or suspicion."[52] The frauds continued until one Raleigh attorney organized a group of detectives to "unearth the roguery" of Hassell, Noe, and the Delamar brothers. At trial, Hassell was found guilty and sentenced to seven years at hard labor in the state penitentiary; Noe and the Delamar brothers each got two years in the Craven County jail and a $300 fine.

Fire insurance schemes, like those involving marine and life insurance, had deep roots in Europe. In the same year that George III signed legislation outlawing life insurance wagering, he also sought to end "mischiefs by fire" in London and Westminster. The 1774 statute was written "in order to deter and hinder ill-minded persons from willfully setting their house or houses, or other buildings, on fire, with a view of gaining to themselves the insurance money, whereby the lives and fortunes of many families may be lost or endangered."

As with the matter of loss of life at sea due to ship-knacking, the business of arson for profit was investigated by a Royal Commission in the late 1860s. At these hearings, one Sidney James Fletcher, a secretary with one of England's largest insurers, noted that, in his fifty-two years of experience, fire losses due to fraud had never been higher. Fletcher estimated that almost one-third of all London fires were intentional, mostly set by bankrupt shopkeepers. "Very often, when a fire was quickly extinguished," one fire adjuster told the commission, "the goods saved were found to be 'dummy' goods, while the naphtha-soaked floor, the piles of papers and other inflammable rubbish scattered about, evidently intended to help on the fire, bore mute but conclusive testimony to incendiarism." The final report of the Royal Commission, issued in 1867, mentioned the activities of "organised gangs of men who made a trade of it to defraud the insurance companies"; but no detailed accounts of such gangs appeared either in Europe or in America until news of the New York "firebugs" surfaced in the mid-1890s.

In early June 1895, Vernon Davis, a young lawyer with the New York District Attorney's office, held a press conference to announce that he had secured evidence "of the most startling character." Davis struggled to keep the details of the firebug gangs under his hat before the grand jury could issue indictments. "Let me just say that there has been evidence laid before me which points toward a firebug brotherhood—a thoroughly organized gang of scoundrels who made much money through their operations. I cannot give you the names now, as that might thwart the ends of justice, but you can depend upon it that by Thursday next I shall be able to unfold one of the greatest schemes ever attempted of that sort."[53] The next week the *New York Times* reported on four arrests that were "expected to uncover the criminal operations of what is said to be the largest gang of incendiaries that was ever at work in New York."[54] Among those taken into custody were members of the Zuker gang—Isaac, the leader, and his brother Abraham, as well as Morris Schoenholz and Abraham Krone, two of the Zukers' arson "mechanics." During the year to follow, Vernon Davis, working closely with city Fire Marshall James Mitchell, would also take action against a number of other major firebugs, including the Herschkopf gang (essentially Adolph Herschkopf and his chief mechanic Max Glueckman), and the Grauer gang, led by insurance adjusters Max Grauer and Samuel Milch, who were said to have controlled "an organized gang of assassins and incendiaries, who had their agents, mercenaries, and firebugs all over the city." Other lesser lights included a number of textile manufacturers who torched their factories and at least one seventy-year-old woman, Mrs. Mary Leddy, who was accused of setting her clothing store on fire for $1,000 insurance (an act that almost got her lynched by the people who lived in adjacent buildings when they found out about it).[55] In all, the New York firebugs of the late 1880s and early 1890s were said to have been responsible for many dozens of fires, yielding an estimated $500,000 to $700,000 in insurance money.

Of all the firebug gangs, Isaac Zuker's was said to have been the most destructive, due mainly to Zuker's partnership with Schoenholz, the arson mechanic. Described by one reporter as "one of the worst firebugs in the country," Schoenholz was a mechanic with a long résumé. Under cross-examination by the famous trial attorney William Howe, Schoenholz recalled just a handful of fires he had set, then asked to consult his arson notebook to be sure. "You keep a memorandum book of your fires?" Howe asked Schoenholz, who replied that he started one in jail. Schoenholz then named four additional fires, all in Brooklyn.[56] "Is that all?" Howe asked. When Schoenholz said that he believed that was all, Howe pressed further, reminding Schoenholz of another case. ("Oh yes, that's so also," Schoenholz admitted with a grin.) "And the fire at Broadway and Great Jones Street in August 1894?" Howe pressed again, forcing a further admission from Schoenholz: "I had forgotten that one also."

Morris Schoenholz was the first major firebug to be convicted. His cooperation with prosecutors became key to convicting several others. At the trial of Isaac Zuker, Schoenholz discussed in fascinating detail how Zuker hired him to torch a storefront on Division Street in Lower Manhattan in January 1892. Zuker had made most of the preparations for the fire himself (moving furniture to a safe house, obtaining flammable liquids, gathering rags), aided by a man named Max Blum, who lived in the property next to the store. The day of the blaze Zuker paid Schoenholz to light the match. "I first had a talk with Zuker about the fire in August, 1891," Schoenholz began. "[Zuker] explained that the Board of Health had condemned his house in Division Street, and said that he had had it insured and was going to start a store in it and then burn it up." Schoenholz then described how the fire was set on January 4, 1892:

> Zuker cut a hole through the wall to Blum's house and pulled a curtain through the hole and saturated it with benzene. Then he poured benzene over the floors and over a lot of clothing scattered around. He fixed a candle on a box in one of the rooms. Around the candle was a rag saturated with benzene and a trail of cloth leading to various parts of the room. A string was tied to the candle and run out through a hole in the wall to the hallway. At 9 o'clock at night I went into the house, and, after lighting the candle, went into the hallway and pulled the string, tipping the candle over. I walked out of the building and saw Bernstein, a nephew

of Zuker's, standing on the corner. The fire broke out in a few minutes, and I stayed about until it was put out. I saw Zuker three days later. He paid me $25 for setting the fire.[57]

Schoenholz was not the only one to finger Zuker as the leader of the gang. Gustav Meyer, another arson mechanic who was once a clerk at one of Zuker's dry goods' stores, testified that Zuker had told him of a plan to set a fire in Newark to be coordinated with the fire set by Schoenholz on Division Street. "[Zuker] talked about the Newark place, and said he had put a 'dummy' named Sulzer in the place to get the insurance and run the store until the time came to burn it," Meyer said. "I asked him why he had to put Sulzer in there, and Zuker said that he had to because Fire Marshall Mitchell had blackened his name with all the insurance companies."[58] On the night of the Division Street fire, Meyer saw Zuker carrying a three-gallon tank of alcohol. When Meyer asked him what he planned to do with it, Zuker reminded him of their earlier discussion. "I am going to do that job," Zuker said. Late that night, Meyer and Zuker met at the corner of Ridge and Division Streets and watched Blum's house burn. "I am afraid that fire is not burning right," Zuker allegedly said with disgust. "Schoenholz didn't do a good job." On the strength of the testimony by Meyer, Schoenholz, and a parade of others, Isaac Zuker, a man who had come to New York from Russia some twenty-five years earlier and had achieved good success as a manufacturer of shoes and clothing, was found guilty of arson. Even the famous criminal defense lawyers Howe and Abraham Hummel could not prevent Zuker's sentence of thirty-six years at hard labor at Sing Sing Prison.[59]

At the time of the highly publicized arrests and convictions of Zuker, Schoenholz, and the others, New Yorkers were already well aware of the firebugs. For years the major newspapers in Manhattan and Brooklyn had featured stories such as "PROFESSORS OF INCENDIARISM" (a shirt manufacturer hires a firebug to light his store to buy new sewing machines)[60]; "THEIR BUSINESS TO BURN" (evidence of "wholesale burning" by arsonists, struggling property owners, policemen bribed to look the other way, insurance adjusters on the take)[61]; and "A STRANGE STORY OF ARSON—A Major Manufacturer Charged with Firing His Factory."[62] One story of an attempt to burn a tenement building during the summer of 1894 was published in the *Times* under the headline "PRICE OF 100 LIVES $2,500—Broome Street House Set on Fire While Tenants Slept."[63] In the article, the tenement was described as a five-story brick building "of the usual type," meaning that it was poorly built of cheap pine wood and was dreadfully overcrowded, with over 100 persons ("poor Germans and Hebrews") sleeping in the structure on the night of the arson attempt. "A fire panic at night in a tenement" was "by no means among the rare experiences in New York," according to journalist Jacob Riis's account from the 1890s." Riis continued: "The surging, half-smothered crowds on stairs and fire escapes, the frantic mothers and crying children, the wild struggle to save the little that is their all, is a horror that has few parallels in human experience."[64] This particular fire had begun in the ground-floor saloon, which had been purchased by a struggling immigrant businessman six weeks earlier, then quickly insured. Fire investigators found small fires in different parts of the saloon and still others in the cellar. Rags soaked in kerosene had been stuffed underneath the wood planks in the cellar and trails of burning paper led from one fire source to another. It was believed that the fire had been set by the owner of the saloon in order to cash in on a $2,500 policy, although the beneficiary of this policy was never found or tried for the attempt.

When a similar incident took place that same summer neither the residents of the targeted tenement nor the firebugs fared as well. On May 31, 1894, at 4:30 in the morning, a fire was intentionally started in Solomon Kleinrock's saloon located in the ground floor of a tenement house at 129 Suffolk Street. Earlier in the year Adolph Herschkopf—one of the leading New York firebugs—had prevailed upon Kleinrock to fully insure the contents of his saloon, then to burn the place down. Soon thereafter, Herschkopf approached Max Glueckman, a Russian-born shoemaker turned arson mechanic, about starting a fire in Kleinrock's saloon at night. Glueckman initially refused to do the job because there were children asleep in the building; he agreed only after Herschkopf raised his price to $50 and insisted that the job be done that night.[65] The fire in Kleinrock's saloon was not the first fire for any of these men. Max Glueckman later told of a number of other fires he set, including the burning of a factory owned by a wealthy shirt manufacturer named Louis Gordon. ("I went to the factory and Gordon and I made the arrangements," Glueckman said of the process of laying muslin strips on the floor and soaking them in kerosene. "I told [Gordon] I could not light the candle on account of the oil on my clothes. He said he would do it and help me, as I was alone.")[66] For his part, Adolph Herschkopf, known on the Lower East Side as the King of the Firebugs, was later shown to have propositioned many shopkeepers to "make a nice pile of money" by torching their stores.

According to Assistant District Attorney Vernon Davis, Adolph Herschkopf "was the mastermind of the group; his brain formed the plan that others carried out; he grew rich on the proceeds of burnings; he and his confederates were hard, ruthless men, who were indifferent to the loss of a life now and then if it put a few hundreds into their pockets."[67] The one such life whose loss most shocked and outraged the prosecutor and the public was that of four-year-old Lizzie Jaeger, who died of burns in her tenement apartment above Solomon Kleinrock's saloon in May 1894. The morning after the fire, Herschkopf's wife was seen crying, scolding her husband for setting the fire, an act that she later said she quickly realized only her husband could have committed. Herschkopf later boasted of the Suffolk Street fire while trying to convince another shop owner to join him in an arson fraud. "You see that burned out building over there?" Herschkopf allegedly asked the man, pointing to the former site of Kleinrock's saloon. "I did that job and we made money. Now we can have a fire in your place and make money also."[68] The appeal was heartless but effective. The man made $50 from the burning of his shop.

In July 1896, Adolph Herschkopf was found guilty of first-degree murder in the death of Lizzie Jaeger. Upon hearing the verdict, Herschkopf sprang from his seat and declared his innocence. He was particularly upset with Max Glueckman and the others who he claimed had sworn his life away to save their own; and he felt betrayed by Vernon Davis of the D.A.'s office whom he had helped by luring Glueckman back from Germany, on the false pretense of needing a mechanic for a fire, so Davis could arrest him when he stepped off the steamship *Rhynland* in New York.[69] Finished with his tirade, one newspaper account stated, "Herschkopf then sat down, pale and panting from the excess of his passion." He was sentenced to life imprisonment without parole.[70]

In all, during the years 1892 to 1897, more than two dozen members of New York firebug gangs had been tried and convicted, earning an aggregate of over 350 years in prison terms. Some gangs operated only in Manhattan or Brooklyn, others traveled to New Jersey or Long Island, and one led by Simon Rosenbaum traveled as far as Boston. At times, prosecutors called Rosenbaum "the shrewdest firebug in the country"; at other times they tried get him to admit he was "Poritz" Rosenbaum, the Hebrew equivalent of a Mafia don.[71] Rosenbaum was typical of the firebug leaders—a forty-year-old Jewish immigrant from Russia. And his "gang" was comprised of some fairly representative characters: a mechanic named Louis Rothman who took care of the torching and an insurance man Max Grauer (who had his own gang) to get the right kind of coverage. Rosenbaum also worked with two female arson mechanics—Mrs. Sarah Silbermeister, who helped Rothman burn a tailor shop, and Mrs. Ida Lieberman, who engineered the burning of a tenement. Silbermeister was sentenced to ten more years than Rothman by a judge who saw the middle-age mother as an integral part of "a gang of the most dangerous crowd of firebugs that has ever existed in this country."[72] Ida Lieberman was sentenced on the same day as Max Grauer. With his eleven children (all girls) standing behind him, Grauer was impassive at his sentence of thirty years at hard labor; Mrs. Lieberman, by contrast, "swayed for a moment, her face turned ashen," then threw "both hands in the air and dropped in a swoon."[73]

Unfortunately for young children living in the tenements of Lower Manhattan during the 1890s, firebug plots were not the only insurance crimes that could be hazardous to their health. Another one was called "baby-farming," and it was made possible by a special line of insurance written on the lives of small children. The very idea of child insurance was highly controversial when it was first introduced in America during the mid-1870s; child advocates, religious leaders, and even some in the insurance industry vigorously campaigned against it as an inducement to "neglectual infanticide." In 1881 an editorial in the New York *Insurance Monitor* stated: "There are thousands in our great cities, steeped in degradation, and ready to traffic in their offspring as if they were horses and goats."[74] A New Jersey newspaper from the time denounced child insurance as a "dangerous incentive to murder." [75]

Jacob Riis, the famous chronicler of life on the Lower East Side of New York in the late nineteenth century, discussed "baby farms" in his 1890 classic, *How the Other Half Lives*. Citing a report by the Society of Prevention of Cruelty to Children written in 1885, Riis offered a definition of the practice: "Baby farms are concerns by means of which persons . . . eke out a living by taking two, or three, or four babies to board . . . outcasts or illegitimate children. They feed them on sour milk, and give them paregoric to keep them quiet, until they died, when they get some young medical man without experience to sign a certificate to the Board of Health."[76] The certificate is then used to submit to the insurer for the $15 or $20 in benefits per child, a handsome profit on policies that had been purchased for just pennies a day. At a hearing on the legality of child insurance held in Massachusetts during the mid-1890s, companies that wrote the coverage were accused of joining poor or mercenary parents in "feathering their own nests at the cost of blood and tears and deaths of human beings."[77]

As with ship scuttling, speculative life insurance schemes, and arson for profit, baby-farming had its roots in Europe: In the 1840s, for instance, baby-farming was vividly described by British political philosopher Thomas Carlyle. "At Stockport, a Mother and Father are arraigned and found guilty of poisoning three of their children to defraud a 'burial society' of some 3 £'s due on the death of each child," he began. "They are arraigned, found guilty, and the official authorities, it is whispered, hint that perhaps the case is not solitary, that perhaps you had better not probe farther into that department of things." Carlyle continued:

This is in the autumn of 1841; the crime itself is of the previous year or season. . . . Such instances are like the highest mountain apex emerged into view, under which lies a whole mountain region and land, not yet emerged. A human Mother and Father had said to themselves, What shall we do to escape starvation? We are deep sunk here, in our dark cellar, and help is so far . . . So the Stockport Mother and Father think and hint: Our poor little starveling Tom, who cries all day for victuals, who will see only evil and not good in this world: if he were out of misery at once; he well dead, and the rest of us perhaps kept alive? It is thought, and hinted; at last it is done.[78]

In subsequent years, the English would probe deeper into the matter. In 1874 a Parliamentary Commission addressed itself to the matter of killing children for insurance, convening hearings that ultimately resulted in the passage of a law to limit the amount of burial benefits paid on the deaths of young children and to mandate that the money be given directly to the undertaker. At the hearings, compelling testimony was heard from a Liverpool coroner who had not "the slightest doubt in the world that an immense amount of parental neglect of a most scandalous character goes on from day to day" with the collection of burial club money as its objective.[79] Further testimony came from a British doctor whose report on baby-farming was read into the record. "In conducting an investigation into the prevalence of baby-farming in Glasgow and in Scotland generally," the doctor wrote, "I came across one case of a baby-farmer who was in the habit of adopting children at a low rate and entering them in a burial society, paying a half-penny or penny per week for them during their life, and when, at the end of the six months or a year, they died by neglect or ill-usage, he pocketed the benefit."

Of this and other accounts of baby-farming, A. C. Campbell was terse in his condemnation: "Here is a trade for ghouls."[80] Other writers based in New York, and apparently unaware of the European roots of the crime, were more specific in their denunciations of both the baby farmers and the firebugs. Both became the objects of a very special kind of derision reserved for foreigners believed to be "importing" new forms of vice to American shores in the 1890s. In an editorial entitled "Our Foreign Criminals" published in July 1896, for instance, the *New York Times* used the occasion of the sentencing of Adolph Herschkopf, the "King of the Firebugs," to remark on the strangeness of the immigrants from Eastern Europe. Burning property for insurance money, when "regarded as a trade," the editorialists wrote, is "alien and remote from any standards or customs with which we are familiar . . . it is of foreign origin and recent importation. In the series of trials of which this is the latest, however, it has been shown that among a part of our foreign population it is a trade as clearly recognized and apparently as much esteemed as any other."[81] The trial of Adolph Herschkopf was typical of the firebug cases. In an editorial that followed the conviction of arsonist Louis Gordon earlier in 1896, the *Times* had characterized the forty-year-old Russian Jew as a "disgrace to his race" in addition to being "an enemy to society" and "a creature for whom a prison cell is the only proper place."[82] And following the sentencing of Isaac Zuker, the most reviled of the firebugs, the *Times* proposed that insurance companies refuse to underwrite the property of immigrants living in the tenements of Lower Manhattan.[83]

The *Times* was not alone in making the arson-for-profit cases of the 1890s a measure of the human indecency of the Jewish immigrants. Editorialists for the New York *Insurance Monitor* referred to the firebugs as "insurance Jews." In August 1895 they wrote: "The typical insurance Jew has no qualms about destroying property, and any incidental loss of life he puts down to the account of the fire, and shifts the burden from whatever semblance of a conscience he may have by considering that it was no part of his intent."[84] The *Monitor* went on to state that Jews had been quick to learn about more deliberate murder-for-profit schemes from the Gentiles. The term "firebug" itself was so synonymous with the Jews that the *Monitor* spoke of the new Jewish life insurance cheats as "lifebugs." But, if all of this was still too subtle a slur, the 1890s saw the coming into the language of another term—"Jewish lightning"—to describe the fortuitous and profitable fire for insurance. Attorney Frank Moss, in his 1897 book on New York, went beyond the mere use of such phrases when he commented on the firebugs who operated in "New Israel." He wrote straightforwardly of the arson schemes of Isaac Zuker as typical of what he saw as the inherent moral depravity of the Jews: "Many of the miserable Poles and Russians make a business of effecting insurance and then setting fire to their stores and homes, and defrauding the insurance companies, regardless of danger to human life."[85]

Moss and others seemed more obsessed with the idea of Jewish criminality and the need to find a basis for racial bias than they were students of the history of insurance crimes. Understood even in gloss, the record of hundreds of years of ship scuttlers, life speculators, arsonists, and baby farmers speaks as equally of ancient Greek shipmasters, British members of Parliament, French aristocrats, and rural Pennsylvania farmers as it does of Eastern European immigrants living in the Lower East Side of New York. On the heels of centuries of schemes to defraud insurers, however, a new kind of insurance cheat was about to stumble onto the scene. Unlike his European forbears in the business of beating underwriters, this insurance cheat would be unique to the United States—the product of a cultural and legal climate found nowhere else on earth.

Beginning the century as a con man, slipping and falling for spare change on rural railroads—beginning, really, as a clown whose exploits A.C. Campbell felt to be merely "a strange development of this humdrum life of ours"—the American accident faker would ultimately find himself at the center of a multi-billion-dollar criminal traffic in faked claims. Since A. C. Campbell's time, American accident fakers have slipped, tripped, fallen, flopped, feigned, fumbled, tumbled, jumped on, hopped off, scratched and clawed, crashed, collided, rammed, battered, beaten, and self-mutilated their way to a place of seriousness on the roster of concern of many big corporations (first the railroads, then the private insurers) and, later, of law enforcement groups at the local, state, and federal levels. All the while the fakers have carved out a strange place in American culture—somewhere between circus freaks and bank robbers, with a touch of the itinerant con man, the streetcorner hustler, the organized mobster, the salesman, the shill, and the entrepreneur thrown in for good measure.

The story of the rise of the accident fakers, and the larger making of a personal injury underworld in America, has been whispered down the lane of the twentieth century: an unrecorded oral history shared mainly by claims people; a steady production of news accounts never before collected. No longer mere clowns, however, the professional accident fakers have moved beyond folklore: They are now seen as the core of a problem whose measure is less to be found in the small change of five- and ten-dollar nuisance settlements than in the round numbers common to big business. Following a decades-long progression in insurance crimes—from the elaborate, often uniquely fiendish or clever plots of individuals or small groups to the more systematic, widespread, everyday business of "ship wrecking cliques," "death rattle cooperatives," and "firebug gangs"—the accident fakers, making principal use of the machines of an increasingly industrial age, would become the most progressive of all.

Where A. C. Campbell left off writing about insurance crimes at the turn of the century, the making of a personal injury underworld in America had just begun.

ORIGINS: NEW YORK (THROUGH THE 1940s)

CHAPTER 1

THE RISE (AND FREQUENT FALLS) OF THE AMERICAN ACCIDENT FAKER

You do not know that there is a profession of being run over, do you? But there is.

—"The Railroad Accident Man,"
New York Times, 1878

HE WAS THIRTY-TWO YEARS OLD, stood five foot six inches tall, and weighed about 150 pounds. He had brown eyes, a high forehead with a slight scar on the right side, and thin light hair that was graying at the temples. His upper front teeth were worn down very close to the gums or entirely missing, and his right forearm was tattooed with a likeness of a hand and a human heart. He told people that he lived in Calera, Alabama, and that he was a barber by trade. But it was not for his work as a barber that F. E. Caldwell would gain a reputation in railway claims offices around the country during the early 1920s.[1]

Warnings about Caldwell's activities were first circulated by J. S. O'Flynn, a claims agent with the Great Northern Railway Company. According to O'Flynn, Caldwell had extorted money from the Southern Pacific Railway Company in April of 1920. Six months later Caldwell struck the Great Northern line near Palestine, Texas. By February 1921, claims man O'Flynn had become sufficiently worried about Caldwell's activities to pen a letter of warning to his colleagues around the nation by way of the *Bulletin* of the American Railway Claims Association—the Bible of the profession, like the *Police Gazette* to the cop on the beat. In his letter, O'Flynn described Caldwell's appearance down to the scar on the forehead. He also made known that F. E. Caldwell sometimes operated under the aliases J. C. James and F. F. Lawley.

In describing the gap-toothed, sometime-barber Caldwell, J. S. O'Flynn might have used the words "train robber," "bandit," "stick-up man," "con artist," "cardsharper," "safecracker," or even "yegg," a term coined before the Civil War to describe a loosely organized order of railway tramps dedicated to all manner of crime against train lines, banks, and post offices. These kinds of crooks were most often associated with crime on the rails during the late nineteenth and early twentieth centuries. These were the usual suspects. Unfortunately, F. E. Caldwell did not fit any of these familiar categories. One phrase did happen to fit Caldwell just right, however—a phrase known only to a small but dedicated group of railwaymen whose business it was to track and capture professional personal injury fakers who traveled the nation's rails staging falls for money. Only in this highly specific context did the words make any sense. For, in the shorthand of the railway claims men, F. E. Caldwell was known as a "banana peel specialist." Or, as O'Flynn put it more precisely, a "banana peel specialist" with "some side lines."

The incident in Galveston, Texas, that O'Flynn pinned on Caldwell involved Caldwell's alleged slip on a banana peel while stepping down from a Southern Pacific train. Later in Palestine, Texas, Caldwell claimed to have slipped on a track bolt that had been lying on the train platform, no doubt one of the claims-faking "side lines" which O'Flynn mentioned in his letter. One week after this, on January 19, 1921, Caldwell was once again banana-peeling for money. Using the alias J. C. James—sounds almost like Jesse James, a true train robber, he might have thought—Caldwell attempted to earn a few dollars from a streetcar company in Texarkana, Texas, by representing himself to claims agents as someone who had slipped on a banana peel on one of the company's downtown trains.

In the first two instances, Caldwell's claims may have been doubted, but they were not denied, and the man was able to leave Galveston and Palestine with a few dollars in settlement money. By the time he reached Texarkana, however, Caldwell had encountered a claims agent for the Southwestern Gas and Electric Company, one W. E. Casey, who had read O'Flynn's earlier letter to the *Bulletin* and so was wise to Caldwell's ways. "On being confronted by Casey with the description contained in Mr. O'Flynn's circular letter," readers of the monthly *Bulletin* were informed later in 1921, "F. E. Caldwell fled North." And nothing more of Caldwell's career was reported.

For a time, this had been the business of F. E. Caldwell: to find the right moment during a train journey to take an old peel from his pocket, then to drop it unobtrusively ahead of him, pretend to slip on it, and later to haggle with railway claims men over the amount of money it would take to forget the whole thing. This kind of banana-peeling offered only minor risks: the physical danger of actually slipping and falling on the peel, and the financial gamble of going through the trouble of staging a fall, then not getting the money. There were also the twin risks of detection—the potentially career-ending humiliation of being found out by claims men, and the possibility of criminal prosecution. F. E. Caldwell was able to flee North before being exposed. Other banana-peelers would not be so lucky, and a few would actually do hard time in jail.

What seems most exceptional about Caldwell's story was how unexceptional it seemed to be; that is, how common it had become for men and women to earn a grifter's living and to achieve quasi-criminal notoriety for the otherwise comic move of pretending to slip on a banana peel. For several years beginning in the early 1920s, in fact, the *Bulletin* reported on a number of different banana-peelers like F. E. Caldwell who operated on rail lines around the nation. The heading chosen for Caldwell's entry, "Another Banana Peeler," referred to this significant subclass of railway injury fakers, and other entries in the *Bulletin* made similarly familiar references to the banana-peelers. Under the heading "Another Banana Peel Case," for example, came a report of the claims-faking activities of an unnamed woman who frequently "alleged that she met with an injury in one of the New York terminals as a result of slipping on a banana peel on the floor."[2] An earlier report named the banana-peeler in question—Mrs. Anna A. Strula, a boardinghouse keeper from Hazlet, New Jersey, who railway claims men dubbed "Banana Anna." Of the seventeen banana peel– related incidents ultimately linked to Banana Anna, the first occurred while Mrs. Strula was riding on a ferryboat operated by the Pennsylvania Railroad. Her last faked fall, a streetcar banana-peeling in 1912, sent her to a women's prison in New Jersey.[3]

It is not clear when banana peels were first transformed from fruit casings, or the occasional prankster's prop, into instruments of a peculiarly American brand of larceny. To be sure, the banana-peelers of the 1920s were not the first to use the peels. One of the earliest recorded outbreaks of banana-peeling for money actually dates from some thirty years earlier and involved not one but an entire family of fakers practiced in the peeler's art.

The Freeman family of Chicago was made up of a father, a mother, and seven children, five of them girls. For a time, the Freemans had worked as song-and-dance artists in second-rate music halls in cities from New York to Chicago. But in the early 1890s the family, especially the women, began working full time faking accidents on steam trains and street railroads.[4] The banana peel was the mainstay of their operation. In June 1894 Jennie Freeman, a teenager, claimed that she slipped on a banana peel that threw her off an Illinois Central train; in September of that same year, she blamed a banana peel for a fall on the Chicago City Railway. Shortly thereafter, a suspicious claims man checked his bureau's regional index cards on the Freemans. Finding more than enough entries to confirm his hunches, he sent circulars around the country asking for additional information on the family. The replies came pouring in. From Boston there were reports of a banana peel fall by Jennie Freeman in May 1894. Later in September, that "same old banana peel story" was used by another Freeman daughter, a "handsome girl" named Fannie, who made a claim against the New York, New Haven, and Hartford Railroad line. Fannie Freeman had also used the banana peel pretext a month earlier in a case against Boston's West End Street Railway Company, in which she claimed partial paralysis and a lack of bladder control as the result of her fall. The banana peel, along with the Freeman girls' theatrics, was usually worth a few hundred dollars in settlement money; sometimes the girls earned as much as $500 per fall.

The banana-peeling Freemans might never have been caught had it not been for Fannie Freeman's failed attempt at a $2,000 claim against the Chicago Rock Island and Pacific Railway on Christmas Eve of 1894. Prior to this, Fannie usually got through the medical examinations with a credible feigning of paralysis. ("When I stuck pins into her legs and feet and touched them with my hands she declared she could not feel any sensation," a doctor once reported to a Boston street railway company. "And I couldn't surprise her into painful expression.") But Fannie couldn't keep up the act all the time. In Chicago railroad detectives, determined to put an end to the Freemans' successful run, rented a room above the family's apartment and fashioned a peephole through the plaster of the girl's ceiling. "To see anything safely it was necessary to crawl under the carpet so that no light penetrated from above," the editors of *Railway Surgeon* magazine noted in 1895. "For five days and nights detectives and reporters for the [Chicago] *Tribune* watched the antics of the 'paralyzed' girl." The account continued:

> They have seen her take exercise by indulging in a hurdle race over all
> the chairs in the place; they have seen her dance more dances than some

people ever heard of, and they have seen her manufacture cold feet and other symptoms of paralysis for the doctors. Most of the Rock Islands' officials, detectives without end, and reporters and artists for the *Tribune* have looked through that hole.[5]

Assured of Fannie Freeman's fakery, the Rock Island detectives sent in two more of their doctors to reexamine her. The doctors tested the girl's muscles and reflexes and shoved needles into her flesh from feet to waist. Then one raised her leg in the air and Fannie, perhaps forgetting what she was supposed to do or, perhaps, improvising a new condition, left her leg in the air, astonishing everyone in the room. Minutes later, detectives eyeing the scene from the peephole above watched as the doctors left and mother Freeman burst into tears: She blamed Fannie for ruining everything, then she showed her daughter how a paralyzed leg should react to being raised in the air. "Mutual recriminations followed," it was later written, "and the mother, finally losing her temper, grabbed Fann[ie] by the hair, dragged the poor 'paralyzed' thing out of bed and pounded her vigorously."[6]

After the Freemans' capture and prosecution, the story of their banana-peeling exploits was written in the form of a pamphlet published by the same group of railway claims men who put out the *Bulletin*. There is no telling how many other banana-peel pamphlets circulated among claims men over the years, although a steady stream were published through the peak years of the 1920s, when the banana-peelers either were more numerous or merely better documented. "The banana peel and step-box artists and other injury faking specialists seem to be working overtime," observed claims man W. L. Alexander in the *Bulletin* in 1921. Alexander, a veteran with the Missouri, Kansas, and Texas Railway Company, seemed to have taken a special interest in the banana-peelers, collecting whatever accounts he could, cross-checking them for similarities, and charting them for trends. Alexander closed his letter with an offer of help to all those who would join him in tracking the activities of these banana-peel "crooks." "We maintain, as you probably know, quite an extensive file on such claimants," he wrote, "and I am anxious for it to be of service and benefit, not only to us, but to the other roads as well. I would like to convey to the other subscribers the fact that we will welcome their inquiries because their information prepares and fortifies us should the same claimant come our way."[7] The imagery was that of a war: on the one side, the railway claims men backed with the extensive resources of the largest corporations in the country; on the other, the professional fakers with their old fruit peels.

By the 1920s banana-peel specialists seemed to have become so common a presence on railroads that Smith R. Brittingham, the author of the definitive book on the railroad personal injury claims, included them as the foremost among five typical classes of accidents that claims men would have to investigate and settle. He writes: "Class A.—A passenger while en route leaves her seat in the passenger coach to obtain a drink of water from the water cooler at the end of the coach and alleges that she slipped on a fruit peel in the aisle of the coach, resulting in a broken hip.[8] Later the author recommends the following battery of questions to ensnare the fruit-peel scammer in her own lies: "Did the passenger carry lunch inclusive of fruit? Was fruit sold on train; if so, did peel correspond to that of fruit sold? Were other passengers eating fruit prior to accident? Could anyone attest to the appearance of peel on floor of car after accident?"

As ridiculous as this banana-peel protocol seems in print to the contemporary reader, it was very real to a banana-peeler named William Hoke three-quarters of a century earlier. Described in the *Bulletin* as a forty-nine-year-old "colored [man] of Louisville, Kentucky," Hoke once claimed to have slipped on a banana peel while a passenger on the Erie Railroad near Marion, Ohio. Under rigorous examination, however, Hoke was found to have been a fraud. The investigating claims man apparently pursued Brittingham's line of questioning and discovered a crucial fact: No fruit had been sold on the train. What's more, the claims man learned, "the banana peel, which was badly worn (apparently indicating its use in other accidents) had not been noticed prior to the accident either by any member of the train crew or by any of the passengers."[9] William Hoke went to jail.

Perhaps the most notorious banana-peel specialist ever documented was Frank Smith—a personal injury grifter who had operated under the aliases Charles Johnson, Charles Jackson, Charles Gotdemus, Walter Scott, and Victor Lamott. Born in Erie County, New York, Smith was the subject of a *New York Times* article published in January 1921 under the unlikely headline "EARNED HIS LIVING BY SLIPPING ON BANANA PEELS."[10] The story's lead attempted to be hard-boiled about the soft-boiled criminal Smith: "Banana peels, which Frank Smith of Philadelphia says have netted him 'easy money,' have today landed him in jail for six months."

The *Bulletin* published their own version of Frank Smith's story. The lead was that claim agent Thomas E. Babcock, of the Public Service Railway Company, had "brought to a close, temporarily at least, the joyful career of one of the most accomplished banana-peel artists the eastern section of the country has come in contact with for some time."[11] The *Bulletin* editors first provided a

FIGURE 1.1. Frank Smith, operating under his many aliases, was one of the nation's most wanted banana-peelers of the early part of this century. Pictured here in mug-shots from the Camden County Prison, Smith was captured in 1921 after a failed fake fall on a banana peel while riding a New Jersey streetcar.

description of Smith—thirty-five years old, "a negro, complexion medium dark, height 5 feet 6 3/4 inches, weight 152 1/2 pounds, scar on the top of his head at the right side and another on his left arm above the elbow." Then they detailed his various swindling successes, followed by a brief account of the one unsuccessful banana-peel incident that eventually landed Smith in New Jersey's Camden County Prison for six months.

Frank Smith's notoriety, and the degree to which he was pursued by claims men around the country, seemed inversely proportional to the sophistication of his methods. On one account, Smith was said to have made a living in the usual way, through the "simple process of slipping on an old banana peel, then exhibiting very shortly afterward to an innocent claim agent a recurrence of a hernial condition." To aid his case, Smith, like many of the other personal injury grifters, often claimed the urgency of his needing to leave town in order to speed the settlement of his claims. He liked to say that he was employed in the port of New York, naming fictitious boats of the White Star fleet, then asking for a quick cash settlement for his injuries before having to ship out. Sometimes Smith represented himself to claims men as a "cow-puncher" from 1710 Smith Street, Cheyenne, Wyoming. Using this pretense, he would plead the same necessity of settling quickly, in cash, before leaving for the West. Perhaps the key to Smith's success lay in the fact that he often worked with a partner named Clarence Hartshorne—"age 44, colored, small black mustache with the initials C.L.H. tattooed on his right arm." Hartshorne allegedly dropped the peels ahead of Smith on the train cars. Later in the claims process, Hartshorne offered himself to the investigating agent as an independent witness to Smith's falls. Convicted as Smith's accomplice, Hartshorne followed his former boss to a bunk in the Camden County jail.

The *Bulletin* editors seemed unusually proud to publish news of the capture of banana-peeler Frank Smith. It is perhaps the only time that the circular published a picture of a claims faker. Two views of Smith obtained from the Camden County Police records are presented. In one, Smith is wearing a button-down shirt under a faux fur-collared jacket. In the front view, a simple cab driver's style cap sits squarely on the man's head. Beneath the mug shots, his name is written along with his many aliases. It is difficult to look at these shots without wondering how Smith explained to his cellmates the reason for his incarceration, or, more intriguingly, how he first came to the notion of earning his living by slipping on banana peels. The *Bulletin* is silent on these points, however, and as with most stories on itinerant accident fakers, nothing further was recorded on Smith after his release from jail.

For a brief time in 1921, Frank Smith, the banana-peel specialist, had come into plain view in the black-and-white pages of the *Bulletin*. Then, just as surely as he arrived, he returned to the shadows—the poorly lit areas of rail stations, the rear of train cars, the margins of midwestern cities—where the business of faking personal injuries for money may once again have taken hold in his mind.

The American accident faker—of which the banana-peeler was only one of many different "specialists"—got his start in the last quarter of the nineteenth century. He began from the fact that real personal injury claims resulting from equally real, frequent, and sometimes horrible train wrecks were being settled by the railroads for real money, often cash. The American accident faker then stumbled upon the unlikely truth upon which his trade was founded: In typical nonserious accidents, it was difficult to tell real claims from feigned.

As a criminal type, the accident faker came onto the scene just as the Great Train Robbers—the Reno Brothers, the Daltons, Black Bart—were passing into legend. The accident faker came onto the American scene not with a bang-bang of gunfire but with a whimper, a simper, a moan, and a crying out about aches and pains suffered as the result of an alleged accident. He carried not a gun but perhaps a screwdriver to loosen the bolts on a train window (which he might later allege to have fallen on his arm); or perhaps a banana peel in his back pocket to occasion a fall. He wore no mask over his face, just a grimace, which all around him could easily interpret as the mark of the injured. He did nothing so dangerous, deeply criminal, or obvious as to blast open a safe for the prospect of the tens of thousands of dollars inside. Instead, he boarded a train at the station like every other passenger, then, at some point in the journey, faked an incident that might earn him five, ten, or twenty dollars in damage claim settlement money. He then slipped wordlessly out of town. By making himself pitiable and a nuisance, and by not asking for a great deal, the railway injury faker was the antithesis of the rough-riding gunman in his manner of thievery. He also distinguished himself from his gun-slinging forerunners in at least one other way: He was often a she.

Not much is known about the accident faker prior to the 1890s. A number of different pioneer accident insurance companies went bankrupt in the 1860s and early 1870s, according to some business historians, so besieged were they with fake claims; but no detailed accounts of the nature or type of frauds survives. One oddball account reported in the *New York Times* in 1881 provides a rare glimpse into the period: The article told of a husband-and-wife team who slipped and fell their way around the nation, amassing a small fortune in bogus claims. Their scheme was said to have been made possible by the wife's rare bone condition, which rendered her limbs susceptible to breakage at the slightest blow. In 1870 the woman, who is referred to only by her maiden name Baker, married a man named James G. Wheelright of Worcester, Massachusetts. The couple moved to Utica, New York, where Mr. Wheelright soon brought his wife down to the railway platform and had her break her leg on a broken plank. Wheelright then sued the railway company for $10,000. Ten days later he accepted $5,000 in an out-of-court settlement. Over the course of the next year, Mrs. Wheelright would break a leg in Pittsburgh and in Cincinnati, netting more than $20,000 for the two faked falls. Later in Chicago, the couple, operating under the name McGinniss, collected $8,000 for an alleged fall in a hotel courtyard. "By this time," the *Times* reported, "Mrs. Wheelright was willing to retire from the business, but her husband had set his heart on making $50,000, and, like a good wife, she consented to break some more bones."[12]

After a failed attempt to collect money from the City of St. Louis in March 1872, the couple planned a slip-and-fall stunt on the ice of a Canadian Railway platform in Detroit. Still $16,000 short of Mr. Wheelright's goal, however, the couple hatched the idea that the fragile Mrs. Wheelright, now "Mrs. Wilkins," would break both arms, netting $8,000 apiece, it was hoped.

Early one morning Mr. Wheelright took his wife out and had her fall on a patch of ice on Canadian Pacific property, where she successfully broke both arms. "Unfortunately, she fell more heavily than was necessary," it was later reported, "and, in addition to her arms, she broke her neck, and instantly expired." Unbowed by grief, Mr. Wheelright raised his demand on the Canadian Pacific to $25,000; he got all that he asked for, exceeding by $9,000 his overall accident faking goal of $50,000.

In 1878 a *Times* editorial made extensive mention of another early accident faker who was said to have profited from a medical condition that rendered his bones brittle and easily breakable. "The least jar, the merest concussion, a car wheel rolling over a pebble . . . he lives on it," a railway claims agent reportedly said. "This wretched creature is always on the go and has cost the different companies in the country, to my certain knowledge a half million dollars in the last ten years," the claims man continued.

> The wretch is married, has a family, and is bringing up that family, who have inherited his cursed wine-glass stem bones. . . . They can, one and all of them, break a bone at shorter notice than any other human beings in this world, and we have to pay for it. . . . If my advice would be taken, I would sacrifice a whole railroad train to him, and once completely annihilated, we might be safe. . . . The wiles, cheats, and impositions put on us are terrible.[13]

Even if such stories were wholly true—and this last one was almost surely intended as a satire of the railroad's notorious tightfistedness in paying claims—such accounts said little about professional accident faking in America before it grew in popularity during the 1890s. A few people with a rare bone disease or double joints or an ability to fake paralysis, in the manner of several "human pincushions" who were also reported on in this era, do not amount to a significant criminal or cultural phenomenon. What is significant about these stories is that they help fix the 1870s as the time in American history when the idea could be clearly articulated that a person, perhaps even a small band of people, actually might travel the country faking accidents for money. It was the idea that was novel, even if it was not actually carried out in these reported cases: Slipping on a fruit peel, pretending to have your elbow smashed by a train window, or claiming to have fallen out of an open train door made no sense as a money-making enterprise anywhere else on earth.

In an earlier age in Europe, people faked accidents and simulated injuries, but not on such a grand scale and not so profitably, as the later American accident faker. Some sixteenth century English beggars would pretend to be accident victims of one sort or another, or sufferers of disease in order to incite pity and to gain charity. Mendicants in Paris feigned blindness, deafness and dumbness, leprosy, epilepsy, and stained their skins to imitate jaundice. Female alms-seekers created the appearance of hideous breast cankers and loose intestines, using blood-soaked sponges and ox bowels; they also simulated the outward appearance of pregnancy with pillows. Impostures of an even uglier sort were recorded in sixteenth century France by a surgeon named Ambroise Paré. He writes: "There have been some who have kidnapped little children and have broken their arms and legs, poked out their eyes, cut off their tongues, pressed upon and caved in their chests, saying that lightning bruised them thus when . . . they themselves have done this to give them the appearance of beggars and to get a few pennies."[14]

More than 300 years before any banana-peelers or step-box artists pretended to slip and fall on an American steam train, a sneak thief named Nicholas Jennings earned his daily bread on the streets of Kent, England, by feigning "the falling sickness."[15] Jennings often presented himself in public areas naked from the waist up save for a tattered, sleeveless leather vest (a jerkin), which hung loose over his shoulders. His head was wrapped in a filthy cloth, and his face, from the eyes downward, was smeared with fresh blood, as if he had just suffered a terrible fall. When he felt he had a sufficient audience, Jennings would cry out about having been laid to waste by "his miserable disease." This was the man's claimed affliction: to suffer falls, chronically and uncontrollably, with the frequent danger of splitting his skull or bleeding to death from his wounds. (Paré later termed it "Saint John's Disease" and tried to describe for other doctors the way fakers often carried it out: "They wallow and plunge in the mire and put blood from some animals on their head, saying that in their thrashing about they have thus injured and bruised themselves; having fallen on the ground, they move their hands and legs about and bestir their whole body, and they put soap in their mouths to make themselves foam, just as epileptics do during their attack.")[16] The apparently injured Jennings carried a felt hat that he placed on the ground before him to receive alms and devotions.

Intrigued or, perhaps, irritated by the noise one morning, a county magistrate named Thomas Harmon called down to ask Jennings what ailed him. "I have the grievous and painful disease called the falling sickness," the man replied to Harmon, who was confined to his second story bedroom by a chronic ailment of his own. Jennings elaborated: "My name is Nicholas Jennings. I was born at Leicester; and I have had this falling sickness eight years, and I can get no remedy for the same; for I have it by kind. My father had it, and my friends before me; and I have been these two years here about London, and a year and a half in Bethlem hospital." When Harmon asked Jennings why the man was so mired in dirt and blood, Jennings explained that, owing to his disease, he had fallen down in the road and lain there all night, having bled almost all the blood out of his body. Harmon asked Jennings whether he would like to clean himself in a tub of fresh rainwater, but Jennings refused, saying that he feared he would only "bleed afresh again."

Harmon suspected that Nicholas Jennings was shamming his falling sickness. Apparently having little else to do with his time but to wonder with "marvelous perplexity" whether Jennings's condition was "feigned or truth," he sent a servant to check the rolls of Bethlem hospital to see if a Jennings with falling sickness had ever resided there. The answer was soon returned that Jennings had never been treated at Bethlem—a division of the awful Bedlam institution that offered a roof and dirt floor to the city's dispossessed poor, sick, old, insane and crippled. Harmon then instructed two boys to follow Jennings and to report on the crank's daily activities. After some searching, the boys discovered Jennings behind an inn, where he was seen preparing for his day's begging activities:

> Jennings renewed his face again with fresh blood, which he carried about him in a bladder, and daubed on fresh dirt upon his jerkin, hat and hosen; and so came back again . . . and begged of all that passed by. The boys beheld how some gave groats [the equivalent of four pennies], some sixpence, some gave more. For Jennings looked so ugly and irksomely, that every one pitied his miserable case that beheld him.[17]

In 1567 Nicholas Jennings was arrested. The "counterfeit crank," as Harmon referred to anyone who feigned suffering for money, soon made a full confession of the ways in which he had long pretended the falling sickness in order to get money. He was pilloried in the village of Cheapside, then was whipped on the back of a cart that was dragged through London. Jennings lived the rest of his days at Bridewell, a house of correction and workhouse for the poor, where his "picture remaineth for a monument." Another memorial came in the form of several woodcut prints—one showing the tattered Jennings with the falling sickness, others showing him pilloried and locked in the stocks.

Whatever was worth memorializing in this counterfeit crank's money-getting practices was apparently worth repeating in another time and another place, centuries removed from the roguery of the Elizabethan underworld. In

Victorian England, for example, the "scaldrum dodge" was popular among professional beggars, who made a living by exhibiting wounds and sores, the fakery of which had become something of an art form in poorhouses. "One simple trick was to cover a patch of skin with a layer of soap and apply strong vinegar, so that what appeared to be large, yellow, matter-filled blisters formed," British historian Kellow Chesney writes. "Another trick was to hide a lump of raw meat under an elaborate clotted dressing." He continues:

> Even beggars with genuine mutilation found that a bit of artifice helped, and before starting work they would touch up the stumps of healed amputations so that they looked inflamed and purulent. Other poor wretches went to the lengths of searing and discolouring parts of themselves with gunpowder, or used vitriol to raise fresh sores and aggravate old ones. In the end, they must have produced a real injury by the means they used to fake one.[18]

At the same time, "cripple factories" and "invalid schools" were springing up in the Lower East Side of New York. Throughout the last quarter of the nineteenth century, mock cripples were supplied with fake harnesses and prostheses and swaths of bandages caked with dirt and fake blood, along with instructions for effective begging, in exchange for a percentage of the money they could collect. Increased competition among beggars in the 1870s led to panhandling specialties in deafness, dumbness, and blindness. "Crumb throwers" waited for the right time to dive at a piece of bread in the gutter, and "mock epileptics" made a living "chucking dummy fits" on heavily trafficked streets.[19]

The only group that may have had a longer record of faking accidents and injuries than beggars were soldiers looking to evade military service. Some soldiers actually combined their military dodge with the beggar's art. A pamphlet published in 1612 described men who posed as soldiers injured in battle, then knocked on people's doors to plead for charitable donations.[20] "Bestow your reward upon poor soldiers that are utterly maimed and spoiled in her Majesty's late wars," they would say as they exhibited their battle wounds while extending their hats for donations. These counterfeit soldiers were reported to have prepared themselves for begging by blistering their skin with a mixture of harsh lime soaps and iron rust aggravated by a piece of rough wood strapped to their arms by leather garters. "Then a linen cloth is applied to the raw blistered flesh, it sticks so fast, that, upon plucking it off, it bleeds," the seventeenth-century pamphleteer continued. "Blood is rubbed all over the arm, by which means, after it is well dried on, the arm appears black, and the sore raw and reddish, but white about the edges like an old wound. Thus, without weapon, do you see how our maundering counterfeit soldiers come maimed."

The full gamut of methods of military malingering were recorded by Dr. Hector Gavin in his 1843 study, *On Feigned and Factitious Diseases*. In this book, Gavin discusses everything from simple dodges to elaborate shams—from the excitation of an existing ulcer to the affectation of a limp, a stammer, a stutter, deafness, blindness, epilepsy, and uncontrollable contraction of the fingers. At the simple end of the spectrum, Gavin explains how soldiers would claim bowel pain for the purpose of evading service. ("This fraud is commonly easily detected by inspecting the soldier's linen," Gavin writes straightforwardly. "If [the man's underwear] be clean we may infer that the bowels are not much out of order.")[21] Gavin also cautions his readers about soldiers who simulate the "pustular eruptions" characteristic of smallpox. ("This imposition consists in puncturing the arms and breast with a needle, and then rubbing in bay-salt and gunpowder. . . . the impostor aids the deception by groaning very dismally during the night time.") Other more exotic feigned and factitious diseases common to malingering soldiers in the early nineteenth century included "ozoena" ("this affection is sometimes simulated by saturating a piece of sponge, or other substance, with some offensive juices, or oils, mixed with decayed cheese, and introducing the imbued substance into the nostrils"); and "foetid transpiration" ("nothing is more easy to simulate than this troublesome inconvenience by anointing the skin with the animal oil of Dippel, asafoetida, the remains of old cheese, or the oily grease from a cart or carriage wheel, or putrefying fish"). Gavin also describes the ever-popular "polypus of the nose" ("attempts have been made to simulate this affection in the nose by introducing the testes of a cock, or the kidneys of a rabbit into the nostril, and retaining them there by means of a small piece of a sponge, which is sometimes impregnated with foetid juices"). Hemorrhoids, of course, were commonly feigned in cavalry regiments ("the bladders of rats or small fish, partly introduced into the rectum, resemble piles so much as to have deceived observers"). Some other conditions described by Gavin—"animals in the stomach," "worms in the urine" (imitated by throwing vermicelli into the chamber pot), and "vicarious discharges of urine"—hardly needed much explanation.[22]

No manner of military malingering was as popular as the simple self-inflicted gunshot wound. The history gunshot wounds self-inflicted by soldiers looking to evade service is as old as the flintlock musket. In one outstanding case, a French author tells of an astounding number of hand wounds experienced by Napoleon's conscripts after several bloody battles fought with the

Germans in 1813. The emperor, suspecting that the unduly large number of wounds had been self-inflicted before reengagement with the enemy, ordered nearly 3,000 of these suspected *malingres* to be confined to a camp separate from the rest of the troops, where his top surgeon examined them. (Although it was widely believed that the wounds were self-inflicted, the surgeon reported to Napoleon that he could not conclusively distinguish real wounds from self-inflicted ones; this disappointed the emperor, who wanted to make an example of these men.) Gunpowder need not only be shot into a foot or hand from a gun; it could also be applied topically, as one chronicler of military malingering explained: "The ingenious Jack or Tommy chew[s] cordite or rub[s] gunpowder into self-inflicted wounds as a more drastic means of giving an air of verisimilitude to otherwise unconvincing symptoms."[23]

With the adoption of the first state workmen's compensation laws in Europe in the mid—to late nineteenth century, civilian malingerers looking to get paid for not working adopted many of the established methods of the military malingerer. Slow death at a mind-numbingly routine factory job could be as much incentive for self-inflicting wounds as the prospect of sudden death on the battlefield. Perhaps no man chronicled in greater detail the various stratagems of civilian malingerers than Sir John Collie, a British doctor who began practicing medicine in the 1890s. In his numerous books, Collie, like Gavin before him, instructed his readers on the different methods of injury simulation particular to his subjects. He detailed how atropine and eserine, drugs derived from the belladonna plant, could be splashed in the eyes of "the astute malingerer" to help simulate the wild eyes of the epileptic.[24] Collie also explained how the mucosal discharge characteristic of otorrhea, an ear disease, could be simulated by inserting butter, oil, or condensed milk into the inner ear;[25] how conjunctivitis might be "easily induced" by tobacco juice, snuff, or small grains of pepper embedded under the eyelids;[26] how abscesses and edema are commonly simulated through the injection of water, paraffin, and turpentine;[27] how a steady diet of picric acid might create the appearance of jaundice;[28] how egg albumen might be injected into the bladder to simulate nephritis;[29] and how sugar similarly injected could suggest diabetes.[30]

As for hemorrhaging from the bowel, the ears, and the mouth, Collie shares instances from his experience in which these symptoms also had been faked in order to prolong sick leave. "It is not difficult to cough up blood by pricking the tonsils," according to the doctor, who complained that "the public is obsessed with the idea that blood coming from the mouth is an indication of a very serious condition."[31] Neither was it difficult to simulate dysentery by producing hemorrhagic diarrhea through "enemas of saturated solution of alum followed by the introduction into the anus of pledgets of cotton steeped in emetic."[32] ("That a fellow human being would deliberately subject himself to such a degrading procedure for monetary gain," observed Collie, would surely be judged "improbable" by all "except those who are accustomed to dealing with fraud in all its contemptible forms.")[33] As for someone faking an accident for money, Collie had heard of a few cases. "Wounds may be self-inflicted for the purpose of extorting damages," he notes. "This is, however, rare."[34]

Collie liked to make surprise visits to the homes of suspected fakers. On one occasion, he was detained at the front door of one man for a "suspiciously long time." Once inside, Collie made sure to look under the man's dining-room table, which seemed to have been hastily covered with a tablecloth. There he found the clothes which the man evidently had just removed before dashing to his bed to play sick, and so ended the claim.[35] Successes like this led Collie to recommend a national system of "lay inspection" of suspected malingerers in which, he imagined, local deputies would be paid by the state to pay periodic surprise visits on their neighbors.

Surprise visits were the least of the tools Collie used to expose welfare malingerers; his physical exams were what really separated the just from the unjust claims. The doctor was especially successful in the way he dealt with the most common complaints of back pain. The "working-classes," he felt, are always counseled "when yer git 'urt, say it's yer back; the doctors can't never get round yer back."[36] Collie sought to reverse this perception by applying an antimalingering method he learned during his military days in the Royal Army Medical Corp (RAMC). "During wartime, when a case is without doubt diagnosed to be malingering," he explained, "there need be no compunction about the forcible application of a very strong faradic current." Several strong men were often required to hold the patient down during this type of treatment. "While the malingerer may stand one or two applications, he cannot stand the daily repetition, and so he quickly gets well."[37]

Collie developed a somewhat less harsh technique for use on civilians that involved an electric charge from a portable battery. He turned on his battery but blocked the flow of current to the calipers, which he attached to areas suspected malingerers claimed to be especially sensitive to pain. The patients, hearing the whir of the battery and anticipating the application of current, would cry out, effectively announcing themselves as frauds.[38] In an opposite type of case, a man claimed loss of all feeling in his lower back, and Collie had almost resigned himself to believing the man's allegations, "when I suddenly bethought me of my trusty friend, the faradic battery." Exploiting "the popular, but of course erroneous, idea that an electric current is not felt even in minor injuries of the spinal column," Collie applied a small voltage of current from his battery, which the man, one bedridden "A.T.," claimed not to have felt. 'The current was then made considerably stronger, and A.T. tried to bear it manfully," the doctor continued. "At last with a howl, he fell in a heap on the ground. There was no one in the room to sympathize, so he was told to get up and not make a fool of himself. It was explained that I now knew what was the matter with him, and that he was to go back to work at once."[39] Collie used similarly stern methods to expose faked deafness, and feigned insanity. Adapting another RAMC technique involving the "introduction of a few feet of India rubber tubing" into men's bladders through their penises, Collie also discovered cases of faked incontinence.[40]

Unlike the beggars who faked accidents, feigned disease, or inflicted wounds in order to elicit charitable contributions—or the malingering soldiers who did the same to evade military service, or the working classes in England who used fakery to get out of work—the American accident fakers were in it for profit from the start. This is not to imply that their means were entirely different, however; only their ends. Railway detectives were just as much on the lookout for "sham invalids" as Hector Gavin or John Collie.[41] And surprise visits and undercover surveillance was still thought to be the best prescription for the faker—be they military malingerers, welfare cheats, or America's new personal injury con men. As one New York doctor put it in 1898: "It matters not whether the malefactor . . . mutilates the body by horribly mangling it by crude and dangerous means, in order to avoid some unsatisfactory duty, or whether it be an individual . . . who feigns disease by simulation, or produces it artificially . . . for the purpose of claiming damages."[42] Another New York doctor writing around the same time thought the new insurance malingerers were even worse than the beggars or counterfeit soldiers of old. He called them "the most contemptible people on the earth," and he advocated a return to the whipping post as the best cure for what ailed them.[43]

One type of early accident faking for money in America popular during the depression years of the 1890s was nothing more than a civilian version of the old soldiers' gunshot-wound dodge. A bullet in the hand or foot could not only get you out of military service, it could also get you a few thousand dollars under the provisions of certain accident insurance policies which could be purchased for just a few cents. At a time when most discussions of insurance crimes tended to be about life, marine, or fire frauds, the gunshot cases became the first accident insurance scheme to merit serious attention. In the revised and enlarged edition of John B. Lewis and Charles Bombaugh's *Stratagems and*

Conspiracies to Defraud Life Insurance Companies, published in 1896, the authors, both surgeons with major American insurers, added a new chapter entitled "Self-Mutilation in Accident Insurance." In it, they documented the surprising phenomenon of self-injury for profit for the benefit of all those readers for whom "it may seem incredible that intentional, self-inflicted wounds, causing mutilation of the person or serious disablement, should ever occur."[44]

Lewis and Bombaugh opened their claims files to report on the striking number of gunshot accident frauds in the early 1890s. One case involved a man identified only as "R. Hicks" who wrote to the Travelers Insurance Company in 1893 to explain that he had suffered an accident while loading his revolver for a July 4th celebration. "While so engaged I dropped it accidentally and it was discharged," the twenty-two-year-old from Chicago wrote. "The ball entered my left hand and literally tore it to pieces, breaking three fingers also." Whatever suspicions sparked the investigation of Hicks's claim proved true: Within weeks, investigators discovered that Hicks had already settled claims with several other insurers over that shooting incident and that he had told different stories about how the accident occurred to each of them. When confronted with this fact, Hicks first stitched together a new story out of whole cloth, then decided to confess. "Completely overwhelmed with the hopelessness of the situation, and in his demoralization," Lewis and Bombaugh report, Hicks "admitted that the whole affair was not accidental at all, but was a scheme deliberately planned and carried out for the purpose of defrauding the insurance companies."[45] In the weeks that followed, Hicks submitted a sworn letter of confession that suggests the state of mind of the willing gunshot victim: "The idea of 'working' the insurance companies developed in my mind last winter," Hicks began. "As the scheme grew, and as I came to see by a careful study of what the policies covered, I recognized a chance to make what I had been looking for, namely 'big money' for myself by losing a hand accidentally, and so I increased my line of insurance accordingly to $20,000." Hicks continued:

> Had I been successful I would have collected $7,500 for the loss of my left hand. I was perfectly satisfied to part with it for that price, and I was disgusted when I found that the shot I had put through my hand had not hopelessly crushed it, and I did all I could to induce the surgeon who attended me to amputate it any way. . . . Now, please do not imagine me a fool, or insane, or a man who has acted hastily, for I have an active brain, a perfectly sound mind, and I gave many serious hours to the perfection of my scheme.[46]

Just a few months before Hicks shot himself for insurance money, the country had sunk into the worst economic depression in its history. In May 1893 the stock market suffered a minor collapse and a major railroad went bankrupt, causing a serious financial panic. That summer other banks and railroads failed. People throughout the country feared a hard currency shortage. Unemployment was estimated at close to twenty percent, and the nation's private and public relief mechanisms buckled under the overwhelming demands for help. "Soup kitchens and cheap or free lodging houses opened," writes social historian Michael Katz on the Depression of 1893 to 1897. "Newspapers created special relief funds and distributed food and fuel; and charity organization societies and settlement houses were pushed into the direct distribution of relief, with only cursory, minimal investigations [of the 'worthiness' of the recipients]."[47] Joseph Coxey's "army" of tens of thousands of unemployed workers marched from Massillon, Ohio, to Washington to protest the government's lack of attention to their plight. Conditions of social upheaval would not be matched until the time of the Great Depression.

The strains of this national economic depression seem certain to have influenced the trigger fingers of at least a few of the hundreds of people around the country who mutilated themselves to collect on accident insurance policies. Claims involving self-mutilation for profit came from an out-of-work carpenter in Pennsylvania, a "financially embarrassed" milkman in Detroit, and an unemployed teenager in Indianapolis. One desperate man from Lyons, New York, borrowed $1 from a friend to buy an accident insurance ticket, then, in the dark of a January evening, allowed his right foot and leg to be crushed by the wheels of a passing freight train. In the same manner—and apparently for the same reasons of dire economic need—a thirty-one-year-old Fulton, Kentucky, man claimed to have fallen under the smoking car of a train that he had intended to board. "In falling, I struck my head against the side of the car, rendering me unconscious for 20 to 30 seconds," the man originally told insurers. "When I regained consciousness, I began to push myself from under the coach and off the track, but before I could do so my left hand was caught by the train carriage three or four inches above the wrist, and crushed so badly as to require amputation, which was done about two hours after the accident occurred." The case proved to be a fraud, as did a similar gunshot claim from two years earlier involving a forty-two-year-old man from Hastings, Nebraska, who told insurers that he had fallen near a railroad crossing late at night. ("I tripped on the sidewalk, pitched forward, and in trying to save myself my left arm was crushed by wheels of a train then passing.") Although the Nebraska man had genuinely sacrificed his hand, he, like the others before him, was shown to have done it on purpose in order to get one-third of a $26,000 short-term accident insurance policy. Nebraska, in fact, was one of the centers of the national "epidemic" of such "cleverly planned self-shooting affairs," according to Lewis and Bombaugh.[48]

Most claims Lewis and Bombaugh cited involved the loss of a left hand by gunshot or by being run over by a train. Thirty-three left hands were lost over four years, according to the authors' count; only four of the more favored right hands were amputated during the same period. Just slightly less popular than the intentional loss of left hands were the losses of fingers and feet through odd circumstances at night with no witnesses present. One man, a "J.B." of Springfield, Massachusetts, hedged his bets by losing both his right hand and his left foot as the result of an alleged fall under a sleeper car at 2:30 A.M. in February 1895. "In some way, but just in what way I cannot tell, I was drawn under the trucks of the sleeper," the man claimed in a story that Lewis and Bombaugh quickly recognized as part of a larger fabrication. "The wheels of one or both sleepers passed over and crushed my right hand and left foot. The injuries which I received were so severe that it was necessary to amputate both my hand and foot, the hand being amputated a few inches above the wrist, and the foot a few inches above the ankle joint." Lewis and Bombaugh are compassionate relating J.B.'s story. Like many people in the mid-1890s, J.B. of Springfield, Massachusetts, had found himself knee deep in the sort of debt that he felt only thousands of dollars in insurance money could satisfy. "Whether the facts were as set forth by the insured or not, it was a terrible loss to him," they wrote. "And it is well to extend him the deepest commiseration and pity, without stopping to inquire too closely into causes and motives."

As late as the mid-1920s, railway surgeons such as Dr. Frederick Mosser of the Third Avenue Railway line in New York would complain of deliberate self-injury schemes and various feigned and factitious diseases to support accident claims. "The purposeful placing of the hand or foot under the wheels of cars is often resorted to," Mosser wrote, adding that, as during the 1890s, most of the wounds were to left hands. He later described the usual stratagems of civilian malingering he encountered in railroad hospitals: "Some have their teeth pulled out, some irritate the skin by various substances, which are sometimes injected under the skin to create abcesses. . . . Crutches, spectacles, strappings, trusses, bandages, freshly applied iodine, are frequently employed to give the appearance of disability."[49] Such schemes were not the norm, however. While some fakers continued in the tradition of the midwesterners of the 1890s, carrying out their morbid, desperate accident schemes—and actually sacrificing hands and feet in the process—the professional personal injury grifters continued their less dangerous simulations. The real fakers were in it for the long haul: they robbed with a banana peel or a rigged train window, not with a gunshot to their hands or feet.

The American accident faker who most occupied the time of railway claims men was a drifter, a career hustler, or a disgruntled railroad employee more than he was a farmer weighing the worth of his left foot against the probability of paying his bank mortgage. His closest criminal contemporaries were the "short-con" artists who first became a fixture in frontier boomtowns during Gold Rush days, making their money with cards, dice, or shells, on steam trains, in streets and saloons, and at fairs and circuses. "There were thousands upon thousands of these short-con workers plying the country in the late nineteenth century," according to author David Maurer.[50] Conning was a way of life for those good enough to last at it, but it was not a way to riches. Most short-conners, in fact, Maurer tells us, lived a hand-to-mouth existence.[51] And the pioneer personal injury grifters of the late nineteenth and early twentieth century were no exception.

Hundreds of accounts in the *Bulletin* underlined the hardscrabble life of the early personal injury fakers. In addition to the banana-peelers and the step-box artists, who faked accidents stepping on and off trains, many of the most successful claims grifters were "nature fakers"—freaks who tried to cash in on their genetic defects, bizarre medical conditions, unique physical capacities, or, in the case of many former railroad employees, preexisting injuries from real accidents. Maud Johnson was a highly successful nature faker active in the early part of this century. Her "chief feats" were said to lie in an ability to throw her shoulder or hip joints out of place and to hemorrhage at will. Finding a pretext in an unusual jerking or lurching of a train, Johnson would press a bottle against her third rib, somehow "causing an awful appearance and producing blood from her mouth."[52] She then would claim that the jerking of the train had caused her condition. For five or ten or twenty dollars, railway claims men could get rid of Johnson by settling her nuisance claims quickly in cash. Playing out this scenario hundreds of times over several years beginning in 1906, Maud Johnson—alias Edith Hayes, Grace Davis, and Kate Dean— reportedly collected damage money in excess of $32,000 from more than nineteen different railroads. Claims men around the country referred to her as the Queen of the Fakers.

Johnson was arrested in 1912. She was convicted of collecting money from the railroads under unlawful pretenses and sentenced to a five-year term in the State Penitentiary in Walla Walla, Washington. When she was released, Johnson reportedly began work as the manager of a traveling minstrel show that moved through small towns in the Pacific Northwest. It was hard for Johnson to stay off the personal injury grift, however. In 1922 a warning about Maud Johnson was published in the *Bulletin*: The Queen of the Fakers is "again at large in the Pacific coast section of the country" and she may attempt to "renew her old acquaintance with her railroad friends."

Persistent, reasonably clever, and often workmanlike, many of the early personal injury fakers did not specialize in any one particular type of accident so much as they made a virtue of variety. Under his various aliases, for instance, Walter Herman Kennedy was identified as the claimant in more than a dozen faked cases in 1922. He had portrayed himself as an "Ed Miller" who made a personal injury claim in Galveston, Texas. He had been "B. F. Smith," injured on a train in Pine Bluff, Arkansas; "R. W. Deason," who tripped and fell in Vicksburg, Mississippi; and "F. M. Huckleberry," who had a window fall on his elbow in Little Rock. He also had been "M. O. Truitt," who hurt his back in New Orleans, and "L. O. Peck" with a sprained wrist in La Fayette, Louisiana.[53] Ironically, Mr. Kennedy was undone under his real name on November 22, 1922 in Dallas; he was arrested then later sentenced to two years in the Texas State Penitentiary. After his release, Kennedy resumed his claims-faking ways. He swore to one railroad employee that he intended to make the railroads pay many times over for all the time he had lost making money on the rails while being confined.

As happened with each of the injury fakers caught by claims men, Kennedy's photograph was circulated to railroads nationwide on the back of an index card that described the extent of the faker's known activities. One of a number of indexing groups recorded the name of almost every person—not just the suspected frauds—involved in a personal injury claim handled by a major accident or health insurer or large transportation company. "We report the name of claimants in every suit, the name of every claimant whom we were suspicious about, and many we report simply because they are crooked," stated William Hooper regarding the policy of his indexing company, the Hooper-Holmes Bureau, established in the 1890s.[54] Urban street railroads organized their own regional index bureaus—first in Boston, then in New York, Philadelphia, Chicago, and the Twin Cities—but often debated at meetings about whether to merge with Hooper-Holmes to make good on their "cherished plan" of a giant national index bureau.[55]

Early on, claims men understood that the information contained on the index cards—physical descriptions, addresses, names of attorneys and doctors, "remarks" about the fakers' routines—would be their best tool. At a 1915 meeting of claim agents, J. J. Reynolds boasted his use of the Boston bureau's

403,000 cards (filed in a number of different ways in twenty-three cabinets) in "checkmating a professional claimant" named Nora Hogan. Reynolds also showed how his use of the cards exposed the claims-faking DeRosa, Spirinsky, Conroy, and Shaughnessy families. "The greatest contribution of claim departments towards unmasking the fakir in accident damage claims is simply the printed card," Reynolds told his colleagues. "The index bureaus are the great forts which guard the portals of the railway treasury [without which] the onward march of the accident fakir and repeater can scarce be stayed."[56] Claims man Cecil Rice of the Pittsburgh Railway Company put it his own way at an earlier claims meeting: "When Mr. Traumatic Claimant of Fakeville is confronted by the record of his previous claims in Malingerers Town and Buncoes Crossing, his surprise and change of home base should alone be worth working for."[57] The index cards on a select group of known slip-and-fall artists got a special circulation among the claims men. They would arrive by mail through the *Bulletin* and would be posted on the walls of railway claims offices, along with photographs of the suspected offenders—a private corporate version of the "Wanted" notices circulated to law enforcement agencies. At one point later in the century, the claims offices of the Chicago Rapid Transit Company were "done in the style of a rogues' gallery" to scare off lightweights in the faking trade. "We posted pictures on the walls of fakers who didn't get away with it and the inscription beneath detailed the unhappy fate that overtook them," claims man A. J. Graham later explained. "It was much better than having magazines in the lobby."[58]

So it was in 1923 that the *Bulletin* announced the "distribution of the cards" on Sam Chalakas, "a Greek, age 40, married, height 5 feet 5 inches, weight 145 pounds, smooth face, sallow complexion, might be taken for an Italian, dark hair, slightly gray, beady eyes."[59] Chalakas was said to have been "expert" at appearing to get his hand caught in a train door, a trick aided by an old injury that gave him the ability to turn out his elbow. Chalakas allegedly attempted to hurry settlements in his false claims on the pretext that he needed to rejoin his wife and children in Greece. The *Bulletin* advised claims men that "this gentleman is now active in Ohio and New Jersey." The index cards were also distributed on a brakeman named Elmer Knoll who reportedly had "a habit of sustaining fractures of the ribs and head injuries";[60] a knitting machine salesman named Clarence Hoffman ("Do you know Clarence Hoffman? Is particularly active in Missouri and Illinois. If he comes your way, wire Trevor Neilson, Claim Agent, East St. Louis Railway Co.");[61] and a Turk named Nicolas Chibisash ("we feel that this man is a professional claimant and that his case should be given the widest publicity possible among the railroads").[62]

Among the most widely reported styles of claim fakery featured in the *Bulletin* was the pretended crushing of a hand or arm by an allegedly broken train window. One particularly bold use of this "broken window pretense" was reported from Lubbock, Texas, and involved a faker named A. C. Castle. Described in the *Bulletin* as being "fifty years of age, chestnut hair (slightly gray and slightly bald on top), brown eyes, and bad teeth," Castle often claimed to have sustained injury to his left hand by reason of a broken window falling on it. On one particular occasion, a claims man checked into Castle's contention that the window in question had a defective latch. "Upon searching Castle," the claims man discovered, "there was found a small screw driver, carried in a special scabbard, which evidently was used by Castle in removing screws and locks from coach windows in order to make them defective."[63] Another practitioner of this scheme, a faker named George McMachin, was said to have worked the broken-window pretense on more than a dozen different occasions. "McMachin is an old offender and has defrauded the claim departments many times on account of his faked injuries," one claims man wrote in the *Bulletin*. "He has had an injury to his left elbow for several years, and his favorite method is to claim that a window fell and injured his left elbow while he was a passenger on a train."[64]

Female accident fakers often were said to be more successful than men, regardless of their particular specialty. In presiding over the trial of a faker named Ila May Boggs, one Los Angeles judge wrote: "The legal records of personal injury show instances of people (usually women) who go about the country here and there and other places under different names suing railroad companies and pretending injury which did not exist. Sometimes they are very clever and they are not found out for a long time."[65] Ila Boggs was one of these women; and so was Mrs. Emanuel Chichester, a twenty-seven-year-old homemaker from Brazil, who reportedly made a living by pretending to fall as she boarded streetcars. Nellie Cummings, one of the earlier women fakers, admitted to deliberately throwing herself from a train in Syracuse, New York, in 1904 and to having done much the same throughout New York State as well as other areas of the country, which she declined to name after her capture.[66] Yet another famous female faker, Betty Lewis—alias Elizabeth Linder, Alice Layton, Victoria Pugsley, and Mrs. Lincoln—was one of the most hotly pursued fakers in the country for a time in the early part of this century. In one instance, Lewis claimed to have fallen from a step-box while attempting to board train Number 23 of the Colorado & Southern Railway. As a result of this fall, Lewis alleged to have sustained a "badly bruised back and hip; strains of the ligaments of the right shoulder; dislocation of right thumb at both joints; and other minor bruises and internal injuries."[67] An investigation by claims man Frank Jones revealed a history of such injury claims, however. Lewis had recently brought personal injury actions against hotels and department stores in Kansas City and Des Moines, Iowa. Jones decided not to settle with the woman. When he announced this decision in the *Bulletin*, the hunt for Betty Lewis intensified.

Soon other claims men started to write of their encounters with Lewis. One revealed that, weeks before Lewis claimed the fall on the Number 23 train in Denver, he had found the woman lying in a heap on the floor of the ladies' rest room in the rail station at Colorado Springs. At that time, Lewis told claim agent H. C. Pribble that she had been seated in a rocking chair in the bathroom, when the rocker gave way beneath her, causing her to fall against a radiator. She also claimed to have been five months' pregnant at the time of the fall, hoping, as did many female fakers, that this would increase the amount of her settlement. Claims man Pribble described Lewis as a "woman of the heavy chubby type" who "is a nice appearing woman, has an intelligent countenance, and knows when to smile." (Pribble added the curious bit of detail that "her nose is straight and small rather than large.") Uncharmed, however, Pribble advised all claims men in the Southwest to watch for the woman's fakery; an earlier letter to the *Bulletin* warned claims men on the West Coast that Lewis might be headed their way. Ultimately, Betty Lewis was arrested in Albuquerque, New Mexico, by a special agent of the Santa Fe Railroad Company. She was taken to Colorado Springs, where she pled guilty to charges of obtaining money from the Santa Fe under false pretenses. That same day Betty Lewis was tried in the district court and sentenced to one to five years in the state penitentiary at Canon City, Colorado.

To read even a few issues of the *Bulletin* of the American Railway Claims Association is to come to share in the claims man's suspicions. It is to begin to understand his pessimistic view of human nature as a job requirement; to tolerate his bias against "beady-eyed" Italians and Greeks, "coloreds," and "Gypsies" as a twin product of 1920s xenophobia and uncritical passion for the eugenical ideals of racial difference then popular. One even comes to indulge the claims men in the few jokes, asides, and rhymes published under the heading "In a Lighter Vein."

The section of the *Bulletin* entitled "Claims of Doubtful Merit" tracked the fakers. Here it was revealed that Robert Alegretti of Chicago, "a poultry messenger," was said to be "getting into the claim-making habit," and that this very much concerned the Minneapolis and Sault Ste. Marie Railway Company.[68] Likewise, the New York Central Lines wrote to warn all Northeast claims men that Patrick Kinney, a brakeman, had confided in some of his friends that he was going to "pull" an accident.[69] Another caution came from the Kansas City Southern Railway Company: "We consider William L. Christenberry one of the smoothest frauds with whom we have ever dealt," the letter began, "and we feel sure he is now plying his vocation on some railroad under some alias." The notice about Christenberry continued with a description of the man whom claims agents were to watch for:

> He is about 5 feet 10 inches tall, slightly stooped, weighs about 170 pounds, has blue eyes, bushy eyebrows, auburn hair almost brown, thick lips, fairly red face. Has just under the corner of left eye a blue skin mark about the size of the end of a lead pencil, possibly a little smaller. Wears open-faced watch in upper left-hand vest pocket on closely-woven chain. X-Ray shows a dark spot on his right lung. He is of Irish descent and shows it.[70]

Since the Bulletin's first publication in 1890, hundreds, perhaps thousands, of banana-peelers, step-box artists, broken-window men, and nature fakers had been described in its pages. Leads were offered and details were pursued. Physical descriptions were rendered by claims men with the purposefulness and exactitude of natural scientists and, sometimes, with a poet's specificity of detail. The goal was to track the itinerant claims fakers across the country and, ultimately, to catch them. And the section of the Bulletin devoted to dubious claims had became one of the favorite tools of this trade. In 1927 author Smith Brittingham recommended it above all other reading matter for "studious use" by the railway claims agent looking to stay current on the literature of a profession which Brittingham believed was fast establishing itself as the equal of medicine, law, and theology.[71]

In fighting the fakers, claims men relied primarily on one another and on their monthly Bulletin; but they also enlisted the help of other departments within the railroad. Company surgeons and doctors were often the first to interview an accident victim and to report to the claims agent on the merits of the case. Although a great deal was written about how railway surgeons should retain their impartiality and not get involved in settling claims, many company surgeons assumed an active role as part of the team whose job it was to beat back the "social menace" of faked and exaggerated personal injury claims.[72]

In addition to the surgeons, claims men also relied on information developed by the railroad police—the "bulls," the "cinder dicks," and the Pinkertons, who collectively formed the largest private policing agency in the

FIGURE 1.2. An accident insurance claims office in San Antonio, Texas, in the 1890s. At offices like this around the country, railway claims men handled the routine business of matching injuries and deaths with dollar amounts. This is also where they tracked the professional accident fakers, reading their monthly *Bulletin*'s and communicating their suspicions and findings to other claims men nationwide. (Photograph courtesy of The Travelers.)

country during the last quarter of the nineteenth century. "As a rule, the railroad police see accidents," one claims man reminded his colleagues at a national claims conference held in 1901. "They know who else saw it, they get you the information, they place yourself and your claim agents in position to know who to see and go to for evidence."[73] Claims men would prepare a case by doing some background "condition work," which entailed talking to neighbors, employers, and coworkers about the plaintiff's condition before and after the alleged accident. ("This work must of necessity be done in houses and flats in close proximity to that occupied by the plaintiff in the case," instructed W. P. Christiansen of the Chicago Railways Co. in 1913. "It is therefore advisable to proceed quietly, and so far as possible, without being seen by the plaintiff, or his family.")[74] Then, if the case warranted it, a separate group of railroad detectives would take it from there. The detectives would do whatever was within their power to see the fakery firsthand. "Your plan must be to see him

serve," one manual of investigation advised. observed? In his own room probably or in any narily see. . . . Sometimes it will be necessary ear-by building and watch the faker until you you will be able to gain admittance as a book eter reader, or some other pretext in order to t."[75]

tically off the train lines—hoboes and tramps, hieves, train robbers, embezzling conductors nabbed by railroad "spotters," and, no doubt, personal injury fakers—feared and hated the railroad police and detectives. But it was the railway claims man who had a special adversarial relationship with the fakers. The claims man's professional identity was intimately bound to the existence of the fakers, like cops and robbers, cat and mouse. Without fakers to crusade against in the pages of the *Bulletin*, the claims man was just a functionary in an increasingly vast corporate bureaucracy; with them, the claims man not only had a job, he had moral purpose. The claims man and the lone-operating faker shared a history. Archenemies, they had grown up together during the late nineteenth and early twentieth centuries. They would also share a common fate. In subsequent decades, each would pass into obscurity as the automobile and the urban accident rings, respectively, pushed them to the margins of the nation's growing personal injury underworld.

While the original accident con game flourished on rural rails during the 1890s, a grander version was being played out on the nation's big cities. The cities offered a number of different targets for damage claims—interurban train lines, horse-drawn streetcars and stages, and electric or cable-drawn trolleys. Cities also offered a unique new target for larceny, a new mark, in the growing numbers of urban attorneys who represented low-income clients in personal injury actions. In a new twist on the old con, accident fakers would appear at attorneys' offices looking as victimized and injured as possible. Attorneys, excited by the thought of the settlement they would probably get from the case, would gladly give the grifter whatever "advance" money was requested, thus completing the con.

The business of conning claims men was often gymnastic, with tumbles and falls and staged incidents. The work of conning an attorney was essentially histrionic: Appearance and dialogue mattered most. Not to be confused with the banana-peel specialist Frank Smith, whose fakery was aimed at claims men, not personal injury lawyers, George Smith was described in the *New York Times* in June 1899: "His right leg was bruised and twisted; his right arm was as crooked as his character was subsequently found to be; he had four newly healed wounds distributed about his head; the index finger of his right hand was missing; he was minus several teeth, and he said his spine was badly sprained and twisted."[76]

According to the headline, George Smith was the "CRIPPLE WHO SUC-CESSFULLY FLEECED MANY CITY LAWYERS." As part of his "clever confidence game," Smith cultivated his appearance as a "a living demand for damages; a permanent hobbling, pitiful protest and testimony against the recklessness and cruelty of a heartless and giant corporation." Smith would enter attorneys' offices looking as bedraggled as possible and would proceed to tell his "plausible story" about "how he had been the victim of the Third Avenue Cable Car." Smith would then say that he wanted to file suit against the cable car company for $50,000 and that he was willing to split the settlement with any attorney who would help him. Having incited the attorney's greed, Smith would ask for his advance, then would leave the office with whatever he could get, having no intention of returning.

The cripple Smith's injury con game was not at all original. Five years earlier, in 1894, the *Times* had published another story, this time on the front page, under the headline "LAWYERS HIS VICTIMS."[77] The article promised to tell how John W. Maurer's "fictions brought him much money." Like Smith, Maurer visited his victims' offices at around 2 P.M. just after the attorneys had returned from lunch. When Maurer was shown in to see the lawyer, "his shoulders would be bent, his head and right hand would be done up in bandages," indicating "that he had been the victim of some horrible accident." He then would tell his "woe-begone" and "heartrending" tales of injuries that had been due to the negligence of Vanderbilt Railroads. "In every instance," the *Times* reported, "the victims signaled their willingness to take the case." Before leaving, lawyers gave Maurer money, "varying from $5 to $40 according to the size of his attorney's purse that day."

The extraordinary number of letters sent to the New York Central and Hudson River Railroads on behalf of John Maurer suggests just how many attorneys had become players in the personal injury game by the 1890s. All the letters were written in regard to an accident that had allegedly left Mr. Maurer seriously injured on August 28, 1894. In their appeals, each attorney restated the facts of the man's fall from a trolley car, as told to them by Maurer during their brief meeting; then each attorney asked that the company settle the case promptly without going to trial. Frank Loomis, the railway claims man investigating the case, collected these handwritten appeals for Maurer from attorneys Louis Lowenstein of 117 West Tenth Street, A. C. Barrett of 71 West Tenth Street, and Edward Krug of Park Row. The letters came to Loomis from the law offices of Wendell and Robeson of 280 Broadway and Kantrowitz and Esburg of 325 Broadway. Loomis also heard from Leopold W. Harburger of 25 First Street, Charles Schnick of 91 Second Avenue, George H. Hyde of 305 Broome Street, and August L. Martin of 30 Broad Street. One John Biddle Clark of 62 William Street was so concerned over the settlement of Maurer's case that he visited Loomis in person at the New York Central claims office. In all, more than a dozen attorneys contacted Loomis on Maurer's behalf.

One reporter commenting on the case took the fact that all the attorneys destroyed their files on Maurer (after Loomis informed them of the con) as a sign of their "chagrin at having been duped." If it was chagrin, however, it was not solely for having been duped. It was for thinking they were successfully playing one game—the new game of handling of high volumes of accident cases on a contingent fee basis—when, in fact, they were being taken by masters of the old fake-injury con.

George Smith and John Maurer aside, most personal injury grifters operating in big cities around the turn of the century victimized the traditional corporate targets with false damage claims. William J. Doran of Philadelphia, for example, concentrated on the streetcar companies. An ex-contortionist and circus tumbler, Doran allegedly knew how to appear to be struck by the trolleys while in fact escaping without injury. In April 1900, he began his accident career with a staged fall from a rapidly moving streetcar—a "mishap" that later brought him $60. In August of that same year Doran began to work his injury con with the help of an accomplice named Myers, who posed as a witness. At other times Doran worked with men named Ritner and Mutschler. "In each of these cases—and there were dozens I have not mentioned, Doran, after performing the acrobatic part of the task, assumed the name of his 'pal' [Myers] while the 'pal' went to bed as the injured person," explained a reporter for the New York Sun in 1902.[78] "This served two ends—Doran, as a witness, escaped arrest each time, and as a professional contortionist he was able to get out the next day and fall from another car . . . No amateur could possibly have undergone the pounding he stood for two years." On off days, Doran might have his wife stage a tumble while he and some friends acted as witnesses.

Not only was Doran an expert tumbler, he also was a good negotiator. Unfortunately, his scheme called for him to assume the role of the witness after the accident, leaving his accomplices to haggle with claims men. To remedy this logistical problem, Doran soon devised a system. "Doran made it a practice to hide himself in a corner, under the bed, from which point he would decide how 'easy' the traction official was, and coach his 'maimed' confederate by raps on the bedstead as to the amount of damages to be asked for."[79] Ultimately the system broke down. In September 1902, he was arrested and charged with the offbeat crime of "having time after time allowed himself to be run down by trolley cars in order to recover damages from the traction company." The next month he began serving a term of several years in a Pennsylvania prison.

Edward Pape was another accident faker who worked the personal injury grift in the traditional way on city streets around the turn of the century. Pape had a "most remarkable deformity"—a seemingly broken neck, according to a magazine account from 1906—"and [he] was not slow to avail himself of it as a money-making device far beyond the figures that might be quoted for him by circus sideshows or dime museums." The account continued:

> Pape can so alight from a trolley-car, slowing to a stop, that he will suddenly fall and go rolling toward the gutter. Instantly there is excitement, and a group of men to pick up the prostrate form of the injured man. He is found to be badly injured, and hurried to a hospital. There the interns discover that he has a fractured neck. A marvelous set of X-ray photographs are made, and the trolley company is usually willing to settle a good large cash sum rather than stand suit. Within a week after the money would be in Pape's hands he would be away and falling off a trolley-car in another city, under a different name, but precisely the same circumstances.[80]

During one particularly successful month, Pape pocketed $75,000 in damage claims against various streetcar companies. The man later recalled one instance in Philadelphia where he had been so convincing in his fake fall that the traction company insisted on hospitalizing him. "I'd just finished my fancy fall, and they got me into the sickhouse," Pape told a reporter. "They put hip-boots on me there in bed with their soles fastened to the footboard, and a rubber bandage under my chin and over my head. They put seventy-five pounds in weights on a cord and pulley-jigger to that bandage, and it nearly killed me all day long. At night I used to wait until it was dark, and then I'd haul the weights and put them under the blanket with me. Otherwise I don't know how I'd 'a got my sleep."

It was with men like Edward Pape, William Doran, and the "cripple" George Smith in mind that representatives from streetcar companies and other large concerns from Boston to Chicago met in the summer of 1905 to form the Alliance Against Accident Fraud. The purpose of the alliance was to share information about accident fakers and to catch them by pooling member companies' resources. The alliance members met in Muskoka Lakes, Canada, in July 1905 to hammer out their charter. They talked about "criminal fakirs" who set out deliberately to have an accident for money as well as the "injury fakirs or malingerers" who exaggerated legitimate accidents.[81] The malingerers were responsible for a lot of the most costly unseen fraud; the criminal fakers caused the most investigative headaches. "A professional accident swindler is hard to locate," it was agreed. "He may get himself knocked down by a trolley in New York this month and tumble conveniently into an open trench in Philadelphia next month; then, his athletic training having kept him immune from actual injury . . . he will threaten suit in both places and the companies will pay him, for their sheer inability to obtain competent evidence proving him a fraud."[82] With all of the accident insurers, streetcar companies, and other corporate interests working together, it was hoped, professional accident claimants would be stopped. If the fakers were going to organize, the logic ran, then so were the claims men. The hopeful mood was captured by a headline in the *New York Times* the day after the alliance formed: "ACCIDENT SWINDLERS TO HAVE POWERFUL FOE—Casualty and Street Railway Men Will Organize Against Them."[83]

To fight the accident swindlers, the alliance established its own "rogues' gallery" of known slip-and-fallers; it also began its own index bureau with 50,000 names consolidated from smaller indexes and organized into neat file drawers by Mrs. Gertrude Welling, the card curator. Detectives were hired to keep an eye on accident cases being tried in courts around the country and to report the names of attorneys who seemed to be full-timers in the accident trade. A committee was even appointed to submit to Congress a bill aimed at "this class of swindler."[84] The alliance was not exclusively concerned with the activities of fake claimants who operated on their own or with one or two accomplices. Of increasing importance to the member companies were the new classes of organized accident professionals—the "shyster lawyers, unprincipled physicians, ambulance chasers, and false witnesses"—who knew how to play the accident game and to win. These accident specialists did not have banana peels in their back pockets; they had law degrees on the walls of their shabby, streetcorner offices. Of the $450,000 that the alliance estimated was lost each year to fraudulent and exaggerated claims nationwide, an increasing share of it was being processed by professionals. "The ambulance chaser and the shyster lawyer are a menace to society, an obstruction to business and a curse to the legal profession," one alliance member wrote. "They prowl around like hungry wolves seeking whose property they may devour. . . . first leveling their guns at steam railroads and street railways, as this class of defendants comes in more frequent contact with a greater number of people than any other public service corporation."[85] While its agents monitored the fakers, the alliance devoted equal resources to working with bar associations and medical societies at the state and national levels in order to prosecute professionals involved in accident swindles. While smaller regional groups used their index bureaus to track the fakers, the alliance was just as interested in using its claims index to bear down on lawyers.

With the founding of the alliance, the investigative emphasis in accident frauds began to shift toward fraud gangs involving doctors and lawyers and away from the exotic doings of a handful of individual personal injury grifters. From this time on, in fact, the accident faker who worked alone or with an accomplice was becoming the exception to the new rule of organized accident faking in New York and in a few other American cities. Accident con men who might have merited front page treatment in the 1890s had become back-page filler. By 1928 the *Times* reported on a nationwide manhunt for an old-style accident grifter named Charles Little, who worked not only on streetcars but also in hotels and department stores. After binding his arm tightly below the elbow, Little would head for his accident destination. "His plan was to pick out a wire leading to a floor lamp, the edge of a rug or an elevator where the car did not stop exactly at the level of the floor. He would then trip and fall, always landing on the left arm, which he had bound up. Because of the binding, this arm would show a decided swelling in the fingers and wrist."[86] Little would use this swelling to barter for settlements with hotel proprietors, store managers, and claims men. He reportedly staged 300 to 400 claims over ten years, accumulating from $35,000 to $50,000, before being arrested in Charlotte, North Carolina, in November 1928. That same year, however, the *Times* reported on two brothers who ran an accident gang believed to have netted over $1 million in less than five years. This was big business, while Charles Little, as even his name suggested, was strictly small time.

By the end of the first decade of this century, the personal injury con artists—that pioneering group of ex-circus performers, "cripples," banana-peel specialists, and various other drifters—had become novelty acts. In the years since their first reported schemes in the 1870s, they had become entertainment for newspaper readers and trophies displayed by railway claims men in their *Bulletin* more than they were the future of the personal injury underworld in America.

As irrelevant to the future of personal injury fraud as the streetcorner monte player in Las Vegas, the early fakers passed unceremoniously into history. Although they followed in the tradition of centuries of beggars, the early American accident fakers were not looking for charity. While they feigned sickness and even self-inflicted gunshot wounds, they were not malingerers looking to avoid either work or military service. Even though they shared the rails with others who lived parasitically off big corporations, the early injury fakers were never the subjects of loving tributes: not of the sort that elevated boxcar tramps and hoboes to "knights of the road";[87] nor of the kind in which frontier con men and train robbers were reinvented as embodiments of frontier individualism.[88] Neither did the early American accident fakers enjoy the same treatment as an earlier group of criminals who robbed on the roads, those "gallant rogues," the English Highwaymen, whose calling card in the seventeenth and eighteenth centuries had been the command for stagecoach drivers to "stand and deliver."[89] There would be no lyric poems written about banana-peel specialists, and few mourned their passage into relative obscurity.

In the end, the history in which the exploits of the early injury fakers bears chronicling is not centrally about the acts of rogue individuals—the kings and queens of the fakers, the nationally known flop artists, the small-time cheats. It is about the culture in which accidents became the foundation of a game, and faking them not only became conceivable (staging a window falling on your elbow? pretending to fall out of a train? shooting off your left hand?), but also, incredibly, profitable.

Early in the 1930s, Annie Platzer, a banana-peeler from San Francisco known widely as Slippery Annie, dropped her peels in one too many department stores and landed in San Quentin prison. When she got out, she dyed her hair red and took up shoplifting in Chicago but was soon caught, tried, and sent to jail again. "She made two mistakes," one claims investigator wrote at the time. "The first was in coming to hard-boiled Chicago. The second was in changing her racket. She should have stuck to bananas."[90]

CHAPTER 2

ACCIDENT RACKETEERS ON THE STREETS OF THE CITY

It is no secret that Jewish criminals did what others did before them and have continued to do, that they all have used crime as another way of moving upward and onward in the American manner. . . . The significant question is what *kind* of underworld each ethnic group established in response to the unique experiences it encountered, who its underworld *dramatis personae* were, and what, specifically, they accomplished.

—Albert Fried,
The Rise and Fall of the Jewish Gangster in America, 1980

IRVING FUHR, a self-described "specialist in vault-light, manhole cover, and cellar-door flops," scouted the streets of New York for promising spots in which to stage accidents during the early 1920s. A crack in the sidewalk, an open manhole in the street, or an unlatched cellar door—all looked good to him. Then, usually in the presence of a policeman, he would pretend to slip and fall in order to create a pretext for a personal injury claim. "In the technical terminology of the business, this was designated as 'taking a flop,'" a panel of judges later explained, "and the person performing the operation, a 'flopper.'"[1] On the first day of his career, Irving Fuhr reportedly took five or six such flops.

He later averaged more than fifty flops a month, and he exceeded seventy-five during one extraordinary month of activity.[2]

Fuhr and his longtime partner, Benjamin Deutsch, maintained a thick notebook in which they recorded the particulars of Fuhr's accident stagings. The two had begun with a smaller notebook, but they filled it with flops in just two weeks. Entries in their accident ledger included the location and date of a flop, the pretense around which the claim would be framed, and Fuhr's alias. One typical flop was recorded in this way: "Harry Schneider in front of Joe's Restaurant, 10 Delancey Street, on December 8, 1925." ("Broken doorstep—broken platform," Fuhr noted to remind himself why he had chosen that place for his staging.)[3] Other entries recorded flops on Sixth Avenue, First Avenue, Canal Street, Amsterdam Avenue, and elsewhere around Manhattan and its boroughs. Fuhr later told police that, as a general rule, he would walk at least two blocks after a flop before making another.

In February 1927, police raided an office in downtown Manhattan and seized Fuhr and Deutsch's flopping notebook. In cross-checking the dates of the recorded accidents with court information, police soon found that attorney Moses Cohen had represented Fuhr in many of the faked cases. The connection was more than mere coincidence. Fuhr, who had been a professional flopper for some time, had made a business arrangement with attorney Cohen in December 1925: Fuhr would do the flopping, Cohen would do the claims filing, and the two would split the settlement money in half. Fuhr had previously flopped for another organization, this one run by a man named Daniel Laulicht and his brother Benjamin. But Fuhr had left the Laulicht brothers earlier in the year in order to try to make more money by working directly with an attorney. "I told him I was working with the Laulichts and I wanted to go out for myself on these flops and would he handle these cases for me," Fuhr later testified about how he had propositioned the attorney. "[Then] we made an agreement."[4]

At trial, attorney Cohen denied any relationship with Fuhr, but Benjamin Deutsch provided convincingly detailed corroboration for Fuhr's story. Deutsch explained how he and Fuhr would call at Cohen's office after the attorney's regular business hours two or three times a week. In these meetings, Fuhr and Deutsch would read to Cohen from their accident ledger. They would give the attorney the time and place and address of the flop; they would describe the defect in the tenement hall or store floor or sidewalk that provided the pretext for the fall; and, if an ambulance had been called to the scene, they would supply the name of the hospital that had answered the call. The attorney would then use this information to bargain for an out-of-court settlement with claims men from streetcar companies or insurers, store owners, and private individuals. Such relationships between attorneys and professional floppers were not uncommon in the first few decades of this century, and they were at the core of the early urban accident rings. After a few months of flopping for Cohen, however, Fuhr and Deutsch began to feel that they were being cheated out of the money that was coming to them.[5] Cohen denied it, and the two men left the office. With hat in hand, they went back to Daniel Laulicht and asked for his help in collecting the money.

To hear Moses Cohen tell it, Daniel Laulicht was the "boss" of an accident ring that the attorney steadfastly refused to join. Laulicht had first come to Cohen's office at 305 Broadway in September 1925; he asked Cohen for work as a process server and left the attorney's office with a few subpoenas to deliver. A week or so later Cohen saw Laulicht enter his office and begin chatting with his secretary. Cohen took the opportunity to ask Laulicht whether he had served the summonses, but Laulicht replied that he had not come to talk about summonses and that he would like to speak with the attorney about another matter altogether. "I took him into my private office," Cohen said, "and Laulicht told me that his real business is not that of process server but as an ambulance chaser who brings cases to a lawyer for a commission."[6] Laulicht, who was in his early twenties, then allegedly explained to Cohen, who was around the same age, a way in which a "young and struggling attorney" might build his practice in a hurry without doing any work. "I have a proposition for you," Laulicht began, according to Cohen. "I am about to take an office in this building, and I want you to come downstairs and occupy it. We will put your name on the door, give you a stenographer and pay you a drawing account of $50." In effect, the deal was for Cohen to become the legal front man for Laulicht's accident gang—nothing more than a name to put on legal stationery for use in extracting settlements from defendants. It was a sweet deal, if an attorney could ignore the ethical and statutory prohibitions against such activity. Moses Cohen claimed to have been one of those who stood his ground against Laulicht and the temptations of the personal injury underworld, however. "I told him I wasn't interested in that proposition," he later asserted. Cohen then said he asked that Laulicht return any undelivered summonses as soon as possible. And this was his last contact with Laulicht, he claimed, save for occasionally seeing the man in the building at 305 Broadway.

Over the course of the next month, however, Moses Cohen struck up a relationship with Irving Fuhr. Fuhr first came to Cohen as an accident victim in need of an attorney, Cohen claimed, and not as a flopper who needed a partner in crime. Cohen accepted Fuhr as a client and also accepted the cases that Fuhr referred to him, including one involving Benjamin Deutsch as an accident victim. Cohen also accepted referrals from other clients that spun off from these earlier referrals. "There was a circle," Cohen explained. "One client recommended another client and that's how I came to be involved in [all of these] cases."[7] Cohen maintained that he believed all of these cases to have been legitimate, and he professed shock when Fuhr and Deutsch began to hound him for payoffs. The attorney claimed to have been even more surprised when Daniel Laulicht reappeared in his office, unannounced, one day near the end of 1925. The two men had not spoken since the time Laulicht unsuccessfully propositioned Cohen several months earlier.

"What is it I can do for you?" Cohen asked Laulicht, who stood "all smiles" in the doorway of the attorney's office. "You owe me money," Laulicht began. What followed, according to Cohen, was an attempt by Laulicht to extort money through intimidating, "abusive" language. ("I'll show you where to get off [trying to cheat me]" was one example Cohen gave at trial; the rest of Laulicht's threats, Cohen claimed, came wrapped in language so crude it did not bear repetition in court.)[8] Laulicht's threats of violence persisted, causing the attorney to fear for his safety. Cohen hired private detectives to protect himself from Laulicht's accident gang while he was at work. Laulicht was either undeterred or unaware of the presence of the detectives, however. Late in the afternoon on the day following his initial visit, Daniel Laulicht, his brother Ben, and a crowd of their cronies entered the attorney's office. At first, Cohen was nervous at the sight of the gang, then, bolstered by the presence of his detectives, he summoned the courage to tell the roughnecks that he did not employ ambulance chasers. Nor did he pay commissions for cases. He then asked the gang to get out of his office.

Laulicht left the office, apparently having been stood down by the incorruptible Cohen; and all of Laulicht's "people" went with him. What appeared to have been a retreat, however, was actually a temporary regrouping. The phone in Cohen's office rang a few minutes later. It was Daniel Laulicht. "Now, Cohen, I know you have detectives up there," he began. Cohen tried to pretend that the men in his office had been clients in a real estate matter, but Laulicht was not buying any of it. "I am a very patient fellow, Cohen," he reportedly warned the attorney. "When I go out to get a man, I get him, even if I wait a week. You won't always be protected by detectives." True to his word, Laulicht and his gang returned to Cohen's office after the detectives left. Only then did Cohen claim to have recognized these ring members as claimants in some personal injury cases that Fuhr and Deutsch had brought to him. "Do you know Daniel Laulicht?" he asked several of them at once in seeming disbelief that his clients could be mixed up in the accident racket. The reply was returned in awful chorus: "Daniel Laulicht is boss."

Cohen had wanted nothing to do with the accident racketeers from the beginning, he later told a courtroom audience, and now he wanted out of whatever he had stumbled into. Against the attorney's protests, however, Laulicht insisted that Cohen remain the attorney of record until all of the phony cases had been settled. When Cohen continued to refuse to have anything to do with false claims, Laulicht once again "became very abusive and cursed." Backed by members of his accident ring, Laulicht renewed his threats of physical harm. "I will knock you down so hard it will take you a year to get up," he said to Cohen, using a taunt that must have sounded scarier in the original context than it read in the court records. Just as the situation looked bleak for the attorney, a detective named Dolen came back to the office, followed a few moments later by the son of one of the Cohen's clients, "a hugely built fellow" who was a member of a local football team. "With fists clenched and arms spread out," Dolen blocked the doorway and challenged Laulicht and his ring members: "Who is going to beat my friend Moe?" Laulicht looked from one to the other of his gang, then asked to use Cohen's phone. He said he wanted to call Kid Flowers, an apparently well-known roughneck who would force the attorney to comply. Sensing that Laulicht was bluffing, however, attorney Cohen claimed that *he* had called Kid Flowers himself for protection and that he was awaiting the man's arrival any moment. ("I winked to Dolen," Cohen later said, "and Dolen said, 'Sure, Kid Flowers was supposed to be here.'") Laulicht seemed to have bought the act. Cohen asked the ringleader to leave, taking his phony cases and his gang with him. And that was that.

According to his version of the events, Moses Cohen had twice resisted the temptations, then the violent extortionate threats, of the new accident racketeers. Judges in the Appellate Division of the New York Supreme Court did not agree. They found that Cohen's story did not stand up to scrutiny— dates of case filings matched more clearly with the testimony of Fuhr, Deutsch, and Laulicht. And the attorney's claimed fear of physical violence was "ridiculous."[9] What's more, the judges felt that Cohen had incriminated himself during the weeks and months after he learned that he was being investigated. He destroyed all of the papers that had to do with Laulicht, Fuhr, Deutsch, or any of the others in the group immediately after an initial interview at the district attorney's office.[10] Cohen also attempted to keep Irving Fuhr from testifying against him, an effort that included meeting with Fuhr's wife Mary and taking her shopping, once for a coat, another time for a set of dishes.[11]

Fuhr ultimately changed his testimony to favor Cohen, but all this accomplished was to add a perjury charge to Fuhr's rap sheet. In May 1930, some five years after first becoming involved with the Laulicht brothers' accident gang—and a few months after returning from New Haven, Connecticut, where he had fled under the pretense of seeking medical treatment for a "nervous breakdown"—Moses Cohen was disbarred.

In the 1920s, the most notorious gangsters in American history—Meyer Lansky, Ben Siegel, Charlie Luciano, "Dutch" Schultz—were inventing the idea of organized crime on the streets of New York, working rackets like bootlegging, loan-sharking, numbers, and protection. At this same time, a lesser known group of gangsters, the Daniel and Benjamin Laulichts of the city, were organizing their own criminal networks of floppers, chasers, shysters, and quacks around a most unlikely, and wholly unexplored, source of revenue: personal injuries arising from street accidents.

In the late nineteenth century, street accidents had become a new fact of daily life for the residents of America's larger, more densely populated cities, of which New York City was the largest and most populous. Mass transportation in New York had evolved from the relatively benign procession of stagecoaches, to the horse-drawn omnibuses that carved neat lines up and down Broadway, to the various mechanized options that became available before the turn of the century: electric railways, elevated trains, and cable cars. Added to this in the decades to follow was the greatest source of accident production the world had ever seen: the automobiles—both privately piloted by pioneer consumers and commercially driven by the early taxi men.[12]

Traffic moved at many different speeds on the disparate byways, lanes, and grand avenues of turn-of-the-century New York. Unfortunately, however, the whole notion of regulating traffic was in its troubled infancy. No procedures existed for licensing drivers, designating rights of way, developing rules about parking, making lanes, installing lights, placing road signs, or establishing etiquette—arm gestures, winks, nods, and whistles—to help govern interactions between pedestrians and mechanized travelers. Initially, there were no sidewalks, only the occasional "isles of safety" in hazardous intersections. One-way streets would not be implemented until after 1910. And traffic lights were not installed until the 1920s. In this climate, trolleys collided with horse cars and motor cars collided with pedestrians and every other imaginable combination of man, machine, and beast collided—and they did so quite often. By the summer of 1922, the City of New York declared the traffic-accident problem an "epidemic" and organized a Bureau of Public Safety to inculcate a sense of safety consciousness through enforcement of new traffic laws.

Members of a Brake Inspection Squad could pull over drivers, take the wheel themselves, and test the brakes. There also were safety parades, demonstrations, and a publicity blitz starring a cartoon character named Aunty J. Walker, a kindly older woman with a sweet smile, a billy club, and a message phrased in the form of "Aunty J. Walker Says . . . " By 1925 the head of the Bureau of Public Safety declared Aunty J. Walker "a hit": "Today she is probably the best known and most popular character, or caricature, in New York City or anywhere else," noted Barron Collier in his history of the bureau. "She writes letters and articles; takes part in parades; appears in person (a police officer, who is an excellent actor and has splendid voice control, making up as Aunty J. Walker) for talks to school children and other groups. . . . The result has been amazing."[13] Still, the bureau did not make much of a dent in the problem.

The first documented automobile-related fatality occurred on September 13, 1899, when a man named Henry Bliss stepped from a New York trolley and was hit by Arthur Smith, speeding by in his new car. Unlike Bliss, most victims of street accidents were injured, not killed, and compensation was left to the back-and-forth of negotiation between antagonistic private interests— claims men and corporate attorneys on the one side, plaintiffs' counsel on the other. While the insurance defense side organized itself according to the norms of corporate, bureaucratic culture, the other side conducted itself in ways common to the streets of Lower Manhattan. There in the jumble of neighborhoods located south of 14th Street, every haberdasher and dry goods man had his own "ropers" and "pullers-in" to hook the unsuspecting passerby into making a purchase, and every personal injury lawyer who expected to stay in the accident business for more than a few months had to have his own runners and chasers. During the first few decades of this century, this was also the stomping ground of the nation's most notorious and most organized criminals: the Jewish gangsters.

If the haberdasher's ropers and pullers-in provided the model for the ambulance chaser, then the Jewish street gangs and vice mobs paved the way for the accident racketeers. During the years in which the accident racket was first taking shape and growing to vast dimensions, Jews were widely seen as the most notorious criminal types in the city. In "Jewtown," as Lower Manhattan was sometimes referred to, one found "guns" and "gunmolls" (male and female pickpockets and petty thieves) along with the "fagins" who organized them. Historian Albert Fried has shown in his excellent study of Jewish gangsterdom that in the back rooms and crowded tenement apartments that served as brothels could be found a number of the city's busiest prostitutes and the "macks" who controlled them.[14] Mixed in with these criminal types were the strong-arm men (the "guerrillas," "schlammers," and "bolagulas") and the gamblers (especially those who set up underground "stuss parlours"). Then there were the gang leaders who cut themselves in for a piece of all the action: Monk Eastman, Max "Kid Twist" Zweibach, Dopey Benny, Kid Dropper, Lefty Louis, "Joe the Greaser" Rosenszweig, and Harry "Gyp the Blood" Horowitz. Similarly organized Jewish criminal underworlds existed on a lesser scale throughout the country, in Chicago, Philadelphia, Cleveland, Boston, Detroit, and Newark.[15]

In the crucible of the Lower East Side, gangs of insurance criminals took shape as never before: first the "firebugs" of the 1890s, then the accident racketeers of the 1920s. The accident racketeers were a lot like their more celebrated criminal contemporaries. They were young, mostly in their twenties or early thirties. They were immigrants, or the sons of immigrants, mostly from eastern and southern Europe. They grew up poor, often in the worst tenements in the city's most congested ethnic ghettos. And they shared a sense, a guiding vision, that the single-minded pursuit of money was its own reason for doing anything, whether it be a brutal mob "hit" or a slapstick flop over a loose manhole cover. For the conventional gangster of the 1920s, the way to make money was to create and manage an illegal market (liquor, gambling, loan-sharking, and the like) or to monopolize a legal business through illegal means, as in the case of the strong-arm control of the trucking industry, poultry and fish processing, dry cleaners, and construction work. For the accident racketeer, the game involved the extra step of first making a business of the professions of law and medicine—high-volume personal injury offices soon began to be called "accident mills." Then the racketeers preyed on the business. "The aspiring neighborhood vice lord and gangster hardly differed from the aspiring neighborhood capitalist," observed Fried.[16] And accident racketeers like the Laulicht brothers walked the fine line between the two, with their accident mill being a place both to process legitimate claims and to manufacture flops illegally when supply slackened.

Although perhaps not as credible with threats of violence as many of their 1920s racketeering contemporaries—was anyone in Moses Cohen's office really going to call Kid Flowers to knock some heads?—Daniel Laulicht and his brother Benjamin nevertheless were among the most successful accident racketeers of their time. Their ring was believed to have netted many tens of thousands, maybe more than one or two hundred thousand dollars, from flops and other false claims in less than two years of operation. The Laulicht organization was credited with having been almost single-handedly responsible for a 20 percent rise in New York liability insurance rates, a figure that may have been possible at the time given the still relatively low volume of accident insurance being written. Perhaps most important, the breaking up of the Laulicht gang led the Manhattan district attorney to provide one of the first estimates of the annual take of the city's new accident racket: $3 million a year.[17]

Even if exaggerated by law enforcement or otherwise inaccurate, these numbers are significant. They indicated the dimensions of an ever-expanding personal injury underworld that had evolved dramatically from the small-change beginnings of slip-and-fall artists operating on trains, inside ladies' bathrooms, and in the poorly lighted corners of hotel lobbies. The story of the immigrant Laulichts' rise to brief prominence in the fake accident trade also hinted at the underworld's future.

Ending ultimately in New York's Sing-Sing Prison, Daniel and Benjamin Laulicht's journey into the fake accident underworld began on Coney Island. At the time, the brothers both worked for the Pure Wet Wash Laundry Company. Restless with delivering laundry and, later, with running their own shop, Daniel Laulicht struck up a relationship with William Weiss, a fellow Coney Islander who was then working as a runner for a Manhattan accident attorney named Charles Sprung. Soon Weiss introduced Laulicht to Sprung as someone who might want to get into the personal injury trade: "Charley, this is a friend of mine just quitting the laundry business and he is OK," Weiss told Sprung. "[Laulicht] will run around and try to get some cases, and you can give him some summonses to serve on whatever cases you get."[18] At this first meeting, Laulicht reportedly asked Sprung how he would be paid, and Sprung explained that runners got one-third of his contingent fee, which itself was roughly one-third of the total settlement. It sounded good to Laulicht: Unlike washing, folding, or delivering laundry for a fixed wage, case-chasing was an opportunity to make "real money." Daniel Laulicht would begin work as an ambulance chaser on the streets of New York near the end of 1924. Soon thereafter his brother Benjamin joined him.

The Laulicht brothers brought twenty-one injury cases to Sprung between December 1924 and July 1925. The brothers were not seeing enough profit from their work, however, and Daniel Laulicht went to attorney Sprung to beef about his situation. "I told Mr. Sprung I wasn't making any money and it didn't pay to hang around," Laulicht later recalled. In reply, Sprung asked Laulicht a question: "Why don't you do what the other fellows are doing. Go out and get some company to 'frame up' a case with you, then I can settle it . . . I can get money from the Ocean Accident Company about ten days after the report goes in."[19] Laulicht claimed not to have really understood what the attorney meant by this, and asked for clarification. "Mr. Sprung then explained to me that the Coney Island Wet Wash Laundry Company was insured with the Ocean Accident Company, and . . . I should know some of the drivers," Laulicht continued. "I said, Yes, I know practically all of them. He said 'Wouldn't it be possible for you to go out there and have the drivers put in a report and state he had an accident?'"

When Laulicht agreed that framing a case in this way seemed possible, Sprung took out a pad and began scripting the details of the kinds of fake cases he wanted. This aroused the curiosity of Daniel Laulicht's later courtroom examiners:

Q: Wait a minute. What do you mean by "he sat down and figured what sort of action should be put in?"

A: Mr. Sprung outlined to me just what the driver should report to his employer.

Q: What did he say the driver should report?

A: I don't remember the correct details, but that it would be four or five people sitting in a taxicab, and as the driver was rounding the corner his horse should run into the taxicab and claim he had injured the people . . . and then the driver should report this to his employer.

Q: And you were to get the driver to put in a report of an accident that never in fact occurred?

A: Yes.[20]

Sprung later said that he had no knowledge of such faked claims and that Laulicht had tried to coax him into ambulance chasing payoffs and accident faking stunts, which he steadfastly opposed. But the record indicated a long list of phony cases that, over time, Sprung must surely have recognized as fraudulent: a half-dozen or so accidents occurring within a few weeks of one another that were remarkably similar. Each allegedly involved horse-drawn laundry wagons and motorized taxicabs on Manhattan streets; each case involved personal injuries to exactly four of the taxi passengers; and each case resulted in full settlement by the Ocean Accident Company within two to three weeks of the claim.[21] There were also several direct links between these separate incidents: Two of the passengers in a taxi hit by a horse-drawn wagon from the Flower Wet Wash Laundry on December 31, 1924, a husband and wife, were also said to have been passengers in a taxi hit by a horse-drawn truck from the Coney Island Laundry Company two weeks later. And ten days after this, Daniel Laulicht used the husband from this pair in another popular scheme: the insertion of fake claimants into real accidents involving public transportation. In this case, Laulicht had seen a motorized truck hit the Sixth Avenue trolley on his way to work, so when he got to Sprung's office he was already thinking of how to capitalize on the situation. "I explained to Mr. Sprung what the accident was and asked what he thought of it, and he said 'I will take a chance if you can put two people on that are really living so that when the investigator comes around and speaks to them they will at least say that they have an attorney and were in the accident.'"[22] Laulicht then told Sprung that he knew two good people to use in the claim—Jack Hirsch, the husband who had been in several of the laundry truck/taxi accidents, and Irving Goldfarb, who also was a veteran of several of the laundry truck accidents under the name Fred Polish. Laulicht also liked to make claimants of his wife Rose, her sister Sylvia, and her sister's husband, Benjamin Deutsch, who later became Irving Fuhr's flopping partner.

Sometimes the Sprung-Laulicht accidents actually took place between laundry wagon drivers and equally complicit cabbies; other times, between laundry wagons and noncomplicit taxis, or between laundry wagons and street trolleys. Sometimes the collisions existed only on claims forms. Sometimes the allegedly injured passengers in the taxi were real people—ring members—and sometimes they were just made-up names, names of friends, names from the phone book, or names from divorce cases Sprung had handled in the past. Everything, anything, seemed to work for some six to eight months into 1925. The money came in regularly, one settlement check after another from insurance companies, from street railway claims men, and from the occasional private citizen (unlucky enough not to have had insurance) who was shaken down for money directly by Sprung's operatives.

If the organized urban rackets of the 1920s provided a "queer ladder of social mobility in America" for successive waves of immigrants, as sociologist Daniel Bell and others have argued, then the Laulicht brothers— laundrymen turned ambulance chasers turned accident racketeers—were fast making their ascent.

Early in 1925 Daniel Laulicht left Sprung's office to go into the accident business for himself. He went to other attorneys to shop around the claimants from his laundry truck accidents, selling cases to the highest bidder. Attorney Morris Katz, for instance, signed on with Laulicht to represent one "Harry Scheiner," a driver of a laundry truck that had collided intentionally with one of the taxis loaded up with Laulichts' friends and relatives. Scheiner was a real taxi driver who had agreed to go along with the faked accidents, but he had died before his claim could be settled, so Laulicht told Irving Fuhr to impersonate Scheiner to get the money. The insurance company investigated the case and interviewed Fuhr/Sheiner. "I asked the man who he was and he said, 'Harry Scheiner,'" the insurance adjuster later testified. "I said, 'We understood you were dead,' and he said, 'No, I'm not, I have been up in the Catskills all summer.'" [23] Attorney Katz, like the claims man, claimed to have been suspicious of Fuhr, wondering aloud why Fuhr did not contact him sooner. Fuhr repeated the story of being up in New York State all summer, too sick even to call the attorney to let him know that he was still alive and pursuing his claim. When Katz doubted him, Fuhr snapped, "What's the difference? Give me my money."[24]

Katz later claimed to have been an innocent victim of flopper Irving Fuhr in the Scheiner case. In several other documented cases, however, Katz proved a much more willing participant in the Laulichts' accident operation, possibly even helping to design different accident scenarios. Katz, like Moses Cohen, the attorney whom Laulicht had allegedly propositioned, then intimidated into joining the gang, had his office at 305 Broadway. Of all of the buildings in Lower Manhattan where Daniel Laulicht would look for attorneys to buy his accident cases—mostly those on Lafayette Street and Park Row—he had the most dealings with attorneys at 305 Broadway, a handsome eleven-story stone building a few blocks from the Federal Courthouse and City Hall. At some point in 1925, Laulicht made this his headquarters. Perhaps tired of doing all the work then paying a lot of the money to his attorney partners, Laulicht hit on the idea of renting his own office and paying an attorney to front for him. He had already propositioned Moses Cohen and Morris Katz when he finally found a taker, Samuel Kopleton, a twenty-three-year-old attorney who had gotten his license to practice law less than a year earlier and had been working for an older attorney elsewhere in the building. By early December 1925, the door of Room 914 read *Law Office, Samuel Kopleton,* with the names of the Laulicht brothers (and a runner named William Spiegel) printed in smaller letters in the lower right.[25]

With an office established to process personal injury claims, the Laulichts now had to chase legitimate cases and, increasingly, to manufacture fake ones. This is when Irving Fuhr of Coney Island came onto the scene as the ring's chief flopper. Daniel Laulicht also kept a small notebook filled with the names of other floppers who would work for $5 a fall: Listed there was Jack Shaw, a boxer from 121st Street in Harlem, who testified that he took ten sidewalk flops under the direction of "Bennie [Laulicht], Willie [Spiegel] and Dannie [Laulicht] of 305 Broadway."[26] Shaw was paid $17.50 for his work before he declined the Laulicht's offer of $100 a week to turn pro as a flopper for the ring. Others like Harry Rich of Newark went out with Daniel Laulicht to select a spot for a fall but could not muster sufficient courage to execute the act when they saw a policeman.

The Laulicht brothers' accident syndicate manufactured personal injury claims like Detroit manufactured cars, instituting their own stumblebum's division of labor. Floppers did not take their own medical examinations, for example. If the insurers asked for them, the Laulichts employed a group of specialists to be examined instead. "'Taking the physical' was the technical term," city judges later explained. "Before each examination, they were informed of their assumed names and addresses, the circumstances of the alleged accident and the nature of their supposed injuries."[27] Chosen for their "ability to persuade the examining physician of the genuineness of their suffering," these men and women were paid $3 to $5 for each physical. Charles Rose, a "pugilist," was one such specialist employed by the Laulichts. In the summer of 1928, Rose told a packed courtroom how he had been approached on the street by Daniel Laulicht in connection with the "fake system." Posing as an injured claimant, Rose submitted to three exams, getting paid $3 for each, before ultimately opting out of the claims racket. David Greenberg was another boxer who told of having been paid by the Laulichts to take physicals. Yet another man, David Sukoff, testified that he had been recruited to take physicals by Daniel Laulicht after meeting him in a downtown restaurant.

People had to be recruited to take fake exams only when insurance company doctors were uncooperative, however. For most cases that were not investigated seriously by insurers, the Laulichts were reported to have maintained their own doctors to write phony reports. In exchange for a share of the settlements, these professionals would allegedly doctor their own paperwork with no need for the sad theatrics of a phony exam by ex-boxers or teenage girls, who also were among the Laulichts' favorite fake claimants. By 1926, in fact, the accident ring headed by two former laundrymen had negotiated business arrangements not only with lawyers and doctors but also with local policemen on the beat, hospital clerks, ambulance drivers, newspaper reporters, insurance claims men and agents, and assorted shopkeepers and neighborhood lookouts. It was a loose coalition of people, most of whom probably did not see themselves as being involved with a criminal syndicate. Nevertheless, this was how city prosecutors would later describe them.

When New York's personal injury underworld worked, money was made through claimed pains, then filtered through many outstretched hands at street level. When the schemes were found out by insurers or law enforcement, however, outstretched hands were thrust quickly back into pants pockets, and memories failed to recall even the most basic outlines of people and events, even in accidents in which serious injuries had been alleged. Perhaps the most outstanding case of denial on the part of a suspected flopper involved Joseph Plastik of Brooklyn, who had made at least twenty-six damage claims during 1926. ("Mr. Plastik was an extraordinarily unfortunate human being . . . he happened always to be around when an accident occurred," one writer observed sarcastically at the time. "It got so that no decent accident, worthy of the name, would ever think of occurring unless it first inquired the whereabouts of Mr. Plastik and then proceeded promptly to the vicinity.")[28] At trial, Plastik claimed not to have been able to recall the facts surrounding any of his twenty-six documented accidents. In his defense, Plastik first offered a flawed tautology—"if the damage suits had been brought, then the accidents must have occurred." He then frustrated prosecutors with his nonanswers to questions: "Can't you remember where any accident happened to you in 1926?" Plastik was asked at the start of an almost vaudevillian exchange. "No," said Plastik, "I've suffered from lack of memory for the last few years."

Prosecutor:	I suppose you are all scarred up as a result of your [twenty-six] accidents?
Plastik:	Well I haven't any scars now.
Prosecutor:	Perhaps, you were hit on the head and that has affected your memory.
Plastik:	I don't remember . . . No, wait, I was hit on the head once and had two stitches taken.
Prosecutor:	When was that?
Plastik:	I don't remember.[29]

When attorneys were confronted with allegations of accident frauds, their policy was almost universally to deny everything—to plead incompetence before admitting complicity, to claim that rogue elements within the office were chiefly responsible, or to claim, with much plausibility, that a high-volume negligence practice precluded detailed knowledge of particular cases. For example, when Charles Sprung was confronted at trial with overwhelming evidence of his involvement with the Laulichts, the court record states simply that the attorney "met these charges with protestations of innocence." Moses Cohen did the same. And even though his name was written on the same door with the Laulicht brothers, attorney Samuel Kopleton also attempted to plead total ignorance of the fake accident operation. He claimed not to have known what the Laulichts were doing until his stenographer, Miss Spitz, told him of their activities; then he immediately phoned an agent at the Alliance Against Accident Frauds.[30] So many of the occupants of the building at 305 Broadway had been openly connected with claims faking at some level, judges later reasoned, that it was completely unbelievable that Kopleton or any of the others could have had no knowledge of this. All were disbarred.

New York was becoming the capital city of America's personal injury underworld in the 1920s, and the building at 305 Broadway, so near the celebrated stock speculations of the Wall Street trading center, was where much of its business was conducted.

Only after having moved into an office suite at 305 Broadway, for example, could a young attorney like Morris Katz have increased his law practice from 30 accident cases in 1924, to 82 in 1925, to 533 in 1926, and, finally, to 1,193 personal injury cases in 1927, at least a handful of which were the accidents between laundry trucks and taxicabs proven to have been scripted by the Laulichts.[31] Like the other attorneys before him, Katz denied any use of ambulance chasers or any involvement in accident faking, but a panel of judges found otherwise: Referring to the Laulicht brothers, the judges spoke of "the shrewdness of these men in the underworld" who knew to take their cases to attorneys like Katz and the others at 305 Broadway and not to outside offices where "honest lawyers acting in good faith" would "denounce their concoctions."[32] Using roughly the same language, the judges reached a similar conclusion about Louis Katz, an attorney who worked for the Laulichts out of his office on the seventh floor of 305 Broadway. Katz's "present predicament," they wrote, is "due to his association with Daniel Laulicht, Benjamin Laulicht, and William Spiegel." Louis Katz, like Morris Katz, was ultimately disbarred "for his connection with the so-called flop cases."[33]

So long as the Laulicht gang stuck with its basic schemes—scripted accidents between laundry trucks and taxis, the insertion of passengers onto legitimately crashed streetcars, and flops on streetcorners and in front of trolleys—they seemed unstoppable. Only when the gang experimented with a new type of accident staging, one mainly using automobiles, did the whole organization come undone. The new auto accident schemes seemed easy enough. In late 1926 Benjamin Laulicht used some of his profits from flop cases and laundry truck stagings to buy a Studebaker. In December of that year, he insured it with the Massachusetts Bonding and Insurance Company under the made-up name of Bernard Lobisch, a variant of his given name.[34] Two weeks later Laulicht authored a letter from the fictitious Lobisch to the insurance company, telling them that he had gotten into an accident resulting in injury to the driver of the other car, "Herman Lotz," as well as to all four of the passengers in Lotz's car. Laulicht had taken the name of Lotz and most of the people alleged to have been injured in the accident at random from Louis Katz's files. The case had been arranged at a restaurant on 23rd Street where members of the Laulicht ring had lunch one afternoon with Henry Lipton, a corrupt claims adjuster who was handling the case from inside the Massachusetts Bonding and Insurance Company.

The Lobisch scheme fell apart when Dr. Alfred Herzog, a doctor hired by the insurance company, visited Katz's office at 305 Broadway to examine the claimants. There the doctor found three young Brooklyn teenagers who had been paid to take the physicals but were badly tutored in the made-up facts of the accident; the girls had been given just a few slips of paper with details on them moments before meeting the doctor. They seemed unfamiliar with the nature of their own alleged personal injuries and, so, announced the whole case as a fraud. Dr. Johnson left the office and went straight to the police. The next day, on February 9, 1927, most members of the Laulicht brothers' accident gang were arrested. Dorris Schimmel, Lillian Levine, and Miriam Freedman, the three girls who botched the medical examination, immediately pled guilty to having accepted money to impersonate accident victims; then they testified against the other ring members. Just over a year later, the Laulicht brothers and their partner William Spiegel were each sentenced to three-year terms at Sing Sing and Great Meadows prisons.

The prosecutions of the Laulichts and the few others involved in the failed Studebaker claim were just the beginning. In the summer of 1928, both Daniel and Benjamin Laulicht were called in from prison to testify for the prosecution against all their former ring members and associates. The Laulichts named all the attorneys with whom they had ever done business—principally Charles Sprung, Moses Cohen, Samuel Kopleton, Louis Katz, and several others whose offices had been in the building at 305 Broadway, on Lafayette Street, or in Park Row.[35] They also named doctors from whom they routinely purchased fake medical reports; and they named Henry Lipton, the insurance adjuster who had helped them with their auto accident cases. All involved were either disbarred, suspended from professional practice, or jailed. It was the biggest blow to the city's personal injury racket since the Alliance Against Accident Frauds first took aim at the fakers more than two decades earlier.

The exposure of the Laulicht ring in 1928 came at a time when the city's personal injury underworld was just beginning to come into full public view. Awareness of organized accident rings in New York, growing since the turn of the century, had begun to peak in the 1920s. A few years prior to the arrests of the Laulichts and Joseph Plastik, the Manhattan district attorney's office brought down the accident-faking Caruso family.[36] Earlier they had nabbed the members of the Brooklyn cripple ring. Converting their biological deficiencies into hard cash, Jacob Itzkowitz, Max Elstein, and Benjamin Greenwald were the principle "cripples" whose fake injury claims would net them more than $100,000 in five years of activity.[37] The three men specialized in staging accidents in which a car, driven by a ring member, would appear to hit another member posing as a pedestrian. The accidents were usually staged near a policeman. One man would fall to the ground, then cry out that a car wheel had passed over his foot, crushing it. Reportedly this was possible because one man had a deformed foot, "the bone of which he is able to dislocate at will and make it appear like a recent injury." The ring staged cases in New Jersey, Connecticut, and Rhode Island. They traveled in two cars with their own witnesses, a doctor to make on-the-spot diagnoses, a negligence lawyer, and a "crooked" insurance broker. When the New York District attorney's office finally captured the Brooklyn cripples, the group was in Boston. By the end of the next year, all would be jailed.

Most likely a *Saturday Evening Post* article highlighting a series of faked auto accidents that had occurred in New England in the early 1920s was based on the Brooklyn cripple ring. The article told how accident fakers would buy "battered old wrecks posing as automotive vehicles" that were lined up for sale along the Boston Post Road with "foolishly low" prices chalked on their windshields, in order to use in their stagings.[38] The *Post* article referred to "a man whom we will call Abe" as one of the principle players in the group. It was Abe's job to buy the used cars. Later in the swindle, Abe also played the role of the injured young man's uncle who pressured the insurance adjuster for a settlement. The reporter imagined Abe's spiel—"I'm this poor boy's uncle, and unless my nephew gets $2,500 before the sun sets . . . " Then the reporter updated readers on Abe's whereabouts: "Anyone wishing to arrange for [Abe's] appearance as a stock actor should write to him in care of the warden of Sing Sing Prison."

Most of the frauds described in the article involved someone jumping in front of a car as the pretext for a damage claim. "More and more these rascals are directing their energies and their plots against the owners of automobiles," the writer observed, "until today they constitute a major element among highway robbers."[39] The trend was typified by the story of a "John Doe" accident faker who was said to have made his living hiding behind bushes or park benches waiting for chauffeured cars to pass in order to jump into their path and, later, claim paralysis. Doe's gimp legs were said to have been "as effective in exciting the tender emotions of juries or the fears of claim agents as the legs of Charlie Chaplin in arousing mirth." Doe was said to have "trapped rich men and women with the same kind of devotion that some hunters give to the search for silver fox [or] whales."[40]

Many of the early urban accident gangs simply worked this same con on a larger scale. One group that specialized in targeting limousines for falls in an unnamed "large city" was reported to have made more than $150,000 in one year. The group's ringleader told how he first trained a member ("a pretty creature," though "her mentality was barely strong enough to sustain her in a position as clerk in a retail food shop"). The man explained his simple fraud in simple terms. "What you got to do is to stand close to the curb and then fall down and holler when a good one passes close to you. Holler loud and take the number of the machine."[41] The trainee grasped what she was being told after a few repetitions, then went out to a busy street for her final exam. "There goes a peach," the ringleader told her as a limo cruised by. "Get busy." And this she did: Within months, her name appeared more than a dozen times in the files of the local Index Bureau, both as an accident victim and as a witness to other flops. Then the woman formed her own flopping ring, which thrived until the Alliance Against Accident Frauds gathered enough information on her to turn her over to the police. (That same year, the alliance was also able to help crack down on a ring operating in an unnamed "Western city" whose members crammed into a cheaply made sedan of early vintage, then went out looking to stop short in front of commercial trucks to generate their damage claims.)[42]

The *Post* was one of the first major magazines to inform a national readership about the work of the new "shabby profession" of "fake-accident swindlers." Noting that the fakers could not be successful over the long term without the help of professionals, the article also exposed the "unhealthy alliance that exists between the scalawag doctors and the accident lawyers" that was becoming increasingly common in the nation's large cities. And no city was larger than New York, where alliances among lawyers, doctors, chasers, and fakers of different stripes had been documented for many years. Organized accident rings involving professionals dated at least to the summer of 1916, when attorneys Benjamin Gunner and Alexander Mandeltort were indicted along with a Dr. Max Loewthan as the heads of a "ring of fake accident insurance swindlers which duped insurance companies out of thousands of dollars."[43] Gunner's group was charged with having "employed women 'patients' whose duties were to fall and suffer 'injuries' on street cars, and in hallways of various apartment houses." One of these women, Lillian Brown, was accused of flopping in front of all manner of motorized transportation—the car of a wealthy woman from Fifth Avenue, a Macy's delivery truck, a street railroad, and even a subway. "There was apparently no limit" to Brown's staging activities, an assistant district attorney told reporters. "She would fall down coal holes in front of buildings owned by prominent people or estates, and she even permitted herself to be dragged by a subway train, according to our information. In the last named case she entered the subway car by the middle door, and was yanked along the platform. She also fell down stairs in tenement houses . . . and did other almost miraculous stunts."[44] Lillian Brown and other members of Gunner's accident ring made more money in a year than any banana-peeler, operating alone or with only one accomplice, could have hoped to have made in a lifetime.

Even before the exposure of Ben Gunner's accident ring, police rooted out Frederick Seymour's gang—sixteen people, including four doctors and a "chorus girl" from New York named Beatrice Graham, all of whom had worked together to fake claims successfully in four states during the years just prior to their arrest in 1904.[45] Readers of *Harper's Weekly* could get an education on the new urban personal injury frauds in the form of Edward Hungerford's cover story, "The Business of 'Beating' Street Railways," published in September 1907. Hungerford's article, illustrated with "remarkable photographs" from the archives of street railway companies, had one straightforward purpose: to document "the men and women who have made a profession of the 'fake' accident business."[46] Much of the article was taken up with the faking activities of loners who claimed serious injuries, then were caught by railroad detectives who had employed them to do strenuous odd jobs in order to snap pictures to prove the frauds in court. The captions beneath the snapshots told much of the story: A "furniture-mover with a 'paralyzed' back, who brought an action for $18,000 damages against a street railroad, is greatly surprised when confronted with this picture of himself." Next to him is pictured "a New Jersey farmer 'incapacitated for life'" who is lofting a load of hay above his head and into a cart. (We are told on the sly that "Two of the company's detectives worked for him as field-laborers to get this picture.") Elsewhere in the article, readers find "a man, the plaintiff in a pending action for 'severe injuries'" moving an enormous box along the sidewalk. A woman who was "supposedly confined to her bed as the result of a trolley accident" is photographed while sunning in Atlantic City. And a boiler-setter is pictured hard at work while he was supposed to be incapacitated with a broken arm. ("The man in black in this picture," we are told once again, "is a detective employed by the company for this very kind of exposure.") There seemed no end to the work that railroad

FIGURE 2.1. An early example of private detectives' photographic surveillance of claims fakers, this snapshot was published in *Harper's Weekly* magazine in 1907. The original caption explains: "A workman with an action for 'permanent injuries' working at house-building for an officer of the street railroad, although he did not know it. The other man in the picture is a railroad detective."

detectives would do, or would pay phony claimants to do, in order to get the pictures they needed, according to one chief claims investigator. "My [agents] have had their carpets laid, their houses redecorated, their household goods moved so many times in the past three years that they say they never know what they are going to do next."[47]

In addition to dishing the dirt on these small-time fakers, the *Harper's Weekly* article also recorded the activities of "several accident gangs which have become known around the country." One incredible story came from Baltimore, where a man named Frank Bobson had taken the extraordinary step of becoming a streetcar driver in order to cause accidents with other streetcars. "His gang would fill his car at a time known to him and he would race madly through the street until he found another car or wagon into which he could smash," Hungerford reported.

> It would not [matter] how slight the collision really was, it would be enough of a peg to hang injury claims by all his confederates who were passengers on the car. If the collision should prove a serious affair it was of no concern to him. He continued to smash trolley-cars until the

traction company became suspicious, and its detectives, unearthing the entire truth of the business, were able to send him to the penitentiary for a term of years.[48]

Before his capture in Baltimore, Frank Bobson had staged accidents in Pittsburgh, Buffalo, and Cleveland with help from his wife, Martha, and one other fellow. The trio reportedly had planned to fake their way out to Los Angeles before they got caught. After being found out by vigilant claim agents of the United Railways & Electric Company, the Bobsons and their friend Edward Moran were tried and sentenced to five years, two years, and six months in prison, respectively.[49]

The Bobsons' complicated style of fakery was uncommon and possibly unprecedented. Try to imagine conductors of an earlier era causing sudden stops of steam trains to benefit personal injury grifters, or contemporary bus drivers seeking out other buses for a collision on city streets. More typical of the organized frauds involving streetcars was the one worked by the John Edwards gang of Buffalo. Edwards would fake a fall and one of his accomplices would witness it. Then he would get himself admitted to a hospital where he would start negotiations with claims men. In the next city—maybe Philadelphia, or Cleveland, where Edwards's gang was ultimately caught—Edwards and his boys would follow the same script, only the gang leader would change his appearance with a wig or fake mustache in order to baffle the claims men who may have tried to circulate his description.[50]

A less organized, but more prevalent, type of streetcar fraud involved ring members or just random passersby, who would jump onto a trolley after it crashed legitimately, then would pretend injury. In many major cities, a streetcar crash set off a scramble in many directions: Truly injured passengers rushed off the car to safety while opportunists rushed on. Runners for plaintiff's attorneys descended on the scene to sign victims (or to insert them on the scene), while the train conductor or motorman sprinted to the nearest drugstore telephone to call the corporate claims men in hopes that they might arrive before all of the others and cut short big claims with small cash settlements on the spot. One early instance of this basic, unorganized fraud occurred in March of 1893 during the aftermath of a trolley accident in the Italian Market section of South Philadelphia. "With arms in improvised slings and heads roughly bandaged with handkerchiefs or any kind of cloth that could be procured in a hurry," began an article in the *Philadelphia Press*, "a crowd of foreigners boarded two cars which had been thrown from the track at the corner of Seventh and Christian Streets, last evening." The account, which appeared under the headline "FOREIGNERS FEIGN TROLLEY INJURIES," began by explaining that two cable cars had collided accidentally and then described the collision between fakers and police:

> The glass in both cars was broken and the passengers were thrown from their seats to the floor . . . Within two or three minutes, the wrecked cars were filled with a crowd of men, all of whom appeared to have received some injury. But as there were several times as many of the injured as there had been passengers in both cars, the trolley men did not give them any encouragement and tried to put them off the cars. The foreigners resisted, and a lively fight was breeding when a couple of policemen appeared and drove the foreigners off.[51]

The difference between these men crowding into already wrecked trolley cars in Philadelphia and the intentional crashing of trolley cars in Baltimore to achieve the same end some ten years later provides one measure of the peculiar progress of the accident racket: Mirroring developments in mass transportation, from the time of the steam trains, to the electric streetcars, to the automobile, the business of faking personal injury claims for money in America had evolved from the random activities of banana-peelers and streetcorner opportunists to the organized business of the urban accident racketeers.

The key figure in the evolution of the urban accident racket in the first decades of this century was the "ambulance chaser." It was the chaser's job to solicit cases for personal injury attorneys—to appear first on the scene of an accident in order to sell a prospective client on the virtues of a given attorney and, it was hoped, to leave with a signed retainer agreement. Competitive pressure among the different chasers and plain greed soon led chasers to the excesses for which they would become notorious: Whether manufacturing evidence, encouraging claimants to exaggerate their medical symptoms, or, occasionally, entirely faking cases, chasers walked the line between the real and the faked claim. "It is but a short step from an exaggeration of an injury to the manufacture of a claim," one transit company official noted early in this century.[52] And the ambulance chaser was the one who actually did the stepping between the unethical act of solicitation and the criminal business of faking.

The practice of ambulance chasing existed long before the term was coined to describe it. England had its "touts" for attorneys since the early nineteenth century, and mention of a "set of low attorneys" who specialized in hunting up high volumes of accident claims against the railroads appeared at least as early as 1870.[53] The term "ambulance chaser" itself, however, is hard to date with any precision; it entered the language at a time when accident litigation increased dramatically in the 1890s but was not really used consistently until the end of the first decade of the twentieth century. In 1897, for instance, a Republican congressman from Iowa quipped on the floor of the House about New York City chasers' always being on hand wherever there is a railway wreck, a street-car collision, or a gasoline explosion.[54] In that same year, a report issued by the American Bar Association did not speak of "ambulance chasers" when discussing the problem of a "system of canvassing and direct solicitation, supported by an army of agents, runners, evidence scrapers and suborners of perjury, which has recently sprung up."[55] And in 1896, the editors of the *Street Railway Journal* did not use the term when railing against the "set of unscrupulous lawyers who make a specialty of [accident] cases."[56] One popular law journal, the *Green Bag*, introduced the term at least two separate times in the early part of this century. In 1902, the journal offered readers "The Evolution of the Ambulance Chaser," a series of lighthearted quatrains that termed chasers "trolleybites" and "a swarming brood of creatures with most rapacious mien."[57] In 1908 the *Green Bag* reprinted an article that warned of a "new enterprise which has grown up, and which has been termed Ambulance Chasing."

No shortage of terms existed for those who would make a business out of street accidents. Chasers might be referred to as "runners," "barkers," "lead men," "middlemen," "accident brokers," "steerers," or, by the popular euphemism, "investigators." And their activities could include everything from the simple signing of clients for a single attorney, to the gathering of retainer agreements in order to auction them off to attorneys for the highest price, cash on delivery. By the end of the first decade of this century, solicitors had become essential to successful personal injury practice in big cities. "A class of lawyers has grown up which attend to nothing else and live upon solicited cases," wrote members of a special committee of the New York State Bar Association in 1908. "It is not possible for any lawyer to have what is called an accident business without building it up by means of solicitation through runners."[58] The situation was much the same in Philadelphia, Milwaukee, and Chicago as well as in the less likely locale of St. Paul, Minnesota (where solicitation of accident cases had reportedly "grown to be a very formidable and well organized business").[59] Chasers were also becoming popular in southern locales like Birmingham, Alabama, and Nashville, Tennessee, where one man reported in 1914: "I was a fireman and was making a hundred dollars a month; I went into partnership with a lawyer and made so much money with him in getting these damage cases that I threw up that job. . . . everywhere men are making money, joining in with lawyers in partnership with them, getting half of the fee recovered in damage suits and doing it as a business. It is a business."[60] In San Antonio, Texas, Frank McCloskey was the regional chaser king. McCloskey bought, sold, and solicited accident claims in the first few decades of this century, employing a stable of chasers who were known to "counsel malingering" and to foist crutches on people who were not injured in order to increase damages.[61] Whichever the term, wherever the city, and whether meant to describe the attorney himself or his emissaries, chasers were roundly despised by transit companies, insurers, and elite lawyers who feared that chasers were degrading the profession, making the bar "a stench in the nostrils of the public."[62]

In New York City, the largest personal injury market of the early part of this century, men and women began to keep one eye on the street they walked or the job they worked and another eye on the spy for accident cases. Some pocketed $5 or $10 on the side with a casual referral; others more intent on making a living engaged in what one writer described as a "daily hunt for the maimed, the halt, and the blind." At any given time in the city, there might be several thousand people exchanging several million dollars in cash referral money: janitors of congested tenements; superintendents of construction enterprises; hospital interns; taxicab drivers; union delegates; disloyal employees of insurance companies, railroads, and steamship lines; truck drivers for department stores; numberless employees of corporations whose businesses regularly produced accidents; and small businessmen and women who devoted themselves to the industry at night.[63] The effect of all of this chasing activity swelled the ranks of the city's personal injury underworld and sometimes made it a meaner place. One description in a 1911 novel described the scene: "The competition for accident cases became so fierce that if a man were run over on Broadway, the rival runners would almost tear him limb from limb in their eagerness to get his cases; and they would follow a dying man to the hospital and force their way on one pretext or another to his bedside."[64]

Those who were only marginally involved in chasing activities were known as "dollar-a-monthers," taking their name from the fee they got for a tip on a client. Others were paid slightly more and were encouraged to join social clubs, labor unions, and community groups in order to make the kinds of contacts that might lead to referrals. The typical case-chaser who was in the business full time was given a base salary, anywhere from $25 to $100 a week plus commissions, as well as a territory to work and perhaps the use of a car. The career chaser carried business cards for his attorney, blank authorizations for police and hospital records, retainer forms, and a collection of favorable newspaper articles and photographs of settlement checks that the attorney had won for various clients. Sometimes the favorable clippings were for a different attorney, but they would be shown so quickly the prospective client would not notice. Louis Moses was typical of these career ambulance chasers, of which there may have been 250 working full-time for some 2,000 attorneys in the 1920s. Moses was hired by attorney Edward Gordon in August 1924, was paid a weekly salary of $55, and used a car owned by the attorney to speed him to accident locations throughout a territory extending from Water Street to Houston Street and from the East River to the Hudson River. At Christmas, Gordon gave Moses a few hundred dollars and a diamond ring. Gordon's chief chaser, Nicholas Ferrante, who went by the less ethnic-sounding moniker Richard Roberts, managed Moses' activities. "Mr. Roberts would call me up, or I would call Mr. Roberts and ask him if there is anything new," Moses later described an average day as a chaser.

> [Roberts] would say to me, John Brown, struck by an automobile, confined to Gouvernor Hospital, compound fracture of the leg. . . . I would go to the family of where John Brown lives, and I would say to Mrs. Brown or to Mr. Brown's son—or if the party happened to be an infant I would speak to the father or the mother—that I represented Mr. Gordon, Mr. Gordon specializes in the line of accident cases, and I ought to take you down to meet Mr. Gordon, you understand, meet Mr. Roberts, this case must get investigated immediately; and I tried to interest them; and that is all there is to it.[65]

If Moses did not get his leads from Mr. Roberts, he would buy them from beat policemen. Prices in New York during the early 1920s between cops and chasers were fairly standard: $10 for contusion cases and $25 for fractures. With increased competition for leads later in the decade, prices rose to $15 on contusions and $50 on fractures.[66] (In Philadelphia, where there was less competition, chasers charged higher fees: $50 for fractures, and $100 to $150 for amputations, or other injuries resulting in permanent disability.)[67] Moses, like many full-time chasers, had to work for more than one attorney in order to make enough commissions to stay alive financially. By the time he was arrested in 1928, Moses was chasing for four or five attorneys. At trial, he reluctantly ratted on only one attorney—Sidney Gondelman, the self-described ambulance-chasing "czar of Kings County Hospital."[68]

In a highly competitive market for personal injury cases—a market made up of "a relatively small number of high-powered, highly organized contingent-fee law machines with hundreds of outside runners and investigators"[69]—successful ambulance chasers had to exploit any advantage they could. Some chasers, such as Mrs. Theresa Braun, a secondhand clothes dealer who had worked as a real estate broker and was active in "Hebrew philanthropic organizations," were successful because of their notoriety within their communities. (Braun liked to brag that she was as well-known as Tom Farley, the sheriff of New York County and Democratic party leader in her district.)[70] Lester Fabricant chased cases for his night law school instructor.[71] And a certain Reverend Johnson, a Baptist minister from Harlem, had an arrangement with a downtown lawyer to refer parishioners who happened to have been in accidents.[72] A great many other chasers, such as Frank Messina, were successful largely because of their ethnicity. In 1922 a Jewish attorney opened a branch office in an Italian neighborhood in Brooklyn, but "almost immediately after he opened this office, and being alone for one or two weeks, he realized he could not speak Italian . . . he then employed Frank Messina, who was not a lawyer, to run his office for him" and success followed.[73] Irish and Italian attorneys acted in much the same way by handpicking Jewish runners to work the Lower East Side. This ethnic foundation of ambulance chasing held true for several other cities, as well: It was stated as a general rule by a Milwaukee judge who observed that most attorneys' "tipsters" were selected "because of their nationality, their ability to speak the native language of the people in their section, and their influence."[74]

For Abraham Gatner, the most famous authority on ambulance chasing in New York in the 1920s—and one of the nation's original chasers himself—all chasers were judged by one standard: the amount of gall they had in pursuing a case.[75] Whether the chaser was "alert and well-groomed" (like "A.S.," who wore a large diamond stud), or like one "P.J.," who looked "more like a waterfront roustabout," success was a function of the right mix of foot-in-the-door persistence, an uncle's affability, and a salesman's instinct to close the deal the minute the front door was opened to him. By his own standard, Gatner measured up as well as any chaser of his time. "I was the most expert 'ambulance chaser' this town ever saw," Gatner began his lengthy confession published for weeks on the front page of the *Brooklyn Eagle* in September 1927.

> I started in the business when it was nothing. I grew with it and I did more than any one else to make it the unrecognized Billion Dollar Industry it is today. . . . I had talents—I believe I still do—and up until a short time ago the legal profession made very good cash value of them. . . . I got into [ambulance chasing] by accident and I got out the same

way. I am so completely finished with it that I am now ready to write my memoirs of it and its leading characters.[76]

Actually, what impelled Gatner to come forward with his story was his frustration in collecting a debt of some $40,000 from two attorneys whose lackluster corporate practice Gatner had transformed into an enormously successful personal injury accident mill.[77] Back in 1924, he had agreed to help attorneys Joseph Levy and Aaron Becker get into the accident business in exchange for a "nice salary and a share of the firm's profits." Gatner's first move had been to spend some $20,000 to $30,000 to secure the services of "the best ambulance chasers in the game"—Tony Sagona, Dave Schaeffer, Eddie Ellenbogen, the two Feinbergs, Irving Wolfe, Sammy Abrams, Max Corbin, Joe Rose, and Ben Roman.[78] It was an all-star team never before assembled, Gatner claimed, and he paid them commensurately, with salaries ranging from $150 to $250 a week. Like the corner policemen from whom they bought information, Gatner's field operatives worked their own beats around the city, phoning periodically to report successes or failures and to get the latest leads. "We gave everybody a good shake," Gatner was proud to say of the way he ran Levy and Becker's chasing operation. "The whole field was systematized," he continued. "Schaeffer and Wolf worked as a team in Brooklyn, which was the territory assigned to them; William Feinberg and Corbin worked in Manhattan; Ellenbogen and Rose in the Bronx and the upper part of Harlem; Abrams and Henry Feinberg worked along the waterfront among the stevedores and longshoremen; Sagona worked primarily on Italian cases."[79]

With Gatner's help, Levy and Becker's practice fast became so successful that neither attorney could hazard an estimate of their firm's annual income within $50,000; and this was at a time when most attorneys successful in private, noncorporate practice made roughly $5,000 a year. Over the course of just a few months, Levy and Becker had largely relinquished their practice to laymen, and they found that they were making more money in law than ever before. While on a vacation at the Grand Union Hotel in Saratoga Springs in July 1924, Becker sent Gatner a postcard saying that he had arrived safely in clear weather. "Hope all the boys are hustling," he closed. "Regards to Schaeffer, Tony, Ellenbogen, Rose, Ben R., Nathan and yourself."[80] Six months later he wrote "Dear Abe" from Atlantic City: "Hope everything is running smoothly and much new biz." That there was: Between the time of the attorney's trips to Saratoga Springs and Atlantic City, the boys had hustled 180 negligence cases, according to Gatner's testimony—none of which had required any attention from Levy or Becker in order to be processed to final settlements.

Despite the evidence of the postcards, and the testimony of Gatner and others during a 1928 investigation, Levy claimed not to have been able to explain how he and his partner had gained such an enormously profitable negligence practice in so short a time. The questioning of attorney Joseph Levy became more pointed as his trial wore on. In the end, Levy and Becker declined to answer almost every question upon the grounds of possible self-incrimination. They denied complete knowledge of all of "the boys," each in their turn. And Abe Gatner? Levy replied, "He was a clerk in my office."[81]

The remark probably offended Gatner. It had been some twenty years since he had begun his journey into the city's personal injury underworld as a clerk in the office of a downtown attorney. The year was 1907 or 1908, and Gatner claimed to have begun with the intention of becoming an attorney himself. "When I was young man, I had an idea that the legal profession was fine," he later wrote. "Within a short time I learned that the law—at least what I saw of it—was a business, just like steel or cloaks or suits. I saw mysterious men come into the office where I was employed and lord it around as though they owned the place. I found out that one was our 'outside man' and the others were his friends, the 'outside men' of other offices." Gatner gave up on his idea of becoming an attorney and persuaded the other runners to teach him the trade that he would later perfect on his own. "I was shown the ropes, which were few at that time," he said. This meant mainly going down to the police headquarters on Mulberry Street to wait for a newspaper reporter to sell him accident slips taken from the police blotter. A typical slip might read cryptically: "John Doe, k.d. [knocked down] while crossing 4th Ave. at 12th Street, abrasions, at home," with maybe some other information about the person's ethnicity, his or her address, and the license of the potentially liable party. With the slip in hand, Gatner would make his way to John Doe's home and try to get him to sign a retainer agreement. "On the first day out I landed an Italian street cleaner who had been run over by a horse-drawn delivery wagon up on 8th Ave., Manhattan. My second call was equally successful." Gatner was hooked. "I found the business very interesting, even fascinating," he later recalled. "It required sharpness of wit, quick judgment and a certain daring. . . . In the early days there was fascination in doing something unethical. . . . I was young enough to enjoy the fun of it—it wasn't sordid then as now—and the coming into contact with the celebrated characters who showed up around police headquarters. You might even call it romance." Gatner's fascination with chasing no doubt also included the prospect of making some $40,000 to $50,000 a year, tax free, with no real boss—and this for someone born outside the country with no real formal education.

The chasing business was too good an opportunity to be confined to the handful of early operators who parceled out the city's best cases among themselves, pursuing leads on streetcars, the elevated railway, and on foot. "The business was carried on as secretly as possible then, in great contrast to today," Gatner later said, "and for three or four years its expansion was more or less confined to those in it from the start." Then he noticed new faces on "Newspaper Row" outside of police headquarters waiting for the day's accident lists from slip boys; and these same new faces were also crowding into a nearby poolroom or the famous café of Keller and Vogler, where the original chasers used to network with police. The 9:00 A.M. visit to headquarters for the accident leads, once a friendly transaction between a few men in the know, now looked like a theatrical cattle call or a soup line. In good weather, Gatner said, the chasers would wait on the headquarters's steps for a slip boy like James "Mc.J." McManus, who had a monopoly and became "quite wealthy." Gatner continued: "We would take out our pencils and papers and take down the information as fast as he read it. Then it was every man for himself, and the palm and the retainer always went to the one of us who knew the best short cuts—surface cars and L connections—that would get him to the home of the injured."[82] Some new chasers, like two sets of brothers nicknamed The Four Musketeers, distinguished themselves from the pack with their quick jump on the information, forcing the others to step up their efforts or get out of the game.

In response, Gatner and some of his close associates moved their hangout to Flanagan's on the other side of headquarters and innovated a number of ways to obtain accident information ahead of the others. In particular, Gatner made arrangements with newspaper reporters in order to obtain the accident lists at 6:00 P.M. on the day the accidents occurred, giving him until nine the next morning to secure the best claims for himself. ("A streetcar collision was the choicest thing on the calendar," he said, "as usually 40 or 50 people were sufficiently 'badly shaken up' for our purposes.") When his rivals got wise, he cut a deal with someone in police headquarters to get the accident lists at 2:00 A.M.; for this, he had to invest in a telephone. A phone was an uncommon device in his Bronx neighborhood during the first decade of this century, but it allowed him to circumvent the newspaper men to get word of accidents directly from police department clerks. Gatner also made deals directly with cops on the beat: For $3 a case, they would phone him with the names and addresses of accident victims, then, in order to keep this same information from other chasers, the patrolmen would change some of the details of the case in their official reports—misspelling the names of the victims or fudging their addresses. (This kind of thing would cause "much howling and groaning, and everybody down the line was accused of 'double crossing,' " Gatner reports.)[83]

Some traffic policemen carried in their hats the business cards of the negligence lawyers for whom Abe Gatner worked. Finding an opportunity to slip the cards into the hands of injured parties, policemen would suggest to accident victims that a particular attorney be retained in the case "with the intimation that if that was not done, the testimony of the police officer as to what he saw at the scene of the accident would not be very favorable."[84] Gatner said he could name a hundred cops and a dozen precincts that did business with the chasers and cited Longabardi's Tailor Shop across from police headquarters as one place where chasers and cops "ducked in" to exchange information through slips in a cigar box "depository." Gatner even knew of chasers "slinking around" the Police Academy to make early contacts. Under the heading "Why Cops Don't Doff Hats," Gatner quipped: "If an inquiring and mischeivous stranger should go along the streets knocking hats off some policemen's heads the sidewalks would be littered with the business cards of 'ambulance chasing lawyers' and other 'literature' of this criminal industry."[85]

The only source of accident information better than police headquarters was the local hospital. "The fat fees in the ambulance chasing game come from cultivating a hospital branch," one writer observed in 1909, the same year when the New York Superintendent of Hospitals noted of Bellevue Hospital "the disgusting condition of affairs in relation to the importunities of the 'ambulance chasers.'"[86] The "least daring" chasers worked through the family to get access to the injured potential client, while the "able chaser" set out on his own first to verify liability in the case, then to use a number of different ruses, misrepresentations, and disguises to get to the injured's bedside.[87] Gatner developed pipelines into several hospitals, sometimes posing as a newspaper reporter himself, sometimes relying on a police officer to get him inside, and other times, "depending on the internal situation in any particular hospital," striking up referral deals with nurses, orderlies, ambulance drivers, interns, surgeons, and even the occasional social worker or candy-striper who worked in the wards. "It is well known that hospital internes receive very little pay, and that this is true also of all hospital employees, from ambulance drivers to nurses," Gatner explained. "Naturally, these people are open to new ways of earning cash, even in small amounts."[88] Some hospitals were controlled by certain runners and lawyers, however, and this could lead to conflicts. In such a hospital where the workers are on the payroll of one chaser, Gatner reports, "a rival chaser, even though escorted by a policeman, is liable to find himself in trouble."

Early on, Gatner understood that, as a chaser, he had two natural enemies: rival chasers, and the corporate claims men who would rush equally fast to the injured's bedsides to head off big settlements with quick cash payments. In 1912 Gatner made a career move that was as bold as it was shrewd: He decided to cross enemy lines by taking a job as a claims man with a New York insurance company. Gatner concealed his experience as a chaser, telling interviewers only that he "had newspaper experience," and was soon awarded the title of "adjuster and investigator" at a salary of $18 a week.[89] Although he admittedly knew nothing of liability or the principles of adjustment or investigation, Gatner was assigned the territory of the entire East Side of Manhattan, from Chatham Square to Harlem. Instructed by his supervisors to make settlements as quickly and as cheaply as the ignorance of the claimants would allow, Gatner, the corporate claims man, walked the city streets with his wad of 1,000 one-dollar bills. ("The bills were of $1 denomination," he said, "so that the poor victims with whom we dealt would be impressed by a stack of 50 of them—or even many less.") Now Gatner bought up accident victims' rights to make claims, while earlier he had attempted to sign on for a piece of their actions against the corporations.

This was what a corporate claims man did: "He purchases claimants' rights of action at the lowest available figure," author Smith L. Brittingham wrote in 1927, the same year Gatner confessed. "He is primarily a salesman" (just as Gatner described the chaser).[90] Brittingham went on to describe the methods for obtaining a quick settlement with poorer, less-educated accident victims that Abe Gatner had learned through personal experience.

> Some claim agents have found that the exhibition of a fat roll of greenbacks has a very compelling effect on the ignorant claimant's mind. Such a claimant proceeds more or less literally upon the fallacy that seeing is believing. His mind doesn't grasp very well the business principle of credits involved in checks, drafts, and bills of exchange, and in such cases it is well enough to employ cash . . . in small denominations in order to create bulk. With the more intelligent claimant the display of cash appears to be absolutely valueless as an inducement to the settlement.[91]

Gatner's success in settling cases underscored the fact that there was little difference between many of the legitimate practices of the corporate claims men and the activities of the ambulance chasers. The claims men, really, were the first chasers of accident victims, a fact that had been noted in magazines and newspaper editorials as early as the 1870s and repeated many times during the subsequent decades.[92] The "fixing" of personal injury cases by the rail corporations, either by settling them cheap on the spot or by rustling up favorable witnesses (who often testified for a fee), was just one aspect of the corporations' larger, organized effort to evade payment in personal injury cases. "It is familiar knowledge that it is the 'policy' of some corporations to fight just claims against them by all, just and unjust, legal and illegal, means, and to pay no damages until the court of last resort has decided that they must pay," a *New York Times* editorial stated in 1905, following the indictment of a New York City Railroad investigator who paid a witness to testify against the claimant. "There is no reason for preferring the powerful corporations to the weak and fraudulent claimants and ambulance chasers."[93] The railroads' "policy" of resisting claims by conducting overtly biased investigations and sometimes creating evidence is precisely what Gatner discovered on the job in 1912;[94] that same procedure led to the disbarment of attorney Henry A. Robinson, the general counsel of the Metropolitan Street Railroad Company. In 1912 Robinson was found guilty of having paid "so-called detectives and investigators" to bribe witnesses and plaintiffs to change their testimony to suit the corporate position. In fact, the Metropolitan Street Railroad paid out thousands of dollars to court officers, clerks, and thirty-four policemen for this kind of favorable testimony.[95] Far from an isolated case in which a defense attorney got fed up enough to adopt the tactics of the plaintiffs—"to fight fire with fire," as Robinson claimed in his defense—judges decided that this was just one example of a massive, and long-standing, "system" by which large corporations ducked making payments to all claimants, legitimate or not. Gatner had wanted to learn this system early in his career; and he did. "In the time I spent with this company, I accomplished all I set out to do," he said. "I learned not only how to judge the value of a claim for bargaining purposes, and all of their tricks, but I also had a good practical course in negligence law practice, and I discovered several channels to exclusive information that were becoming imperatively necessary to the other side of the business."

In 1913 Gatner went back into the chasing business for himself; the next year he was arrested for his involvement in Ben Gunner's accident ring. Gatner claimed to have first learned of faking cases from his fellow corporate claims men. At a 1916 trial, he justified his action on purely economic terms. In the ambulance-chasing business, sometimes he had to fake cases to keep up with competing chasers. In the aftermath of his arrest, Gatner gave his first confession, naming fifteen attorneys for whom he solicited cases.[96] A grand jury investigation was begun at once and several arrests and prosecutions followed.

By 1926, after a falling out with Levy and Becker and other attorneys he had worked for in the past, Gatner decided to expose them. After getting no response from a major New York bar group, the following year Gatner offered his confession to the *Brooklyn Eagle*; and a year later he was called to testify at a citywide hearing into local ambulance chasing practices. Once more Gatner made headlines for his frank confessions about the inner workings of the accident business. Before a packed downtown courtroom, Gatner named all of the accident attorneys for whom he had chased cases over the years, among them Sammy and Jack Malts, George and Jack Savits, and Emil Reichman. He listed the names of those police stations controlled by runners—Clinton Street, Fifth Street, East 51st Street and East 104th Street—and he named the corrupt newspaper "slip boys" who slipped him some information about accident cases for a few dollars apiece.[97] Gatner also named the public hospitals where information about accident victims was regularly secured from clerks and interns, and where staff members were paid to facilitate the runners' access to potential clients: Bellevue, Harlem, Gouverneur, Lincoln, Fordham, and Beekman Street.[98]

Gatner revealed the most about the workings of the early accident trade, perhaps, when he told a courtroom audience how he had transformed the office of Levy and Becker into the world's most successful chasing operation. The court disbarred the two attorneys in 1930. By this time Gatner had been in city prison off and on for two years on charges stemming from a dispute he had had with another attorney. At his trial, Gatner had conducted his own defense.[99] He called no witnesses, nor did he hide two prior convictions, one for juvenile delinquency in 1903 and one for grand larceny stemming from his accident faking with Lillian Brown in 1916. Before the jury, he may have argued that he had overcome his youthful indiscretions, and his brief experiments in accident faking, to enjoy success in managing a law office. He had systematized the methods of a personal injury practice to keep pace with the high volume of accidents in the machine age—at times, taking the lead in manufacturing accidents and injuries on his own—and, on the whole, he was proud of it.[100] Indeed, Gatner had self-righteously initiated the legal actions that ultimately landed him in jail and ended his career.

Abe Gatner's lengthy public confession in 1927 had been much anticipated—the *Eagle* trumpeted the coming of his sensational "revelations" for several weeks, as if the text to follow had almost religious significance. And when the confession finally ran, it did indeed become the central text in a crusade.

Eagle reporter Joseph Lilly built up the publication of the confession as an unprecedented glimpse into the city's damage suit racket "from an individual who knows from his own operations the principal law firms and lawyers involved, the various channels of petty officials and hangers-on through whom they operate, and their exact methods."[101] Ambulance-chasing lawyers and their cohorts throughout the city were reportedly "thrown into consternation" by the announcement of Gatner's willingness to come forward. And their anxiety was heightened by reports that Gatner had supplied detailed lists of attorneys, runners, policemen, doctors, hospital employees, politicians and others involved in the city's personal injury underworld. By contrast, William Clarke of the Alliance Against Accident Fraud greeted the news of the coming confession with unbridled enthusiasm. Clarke thought the Gatner confession should be the turning point in his group's long-standing war on the fakers, saying: "Now, if ever, is the time to get to the root of this nefarious traffic."[102]

During the weeks to follow, a number of others joined Clarke and the *Eagle* in their crusade. Midway through the publication of Gatner's confession, the members of one association of movie theaters, a group particularly hard-hit by slip-and-fallers making use of spilled drinks and sticky floors, held a meeting in Times Square to join the campaign against fake claims and chaser lawyers. ("Before we get through with this campaign," one theater owner vowed, "we are going to put somebody in jail.")[103] Soon they were joined by the Vaudeville Mangers Protective Association, including the giant Fox and Loew's theater chains;[104] the largest taxi trade group in the city;[105] a number of insurance organizations, such as the New York Claim Association, the National Bureau of Casualty and Surety Underwriters, the Spectator company, an insurance trade publisher; and a dozen or so "civic groups" made up mainly of men friendly to corporate concerns—all of whom met at the Hotel Martinique one evening in late September 1927 to declare a "city-wide war" on ambulance chasers.[106] At the meeting, the leader of the Greater New York Taxpayers Association announced his belief that 50 to 90 percent of tenement accidents were staged for the purpose of making personal injury claims. "We are going through a more dangerous period of moral hazard than I have ever known," the man said, "and I have spent all my life in the real estate and insurance business. We have now more fraudulent accidents and claims than I have known in my experience." The sentiment had been voiced earlier in the week by John L. Belford, the monseignor at the Brooklyn Church of the Nativity, who wrote to the *Eagle* to say "Well done!" and to spur them on in their crusade.[107] By the end of September, several other newspapers had joined the anti-chaser campaign also.

Near the end of his confession, Gatner had blamed "big corporations" for allowing the city's personal injury underworld to persist, despite knowledge of the work of its biggest players. "Rather than fight padded and faked claims and put these crooked lawyers out of business, if not in jail, they settle suits which they know to be worthless."[108] The corporations responded with their announcements of a new resolve to fight the fakers. The organized bar groups were silent, however. And this became the new focus of the *Eagle* crusade, with each successive article capped by a statement of the number of days since the *Eagle* first called for action and the plain, boldface statement that THE BENCH AND BAR ASSOCIATIONS DO NOTHING. "The purpose of these articles was to obtain action for reforms that only can flow from the Bench and Bar," reporter Joseph Lilly wrote near the end of September, "and no move has come from them." A few days later E. J. Byrne of the Brooklyn Bar Association pledged to devote his time and ability "to cut out this rotten sore on our profession," after which Lilly noted that the "daily challenge of the *Eagle* . . . had impelled him to speak earlier than he had anticipated."[109] The next night, at the Association's monthly meeting, however, Byrne was silent on the chaser issue, and only one person even mentioned it.[110]

The *Eagle* series had come about through the urging of several corporate lawyers "who had studied the subject and were tremendously interested in carrying on the warfare against the [Ambulance Chasing Fraternity]," according to Frank Carstarphan, one such attorney. And when the bench and organized bar failed to take up the issue initially, this same group of lawyers formed their own group to lobby for action. Although named the Citizens Committee Against Fraudulent Claims, the group's membership included few laypeople, mainly representatives from eighteen mutual casualty insurance companies, eleven railroads operating in New York City, five local street railway and taxicab companies, six food manufacturers and distributors, and numerous real estate companies.[111] The language used by the Citizens Committee was extreme: It spoke of evils, purges, and war. "Our committee stands as an army of sentinels prepared and ready to carry on a militant and aggressive warfare against any persons or groups that shall undertake the fraudulent and criminal promotion of claims and civil damage suits."[112] At one point Carstarphan likened his committee to a group called The Vigilantes who banded together to work against the Axis powers during World War I. Elsewhere, he proposed to look at the problem of chasers and accident fakers "eugenically," a point that he followed with a brief digression on the merits of sterilizing criminals and insane people "who have neither the intelligence nor the background to know what law means." When the organized New York bar associations finally began their own campaign against the chasers, they expressed similar sentiments in the less explicit terms of "weeding from the profession" certain "undesirables" among personal injury practitioners who had neither the character nor education to be lawyers.[113]

The venomous campaign against the chasers that began with Abe Gatner's confession in the *Brooklyn Eagle* seemed to be about more than corporations simply banding together to limit damage suit payments, or bar associations endeavoring to clean house. Questions of the ethics of soliciting legitimate cases would be confounded with the criminal matter of accident faking. Abe Gatner's personal injury business would be swiped at with the same hand that took aim at the Laulicht brothers' accident mills. Chasers, who served some legitimate social function (albeit for reasons of self-interest) in opposing the corporate claims men in their attempt to exploit poorly educated accident victims, were seen on a continuum with the accident racketeers—and all were seen more generally in the context of "immigrant vice" that was weakening the city's social fabric. A unique combination of the general notion of Jewish organized criminality (popular early in the century) with historical contempt for the ways Jews seemed to succeed in America seemed to have helped conflate the activities of the ambulance chasers and the accident racketeers into one "foreign" evil. According to historian Oscar Handlin, Jews had deep, mysterious, sinister associations with the city, trade, and finance. When Jews were successful—and this happened to an infuriating degree, as far as many "native-born" Americans were concerned—it was widely believed to have been the result of the labor of others. Characterized as members of "a parasitical race who produces nothing," Jews were "credited with the capacity for profiting from every contingency."[114] And the ambulance-chasing practices of the contingent-fee accident lawyers seemed to make a perfect case in point. Located in the cities, associated with mysterious, greedy foreigners, and symbolizing a decline in American values, the business of faked personal injuries was not only costing policyholders money in the form of higher premium payments, it was also seen as potentially "ruinous" to "our" civic life, much like the long-term effects of immigration itself, according to writers like Frank Moss. "That the Russians, Poles and Slavs are going to remain with us is perfectly plain," Moss once wrote. "That their great numbers and their multiplying habits are going to continue as large factors in our City life needs no demonstration; and that they are a danger, a detriment, a drag to our City's progress, is self evident."[115]

The practices that Moss believed made immigrants a drag on the city's progress, however, represented progress itself to men like Abe Gatner and the attorneys he worked for: many had begun practice in ground-floor tenements on Rivington Street with offices in the front room and children crying in the back, then graduated to nicer offices near city hall. Blocked entry to more prestigious corporate practice, the early personal injury lawyers began to succeed by doing the dirty work of accident cases. By the first few years of this century, when the automobile was transforming the nation's cities and reconfiguring people's lives—all for the better, it was believed—a distinctly American form of enterprise grew out of the wreckage it left behind. Those willing to chase accident cases and process them to settlement were rewarded with livable wages, if not always outrageous fortunes. Inhabitants of the personal injury underworld were able to take a few steps on a queer ladder of American social mobility—to get ahead in a country where they might otherwise be left in the dust of a nation speeding ever-forward without them.

The career paths of those who dwelt at the bottom of the metropolitan bar were not centrally on the minds of the nation's leading law groups, however. In 1928 bar associations in New York and several other cities would attempt to put an end to all of this accident business once and for all: a "nationwide war" would be declared on the ambulance chasers.

CHAPTER 3

THE NATIONWIDE WAR ON AMBULANCE CHASERS

If the house is to be cleaned, it is for those who occupy and govern it, rather than for strangers, to do the noisome work.

> —Judges of the Appellate Division of the New York State Supreme Court in Answer to a Petition by the City Bar Associations to Conduct an Investigation into Ambulance Chasing Practices, 1928

Nothing plunged the professional elite deeper into despair than contingent fees and the proliferation of negligence lawyers whose practice depended upon them. Rather than cure the doctrinal disease, and adversely affect their corporate clients, bar leaders and authors of treatises on legal ethics preferred to denounce the symptoms: contingent fees and ambulance chasers.

> —Jerold Auerbach, *Unequal Justice*, 1976

ISIDOR JACOB KRESEL ARRIVED IN NEW YORK IN THE 1890S, an immigrant. As a young man, he lived with his family in a crowded tenement building on Stanton Street in the city's Lower East Side. He put himself through college at Columbia University, then through law school there, by tutoring other students. In 1901, at the age of twenty-three, Kresel got a job in the Manhattan District Attorney's office; there he began to build a reputation as a relentless public prosecutor who probed into every facet of cases in pursuit of a conviction. Over the years, he played a key part in major antitrust and bankruptcy prosecutions, and he was part of the team of lawyers who impeached the Governor of New York in 1913. Kresel "knew where facts were buried and how to dig them out," one writer would later say of him. And many felt that his personality matched his physical appearance: Diminutive and slight in build, Kresel, it was once joked, could "run under a table wearing a high hat."[1] From his earliest days at the D.A.'s office, Kresel was referred to as the Ferret.[2]

In February 1928, Isidor Kresel was named to head an investigation into ambulance-chasing practices in New York City. The investigation had come about through the efforts of the city's most elite bar group, the Association of the Bar of the City of New York. Over the years, the association had expressed concern over a "well-organized system" of soliciting personal injury claims that brought with it a number of abuses, chief among them the exploitation of "poor and ignorant" clients who paid fees that were too high or were cheated out of settlement money in some way. In a broader way, the group asserted, the chasers had become a public scandal, degrading the quality of justice in the city and lowering the public's estimation of the legal profession. In 1926 association leaders began crafting reforms of the rules governing personal injury practice in the city. Early in 1928, they were pushed into more drastic action by public pressure resulting from Abe Gatner's detailed confession about the city's chasing culture published in the *Brooklyn Eagle*. They petitioned the State Supreme Court for the authority to conduct hearings into what was referred to generically as "chaser evils." The next month the court responded favorably to the petition, agreeing with the bar elites on all major points.[3] Writing under the headline "CHASING THE CHAS- ERS," editorialists at the *New York Times* praised this effort to clean up all of the "unprofessional, obstructive, and corrupt practices of the ambulance chasers, and their squads of runners, henchmen, and go-betweens."[4] With court approval and the press's encouragement, bar leaders set dates for the hearings to begin. And the Ferret took it from there.

Kresel was vacationing in Palm Beach, Florida, when he was officially named to head the chaser probe. He sent a telegram to the major papers, however, to let New Yorkers know that he was pleased with the appointment, that he saw it as his duty to serve the public and the legal profession, and that he was looking forward to purging the bar of its undesirables. When he returned to the city, Kresel hand-picked his assistants from hundreds of volunteers, choosing mainly former federal prosecutors; later the staff would be augmented by young corporate lawyers volunteering their time.[5] In late February 1928, the hearings on ambulance-chasing practices in New York began and Isidor Kresel went to work, first in closed-door sessions, then before the public. Under his persistent questioning, one aging attorney broke down and resigned from the bar. He reportedly "shook his gray head" in shame and declared himself to be "under a great mental strain" before finally "wincing and acquiescing" to Kresel's charges.[6] Another attorney claimed to have suffered a nervous breakdown as a result of Kresel's ceaseless excavation of his business affairs, but then submitted to questioning and was ultimately disbarred. Still other attorneys fled the city before facing the Ferret's examination: Lawyers were rumored to have taken night trains to Miami or to Los Angeles, or to be "hiding somewhere in New Jersey." Samuel Goldberg, for one, was alleged to have fled to Europe at the start of the chaser hearings but then to have returned surreptitiously in order to conduct his practice from Hoboken with the help of a law clerk named Sidney Grayson. Apparently frustrated at attorney Goldberg's defiance of the inquiry, Kresel grilled Grayson: "Isn't it a fact that you know Goldberg returned a week ago and that you have an appointment to meet him in Hoboken tonight before he leaves for California?"[7] Grayson denied it, but Kresel persisted: "You have no appointment to meet him tonight?" he asked. Grayson again denied it, and Kresel again pursued. "But is it not true that you drove to Hoboken a week ago and met Goldberg?" Grayson continued to deny that he had made contact with Goldberg, but Kresel ultimately forced a minor admission from him. The next day the Ferret would probe for more.

After almost six months of hearings on ambulance chasing, Kresel and his colleagues had elicited an incredible volume of testimony: 11,000 pages from some 1,100 witnesses. Kresel had spoken to enough people—pushcart peddlers, taxi drivers, hospital clerks, runners, floppers, doctors, attorneys for the defense and for plaintiffs—to develop a picture of the illicit networks that had developed around personal injuries on the streets of New York. "There is a relation between the police and the ambulance chasers," he concluded before a crowded courtroom on the last day of the hearings in July 1928. "There is a relation between the hospitals and the ambulance chasers; there is a relation between the physicians and the ambulance chasers. Even some of the newspapermen have not escaped the contamination."[8] Kresel also cited the equally reprehensible practices of the insurance companies whose representatives rushed to accident sites and to hospital bedsides in order to secure "cheap" and "paltry" settlements. But, for the most part, he concentrated on the plaintiffs' lawyers. In particular, Kresel stressed the moral failings, educational shortcomings, and the base commercial instincts of the chasers: "The root of the evil lies in the fact that some lawyers who are admitted to the bar never should have been admitted to the bar," he told the court. "These are men who have no background, no character, not sufficient preliminary education, no idea of the ethics of the profession, and no distinction in their minds between business and profession; men who consider these cases as business, treat them as business, just as if they were selling shoes or clothes." Again Kresel acknowledged that insurers had been the first to make an unseemly business of accidents; and he conceded that the plaintiffs' chasing practices had grown up largely in response to these defense techniques.[9] But the ambulance chaser hearings of 1928—hearings that took place not in only in New York, but also in Milwaukee, Philadelphia, and several other major cities around the country—were not about the practices of the casualty insurance industry, its agents, adjusters, or attorney defenders.

In October, Isidor Kresel's findings were summarized in a final report on the chaser hearings written by Judge Isidor Wasservogel of the State Supreme Court, who had presided over the hearings. Relying on evidence developed by Kresel, Wasservogel characterized ambulance chasing as an "industry" operated according to the "highly organized business methods" of a minority of personal injury specialists.[10] The judge recommended that seventy-four of these attorneys be disbarred or cited for some kind of disciplinary action. In the subsequent months, Kresel himself began to conduct the disbarment proceedings. Among the first to lose their licenses were the attorneys who had been associated with the Laulicht brothers' accident ring at 305 Broadway. Then came the disciplining of attorneys who were shown to have paid runners for cases. Of these, some were disbarred, others were suspended from practice for one or two years, and still others were censured.

Even the Ferret could not dig up evidence enough to support all of his accusations against the chasers, however; and in the year following the hearings, more than a quarter of all of the charges were dismissed.[11] At the same time, in the State Legislature, much of the initial momentum for legal reform of personal injury practice had also dissipated. By March 1929, all of the antichaser bills that had been introduced during the previous year, and strongly supported by Governor Franklin Roosevelt had been voted down by upstate Republicans, who saw them as products of "hysteria" in New York City that would soon quiet down on its own.[12] In the end, the only institutional reform coming from the countless man-hours of prosecution and legislative wrangling, and from some six months on the hot seat for every small-time negligence attorney in Lower Manhattan, was a relatively minor matter of court procedure—Rule 4-A—which required attorneys for plaintiffs in personal injury cases to report their fee arrangements to the courts within ten days after signing a client. This rule would last a few decades, until Judge Wasservogel again presided over hearings on contingent fee law practices in the mid-1950s; then Rule 4-A too was scrapped.

While the fireworks of the 1928 New York chaser probe fizzled, Isidor Kresel's star soared. He was a reformer at a time when reform was on the minds of New Yorkers; a success in the private sector (after leaving the D.A.'s office) who nevertheless maintained an abiding interest in doing the people's business; an indefatigable fighter for what was right in his frequent role as citizen-prosecutor. During the chaser hearings, a flattering photograph of Kresel had appeared in the Sunday *New York Times* as part of a feature on "the leading lawyer who set aside a year out of a busy practice to supervise the chaser investigation without a fee."[13] When asked why he had returned so often from private practice to serve as a special public prosecutor, Kresel again stated that he felt it to be his "public duty" as an American. Later, in an unpublished autobiography, Kresel would name the credo that had driven him to success from his humble beginnings as an immigrant on the Lower East Side: "America," he said, "is my passion and my religion."[14]

In 1930, after completing the last disbarment actions against the chasers, Isidor Kresel returned full time to private practice, where he had been one of the city's major corporate attorneys for almost twenty years. Within months, however, he was called back to public service by another of the city's major bar leaders, Judge Samuel Seabury, who wanted Kresel to be his right-hand man in a massive investigation into corruption in the magistrate's courts. With his appointment to the Seabury Commission, Kresel had reached a new height in his already stellar career. During the initial months of the Seabury inquiry— an historic probe that ultimately led to the resignation of Mayor Jimmy Walker—Kresel's good reputation continued to grow. Again he worked without compensation, achieving results quickly through methodical investigation. After only eight months of public hearings, the Ferret had secured indictments of several corrupt magistrate's judges and politicians.

The great rise of Isidor Kresel from hustling immigrant to esteemed public prosecutor to successful corporate attorney had taken some thirty to forty years. The fall, however, when it came suddenly in 1931, would take considerably less time. In a startling turn of events, Kresel had been forced to resign from the Seabury investigation after being indicted for his alleged role

FIGURE 3.1. Isidor J. Kresel (second from left) is pictured here as part of the team of lawyers who impeached the Governor of New York in 1913. In 1928, Kresel conducted hearings on ambulance chasing in New York on behalf of one of the city's elite bar groups. Early in his career, he earned the nickname "The Ferret" for his tenacity as a public prosecutor. (Photograph from the *New York Times*.)

in a major banking scandal involving one of his corporate clients, the Bank of United States.[15] By November 1933, Isidor Kresel had been found guilty of securities fraud in connection with a complicated financial scheme known as "the Bolivar Plan"; then he was sentenced to thirty months in prison. Although Kresel was set free on bail before serving any prison time, the long public trial and the ultimate conviction destroyed him personally. His health had begun to fail in the first months following his indictment in 1931, and it continued to worsen. After paying his share of a civil judgment against him resulting from the case, he was penniless. To make matters worse, Kresel's wife died that year. Her friends conjectured it was due to despair over the trial; Isidor later declared that she had been killed by attacks upon the couple's good name. As if this were not bad enough, the former special prosecutor of ambulance chasers was himself disbarred after being found guilty of a felony.[16]

While Judge Seabury had become a national figure by the close of the magistrate's probe—and some political strategists were even considering him over Roosevelt for the Democratic presidential nomination in 1932—Seabury's chief assistant, Isidor Kresel, had become a footnote to the proceedings, a victim of its politics. In the years following his trial, Kresel fought doggedly to overturn his conviction and to be readmitted to the bar; in January 1935 he succeeded. The day after his exoneration, Kresel reportedly sat "dazed" behind a "huge desk in his office on the thirty-fifth floor of 15 Broad Street, receiving the congratulations of his friends and well-wishers."[17] He was heard to have repeated the same phrase throughout the afternoon—"Isn't it grand?"—while "sipping a glass of port wine that someone thrust into his hand." When a relative of his deceased wife phoned, he again remarked "Isn't it grand?" before adding that it would have been wonderful if his wife had lived to see his name cleared. "I do not want to be melodramatic," Kresel said at the time, "but this means more to me than life itself. It is a vindication, professional and personal." Headlines in the next day's paper announced that Kresel was preparing to rebuild his career, but this would be one project immune to his perseverance. The damage to his reputation could not be reversed: Never again would Kresel be called on for his passionate brand of public reform; and this was a bitter pill for the Ferret to swallow. When he died decades later, Isidor J. Kresel's obituary did not even appear in the paper that had for so many years sung his praises.

To the ambulance chasers whom Isidor Kresel had prosecuted for marginal ethical infractions in 1928, the wrecking of his public career must have seemed like justice. The fact that the case against Kresel was mostly trumped up as political revenge did not detract from the chasers' glee, most likely, but, rather, enhanced it—like the final accent in a collective touché.

For decades prior to the war against the chasers, legal elites had made a hobby out of wringing their hands over conditions in the ghetto of the legal profession: the personal injury bar. The elites did not like the way that most personal injury lawyers got their cases (through streetcorner solicitation). Nor did they like the manner in which accident lawyers were compensated for their services. (Almost from the moment the contingent fee was legalized in New York in 1848, the elites believed it would transform the law into a lottery by giving the lawyer a percentage stake in the outcome of a case.) And they did not like the high volume of litigation that contingent-fee lawyers seemed to encourage. (Minor accident cases cluttered the court dockets and slowed the same civil justice system that they had to use in their own corporate law practices).

Beyond these structural points, the elites had more serious beefs with the individual attorneys who handled accident cases: Personal injury attorneys were thought to be "commercializing" the legal profession, corrupting it away from the profession's nineteenth-century norms. The chasers' brazen solicitation of accident victims threatened legal elites' misty-eyed sense of themselves as Abe Lincoln–types to whom clients came "naturally" without need for "touting." The elites saw little wrong with their own business-getting practices, of course—hobnobbing at country clubs, networking at social gatherings, exploiting business contacts—and somehow they found nothing overly commercial about their own "law factories" set up to serve big business. The Wall Street lawyers, in fact, had their own "trappers" and rainmakers who were able to bring in business through their background and broad social contacts.[18] These corporate attorneys were at least as responsible as the chasers for commercializing the profession during the early part of this century. But as corporate lawyers were the ones who ran the bar associations, there would be no public campaigns against the Wall Street lawyers.[19]

As much as anything, the elites objected to something about this new breed of accident attorney that was hard to define but that everyone agreed the chasers lacked: character. The elites denounced the chasers as "unlearned, unlettered, and utterly untrained young lawyers with no esprit de corps and little regards for the traditions of the profession." In translation, legal historian Jerold Auerbach later explained, this meant that they were immigrant attorneys and, in particular, Jews: "A veritable flood of lawyers, with foreign names, concentrated in cities, who often entered the professional portals through night law schools or even correspondence courses, threatened the image of the legal profession as an aristocratic enclave," Auerbach writes of the conditions that led to the adoption of a code of ethics for lawyers in the first decade of this century. "As the children of new immigrants entered the legal profession in unprecedented numbers, only the Canons of Professional Ethics separated the bar's best men, Protestants of English and northern European origins, from the 'unfit'—Jews and Catholics from eastern and southern European backgrounds."[20]

The adoption of the ethical canons in 1908 along with new requirements of education, citizenship, and character, in fact, were all part of an effort by the elites to regain control over who could become a lawyer in America. Auerbach explains:

> The ethical crusade that produced the Canons concealed class and ethnic hostility. Jewish and Catholic new-immigrant lawyers of lower-class origin were concentrated among the urban solo practitioners whose behavior would now be unethical because established Protestant lawyers said it was. . . . Ambulance chasers became the scapegoats in a heterogeneous profession increasingly populated by foreign-born lawyers.[21]

Twenty years after the adoption of the canons, a full-blown war against the ambulance chasers had taken shape in courtrooms around the country. Often denoted by the phrase "the sanitation of the bar," which faintly suggested the eugenical ideas of "native white" racial superiority popular in the 1920s, the war against the chasers would provide the dramatic culmination of decades of efforts by legal elites to reduce the city's swelling numbers of immigrant practitioners. For those lawyers who saw themselves in the tradition of be-wigged barristers perorating eloquently at the ancient Inns of Court, most personal injury lawyers were not only vulgar and a disgrace, they were not even real lawyers. That many of them "could not speak the King's English correctly," in fact, was one of Isidor Kresel's principal knocks against the chasers, along with the fact that the chaser-lawyers played cards at cafés near police headquarters and not at places like the University Club.[22] For those who worried that tough new restrictions on entry into the legal profession might "create an aristocracy in the law," Kresel told an audience of bar members after the hearings, "I frankly confess that criticism holds no terror for me." The Ferret also dismissed questions about his method of inquiry—public hearings: "To the cry that individual liberty was unreasonably invaded when a whole class was laid under inquisition without any specific charges and solely upon allegations based upon mere information and belief," Kresel countered with his belief that membership in the profession was a privilege and not a right, making the chaser tribunal necessary and justified by the profession's need to police itself.[23] (A subsequent note in the *Harvard Law Review* found the language of Kresel's argument and the court opinion on which he relied "worthlessly vague." The note suggested that the court should not have sanctioned the chaser hearings due to: the possibility of abuse of power in such inquisitions; the creation of jury prejudice against personal injury litigation; and privacy concerns for the falsely accused attorneys.)[24]

The degree to which class and ethnic resentments fueled the crackdown on the ambulance chasers in 1928 was starkly evident during the later case against Isidor Kresel himself for his involvement in the Bank of United States scandal. The lawyers who prosecuted Kresel, almost all of whom bore a personal grudge against him of one sort or another, played up the corrupt doings of the city's "Wall Street" legal establishment just as Kresel and the elites had played up the sordid dealings of the ambulance chasers back in 1928. On the first day of the trial, an assistant district attorney read 163 pages of charges against Kresel, an oratorical feat that took more than eight hours. In this extraordinary opening, the prosecutor told the jury that Kresel was a "pilot fish" who guided the Wall Street "sharks that scour the financial seas" in order to steal depositors' money. Kresel attempted to defend himself by producing people of known public quality to testify to his good character, but this only played into the politics of the prosecution strategy. The prosecution dismissed these eminent state and national officials as "a veritable parade of wooden soldiers" and "Bar Association pundits" who tacitly condoned people of their elevated status operating above the law.

Recalling Kresel's role in the chaser investigation, the prosecution floated the theory that Kresel had been "used" by the city's leading legal elites, who shrewdly put him, a Jew, forward to do the work of cleansing the bar of the mostly Jewish negligence lawyers. Kresel was a sellout to his race, a Jewish Uncle Tom, the prosecutors hinted. "Certainly he has his friends among the Bar Association lawyers," the prosecution hammered at the relation between Kresel and bar elites such as Charles Evans Hughes, a longtime friend who had once been Governor of New York, the Republican nominee for president, and secretary of state, and who, in 1928, while serving as head of the Association of the Bar of the City of New York, helped pick Kresel to head the chaser probe. "They have used him," the prosecution continued. "He has been the bloodhound that tracked down the little shysters, the little lawyers. He was cold, he was relentless, he was implacable, in the pursuit of the little shyster, the little ambulance chaser."[25]

Kresel's animus against the chasers had been twofold, it was suggested: Not only was it a matter of elite versus nonelite lawyers, but also, more subtly, of Jews of older German heritage (like Kresel) versus Jewish immigrant attorneys more recently arrived from Russia and Poland (like most of the chasers). Such enmity between German and Russian Jews ran deep during the early part of this century, according to historian Oscar Handlin. "The outraged German Jew saw, shuffling down the gangplank, himself or his father, stripped of the accessories of respectability. . . . This was what he had escaped from, been Americanized away from and he did not like its catching up with him. A fear came over American Jewry lest it be Russified."[26] Kresel's autobiography was soaked through with such fear. One writer who read the unpublished manuscript found it to be "filled with invective against radicals and immigrants less assimilated than he was."[27]

In the end, the prosecution succeeded in demonizing Isidor Kresel. They had remade his largely ethical legal conduct in the Bolivar scheme as unethical and had reinvented the Ferret's virtues as character flaws. Many of the chasers knew the experience: Back in 1928, their desire to succeed as lawyers in America—to rise from the ghetto of the legal profession by handling high volumes of personal injury claims, if they were not allowed to do more sophisticated work—had been redefined by Kresel and the bar elites as undignified, unethical, and intolerable. At that time, more than a few personal injury lawyers whose worst infraction was offering a minor non-cash gratuity for a case-referral were lumped in with the attorneys at 305 Broadway who had helped Daniel Laulicht build a fake accident empire. And many reputations were unfairly destroyed in the process. The war against the ambulance chasers was not about the crimes of the accident fakers any more than the initial conviction of Isidor Kresel was about securities fraud; each was a more subtle affair of ethics and the kinds of behavior acceptable in different legal cultures. Seen in the larger context, the wrecking of Kresel's career in 1933 was more than an incidental postscript to the chaser hearings. It underscored their central meaning: The war against the chasers was personal.

In the long history of antilawyer sentiment in America, which stretched back at least to colonial times when Cotton Mather preached against "knave" attorneys and continued through the eighteenth- and nineteenth-century plaints to "annihilate" a growing legal aristocracy, the war against the chasers of the 1920s represented something of a first: lawyers publicly attacking other lawyers.[28] Antilawyer sentiment of old might have involved citizens' groups petitioning state legislatures to "check and controul [sic]" the "horrid extortion, tyranny, and oppression" inflicted on them by elite lawyers who were feared to be secretly running the country. But the elites of the 1920s would take action themselves against the shufflers at the bottom of the legal hierarchy, the personal injury attorneys, who also happened to be among the most vulnerable members of American society: the immigrants.

Back in 1908, at the ABA convention where the Canons of Professional Ethics were being debated and where it was suggested that accident lawyers be more closely overseen by the courts, one delegate objected on the grounds that "no self-respecting lawyer in America" would submit to such an "inquisition" over the conduct of his practice. Twenty years later, however, many of the nation's major bar groups were petitioning the courts for the right to conduct just such inquisitions. In October 1928 the cover of the *ABA Journal* announced: "THE NATIONWIDE WAR ON AMBULANCE CHASERS." The accompanying text made plain what everyone involved had known for many years: "The Bar's effort to suppress 'ambulance chasing' and 'ambulance chasers' has attained the proportions of a national drive."[29] In the late 1920s, the same forces that forced immigrant attorneys into the professional ghetto of personal injury practice, then blocked them from moving up into more lucrative corporate work, had organized to drive them out.

The original idea of holding citywide hearings into ambulance-chasing practices, as well as the legal precedent, had come from Milwaukee, where the leaders of the Lawyer's Club began holding lunchtime meetings about the chasers in 1926. Months of the club's lunchtime strategizing finally took the form of a novel idea that would lie behind all subsequent chaser probes around the country: The Lawyer's Club would petition the State Supreme Court for the right to compel personal injury lawyers to come before members of the club and explain how they conducted their law practices. That the club, acting alone, had no authority to ask nonclub members to do anything of the sort was clear. The question was, first, whether the court itself had the authority to conduct such hearings and, second, whether the court could lend its authority to the Lawyer's Club for as long as it took to get the job done. The club's lunchtime meetings were spent researching these questions and sharpening the arguments in favor of the hearings. The *Milwaukee Sentinel* later characterized these months as "a time when both the Lawyer's Club of Milwaukee and the Milwaukee Bar Association were engaged in militant campaigns to suppress ambulance chasing in all forms."

If the Lawyer's Club needed a pretext for the hearings, an outrage around which to galvanize public opinion about personal injury abuses, such a pretext came early in March 1927 when "the King" of Milwaukee ambulance chasers, Edward Buer, made the mistake of describing his business activities in court. Testifying in a case that he himself had initiated against a newspaper reporter who failed to give him the accident tips he had paid for, Buer explained how he conducted a "wholesale business" in personal injury claims. Like the New York chasers, Buer, a member of the county election commission, claimed to have business relationships with members of all of the Milwaukee papers plus the usual array of tipsters in police stations and hospitals. Buer also had partnered with a handful of attorneys for whom he solicited, and he boasted of having handled more than 1,000 cases during the few years prior to his testimony. At the time he testified, Buer had no idea that what he was saying was significant beyond the $167 action he had initiated. In the next day's *Sentinel,* however, his admissions were published under a front-page headline that screamed "BIG AMBULANCE DEALS RE-VEALED—Socialist Admits He Had an Organized Band of Runners."[30] The text stated simply: "Ambulance chasing, long a cancer in the legal profession in Milwaukee, was brought into the open yesterday."

The board members of the Lawyer's Club did not miss the opportunity to capitalize on Buer's missteps; in fact, it seemed, the club had made a special effort to provoke his testimony and to record it in order to build momentum for citywide chaser hearings. A board member who had participated in the lunchtime strategy sessions about the chasers cross-examined Buer on behalf of the newspaperman. The Lawyer's Club had also arranged for a stenographer from the mayor's office to be present for Buer's testimony.[31] Both were unusual measures to take in an otherwise insignificant civil action. As soon as Buer's testimony was transcribed, the Lawyer's Club annexed it to their petition to the Wisconsin Supreme Court. And the court, acting almost as quickly, returned a favorable reply. A majority of the judges agreed with the Lawyer's Club petitioners that the chasers were furthering "public contempt and ridicule" for the courts and for the legal profession. To use the metaphor most popular at the time, it was time to clean up the metropolitan bar.

On April 30, 1927, just over a month after Buer's court appearance, forty subpoenas were served on the city's most prominent personal injury attorneys, compelling them to appear at a tribunal like no other in the nation's history up to that time.[32] Samuel Kops, described as an "ambulance chaser de luxe," was not called to testify initially, but almost every other major personal injury lawyer in the city was. Some chasers fled, as would later happen in New York, with the only difference being their destination of Chicago rather than New Jersey.[33] The bulk of the Milwaukee testimony, like that which would later be taken in New York, involved stories of citizens being duped, shortchanged, and generally overreached by greedy personal injury lawyers. One particularly pathetic tale involved "a negro baseball player" who had lost a leg and an arm in a railroad accident, then, at the hospital, was cheated out of the money he needed to buy artificial limbs.[34] In another case, this one discussed on the first day of testimony, a sixty-six-year-old man told how "a lot of persons came to my home to get my case" after he fractured his skull in an automobile accident in June 1925.[35] These persons were later revealed to have been attorneys' runners who had learned about the accident from paid informants at Milwaukee's Emergency Hospital. Other disgruntled citizens also described the practices of the Milwaukee chasers and runners working for different personal injury lawyers explained their networks of police, hospital, and lay tipsters. Commenting on these early disclosures, one local law review reported that, although the hearings were just getting started, "the inquisition has already served to open the eyes of the public in general to a condition which had grown up, cancerous-like, as a menace alike to the public and to the profession."[36]

The Milwaukee chaser hearings were going as planned by the Lawyer's Club until, in early May 1927, one lawyer, William B. Rubin, a chaser only in the broadest sense of handling workmen's compensation cases but otherwise one of the state's most prominent figures, refused to appear at the Lawyer's Club tribunal, grinding the proceedings to a halt. From this point on, Rubin would be described in the press as the lone "chaser" who defied the "quiz heads."

By the time he challenged the legality of the hearings, William B. Rubin was already widely known in Milwaukee. In the late 1890s, when he was just out of law school, Rubin had made a name for himself during a run for Congress, which he lost by a narrow margin. Later called "the storm center of Milwaukee politics," he would be the Democratic nominee for governor of Wisconsin. [37] In his private practice, Rubin had distinguished himself locally and nationally as an advocate for the rights of labor, settling strikes around the country as well as helping to craft a major piece of federal labor legislation. Having come to Milwaukee from Russia in the 1880s when he was only nine years old, William Rubin was known throughout the city's immigrant quarters as "the first Russian Jewish lawyer in Milwaukee."[38]

In the summer of 1927, however, William Rubin made frequent front-page headlines because he refused to tell a panel of elite, corporate lawyers the nitty-gritty details of how he conducted his law practice. Rubin believed that the hearings conducted by the Lawyer's Club were an illegitimate "fraud on the courts," and he wanted nothing to do with them. Not only did he refuse to be sworn to testify, but he also filed a $2,000 damage suit of his own against the club members who were conducting the hearings.[39] According to Rubin, these attorneys, "actuated by jealousy, envy, and hatred," had "used the pretext of exposing 'so called ambulance chasing' in Milwaukee" to enter into a conspiracy to injure the good names and reputations of all negligence lawyers in the city. What's more, Rubin claimed to "have the goods on the lily whites" who were conducting the chaser investigation, meaning that he had evidence to implicate his accusers in unethical solicitation activities of their own.[40] Rubin's defiance was characterized by the *Sentinel* with the same word—"militant"—that the paper had earlier used to characterize the Lawyer's Club campaign against the chasers. Completing the picture, the paper reported that "the stage had been set for the legal battle of the century."

In the days after Rubin initiated his action against the Lawyer's Club, lawyers and laymen alike were intrigued by his charges. Rubin was expected to appear in court on the Friday following his allegations, and, as the hour approached, a standing-room only crowd filled the city's largest courtroom. "Excitement was at a high pitch as the hands of the clock crept toward the designated time," but, at ten minutes past the hour, Rubin telephoned the court from Madison to say that he had been delayed in another matter and would not return until after the weekend. To his supporters in the Milwaukee courtroom, Rubin relayed another message of his defiance of the lily-whites: "I will merely say I am ready for them and not afraid of them."[41] On the following Monday, a crowd comprised of "virtually every attorney in the city, together with as many additional spectators as can crowd their way in" was again expected for the "denouement in this dramatic battle." The mixed imagery of war and theater was appropriate to the events that would follow.

Rubin's courtroom appearance on Monday, May 10, 1927, ended, perhaps anticlimactically, with his being sentenced to a thirty-day term for contempt for not testifying before the tribunal. "Before the largest crowd which ever jammed, packed or fought its way into a Milwaukee courtroom," Rubin had "hotly contested" the forces that he believed were attempting to unfairly curtail, oversee, and, ultimately, destroy the law practices of a select group of personal injury attorneys. Over the course of the morning, he was reported to have "matched strategy and skill with a formidable phalanx of attorneys" who presided over the special proceedings, including Francis Mc-Govern, a former Wisconsin governor, and five others "whose names read like a blue book of the Milwaukee bar."[42] Although Rubin was not cowed by these formidable interlocutors, his dilemma in opposing them soon became clear: How could he testify in the same forum that he declared in his suit to have been illegitimate? Even if he could produce evidence of the Lawyer's Club's conspiracy to defame him and other negligence lawyers, why would he waste it in a forum that would be judged a fraud if his arguments proved right?

As this circularity of logic played out in the courtroom, Rubin seemed at times to be toying with the crowd. "Necks craned, and an expectant hush fell over the courtroom" as Rubin declared that he would "now disclose the facts" against the Lawyer's Club board; but then he declined to do so. At other times, Rubin fashioned himself as a conscientious objector to unconstitutional proceedings. "Without intending any personal affront or in anywise acting as disrespectful to authority or law," he began, "I desire to state as a lawyer, that under the constitution and laws, this body, as it is now proceeding is not a judicial tribunal or court, and I cannot provide testimony here without prejudice to my rights." Finally Rubin appeared to be just the sort of person he claimed not to be when he warned that "no one for a moment should think that I have set up a smoke screen of legal technicalities to conceal myself behind them."

It was precisely a man appearing to hide behind a smokescreen of technicalities who gathered his papers and began to leave the courtroom, claiming that he could not conduct his own prosecution of the lily-whites without the testimony of a missing witness. When it was pointed out that the missing man was in the courtroom, former governor McGovern asked Rubin why the examination could not take place right that moment. Calls again emerged from the bench for Rubin to present his case against the Lawyer's

Club and then to submit to sworn testimony himself. Lawyer's Club members whom Rubin was accusing in the chaser "plot" then stood up and offered to allow themselves to be cross-examined. When Rubin declined, the tribunal finally ran out of patience. Rubin asked if he "might be permitted to say just a few more words on the record," and Judge Aarons fired back that "the record would speak for itself." Rubin was cited for contempt—the first major obstruction to the nationwide war against the ambulance chasers was cleared—and the hearings in Milwaukee resumed the next day.

The decision in the case of *Rubin v. State of Wisconsin Bar* inspired bar groups around the country to use the authority of the courts to help their decades-old ousting of the immigrant, accident lawyers from the profession. This use of *Rubin* was what Justice Crownhart of the Wisconsin State Supreme Court had feared when he wrote his impassioned dissent to the majority opinion in that case.[43] Crownhart began by noting the fact that the proceedings against the chasers in Milwaukee had been initiated and carried out by a private corporation, the Lawyer's Club, which was "composed of attorneys in competition with other attorneys in Milwaukee County."[44] Then he brought out the particular bias that the Lawyer's Club had shown against personal injury lawyers: "Unethical practices are not confined to attorneys who appear in personal injury cases," Crownhart reminded his colleagues before asking why similar "inquisitions" could not be instituted against corporate counsel or in other branches of law. The justice seemed most disapproving of the great "hue and cry" that attended the hearings through newspaper coverage: Why had the forum of public hearings been chosen over the customary use of the grand jury system, which offered a way to help substantiate charges before shattering reputations so valuable to attorneys practicing in a competitive climate? he wondered. Such an inquisition as the Lawyer's Club had planned for the chasers, Justice Crownhart wrote toward the close of his dissent, violated attorneys' personal and professional rights and was "illegal from its inception."

Most observers at the time did not view the nation's first chaser hearings in this light, however. One writer for the *Atlantic Monthly* spoke glowingly of the Milwaukee chaser hearings as "an interesting recent experiment in the suppression of ambulance chasing" that "indicates what can be done" to fight an evil system. ("What we have to deal with here," the author exhorts, "is a major problem of house cleaning, of driving the traffickers from the temple of justice.")[45] Bar leaders and newspaper editorialists around the country also praised the efforts in Milwaukee, asking themselves whether they had a chaser problem locally that might necessitate hearings. For its part, the *Saturday Evening Post* prescribed a healthy dose of Milwaukee-style medicine all around:

"There is scarcely a populous jurisdiction in the United States whose bar does not need a thorough house-cleaning."

As the hearings played out in Milwaukee, nine lawyers pled guilty to employing runners to solicit cases. Three attorneys were classified as having conducted themselves in a way that "caused the court to seriously question their fitness to continue the practice of law." And four attorneys, including William Rubin, had been requested to appear in court once more in order to defend themselves against the testimony of sworn witnesses. In sum, bar leaders concluded in 1929, the hearings had served to expose the "nefarious acts" of the chasers, and largely to end them, not only in Milwaukee but also in other parts of the state where newspaper reports of the hearings had been followed with great interest. Back in May 1927, after Rubin first squared off against the chaser quiz heads, one reporter had noted that what began as an inquiry into ambulance chasing "had suddenly developed into a question of the personal honor of several of the men who have been its moving spirits." It was true. Rubin, a maverick and a grandstander, merely amplified the central fact of the nationwide war against the chasers that would be borne out again in New York and Philadelphia: It had been personal from the beginning.

The Milwaukee tribunal would not only set the legal precedent for chaser hearings, it would also begin the obsession with the names of the chaser-lawyers—or, rather, the obsession with the ethnicity of the names—that was to become characteristic of the nationwide war that followed.

The focus on the chasers' ethnicity was not just the preoccupation of legal elites. It derived in part from the street-level work of the chasers themselves, where success often depended on the name of the soliciting attorney. As in New York, the ideal combination was a lawyer with an Anglo-sounding name whose runners were the ethnicity of the neighborhood in which the solicitation took place. Immigrant accident victims looking to retain an attorney must have doubted the ability of one who was too much like them, as if that person was sure to be as unconnected or unfamiliar with the networks needed to secure the best settlement, or, worse, that the attorney might be as equally desperate for money and so might be likely to shortchange or cheat. One woman who was injured in a bus accident told the Milwaukee tribunal how she had been solicited by runners for an attorney named Adamkiewicz, for instance, but then was told by another runner that she had made a mistake. "Why don't you get a decent lawyer?" the runner asked the woman. "A Polish lawyer don't stand a show in court," the man continued. "Why don't you get Joseph Padway?"[46] On the runner's advice, the woman switched from Adamkiewicz to Padway—who was himself an immigrant, but from Leeds,

England, not from Eastern Europe—only to be shortchanged at the time of the final settlement. A non–Eastern European surname was no guarantee of fair treatment by contingent-fee lawyers, the woman in this case learned. But the perception of reliability engendered by Anglo-sounding names was what mattered on the streets where the business of personal injury was conducted.

Louis Saichek, another chaser who testified at the Milwaukee hearings, was well aware of the importance of nonethnic-sounding names when he set up an ambulance-chasing operation to look like a Legal Aid office. To start, Saichek gave his business a name, The National Claim and Adjustment Bureau, that conveyed just the right suggestion of officialdom, with the ring of good old American, bureaucratic neutrality and not a hint of the fledgling immigrant enterprise that it was. Saichek then explained how he would tell accident victims that he could most likely settle their cases himself, but that if he should need to involve a lawyer, clients would have a choice of the best attorneys in the city. "I told them to let me settle the cases out of court—that the matter would be handled in a shorter time and with better results," he said. "But I always said that if I couldn't get a settlement they could have their choice of any attorney they wanted."[47] To secure clients, Saichek frequently used the names of the elite Lawyer's Club attorneys who were examining him at the hearings. "Yes, I used the names of many of you attorneys," Saichek replied to a question from H. O. Wolfe, the president of the Lawyer's Club. "I used Bennett's name and Fawcett and Dutcher, and Cannon, and your name, Mr. Wolfe." This provoked an angry line of questioning from presiding Judge Gehrz:

Judge Gehrz:	Why did you pick out those names?
Saichek:	I always used the names of good attorneys.
Judge Gehrz:	Did you think it was proper to use such names?
Saichek:	Yes.
Judge Gehrz:	Did you have any authority from any of these attorneys?
Saichek:	No.
Judge Gehrz:	Well, it is the use of this kind of method which gives the profession of law a bad name.[48]

The personal injury trade was driven by names—names of accident victims to put on claims forms, names of tipsters, names of attorneys—so it was no surprise that names would become central in the war against the chasers. Names dominated the proceedings in Milwaukee, New York, and Philadelphia, where chaser probes were conducted not only in the 1920s but also in the 1930s and 1940s. Fed up with chaser evils of their own and inspired by the urgings of Charles Evans Hughes of New York, who made a special visit south to encourage a cleanup of the Philadelphia bar, the law association there finally decided to take action.[49] In March 1928 the association passed a resolution calling for a remedy of "the ambulance chasing problem" that was said to be "debauching hospitals and the police force, and causing the Philadelphia Bar to lose repute." Citing the usual abuses—outrageous contingent fees, rapacious chasing on streets and in hospitals, the debasing of the legal profession—the association took encouragement from their counterparts in other cities. "New York has taken the evil by the throat and Milwaukee has stamped it out entirely," it was written of the chaser probes that had already been successfully prosecuted. And Philadelphia would be next.

Chasing conditions in Philadelphia were said to have been "vile," but were nevertheless "many shades less dark" than in New York; and accident faking of the sort practiced by the Laulicht ring was not known to have existed much at all.[50] Indeed, some ten years earlier, at a meeting of the Pennsylvania State Bar Association, one lawyer commented that the "ambulance chasers in Philadelphia are mild, gentle, totally innocuous, compared with those who are located in New York," and another lawyer, this one from Pittsburgh, expressed disbelief that chasers operated in Philadelphia at all. "I do not believe very much in this ambulance chasing," Frank McGirr began. "You hear about it in the newspapers once in a while, but my experience has been that it is the corporation agents who are the ones who rush to the hospital, or bedside of the dying, and try to get their releases from them. I do not think *any respectable lawyer* has anyone out looking for cases for him, and the few, if there are any such, are *lawyers that do not amount to anything anyhow.*"[51] McGirr was shouted down by one delegate who spoke about chaser evils in Philadelphia and by another who suggested that McGirr had been playing too much golf to know that ambulance chasers operated on the streets of Pittsburgh, as well. McGirr backed down and the state bar proceeded with the passage of some minor antichaser measures. The outcome of the meeting was reported in 1920 under the heading "Sanitation of the Bar," but the real cleansing action would not begin until the end of the decade.

In October 1928, after seven months of "intensive research into ambulance chasing and allied abuses," the final report on chasing practices in Philadelphia was delivered to City Hall, stirring interest in ambulance chasing to the level of intensity that marked the Milwaukee and New York tribunals.[52] "Not in the memory of the oldest member of the bar association has there been such a throng of lawyers to attend one of the quarterly meetings," the *Philadelphia Inquirer* reported. The crowd had come mainly to hear the names of the accused, which had been kept secret until the report was issued; and even then, the names were not reported in the press.[53]

In Philadelphia, unlike Milwaukee or New York, investigation into the activities of the chasers had not been conducted through public hearings; it was done more "scientifically," as one law journal put it, through question-naires, a study of over 5,000 personal injury claims settled in the city, and dozens of private hearings.[54] Perhaps the methods of the Philadelphia inquiry came about from a deeper commitment to those who might be unfairly smeared in a public investigation, or maybe there was just a different sense of propriety in the city of brotherly love. Equally likely, however, was a reluctance on the part of the Philadelphia bar to expose many of the more prominent lawyers, including some of their own members and some local politicians, who traf-ficked in personal injury cases solicited by runners just as much as the night school–trained immigrant practitioners.

In a summary of the final report on chasing in Philadelphia, one writer expressed some sympathy for "established" lawyers, presumably nonimmi-grants, who were gradually pushed into handling accident cases by economic necessity. Over time, it was suggested, these otherwise reputable lawyers had become "debased" by their dealings with the immigrant types who did the actual dirty work of solicitation, the point being that the immigrant "runners" and "lead men" were the real source of the contagion. Outside of the official report, Henry Drinker, the leader of the Philadelphia probe and a respected authority on legal ethics, spoke more frankly, and more specifically, about the true targets of his investigation: He complained about the "Russian Jew boys" who came "up out of the gutter," conducting their law practices by "merely following the methods their fathers had been using in selling shoe-strings and other merchandise."[55] A few years before the Philadelphia chaser probe, Drinker's committee had met to discuss the problem of the "overcrowding" that threatened the "honor and dignity" of the Philadelphia bar. "To identify the problem," historian Jerold Auerbach writes, "names were read from a *New York Times* list of graduates from New York Law School; by the reader's estimate, 250 of 279 were men 'who perhaps by their disposition, their character and their training, would be naturally disposed to move along the line of a commercial or industrial life.' They were, in a word, Jewish."[56] Two weeks after issuing their final report, Drinker's committee announced five tough new rules for the regulation of personal injury practice in Philadelphia. The headline in the next day's *Inquirer* read "Lawyer's Runners Get Death Blow,"[57] but just six years later, in 1934, the Philadelphia chasers, apparently risen from the dead, would be probed again.

In the early 1940s, Philadelphia conducted its third chaser inquiry in fifteen years, and once more the issue of the disclosure of the names would ultimately eclipse all other interest in the probe. This time, the law association conducted private hearings, then issued a report circulated only to select members of the association's leadership and to a panel of judges.[58] Once again, because no names were revealed publicly to match to chaser evils, suspicion was directed at the whole professional group. In the weeks surrounding the issuing of the report, "whispers, rumors, and hush hush" helped build momentum for the release of the names of the accused chasers.[59] On May 8, 1942, one Philadelphia paper broke ranks and printed some of the names; another paper described the abuses of one lawyer accused of "forcing his way into the homes of damage claimants, offering them jobs if they would give him their business and showing them how to 'fake' their injuries to impress the trial jury." Judges and the leaders of the organized bar groups in the city criticized the newspapers for their "premature and unauthorized publication" of the law association's final report before the attorneys named could be questioned about their actions.[60] The newspapers shot back with a reminder to their detractors that the final report from the 1928 investigation was ultimately made public, but no one minded because no names were included in it.

The real question seemed to be why the names were included at all in the 1942 report, although not publicized, and not in the 1928 one. Again, the answer may have been in the names themselves. In 1928 the names of the accused seemed to have been kept secret because their public disclosure might have damaged the reputations of some "established" lawyers who were involved with chasing in the city. But, in 1942, the names released were predominately those of lesser-regarded practitioners—immigrants; *not* releasing them would damage the reputations of most of the city's established attorneys, who had since cut down on their chasing activities. ("After all," one newspaper editorial rationalized, "no client could be blamed for wondering if his counselor was included in the 'secret' list.") The headline of the article in which the names had been leaked mentioned the chasing activities of one John R. K. Scott, a "well-known Philadelphia socialite attorney, Republican leader of the 14th ward and candidate for Congress in the 3d District."[61] But Scott's name was news partly because it was the exception to the ethnicity of most personal injury lawyers in the city: Most of the forty-six other names listed in the leaked report were those of Jews.

Thirty years later, in the early 1970s, the Philadelphia bar conducted yet another chaser probe in which the names were initially kept secret, then leaked to the press. This time complaints came from inside the association's own Board of Governors, one of whose members called the probe a "witch hunt."[62] The board member charged that the probe unfairly targeted plaintiff's lawyers in accident cases (most of whom were not Association members), on behalf of the defense attorneys who worked for insurers (many of whom were members). The lawyer also charged that the investigation was laced with anti-Semitism from the start. Ninety-seven percent of the lawyers named as chasers in the association's final report, all Jews, were listed there in black and white, the lawyer claimed, not because they were the only ones to deal in high volumes of personal injury claims but rather because the association wanted those to be the only names listed. The "investigation" reportedly involved asking personal injury claimants, "Why did you pick that Jew as a lawyer?" Some investigators were said to have begun their interviews with the statement: "We are investigating your shyster lawyer."

In the war of names that the nationwide war against the ambulance chasers proved to be, no name was more powerful a weapon than "shyster," which bound up the sense of a legal cheat with that of the Jewish immigrant. The shyster image was that of an oily character, a swarthy type who lived downtown, or wherever the ethnic ghetto happened to be, and who worked near the courts. The shyster was going to use unethical or unlawful means to get what he wanted, usually money, but since his interest and yours might be the same, he was not necessarily to be avoided, just to be publicly denounced. One of the shyster's most important characteristics, his Jewishness, was rarely stated outright, but this is because it was unnecessary to state what was already understood.

Although untrue, the popular story of the origin of the term "shyster" had its beginnings in a book filled with anti-immigrant and, specifically, anti-Semitic venom: a three-volume "historigraph" of New York written by an attorney named Frank Moss, who had worked closely with the Reverend Charles Parkhurst and had served on the Lexow Committee, which investigated vice and police corruption in New York. Throughout his book, Moss seems disgusted by the way that Manhattan, a city once inhabited by "sturdy Dutch," was now teeming with immigrants whose penchant for crime threatened its future. Near the end of the book, Moss takes a tour of "New Israel," explaining the origin of New York shysterhood along the way by telling a story about a Jew named "Scheuster" who worked as a criminal lawyer in the city's major prison, The Tombs, during the 1840s. Scheuster was what Moss called a "Clinton Street lawyer," by which he meant one of the Irish or German Jewish immigrant attorneys "who may be seen about the two local courts, buzzing like flies at a meat shop."[63] In the district where the Clinton Street lawyers operated, as Moss tells it, there was "a little Irish" judge named Barnabas Osbourne.

Scheuster frequently appeared in Judge Osbourne's courtroom, often acting in ways that were "reprehensible and obnoxious." This behavior persisted to such a point, Moss says, that "when another lawyer played a mean trick, the judge would call it a 'Scheuster practice.'"[64] Those lawyers who emulated Scheuster— either by playing "mean tricks" or by being Jewish, Moss does not make it clear—soon came to be called "shysters." (For extra anti-Semitic emphasis, Moss follows this Scheuster story with an aside about a Jew named Moses Borachek whose "foul stench" preceded him into the Clinton Street courtroom, forcing the judge to cry out, "Fresh air! Open the windows!")[65]

Unfortunately for Moss's account of the origin of the word "shyster," there was no Judge Osbourne serving on the bench at the time he is alleged to have coined the term; and, what's more, as linguist Gerald Cohen learned when he made an exhaustive study of the subject in the early 1980s, there was no Scheuster. "Shysters" did exist, however, Cohen points out in his remarkable study. In an 1859 dictionary, "shyster" was defined to include: "All men who hang around the police courts of New York and other large cities and practice in them as lawyers, but who in many cases have not been admitted to the bar. They are men who have served as policemen, turnkeys, sheriff's officers, or in any capacity by which they have become familiar with criminals and criminal courts."[66]

These original shysters who worked out of the criminal courts were notorious for their lack of legal training, their avoidance of ever taking their cases to trial, and their bribing of officials in the few cases they did handle through the courts. The original shysters were confidence men, more or less: They would promise to represent incarcerated clients in exchange for money and goods given up front in good faith. With the goods in hand, however, the shyster would leave the prisoner, never to return. Most original shysters were not licensed in any way, and few stayed around long enough to become as notorious as Moss's "Scheuster" was said to have been.

The true story of the passage of the term "shyster" into the language has its origins in the journalistic ravings of Mike Walsh, a man alternately described as a political radical, a visionary, a crusader for lost causes, a demagogue, and a drunk. On July 22, 1843, in the pages of a radical newspaper, the *Subterranean*, which Walsh founded and edited himself—a paper whose logo was a pen-and-ink sketch of an eye above a caption that read "Knaves and Thieves beware this [eye] is on you"—Walsh began a personal campaign against the shyster lawyers who operated in the Tombs. Walsh denounced these men as a "horde of professional scoundrels, thieves and swindlers, who, with a superficial knowledge of the forms of the courts . . . set themselves up for lawyers and on that pretense cheat and rifle every unfortunate wretch who falls within their clutch." Walsh stretched his imagination for whatever terms of opprobrium he could attach to these lawyers: "ignorant blackguards, illiterate blockheads, besotted drunkards, driveling simpletons, *ci devant* mountebanks, vagabonds, swindlers, and thieves."[67] But, in these early stages of his campaign, he still conceived of them as American species of the English "pettifogger," a name he used for the title of his article.

A week after the publication of the original article, Walsh authored a sequel, also under the heading "The Pettifogger," which focused on the excitement generated by his earlier treatment of "this annoying species of vermin." Principally, the article concentrated on a meeting between Walsh and a lawyer named Cornelius Terhune. At eighty-two years old, Terhune was known as the "Centre Street Blackstone," the grand old master of the Tombs criminal lawyers. As Walsh tells it, Terhune confronted him in Jack Martin's bar late one evening in July 1843 to discuss Walsh's first article on the pettifoggers. Terhune, who was known to cheat a client or two, but who was also revered for his shrewdness at trial, resented being lumped with the incompetents and outright con men who also worked out of the Tombs. "Ven you put sich pieces as that 'ere in the paper," Terhune admonished Walsh in his apparently German brand of English, "you ought to make the exceptions—ought to lay it down straight—you understand. There's plenty of 'em around [the Tombs] that wants [publicity for their misdeeds]—wants all you can give 'em; *but ven you do it, just give the names,* so I won't be confounded with sich *shiseters* as Magee, Peck, Camp, and Stevenson, because I'm down on sich suckers as them—I am."[68]

Terhune went on to provide a definition of the previously unheard of term "shiseter;" it involved the word's relationship to the German words "scheisse," the equivalent of "shit" in English, and "sheisser," meaning someone of no worth. Walsh loved the word, which he bastardized into "shyster," but did not begin to use immediately. For most of the summer of 1843 Walsh made no mention of Terhune's term. Then, in September, Walsh was charged with eleven counts of libel resulting from articles he had written in the *Subterranean.* Angered, Walsh reached deep into his bag of pejorative terms for lawyers and came up with "shyster." At first the word showed up twice in the same issue, then, a week later, four times, then, the next week after that, Walsh used "shyster" eleven times in one issue. Terhune had given Walsh a hammer in the form of the term and every lawyer in the vicinity of the Tombs became a nail. William Wood was denounced as "an egg-headed ferret-eyed shyster," and John Tilyou was presented to readers as an "unmitigated white-livered shyster."[69] Others were swiped at as a group—a "swarm of shysters," a "committee of shysters," and a "gang of shysters, Old Hunkers, police officers and other thieves" whose "touch is pollution and breath is a pestilence." After his libel trial began, Walsh expanded the use of the term to mean not just the transient group of incompetents who preyed on Tombs convicts but also public officials who were political puppets or corrupt. Manhattan district attorney James Whiting was a particularly favorite target of Walsh's attacks: "Is it not a disgrace to a city like New York to have such a mercenary lying 'shyster' for its prosecuting officer?" Walsh asked his readers, rarely referring to Whiting thereafter without adding "the shyster" after the D.A.'s name. Walsh's persistent and, sometimes, reckless attacks landed him in the Tombs for stretches at a time, but this only gave him more material for his antishyster jeremiads in the years following his release. Over the course of the 1840s, Walsh's one-man crusade against the shysters gave way to a career in politics of his own, but, by this time, the word had a life of its own in the popular press and daily conversation.

Somewhere between the time of Walsh's campaign against the shysters and the 1928 campaigns conducted by Kresel and organized bar groups, the term "shyster" had come to refer less to incompetent criminal lawyers than to crafty or greedy lawyers, of which the low-level, Jewish personal injury attorney was the most representative.

No doubt Frank Moss's Scheuster story helped to transform the image of the shyster from an incompetent Irishman or German into a crafty Jew. Decades earlier, however, the change was already taking place. One article from 1871, "Sharks and Shysters," described the practices of the transient con men who had outraged Mike Walsh. The article also mentioned the new "legal sharks."[70] Supposedly, the new shysters of the 1860s and 1870s were clever and known for their repeated successes at trial, not their ignorance of trial procedure and their failures to show up at court. "The shyster of today appears in many varied forms and phases," another writer later wrote. "We have the stupid, lazy shyster whose chief offense is his lack of knowledge and industry. He merely ekes out a living in the scums of the law. He is a disgrace, but not merely so dangerous as the smart, energetic shyster, who is able to hide his true character and is keen enough to succeed."[71]

The differences between the old and new shysters were most graphically embodied in the law partners William Howe and Abraham Hummel, the two most infamous shyster attorneys of the nineteenth century. The two men were perhaps more responsible for popularizing the shyster attorney than any other lawyers in history. Like the shysters of old, Howe and Hummel set up shop across from the Tombs prison. Unlike the old itinerant shysters, however, they were prominent fixtures on the New York scene for decades. A sign in front of their office measured forty feet long, with the words Howe and Hummel's Law Offices written in three-foot-high, block letters that were lit up at night; their cable address was LENIENT.[72] Howe, the older of the two, was the embodiment of the original shysters whom Walsh had campaigned against. Described as having "the voice of a pre-Stanislavsky tragedian and the personality of an accomplished carnival grifter," Howe had actually worked for years in various American cities as a confidence man; his ability to weep on cue, cultivated in these early years, later became a staple of his courtroom tactics.[73] Most likely, he first became familiar with the procedures of the criminal courts by being jailed himself. Such an evolution from criminal into criminal lawyer, Arthur Train once wrote, was natural enough "in a period when the criminal bar consisted mainly of unfrocked priests, drunkards, ex-police magistrates, and political riff-raff of all sorts."[74]

During the decade following the Civil War, William Howe became one of the most sought after criminal attorneys in the city. By the late 1860s, his client base had widened from "streetwalkers, pickpockets, and sundry misdemeanants" to include the most prominent underworld figures of the day: "General" Abe Greenthal's national pickpocket ring; Chester McLaughlin's forgery gang; and members of the Whyos, the leading downtown New York gang of the time. Howe was so inundated with legal work that he made a partner of his one-time office boy, Abe Hummel. Hummel, the son of recently emigrated German-Jewish parents, had moved with his family to New York when he was two or three and grew up in what is now Tompkins Square.[75] After graduating from public school in 1863 at age thirteen, Hummel looked for work, which he ultimately found in Howe's Centre Street office. Just a few years later, when Hummel was still just a teenager, Howe made him a partner.

Howe and Hummel could not have been more opposite in appearance. "Howe was big and flamboyant," writer Richard Rovere wrote of the law partners. "He was a man of enormous frame and girth, deep-chested and lion-handed, with a quantity of wavy gray hair, walrus mustache, and a ruddy alcoholic complexion." By contrast, Hummel "was small and owlish with a black mustache, more closely cropped than Howe's, shifty black eyes, and an unchangingly noncommital expression. Howe was a ponderous, though forceful man, mentally as well as physically; Hummel was quick and fussy and crafty. Howe was coarse and expansive; Hummel was sleek and foxy."[76] A division of labor developed between the old and new shysters, Howe and Hummel, that corresponded to their different styles, backgrounds, and appearances: Howe handled all of the trials of murderers, bank robbers, and brothelkeepers, and Hummel took on the more complex criminal frauds. "While Howe was down the block dazzling jurors with his diamonds and fouling their thought processes with his sonorous oratory," Rovere observed, "Little Abie holed up in his office and put his brains at the service of bookmakers, bucket-shop proprietors, and all the fancier elements of the firm's criminal clientele."[77] Unlike the new breed of shysters whose bread and butter was pain and suffering, Howe and Hummel were never known for their handling of personal injury cases.

By the end of the nineteenth century, Hummel had eclipsed Howe in terms of notoriety. "His name had become, among lawyers, almost a synonym for crook and shyster." Now it was Hummel who was said to conform better than Howe to the term's literary stereotype. With Abe Hummel in mind, author Arthur Train created the character of Abraham Gottleib, a "hawk-faced little man" who is taken under the wing of an older attorney, Artemas Quibble. Gottleib and Quibble work out of an office across from the police station that has an enormous sign out front just like that of the real-life Howe and Hummel. In Train's famous 1911 novel, *The Confessions of Artemas Quibble*, Gottleib is portrayed as the "consummate shyster." With Quibble's help, Gottleib handles criminal cases, like the old shysters, but also personal injury cases, like the newer ones. Frank Moss, the originator of the Scheuster story, may have had Abe Hummel in mind as the model shyster. Moss was personally familiar with Abe Hummel at the time he wrote the *American Metropolis*, having bitterly opposed him in court several times during the late 1880s and early 1890s.

The fact that Moss's Scheuster story survived for so long unchallenged demonstrates the depth of the prejudices that willed it into being in the first place; and traces of the term's history have persisted ever since in American attitudes toward personal injury lawyers.

As it issued from Moss's mind in 1897, the activities of the "Scheuster" shysters were just another example of a long tradition of Jewish villainy dating back several centuries to "Shylock," the Jewish moneylender portrayed in Shakespeare's *Merchant of Venice*. In late nineteenth century readings of the Shakespeare character, according to writer John Gross, Shylock represented the "successful Jew trying to break into social circles where he wasn't welcome."[78] This sense of the meaning of Shylock came to national attention in 1877 when Judge Hilton, the owner and chief executive of the Grand Hotel in Saratoga Springs, New York, accused banker Joseph Seligman of having risen to prominence in banking through the "practice of the veriest Shylockian meanness." The comment was made just after Hilton had denied Seligman a room in his hotel. When Hilton was later interviewed by a newspaper reporter, the hotel baron attempted to draw a distinction between upright, established (most likely German) Jews and Seligman's brand of "vulgarity": "Seligman is to the Hebrew what the Shyster is to the law profession," Hilton said. "He is the Sheeny," he added, using one of the more popular derogative terms for Jews of his day. Most newspaper editorials supported Hilton's action. Despite the sensation it caused, the first meeting of the American Bar Association (ABA) took place at Hilton's Grand Hotel in Saratoga Springs in the summer of 1878; and Part I of the official history of the ABA, covering the years leading up to the drafting of the Bar Canons that were so heavily slanted against solo-practicing negligence attorneys, is referred to nostalgically as the "Saratoga Era."

The sense of the shyster as a Shylock surfaced in many of the writings of elite legal fraternities of this time, often being used as a more venomous, angrier, cursed substitute for ambulance chaser. The theme of the Shylockian shyster emerges in the minutes of the annual meetings of the State Bar Association of Alabama, whose code of ethics drafted in 1878 became the model code for the ABA Canons adopted in 1908. As early as an 1897 meeting of the Alabama State Bar, R. L. Harmon read a paper entitled "The Lawyer and the Shyster," which pronounced an informal war on Alabama shysters. At the time, the shysters Harmon had in mind were working around the criminal courts, like the original shysters of the 1840s, "watching for an opportunity to fleece some poor fellow who is in trouble."[79] Personal injury lawyers were not yet established in any numbers in Birmingham, and Jews were just settling in the state. Although a rarity through the 1880s, Eastern European Jews began arriving in significant numbers during the 1890s; in the subsequent two decades, they shaped the muddy frontier of central Alabama into one of the major southern centers of Jewish life.[80] These new Jews of Birmingham settled in a ghetto area on the north side of the city, making a living as peddlers, butchers, dry goods salesman, and, undoubtedly, runners for criminal and personal injury attorneys and then attorneys themselves.

Even if Harmon did not have in mind the Jewish personal injury lawyers and their runners, he nevertheless laid down the logic that would be used in the professional house-cleanings of the accident shysters that took place over the next thirty years. He writes: "We need not hope that the law can be made absolutely perfect, nor need we expect to be able to disbar, or keep out of the legal professional, all of the shysters and pettifoggers, but it is the solemn duty of every honest and able lawyer to do his part in the endeavor to perfect the law, drive out the shysters and pettifoggers, and purify and elevate the legal profession."[81] In 1916 the Central Council of the Alabama State Bar took just this sort of action against disreputable personal injury attorneys of

Birmingham, disbarring several "shysters," an act that had "a very healthy effect in the state."[82] A report from 1924 noted that the "'ambulance chaser,' so active ten or twenty years ago, has well-nigh disappeared";[83] nevertheless the damage done to the bar's reputation by the very presence of the personal injury attorneys continued to be a source of anger and concern. "If the bar is regarded as a bunch of shysters and tricksters, it is simply because we have admitted into our gates too many who disregard the high principles and purposes of this time-honoured profession," Fred Johnson of Birmingham stated at an annual meeting of the Alabama State Bar in the mid-1920s. Johnson went on about the public perception of lawyers as "money-grabbers and skin-flints," a perception that could be changed only by the organized Alabama bar's "clean[ing] and restor[ing] the profession to the high position of honor and trust it held in the days of old."[84]

In 1926 Oscar Tompkins, a one-time state legislator and outspoken Alabama bar leader, sounded this theme again, speaking about the personal injury "shysters and tricksters who had wriggled their way into the profession for gain solely . . . in New York, Wisconsin, and Ohio."[85] In contrast to those northern cities, still plagued by chasers and shysters, Tompkins noted, "Alabama had struck right at the tap root of a large part of the trouble." As he elaborated, Tompkins moved closer to naming the ethnic group that all members understood to be the offending party when shyster practices were described. Thompson warmed up the crowd of bar delegates with an anecdote whose laugh line was "Rastus, you low down count nigger, why didn't you send that goat on like I told you?" to which Rastus replied, "Befo Gawd, Cunnel, that fool goat done et up whar he's gwine before he got started."[86] Apparently this kind of story went over well at the annual meetings: A few years later, an Alabama State Bar member would address himself to Tompkins, who was then the outgoing president of the group, and tell a story about "a Jewish friend I have by the name of Abe Goldstein" who "tried his best to get in the Ku Klux Klan." In the story, "Brother Goldstein" is blindfolded, thrown over a barrel and given fifty lashes by the Grand Kligraf, 75 lashes by the Grand Dragon, and 100 lashes by the High Mogul, all of whom told Goldstein that this was just the "first degree" of initiation.[87] The laugh line of this story was Goldstein saying that he was grateful for the right to join the Klan, but if he was not at next Friday night's meeting, the group need not wait for him. The delegates loved the story.

This was the atmosphere in which Oscar Tompkins discussed the way in which big-city Birmingham shysters had come to infest his small town of Dothan in the southern part of the state. "I come from a section of the state that has practically no damage suit practice done locally," he began.

> It is about 225 miles from Dothan to Birmingham, and I will say in passing
> that someway or other the news of a railroad accident or a boy getting
> his foot cut off at a saw mill that is not under the workmen's compensa-
> tion act has a strange way of coming by grapevine immediately to
> Birmingham, and a strong, capable, honest Birmingham lawyer gets hold
> of the case—only 225 miles—but it is transmitted by grapevine, it is
> faster than radio, it is faster than telegraph or telephone. I know it is so,
> because it never fails to get here.[88]

Tompkins, building toward his point, momentarily assumed a posture of fair-mindedness by saying that "not all the crimes in Alabama have been committed by damage suit lawyers," although the implication is to the contrary, and the term "damage suit lawyers" probably stands in for Jew. Earlier in his remarks Tompkins had asked rhetorically about the present "aims and purposes" of the state bar; now he returned to this theme by stating that "the purpose of this organization is to try to clean house, if we can." Who were the intended targets of this house-cleaning? Who was the source of the trouble that came from the city to disturb peaceful Dothan, Alabama? Again with tongue in cheek, Tompkins cautioned that the members of the bar "ought not to rush headlong" in ousting the predominately Jewish Birmingham negligence lawyers from law practice in the state. "No man ought to be cast out of the Synagogue, Brother Monte," he said, addressing himself to a fictional Jew, "or from the Klavern," he added, referring to the local chapters of the Ku Klux Klan and addressing himself to "brother somebody else."[89] ("I mean brother most of you boys," Tompkins quickly amended his comment to reflect the fact that most of those in attendance were Klan members.) Again laughter. Tompkins then continued talking about the fate of the ambulance chasers and shysters in Alabama: "He is entitled to his day in court, to a fair and impartial hearing, and I believe he will get it at the hands of the present State Bar Commission, if all of the other boys on it are as straight and honest as I am." As he finished, laughter among the mostly Klansmen delegates once again filled the room.

And there it was out in the open: laughter. Sham justice for the negligence attorneys as performed by a bar commission of "the boys," who, when they were not passing ethical judgments on personal injury lawyers, were helping to revive the Klan in the South with its new emphasis on "those whose European accents and places of residence marked them not only as Jews but also as immigrants."[90] For many of the members of the Alabama State Bar in the 1920s, the war against the chasers might have seemed like just another skirmish in this larger battle against alien threats to their "native" way of life.

Taken together, these meetings in Alabama form something of an emblem of what the nationwide war on ambulance chasers was really about. Far from the courtroom in which necks craned to hear the evidence William Rubin failed to produce, here was a strong suggestion that at least some of the "lily-whites" of at least one bar association had loosely conspired against the immigrants who crowded at the bottom of their profession. Far from the mahogany-paneled courtrooms in which Charles Evans Hughes had announced the campaign against the ambulance chasers and Isidor Kresel had named seventy-four attorneys for prosecution, here was the counterbalance to high-minded rhetoric about court reform or the relief of court calendar congestion.

"The minister in his opening prayer gave us some good thoughts," so it was said in the annual address to the Alabama State Bar in 1927. "He used the word 'shyster,' which we have heard before, but that doesn't apply to us," he added. "It means the fellow who didn't come here."[91] The president's remarks, like those of Tompkins the year before, were followed by laughter.

"Ambulance chasing, I say, is dead," Isidor Kresel told reporters after submitting his final report in the New York chaser probe of 1928. "As a system it is broken up and is dead," he added before noting that the bar should still be "watchful that the same forces do not reassemble and re-establish this nefarious business."[92] Some sixteen years earlier, another bar leader had pronounced the end of the ambulance chaser. "It is a fact indisputably proved that no shyster, barrator, or ambulance-chaser, by whatever name he be called, ever thrived long," it was written in the Yale Law Journal in 1912: "They have made progress for a while, have amassed snug fortunes at times, but in the end they die failures and disgraces, having not only ruined their own lives, but brought reproach and dishonor upon their profession."[93]

However true this may have been about the practices of the old, transient shysters of the criminal courts, the new personal injury shysters' practice was supported by too many institutional facts to be stamped out, cleansed, purged, or done away with by the boys of the organized bar. The contingent fee was legal, accident rates were rising, and immigrant attorneys crowding at the bottom of the bar, in the ghetto of the profession, who were doing the work no other attorneys would do—not even those who worked for Legal Aid Societies—actually were beginning to find a measure of success in America by handling high volumes of personal injury cases. The war against the ambulance chasers had been personal, fought over names, largely a sideshow that was more about the internecine politics of metropolitan bar groups and general anti-immigrant feeling of the 1920s than it was about unearthing the deep-rooted underlying issues. The difficult ethics of solicitation, the problem of the fair compensation of accident victims, the question of the social utility of the contingent-fee system (proscribed since medieval times and still illegal in almost every other country in the world),[94] and the growing criminal traffic in faked or exaggerated personal injury claims were not evils imported from overseas, as convenient an explanation as this may have been for bar elites nervous over their own professional standing. Like the contingent fee itself, which sat at the root of both the free and illegal markets in personal injuries, these were conditions unique to American shores, and they were here to stay.[95]

By the mid-1930s, accounts of the ethical infractions of the ambulance chasers had receded once again to the minutes of private bar groups. During the years of the Great Depression the criminal violations of the accident racketeers resurfaced on newspaper front pages, their schemes having taken a turn for the worse.

CHAPTER 4

INSIDE THE HOUSE
OF PAIN

He has seen but half the Universe who has never been
shown the House of Pain.

    —Ralph Waldo Emerson, "Essay on Tragedy"

J OHN BUTZIK RAN HALF-NAKED through the streets of Passaic, New Jersey.
It was late on a Monday night in January 1932, and it was cold. Butzik
hadn't had time to worry over the temperature. The man thought only of the
Passaic Police Station and how to get there quickly despite the drag of his left
leg, which was partly encased in a plaster cast. Stitches hung loose from
underneath bandages covering a deep gash on his left arm. This was no
midnight jog; Butzik believed he was running for his life. When he finally
reached police headquarters, Butzik sat down with the first officer who would
listen to him. He then spilled the details of how he had escaped from a nearby
roominghouse, where a doctor and some others had just conspired to kill him.
The episode was reported the next day in the *New York Times* under the headline:
"MUTILATED, HE SAYS, BY 'ACCIDENT RING'—Passaic Man, Fearing Further Torture,
Tells of Conspiracy to Collect Auto Insurance."[1]

  John Butzik told the police that, a week and a half before running "fear
crazed and wounded" through the streets of Passaic, he had been lured by "easy
money" to the office door of a local doctor named Samuel Lustberg. On this
Saturday morning, Butzik, a forty-year-old man sometimes known as John
Woznak, told Lustberg that he had heard that the doctor could help him make

a few dollars by doing an accident. Lustberg waited little before preparing Butzik for his first faked claim: After placing Butzik's uninjured left leg in a cast, Lustberg made a deep incision into Butzik's left arm and stitched it closed. The next day Butzik would call his insurer and falsely claim that the injuries had been the result of a car accident; he would also claim that his passenger at the time of the accident—twenty-one-year-old Frank Stamato, who had also been gashed by Lustberg—had been injured in the crash, too. This was how Dr. Lustberg's accident ring worked: The doctor deliberately injured healthy limbs to substantiate claims from made-up accidents. A Passaic prosecutor described Dr. Lustberg's operation as "one of the most monstrous attempts to defraud insurance companies ever perpetrated in New Jersey."[2]

In the week that followed the laceration of his arm and plastering of his leg, John Butzik successfully exhibited his injuries to an insurance company medical examiner. For all his good work, though, Butzik did not receive any money promised to him by Lustberg; worse, he began to suspect that something had gone terribly wrong with the incision on his arm. On the next Monday night, Butzik returned to the doctor's office—this time for a real examination of his arm. While he waited in one part of the office, he overheard the doctor talking to one of the ring members in another room. "We'll do it here," the doctor reportedly said. "You won't do it in this house," a woman's voice shot back. "Okay," the doctor agreed, "we'll do it in the back room." According to Butzik, Lustberg and the woman were discussing the possibility of murder and Butzik was their target. Evidently, Butzik's arm had become so seriously infected that it required attention beyond what Lustberg was willing or able to provide from the room that served as his office that evening, and murder may have seemed like the simplest solution. Terrified, Butzik bolted from the room and headed straight for the police station.

John Butzik's inclination toward easy money could very well have killed him. (A year earlier Dr. Lustberg had been publicly accused of involvement in the murder of Frank Waganaar for insurance money.)[3] Instead, Butzik landed in Passaic's St. Mary's Hospital with some infected cuts. While Butzik recovered from complications arising from the infection, Bergen County police arrested fifteen people, including two young lawyers, all of whom had been members of Dr. Lustberg's ring.[4] The doctor himself was also arrested, tried, and, convicted. In March 1932 Dr. Lustberg began serving eighteen months in state prison.[5]

After his parole in 1934, Sam Lustberg moved to Washington, New Jersey. He had lost his medical license, but only thirty-three years old, he was ready for a new career. He established an optometry practice. The office turned out to be another front for accident faking: A little more than two years after John Butzik's midnight run through Passaic, Lustberg was indicted again. This time police connected him to two different young Passaic lawyers and to several other self-described "dupes" who allowed themselves to be operated upon unnecessarily to create real-seeming injuries in support of manufactured accident claims.[6] Lustberg had realized that, during these black Depression years, there was no end to the number of people who would submit to bodily mutilation for money.

The Great Depression. The images are of desolation and desperation, suffering and ruin: People waiting in long lines on city streets for a hot-soup lunch; others on the hunt for secondhand coats in winter, for a job, or just waiting for waiting's sake. Families recently evicted from their homes sitting on curbsides next to their hastily packed and overstuffed suitcases and trunks. "In 1933 and 1934 there were so many evictions on the East Side of New York, you couldn't walk down the streets without seeing furniture on the sidewalk," one woman remembered.[7] Some people got by during these years by doing odd jobs or public works projects, repairing roads and bridges, building dams. Others got by less well by relying on money from relief groups or local community chests or by living in makeshift Hoovervilles on the fringes of the towns which had once sustained them with jobs. Some young men fled, hopping freight trains in any direction away from home. In the rural South and Appalachia, sharecroppers faced dry harvests. Some left in search of literally greener pastures elsewhere; others toughed it out on the hopelessly unfruitful plains. John Steinbeck's Joad family from the *Grapes of Wrath* packed all they owned onto the back of an old Hudson truck, then headed west away from their Dust Bowl farm for a government encampment at Weedpatch, California. Steinbeck observed of Depression-era families like the Joads:

> The dispossessed were drawn west. . . . From Kansas, Oklahoma, Texas, New Mexico; from Nevada and Arkansas families, tribes, dusted out, tractored out. Carloads, caravans, homeless and hungry; twenty thousand and fifty thousand and a hundred thousand and two hundred thousand. They streamed over the mountains, hungry and restless—restless as ants, scurrying to find work to do—to lift, to push, to pull, to pick, to cut—anything, any burden to bear, for food.[8]

Staging accidents and faking personal injuries for money or food in increasingly dangerous and gory ways is not a familiar image of the Great Depression, but it was a significant reality for many Americans at the time. "[This was] one business untouched by the Depression," remarked New York claims man William Cavanaugh at a 1933 international claims conference.

As a matter of fact, the claim fraud business of the United States grew in hard times and flourished in adversity. . . . This racket has come to the forefront so tremendously within the past two years, I say to you today . . . that with the elimination of Prohibition, with the return to the ranks of earning easy money in some other field, with the vast number of crooked minds that have been engaged in this industry, the increase in the fraudulent claim field will become even greater . . . We call this an age of rackets, and the claim racket is coming to be regarded as one of the most profitable. And I actually mean that. I think that the claim racket in the insurance business today . . . would compare with any of the major rackets in this country."[9]

Economic hard times did not give birth to new accident schemes so much as they increased the number of people attempting the old schemes; this, in turn, raised the threshold for what insurers would consider a believable claim. Unlike the "paper" accidents brought off by the Laulicht gang in the 1920s, which typically involved punch-drunk boxers standing in for medical exams, now claimants often had to create "real" injuries. This meant crude self-inflicted wounds of the sort administered by doctors such as Sam Lustberg in Passaic or Samuel Kauffman of Rochester, New York, whose accident faking increased in the early Depression years as his legitimate suburban medical practice flagged. In one claim Kauffman scripted an accident involving a man named George Neidert, who had a preexisting skull fracture to exploit, and a few members of the Kelso family, who were "poor" and "eager" to make money any way they could. All were to claim to have been hit by a passing car while waiting to cross a busy intersection.[10] After some streetcorner theatrics on the day of the claim, the group returned to Dr. Kauffman's office. Neidert had his old head wound refreshed by the doctor, who beat his skull with a ruler and rubbed acid into the cut to cause bleeding; George and Mary Kelso had their shoulders rubbed bloody with sandpaper. Then all three were taken to the hospital for treatment.

Dr. Kauffman was tight with the money he collected from insurers, passing along only a small fraction of it to the people he used as victims. "After cracking my skull, that dirty crook takes most of my dough!" an angry George Neidert later fumed to a grand jury. The doctor's methods of doing business kept him ever in need of new recruits as accident victims. Once Kauffman placed a newspaper advertisement for a nurse, then, when a woman named Mildred Wilson came to his office to apply, he said that he did not need a nurse so much as he needed someone to play the part of an injured pedestrian in one of his schemes. In short time Kauffman was instructing Wilson on how to fake being "run down" by a car on the street, drugging her, and inflicting bruises and other injuries that left her hospitalized for a week.[11]

In another of Kauffman's cases, a man named Alessandro Turri complained to the doctor that his elderly in-laws were costing too much to support. Kauffman prescribed a fake accident in which the old couple would pretend to be brushed by a speeding car on their way to church. Turri's in-laws agreed: They faked their incident in the street, then visited Dr. Kauffman at his office. Kauffman reportedly "battered the old man so that he looked as if a runaway truck had hit him." When Turri's mother-in-law worried over having no bruises of her own to show the insurers, Kauffman obliged her with a punch in the nose and a promise that she "would get much money for that." Dr. Kauffman himself once got a scare from hitting an old woman to further a claim. After rapping Mrs. Sarah Ritterson on the head with a baseball bat wrapped in a towel, the woman fell to the ground and remained there, unconscious, for five hours. When Mrs. Ritterson returned to her senses, Kauffman was relieved to find the woman "brave" and "money hungry" enough to go ahead with the plan. He sent her out on the street for her staging with "Honest" Jake de Fisher, a crooked garageman who helped the doctor with the mechanics of many of the frauds. With Jake taking care of the body damage to the cars and Kauffman doing the same for the people, the doctor was said to have generated more than $50,000 in just a few years before a handful of disgruntled former associates helped land him in jail.

This newly desperate type of accident faker was the most prevalent personal injury faker of the 1930s. According to a *Saturday Evening Post* feature from the period, the self-mutilator joined the ranks of the accident flopper, the food artist ("who slips foreign objects in his pie or soup, objects, ranging from glass and metal parts to, believe it or not, parts of mice"), and the acrobat ("who falls in front of, and in and out of, moving vehicles"). It was the function of the expert in self-mutilation "to submit to terrific beatings—beatings which break and fracture bones—then to be smeared with blood, battered with bruises, and covered in abrasions and lacerations."[12] Divisions existed among those fakers who exhibited real injuries: First there was the opportunist who capitalized on a preexisting injury such as a hernia, an unknit bone, an unhealed fracture, an abnormal joint condition. Then there were those like the members of the Lustberg ring who were willing "to be battered and gashed on order."

A reporter for the *Saturday Evening Post* alluded to Dr. Sam Lustberg when he wrote of a doctor who had given "a man a shot of cocaine, then gashed his arm so thoroughly with a scalpel that the frightened man jumped right out of the window and ran to a police station half dressed." The Lustberg story was just one example of what the writer characterized as "a racket of enormous proportions and far-reaching civic significance" that "blankets the entire country."[13] In the 1936 article, the *Post* writer estimated the value of the nation's personal injury underworld at $15 million a year, up from $3 million a decade earlier. Then the writer sketched the basic organization of the fake accident enterprises that grew up during the Depression—"Fake Accidents, Inc.," he called them. At the top were "the brains" ("one or more lawyers of the ambulance-chasing type, a doctor of equally easy conscience, and, perhaps, a crooked insurance adjuster"). Working under the brains were the "runners, professional witnesses, expert flop artists, and dupes." Then there were those who dwelt in the bottommost levels of Fake Accidents, Inc.—the "illiterate and unscrupulous folk who have recently had amputations or hernias or fractures" as well as those "emotionally subnormal individuals who will allow themselves to be 'injured' for purposes of evidence." The gruesome injury-faking techniques practiced by this latter group were later described: "Jagged bits of tin make lovely abrasions on the back or legs; a sandbag or a sack of oranges makes black-and-blue marks that are very satisfactory. Belladonna in the eyes and chicken blood in the ears and nostrils help simulate a case of fractured skull, while mineral oil injected into a joint gives all the swollen appearance of a bad sprain."[14]

Stories of self-mutilation for insurance money came from all over the nation during the 1930s. In Oakland the police inspector, John MacDonald, published a book that included a description of Bay Area accident rings that employed "mob surgeons" to help make convincing fake claims. "At a chosen time an accident will occur," MacDonald wrote, "and one of the operators will suffer an apparent injury to his back, head, or body."[15] The patient will later be "prepared" for the claims adjuster's visit by being put into a plaster-of-Paris cast and bandaged—all hallmarks of a very serious case. In some cases, however, MacDonald noted, a doctor was not needed to help simulate believable injuries. "It is a fact," he wrote, "that some persons have the ability to throw their eyes out of the sockets; some can bleed at will from eyes and ears; some can throw their joints out of adjustment; others can simulate internal injuries. All of these are aids in this swindle." In Portland, Seattle, and throughout the Pacific Northwest, the Foster Gang operated, pushing old automobiles off cliffs, then running down after them and positioning themselves as if they had been inside during the crashes. The "victims" would prepare for their roles by beating each other with rubber hoses for bruises, scraping themselves with stiff-bristle brushes, rolling on broken glass, doping their eyes with belladonna, and, finally, inducing unconsciousness with sleeping powders.[16] In Cleveland, a "gigantic fake claims racket" was uncovered; it involved the self-infliction of injuries and was estimated to have earned lawyers, doctors, and phony accident victims more than $200,000 a year.[17] In Kansas City, Missouri, the Chamber of Commerce completed a study of that city's "claim racket," citing, among other things, evidence of an inordinate number of people who claimed to have hurt themselves while getting on and off elevators in apartment buildings and offices, and who had the cuts and bruises to prove it.[18]

Early in the 1930s, this uglier and often more dangerous fake claims business was uncovered in cities large and small throughout the country, but was especially active in the rural South and Midwest. One group of brick-masons by trade before the Depression was based in Birmingham, Alabama, and operated throughout Georgia, Alabama, Mississippi, and Louisiana. The group staged hundreds of accidents in which an insured driver was said to have spun out of control and hit a pedestrian. For insurance policies, the ringleaders recruited the "otherwise respectable citizen who needed ready cash." To fake injuries, the ringleaders often operated on themselves and a dozen or so members of their inner circle, many times using bricks in their fakery, according to one account. "Before going on a job, they would scald their bodies with hot towels until the skin was tender. Then they would scrape bricks across the sensitized part, causing a convincing abrasion. Usually this was done to the back or abdomen." The account continued: "[This] was not enough. Our masons were perfectionists. On the way to the hospital they would lacerate their gums so that they could expectorate blood. Another favorite clincher was to devour a cake of laundry soap which, not unnaturally, caused nausea and fever." Two different rings operating out of Omaha, Nebraska, and Kirksville, Missouri, were somewhat more sophisticated. The Omaha ring, run by a middle-age man who dealt in real estate before the Depression, made a routine of two-car accidents in which one car pushed another into a ditch or down a slope. The car's occupants then tore their clothes and gashed themselves. Then the "serious realism" began: "This sometimes was administered with a baseball bat, sometimes with a rock, sometimes with a rubber hose—sometimes even with razor blades." The Kirksville ring was also run by a former real-estate man who took a personal interest in administering injuries to bolster fake claims: "He is known to have broken a man's wrist with a crank handle and to have smashed his hand with a hammer," one account stated. "Another man permitted the leader to break his leg with a 16-pound sledge hammer, then alleged he had been run over by a truck." According to a detailed investigation by federal investigators, two members of the Kirksville ring permitted the amputation of their arms, one allowed the removal of an eye, another the amputation of his toes, another the extraction of five teeth, and one feigned insanity.[19] The Birmingham, Omaha, and Kirksville rings were thought to have filed thousands of fake claims, continuing through the 1940s, amassing hundreds of thousands, perhaps millions, of dollars. Of all this, however, the self-mutilators themselves usually pocketed less than $500 per accident.

In Brooklyn, newspaper reports told of the injury simulations of the Tagliaferri brothers. Mario Tagliaferri made a practice of injecting his brother Gaetano's wrist with mineral oil in order to cause inflammation and thickening of the tissues. The brothers then would fake accidents by pretending Gaetano had fallen down a stairway or tripped on the sidewalk. The Tagliaferris' accident ring was alleged to have defrauded insurance companies of more than $40,000 through the faking of bone fractures to wrists, elbows, and knees.[20] Thirty-five and fifty years old, respectively, Mario and Gaetano had been working as butchers at the time of their arrests in the summer of 1934. Other members of their ring included two other butchers, a hat cleaner, a glazier, a real-estate salesman, two housewives, a lawyer, three doctors, and several unemployed neighbors. The actions of these ordinary Americans in difficult economic times shed new light on the alleged moral depravity of the "foreigners" who feigned trolley injuries during the depression of the 1890s. When pushed by dire necessity, the newly arrived immigrant was not the only American to reach for the phony arm sling, the baseball bat, or the razor blade.

In Pittsburgh during the early 1930s, as elsewhere around the country, the name of the game was self-mutilation for money. Pittsburgh was harder hit by the Great Depression than many cities in the country, with its economic well-being linked almost exclusively to the production of steel. As the nation's largest steel center, Pittsburgh had attracted masses of unskilled and semiskilled labor early in the century. The residents of "Polish Hill" had come from failing agricultural villages in Eastern Europe; "Hill District" African Americans had migrated north to Pittsburgh from rural southern towns in the 1920s; and Italians settled in the East Liberty and Bloomfield sections of the city.[21] When the bottom dropped out of this manufacturing economy, these people fell quickly into the ranks of the city's unemployed, relying on private charity and public relief.

While the production of steel ground down significantly in Pittsburgh, the manufacture of fake personal injury claims boomed: Locals referred to it as "the oil business." In 1936 writer Elliott Arnold of *The Nation* took readers inside Pittsburgh's "House of Pain," which he described as "a unique establishment where the manufacture of injuries later to be attributed to automobile accidents was carried on wholesale."[22] The House of Pain was run by a man named Frank "Duke" Gemellaro, a "likable middle-aged man who occasionally posed as a lawyer." Gemellaro handled all aspects of his injury manufacturing operation, from procuring policies and policyholders for use in fake claims, to office administration, to settling the claims with insurance adjusters, taking as his fee half of all he could get for his clients from insurers.

In Duke Gemellaro's House of Pain, accident victims were prepared for their accidents and for their examinations by insurance company doctors. In an assembly-line version of what went on in Dr. Lustberg's office, visitors to the House of Pain had their limbs rubbed raw by graters crudely fashioned from punctured tin cans, sandpaper, knives, razor blades, and other everyday instruments capable of lacerating skin. ("A half dozen good rubs on the neck and shoulders," writer Arnold remarked, "and the 'victim' would look as though he had just passed through a meat grinder.") To simulate bruises, people reportedly beat each other with their bare fists and with sacks filled with apples, potatoes, and oranges. Chicken blood in the ears and rough metal wire wrapped tightly around the head would later help make a convincing case for concussion and skull fracture.

With clothing ripped and sullied in a believable way, the would-be crash victims left the House of Pain for the streets of Pittsburgh. They cruised the city's streets, sidewalks, and department stores, looking to get into accident situations on which to base their damage claims. (Hot paraffin was reportedly spread over the scabs to keep them soft and prevent them from healing until the case was settled.) During four years of operation, Frank Gemellaro and the visitors to his House of Pain were believed to have earned more than $1 million. By mid-1936, Pittsburgh police finally closed the house, arresting the principal members of Duke's group. Frank Gemellaro was sentenced to five years in state prison. Far from being "emotional subnormal," as magazine accounts of the fraud would later claim, the "dupes" who submitted to unnecessary operations and self-maiming at the House of Pain were most likely using their limbs in one of the few profitable ways then available.

The grim economic logic of self-maiming for insurance money during the 1930s had not changed very much since the depression of the 1890s. In both depressions, left hands and feet seemed more vulnerable than right ones; and the left hands of farmers, stockbrokers, and real-estate men were among the most susceptible of all to voluntary amputation. As one writer would later observe: "The bottom of the Depression was also the peak, for most companies, in [self-mutilation] claim[s]."[23]

In 1896 insurance examiners John Lewis and Charles Bombaugh discussed a rash of cases of fake gunshot wounds in Nebraska and other rural areas, which they lumped together under the heading "Self Mutilation in Accident Insurance." Some forty years later, claims agent Burt A. Richardson of Atlanta would update the story. As Lewis and Bombaugh had written about men who shot off their left hands and feet, or allowed their limbs to fall under train wheels, in order to collect on their accident ticket insurance policies, Richardson wrote similarly of men who willingly sacrificed their left hands to put food on the tables or to pay outstanding debts in the early 1930s. In a scene sadly reminiscent of the plots described by Lewis and Bombaugh, Richardson tells of one Pennsylvania man who purchased a railroad ticket policy for 25 cents, then, at midnight, pretended to have fallen from the platform and onto the tracks before a departing train. "One of his arms was thrust beneath the wheel of the last Pullman, which completely severed it above the wrist," Richardson writes. "The injured man made a tourniquet himself, as there was no one present to aid him, and walked to his brother's home about a half block away. A doctor was hastily summoned and he completed the amputation as best he could in the kitchen of the brother's home."[24] In Oklahoma City, an oil worker named Dillon Smith contrived a fall in order to lose a hand beneath the wheels of a streetcar. The accident was supposed to bring Smith $375 cash, but, instead, earned him a year in the McAlester penitentiary, the same jail from which Steinbeck's Tom Joad is released at the beginning of the *Grapes of Wrath*.

In the early 1930s, the idea of trading one's limbs for hard cash was pervasive in America—even "contagious," according to claims man Richardson. Why a person would commit the unthinkable act of self-mutilation, Richardson believed, boiled down to three principal motives: religious frenzy ("the evangelist who permits a rattlesnake to strike him repeatedly"), fear (as in the case of the wartime malingerer), and dire financial need.[25] This last category of self-mutilator appeared during times of economic depression. The loss of a thumb and an index finger of the same hand was usually worth $1,500 under the standard accident policy. Loss of sight in either eye? $2,500. Loss of a hand or a foot? $3,000. An arm or a leg? $3,750. Any combination of the loss of both hands, feet, or eyes, or a hand and a foot, or a hand with a foot and an eye? $7,500.[26] As to how the self-mutilation was most often accomplished, Richardson writes: "Having an arm or a leg sheared off by a streetcar or a train, or shattering the member so badly by gunshot wound that immediate amputation is necessary are the two most common forms."[27] One outstanding case of this type of self-mutilation involved a life insurance agent who was seen to dive under a streetcar, with the intention of causing the amputation of both of his arms. ("This individual seemed to have had a self-mutilation complex," Richardson writes, "as indicated by signs of a previous mutilation of the man's fingers" and by the fact that he claimed fractures to both of his arms, which he had already reduced to stumps in earlier faked claims.)[28] Another case took place in a hotel in a small city where a man shot off his left arm to collect on four different accident policies that he had managed to secure in the weeks immediately preceding the incident. The man, who was later shown to have been hopelessly behind in his bills, had entertained "rosy dreams" of obtaining cash payments of more than $30,000 from the loss of a limb.[29] Insurers settled with him for next to nothing, however, having been convinced by a mass of physical evidence that the "accidental" gun misfiring had been on purpose.

Perhaps the most strikingly desperate accident scheme described in Richardson's book involved an attorney named Carl Wilson, who claimed to have lost both his left foot and his left hand during a hunting expedition. Wilson told insurance agents that he had climbed into a tree to get a better shot at a squirrel when he lost his footing and fell. He said that he "flung his wrist against the blade of a sharp ax, severing his hand from his arm; and at the same instant his shotgun striking the ground, discharged both barrels into his foot."[30] An insurance investigator who visited the scene of the accident later that week discovered the real story after noticing a tree stump covered by debris nearby. "With careful hands, this debris was removed bit by bit, and there beneath it, buried in the decayed center of the stump, was a hypodermic needle, which chemical analysis indicated had contained some form of local anesthetic." Carl Wilson, an attorney who was well aware of the double dismemberment clauses of his multiple accident and life insurance policies, had deadened his limbs with the anesthetic, then cut off his arm with an ax and shot himself in the ankle. The case was tried three different times, with the jury deadlocking each time before a nominal settlement was finally reached out of court with Wilson. The double amputee attorney limped away from the incident with only $50 to show for his efforts.

While accident frauds, especially those that involved self-mutilation, were the most prevalent type of insurance crime during the Great Depression, they were not the only schemes to flourish.

Countless merchants with failing businesses set fire to their stock at a rate unseen since the time of the firebug gangs in the 1890s. And regular folks in need of quick cash joined the "Burn Your Own Home Movement," as one writer in 1933 termed the rush to set insurance fires.[31] To handle all the new arson business, Sam Sapphire, a former woolens manufacturer from Brooklyn, started his own arson-for-profit service. "In the late Twenties, Sapphire had set only a few fires, mostly for friends," one account stated. "But once the Depression hit, and just about everyone was on the edge of financial disaster, he teamed up with a firm of dishonest public fire adjusters and began setting fires almost as fast as he could obtain the celluloid and the plumber's candles he used to ignite them."[32] Sapphire's standard fee was $500 per fire, but he offered a special for factory owners who also wanted to cash in on their residences: $50 to burn an apartment.

Another arson service that thrived during the Depression era operated throughout White Plains and Yonkers, New York. Forty-five-year-old George Mondello, the group's ringleader, advertised that he would burn down the house of anyone who was willing to part with 10 percent of the resulting insurance settlement. Mondello's arson service was believed to have burned more than $400,000 worth of property in New Rochelle, Mount Kisco, Port Chester, and parts of Connecticut before being exposed by a private detective who recorded incriminating conversations with Mondello on thirty-eight phonograph records.[33] In late 1936 New York State attempted to address the reemergence of such widespread arson-for-profit schemes by passing a new law increasing penalties for willfully burning property with intent to defraud an insurer. Like similar arson statutes dating back to eighteenth-century England, the legislation proved ineffective.

As surely as fire insurance frauds returned on a grand scale during the Great Depression, so did speculative life insurance frauds of various sorts. Some relatively benign schemes began with newspaper ads offering to collect on lapsed insurance policies: "Insured may be dead for years, may have disappeared, or be disabled. Let us investigate. Bring or mail policies to us."[34] Other more intricate plots were reminiscent of the life frauds popular during the depression of the 1890s, where the old, the sick, or the stupid were preyed upon by people who took out policies in their name. Last seen in rural Pennsylvania and North Carolina, such speculative life frauds reappeared in Brooklyn early in the 1930s, when six different people purchased forty-three life insurance policies on Fred Ewald Bottger, a man who had long suffered from terminal cancer. To secure the policies, a healthy, forty-two-year-old man named Walter Forster took the medical examination under Bottger's name. Forster and his wife, Anita, had owned the home in which Bottger had lived since his separation from his wife. They were the first to insure his life; ultimately policies amounted to over $500,000.[35] In January 1935 Fred Bottger finally succumbed to his illness (with a little help from his friends), dying alone in his rented room. Among those in line to collect on his life were a local doctor, a butcher, a former insurance agent, and dozens more. In the months following the initial exposure of the case, more arrests showed the extent of the life frauds in New York. Thirty-eight people from Brooklyn were charged with participating in similar schemes to defraud more than 100 life insurers by insuring the lives of chronically sick or aged people in the community. Tips had come from druggists who identified the best prospects through the prescriptions they filled. In other cases, relatives and acquaintances of the sick and dying conspired with others who would take the medical exams. By January of 1937 all thirty-eight Brooklynites who had been arrested and tried for life insurance speculations had been found guilty and received suspended sentences. Only two people served prison time for the frauds.

The history of insurance crimes has shown that, where pretended death and speculative life insurance frauds flourish, outright murder for insurance is not far behind. This proved as true during the Depression of the 1930s as it had in the 1890s. In Philadelphia during October 1934—almost forty years after H. H. Holmes had killed Benjamin Pitezel for insurance money in that same city—a brutal murder-for-insurance plot was uncovered. Adam Ambrose, a South Philadelphia butcher in his early forties who was having trouble supporting his three sons, had insured his own life for $10,000, then went about finding someone of roughly his size and appearance to stand in for his corpse. Ambrose soon found his victim, a drifter named Joe Jesbutis who was a resident of one of the tin-and-tarpaper shacks on the outskirts of the city. By promising Jesbutis work as a housepainter, Ambrose lured the man to a New Jersey beach town where he planned to kill him, then to use the body to stage his own death. Ambrose killed Jesbutis but then, for some reason, could not go forward with the plan to make the insurance claim.[36] After surrendering to Philadelphia police, Ambrose returned to the Cape May County sand dunes where he had buried homeless Joe. He waited while police and some Coast Guardsmen dug through the sand. "Are you sure the body is here?" one of the officers asked after a half hour of searching had uncovered nothing. "Sure it's here," Ambrose replied before he grabbed a shovel himself and dug four feet into a dune. "Here it is," he declared after a few minutes. "My conscience is clear, now give me a cigarette." The next morning Ambrose was found dead in his cell in the Cape May Court House: He had hanged himself from a rope fashioned from strips of his mattress cover.[37]

During the darkest years of the Great Depression, economic hardship put price tags on the heads of the nation's most vulnerable—the old, the sick, American Indians from the West (some of whom were targeted by a group of "fake" New York Indians who ran a murder-for-insurance gang),[38] and, occasionally, children. One of the many stories of child murder for insurance came from Houston, Texas, and involved a father who killed his four-year-old girl in order to collect on a $400 policy.[39] In July 1934, E. H. Stuart, an unemployed laborer, drove his twin daughters to a bridge seventeen miles outside of the city. While the girls slept, Stuart parked by Cypress Creek, took one of his daughters from the car, then drowned her in the shallow water. For weeks before finally confessing, Stuart claimed that his daughter had been kidnapped from his car while he went into a store to buy some sandwiches.

During that same summer, a crippled alcoholic named Harry Wright was lured out to a highway near Cooperstown, New York, then was beaten with a mallet and run over "accidentally" at the direction of Mrs. Eva "Little Eva" Coo, a broke bootlegger and sometime madam looking to collect what she could on the man's life.[40]

Not to be outdone by Mrs. Coo, four New York men known collectively as the Murder Trust carried out one of the most horribly protracted murders for insurance in history.[41] In attempting to do away with Mike Malloy, an unemployed fireman who was a regular at Tony Marino's Mermaid Tavern in Lower Manhattan, the Murder Trust used a number of usually reliable homicide techniques: They tried to get Malloy to drink himself to death through a mixture of alcohol, turpentine, and horse liniment; they tried to freeze him to death by stripping him to the waist, pouring cold water on him, then leaving him for dead in Central Park on a frigid winter's day; they fed him a sardine sandwich laced with slivers of the sardine can itself; and they put his unconscious body in the middle of a busy street and offered a taxi driver from $200 to $400 to run him over. Finally they succeeded in poisoning "Malloy the Mighty" (as one account referred to him) by running a gas tube from a heater into his mouth. Members of the Murder Trust were later executed in just one try in the electric chair at Sing Sing Prison.

While murder for insurance was, perhaps, the more dramatic or widely publicized life insurance scheme, the real shame of the Great Depression was the boom in suicides for insurance committed by financially strapped middle-age, middle-class men. "When I attended Berkeley in 1936, so many of the kids had actually lost their fathers," film critic Pauline Kael later told oral historian Studs Terkel. "They had wandered off in disgrace because they couldn't support their families. Other fathers had killed themselves so the family could have the insurance."[42] Dr. William Muhlberg of the Union Central Life Insurance Company wrote about the increase in suicide for insurance: In an article published in the early 1930s in the *Claim Investigator*, Dr. Muhlberg cited "loss of fortune or reputation and dishonor" as the leading cause.

As far as we could determine through post-mortem investigation, the increase of the suicide rate in 1932 was largely due to injured vanity and was noted principally among policyholders carrying large amounts of insurance. The victim had been very successful in business, usually a self-made man. He accumulated much wealth and prestige and a reputation of being a financial wizard during the boom period. The economic crash ruined his reputation as a financier, and although he may have had enough money left to live comfortably or to rehabilitate, he was evidently ashamed to face his family and friends and chose the easiest escape.[43]

Claims man Burt Richardson also wrote about the increase in suicide for insurance during the early 1930s. He tallied up the latest "fashions in suicide," noting that pistols, shotguns, gas asphyxiation, and hanging led the way before and after the Depression, but that carbon monoxide poisoning and falls from windows had increased significantly in the early 1930s. In a section entitled "Falls From Windows," Richardson fleshes out the truth behind the popular joke that it rained stockbrokers and traders after the stock market crash of 1929. "The drastic and thoroughly conclusive act of jumping from a height reached a popularity which it had not previously known," Richardson writes. "Managers of tall buildings engaged guards to patrol about in the upper regions to watch out for individuals who might be acting strangely. Even at points far removed from Wall Street, special precautions were taken; 'suicide-proof' screens were installed in several buildings in Midwestern cities."[44] One Aetna life insurance statistician went so far as to develop a mathematical formula for determining whether the deceased jumped or fell from the window in question. "The starting point in this calculation is the exact distance between the spot where the body hit the ground and the foot of the building," Richardson tells us, with the rest of the calculation apparently being too complicated to summarize.[45] One case of a suicidal leap from a roof-top was solved without need of complicated math, however, after a dogged insurance company attorney located two eyewitnesses. In court documents the couple, referred to only as "Mr. and Mrs. Smith," tell what they saw from their porch in the summer of 1930: "We were sitting here, just like today, not talking any—just watching the neighborhood boys playing in the street," Mrs. Smith began. "I saw him first—I looked up to see whether there were any clouds when father said something about rain; and there that man was, walking up on top of the First National Bank Building." Mrs. Smith continued:

I pointed him out to father for no reason at all. I told him, "There's a man up on the roof over on the bank building." . . . He would walk to the edge of the roof and look over at the street. And then he would walk away again over to another part of the roof. And finally—he seemed to make up his mind. We saw him take off his coat and his hat and lay them down. Then he stepped up on that kind of a ledge around the roof, just stood there a minute, and before we knew what he was going to do, jumped off![46]

With stories like this in mind, Burt Richardson rejected the notion that most of the insurance schemes of the Great Depression were backed by "sinister organizations" or by "one directing genius" who controlled the operation. While this was the kind of talk that some newer claims men put in their reports, then passed along to reporters looking to spice up a routine news story, Richardson had no time for it. Experience had taught him better. "Most of these [frauds] have their genesis in bad financial conditions," he wrote. "The urgent need for money and the success of the first few attempts to collect on insurance build up a community frame of mind which sees no wrong in a false claim. Individuals become obsessed with the idea of getting money from the insurance companies, and all cooperate in helping to get the other fellow's claim through."

This explanation was a welcome antidote to much of the overblown reporting on arson and life insurance scams from the era, but it did not really apply to the accident rackets. In the early 1930s, newly intensified investigations revealed that accident faking actually had become organized beyond all previous understanding. In response, the insurance industry had organized like never before to combat it. "The activities of fraudulent plaintiffs and unethical lawyers cannot be suppressed by a casual blow," an editorial in an insurance publication stated in 1927. "These people have actually built up an intricate, many-sided organization to carry on their bad practices and it will take an equally smooth running machine with which to combat it."[47] The Alliance Against Accident Frauds established in 1905 was doing a "commendable" job but was underfunded and "toothless." To fill the void, the National Bureau of Casualty and Surety Underwriters in New York set up its own permanent body late in 1927—reorganized as the "Claims Bureau" in 1937—dedicated to fighting "claim evils."[48] The bureau's two main goals were "(1) to checkmate the lone wolves and other claim 'repeaters'; and (2) to smoke out the ambulance chasers and fake claim syndicates."[49] Initially the bureau established secret offices in six "strategic" cities around the nation—New York, Newark, Cleveland, Chicago, Los Angeles, and Atlanta. The bureau employed a dozen full-time agents, most of whom had come from the Federal Bureau of Investigation (FBI); by 1940 the number of agents had doubled and bureaus had been added in a half dozen more cities. An index card system included information not only about chronic claim fakers but also about the lawyers and doctors who seemed to be managing their careers; by the end of the 1930s, the bureau had more than 2 million cards in its eight regional indexes. The bureau also published its own version of the railway claims men's *Bulletin*: The Claim Information Bulletin Service, which soon developed into a "full fledged rogues' gallery of crooked or suspected claimants . . . Photographs of the subjects, descriptions, fingerprint classifications, accounts of their claim history and their particular kind of racket, together with other pertinent information, are contained in these bulletins." During the early part of the decade, bureau agents brought about investigations in cities across New York State—Buffalo, Rochester, Albany and Syracuse—as well as cases in Girard, Kansas, Portland, Oregon, and San Francisco.[50] In Boston a five-year accident fraud investigation initiated by the bureau resulted in the exposure of hundreds of fake claimants and "quack" doctors as well as the disbarment of over eighteen lawyers.[51] In Atlanta a "secret committee of adjusters" armed with records from the Index Bureau were the impetus behind an accident fraud investigation that culminated in the successful prosecution of four lawyers, who traded seats in their comfortable offices for places on a Georgia chain gang.

Unquestionably the greatest case in the early history of the Claims Bureau, and one of the most famous cases of its time, the capture of fake accident entrepreneur David Schiffer required years of undercover investigation. Wayne Merrick, the former FBI man who ran the Claims Bureau in the 1940s, celebrated Schiffer's capture in 1948 with an article entitled "A Guy Who Never Had a Chance,"[52] but, actually, Schiffer had eluded investigators for over sixteen years. The son of a tailor from the Lower East Side, he had spent time in reformatories during his teens for pickpocketing and had served time in an Atlanta penitentiary for dealing heroine and morphine. Schiffer slipped into the accident racket in his late twenties when he began work as a chaser for attorneys in The Building of the Forty Thieves—"a building," he later said, "where a lot of lawyers had offices and a lot of guys hung out looking to make a buck." For Schiffer, chasing was just business. In 1933, though, Schiffer crossed the line from unethical solicitation business to accident-faking crime. "I faked accidents on New York streets," he later said in the beginning of a two-part confession published in *Collier's* magazine. Dictated to reporters "from seclusion in Coney Island" and billed as "probably the most unusual true story of its kind ever told,"[53] Schiffer continued:

> I think I was the biggest operator in this line in the country. I hired "floppers" and "divers" to make out they had been hit by cars, and then I collected from the insurance companies. I kept a stable of six or eight floppers and divers all the time. I would pick them up on corners where I knew guys hung out looking to pick up some change. The floppers [would] pretend to get hit by cars that were going slow around corners. They dash out to cross the street as the car comes around the corner, put their hands on the front fender, flip over backward, and lay in the street groaning. The divers [would actually] jump into the side of cars going straight up the street at thirty miles an hour. They stand several feet off the curb and as the car approaches, run out and sort of crouch while slamming their hand against the door, making a loud noise. The car stops, and from there on the routine is the same as it is with the flopper. Once, the Chicago mob sent me a flopper with a big reputation. This flopper was the best actor I ever met. He was so good I had to pay him $75 a flop, which was top money as I was paying my other floppers $25. In 15 years I never saw a flopper or diver even get bruised.

The key to Schiffer's success, as he told it, was to never give anyone else anything more than bit parts in his schemes. Schiffer would not use his floppers or divers to fake medical exams, for example, because he "did not want [them] to feel too important to the set-up." He also did not make deals with doctors and lawyers, choosing instead to make them believe that the cases he brought them were legitimate. Schiffer accomplished all this mainly by building a library of X rays of fractures and breaks of elbows, arms, legs, hands, and skulls. "I saw immediately that I would need a file of X rays to build up my pattern of operation," he later explained. "My first step was to got to the Municipal Lodging House, which had bums and derelicts." Posing as a medical student, and offering bottles of whiskey for cooperation, Schiffer persuaded countless homeless men to have X rays taken for use in his claims. ("I could do more tricks with my X rays than a monkey with a peanut.") Later he sometimes used these same men to submit to the medical exams, giving them home addresses by arranging with prostitutes to use their apartments as mail drops for settlement checks.

> I sold doctors and lawyers a bill of goods. I fooled insurance investigators. I made the cops work for me. With nothing but a library of phony X rays,

FIGURE 4.1. This photograph of a professional flopper being arrested was taken in the late 1940s. The man, who was part of David Schiffer's flopping ring, faked falls in front of cars. Surrounding him are New York City Police Detectives and agents of the Claims Bureau. (This photograph was published in a 1949 issue of the *Casualty and Surety Journal*.)

> I beat every insurance company on the street. In all, I cashed over a million dollars' worth of insurance-settlement checks, but I never kept any records. My files were in my head. I never put a cent in the bank. Sometimes I had as much as $20,000 in my apartment in the Bronx which I paid $60 a month for. I kept the money mostly in $500 bills and concealed them in a book called Ivanhoe, which was in a stack of other books in a closet.

As he got deeper into the accident racket, Schiffer lived in a state of hyper-vigilance and unrest. "I had to be thinking all the time as it would have been fatal to backtrack on myself. I had to be careful that a flopper did not take two flops in front of the same cop or be picked up by an ambulance and taken to a particular hospital where he could be recognized as a repeater." In the end, Schiffer became increasingly paranoid that he was under investigation. And he was right. While private detectives filmed him in a supermarket in 1946,

Schiffer became aware that at least some investigators were on to him. At the same time, investigators from the Claims Bureau and two New York City detectives began what turned out to be almost three years of surveillance on Schiffer, who seemed at least partly aware of what was going on. "On leaving his house, he carefully looked up and down the street and then walked rapidly away from the house," the *Collier's* reporters noted. "The two detectives could never tell whether he was going out to bilk an insurance company or buy a pound of butter." Schiffer's phone lines were tapped, forcing him to invent a coded language that detectives never deciphered. That is, until one day in 1948, he broke his own code and spoke openly about a flopper named Daniel Cozzi. In April 1948 Schiffer was arrested near his home in the Bronx while driving to a doctor's appointment; arrested on the same day was Isidore Leder, one of Schiffer's longtime floppers, and Meyer Segal, a twenty-seven-year-old punch-drunk prizefighter whom Schiffer used for medical exams.[54] With some of his floppers agreeing to testify against him, Schiffer was forced into pleading guilty to many of the charges. "I tried to make a deal with the D.A., but they would not play ball," he wrote near the end of his published confession. "The judge gave me four-to-eight in Sing Sing. This sentence was more than I anticipated but I am man enough to take it as all my life I lived with the adage that in playing with fire I will get burnt some day."

While the work of the insurance industry's "card index detectives" was significant in uncovering the extent of the accident-faking industry around the country in the 1930s, New York was a country of its own. The situation in Manhattan, especially, required greater attention than private police could provide. By the end of the decade, three different probes of the accident rackets would be carried out by city, state, and federal agents and prosecutors that revealed not only the reappearance of accident gangs, but also the rise of the new rings of disease simulators who targeted workmen's compensation and related relief plans begun during the Depression years.

Less than a decade after Isidor Kresel's chaser probe had shut down the Laulicht brothers' ring, the accident racket had returned on a grand scale to the streets of New York. In fact, all of the newspaper and magazine attention to the 1928 chaser inquiry actually may have led to a worsening of conditions. "Initially, it made public the whole traffic in claim faking and its attendant evils, and for a time at least New York was comparatively free from the racket," one insurance executive observed in 1936. "But no sooner had the investigation stopped than the racketeers boldly reopened for business on a more dazzling scale than they had ventured to dream of before. It would almost appear that they too had

FIGURE 4.2. Pictured here in 1948, David Schiffer began managing a ring of accident floppers and divers during the Depression. Schiffer claimed to have kept a "stable" of men who would dive in front of cars. Schiffer also kept a "library" of X rays of fractures and broken bones for use in building the floppers' claims. After his arrest, Schiffer published a two-part confession of his fake accident career in *Collier's* magazine. (Collier's photo by "Giles.")

profited from the investigation by learning what errors to avoid in order to escape detection in the future."[55] The sentiment was echoed later, in 1936, by one of Isidor J. Kresel's former associate counsels. Despite all the publicity surrounding the disbarment of a few "small-fry" shysters, the man wrote, "the ambulance-chasing investigation of 1928 accomplished little or nothing of permanent value."[56]

In their rebirth, the accident rackets of the 1930s were characterized by a new ugliness, a new desperation, and, often, in these years following the suppression of the "shysters," a new ringleader drawn from the ranks of the medical profession: the "quack" doctor. The history of the organized medical profession's drive to rid itself of quacks stretches back many more centuries than the lawyer's campaign against the shysters. In England, during the mid-sixteenth century, the Royal College of Physicians summoned London's most infamous quacks before its Board of Censors and questioned them, with the authority to put the worst quacks in prison.[57] In America, quacks and "empirical pretenders" were rooted out by doctors in Norwich, Connecticut, as early as 1763. Throughout the nineteenth century, when quacks may have included anyone not in the medical mainstream—practitioners of herbal treatment, homeopathy, hydropathy ("wash and be healed"), osteopathy, and chiropractic medicine—they were consistently campaigned against. The quacks most hated by the organized medical profession in the nineteenth century traveled with medicine shows dispensing home-brewed potions with such names as Swamp Root, Liquozone, Dr. S.P. Townsend's Extract of Sarsparilla, Roger's Cocaine Pile Remedy, and some other remedies that were mainly grain alcohol with coloring or else contained lethal toxic acids.[58]

A new kind of quack emerged in America during the first few decades of the twentieth century and he proved just as annoying to the organized medical profession. This new quack was taking payoffs from personal injury lawyers in order to falsify medical certificates or to provide "expert" testimony-to-order in personal injury actions. This new quack was also, increasingly, working the accident racket on his own, counseling claimants in fraud, supplying fake medical reports, or inflicting injury to back up claims. In 1937 the Medical Society of the County of New York publicly acknowledged this new type of insurance quackery. With a "flush of shame," the group's president announced that he had become aware that "some of its members, fortunately very few, however, have joined hands with unscrupulous lawyers and insurance agents to defraud insurance companies of large sums of money." Adding that "this sort of practice must stop," the president concluded with a promise that stern measures were going to be taken: "The Medical Society of the County of New York is launching a movement to eliminate and abolish insurance racketeering."[59] That year some fifty doctors were arrested, jailed, or stripped of their licenses for having aided fake accident gangs or for running their own workmen's compensation rings.

The Medical Society's drive against insurance quackery came near the end of a massive new campaign against the accident rackets in New York. No longer just a matter of ethics to be handled by private professional associations, the accident fakers now constituted a major criminal enterprise to be prosecuted by the city's top crime fighters. Early in 1936 William Dodge, the Manhattan District Attorney, acted on information that a ring of lawyers had "revived" the accident racket in the city. Dodge created a special Accident Fraud Bureau to be funded with $50,000 from the city and staffed by a few experienced prosecutors with help from a dozen or so young corporate attorneys who donated their time to beat back the "evils" of "wholesale accident faking."[60] After several months of closed-door examinations and grand jury testimony, the bureau began handing down its first indictments. Among the accused were some of the same people who had been named in the 1928 chaser probe: Nicholas Ferranti (aka "Mr. Charles Roberts"), who had been the lead chaser for attorney Edward Gordon in the 1920s, was accused of doing the same for another attorney; Max Korbin, once one of Abe Gatner's star chasers, was arrested for his solicitation work in Harlem Hospital; and attorney Irving B. Linden, who had been suspended for two years for chasing in 1929, surrendered to the Accident Fraud Bureau on similar charges in October 1936.[61] As in 1928, some of the attorneys named in the inquiry had employed chasers, and these chasers still hunted up the same types of clients—"the foreigner, the illiterate son, the frightened denizen of the slums."[62] Once again those attorneys who were more seriously involved in accident faking fled the city until the probe blew over. The only new disclosure involved the new multiethnic alliances between Jewish personal injury lawyers from downtown and Puerto Rican chasers from Harlem and the Bronx.

Although assisted by members of the city's elite bar associations, the District Attorney's Accident Fraud Bureau was no tool of the corporate attorneys. Bernard Botein, the assistant D.A. in charge of the bureau, went beyond Isidor Kresel's mere naming of abuses in claims settlement by insurers and actually prosecuted two officers of the Yorkshire Indemnity Company who took kick-backs from plaintiffs in exchange for inflated settlements. What's more, one of these Yorkshire officials, Chester W. McNally, had actually served as an aide to Isidor Kresel during the ambulance chaser investigation of 1928.[63] Botein was as proud of these prosecutions as any he would later achieve. Early in September 1936 he held a press conference to discuss the sentencing of McNally and his partner to up to three years in prison: "Three months ago when the Bureau was organized," Botein said, "we announced we would go into cases of suspected collusion between indemnity company officials and others in settlements of accident claims, as well as bogus claimants and ambulance-chasing lawyers and their 'runners.' And now we have begun."

True to these intentions, Botein aspired to conduct an inquiry in 1936 that was more than just a front for purging marginal personal injury lawyers by professional elites. Beginning early in the year, Botein's bureau reviewed tens of thousands of the contingent-fee agreement cards filed with the courts since the 1928 investigation. Besting even Isidor Kresel's "ferreting" of the chasers, Botein's bureau examined more than 12,000 witnesses and gathered evidence from many others. His bureau was aided by a special squad of sixteen policemen hand-picked by Police Commissioner Lewis Valentine, some of whom, unfortunately for the credibility of the effort, were later proven to have been taking payoffs from personal injury attorneys in Queens in exchange for accident case referrals and information.[64] Several insurance industry groups, including the Alliance Against Accident Frauds and the Claims Bureau, which both provided a great deal of the paperwork needed to zero in on the worst offenders, also assisted Botein's bureau.

In its few years of existence, Bernard Botein's Accident Fraud Bureau issued over 200 indictments involving 133 individual lawyers, doctors, runners, accident ringleaders, professional claimants, and insurance company officials. In the overwhelming majority of cases, they obtained convictions, admissions of guilt, or forced the resignations of doctors and lawyers. Botein had tried as hard as anyone ever had to squash the accident rackets, and then he tried some more. But, like others before and after him, he would make no lasting impact, a fact that Botein himself later acknowledged. In an interview conducted in the late 1960s, Botein, then a distinguished justice on the New York State Supreme Court, looked back on his career in public life and spoke about what he called the "ten-year rule" governing municipal interest in ambulance chasing and its associated evils: "Suddenly there's a great hue and cry and investigation, and the papers are filled with details of lawyers and their chasers and accident faking and the padding of medical and hospital bills. A few lawyers are disbarred, several doctors get their wrists slapped, the bar issues an earnest statement and a month later—things are back to normal."[65]

As head of the district attorney's Accident Fraud Bureau, however, a younger Bernard Botein was considerably more sanguine about the prospects of obliterating the city's underworld trade in accidents and injury claims. In his final report, Botein suggested that the city's burgeoning personal injury underworld could be pulled up by its roots by going after the attorneys' runners, subrunners, freelancers, and "entrepreneur chasers" who did most of the dirty work in solicitation and faking.[66] Botein also named the rest of the usual suspects: the small but dedicated portion of the legal profession that aggressively maintained a high-volume accident business; the doctors who either played a supporting role to the lawyer's lead or were themselves the ringleaders of fake accident rings; and the insurance company adjusters and investigators who often showed a "shocking lack of fairness" and a "deplorable lack of ethics" in dealing with "ignorant and credulous victims of accidents."[67] Like the earlier author of Fake Accidents, Inc., Botein sketched the basic organization of Depression-era accident rings that usually manufactured claims of three types: industrial workmen's compensation cases; auto accidents; and tenement house slip and falls. Whatever type of ring, Botein noted, there was always a central figure who "blueprints the proposed claim, engineers its progress and drives it through to consummation; he makes the necessary cash advances, pays other participants out of the recoveries, and retains the balance as profit."[68] The ring members are trained to be versatile enough to play the claimant one time, the witness another, and to solicit cases if needed. Hotel owners and roominghouse keepers were often given a piece of the action in exchange for the use of their addresses as mail drops for settlement checks or as residences for claimants acting under assumed names.

Most convictions generated by Botein's Accident Fraud Bureau involved members of two accident rings that had operated in New York throughout the 1930s. One was run by a forty-four-year-old layman, Samuel Bornstein, the head of a group of lawyers, doctors, and accident-staging "stooges" that had defrauded insurance companies of hundreds of thousands of dollars over the previous eight years. Bornstein, who was ultimately trapped by detectives in a Brooklyn phone booth in December 1936, was charged with helping to create more than 500 fake claims in the early 1930s. Bornstein frequented coffee shops on the Lower East Side to induce regulars into playing the injured "dummy" in his claims.[69] He also was observed spending the better part of his days "wander[ing] about the streets spying out defective steps in front of buildings, broken vault lights in the sidewalks and other conditions affording an opportunity to file fake claims."[70] Sam Bornstein handled as many as 500 personal injury cases in 1935 and 1936, three fourths of which involved faked or made-up claims, substantiated by medical certificates purchased from physicians for $3 a piece.

The other major ring exposed by Botein's bureau, the Hurwitz gang also involved extensive alliances with doctors and lawyers from the Lower East Side.[71] Run by a thirty-one-year-old "pseudo insurance broker," Jacob Hurwitz of the Bronx, the gang was said to have defrauded insurers of an estimated $500,000 annually in its three years of existence. Both Hurwitz and Bornstein pled guilty soon after being indicted, were sentenced to prison terms on Hart's Island and at Sing Sing, respectively, then were brought back to the city to testify against all of their confederates in exchange for reductions in their sentences. Together, the Bornstein and Hurwitz accident rings were believed to have defrauded insurers of as much as $1 million a year over the ten years preceding their arrests.[72]

Before uncovering these larger organizations, however, the renewed campaign against the accident rackets in New York focused on the relatively minor activities of one aging doctor from the Lower East Side. Dr. Abraham Benjamin had practiced medicine for more than twenty-five years before being indicted, arrested, and, ultimately, tried for accident faking in July 1936.[73] At a time during the Depression when lawyers netted less than $2,000 a year and joked about their profession being a "dignified road to starvation,"[74] and when most doctors were not doing much better, Dr. Benjamin had become involved with a Brooklynite, Edward Hausman, who posed as an attorney to handle fake accident cases. Hausman organized slip-and-fall accidents, then got doctors to help him substantiate the claims. In the case leading to the arrest of Hausman and Benjamin, Hausman had made floppers out of a Brooklyn fruit dealer and his wife, the mother of two children, whose pregnancy often was used to increase belief in the fake accidents. The trial judge who sentenced Dr. Benjamin had apparently never heard the name Lustberg: He referred to Benjamin as "about the worst scoundrel" ever brought before him and then expressed regret that he could not sentence the doctor to more than fifteen to thirty months in Sing Sing prison.[75]

Details of Hausman and Benjamin's accident operation figured prominently in a report submitted to city bar leaders intended to demonstrate that the accident rackets had returned to New York and that some action needed to be taken. The findings, which were reported on the front page of the next day's *New York Times* under the heading "Bar Inquiry Asked on Huge Fraud Ring," caught the eyes of more than just city bar leaders. In the months that followed, District Attorney Dodge intensified his efforts to fight the accident racketeers, securing the additional funding needed to formally establish his Accident Fraud Bureau. The resurgence of the accident racketeers also caught the eye of the city's number-one racket-buster and Dodge's archrival for control of criminal justice in the city, Thomas Dewey.

As he pressed for city funds to start his Accident Fraud Bureau, William Copeland Dodge, the Manhattan District Attorney, needed to combat doubts about his crime-fighting stature in the city, and the accident rackets proved to be a perfect target for investigation. For years, many reformers had thought of Dodge as a do-nothing Tammany hacker who hindered organized crime probes and blocked political reform. He had been openly under attack since 1934, when Mayor Fiorello LaGuardia commissioned a report that concluded that Dodge's office was one of the last "nests of the spoils system, reeking with incompetence and favoritism, and expensively operated by gentlemen of obvious unfitness." LaGuardia wanted Dodge out, and everyone knew it. By the end of 1935, LaGuardia took action: He persuaded Governor Franklin D. Roosevelt to take the unprecedented step of appointing a special prosecutor for Manhattan, making it possible to circumvent Dodge almost totally in the administration of criminal justice in the city.

By early 1936 Dodge sorely needed credibility as a law enforcement officer. The fake accident trade proved to be one of the few citywide rackets that the public would be glad to see wiped from the city streets, while, importantly, it was safe to probe in that it didn't threaten the city political machine that had helped elect him. Having no connections to Tammany Hall or to known mobsters, the accident racket was unlike the many "industrial rackets" that the D. A. had been reluctant to fully investigate. And this—along with the fact that accident faking had increased exponentially in New York during the 1930s—made it a racket ripe for probing. During 1935 and 1936, in fact, both District Attorney Dodge and his equally embattled political counterpart in Brooklyn, William Geoghan, were reported to have "pushed" their respective "wars on fake accidents," allocating significant special funds to initiate and sustain the investigations.[76]

The idea of probing the accident rackets also attracted Thomas Dewey, the man who had been named Manhattan's special prosecutor in 1935.[77] Unlike Dodge, Dewey had never been afraid to probe this or any of the other more serious rackets of the day. From 1935 to 1937, the thirty-three-year-old political appointee had earned a popular reputation as the city's "racket-buster," obtaining seventy-two convictions in seventy-three tries. Among his most famous prosecutions, Dewey had successfully combated Dutch Schultz's restaurant cafeteria extortion ring; and he ended the control of the bakery and flour trucking industry by notorious gangsters Jacob "Gurrah" Shapiro and Louis "Lepke" Buchalter. Perhaps the most important prosecution for a man who would become Governor of New York and make his first of three runs for the presidency by his fortieth birthday was that which ended the racketeering dominance of Salvatore "Lucky" Luciano.

Late in 1936, amid all of these high-profile cases and the heightened politics of criminal justice in the city, the *New York Times* reported that the relatively unimportant accident racketeering of runner Edward Hausman and Dr. Abe Benjamin had "engaged the interest" of Special Prosecutor Thomas Dewey. During this important election year, then, two major inquiries into accident racketeering would be conducted concurrently in New York—one through Dewey's agency, the U.S. Attorney's office, the other by the Accident Fraud Bureau of the embattled office of the Manhattan District Attorney. While Dodge's bureau concentrated on the traditional accident frauds of the Bornstein and Hurwitz gangs, the federal prosecutors looked elsewhere, uncovering a previously unknown network of doctors, lawyers, and laymen who victimized state and federal workmen's compensation funds by feigning heart disease.

In May 1937, a two-column headline on the front page of the *New York Times* announced the beginning of the federal investigation into personal injury frauds: "HUGE INSURANCE RACKET BARED BY 14 ARRESTS HERE; U.S. OPENS SWEEPING DRIVE ON DISABILITY RINGS."[78] The body of the report told how Lamar Hardy of the U.S. Attorney's office had directed a squad of forty-seven postal inspectors and city detectives to move "swiftly and secretly" against members of an injury ring accused of "schooling" middle-age men in how to fake heart disease. "Human beings have been doped like race horses," Hardy later told a courtroom audience of the ring's methods; the comment was repeated in almost every article subsequently written about the prosecutions, lending a sensational aspect to the story. Hardy also told reporters that ring members had feigned brain diseases, paralysis, and tuberculosis with astounding medical skill, producing symptoms convincing enough to fool state and private insurance examiners into approving claim payments as high as $100,000. Parceled out in weekly installments, the money could sustain ring members for years.

Hardy's investigation of Depression-era heart disease schools took federal agents to the building at 305 Broadway—the same building that, a decade earlier, had been the headquarters of the accident ring run by Daniel and Benjamin Laulicht. Now two other brothers, Elias and Joseph Garrow, both attorneys, had set up offices there as fronts for their $3 million-a-year fake heart disease mills. Like the Laulichts, the Garrow brothers managed a network of chasers who recruited claimants for the frauds. The real work of the Garrow brothers' ring was done by the doctors, though. The Garrows paid their doctors to administer shots of a cardiac stimulant, digitalis, sufficient to produce increased heartrates in the ring's claimants. The digitalis was used in conjunction with "rigorous drilling" and fatiguing exercise ("endless dashes up and down flights of stairs were prescribed").[79] The combination of a tortuous regimen of exercise plus a nearly toxic dose of digitalis was designed to generate spasmodic heart palpitations in ring members before they submitted to electrocardiograph monitoring by insurance company examiners. Sometimes the show was convincing enough to start the adjuster writing checks immediately. Other times examiners insisted on hospitalizing the claimants in order to monitor their condition over time. When this happened, ring doctors would have to step in to save the claim: They would fabricate a medical chart and get it into the hospital files, then they would surreptitiously give the fake claimant enough digitalis to maintain heart palpitations for the duration of the hospital stay. Some claimants were also coached in the theatrics of how to simulate heart attacks while hospitalized.

The Garrow brothers' heart attack ring was extensive, involving dozens of "dupes" and doctors. (One dupe, the dean of a New York teaching hospital, had a real heart attack and died when he realized that the Garrows had attached his name to fake cases without his knowledge.)[80] But the Garrow ring was only one of several disability rings operating in New York at the time. Its chief competition, according to federal prosecutors, came from an operation run by another team of attorney brothers, Joseph and Alfred Weiss of Brooklyn.[81] In a second wave of arrests later in the summer of 1937, the Weiss brothers had been charged by federal and city authorities with having set up their own "heart trouble school" that generated hundreds of thousands of dollars. Like the members of the Garrow ring, fake claimants in the Weiss brothers' group were coached to complain of the telltale signs of cardiac arrest: squeezing pains in the left chest, numbness in the fingers, cold sweats, shortness of breath, frequent attacks of dizziness, weakness, recurring tired spells, palpitation of the heart, and discomfort at night. As a way to make a living, this kind of pathological playacting was not for everyone. But to a number of middle-age men down on their luck in the early 1930s, the shame in pretending heart attack symptoms seemed less significant than the embarrassment of not being able to provide for their families, and the disability rings were as steady a source of cash as anything going.

As potentially comic as the methods of fakery seemed to be, the business of faking heart attacks for money during the Depression could be deadly. There were threats to the personal safety of fake claimants from an adverse reaction to the digitalis, of course. But this was nothing compared to the intimidation by thugs who came after them if they considered ratting on the gang. After the initial arrests of members of the Weiss brothers' ring, reports soon appeared of "gangster threats of murder" against members who considered helping government prosecutors.[82] One man whose life was "menaced" by henchmen from one ring chose to remain in jail rather than face the outside parties he feared were waiting for him in front of the Thirty-Seventh Street Prison. Another man was reportedly being sought by "a carful of gunmen cruising around" for an opportunity to "bump him off" before he could testify against the Weiss brothers. Most witnesses led a nomadic existence, sleeping at a different hotel each night during the six weeks after they had first been indicted. Veteran detectives provided twenty-four-hour protection.

As arrests mounted in the fake disability cases, reporters continued to write of "an underworld element" that had "crept into the background" of the investigation. Whether the criminal element involved in the accident rackets was any more dangerous in the 1930s than it had been in the 1920s, when attorney Moses Cohen threatened to call Kid Flowers to take care of Daniel Laulicht, is anyone's guess. But there was no mistaking a heightened awareness and an increased emphasis on the criminal aspects of accident faking by prosecutors and the press. As Botein's Bureau pursued the Bornstein and Hurwitz gangs, and federal prosecutors shut down the Garrows' and the Weiss's, popular magazines cranked out the copy—from "Fake Accidents, Inc.," to "Beware the Accident Fortune-Hunter,"[83] which spoke of accident faking as "America's most popular racket." Other features included "Racketeers by Accident," a center spread in *American Magazine* on "the new Goliath among underworld professions, the fake accident insurance racket."[84] This last article promised readers "the inside story of criminal gangs that collect fortunes by faking injuries in elevators, motorcar crashes, and even by falling down your cellar stair." Another account from the period referred to the ambulance-chasing attorney as the "Al Capone, the 'higher up' in the accident racket."[85] And a book published in the mid-1930s titled *Insurance Racketeers* provided an account of one insurance investigator who found dealing with the ambulance chasers of St. Louis to be an increasingly dangerous occupation. "Every day I was threatened with injury and sometimes death," he wrote. "Had I been working alone, I am not sure that I should have gone on in the face of these threats."[86]

While some written accounts focused on the sexier organized crime angle, the accident rackets were just as often covered as a bread-and-butter consumer issue for people who paid car insurance. One magazine feature from the late 1930s blended the two themes. Illustrated with a sketch of a giant arm representing "fraudulent and exaggerated claims" holding up a car marked "insurance rates," the article, like so much of the later writing on the accident fakers, illustrated the way in which insurance premiums rose in relation to the number of fraudulent claims paid. "After weeks of research among the files of the nation's rate-making bureaus, police records, and the offices of insurance executives and investigators," the reporter came to the "shocking truth" that "rates might be one third lower if fraudulent and exaggerated claims had not swelled the total cost of damage payments and settlements."[87] This reporter countered the popular notion that accident frauds victimized big corporations: "It is you and I, the great American premium payers, who are the ones who are being fleeced," he concluded, "and it would mean money in our pocketbooks to get hard-boiled with insurance-racket crooks, big and little."

Elected officials who did, in fact, get "hard-boiled" with New York's accident racketeers found themselves with a good issue to run on. Harold Hastings, an assistant in Botein's Accident Fraud Bureau, for example, campaigned to become District Attorney of New York in 1937. Running against racket-buster Thomas Dewey, Hastings promised voters that he would continue his own "warfare against the fraudulent accident racket." He realized voters were fed up with the high cost of their auto insurance policies, and was one of the first politicians to campaign squarely on this issue. "Prior to the very successful campaign which Mr. Botein and I directed, you were milked to the tune of millions every year through fraudulent accident claims," he began the first speech of his campaign. "One fake accident ring we smashed collected $200,000 yearly on spurious claims. Another combination was responsible for 300 fake cases a year." He continued: "I am reliably informed by insurance statisticians that the successful crusade conducted by us will be reflected in next year's insurance rates. You can be assured that your insurance bills will show a considerable reduction. . . . [I also] pledge to prosecute vigorously and efficiently not only fraud investigations, but all other criminal cases irrespective of their headline value."[88]

At the emotional center of the "crash racket" stump speech, news story, and magazine feature was a simple point: namely, that people who played by the rules by dutifully paying their insurance premiums were forced to foot the bill for the activities of flop artists, ambulance chasers, shysters, and quacks. And the stories about the disability fraud rings—principally, the heart attack schools—added a new source of outrage to the story: Unlike the early injury con men, or the "foreigners who feigned trolley injuries," or the Laulicht brothers' automobile insurance frauds, the New York disability rings of the 1930s did not victimize private corporations. These new frauds were drains on the institutions of the newly expanded welfare state supported by tax dollars. Everyone, not just insured automobile owners, could feel equally upset about seeing tax dollars squandered on frauds. The theme of rage at welfare cheats was as old as public welfare itself, showing up in the work of British Poor Law Commissioners in the 1830s, who used a battery of "unerring tests" to separate the undeserving frauds from the truly needy. Even earlier, in France during the sixteenth century, church rectors made surprise visits to the homes of suspected welfare cheats and routinely found evidence of malingering.[89]

The idea of abusing public relief was by no means new to the activities of the fake disability rings of the 1930s, and their method of fakery was no more creative, or outrageous, or dangerous than anything that might have been described by Sir John Collie or Dr. Hector Gavin fifty or a hundred years earlier. The novelty lay in the scale of the Weiss and Garrow operations and their extensive organization for profit—hundreds of thousands of dollars, millions—not just isolated instances of individuals avoiding work. By the time state, and later federal, worker's compensation plans first went into effect during the second and third decades of this century, a significant personal injury underworld had already been developed. Networks of runners, chasers, shysters, and quacks had already been formed to take advantage of fake claims, no matter if the target be public or private. When economic depression came, it was a case of new wine into old bottles with public relief providing as sure a payoff as private insurance. For many people during the Great Depression, houses of pain and heart attack schools became as important a set of institutions as banks and workplaces had been before the stock market crash.

The prosecutions of the Weiss and Garrow disability rings dragged on for some five or six years. But when guilty verdicts were finally upheld in the early 1940s, the first era in the development of a personal injury underworld in America was at an end. By this time, it had all been done—from the slapstick of the banana-peelers to the tragedy of intentional dismemberment for accident insurance money—and it had all been documented and laid before the public. Later generations of American accident fakers would not do things radically different. The novelty of the fakery would not be what distinguished the later chapters of the making of a personal injury underworld in America, despite breathless news accounts to the contrary. Rather, the continued vitality of the underworld lay largely in the persistence of the same time-worn schemes across vastly different ethnic groups arriving at the beginning and end of the century, all of whom found their way to the idea of faking accidents for money as a way of getting ahead in America.

Just before this initial era of accident faking in America slipped from newspaper front pages to back pages, a few last words were recorded. "I am telling you before we go any further that there is no use of us kidding each other," a federal prosecutor told a member of the Weiss brothers' disability ring at a 1937 trial. "We have watched your telephone, we have watched all these lawyers' telephones, we have had rooms tapped," Assistant U.S. Attorney John Dailey told Dr. Hirsch Messman in attempting to persuade the doctor to testify for the government against the other Weiss ring members. "We know what is going on," he assured Messman. "We are not stabbing in the dark." He continued:

> If you want to hear your voice on a record we will be glad to play it. In your instance, Doctor, there is so much to cover. You have been in this for so many years that we feel that in order for you to help yourself, since you are considered one of the principals here, it would be wise for you to indicate to us whether you intend to tell us everything and come clean,

or whether you intend to play ball with the Garrows and the rest of the crowd. We feel that you can be of great value and you want to help yourself. That is straight talk.[90]

Dr. Messman confessed, saying that he and another physician, Max Goldstein, had been involved most deeply in the activities of both the Weiss and the Garrow rings. (Goldstein was a heart specialist who had once headed the cardiac division of Sydenham Hospital, and he had become important to the rings because he could supply the electrocardiograms necessary to substantiate fake claims.) Messman then described a typical fake heart disease case in which a "patient" was put through the full regimen of fabrications. "This fellow outside, his name is [Benjamin] Nelson," Messman began to Goldstein in December 1934. "Nelson is going to be a disability case."

> I said to [Dr. Goldstein], "You remember the Weisses are quite liberal with payments to doctors, not like the Garrows" . . . He said, "What are you going to claim?" I said, "It is a heart case, not a t.b. case." I said, "The reason I brought him here is that I expect to take him to the hospital, and what is on my mind, I want you to take his electrocardiogram to see if he is ready to go to the hospital, because I have given him digitalis in the past four or five days." He said, "How much digitalis did you give him?" And I said, "Two tablets three times a day". . . . He said, "The situation is this. Apparently he is ready if he took what you say he has taken. Assume that the electrocardiogram I am going to take right away is not positive enough, then he will stay in the hospital, take another few tablets and then I will take another electrocardiogram in the hospital anyway, because that is part of the buildup."

Messman's testimony was later complemented by that of Nelson himself, who made an appearance at Dr. Goldstein's initial trial in 1938: The forty-two-year-old dairyman from the Bronx testified that he had been given digitalis pills by the doctors and was told to hide them when he was in the hospital and to scream in simulated agony every now and then to support his claim. At the time of his alleged heart disease, Nelson later said, he was healthy enough to have tossed sixty-two-pound butter tubs from his truck, before lifting them into customers' iceboxes.[91] Later in the trial Messman and Goldstein were said to have given the same "treatment" to Morris Spitz of the Bronx.

In March 1938 Dr. Goldstein, Joe Weiss (the "general" of the Weiss ring), and most of the others were convicted of fraud largely due to this testimony.[92] A few months later most of the principals in the Garrow brothers' ring pleaded guilty to fraud and conspiracy charges.[93] Everyone who did not plead guilty appealed the convictions on complicated grounds having to do with the constitutionality of the wiretaps—at that time they were a novel and untested method of gathering evidence in criminal cases. Most of those arrested in both the Weiss and Garrow rings had been incriminated by phonograph records made by postal inspectors "watching and listening in secret places." The taps were placed on business phone lines, in restaurant booths, and at other locations frequented by ring participants. For six months federal authorities had compiled the records. Transcripts of all intercepted conversations had been made by stenographers working in both English and Yiddish; they were then presented to the prosecutors in the U.S. Attorney's office. At trial, transcripts of the conversations were supplied to witnesses and the recordings were played for the jury. In considering the legality of the wiretaps, the Supreme Court flipflopped, rendering two different decisions over three years. In the end, the wiretaps were held to have been legal, and Dr. Goldstein and the Weiss brothers were put behind bars.[94]

By 1942 all of the litigation arising from disability fraud rings of the late 1930s had come to an end. Four lawyers involved with the disability rings had been convicted along with nine doctors, seven chasers, and twenty-four heart-disease claimants who either pled guilty to federal charges or had been convicted in jury trials. Of the ringleaders, Joseph Weiss had pleaded guilty to fraud; the charges against his brother Alfred had been dropped as part of a plea bargain. As for the Garrow brothers, both eventually were given prison terms. At sentencing, Elias Garrow was on the verge of tears as he complained that his help as a government informant had not further minimized his twenty month prison term. "Your honor," he pleaded, "I was raised in the direst poverty and worked in sweatshops. I did everything possible to become a lawyer, and I say to you now that not until this thing happened did I realize the full iniquity of it all."[95] The judge refused to reduce the sentence any further; he intimated that, all things considered, Garrow, who faced up to 640 years in prison, had gotten off well.

The world of the U.S. Supreme Court, where the fate of the disability fraud ring members was finally decided, was a great distance from the personal injury underworld where the rings had operated during the 1930s. Back on the streets of New York, Thomas Dewey, the former Special Prosecutor of Manhattan, who had since been elected officially to serve as District Attorney, was busting up an all new set of accident gangs. Dewey had begun his own ten-month accident fraud investigation just after taking office. In March 1939, he was proud to announce the indictment of twenty-four people.

In his investigation, Dewey did not rely on controversial wiretaps for his information, as his colleagues at the U.S. Attorney's office had done. Instead, he innovated an even more powerful tool for gathering evidence for prosecution of the accident rackets: Police trucks were fitted with canvas sides, then outfitted with a motion-picture camera and a still camera with a telescopic lens. "Through holes in the sides of the truck," prosecutors later explained their innovation, "Police Sergeants made pictures of the various defendants at gathering places in lower Broadway, Canal and Duane Streets, and some moving pictures of defendants entering the homes of accident victims."[96] The camera-wielding police surveillance team parked most frequently in front of a roominghouse on St. Marks Place. It was said that "Bowery derelicts" who had been employed as victims of staged accidents lived here when they needed to have a permanent address where insurance settlement checks could be sent.

The results of Dewey's probe were predictable: prison terms for the few unlucky chasers, lawyers, and doctors who could not explain their way out of the charges. Dewey's determination even landed him some fish who had slipped out of several earlier nets—notably, a few chasers who had been part of Abe Gatner's stable of prize chasers in the early 1920s. It was the methods of Dewey's probe, however, that really proved important. Just as the fakers had adapted to each innovation in mass transportation over the decades since the late nineteenth century—the steamtrain, the trolley, the automobile—so, too, did law enforcement appropriate the latest means of recording equipment to document the frauds: the still photograph, the phonograph records, and, finally, the motion-picture camera. Forty years later, it would be videotape.

Inside the House of Pain no movie cameras recorded anything and no still cameras captured even a snapshot of anyone entering or leaving. No walls were bugged, and few written accounts detailed its three years of operation. In the end, its actual existence is not as revealing as the fact that, by the 1930s, America had a lengthy history of accident faking for money in which a House of Pain would have made perfect sense.

INDUSTRY
(AT MIDCENTURY)

CHAPTER 5

WHIPLASH CULTURE

There seems to be a wave of fraud, of malingering and perjury sweeping over the land. The effort to gain something for nothing, to get the money of others by false swearing, is absolutely degrading men, women, and children all over the country . . . Does it not seem as if somebody should hold up a hand and cry, 'halt'?

—Willis King, Missouri Pacific Railway System, 1906

The sordid gamut of gouging insurance companies, ranging from organized, professional fraud to petty, amateur padding of claims, together with the tawdry tactics of certain claimants' counsel, may be symptomatic of a sick society. Is it just another aspect of the something-for-nothing syndrome? Or is it more support for the dismal thesis that we are living in an age of declining morals?

—Address to the Federation of Insurance Counsel, 1964

IN 1964 AND 1965, visitors to the World's Fair in Flushing Meadows, New York, could ride an eighty-foot Ferris wheel in the shape of an enormous whitewall tire built by the U.S. Rubber Corporation. Fairgoers could also rise through a glass-tube elevator to the top of the 7-Up observation tower, emulating the bubbles in a glass of their favorite clear soft drink. Other popular attractions in this corporate theme park included Chrysler's

Autofare (a tour through "the biggest car in the world"); General Motors' Futurama, the largest pavilion at the fair; and General Electric's Progressland, the most widely attended exhibit with 29 million visitors, which invited people into one of four revolving auditoriums to see stage shows on the history of electricity. Photographs of these exhibits were printed in the Fair's Official Souvenir Program beneath the heading "Testimonials to America's Industrial Strength."

Just across the way from these exhibits—on the other side of the shimmering Pool of Industry—was a bright red-roofed building in the shape of an umbrella. The sponsors hoped that this outsize umbrella rooftop would be recognized as the new corporate symbol of the Travelers Insurance Company. For much of the company's 100-year history, the Travelers' symbol of "security through insurance" had been a nameless knight in armor who bore a shield reading "Tuebor" (Latin for "I will defend").[1] From 1870 through the 1920s, the Travelers' knight in armor had been memorialized in cuff links, watch fobs, tie pins, statuettes, and bookends. During the 1950s, Travelers resurrected the symbol, enrolling its most successful salesmen in the Knight in Armor Club. In 1960, for reasons unexplained by the company historian, Travelers debuted the red umbrella symbol in a magazine ad. After its immediate success, the company began a massive giveaway of red umbrellas of all sizes bearing the Travelers "T." The rest is history. Red umbrellas began to appear on company stationery, in newspapers, and in glossy magazines. Red umbrellas were laminated onto giveaway brooches, lapel buttons, pendants, and earrings; they were woven into neckties, vests, sports shirts, and head scarfs. In a short time, the Travelers' red umbrella, like the long-shot idea of accident insurance itself launched a century earlier, had become part of the fabric of American life.

While the exterior design of the Travelers' World Fair pavilion marked the final victory of the red umbrella over the knight in armor, a different sort of triumph was being celebrated underneath the giant umbrella: "The Triumph of Man," as depicted in thirteen enormous dioramas. These interpretive exhibits included such favorites as "Man's Discovery of Fire as a Useful Element" and "Man's Learning to Raise Food for Himself." The exhibits culminated with a final show of man's "great scientific, explorative, and mechanical achievements." In the view of the exhibitors, insurance itself was an integral part of this story of the "triumph of man" over the random forces of nature: Insurance had been the "handmaid" of Western progress. Without it, maritime explorers and traders in the eighteenth century may have been less willing to risk the perils of sea travel; railroads and major manufacturers of the nineteenth century may have expanded at a slower rate; and, during this century, the daily navigations of the suburban automobile owner may have been that much less worth taking for fear of the economic consequences of an accident. Insurance had literally helped Americans get to Progressland in 1964; and, just as certainly, insurance would help propel them into a brave new Futurama. In case visitors to the red umbrella pavilion missed this point, however, it was underscored by the author of the Travelers Centennial volume published in conjunction with the fair: "The role played by the insurance industry—and by the Travelers Insurance Companies in particular—is not directly expressed in the exhibit," the historian noted. "But it may be inferred readily by the visitor to 'The Triumph of Man.'"[2]

Joseph Appleby, a forty-year-old gas station attendant, was not able to attend the Triumph of Man exhibit during the summer of 1964. In fact, he missed the entire New York World's Fair while he sat in a Kansas City jail awaiting a prison term for accident faking. During the early 1960s, Appleby had found a profitable sideline to his gas station work: He would drive junk cars off his lot into traffic, then he would stop short in front of commercial trucks, which he could be sure were well insured. Appleby admitted to having staged more than thirty-five of these truck accidents and to having subsequently filed an equal number of phony personal injury claims that brought him more than $10,000 over the years. For Appleby, the great institution of accident insurance had been the handmaid of his own peculiar kind of progress through life: He used the money to help support himself, his wife, and their eight children.[3]

LeRoy Anderson of Chicago did not have time to visit the World's Fair in 1964, either. Like Joe Appleby, Anderson was in jail facing charges resulting from his years as a leader of one of the biggest accident gangs in the country. Anderson, who weighed 250 pounds and was nicknamed "Big Red," helped stage as many as 500 car wrecks in cities across America, from Buffalo to San Diego. Anderson and his associates were examples of a new kind of auto accident gang that emerged in the 1950s. No longer content to dive in front of cars, the newer accident fakers were behind the wheels themselves looking to stop short in front of people who stood a better than even chance of being insured. Anderson's gang would then use a time-tested technique of building up claims with self-inflicted wounds. "Before setting out to work," an account in Newsweek magazine noted, "members of the gang occasionally broke a limb or two to guarantee a sizable settlement."[4] Members of the Feliciano ring, based in the Bronx just miles from the Flushing Meadows Fairgrounds, were also major practitioners of the new sudden-stop accident fakings. Typically, the eight Felicianos would buy a used car for $100 or less, stuff it with four or five people, then position themselves in front of a slow-moving truck until they trapped the truck into ramming them from behind. "Crash, complain and collect quickly, that's their *modus operandi*," explained Robert Dick, an investigator with the Claims Bureau, the insurance industry's fraud police.

During the early 1960s, special agents of the Claims Bureau continued their work against the fakers begun several decades earlier by Wayne Merrick, the former FBI man and New York City racket buster. In a 1945 report, Merrick noted the end of the quietus on fake claims during the World War II years. "With the return of peace, the casualty insurance industry may reasonably expect some return of the ambulance chaser and claim faker," Merrick stated: "The Claims Bureau is on guard."[5] Indeed. The bureau now maintained 15 million index-card records of possibly faked claims, stored in great walls of "modern power files" located in ten regional index bureaus throughout the country. Claims Bureau agents met regularly with local claims departments and with local law enforcement and federal postal inspectors to "flush out" accident gangs. During the late 1940s and 1950s, the bureau helped uncover organized fakers in every major town from Akron, Ohio, to Panama City, Florida, with the most cases coming from New York, Chicago, and the poorest regions of the rural South. One gang was even discovered in Walla Walla, Washington, the territory that, fifty years earlier, had been the domain of Maud Myrtle Johnson, the Queen of the Fakers.

By 1964, accident claims that were in some way fake or exaggerated were estimated to amount to some $350 million nationwide. This was a dramatic increase from an estimated $150 million ten years earlier, which, itself, was considered a high-water mark for fakery. The most popularly reported case from this time involved a family from St. Louis, the Tumbling Womacks, who feigned slips on banana peels and falls down elevator shafts, and contrived stumbles in front of cars all over the Midwest. (Blanche Womack alone was cited on fifty-seven cards on file with the St. Louis Index office.)[6] And no feature from the era could resist mention of the claims-faking career of Grace E. Walker—alias "Rimrock Annie," so named for her early career as a hard-rock miner. Rimrock Annie, always described as "buxom" and once pictured in *Time* magazine dressed in western garb like a slip-and-fall Annie Oakley, bragged of having been hospitalized over fifty times in cities across the country. Her success was based on her convincing theatrical falls and her even more convincing contrived medical symptoms: She could dilate her left pupil at will due to an old mastoid operation and could make it look like blood was coming from her ear (an indication of skull damage) by biting her lip and shaking her head quickly from side to side in apparent convulsion.[7] Some commentators mentioned Rimrock Annie, the Tumbling Womacks, Maxwell Rifkind (Chicago's "master of the one-man car accident"), and, later, the new car accident rings, as examples of a rising level of fakery, which was at an "all time high."[8] One writer from the time took a longer view of the accident insurance faker as a "peculiar predator who is as active today as he was a half a century ago and who, in all probability, will continue to flourish as long as the institution of insurance exists."[9] But more typical has always been the contention that, whatever the claims excesses of the past, they were nothing compared with the present state of things.

N. Morgan Woods, the head of the Claims Bureau, was one of the most-quoted authorities on faked claims during the 1950s and 1960s. Woods knew his topic well: He had helped uncover the Kirksville, Missouri, accident gang shortly after coming to the Claims Bureau from the FBI in the early 1940s, and he continued to fight the fakers for the next twenty years.[10] By the time he took the top job at the bureau, Woods had seen it all. Over the years, his view of what constituted a fake claim had expanded dramatically. The organized gangs, once central to his concerns were now to him just the hard core of a more widespread problem—a problem difficult to name and even harder to fight. The problem, as Woods came to see it, was less about the law than about morality; more about some kind of general societal sickness than about the activities of individual wrongdoers. Like many of his colleagues in the insurance industry, Woods had turned his attention squarely on the problem of "skyrocketing" car insurance rates—a subject chronicled in frequent features such as "Why Your Auto Insurance Costs So Much" (for all those readers "angered and puzzled by this mystery of soaring rates"); and "Why the Cost of Auto Insurance Goes Up and Up" ("If you are shocked by your latest bill for auto insurance, you need to know this").[11] Some reasons cited for rising rates involved impersonal forces—rising rates of accidents and inflation. Edward Rust, the head of State Farm, for example, told a reporter in 1964 that the increase in fakery and frivolous claims was due to the fact of "more opportunity" resulting from "more cars, more drivers, and more accidents."[12] Some of these same impersonal forces also interested policymakers and legal theorists who looked at the problem of rising rates in the larger context of the historical failure of tort doctrine to function effectively as an insurance scheme. As early as 1916 such considerations prompted suggestions that "an altogether simpler method is available for the adjustment of claims" on the model of Workmen's Compensation, and a similar contention was behind the push for no-fault insurance in the 1960s. Critics of the insurance industry often cited a different set of impersonal forces to explain rising rates, however: Insurers were essentially investors of premium dollars who had to raise rates to cover losses during periodic downturns in the market business cycle, it was frequently pointed out, and the "crisis" in auto insurance was really manufactured through insurers' tricky bookkeeping.

Morgan Woods's sense of the underlying problem of rising rates did not involve impersonal forces. Rather, he blamed the increase on the public. More specifically, he focused on what he and others in the insurance industry termed the public's growing "claims consciousness." Woods spoke of damage suits for personal injuries as part of a "sordid picture" of what he saw as a larger moral and ethical decline in the country. In 1960 he delivered a speech to the Federation of Insurance Counsel entitled "Combating the Fraudulent Claims Menace" in which he said that such suits had become "a national pastime" for a certain unnamed segment of the public. "We find many claims-conscious people, working in collusion with certain lawyers and doctors, who forget about morals and fairness and try to get as much money as they can from built-up injury claims."[13] Several years later Woods was quoted again on this subject: "People are making claims for things today that years ago they would have dismissed with a shrug of the shoulder," he said before adding that "amateurs who engaged in a little theivery" had more to do with the rising tide of faked claims than did accident gangs and flop artists. "Nowadays reputable business men, little old ladies and otherwise honest citizens are filing padded claims and resorting to out-and-out frauds that once were almost the exclusive domain of ambulance chasers, unethical doctors, and highly organized fraud rings."[14]

In 1967, the same year that Woods's comments were reported, movie-goers could see two Academy award-winning actors in a comedy that seemed to make his point about amateur involvement in phony personal injury claims. In *The Fortune Cookie*, Jack Lemmon played Harry Hinkle, a CBS cameraman knocked down by a football player in the course of filming a game. Walter Matthau played William "Whiplash Willie" Gingrich, a "cheap chisling shy-ster" who, when we first meet him, is talking to a potential client about the man's alleged slip on a banana peel. ("Interesting case," Willie muses, the spirit of litigiousness ladled like sauce over his every word. "I am considering suing the United Fruit Company. There should be a printed warning on those things [banana peels]; they can be bad for your health.") Later, Willie is watching the football game in his office when he sees Hinkle, his brother-in-law, taken from the football field on a stretcher. Soon he is at the hospital where he announces to a crowd of reporters that he is suing for $1 million on Hinkle's behalf. Then Willie has to get Hinkle to go along with the suit:

Willie: I hate to break it to you kid, but you got a spinal injury.
Hinkle: What?
Willie: Your left leg is numb, and you got no feeling in the first three
           fingers of your right hand.
Hinkle: You're crazy. I can move my hand . . . and my leg.
Willie: Sure you can—if you want to blow a million bucks.
Hinkle: A million? What are you talking about?
Willie: That's what we're suing for. They'll offer a hundred thousand,
           and we'll settle for a quarter of a million.[15]

Reluctantly, and for reasons that have more to do with the love of a woman than with a lust for insurance money, Hinkle agrees to help Willie with the personal injury scheme. Within days, a phony doctor from Chicago arrives on the scene to help prepare Hinkle for the insurance company examiners. The doctor enters Hinkle's hospital room disguised as a Chinese waiter and administers pills concealed in fortune cookies to help Hinkle simulate paralysis. Upon first seeing Hinkle with Whiplash Willie, the insurance company doctors are skeptical. They move carefully over Hinkle's body, probing for signs of fakery in the manner of the real-life Sir John Collie detecting malingerers during the first decade of this century. At one point, one of the insurance examiners suggests a healthy dose of rough justice for what he is sure to be Hinkle's imposture. ("Throw him in the Snake Pit and see if he is well enough to crawl out.") The insurance company defense lawyers are equally skeptical of any claimant represented by Willie. They talk briefly about settling the claim before it goes before a jury; but one of the lawyers objects in principle: "Settle? It's not just the money," the lawyer says, adding that it would be dangerous to society if "shysters like Gingrich ride roughshod over the laws of this land." Gingrich, for his part, also talks in terms of principle, not money, albeit histrionically, as he voices worry over the unchecked power of big corporations to "stick it to" little guys like Harry Hinkle.

In the end, Willie's $1 million personal injury claim comes to nothing thanks to the combined reemergence of Hinkle's good character and the persistence of "Perky" the detective, who does surveillance work on Hinkle for the insurance defense team. In the real world of America in the 1950s and 1960s, however, such endings—happy endings, at least from the insurance industry's perspective—seemed to be unlikely. "Even exemplary citizens are under continuous pressure by their friends to exaggerate claims in accident cases," one insurance executive told a reporter in 1958. The high cost of auto insurance, the same executive explained, was a direct result of a "shifting standard of morality" in America. The executive's comments were reported under the headline "MORAL BREAKDOWN SEEN IN AUTO CLAIMS," but the idea he and his colleagues were trying to get across was more frequently expressed by one simple word: whiplash.

Whiplash, a term first used in the early 1920s to describe neck injuries experienced by pilots on aircraft carriers, which was then applied to a similar syndrome experienced by people involved in rear-end automobile collisions, had, by the 1950s, come to be the centerpiece of a hotly contested debate over "skyrocketing" rates of personal injury claims in the United States. While whiplash began as a medical diagnosis, sometime during its course through the middle decades of this century it became a kind of universal diagnosis of the sick state of the national morality. It had become a putdown, both of the individuals who made the claims and of the society in general that tolerated those claims.

To trace the word's accumulated meanings and sinister associations to their roots in American culture would be to go beyond factual questions of real or faked claims, to step outside of the charged debate over the causes of rising insurance rates, and to put aside doctrinal questions about tort law or no-fault remedies. The elusiveness of whiplash begins with the meaning of the medical syndrome itself. Since it was first introduced, almost nothing about the diagnosis has been uncontroversial. While most medical researchers working in the 1950s and 1960s agreed that whiplash involved a neck sprain resulting from a rear-end collision, for instance, there was no general agreement on how exactly the injury occurred. Some believed that, upon impact from behind, a car passenger's head first snapped back (hyperextension), then "whipped" forward (hyperflexion); others who were equally well qualified argued the opposite (first hyperflexion, then hyperextension). Over the years, consensus formed around the hyperextension, then hyperflexion mechanism of injury.[16] Engineers who researched whiplash injuries in simulated car crashes measured the precise angles at which human heads snapped back and whipped forward at different speeds of impact. (According to one such study, the head of an average-size adult, weighing from seven to eight pounds, would snap back at 78 degrees upon rear-end impact by a 3,500-pound car traveling 30 miles per hour if there were no headrest to stop it.)[17] By the end of the 1960s, engineers at General Motors had developed "Sophisticated Sam" manikins for use in the whiplash tests. Sophisticated Sam was guaranteed to fracture, rupture, sprain, and break at human tolerance levels. Unlike real whiplash sufferers, however, Sophisticated Sam did not get dizzy or vomit or suffer chronic soreness or just feel "out of sorts" days or weeks or years after a simulated crash. This disappointed auto manufacturers: Under attack from Ralph Nader's auto safety movement as well as from accident insurers, they hoped that engineers would be able to say something conclusive and objective about endlessly subjective (and costly) pains in the neck and back and head. No amount of expensive crash research seemed to settle the question of the truth of whiplash complaints, however. "This is the sad part of our plight," complained one insurance executive in 1964. "For there appears to be no absolutely sure way of separating the fake from the real."[18]

If engineers tried unsuccessfully to prove something about whiplash through crash tests, medical researchers would attempt to get a handle on the problem by reviewing the literature on the subject and studying the people who complained of it. The most superficial of these reports were nothing more than angry editorials on the word *whiplash* itself. In 1957, for example, two doctors from Michigan wrote that they disliked the term "whiplash injury" because, they believed, it was becoming "a master hoax diagnostically," like the terms "headache," "bellyache," or "slipped disc."[19] In 1958 two different doctors also raised a beef over the word. "The term whiplash injury covers a multitude of diagnostic sins, as did the term indigestion 30 odd years ago," they observed. "However, we believe that whiplash is with us for a long time, since it has come to signify something that the patient thinks he understands, and that lawyers relish."[20] The following year another doctor attempted to "lay bare" the uses to which the whiplash diagnosis was being employed: "The term to the honest is merely a bulwark behind which ignorance skulks; to the dishonest, it is a mirage with which to confuse and delude."[21]

One review of the whiplash literature from the late 1950s and early 1960s concluded this way: "The medical profession created a 'Frankenstein['s monster]' when they fathered and popularized the term 'whiplash injury.'"[22] Interestingly, "Dr. Frankenstein" himself, orthopedist Harold Crowe, agreed with his colleagues: Dr. Crowe had coined the term *whiplash* in a speech delivered at a meeting of the Western Orthopedic Association in 1928, but, over the years, he had come to take a dim view of the whiplash syndrome. Thirty years later, in fact, Crowe wrote that "the coinage was counterfeit."[23] Often, during his later years, Crowe spoke against the whiplash genie that he let out of the bottle. "As most of you are aware, I presented eight cases of neck injuries resulting from traffic accidents in 1928 before the Western Orthopedic Association in San Francisco," Crowe said in 1963 at a meeting of his colleagues at the Academy of Orthopaedic Surgeons.

At the time of that presentation I used the unfortunate term "whiplash." This expression was intended to be a description of motion. It was not thought to be a name of a disease. The name "whiplash," however, has been accepted by physicians, patients, and attorneys as the name of a disease and the term "whiplash" has been published subsequently by many physicians with this unfortunate misunderstanding of the word.[24]

Later that year Crowe addressed the same body of orthopedists before which he first offered the term. In his comments, Crowe seemed to side with those doctors who believed the joke, then popular, that whiplash could be defined as a pain in the neck that persists until all litigation has ended. In his remarks, Crowe cited the work of a team of neurosurgeons from Tennessee who, in 1956, attempted to demonstrate the truth behind this joke with a study of 100 whiplash patients. The Memphis Study, as the work of Dr. Nicholas Gotten was later referred to by insurance industry partisans, purported to show that 88 percent of whiplash patients ceased to suffer symptoms after the settlement of their insurance claims. Other studies on whiplash from this era also concentrated less on the nature of the syndrome than on what became of patients after they ceased to be plaintiffs. In 1957 two doctors from the Midwest published a review of 5,700 auto accidents that resulted in 9,000 injured people. Only 1.1 percent of the injured passengers were found to have suffered some type of "whiplash injury," and 80 percent of these cases were deemed to be clinically insignificant. Another study of whiplash victims from the late 1950s, this one by a British doctor, began with the review of the doctor's research on "psychosocial" causes of the syndrome but ended as a political tract on the demoralizing, corrupting effects of social insurance inducements to prolong injury. "The exploitation of his injury represents one of the few weapons available to the unskilled worker to acquire a larger share—or indeed a share of any kind—in the national capital," Dr. Henry Miller concluded in the *British Medical Journal.* "Its possible yield may not bear comparison with the weekly recurring fantasy of a win in the pools, but it is more clearly within his grasp, and it may yet endow him with a capital sum such as he could never have saved during a lifetime of unremitting labour."[25]

Both Gotten's and Miller's studies were later criticized for using empirically unsound research procedures and for misstating their belief that the majority of whiplash patients returned to work immediately after the settlement of their claims as fact.[26] But such criticism did not keep these studies, and many others like them, from carrying a lot of weight in the whiplash wars of the 1950s and 1960s. Insurance companies wanted to read these findings and, perhaps more important, wanted others to read them. In 1960 insurers collected a number of these writings, together with articles by insurance defense lawyers and company executives, and sent them to more than 11,000 judges, legislators, and lawyers in what was to be the first volley in what they termed *The Revolt Against "Whiplash."* The stated purpose of the volume was to "demonstrate that the term 'whiplash injury' has been thoroughly discredited and cannot be utilized for any proper purpose in personal injury litigation."[27] In 1964 the case obviously had not been demonstrated sufficiently, as the Defense Research Institute (DRI), the insurance industry organization that produced the initial volume, published *The Continuing Revolt Against "Whiplash."*

Most writings marshaled for the DRI-led revolt started from some form of the proposition that whiplash was not a medical syndrome, but the contrivance of a syndrome for gain. The source of the contrivance might be conscious and willful, in the case of greedy lawyers or accident victims. Here it might be referred to as "profit neurosis," "greenback disease," or "compensationitis." Or the contrivance might be a less willful psychosomatic conversion of a desire for gain into the symptoms that would merit it in the eyes of the law. Here it is referred to as "accident victim syndrome," accidentitis," or "aftermath syndrome." The term "whiplash" itself, on one psychoanalytic version of this general idea, acted as a "traumatizer, operating at the subliminal, the subconscious, and the conscious levels" of the injured person, convincing him that he has a serious medical condition rather than just some minor aches and pains.[28] Dr. J. E. M. Thompson put forward his own version of this view. "Emphasis on this 'whiplash' idea misguides the emotional make-up of a patient," he wrote after noting that his "esteemed friend" Dr. Crowe had coined the term "when he was too young to know better." Thomson continued: "By planting the implication of 'whiplash' in the patient's mind, perhaps a very innocent minor soft tissue pathology might stimulate vicious legal damage claims."[29] Most symptoms associated with whiplash, another doctor wrote in the same vein, were due simply "to abnormal fear present in the minds of the patients as a result of having heard the dread term 'whiplash injury' after the accident."

This theory that whiplash was either a psychological contrivance or a cultural construction perpetuated by word of mouth—and not a medical syndrome initiated by a rear-end collision—was a mixed blessing for those who believed in it. On the one hand, it helped explain one of the most baffling aspects of whiplash claims—namely that symptoms often did not appear for days, weeks, or even years after the accident. (The "incubation" period, on this view, was a measure of the amount of time after an accident in which people come to realize, consciously or not, that it was in their financial best interest to claim pains in the back and neck.) The down side of this cultural view of whiplash, however, was that the more the term was accepted in the culture,

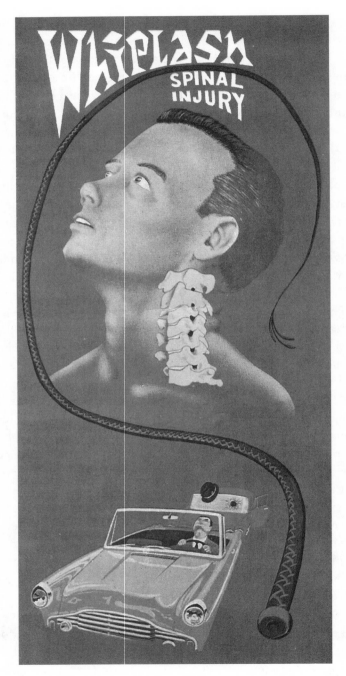

FIGURE 5.1. Distributed in doctors' offices in the 1950s and 1960s, this pamphlet was part of an attempt by medical groups to educate the public on the connection between neck and back injuries and rear-end automobile collisions.

the harder it was to defeat. Whiplash was on people's minds after an accident—this much was clear. It was out there in the culture like a virus, the DRI believed; one doctor went so far as to suggest that the whiplash "plague" be described in quasi-biblical terms: "It was manna for the plaintiff's attorney, pestilence for the defense attorneys, and a paid vacation for the patient without any scruples."[30] And the vaccine—a campaign of "public education" by the insurance industry—was not really working. If it were, why had it been necessary to continue the whiplash revolt four years after the "fallacy of the term" had been amply "demonstrated"?

While murkiness lay around every corner of the debate, this much was clear. No word frightened the mighty monolithic insurance industry right down to their bottom lines as much as whiplash did in the 1950s and 1960s. As a practical matter, insurers could not keep all injured people from hearing the word any more than they could keep them from consulting attorneys or talking to their friends. But insurance defense lawyers were instructed to restrict their own usage of the term, especially in writing to the plaintiff's attorney. "Don't at any time, think, speak or write 'whiplash' except within quotation marks," attorney Harley McNeal advised his colleagues in the first revolt against whiplash. Another attorney, a past president of the DRI, advised insurance defense lawyers to not let the jury hear the word "whiplash" for fear of its powerful associations. (In his article, "How to Forestall the Use of the Term 'Whiplash' in the Hearing of the Jurors," the attorney recommended that defense counsel file a pretrial motion to restrict the plaintiff's attorney from using the term.)[31] Other defense lawyers concentrated on stocking juries with those most likely to be unsympathetic to plaintiffs: "The traditional man from Missouri who says 'show me' and believes nothing that he can't see," lawyer Harlan Dodson described his ideal juror, contrasting him to liberal eggheads "whose greatest physical activity consists of lifting the morning paper."[32] As for prospective jurors who may have had an actual experience with soft-tissue injury and the resulting complications, Dodson definitely did not want them around, for fear that their experience would render them hopelessly empathetic to claimants. (The experience of actual accident trauma could prove sufficiently powerful to change the mind of even a fellow insurance defense lawyer like Bert Strubinger. In the early 1950s, Strubinger was skeptical enough of accident fakers to write an article entitled "Unmasking of Fraudulent Claimants and Malingerers," but he was fair enough to admit that his own accident experience convinced him that some soft-tissue injury to the back was bona fide.)[33] If the word "whiplash" could not be kept from the courtroom, and the right jurors could not be settled on, insurance defense lawyers could always go to the source of the problem by digging into the claimant's moral character. "Is the party a stable individual?" one attorney talks through his questioning of alleged whiplash victims. "What is his work record? What is his family life? Is he claims-conscious? What is his standing as a citizen? Is he neurotic? Is he prone to exaggerate? Has he run afoul of the law?"[34]

Both DRI volumes began with an essay entitled "The Genesis, Growth and Destruction of the 'Whiplash' Myth." For the "genesis" of whiplash, the author refers to Dr. Crowe's 1928 speech in San Francisco; for the "growth" of whiplash, the author credits plaintiff's lawyers in the 1950s who found in whiplash a "jack-pot winning 'hidden persuader'" of juries. As for the "destruction" of the "whiplash myth," the editor of the volumes simply declares that the term "has fallen entirely into disrepute." Unfortunately for the insurance industry, however—and for the one whiplash revolter who prophesied the term would soon "be relegated to the fad status of the Hula Hoop"—whiplash was not so easily defeated. That the person who first coined the term as a young man publicly voiced skepticism about the phenomenon in later life is certain; but that this admission failed to have a major impact on the legitimacy of the whiplash concept in medical and legal contexts is equally certain. Thirty years after the alleged destruction of the whiplash myth, the DRI was still publishing features like "Whiplash: Big Business & Serious Problem."[35] And, in the early 1990s, an editorial in the *New England Journal of Medicine* still used the terms "whiplash injuries" and "whiplash syndrome" to describe what has remained "one of the most controversial conditions in medicine."[36]

The war on whiplash was not a one-sided affair by any means. Even at the time that Dr. Crowe was recanting on whiplash and the DRI was revolting against it, the organized personal injury bar was rounding up its own medical experts in its defense. In early 1965, for example, an article on "the whiplash controversy" appeared in the premiere volume of *Trial*, the official magazine of the fledgling Association of Trial Lawyers of America. The author of the article, Dr. Atha Thomas, a distinguished orthopedic surgeon, argued against the misleading DRI pamphlets that, he believed, were part of an "intensive and well organized effort on the part of insurance companies and defense attorneys" to discredit the term "whiplash" unjustifiably.[37] Thomas's own study and review of the literature led him to believe that, whatever the name (he did not defend the term "whiplash"), the whiplash syndrome was not primarily a product of persuasive suggestion, neurosis, or lust for insurance money. Rather, whiplash could be explained by actual damage to nervous and vascular structures.

Thomas's position on whiplash was supported by the results of a number of other studies, including those by several doctors who spent years investigating injuries suffered by people in train accidents. These doctors discussed the phenomenon of people who escaped a railway accident without serious injury (loss of life, broken limbs, and other "wounds of consequence") and yet sometime later, experienced a steady decline of health that often ended in death, shock, concussion, or contusion. The doctors' results were summarized in a newspaper editorial:

> A hurt, apparently trifling, to the back or sacrum may occasion an inflammatory process which may, even after years, terminate fatally. It is impossible to tell from external manifestations what hidden injury may have been wrought. It happens not infrequently that the severest primary lesions present outwardly only slight, unimportant symptoms. Persons often die directly from railway accidents who have imagined at the time that they have not been injured a whit. [38]

At the time the doctors were researching this surprising aftermath of railway accidents, the "whiplash myth" had not yet been created. In fact, in 1879, when their results were summarized in the *New York Times*, the doctors were involved in a debate over a different phenomenon—"railway spine"—which had become as controversial in the mid-to-late nineteenth century as whiplash would become in the 1950s and 1960s. In its time, railway spine was debated at conferences of claims men; worried over by railroad executives and their lawyers; and battled on the front lines by surgeons and doctors working in railroad-owned hospitals. Research on railway spine often was crude. (Lacking Sophisticated Sam manikins for crash tests, Dr. B. A. Watson of Jersey City, New Jersey, dropped dogs from a fifth-story rooftop and struck others at the base of the spine with a sledgehammer, then did postmortem experiments to see if actual, observable damage had been done to the spine by concussion.) But the pressing need for conclusive facts about railway spine was every bit as strong as it would later be for whiplash, driven as it was by the equally enormous medicolegal consequences of the research in personal injury cases.

Almost all of the themes that emerged in the revolt against whiplash were first rehearsed during the late nineteenth century in the debate over railway spine. Its unseen and elusive mechanism of injury was seen as a mystery whose solution was less medical than moral. "The almost entirely sensory and consequently subjective character of the symptoms in this disease, and the uncertainty of its pathology," one doctor wrote in 1891, "have opened wide the door for malingerers to make legalized depredations on the treasuries of railway corporations, and has afforded a nice harvest to shyster lawyers and conscienceless physicians."[39] Like whiplash, railway spine was characterized in sinister terms by detractors and disbelievers. One writer decried it as "an evil which is fast spreading and sweeping our country like the flames of a prairie fire."[40] Another writer, an outspoken defense lawyer named Clark Bell, preached often, and passionately, against the evils of railway spine. "Railway spine is the Nemesis of the modern railway," he began an address before the National Association of Railway Surgeons in 1894: "[Railway spine] has baffled both railway surgeons and counsel, and, vampire-like, sucked more of the blood of corporate bodies and railway companies than all other cases combined. It is the ready refuge of the malingerer, the weapon always burnished bright and sharpened, of the unscrupulous attorney and his partner in profit, the medical expert, and affords advantages for the scheming, avaricious claimant. "[41]

Like the later whiplash revolters, Bell found railway spine "most elastic in definition and most elusive in description," qualities that made it hard to attack. He ended his speech with a plea for research by railroad surgeons, a plea that could equally have been the preface to the DRI volumes on whiplash. "[Railway spine] should be brought out of the shadow into the sun, out of the darkness into the light, out of the mysterious into the actual—the real," Bell exhorted. "I call upon [you], in the name of the judges and of the bar, to frame a correct definition of this disease, if it exists. . . . How many more millions of dollars must follow in the same channel before a halt is called?"[42]

Controversy in America over railway spine first began in the 1860s following reports from England that an eminent professor of surgery named John Eric Erichsen had published six lectures "on certain obscure injuries of the nervous system commonly met with as the result of shocks to the body received in collisions on railways." In mid-October 1866, the *New York Times* announced Dr. Erichsen's research with the headline "Railway Spine—A New Disease." The accompanying text told how Erichsen had finally explained a syndrome that had become increasingly familiar to rail travelers over the years: A train passenger emerges from a collision with no apparent injuries, except for some general weakness and confusion. In a few days, however, the picture changes. 'The passenger finds 'that he is not the man he was;' he has lost bodily energy, mental capacity, business aptitude; he becomes ill and irritable, grows pallid, loses his memory, finds his sleep disturbed, frets about the state of his eyes, loses his delicacy of thought, and, finally, displays all the symptoms of paralysis."[43]

Just a year before Erichsen published his work on railway spine, English novelist Charles Dickens described his own experience with this condition after being in a rail accident at Staplehurst in Kent, England. Four days after the crash, Dickens wrote a letter to a friend in which he told how he had been in his compartment with two women at the time of the crash. The women screamed and Dickens tried to calm them; then, after instructing them not to move, he climbed out the window to safety. Dickens and his two fellow passengers had been lucky; some of the cars had ridden off the bridge when the train derailed, while Dickens's compartment caught on the side of an embankment. In his letter, though, Dickens comments that he was still "shaken" by the experience and that his hand was "unsteady"—not from the crash itself, he tried to convince himself, but from the experience of "working among the dead and dying" for several hours afterward. In a later letter, Dickens admits that he is still "not quite right within."[44] He is baffled as to why the shaking and uneasiness has grown "more and more" and not "less and less" over time. He continues: "I am curiously weak—weak as if I were recovering from a long illness. . . . I begin to feel it more in my head. I sleep and eat well; but I write half a dozen notes, and turn faint and sick." Dickens then ends his letter in an uncharacteristically abrupt manner: "In writing these scanty words of recollection I feel the shake and I am obliged to stop. Ever faithfully, Charles Dickens."

Erichsen seemed to make sense of Dickens's experience in his book on railway spine published the following year. He writes:

> One of the most remarkable phenomena attendant upon this class of cases is that, at the time of the occurence of the injury, the sufferer is usually quite unconscious that any serious accident has happened to him. He feels that he has been violently jolted and shaken . . . but he finds no bones broken, merely some superficial bruises or cuts on the head or legs, perhaps even no evidence of external injury. He congratulates himself upon his escape from the imminent peril . . . assists his less-fortunate fellow-sufferers . . . When he reaches home, however, the effects of the injury that he has sustained begin to manifest themselves. A revulsion of feeling takes place. He bursts into tears."[45]

Erichsen allows that a similar syndrome might result from other types of "ordinary injuries of civil life"—falling from a ladder, overturning a horse carriage, tripping on a tree root. But he argued that railway accidents deserved special scrutiny because of their increasing frequency, the severity of the injuries, and the insidious progression of obscure initial symptoms to matters of life-threatening urgency. "It must be obvious to you all," he wrote, "that in no ordinary accident can the shock be so great as in those that occur on Railways."[46] As for the name of the syndrome itself, Erichsen agreed with some of his early critics that the term "railway spine" was an "absurd appellation"; but he accepted it finally as a decent paraphrase of a vast body of research. Within a few decades, some medical textbooks would refer to the syndrome as Erichsen's Spine.

Even in the 1860s, Erichsen was aware that his work would be relevant not only to fellow doctors, but also to lawyers and railroad officials who were being confronted with increasing numbers of personal injury cases. "There is no class of cases in which medical men are now so frequently called into the witness-box to give evidence in Courts of Law," Erichsen writes. "And there is no class of cases in which there is more discrepancy of surgical opinion."[47] The editors of the leading British medical journal, The Lancet, agreed with Erichsen about the importance of these cases and about the generally negative effects of extended rail travel on workers (who often stood on tiptoe to absorb the shock of the rails on their spines) and passengers (who suffered terrible fatigue and soreness in the years before railway seats were cushioned). In 1862 the journal published a pamphlet on The Influence of Railway Traveling on Public Health in which it concluded that the railway traveler's "entire organism is subjected to a degree of wear and tear that did not exist in preindustrial travel."[48] The Lancet editors broke with Erichsen on the matter of whether such "wear and tear," when compounded by the shock of a rail accident, constituted a compensable injury. They expressed a very definite skepticism about the underlying cause of claims arising from seemingly minor rail accidents. "The temptation to persons of low moral sensibility to trade upon [rail accidents] is very strong," the editors wrote in March 1866, "and it behoves the medical profession, whose part in these actions is a most important one, to guard, by every means in their power, against lending a help, which is very powerful, to the designs of fraudulent individuals."[49] Dr. Thomas Buzzard, writing a few months earlier in The Lancet, shared this distrust of the motives of accident litigants. He observed how a plaintiff's desire for monetary compensation might lead to the fakery of symptoms that doctors like Erichsen mistakenly interpreted as a bona fide condition: "There are not wanting cases of apparent injury in which the imagination of the sufferer, and sometimes even a less honest influence, plays a very important part in the production of symptoms."[50]

What made Erichsen's research so worrisome to railroad claims departments was not so much his naming of railway spine—others had written of it previously—but his explanation of its root causes. Erichsen located the source of railway spine symptoms in microscopic changes to the spine that could not be seen but that were nevertheless as demonstrably real as when a hammer blow to a magnet knocks out the magnetic forces. At the time, this pathological explanation of railway spine fit well with the legal notion that only "real" physical injuries (and not "hysterical" mental distresses) qualified an accident victim for compensation. During the late nineteenth century, Erichsen's railway spine diagnosis, in combination with greater numbers of rail accidents, proved to be a one-two punch that stung the railroads with increasing numbers of damage claim cases. Most plaintiffs' lawyers who litigated accident cases during these years were said to have entered the courtroom with a copy of Erichsen's *Surgery* under the arms. One American medical professor would later write: "Erichsen's little volume became a guide book that might lead the dishonest plaintiff, if he felt so disposed, to set out upon the broad road of imposture and dissimulation with the expectation of getting a heavy verdict."[51]

The story of railway spine became more complicated after Erichsen's work was seriously criticized and, ultimately revised, by Dr. Herbert Page in the 1880s. Although Page was affiliated with a British railroad, his attack on Erichsen was founded on purely medical grounds. Page began with the fact that few postmortem studies of accident victims showed the microscopic spinal lesions that Erichsen claimed existed. Page was not simply interested in tearing down Erichsen's disease; he had an alternate theory to explain the nausea, dizziness, and anxiety experienced by people involved in railway collisions. His theory stressed psychological factors, which were better understood in his time than in Erichsen's, rather than organic pathological ones. In short, Page believed that Erichsen had confused mechanical shock to the spine with psychological shock. Page granted that there was a difference between suffering a conventional collision on the street and suffering a modern railway collision; but he believed that the difference lay in the terrible, *psychical* fears that were unleashed when the mechanized order of steam train travel was violently disrupted by collision or derailment. "The vastness of the destructive forces involved, the magnitude of the results, the imminent danger to the lives of great numbers of human beings, and the hopelessness of escape from the danger," Page believed, "gave rise to emotions which in themselves were quite sufficient to produce shock or even death."[52] While holding that "railway brain" was a more accurate description than "railway spine," he also suggested other terms—"nervous shock," "traumatic neurosis," or "neurasthenia"—as more descriptive of the syndrome. Page's thesis was furthered in the 1890s by the work of the pioneer psychiatrists of Europe, including Jean Martin Charcot and Sigmund Freud, who studied post-traumatic neuroses following rail accidents as a way of making sense of the idea of men exhibiting "hysterical" symptoms of the sort previously thought specific to women. Freud, for one, believed that a condition like railway spine was the product of a complex psychosomatic conversion of fright into physical symptoms. In 1895 he wrote: "During the days following a railway accident, the subject will live through his frightful experiences again both in sleeping and waking, and always with the renewed affect of fright, till at last, after this period of 'psychical working-out', or of 'incubation', conversion into somatic phenomenon takes place."[53]

The news that railway spine might be psychological rather than pathological—and, so, potentially less legally compensable—must have come as welcome news to the railroads. "Presumably Mr. Page's book, like that of Mr. Erichsen before, was soon a familiar sight in courtroom trials," one contemporary writer on the subject speculates.[54] But just how Page's work influenced the outcome of railroad accident cases, or how it affected the legal concept of injury, is not clear. At least one doctor quoted at a 1901 claims conference believed that neurasthenia—"What a beautiful word! How classic! How scientific! How musical and poetic to one with a smattering of Greek"—was much more pernicious than "railway spine."[55] The Oklahoma doctor believed that the term "neurasthenia," because of its "superficial, scientific catchiness," would "for a long time remain a member of the gang to rob railroads before it is found out." L. L. Gilbert, an attorney with the Pennsylvania Lines Railroads, agreed with the doctor, adding, in words that would resound in the later revolt against whiplash, that "neurasthenia covers a multitude of sins, lies, and frauds." In Gilbert's view, the "incubation" period between accident and the first appearance of injury was not a time of "psychosomatic conversion" of fright into organic illness. Rather, it was a measure of the amount of time it took an accident victim to realize his or her opportunity to cash in at the expense of the railroads. Attorney Gilbert explained his view further:

> You take a person, a practical man or woman, let them be subjected to
> a railroad accident, especially a railroad accident because the public have
> learned to believe that they alone are causing Neurasthenic trouble, let
> a person of this character be in a collision—do not care how slight that
> collision is, there will always be a little soreness after the accident. The
> mind works upon the body until ninety-nine out of a hundred, although
> not actually injured in any way, and though you would expect that they
> would recover absolutely within a week or two weeks, [claim to be]
> temporarily or permanently disabled.[56]

A few years later Dr. Willis P. King, a surgeon with the Missouri Pacific Railway system during the 1870s and 1880s, also expressed skepticism about both the organic and psychological theories of railway spine put forward by Erichsen and Page. Like many of his colleagues in railroad claims work, King preferred instead to focus on individual greed encouraged by a society with lax morals. "The truth is that, when persons come out of a wreck unhurt they are usually jubilant about it at the time and are disposed to boast of their good luck," King wrote in a passage that seemed like an explicit revision of Erichsen's original formulation of railway spine. "But, after the lapse of several days, during which they have had time to hear of the fabulous sums that have been paid to others, begin to 'kick themselves,' to use a slang phrase, for being such fools, and for not making complaint of injury and putting in a claim for damages. They feel as if they had lost their pocketbook, which contained a large sum of money."[57] This is when claimants start talking about "taking old Jay Gould [the railroad baron] for all he's worth." Dr. King had worked initially in the Missouri Pacific Hospital in Sedalia, Missouri, where he dealt with injuries ranging from "mere abrasions of the finger up to injuries requiring the amputation of a leg, thigh, or an arm, to trephining the skull, and even returning extruded intestines and other viscera, then closing up and treating the wound by which they made their exit." King's concern was not with these cases brought about by employees, however, but rather with the more than 200 cases involving passengers in which he personally had been asked to testify. In King's opinion, only six or seven of these cases merited compensation. The rest (the discussion of which forms the bulk of 300 pages) were sustained by malingering, fraud, and perjury—a disgrace to humanity, he felt, and also to "American manhood and womanhood, and even tender and innocent childhood."[58]

In the introduction to his 1906 book, *Perjury for Pay: An Exposé of the Methods and Criminal Cunning of the Modern Malingerer,* King explained that he was writing at the behest of his own conscience, not at the request of the railroads. In fact, King says that he himself had begun working for the Missouri Pacific with the popular prejudice that the "railroads hurt people and then kicked them aside and passed on . . . but, oh, what an awakening, when I came face to face with the facts." And "the facts" were plain to King: He granted that a great many people actually got hurt in train accidents and that, in other cases, "the dishonest schemes to make money out of the accident" come to people only after the accident. "But," he added, "if we could know the truth about the number who go to work and deliberately create the accident, if the reader will pardon the bull, he would be astonished more than ever."[59]

To the extent that his book was about solutions, King offered a modest proposal that all personal injury cases should be tried before a jury of "intelligent physicians." Laymen were not competent to judge the medical testimony in most cases, King believed, especially when Dr. Erichsen's railway spine was being debated. "Every lawyer who makes it a business to hunt up cases and sue corporations either has a volume of Erichsen's Surgery," he wrote, "or else the weak doctor whom he employs to do the swearing for his clients has one which is easily accessible to the lawyer and, in either case, you will find the chapter on 'Railroad Spine' well thumbed."[60] King did not mince words when it came to Dr. Erichsen, who, although once an eminent physician, was now, in King's opinion, a "credulous old granny." In fact, Erichsen, who had served as the president of the Royal College of Surgeons and had also been Surgeon Extraordinary to Queen Victoria, had died ten years before the publication of King's book.[61] Dead or alive, it mattered little to King: Erichsen "had done more to injure corporations and to help rogues and perjurers rob railroad companies than all that has ever been written on the subject of injuries to the spine, before or since."

In many ways both the railway spine and the whiplash controversies functioned as ways to talk about something larger in the culture: namely, what many felt to be an "explosion" in the use of courts to solve problems (especially those involving injury) that Americans used to work out among themselves or just accept stoically. "In my personal judgment, it is an unmanly thing to make such a claim [for personal injury]," one judge wrote in the 1860s. "Such injuries are part of the ills of life of which every man ought to take his share."[62] Twenty years later, in 1881, Judge Oliver Wendell Holmes would put words to a similar sentiment, effectively summarizing the state of accident law in America: "The general principle of our law is that loss from accident must lie where it falls." Willis King lived this judicial philosophy: "I grew to almost middle manhood before I ever heard of a lawsuit for damages on account of personal injuries," he wrote in 1906; and the few cases he did know of involved people who refused to take the money they were awarded, having felt reward enough in being proved right. "Just think of it, reader!" King continued. "Think of it and then compare such action with what you and I witness or read about every day."[63]

King was better at describing the personal injury frauds that were "sweeping the country" and at expressing his indignation at how much conditions had changed from the time of his youth than at offering some account of the cause of the change. He mentioned only what he believed to be Americans' new "speculative turn of mind." By this King meant a change in general attitudes about what ways of making money were valid, and, specifically, a change in attitudes about accidents—from the accident as some form of tough luck to the accident as an opportunity for gain. Many in King's line of work attempted to articulate the same idea. At the 1901 railway claims conference in Cleveland, for example, one doctor spoke of the "increasing disposition of the public to bring damage suits for personal injury, not only against the Railroad Company, but against all corporations." The doctor later expanded on this new disposition: "It has come to be almost the first thought of injured passengers, as well as employees to ask—'How much can I secure for this injury?'—even before the doctors have been able to estimate the amount of injury sustained."[64] Blewett Lee, an attorney with the Illinois Central Railroad, delivered a blistering speech on the new "damage suit disease" in America: "People catch personal injury suits from one another just like an infection," he said. "Indeed, sometimes I imagine that it is a horrible disease which attacks the moral fibre. It is called 'easy money' . . . [and] it is the death of honest labor."[65]

Talk of a new disposition toward easy money, a speculative turn of the American mind, would later be recast by the whiplash revolters as the lament over "claims consciousness." To put the original formulations of this idea back in their mid-nineteenth century context, however, is to confront America's deeply confused and contradictory attitudes toward gambling and speculation. Through the late nineteenth century, money made through any speculative means was suspect—the stigma did not just attach to the particular form of personal injury prospecting that later worried railroad men. Speculating in stocks or real estate was as taboo in nineteenth century America as usury was in the Middle Ages. Money should accrue naturally, many believed—that is to say, slowly and honestly, through productive labor, not quickly and effort-lessly through abstract gambling. Farmers, whose idea of wealth was tied to the dirt and roots of their crops, grew incensed at the "devils" who came into their towns to profit through speculation on grain futures.[66] Later those who pursued personal injury claims were often cast in the same light: as sinister outside threats to a simpler way of life that was getting harder and harder to maintain against the socially destructive assaults of "modern" individuals—people who saw no harm in pressing their personal claims or pursuing their private speculations at the expense of the greater good. As the American economy diversified and became more complex in the late nineteenth century, however, some amendments had to be made to this thinking. Distinctions were now necessary between good speculation, which benefited society, and bad speculation, which was all reducible to some form of selfish gambling.

"Gradually through the nineteenth century, through a reconstruction of ethical standards of capitalism," historian Ann Fabian explains, "speculators managed to shed their aura of evil."[67] Stockbrokers ultimately made the cut, for instance, but personal injury litigants and contingent-fee lawyers did not. This was abundantly clear in the remarks of Ilinois Central attorney Blewett Lee, who defended the land and stock speculations of American capitalists and denounced the "damage suit disease" as the "death of honest labor." Lee makes this point more explicitly after telling a story of Mississippians pressing damage claims for cold feet in unheated cars ("coldfeetos," he calls them derisively): "Any man who by his labor and self denial has accumulated the sum of twenty thousand dollars will not enjoy this story," Lee says. "How long did it take you [to earn the money being given away to complainers]?"[68] The conflict was not simply between good speculators and bad, investors versus gamblers, in this view; but also more fundamentally about two rival views of American individualism: the rugged, self-sufficient pioneer who could shrug off a little pain and suffering versus the new rights-oriented (read "claims-conscious") individual who believed that misfortune was not always just a sign of God's disfavor but might actually be the product of another's negligence and who could be aggressive about pursuing remuneration. For many who could not hold these two views in balance, the apparent contradiction between them was resolved in a rough way: the pioneer ideal was romanticized, while aggressive rights-claimers were stigmatized as greedy troublemakers threatening simple, pastoral, American social cohesion.[69]

In his 1913 address, Blewett Lee saw himself speaking not only for the farmers whose freight rates would increase due to damage claims, or the honest ticket-buying (and no-claims-filing) passengers who would have "to foot the bill for the damage suit business." He also saw his mission as a warning about the potential downfall of big business in America at the hands of damage-suit claimants. "Every form of capital has reason to fear the treatment which is now being meted out to railroad companies," Lee warned. In the face of increasingly baseless damage-suit assaults, corporate America stood like a "huge buffalo surrounded by Indian hunters, shooting arrow after arrow in the poor beast while it staggers along with blood pouring from its nostrils."[70] Never mind that it was Anglos, not Indians, who exacted the most wasteful, wanton slaughter of American buffalo (as "frivolous" or mercenary as any damage suit ever was). The image was potent nonetheless, every bit the companion of the often expressed image of fraudulent and frivolous claimants sucking the lifeblood out of corporations. And it guided earlier generations of railroad men in their efforts to do all they could to prevent the damage-suit disease before it got started.

In the context of personal injury claims, nostalgia for a simpler time when Americans were thought to have settled disputes without recourse to courts and lawyers, one self-sufficient pioneer to another, often was cover talk for a corporate legal culture of noncompensation for accident victims. Beyond a campaign against marginal, perhaps fraudulent, railway spine claims, the railroads fought hard against payments in even the most tragically legitimate cases. And when settlements were offered preemptively to avoid litigation, the railroads made sure to frame them as charity: No one had a right to charity, it was to be understood; at the same time, everyone had a responsibility to bear up "manfully" under the weight of their share of the "ills of life." What this view failed to comprehend, however, was that the average person's share of the ills of life had been increasing dramatically, both in England and America, and that the rail corporations bore some responsibility for them. In the age of the steam railroad, accidents had become a new fact of life, impressing themselves negatively on a public that was otherwise enamored with the promise that industrial technology was transforming their everyday lives for the better. In 1853 alone, the year from which railroad historians date an initial era of accidents, some 234 train passengers died in accidents in America. By contrast, during the preceding twenty years, only 50 people were estimated to have died in train crashes, and no more than 6 people had ever died in a single incident.[71]

For those people who did not experience directly the downside of industrial progress—accidents—a distinct brand of journalism developed to document the horrors of rail travel. Rail accidents were the frequent cover story in the illustrated newspapers of the mid-nineteenth century; in the aftermath of many rail tragedies, enterprising publishers printed "accident broadsides" painted in lurid detail and color. In 1865 *Harper's Weekly* painted a typically grim portrait of the safety of the rails. "During the present year Death appears to have set his mark on the traveler," the *Harper's* article stated. "Everyday the record of mortality is continued. Now it is a collision; now the explosion of a locomotive, and then again the sudden precipitation of an entire train down a steep embankment or perhaps into some river. There has come to be a general insecurity and distrust, and every man or woman who steps out of a railway car unhurt does so with a feeling of sensible relief."[72]

The *Harper's* editors ended by noting that more lives had been lost in rail accidents in 1865 alone than had died in some of the bloodiest Civil War battles. The analogy resonated throughout the century, as the names of the very worst rail disasters were discussed with the same awful reverence that was otherwise reserved for the worst war battles. In the summer of 1856 the nation came to know Camp Hill, the small town in Pennsylvania where a head-on collision had caused the deaths of sixty-six young children who had been on a church picnic earlier that day.[73] Twenty years later, in December 1876, word spread about Ashtabula, named for the site in Ohio where the *Pacific Express* fell through a bridge one snowy night, killing all eighty passengers on board. The wreck at Ashtabula had been the deadliest railroad accident in American history up to that time; it so captured the public's imagination that a memorial lithograph was published in addition to a book, *The Ashtabula Bridge Disaster*, which detailed the incident in all of its bloody particulars. In between Camp Hill and Ashtabula, the nation's attention fixed on the Angola Horror, named for the site in New York State where a defective axle, combined with a faulty bridge, derailed the *Lake Shore Express*: Forty-two passengers burned alive inside an old wooden coach at Angola.

Other well-known railroad wrecks included Busey Bridge and Mud Run, both of which were the subject of extensive coverage in the illustrated magazines of the 1880s; pen-and-ink drawings depicted rescuers digging bodies from the wreckage of each crash, then stacking the dead in funeral cars. The wreck at Chatsworth in 1887 was named for the farm country of central Illinois where eighty-two people died when a small wooden bridge gave way over a dry creekbed. News of Chatsworth gripped the Midwest, where it was soon memorialized in a folk song that included the stanza 'The dead and dying mingled/ With broken beams and bars/ An awful human carnage/A dreadful wreck of cars." The victims of Chatsworth were depicted in an illustration in *Harper's Weekly*—some in shock, some in pain, others running in fear, "the air resounding with the shrieks, groans, and prayers of the sufferers." A photograph taken at Chatsworth shows surviving passengers, aid workers, and sightseers impelled by morbid curiosity to see the train cars that had "telescoped" one into the other, killing most of the passengers inside earlier that week.

When the railroads first appeared, they radically changed people's perceptions of space: Places once thought remote now were only hours away. Cities themselves were restructured around rail lines. Perceptions of time were also altered with the standardization of time zones throughout the country to conform to the demands of rail schedules. Fear of changes brought about by the railroads, as well as deep concern over the smoke-belching leviathans themselves, was gradually set aside in the name of progress. In psychological language, writer Wolfgang Schivelbusch theorizes, the fear was sublimated— at least until an accident occurred. Then every repressed reservation about industrial technology and the type of progress it represented was released. In this sense, railroad accidents became an unpleasant reminder of the fragility of a modern life balanced precariously on two steel rails, a glimpse into the dangerous forces of mechanized progress that can come unharnessed at any moment. "Only the accident reminds us of this," writer Ernest Bloch once observed. "The crash of collision, the roar of explosion, the cries of maimed people—a production that knows no civilized schedule."[74]

The nationally known rail accidents of the last quarter of the nineteenth century occurred toward the end of a horrible wave of railway disasters that continued for more than thirty years. The accumulated effect of these railway horrors on public perceptions of train travel was enormous, even if sometimes overstated and exploited by the press. Horse-drawn railcars had rarely caused serious accidents; and, before the horse-drawn railways, in the late eighteenth and early nineteenth centuries, the typical transportation accident had been a simple matter of a stagecoach overturning at a low speed on a deeply rutted mud road, perhaps dumping out some of its half-dozen or so passengers. ("Usually a vehicle overturned and its occupants received a bad shaking up and some bruises," according to one account, "and occasionally someone suffered a broken limb.")[75] One story surviving from this era relates how a coach carrying Henry Clay, the senior Senator from Kentucky, overturned in Uniontown, Pennsylvania. After the crash, Clay was dragged from under the coach, having sustained no serious injuries. While dusting himself off, the gray-haired senator was said to have remarked good-naturedly that "the Clay of Kentucky had been mixed with the limestone of Pennsylvania." The driver of Clay's coach, who had been thrown from his seat and suffered a broken nose, finished the journey—the typical aftermath of a preindustrial transportation accident.

When serious railroad accidents finally began to occur regularly in the early 1850s, they were overwhelmingly the result of the fact that, during the preceding two decades, the American railroads had been poorly constructed with the worst materials available. Unlike the British rails, which had been built to last, the American rail lines ran over wooden bridges, not stone or metal ones; the track was not maintained; and due to a lack of time and money, sharp curves and steep grades had not been straightened or flattened. Fortunes had been made from this hasty progress of the railroads across the nation— great fortunes measured in almost magically large numbers, quick fortunes amassed in a single generation by a handful of Huntingtons and Vanderbilts and Jay Goulds. These were the men who made the deals to lay the track, to mine the coal for fuel, to build the cars and the stations, and to buy the land at bargain prices over which a restless nation was pushing forward toward its future—its "manifest destiny"—now at twenty-five miles an hour, now at thirty-five, now at fifty. All of this progress was not without its price, however.

Neither the technology of the cars nor that of the roadbed kept pace with the new volume or speed. The result was stated straightforwardly by one railroad historian: "This cheap, hasty construction, coupled with increased traffic and speed after 1852, produced half a century of frightful carnage."[76]

Early in this new era of accidents, the mood of the public seemed to be one of unqualified antagonism toward the railroads. Stories about even minor railway accidents were reported under headlines that screamed "ANOTHER RAILWAY HORROR"; more serious accidents earned the label "RAILWAY MURDERS." One article, "Nobody's Murders," published in *Harper's Weekly*, reflected sardonically on the way that the railroads profited from operating the rail lines, while innocent passengers increasingly paid the price with their lives. "A train thunders along a down-grade around a curve above a precipice at the rate of forty miles an hour—a rail snaps—two cars are hurled off the track down the bank, and six or seven corpses and a score or so of maimed victims are taken from the ruins," the account from 1858 began.

> [Then], the President or some other officer "hurries to the scene of the disaster"—an inquest is held—the officers of the road swear that it was in "good enough" condition—that the rate of speed was not unusual; that the same thing had been done a hundred times before safely; and as many other absurdities as occur to them—and a jury returns, of course, that nobody is to blame. Nobody ever is. Boilers are bursting all over the country—railroad bridges breaking and rails snapping—human life is sadly and foolishly squandered—but nobody is to blame.[77]

Such talk about "nobody's murders" was one way of summing the legal climate of the middle nineteenth century, which generally favored corporations over individuals and made it hard to successfully pursue a personal injury action against the railroads. In general, railway workers and, later, passengers injured or killed on American railroads had to go it alone after an accident throughout much of the century. A cluster of legal principles had formed like a clot in the channels that may have carried compensation to accident victims. Workers, especially, faced the dread trio of the "fellow servant rule," contributory negligence, and the doctrine of "assumption of risk." Taken together, these common-law principles told workers that they had no case if their coworkers were responsible for the accident; or if they themselves were even partly responsible; or if the nature of their job made it clear that significant danger was involved, the principle being that the higher wages that workers got for doing dangerous jobs was, effectively, compensation in advance for any accident that might occur. Very few litigants could negotiate this legal obstacle course.

"Workers disabled in accidents and the widows of deceased railway men faced a grim and uncertain future," observed historian Walter Licht in his study of the lives of the early railwaymen. "In making claims for compensation for their losses, the legal system offered little or no relief. Railroad companies often granted gratuities to injured men and sometimes paid hospital and funeral expenses, but only in an informal and unsystematic fashion."[78] The informality was the center of the railroad's (non)compensation policy. "Avoid any particular practice lest it might become a common law," one railroad executive warned his line's officials; many companies stated explicitly in employee manuals that they were not under any obligation to award "gratuities" to injured railwaymen or their families.[79] In a way that was purposely unpurposeful—"informal, discretionary, and completely voluntary"—the railroads made car cleaners of the brakemen who lost their legs in a fall from the top of the cars in winter snow. They found desk work for the "couplers" who routinely lost fingers joining car to car manually in the old link-and-pin style, or the cabmen who suffered frostbite in the cold and were burned by sparks from the fire stacks of the engines. Sometimes, however, the injured railwayman would get nothing from his former employer except a trip to the local poorhouse. There the injured worker ate and slept alongside the mentally ill, the chronically sick, the elderly poor, the orphaned child, the pauper, the tramp, the families dependent upon seasonal work, and the homeless men who could not find a place to sleep that night in the local police station. Poorhouses of the nineteenth century were the "backwaters of social policy. . . . stagnant festering exceptions to the progressive spirit in American life"[80]—themselves the product of a purposely informal and punitive system of social welfare in America— and the discarded injured railwayman, no longer productive, fit right in. In short, injured railway workers took what they were given; and, when they were given next to nothing, they took that, too. Licht summarizes the situation this way: "Railway workers either had little access to legal assistance, did not want to jeopardize their chances of receiving voluntary gratuities from their employers, feared for their future employment, or else calculated quite rationally that the possibilities of ultimately winning in court were quite slim."[81]

The story of what happened to passengers injured or killed on the rails followed only a slightly different arc across the nineteenth century. Passengers had less disincentive to sue, and so sued more often, even though they were largely unsuccessful in obtaining compensation. "Although the law as now established by our Courts seldom enables a man to recover, or even to get his case before a Jury," it was noted by a *New York Times* reporter back in 1866, "there seems to be no end to the attempts to make railroads responsible for the accidents that are daily occurring." In New York City, only thirteen people brought personal injury suits to the Supreme Court in all of 1870, legal historian Randolph Bergstrom points out. In 1910, by contrast, this figure would catapult to 595 suits, and these numbers were only a fraction of the increasing numbers of cases being settled out of court. During the crucial forty years between 1870 and 1910, Bergstrom has shown, the frequency with which New Yorkers brought their personal injury cases to court had increased 4,500 percent; other researchers have recently demonstrated that a similar situation existed in several other large cities.[82] Somewhere during the late nineteenth century, with railway disasters becoming more frequent and corporate attitudes toward compensation lagging behind like the technology of the rails and roadbeds that caused many of the accidents in the first place, Americans had discovered the personal injury lawsuit.

That the increasing number of personal injury lawsuits in the late nineteenth century had something very much to do with the increasing number of accidents is beyond question, but it is not the whole story. Modern living had certainly brought with it more dangers: The streets of America's largest cities were especially crowded, with new ways to get hurt by man, beast, and machine. But, during this time, increasing numbers of damage suits were also being brought based on old dangers—preindustrial types of accidents such as simple sidewalk falls and horse-related mishaps. Americans, especially those who lived in or near major cities, were filing more personal injury actions—not primarily due to increasing industrial dangers, or the absence of changes in the law (thereby making such suits easier for plaintiffs to win), but because their basic idea of what an accident was had changed.

No longer simply the fault of careless individuals, an accident was now seen as potentially having a complex cause outside of the control of individuals, and expectations that corporations might be held to an increased standard of care began to rise. People began to understand that the shoddy workmanship of the railroads, not the fabled "drunken switchman," had caused Camp Hill, Ashtabula, Chatsworth, and most of the other "railway horrors" of the day. No longer the prosaic overturning of a stagecoach, an accident was now seen as having long-term consequences for its victims. Sometimes these consequences were as immediate and tangible as a lost limb; other times, as in the case of railway spine, the consequences of an accident could go unseen for weeks, months, or years; and this did not mean that they were any less real, or less worthy of compensation. Unfortunately for injured passengers, however, this new attitude existed long before it was recognized by law. Legal historian Lawrence Friedman summed the state of tort law in the nineteenth century this way: "There was almost certainly no conscious conspiracy to cut liability down to size, no conspiracy against injured workers, passengers, pedestrians. But the spirit of the age was a spirit of limits on recovery. People lived with calamity; they had no sense (as would be true in the 20th century) that *somebody* was always responsible—either the state or some private party."[83]

The discovery of the personal injury lawsuit was one response to the era of accidents that began in the mid-nineteenth century; the invention of accident insurance was another. In fact, it can be argued that accident insurance itself, in offering predictable monetary outcomes to otherwise random accidents beginning in the 1860s, helped to create the new expectations about monetary rewards for accident victims—the new "claims consciousness"—that the railroads tried to frustrate with their informal compensation strategy in the late nineteenth century and that the insurance industry itself would later campaign against during its revolt against whiplash.

As increasing numbers of accidents came to be the negative by-product of America's industrial progress, the accident insurance business emerged to transform this negative into an enormous positive. While insurers would later come to denounce all those who profited from accidents, portraying personal injury attorneys as vultures making a fortune from the misfortunes of others, the industry itself was built more squarely on the idea of profiting from accidents. The more horrible were the train wrecks of the mid-nineteenth century, the more people came to understand why they might need to buy accident protection. Railroad calamities were personal tragedies for the victims and publicity nightmares for the rail lines, but they boosted sales for the pioneer accident insurers. It is fair to say that Dick Johnson, an early accident insurance salesman sent from Hartford to sell the idea in New York, made more lucrative use of newspaper coverage of accident horrors than any ambulance chaser ever did. "We capitalized strongly on current events," he later said. "After reading the morning paper on my way to the office, I would sketch an imaginary picture of a hotel fire, a ferry boat collision, a railroad wreck or what not. I would rush the sketch to 'Ringle,' who would convert it into chalk plates in time to get them into the paper the same day. Oh, we had a grand old time."[84] Harry Porter, an ad man who worked for the Travelers several years later, stated the connections among tragedy, fear, and insurance profits more clearly. "Because the elementary and common emotion in the sale of accident insurance is fear, the advertising itself must be planned and written to take advantage of that emotion," Porter said in a 1915 address. Later he added an important word

FIGURE 5.2A. This ad for Travelers Insurance company appeared in popular magazines in the 1860s. Drawn by Thomas Nast, the famous cartoonist who created the donkey and elephant symbols for the Democratic and Republican parties, this cartoon capitalized on popular fears of increasing numbers of railway disasters in order to stimulate sales of accident policies. Death, according to the original caption, is "our constant traveling companion." (Courtesy of The Travelers.)

about strategy: "The fear must not be approached with the explosion of a bomb, but in an insidious and careful way, for we are talking to people with intelligence, and, in fact, this very intelligence is a stimulant to the fear itself."[85]

The early selling of accident insurance may have been insidious, as Porter later suggested, but it was not very careful in how it stimulated fear about accidents to sell the Travelers' particular brand of security. One favorite Travelers' ad from the 1880s, for example, was a Thomas Nast cartoon depicting a skeletal grim reaper in a dark suit and top hat in the center of a rail car flanked by two concerned family men. Each man is reading a newspaper

FIGURE 5.2B. This early ad for Travelers Insurance Company was part of a sales strategy to exploit the increasing dangers of everyday life in modern, industrial America in order to sell an unlikely commodity, accident insurance, to a public that did not yet know why it was necessary. (Courtesy of The Travelers.)

with headlines evocative of the much-reported "railway horrors" of the age—one reads "Railroad Slaughter," the other, "Boiler Explosion." Another early advertisement entitled "The Dream of the Man Not Insured" shows a man in bed with eyes wide open and hair raised in fright, apparently suffering through troubled sleep. Surrounding him in the cartoon frame are visions of the accident fates that might befall him during the day—falling headfirst downstairs, being trampled by a team of horses, running a hand through a circular saw, slipping on an orange peel. ("Thank heaven! Tis only a dream," the man says. "But if I live till morning I'll have a policy in the Travelers.") Other early Travelers' ads were less bald in cashing in on the public's general fear of railway accidents: A man walking by a body of water has his nose bitten by a crocodile, as the bottom of the frame offers the admonition to "Insure Against Accidents." A series of ads appearing in the 1870s featured "Mr. B. Careful," a man with a leg in a cast, arm in a sling, and a bandaged head who failed to get accident insurance because he felt he "didn't travel much." Other early ads simply depicted terrible accident situations or offered testimonials from P.T. Barnum or "Chang," the famous "Chinese Giant," followed by the slogan "Moral: Insure in the Travelers." Travelers' ads appeared not only in the most popular magazines of the day—*Harper's Weekly, Puck, Frank Leslie's Illustrated Weekly*—but also in the company's house organ, *The Travelers Record*, whose subscribership of 50,000 reached more readers than any other.

Print ads were only one aspect of the selling of accident insurance in America; the work of the company's pioneer sales agents was just as integral. One of these agents, Edward V. Preston of Hartford, began working for the Travelers after returning from service in the Civil War. Preston, who worked on a combination of commission and salary like all of the early agents, later tried to recall how he first convinced people to buy policies from him. "I first besieged my friends and acquaintances for their favor," his words were later recorded. "I recited accidents I gathered from the street and from the newspapers. Every morning and every evening I loaded up with items. No merchant, banker, traveler, or stay-at-home could escape my ammunition."[86] Preston's big break came when it was widely reported that the Travelers paid $2,000 to the widow of an insured man who died after being stung by a poisonous insect. ("How we crammed that payment down the throat of the skeptics!" Preston recalled. "From then on, the work widened and prospered.") Another pioneer Travelers agent, John Way, rode a handcar along thousands of miles of track in Iowa and Nebraska selling railroad workers on the idea of accident insurance while trying to not get killed himself by approaching trains.

Despite the work of these pioneering insurance agents and the prevalence of the print ads and the giveaway items—free lunches, umbrellas, entertainment—accident insurance was not a profitable business in America for several decades after its introduction in 1864. "For a while we were not in general taken seriously," Travelers' founder and visionary James Batterson later recalled. "We were more a subject of jeers and flat witticisms."[87] To understand why people were not buying accident insurance initially is to look again at what exactly was being sold. Clearly, accident insurers were selling the hope of security in an age of increasing dangers. On a more abstract level, though, they were selling something much more controversial—a nonfatalistic view of accidents in which money could be equated with the loss of human limbs. This view was the logical extension of the nonfatalistic view of death that, sociologist Vivianna A. Rotman Zelizer shows, life insurers sold tirelessly during the first half of the nineteenth century. The idea behind both life insurance and accident insurance was as profoundly scientific, rational, and commercial as it was potentially disturbing or dangerous: cash for human life.[88]

Initial opposition to accident insurance and to the underlying idea of cash for life was a watered-down version of the strong initial rejection of life insurance earlier in the century. Prior to 1843, the magical year in which life insurance was said to have finally caught on in America, the business of insuring lives had not been received enthusiastically. At best, people did not understand why they needed to insure their lives. At worst, people objected to the idea of gambling on life—evidence already existed that this could lead to murder for insurance. (Similar reports of widespread malingering, fakery, and perjury would cause at least one railway surgeon to recommend that accident insurance be prohibited by law.)[89] Many academics wondered whether insurance in the event of death would replace the traditional support of family and community with the purely monetary support of an impersonal corporation. Clergymen sermonized about the sacrilege of reducing death to an economic event. The more people trusted in the life insurers, the author of *The Evils of Life Insurance* believed, the less they would look to God. ("We believe Satan never fitted so keen and sharp pointed an instrument to pierce the soul of a saint as Life Insurance, to induce him to loosen his hold on his heavenly father.")[90] Many religious leaders went so far as to forbid their parishioners from insuring their lives; Mennonites excommunicated any member who insured; and as late as 1899 a group of Lutheran ministers vilified life insurance as "antagonistic to Bible teachings." "Many people think that there is something sacred in human life which should not be made the subject of a policy of insurance," one life insurance pioneer acknowledged. "It is regarded as almost as bad as man-stealing or dissecting a human corpse."[91] To this day life insurance is banned in some Muslim countries.

Even when life insurance finally succeeded in America—between 1840 and 1860 the total dollar value of life insurance in force jumped from $5 million to $205 million—it did not do so by directly meeting the objections against it. Rather, life insurance ultimately succeeded by showing itself to be in line with the idea of insuring property, a practice that was, by then, centuries old. In their sales pitches, life insurers tried to point up an inconsistency in the fact that men insured their homes, their stores, and their merchandise against fire, and their ships against danger, but would not insure their lives for the benefit of their families. ("There are some men who insure their property against loss by fire who seem to be opposed to life insurance," the writer of one popular insurance sales book noted, "as if a man's house or his store could be worth more to his family than his life.")[92] This equivalence between a life and an article of merchandise was precisely what opponents of life insurance felt to be wrong with the whole institution: "A man may barter and banter where mere goods are concerned," one writer maintained in the 1860s, "but what a degradation to bring life operations to this low level."

The ultimate success of life insurance in America was due to a powerful, innovative, two-pronged marketing strategy. Company literature chiseled into stone a sense of the high moral purpose of those who insured; it touted the companion virtues of providing for one's family and not letting oneself become a burden to society. Several major insurers even successfully courted religious leaders to do their bidding from the pulpit. ("Once the question was: can a Christian man rightfully seek Life Assurance?" one minister proclaimed in the 1880s. "That day is passed. Now the question is: can a Christian man justify himself in neglecting such a duty?")[93] Meanwhile, on the streets, the pioneer life insurance agents did the "dirty work" of selling Americans life coverage one person at a time. As a group, these agents were men who had failed in other professions. The life agency of the mid-nineteenth century was likened at the time to an "asylum, a last refuge on the road to the poor house, a sanctuary for the lame, the halt, the blind, and the refuse of every calling."[94] If these men were not already at the bottom of the occupational ladder, they were further stigmatized by their connection with the life insurance process of secularizing, commercializing, and bureaucratizing death; and insurers let the stigma lay where it fell. From the increasingly lavish comfort of their home offices—in 1886 Chicago's Home Insurance Building became the nation's first skyscraper—insurers removed themselves from the ugly work of their streetcorner emissaries.

Accident insurers also made their initial appeals in thinly moral terms. "It is the most enlightened and benevolent form which the projects of self-interest ever took," one pocket sales manual stated. "Those who give their money ostensibly to benefit themselves, may be thus providing that which will certainly benefit others."[95] The manual was published in 1851 to help sales agents of the world's first accident insurer, the British Railway Passengers Assurance Company. The book begins with a number of reasons to insure, one of which is an appeal to the "benevolent mind" that, even if they are not in want of relief themselves, their premium dollars would help create a fund for others less fortunate. None of the letters from satisfied customers that form the bulk of the little chapbook mentions this as a reason for their satisfaction, however; and few write to say that they were just so satisfied with the peace of mind they got from insuring that they just had to write. Rather, the portrait of the satisfied customer is the person who was skeptical about the idea of accident insurance until the investment paid off in the form of a settlement. The same would later be true for the pioneer American accident insurer, The Travelers, which was modeled directly on its British forerunner. In its early years, *The Travelers Record* published booklets of testimonial letters from satisfied customers thanking the company for prompt payments and advising all readers to get insured. Once The Travelers proved its credibility by paying claims (unlike a spate of fraudulent early insurers), the company was faced with the challenge of instilling the virtue of paying into the insurance fund but not drawing out. "When a man has been insured against accident for several years, and in all that time has escaped injury, he sometimes concludes that it is useless throwing money into a mill which grinds no grist for him," an editorial in *The Travelers Record* stated in 1879. "The man wants to see some tangible return, some share in those 'cash benefits' he has heard so much about."[96] The editorialists argued that peace of mind was a benefit not to be undervalued and that premiums unused by one subscriber provided for unfortunates. But salesmen were sent in the field with lists of the dollar figures paid to individuals for everything from bee stings to falls from ladders to train wrecks. (Only suicide and injuries caused by Indian attack were excluded from the earliest standard policy.)

Just as life insurers ultimately dropped their moral appeals in favor of economic rationales, accident insurers came to tout their cash benefits and the underlying science of distributing risk that enabled them to match body parts with dollar equivalents. The author of "What Is the Value of Human Life in Dolllars?" for one, was impressed enough by the actuaries' efforts to look forward to the day when "scientists would succeed in having established a standard money value for each man and woman, boy and girl, dead or maimed."[97] Science and technology had generated accidents as an unwanted by-product of progress, the story seemed to go, but, given enough time, a new actuarial science, and later a science of "accident prevention," would set things right again. In the meantime, the accident insurance industry also seemed to imply, unscrupulous people—shyster attorneys, quack doctors, malingering claimants crying "railway spine" or, later, "whiplash"—would continue to exploit the cultural confusion about how much human life and pain and suffering was really worth in dollar and cents. "The past ten years have witnessed the rise of a certain class of shyster lawyers who find their livelihood by preying on corporations and private individuals," the editorialists at *The Travelers Record* wrote in 1897. With no trace of hypocrisy given their own sales strategies, the editorialists went on to lambaste this "swarm of rats" that combed the newspapers for records of accident tragedies on which to capitalize. Blinking not at all at their own initially manipulative appeals to customers (portraying themselves as a benevolent society benefiting unfortunates), The Travelers' editorialists excoriated the plaintiffs' lawyers who "pose as the champion of some poor person oppressed or injured in some way . . . while inwardly licking their chops over the rich morsels they are about to devour."[98]

Americans, following cues from the accident insurers, seemed to have taken all of their original discomfort with the very idea of insuring lives and limbs for cash rewards—all of the negative feeling that originally stigmatized the life and accident insurance businesses themselves—and transformed it into a preoccupation with the goings-on of the plaintiffs. All that may have once seemed irreligious or threatening to tradition about insuring a life against accident or death was gradually displaced onto those who made it their business actually to collect on an insurance contract: personal injury attorneys and their soliciting agents, especially. Being awarded money for an accident, once "unmanly," "unheard of," or a sign of moral weakness, was now all right; but collecting an "excessive" amount was now the central problem.

During the fifty or sixty years preceding the revolt against whiplash in the 1960s, an entire journalistic genre evolved to record the stories of outrageous damage claim verdicts and spectacular personal injury frauds, just as an earlier journalistic genre documented the injustice of "railway horrors" that left people injured or killed and destitute. The details of these "damage-suit disease" stories are not important, only the spirit in which they are told. Like the earlier journalistic genre of stories that emphasized the railroad octopus that was devouring profits while leaving behind the wrecked lives of workers and passengers, the standard damage-suit disease story was essentially a lightning rod for two angry moods: the one, outrage at corporate indifference to personal pain and suffering, the other outrage at individuals who tried to profit from their pain and suffering at the expense of corporations. Over the years—from the era of railway horrors and railway spine, through the damage suit disease stories and the whiplash revolts—these two contradictory attitudes about personal injury claims in America have not been resolved; they have only become more pronounced.

If Americans have been of two minds about accident claims since the middle of the nineteenth century, by the middle of the twentieth century those two minds had grown into two distinct, opposing bodies. On one side, the insurance industry, a corporate giant that had finally taken its place beside General Motors and General Electric at the 1964 World's Fair. On the other side, a self-styled giant tamer, the personal injury bar, which first organized in the late 1940s, when a group of attorneys in Boston formed the National Association of Claimants and Compensation Attorneys (NACCA) in reaction to the inequities of the chaser tribunals of the 1920s and 1930s. The battle between plaintiffs and corporate defendants began in the time of the railroads. ("The personal injury lawyer and the personal injury doctor, with his 'traumatic neurosis,' stand in the ring and fight the railroad doctor and the railroad lawyer, with his 'contributory negligence,'" it was written in the *Yale Law Journal* in the 1890s. The two sides go at it "from start to finish with a jury for the referee and a judge who is reduced by legislation to be a mere official time-keeper."[99]) In the late nineteenth century insurers gradually assumed greater and greater shares of railroad liability, and then, with the rise of the automobile, replaced the railroads as the major corporate defender. War against railway spine gave way naturally to the revolt against whiplash. Just who threw the first punch between these two institutionalized adversaries is as unanswerable a question as it is irrelevant; what is clear is that the blows really started to land in the 1950s.

By 1959 Jacob Fuchsberg, one of the pioneers of the plaintiffs' movement, had had enough with the insurance industry's propagandistic "revolt" against personal injury claims. He wrote to a Long Island newspaper to protest the publication of an article—"INSURANCE CHISELERS COST YOU MONEY"— that he felt was part of a "carefully planned press campaign" to "cast doubt and suspicion" on even the most meritorious claims in order to bring down damage settlements. In his letter, Fuchsberg passed along a confidential memo circulated among insurance underwriters in 1958. The memo, written by a consultant to the insurance industry, began by noting its pleasure at the recent publication of several magazine articles that stressed the insurance industry message: high damage-claim settlements for a few people meant high insurance premiums for everyone else. The insurance executive then went on to suggest a full-blown media blitz to get this message out: "Let's see more articles like these in *Life, Saturday Evening Post* and *McCalls,* a few network TV shows built around the theme, a couple of movies and a Broadway show." This "could be done and still be entertaining," the executive suggested, "if the right people are romanced."[100]

The executive's plan seemed to have been carried out. In February 1959, for instance, an episode of the police drama *Dragnet* featured a plot to fake an accident for money; it concluded with the insurance industry message that false claims hurt all premium-payers, not just insurance companies.[101] In November 1962, another NACCA president expressed his great distress at a network TV show—*Smash-up*—which, once again, used a story line of fraudulent claims to undermine the believability of all personal injury claims. The president of the NACCA described the program as a "great calumny" on the legal and medical professions; in the next month's *NACCA Newsletter,* he began by indicating that much of his time over the previous month had been occupied with the "nefarious" TV program *Smash-up.* He continued: "We have been vigorously prosecuting our claim that the program was instigated as a propaganda device designed to unduly, illegally, and improperly influence prospective and active jurors to the great harm and detriment of literally millions of honest claimants."[102] A few years after this, yet another NACCA president would take issue with attacks on personal injury claimants and their lawyers that he felt were orchestrated by the insurance industry. Writing in response to such features as "AUTO CLAIMS—75% PHONY?" and "DAMAGE SUITS—A PRIMROSE PATH TO IMMORALITY," attorney Herman Glaser argued that it was only "reasonable to conclude that these attacks were deliberate, calculated, and intended to destroy a branch of the law which has always been concerned with fair and just compensatory damages."[103]

While none of the NACCA presidents' suspicions was ever proven, the accident insurance industry made it plain in its own newsletters that it had indeed hired a public relations director; although it was not the job of this PR man to "plant" stories in the press, his office did prepare articles and features for publication in national magazines.[104] The hiring of a PR man was only one part of a campaign by casualty insurers to "educate" judges, lawyers, and the public about the social harms of unchecked damage awards. Throughout the 1950s, this educational campaign took the form of a series of advertisements in national magazines. In one of the ads, a puzzled housewife asks herself, "ME? I'M PAYING FOR EXCESSIVE JURY AWARDS?" She is answered in the text of the ad: "Yes, Mrs. Jones, you pay for liability and damage suit verdicts whether you are insured or not. . . . So next time you serve on a jury, remember this: When you are overly generous with an insurance company's money, you help increase not only your own premiums, but the cost of every article and service you buy." The formation of the Defense Research Institute, whose first publication in 1960 was the *Revolt Against Whiplash*, was also important to the success of the accident insurance industry's informational campaign to deflate "ballooning" jury verdicts.

Just as the NACCA had branded all of the insurance industry's "educational" campaigning as an attempt to "brainwash" prospective jury members, the members of the Federation of Insurance Counsel and other insurance defense groups said just the opposite: namely, that their efforts were an attempt to counter the *real* brainwashing campaigns being conducted by the NACCA. "The activities of the organized plaintiffs' bar have made the American people increasingly claim-conscious," one lawyer told an audience of insurance counsels in 1964. "A general feeling has developed that whoever is injured in his person or property ought to receive compensation, whether or not he was to blame for his own loss. This cannot be!"[105] The DRI's mission was to "vigorously fight" all of this, according to director James Ghiardi. "In my opinion this is the organization that can meet the onslaught of the organized plaintiffs' bar and present to the public the truth about the personal injury picture."[106] Six months earlier William Knepper, the president of another insurance defense group, also spoke of the "NACCA onslaught"; he then trumpeted the "mission" of insurance defense lawyers "to present to the public the truth about the insatiable appetite of the plaintiff's bar for ever-larger verdicts regardless of fault." In a 1963 speech, Knepper tried to rally his troops to face the opposition: "The organized plaintiff's lawyers have concentrated their efforts and their enthusiasm in a single association, one which has grown to a membership of more than 12,000 and seeks to be recognized as 'the second largest bar association in the United States.' We cannot meet that challenge unless we work together."[107] At the next year's meeting of the Federation of Insurance Counsel, another call to arms was delivered: "If we can't prevail upon NACCA to change its course and renounce the objectionable doctrines it stands for, then let us repudiate them forthrightly, lest they blot the proud escutcheon of the legal profession. It can be done. It must be done. And with your help, it WILL be done!"[108]

That plaintiffs' lawyers were now seen as a formidable force must have provided some satisfaction to all those who could still remember the days of the nationwide war against ambulance chasers. Indeed, several NACCA founders had begun their careers when elite corporate lawyers in major cities around the country were attempting to disbar, suspend, censure, publicly embarrass, and generally discredit the "little shyster" personal injury lawyers who were pressing minor accident cases against colossal corporate clients. Many leaders of the personal injury bar in the 1950s and 1960s were men who might have been senior partners in corporate law firms had the opportunities been open to them when they were just starting out, one insurance executive conceded at the time. "But they didn't go to the fancy law schools, they're Jews, the jobs weren't open to them when they started," he added. "I admire them."[109] Now, at the top of the personal injury bar, these lawyers were litigating cases that were every bit as complex, and potentially lucrative, as their corporate counterparts—products liability, medical malpractice, aviation accidents. In fact, the class divisions that used to exist most dramatically between corporate lawyers and solo-practicing accident attorneys now pertained as much to the divisions between these new personal injury attorneys and the ones who still made a living primarily from lower-level auto accident litigation—"the dissatisfied and hungry end of an extremely varied occupational spectrum."[110]

By midcentury, those attorneys who dealt primarily in high volumes of low-level accident claims operated in a legal world, or underworld, entirely of their own—not welcomed by their fellow plaintiff's attorneys or by the larger profession. They remained behind as the businessmen of a personal injury bar undergoing dramatic change. As much personal injury work became more complex, the low-level accident lawyer's functions became more bureaucratized—a combination of bookkeeping and brokerage, requiring little or no reading of legal material or any actual litigation. "The personal injury practice of half of the specialists in this area—the lower-level practitioners—is restricted to building up a file and to effort at negotiation with claims adjusters," according to one study of Chicago solo lawyers in the 1960s. "The bigger cases are referred out to other lawyers if they cannot be readily settled."[111] Even the nonlawyers who made a business of soliciting personal injury cases were becoming stratified. No longer just "small fries" who "climb hospital fire escapes to get to a victim's side," these new chasers might dress in expensive conservative suits, double-breasted overcoats, and homburg hats, and make more than $50,000 in areas of more substantial liability.[112] These new chasers—like the new elites of personal injury practice and the members of the other national bar groups—often scorned those who still dwelt in the legal backwaters of high-volume, auto accident practice. The nonlawyers who remained in high-volume personal injury occasionally bought their attorneys outright. "These chasers put you under pressure," one Chicago lawyer complained in 1958. "They run the lawyer, the lawyer doesn't run them."[113] Some fifty years earlier, a legal ethicist had looked at the growing trade in high volumes of accident cases and asked worriedly if the law were not becoming a business. By midcentury, the answer was clear: Accident claims were a major business just as much as the manufacture of cars or the institution of accident insurance. Some low-level personal injury attorneys were stigmatized as dirty workers trading in death and misfortune, just as the early accident sales agents had been; but many attorneys who got into high-volume personal injury embraced their roles as businessmen and not professionals, and operated their "accident mills" as such. In this underworld of tort, lawyers were not really lawyers and the law was really a business. "The client may be, in the eyes of the lawyer, only the source of a piece of lucrative 'raw material' to be processed to a settlement," one study from the early 1960s concluded, "while the lawyer is, in the eyes of the client, only a necessary professional aid in extracting from the insurance company enough money to compensate him for expenses and suffering."[114] The idea of a personal injury underworld resulted from this surprising reality of legitimate claims settling practices in the United States—itself a netherworld of business opportunity, where a visionary, like The Travelers' founder James Batterson, and a rag-tag army of accident insurance agents pioneered a billion-dollar business in the

1860s, and Abe Gatner and an equally vast group of pioneer chasers later converged on accident sites to do the same.

When the insurance industry and the popular press continued to paint all of personal injury law with the broad brush of the bottom-rung ambulance chaser during the 1950s, the newly organized plaintiffs' bar fought back in a way which had not been possible in 1928. "The NACCA is doing the most to rid the American legal scene of the unscrupulous few," one of group's leaders stated at the time. "Yet, ironically, people with an ax to grind (usually an insurance ax!) seek to vilify NACCA members themselves with the handy nasty name of ambulance chasers."[115] The speaker of these words, Melvin Belli—a man proclaimed the "King of Torts" by *Life* magazine in 1954—had done perhaps more than anyone to raise the dollar amount of personal injury awards in America. In a book that endeavored to tell the story of the evolution of the tort lawyer from colonial times through the 1960s, lawyer Stuart Speiser would later write an entire chapter on "The Importance of Melvin Belli." Championing the injured, Belli pioneered the idea of the "more adequate awards"; he also helped liberate those personal injury lawyers still "shackled" by nineteenth-century concepts that limited the areas in which a damage suit might be brought successfully.[116] Speiser recognized that Belli was sometimes a "clown": He played practical jokes at bar meetings; he was a tireless self-promoter who publicly mixed with movie stars (he spent months at a time in Europe with Errol Flynn), mobsters (he counted Mickey Cohen among his dearest friends), and prostitutes (a San Francisco madam gave him a weekend with two hookers for Christmas one year); he worked in an office decorated with San Francisco Gold Rush paraphernalia and was a stop on the city's Gray Line Tour; he used to raise a Jolly Roger pirate flag from the rooftop of his office every time he won a case. But Speiser came to realize over the years that, whatever his manner, Belli had been "the apostle and the deliverer" of the plaintiffs' movement in America.

Belli also liked to see himself in these heroic terms. "I was a missionary giving these lawyers a new gospel," he later wrote in his autobiography, speaking of the "Belli Seminars" he conducted for his colleagues during the 1950s.[117] "I felt our economic system was stacked against the little man," he wrote of his motivations for becoming a personal injury lawyer. "The insurance companies had entire firms of lawyers to help them in their struggle. But the people-at-large had damn few attorneys ready to fight on the other side." The problem, as Belli saw it, was that "it just didn't pay" for attorneys to risk getting no fee in the event they lost their case. The answer that Belli offered in a law review article published in 1950 and during a subsequent nationwide lecture tour was to raise the size of damage awards from levels that were set a half-century earlier so that they were in line with contemporary values. "Maybe I could make these cases pay," Belli wrote. "Then maybe the poor man in America could have as much justice as the rich man. Once I began to see the struggle in those terms, I was on my way."[118]

Within a few short years, Belli had made a national reputation for himself—both with his fellow lawyers and with the public—and, in cases where his techniques were being used, the trend in damage awards in jury trials was upward. In 1951 the founder of the NACCA, Sam Horovitz, called Belli and asked him to lend his name to the organization by becoming president for a year. Belli, who was in Europe leading the life of the international playboy with Errol Flynn, later described the call: "Look, you're the guy we need in Cleveland [to participate in an annual NACCA conference]," Horovitz allegedly began in words that sound more like Belli's than his own. "For years this personal-injury stuff has been a chicken-shit affair. They've been robbing cripples and widows. In 1927 the Massachusetts Bar tried to disbar me on the grounds that I couldn't be doing all the claimants' work I was doing for thirty-five dollars a week. They thought I had to be on the take."[119] Horovitz's own story, more than Belli's, was the story of the rise of the personal injury lawyer in America in the first half of this century. But, as Stuart Speiser observed, it was Belli who brought it all together and "fomented a revolution." For every revolution in liability, however, there would be a counterrevolution; and this is just what the Federation of Insurance Counsel, the DRI, and the other industry groups had begun to do in the mid-1950s.

Since the middle of this century, the NACCA, later renamed the American Trial Lawyers Association (ATLA), and the various insurance industry interests have embodied the nation's two minds about the aftermath of accidents. They are the cartoon opposites of the tight-fisted, cold-hearted insurer on one side and Whiplash Willie on the other. They are the sword-carriers for our two most cherished self-images as Americans—the one, born in the nineteenth century, built on the back of the rugged individual who is responsible for taking care of himself without making burdensome claims on the larger society; the other, new to the twentieth century and born of the higher expectations of a progressive age which imagined the continual perfection of everyday life, celebrated the individual with rights and liberties and fought the system that tried to take them away.

In this culture, where the notion of what constitutes a *legitimate* personal injury claim continues to be controversial, the problem of fraudulent claims has perhaps been the only constant. First fought by the railway claims man in the late nineteenth century; then exposed by various law enforcement groups in New York and other major cities throughout the first half of this century; and then, in the 1950s and 1960s, becoming a key part of a publicity campaign by the insurance industry, the activities of the fake claim artist (aided by the usual professional accomplices) have been the one point on which all parties can find some agreement. Fakers cost everyone money by raising rates, eroding credulity in honest claims, and, to the extent the claims involve doctors and lawyers, casting a shadow on the professions. The *idea* of the personal injury faker, sometimes more than the actual fakers themselves, serves a further function, however: For a society that has always been uncomfortable with the basic idea of cash for life (first put forward by insurers), the faker allows the honest claimant to believe that personal injury compensation is dirty in all of its aspects—from chisling insurers, to unctuous lawyers and quack doctors, to the stereotypical shady garageman.[120] Distanced from the dirty work of settlement, personal injury claimants can then feel that exaggerating a claim or authorizing their attorneys to make outrageous demands on their behalf or conspiring with a garageman to inflate the damage estimate and split the difference, is neither morally murky, socially destructive, or, in the case of outright faking, deeply criminal.

Whether insurance companies (and railroads before them) circulated stories of fakers in order to justify raising rates is not the central point. Rather, Americans themselves seem to need stories of fakers to justify their own petty larcenies, or to confirm some general, inchoate sense that, since American institutions are corrupt and in decline, why not get what one can while the getting is good. So long as someone is clearly abusing the personal injury compensation system, questions about the (non)system itself—and our un-mentionable attachment to its lottery-like potential benefits—can be put off, diverted. The matter of compensating accident victims in America has, from the time of the railroads, been *purposely informal*—not because of any corporate conspiracy but because Americans seem to want it that way just as they have allowed increasing institutionalized casino gambling—first Las Vegas, then Atlantic City, then the fringe exceptions of Indian reservations and riverboats, and, soon, anywhere with a significant enough "feeder pool" of potential gamblers to justify construction costs. So long as accidents remain an open-ended opportunity (and not a scheduled payoff under some state insurance scheme), everyone involved, acting through institutional proxies, can poten-tially get more than he or she deserves, the proverbial something for nothing. It is no accident that accidents, initially the by-product of industrial progress in a booming, late-nineteenth century America, became their own free market opportunity for pioneer insurers and the early chasers. (In a 1964 study, one writer investigated the question of why Americans have followed their unique course in choosing the contingent fee to link accident victims with their proper compensation "in view of [its] almost complete condemnation in other times and in other parts of the world." In that study, F. B. MacKinnon explained the free market faith behind late-nineteenth century arguments in favor of the fee: "[T]he economic relationship between lawyer and clients should be governed by the same principles which establish the price of goods and services generally in a laissez faire economy."[121]) Once this is dug out from the history in which it has been deeply embedded, the personal injury underworld of the twentieth century seems almost logical in its broad expansion, businesslike in its exponential growth, and democratic in its wide recruitment of inhabitants.

Over the last century, whiplash and railway spine stories, like the related hand-wringing over the "litigation explosion," have functioned primarily as a peculiar form of nostalgia: a "ceremony of regret" about the vanishing of a simpler, noncontentious, early industrial world that enjoyed all of the benefits of economic progress with none of its negative by-products—the fact that no such time ever existed notwithstanding. The story of the growth of an actual fake accident underworld, however, tells us about the meaning of progress in the other direction: chiefly, the deep American impulse to make a market in anything (even fake accidents) in order to get ahead. Somewhere outside the boundaries of the ongoing battles between the insurance industry and the organized plaintiffs' bar (in which the fakers have been something of a diversion), the story of the making of a personal injury underworld in America was becoming a topic unto itself in the 1970s.

UNDERWORLD: LOS ANGELES (TO THE PRESENT)

CHAPTER 6

THE FRIENDS OF THE FRIENDLESS

Cappers prowl the freeways and highways of this
County around-the-clock in radio-equipped cars,
waiting for word of an accident. . . . Once embarked
upon a course of fraudulent activities, it is but a simple
step for the unethical attorney to sponsor or condone
the fabrication of accidents.

—From Public Hearings on The Friends of the
Friendless, Los Angeles, 1974

FATHER THOMAS MATIN was seated at a table in La Siesta restaurant in East Los Angeles when he gradually came to a realization: The charity he had helped found several years earlier—a charity that had never fully come into being because its application for tax-exempt status was never completed—actually was functioning quite well. Earlier that day in April 1973, he learned, the group had conducted an Easter festival at the County Medical Center in which volunteers from a local high school dressed in cotton-tailed bunny costumes and distributed goody baskets to young children. And this was just the latest example of the kind of work that had earned the charity awards and commendations from the hospital and the city during the preceding few years.

For much of his adult life, Father Matin had been the pastor of a church located in Chavez Ravine, near Dodger Stadium, where he had come to know intimately the struggles of the Latino immigrants, legal or not, who were trying to make a go of it in L.A. Matin did what he could through the church, but he always felt that he could have been doing more. For years he dreamed of founding a charity organization that would "help the poor Mexican immigrant who has nothing."[1] By 1970 Father Matin had come up with a name for his group—The Friends of the Friendless—but what he needed was a lawyer to help him through the legal process of establishing a charity. Matin turned to George Hatcher, a young entrepreneur born in Mexico and raised in East L.A., who often boasted about how much money he had and how politically connected he was. Although not a lawyer himself, Hatcher was known by many in the community as someone who made a lot of money through his connections with a law office; exactly what the connection was, few people were certain and no one asked.

With George Hatcher's help, Matin's Friends group was on its way. Pleased with the partnership, Matin offered Hatcher the job as the director of the charity, but Hatcher declined, installing his wife in the position instead. The Hatchers' home became the group's official address. For Father Matin, all of this activity seemed to be progress toward the fulfillment of his hopes. Yet many months passed with no further action. There were no meetings, and no officers or board members were elected; there was no fund-raising activity, and no community programs were planned. Matin tried to contact Hatcher several times at the Friends headquarters, but Hatcher was rarely in the office and he did not return calls. "I thought the organization was dormant," Father Matin said of his state of mind back in 1971. Two years later at La Siesta restaurant, with volunteer Easter bunnies, Hatcher, and a number of others toasting their achievements around him, he would learn that the "Friends of the Friendless" had just been getting started.

Over the years, ambulance chasers have used all manner of artifice, subterfuge, and bribery—not to mention the occasional cheap disguise—to get to accident victims ahead of the competition. Early chasers cultivated contacts at the richest sources of information—police precincts, newspaper offices, and hospitals. And they greased palms at every step along the way to the bedsides of possible clients, starting with the first tip from the cop on the beat, the news reporter or the local merchant, and continuing through the hospital orderlies, nurses, or interns who smoothed the way into an emergency room or recovery ward. The best operators, in the opinion of Abraham Gatner, the grand old man of the solicitation trade, were those "with the 'facilities' that enable [them] to glide in the front door of the hospital, walk boldly to the ward, and get down to open business with the client."[2] Individuals might resist a payoff on any given occasion, Gatner had found in his long career, but professional groups who came in regular contact with accident victims were eventually sucked into the attractive orbit of the solicitor's roll of bills. Back in 1927, Gatner put this point in terms of the "progressiveness" of the "ambulance chasing industry," which "kept up with all developments," and he used hospital social workers as an example. "A few years ago," he wrote, "when social service workers began entering the hospitals to benefit the patients, the 'industry' went with them, and, today, a number of these workers, some innocently and some not, have become very valuable assets." The "ambulance chasing industry," he concluded, "corrupts everything with which it comes in contact."[3]

Abe Gatner, the son of Russian immigrants and lifelong inhabitant of the Lower East Side of New York, probably could not have imagined operating successfully in a city like Los Angeles in the early 1970s: The region's famous sprawl, especially, would have made it difficult to cultivate the necessary street contacts and nearly impossible to divide into regions small enough for single chasers to work by themselves. Still, with progress as his watchword, Gatner would have kept up with developments—the police scanning car radio, for one thing, could end his reliance on the beat cop or newspaper hack. He also would have recognized opportunity: East Los Angeles in the last few decades of the century was a lot like the Lower East Side of New York in the first; an immigrant quarter, largely self-contained, whose inhabitants might not know their rights to compensation if they were involved in legitimate accidents (and so could be exploited) or else might be willing to fake an accident once it was explained that this was one of those famed ways to make easy money in America. "Progress" would almost certainly have been Abe Gatner's judgment had he been asked to comment on the work of the Friends of the Friendless. This group did not bother with the hit-or-miss business of corrupting individual hospital workers for access to accident victims. The Friends, accident case solicitors masquerading as do-gooders from a Catholic charity, were taking matters into their own hands. In a business built on stealth, the Friends were a step ahead.

In their brief but highly successful run, the Friends not only controlled the largest hospital in Los Angeles County, aided along the way by local political leaders and their staffs, but diplomats at the Mexican consulate also fed them referrals. Hatcher's agents did not lurk in hospital corridors like previous generations of chasers, waiting for tips from orderlies or nurses. The Friends walked freely down the center of hallways in the County Medical Center. They wore lab jackets emblazoned with a patch containing all sorts of official symbols—the American flag, a red cross, the medical caduceus, an eagle—underneath which were printed the words "In God We Trust." On the

outer ring of the patch were the words "Friends of the Friendless: Volunteer".
Despite their carefully cultivated appearance of legitimacy, the Friends had
never been fully recognized as a charity by the state. And by the time they
were given permission to work in the hospital, they had lost all contact with
Father Matin. None of this seemed to matter. "In the sprawling, anonymous
hospital, no one seemed to question who they were or what they did," observed
the *Los Angeles Times* reporters who first publicly exposed the group's illegal
activities. "They cruised the wards with authority."[4]

Outwardly, the Friends were a benign, even welcomed, addition to the
hospital landscape in the early 1970s. They distributed candy and cigarettes,
magazines, cosmetics, and other comforts to patients who had been brought
in from car wrecks and from various other accident sites around L.A. County.
They concentrated mainly in the orthopedic ward and limited themselves
almost exclusively to the most injured people and to people who spoke
Spanish, preferably illegal aliens. Far from causing suspicion, these practices
seemed to reinforce the Friends' charitable mission: to be friends to the
friendless immigrants who were otherwise lost in a strange, impersonal Anglo
institution. In a county fast becoming as populous as a small nation, and more
heavily trafficked with automobiles than anyplace on earth, accidents were
inevitable. At the county hospital, the Friends were needed and, when they
arrived, they were praised: "Mr. Alejandro Barriga makes his living in the
export-import business," the hospital newsletter wrote of one of the Friends.
"But two or three times a week, he still finds the time to import a special brand
of cheerfulness to patients on Ward 3800."[5] The article went on to quote Mr.
Barriga about how much he had come to look forward to his visits to the
medical center. "I get as much as I give," he explained. "I get spiritual fulfillment
with the knowledge that I'm able to help and be of service to someone. This
way both the patients and I are rewarded." Alejandro Barriga's rewards as a
Friend of the Friendless may not have been wholly spiritual, however. In a
series of articles published early in 1974, investigative reporters George
Reasons and David Rosenzweig exposed the real business of the Friends as
solicitors of personal injury cases for George Hatcher.

A listing of the Friends' abuses reads much like complaints about chasers
from earlier in the century, with the only significant change being a shift in
ethnicities of those involved. Some people signed away their rights to compensation for their accidents at a fraction of their worth; others were not even
aware that claims had been filed on their behalf, having signed documents
without understanding them or, in a few cases, without being fully conscious.
(One woman, still groggy from anesthesia and lacking the use of both her arms

due to injury, was reportedly approached by a Friend who "entered her room, glanced around to make sure they were alone, and then reached under his smock, pulling out a pink piece of paper and an ink pad." Without identifying himself, the Friend stuck the woman's thumb onto the pad, then pressed her print onto a retainer form and left.) At one point, the family of an accident victim became suspicious of one of the Friends, an attractive former cocktail waitress named Linda Berni. Wearing her Friends patch, Berni had wheeled her cart into the patient's room and introduced herself as "an assistant director of volunteer services," but nevertheless watched the door nervously as if fearful of being detected by someone with real authority. In another case, the sister of one accident victim thought she detected a "funny" incongruity in Berni's story when she saw the woman pull into her driveway in an expensive Cadillac, then introduce herself as a volunteer with a Catholic charity. "She said she wanted to help Mexican people and wouldn't help anybody else," the accident victim's sister said of Berni. "She acted very interested and talked a lot, but she wouldn't give me straight answers."[6]

In a 1977 novel, Linda Berni and the Friends showed up in fictionalized form as The Protectors of the Poor—a front for ambulance chasing in Los Angeles set up as a "charity for the Mexicans at County General," with "candy and rosary beads and someone to talk to them in Spanish."[7] The author embellished on the facts by having a local madam send girls into the hospital to get signed retainers for $50 apiece: The prostitutes rub up against male accident victims, then let them look down their dresses. ("That's when she flashes the insurance form at him," the madam explains. "'Sign this, I'll get you a lawyer who'll sue the bastard who hit you.'") Linda Berni was no prostitute, and none of the Friends were said to have used suggestions of sex to sign clients—especially not Alejandro Barriga, a mildly obese man of middle age. But the fictional madam got the hospital scheme right on a broader level. "Ambulance chasing is what you'd call it," she said. "It's worth a fortune. They can't complain, the wetbacks, they don't get their money, because they're illegals, most of them."[8] It was true. The Friends often played the part of benign confidants, like trusted aunts or uncles, passing along some good advice about how not to get screwed out of just deserts from *gringo* insurers. When patients seemed unwilling to sign up with a lawyer to get money for their injuries, though, the Friends might use coercion, suggesting that the immigrants would be deported if they did not sign up for their particularly friendly brand of legal protection.

In the early 1970s, the Friends were just another in a long line of groups profiting from the precarious plight of newcomers to Los Angeles. From the time they left their homes in Mexico or in countries farther South, Latino immigrants to America were easy prey for all sorts of con men, shake-down artists, and outright thieves. And this was especially the case with illegals. In their journey north by car, bus, foot, or stuffed in the backs of trucks or train cars, Luis Urrea writes, the immigrants might routinely encounter "police corruption; violence in the forms of beatings, rape, murder, torture, road accidents; theft; and incarceration."[9] Those with the money and the intention to cross the border illegally might gather in Tijuana then strike some hard bargain with a *coyote*—later called *pollero*, or "chicken wrangler"—to smuggle them across the border: "When the appointed hour comes," Urrea says of the crossing

> you join a group of *pollos* (chickens) who scuttle along behind the coyote . . . If the *coyote* does not turn on you suddenly with a gun and take everything from you himself, you might still be attacked by the *rateros* [thieves who hide in the hills on the American side]. If the *rateros* don't get you, there are roving zombies that you can smell from fifty yards downwind—these are the junkies who hunt in shambling packs. If the junkies somehow miss you, there are the *pandilleros*—gang-bangers from either side of the border who are looking for some bloody fun.[10]

Once the initial part of the passage is over, other dangers still await: vigilante posses of "Aryans" out to combat illegal immigration, scorpions and snakes out for blood, and the United States Border Patrol, which conducts the most legitimate pursuit but is still a terrifying presence in the borderland arroyo at night.

For those who made it to the relative safety of friends, family, or other contacts in areas like East Los Angeles, perils still existed; although they were now more economic than physical: Fraudulent moving companies took money and goods up front and gave nothing in return but an empty promise to deliver them back to addresses south of the border; car dealers unloaded lemons on people who could not read the fine print; and "immigration consultants" charged big fees to do routine paperwork. And then there were the Friends at County Medical Center waiting for accident victims. (Later there would be the accident cappers: For all those who had jammed themselves into the backs of trucks or railroad cars to reach the fabled land of opportunity, it would be perhaps just a short conceptual leap to the notion that making it in America might involve sitting four to a car to absorb a rear-end collision on a freeway.) So many cheats and schemers focused on immigrants that the Los Angeles

Police Department assigned several detectives to an office in an old tortilla factory in Boyle Heights to conduct *Operacion Estafadores* (Operation Swindlers). Originally funded as a temporary program in 1972, the office remained open through the 1980s.[11]

In the vast landscape of people who victimized the new immigrants under the guise of helping them, the Friends of the Friendless were scarcely noticed; and in the official history of the County Medical Center, they would merit just a few paragraphs.[12] But in the making of a personal injury underworld in the second half of this century, the Friends stood out. The scheme itself was inventive but probably not entirely unprecedented; and certainly other equally lucrative chasing schemes could be found running at the same time around the country: in Washington, D.C., Newark, and Miami, to name a few cities. What made the Friends important was the Friends themselves and the parallels between the chasing culture they developed and the one first forged by the original chasers: The Friends were a clear example of the ethnic succession in the underworld, from the time of the original chasers—the Irving Wolfes, Sammy Abrams, the Feinberg brothers—who saw themselves as pushcart peddlers hawking personal injuries like pants or hats, to the rise of a new group of agents—Roy Ramos, Sammy Chavez, Alvaro Tamayo—who also made a business of personal injuries but who liked to regard themselves as coyotes. As the names changed over the years, a few basic constants remained: accidents occurred in greater and greater numbers and private insurance offered the open-ended opportunity to profit from them. The immigrant simply had his ear closer to the street than most other Americans: He could hear more clearly what was being said to him by the rumble of the cars, the hum of the legal system, and the buzz in his ear of Anglo professionals.

Like many of the original chasers, George Hatcher began his journey into the personal injury underworld as an attorney's "investigator". Hatcher reportedly set himself up in the attorney's office, formed an investigative front company, Aztec Industries, and then recruited a number of coyotes to help solicit personal injury cases. A few of Hatcher's coyotes had criminal records, and some carried guns; all were equipped with beepers to receive the latest tips on accidents from paid informants, and all spoke Spanish. In a short time, Hatcher and his coyotes took over the attorney's office—as Gatner and "the boys" had done in Levy and Becker's office in the 1920s—bringing in hundreds of cases where formerly there had been only a few dozen. "George Hatcher exercised such an influence that we didn't know what was going on," the attorney's law partner later stated. "It was a circus in the office. [The attorney] lost control."[13]

By 1972 Hatcher, a high school dropout, was making it big in the accident business; he had multiple houses, drove luxury cars, and threw lavish parties. Trading in high volumes of illegally solicited and built-up personal injury claims was not what Hatcher had planned to do with his life, and later he would go on to other things, looking back on that period of his life as "a bad time." But in the early 1970s, this was his business, and he brought to it the extraordinary energy and innovative spirit of a latter-day, Latino Abe Gatner. Hatcher began with the fairly traditional step of buying the use of an attorney's name in order to open a law office to process increasing numbers of referrals coming in from the Friends and his freelancing coyotes. When pressure from state bar investigators scared one attorney out of town, Hatcher bought another law office and transferred the cases from one to the other. Medical reports were the backbone of any successful personal injury claim, Hatcher soon discovered, and this is where he began to show some genius for invention. Hatcher started a business, Doctor's Service, which began by transcribing medical reports for understaffed physicians but ended as a mill to generate the reports that Hatcher needed for his claims.[14] Hatcher also found a doctor, a middle-age man with a drug problem, to front for him in a clinic in East L.A.

Back in 1920s New York, an attorney named Silas Axtell had been disbarred for soliciting personal injury cases from foreign sailors by sending out agents who wore badges that read "Patrolman" (made to look like those worn by policemen) and by creating the impression the cases had been referred to him from officials at the American embassies of the sailor's country of origin: in one case, it was the German consul general; in another, it was the consul general from Spain.[15] Fifty years later, George Hatcher would not advertise any affiliation with the Mexican consulate in Los Angeles; his referrals from the consulate's legal officer were real and they were secret.[16]

Hatcher's political connections did not stop at the Mexican consulate; they also reportedly included the state senator who represented Hatcher's district. These connections helped get the Friends into the County Medical Center in the first place; and two years' worth of pressure from the state senator's office reportedly kept the Friends in the hospital, despite several reports to administrators that the charity was really a front for ambulance chasing.

Under the weight of several simultaneous investigations, Hatcher's personal injury empire first began to crack during the summer of 1973; it began to crumble the following year. Legitimate clients began to complain to the police, the district attorney, and the state bar that they were not seeing any of the settlement money promised to them by Hatcher's people. Hatcher report-edly responded to complainers by attempting to pay them off in cash: Coyotes drove to the clients' homes and asked them to ride to a drugstore; there they cashed a check while the frightened clients waited in the car.[17] These lame efforts were not enough to keep investigators from probing the legitimacy of Hatcher's outfit further, however. Late in 1973, Hatcher got word that the *L.A. Times* was looking into his operations at County Hospital and elsewhere. Hatcher's creditors, investors, and associates seemed to lose confidence in him or were afraid to be linked to him, and everything they had supported for Hatcher began to fall back to earth. As quickly as Hatcher had accumulated the cars and houses, his boat and his restaurant, he just as quickly sold all of it and filed for bankruptcy. Rumors circulated that, for creditors associated with the Mexican Mafia, Hatcher was a marked man.

In May 1974 Hatcher was indicted by a grand jury.[18] Later that month the district attorney's office raided his office on Bunker Hill, seizing the contents of a massive safe. Three ledgers were removed from the safe that contained the details of Hatcher's business dealings with doctors, lawyers, solicitors, clients, and politicians.[19] In August 1974, following a preliminary hearing that took six days and involved testimony from more than forty-five witnesses, all of the major players in Hatcher's personal injury ring were indicted.[20] At the Mexican consulate, both the consul general and the legal officer were summoned immediately to Mexico City for disciplinary hearings, then each was reassigned to a lesser diplomatic position.[21]

While Hatcher awaited trial—he would ultimately be sentenced to two years in county jail on charges related to his Friends business enterprises[22]—several of his former coyotes were now chasing cases for other people. Late in 1974 *Times* reporters observed them at the scene of a horrible crash of a school bus that had been carrying migrant workers across the Mexican border. The coyotes who descended on the accident scene looking for case referrals told victims and their families that "they were doing an investigation into all the terrible ways Mexicans were being treated in this accident and that they were there to help the people." No longer working under the umbrella of the Friends of the Friendless, the men now claimed an affiliation with an outspoken champion of farm workers' rights: They referred to themselves as the friends of Cesar Chavez.[23]

From the moment reports about Hatcher and the Friends were first published in the *Los Angeles Times*, officials of all kinds began to hurl accusations of blame at one another. Kenneth Hahn, the chairman of the Board of Supervisors, called the disclosures a "bombshell" and expressed anger with the city hospital administration. "I want to know how a ring could operate for two solid years without anyone knowing about it?" he asked.[24] (A hospital official later replied that he feared that asking the Latino charity workers to leave would be seen as racially discriminatory and would have "a severe negative reaction" in the Mexican American community.)[25] Hahn also condemned the state bar for ignoring complaints about the lawyers involved in Hatcher's ring. The state bar president shot back that Hahn was "considerably misinformed and grossly in error" about what the bar knew of Hatcher's group.[26] For his part, the state senator involved in the case wrote a letter to the *Times* denying any firsthand knowledge of Hatcher's illegal activities, admitting only that he knew Hatcher as an "eminently successful young businessman" and that, regrettably, he had accepted gifts from Hatcher—many of which he claimed that he ultimately had to pay for himself.[27] Commenting on the larger policy issue of providing genuine low-cost legal help for low-income people, editorialists at the *Los Angeles Times* recommended that the state government and the organized bar patrol "the legal wasteland in which coyotes prowl."[28] And Warren Christopher, the future U.S. Secretary of State who was then president of the L.A. County Bar Association, responded by setting up a legitimate lawyer-referral service for patients in the county hospital system.[29]

Revelations about Hatcher and the Friends continued throughout the summer of 1974, culminating in a week of hearings conducted by Baxter Ward, a former TV anchorman who was then a member of the County Board of Supervisors. Just as investigators on the other side of the country were following up Woodward and Bernstein's leads on Watergate, Baxter Ward was led by reporters Reasons and Rosenzweig to puzzle through the interconnections among a Catholic charity, a hospital, several legal and medical offices, a state senator, and the Mexican consulate. In August 1974, Ward published his findings. On the political side, he denounced the "ignorance and apathy of a number of agencies" who stood by as the Friends and thirty-five to forty other law firms that used chasers thrived. The county hospital in particular, Ward believed, had suffered "an administrative breakdown bordering on paralysis" caused by "real or imagined political interference" from aides to a county supervisor and a state senator.[30] Ward was known throughout his career as a political gadfly who often cast himself as a lone crusader out to clean up government corruption, so his conclusions about administrative failures and apathy were not altogether unexpected. Not so, however, his conclusions about the spread of ambulance chasing—"capping" was the word used in the criminal code—which he outlined at the start of the hearings. "Our investigation has revealed that capping is widespread, not only throughout the County hospital system," Ward told a packed hearing room,

> but in private hospitals as well; that it is not a new problem but one which has been around for years or even decades; that while capping may appear innocent and benevolent, it often breeds a broad variety of other crimes, such as bribery, forgery, grand theft, fraud, and even violence; that the loss to the County and insurance companies caused by capping rings engaged in fraudulent claims is estimated in the tens of millions of dollars a year; and, finally, and perhaps most importantly, that poor people, many of them minority group members unfamiliar with the legal system, are often cheated out of all or part of the accident settlements they deserved by cappers working with crooked attorneys and doctors conspiring together.[31]

In their months of preparation for the hearings, Ward and his committee had correctly situated the Friends in the larger context of L.A. County's personal injury underworld; and their conclusions were fleshed out in compelling detail. But it was not until the hearings actually began that testimony emerged about crashes being staged around L.A. County by accident rings. Just as the confession of chaser king Abe Gatner in 1927 led to hearings that exposed the Laulicht brothers and other accident rings of old New York, the investigation into the Friends opened a window onto L.A.'s emerging fake accident culture. On the second day of testimony, Commissioner Ward listened as an investigator named Milton Crawford described the staging of a "typical rear-ender" on an L.A. freeway. Ring members would use two cars: one car filled with passengers, the other driven by an "expert" driver who would help trap a third car—a victim likely to be insured—into rear-ending the car stuffed with ring members. "They will pick out an unsuspecting person on the freeway system," Crawford said of the scam, which would later be termed a swoop-and-squat.

> The automobile to be rear-ended will maneuver its way into the front of the victim who will hit them. As they are proceeding along at a speed of 55 or 65 miles an hour, these two cars are traveling parallel. Then, the car to the right of the car to be hit will effect a speedup and make a sharp turn in front of the victim's car . . . then he will jam on his brakes. The reaction time on the guy that's following usually isn't quick enough to avert a collision.[32]

Crawford provided Ward's committee with an example of a freeway swoop-and-squat that he had successfully investigated. Crawford, it seemed, had gotten information about an accident that was to be staged; when it was set to be carried out just as planned, Crawford moved in on the stagers and forced confessions from several of them. One woman in her early twenties with two children told Crawford how she got involved with the staging one night when a friend named Nancy asked her to join her and some other friends for dinner. "After I was in the car with two men and Nancy, I was told that they were going to stage an accident," the woman explained. "We went onto the Freeway, and while on the Freeway, Lorenzo made a quick stop and the car that was behind him hit us, and after this car hit us the car that was following him then hit the car that hit us."[33] That night the woman and her fellow passengers were taken to an attorney's office and then to a doctor. "The doctor did not examine me nor did he give me any x-rays," she said. "I did not even undress or go into an examining room." And she never met with the lawyer, either. When Ward asked whether swoop-and-squats were common, Crawford said that he was currently investigating a half-dozen of them.

A few years after the Friends hearings Crawford introduced Dan Rather of *60 Minutes* to a capper who staged swoop-and-squats on L.A. freeways. The capper talked about the mechanics of the schemes. Then he discussed the money: a few hundred dollars for the people who sit in the cars for the stagings; a few thousand per accident for the capper who scripts it; and twice as much for the doctors and lawyers who run the rings, all of which amounted to many millions, perhaps even $500 million a year for rings nationwide. Rather took a moment to be stunned by the numbers. "That's one-half billion dollars a year, with a 'B'—about the same as Ford Motor Corporation's profits last year, when Ford ranked as the third largest corporation in the United States." As he learned from the capper, however, it was a sad-luck fortune at the lowest levels of the accident rings, where claimants risked their lives for a few hundred dollars while the lion's share of the money went to lawyers and doctors. All of this was as new to Rather as it had been to Baxter Ward, and Rather probed the capper specifically on what he felt to be the most incredible part of the schemes: the special emphasis on the recruitment of pregnant women as passengers for the stagings.

> Rather: Now how do you get a pregnant woman to do that? . . . Do you have any trouble finding people to take part in these accidents?
>
> Capper: It's not hard. It's never hard. It's not at all. They usually be down and out or against the world at the time . . . A lot of

people—a lot of people are broke. A lot of people like easy money.[34]

Then Rather asked about this capper's own staging habits:

Rather: On a good day, how many accidents do you set down?
Capper: Have I set down? Three, four . . .
Rather: A day? And in your best week, how many accidents have you set down?
Capper: All week long. I don't know. All day, all week long.

At the Friends hearings, Milton Crawford's findings about accident rings in Los Angeles were supported in large part by James McMullen, the director of investigations for Farmer's Insurance Company. McMullen told Baxter Ward and the committee how he had uncovered a series of twenty-two accidents that had been planned by one capper—a man who called himself David Roxton—over two years. Roxton's accidents were not swoop-and-squats on freeways, according to McMullen; they were "paper" accidents made to look like real crashes.[35] One man later confessed his involvement with Roxton's accident ring. One afternoon he and some friends met one of Roxton's aides, who told them their parts in the fake accident. Then the man's car was taken away and returned a half-hour later with extensive damage done to it by a tow-truck driver who backed into it repeatedly. By scripting dozens of these paper accidents, Roxton, who was in league with a few attorneys, had generated more than $300,000 in fake claims, according to McMullen. But when McMullen took his evidence to the L.A. district attorney, he was told that there was nothing to be done about it, partly because the evidence was not sufficiently solid, but mainly because even perfectly prepared cases of this sort were not very high priorities for prosecution. Private investigator Milton Crawford also claimed to have encountered apathy from the D.A., from local law enforcement, and from the state bar. District Attorney Joseph Busch shot back with an angry denial: "I've got a team of guys who do nothing but chase lawyers," he said. "We prosecute more lawyers than any other profession."[36] In the previous two years, Busch had announced the indictment of several groups and asserted that lawyers were involved in the schemes, but chiropractors were the only professionals named.[37]

The plain fact was that official public interest in ambulance chasers or accident fakers was cyclical, as judge Bernard Botein of New York once observed, and the era before the Friends scandal had been yet another low point. This made Baxter Ward angry during the summer of 1974—he widely charged every major county agency that had failed to do something about the

Friends or accident fakers with ignorance, apathy, or conspiracy. But his anger was short-lived and he soon moved on to other matters: After serving a few more years on the Board of Supervisors, Ward briefly returned to TV news then left public life for most of the 1980s to write a murder mystery. In 1994, when asked about the hearings he had conducted into the Friends of the Friendless Ring and the subsequent disclosures about the early accident-faking gangs operating in L.A. County, Ward could not recall anything that was not in his final report. And when asked whether he still had a copy of the report, Ward thought for a moment before concluding that he probably did not.

Precisely because insurers knew that public officials could not be relied on to gather evidence consistently on ambulance chasers and accident fakers, and especially not to prosecute them regularly, the industry formed its own police agency in 1971. At the time, it was the only industry-wide private investigation squad in the U.S.[38]

The idea of private police conjured up images of the old railroad bulls who were infamous for their strong-arm protection of big industry, and some insurers were scared away for fear of a public relations backlash. The reality was far different from the idea, however: The agents did not carry guns, wear badges, or have any police powers. Most were men with law enforcement backgrounds, many of them supplementing their early retirement pensions with a solid "industry" job. Agents worked out of their homes in cities around the country and sent their reports to regional offices in New York, Chicago, and Los Angeles. After getting referrals from claims adjusters at member companies, they would try to develop the case—send for cards from the Index System, make phone calls, check out names and addresses. Then, if it looked good, they would use their contacts with law enforcement to get the case investigated officially. If law enforcement was interested, agents would assist in shepherding the case through to prosecution, mainly by assembling "historical" charts of possible fake claims taken from industry databases. Field agents quickly found that they worked not only against the chasers and fakers but also against a brick wall of disinterest from public officials. The job required agents to be part sleuth and part Jimmy Stewart—tireless advocates for their own particular just causes. "We have to be absolutely perfect when we walk into a prosecutor's office," the group's legal counsel said back in 1971.[39] And perfect was never an easy standard to live up to, especially when most agents had never heard of a swoop-and-squat or a slip-and-faller before they were handed a stack of files to investigate.

The idea of a privately funded insurance fraud police force was not new, of course. In 1905 the Alliance Against Accident Fraud had been formed in lower Manhattan to gather information on fakers and floppers. In 1937 the Association of Casualty and Surety Underwriters set up the Claims Bureau to deal with the fact that "fraudulent and exaggerated personal injury and other damage claims were becoming a real 'racket.'"[40] Staffed with former G-men and headed initially by one of New York City's top "racket-busters," the Claims Bureau operated field offices in most major cities across the nation. By the late 1960s, it and its successor organization, the Fraud and Arson Bureau, had outgrown the insurance trade group that had established it. The idea was finally hatched to create an entirely separate entity to deal with the growing problem of personal injury frauds, a companion to the industry's auto theft bureau, which had been in existence since 1912. Insurers originally called their group the Casualty Insurance Fraud Association, but the group's first director thought the name too bland and technical to interest anyone outside the industry, so he pushed to change it to the Insurance Crime Prevention Institute (ICPI).[41] For many field agents, an "institute" was worse than an "association," and both were steps down from the original idea of being a "bureau," which had a familiar ring to all agents who had come from the FBI or who liked to think of their agency as being modeled after it. Critics from outside the industry did not care what the group was called: Whatever the name, they felt, the ICPI was just another body through which insurance companies could chisel down payments to accident victims. To this claim the ICPI director responded by making clear that the group's emphasis was criminal prosecution, not the settlement of claims, a process with which agents were forbidden from getting involved. The focus would not be on the little guy, the director clarified, but rather on the organized rings that were thought to be the largest contributors to the cost of personal injury frauds nationwide, then estimated at $1.5 billion a year.

While the ICPI board of directors may have chosen a bland name for their group, for their first leader, they chose boldly. James Francis Ahern was a charismatic young police chief with a national reputation, a commanding physical presence (only slightly above average in height, but with a thick wave of prematurely gray hair, a square jaw, and, often, a sharp pin-stripe suit, which said he meant business) as well as a personal mystique: Some found him unapproachable and distant; one agent later referred to Ahern's "J. Edgar Hoover quality." As a teenager growing up in a family of nine children, Ahern had studied to become a priest, then went to college with plans of going to law school. Ultimately, he joined his brothers at the New Haven, Connecticut, Police Department. (Not long thereafter, it would be referred to only half-jokingly as "the Ahern Department.") Ahern rose fast through the ranks.

While still only in his mid-thirties, he became the youngest police chief in the city's history, getting the job over the heads of dozens of men with more seniority.[42]

"During the 1960s," an ICPI training film stated, "insurers decided they could no longer deal with the fraud problem on a case-by-case basis." A "new approach" was needed to shut down the organized rings, the film went on to explain, and James Ahern, a man praised by the president for his innovative policing, was the man for the job. During his years as a police chief, Ahern worked hard on reforming old police methods, and he was not afraid to take on those elements of the force that had been linked to organized crime. Ahern first came to national attention when a Black Panther rally on the campus of Yale University threatened to become a race riot. His nonconfrontational style of brokering peace was hailed as a model of "new policing." The experience helped land him a seat on the President's Commission on Campus Unrest, where he played an active and outspoken role. At a time when many believed he would run for mayor of New Haven, however, Ahern announced his retirement from the police force, saying that the "fun was gone" and alluding to harassment from elements of the city government who were opposed to his reform policies.[43] One week later, in early January 1971, Ahern accepted the job to lead a nationwide drive against accident insurance frauds.[44] The industry was so excited to get Ahern that they agreed to move the headquarters from the planned space in Chicago to an unlikely outpost closer to his home in Westport, Connecticut, where it remained until the early 1990s.

James Ahern was the public face of the ICPI for much of the first decade of the group's existence, and was often featured in magazines or on television talking about the subtle social menace of insurance crime. (One flattering *People* magazine profile came complete with color shots of Ahern talking with prosecutors, reviewing a file at ICPI headquarters, and as a handsome new bachelor, sitting pensive on the beach near his Connecticut home "after a hard day of sleuthing.")[45] Ahern set the tone within the organization also— the tone of a law enforcement agency that lacked the badges and the guns but otherwise was as serious about jailing insurance criminals as the FBI was in nailing mobsters. One of Ahern's top aides, in fact, had been considered as a possible successor to Hoover as director of the FBI, and another man, the ICPI's eastern regional director, was a former chief inspector with the New York City Police.

As surely as Ahern the police chief had attempted to undo the hold of organized crime on New Haven, Ahern the ICPI director would go after organized fake accident rings. Ahern believed that insurance fraud, traditionally dismissed by law enforcement as white-collar and innocuous, was becoming as "menacing and threatening" to national values as street crime was to personal safety.[46] He often expressed his belief that doctors, lawyers, and chasers were joining forces with traditional organized crime, who used the money from personal injury frauds to fund their other enterprises—loan-sharking, drug trafficking, and gambling, among other things. Working together, Ahern felt, the white-collar professionals and the mobsters were better organized than any of the groups set up to fight them. "White-collar crime has joined the syndicate," he wrote in 1973. "That is the challenge we face. And it is not an easy one."[47]

Throughout his years at the ICPI, Ahern was concerned with these more "sinister aspects" of what the public and press often thought of as a victimless crime against big, soulless corporations. Reviewing his first year's experience at ICPI, Ahern told reporters that he felt that "organized crime elements" were involved in at least a quarter of the 800 cases that the ICPI was actively working.[48] The previous year the ICPI had arrested several interconnected rings of chasers and stagers said to have been tied to the "Black Mafia" in Detroit. In early 1973 the ICPI announced its role in the uncovering of a Mafia-controlled ring of Italian immigrants brought in from Palermo and other towns in Sicily to stage accidents on Chicago's West Side, collecting over $700,000 during the course of five years. The accidents were remarkably similar: A car driven by one member of the group would ram into the rear of a car containing four or five other members. When questioned by insurance investigators, the driver of the at-fault car almost always used the excuse that he had dropped a lighted cigar and bent over to pick it up when the collision occurred. Investigators called it the "dropped stogie ploy," and it was said to have originated with the group's ringleader, an Italian hairdresser.[49] The more dangerous fake collisions involving higher speeds were reserved for people who were trying to pay back money owed to ring-connected loan sharks.

The story of the Sicilian accident "dons" helped to make Ahern's point about the involvement of traditional organized crime in large-scale personal injury frauds. Another case of accident stagers from Providence, Rhode Island, also had links to organized crime (and, oddly, also involved an Italian hairdresser) and was one of the ICPI's most publicized early stories.[50] More common, however, were the rings of varying nationalities organized specifically to stage accidents. In Chicago alone, a ring of Nigerian "students" was as big on the South Side of the city as the Sicilians were on the West. Led by a twenty-five-year-old who fled the city after he learned that he was being investigated by the ICPI and the immigration service, some fifty men and women were arrested early in 1974 and charged with having caused street accidents on purpose.[51] Sometimes ring members inflicted knife wounds on themselves to impress insurance adjusters; other times they just created their own medical reports with the help of a rubber stamp borrowed from a South Side doctor. What first led ICPI agents to look into the case was the recurrence of the doctor's stamped signature, which ultimately provided the evidence that led to convictions. This kind of mundane detail often caused the downfall of a fraud gang. A few years earlier, a rubber stamp played an equally pivotal role in an ICPI investigation in Philadelphia. There ring members made the mistake of stamping their fake medical reports with the name of a doctor who had been dead for several months. Forged signatures on doctors' reports also helped the ICPI to uncover an accident ring working Cleveland's East Side.[52]

When neither traditional organized crime groups nor ethnic ties formed the backbone of a ring, ICPI agents looked for family ties—cousins running into cousins at an intersection, uncles serving as "independent" witnesses to a crash, husbands and wives vouching for the other's employment in order to collect wage losses on certain policies. Over the years, brothers were often found at the center of accident rings: the Laulicht brothers in New York in the 1920s and the Garrow and Weiss brothers' disability rings of the 1930s both come to mind. Then there were the Barnard brothers in Portland, Oregon, in the late 1950s and early 1960s. George Barnard arranged all of the collisions himself. Each was a two-car crash between "weapon" and "target" cars. George drove the weapon car himself on five occasions, while other times the cars were driven by a rotating group of friends such as Leland and Geraldine Deegan, a lounge singer and cocktail waitress duo who often worked with the Barnard brothers. With advances of several hundred dollars from a Portland attorney, George Barnard would buy old cars (a 1941 Chevrolet, a 1951 Oldsmobile), then round up friends to crash them. If the damage wasn't good enough, often the attorney would instruct Barnard to crash the car into a tree. "I'm not an attorney, I am just a banker," the attorney reportedly said. "They will never get me. They will get some of the small fry in this matter, but they will never get me." The attorney was right. After a number of appeals, he got off without prison time, while postal inspectors and FBI agents were able to develop enough evidence on the Barnard brothers to send them to federal prison for several years.[53] After the initial indictments in 1961, the Deegans fled to Bend, Oregon, where they got jobs in a restaurant. But when the FBI located them, agents rushed to Bend "with as much as alacrity as if Deegan had been No. 1 on the list of ten most wanted; they got their man even though it required the interruption of the orchestra and the dance" when they yanked Mr. Deegan off the bandstand and rushed him and his wife to Rocky Butte Jail.

During the first few years of the ICPI, several more teams of brothers would be added to the list of famous fraud families. In Columbus, Ohio, for instance, the Reynolds brothers—Clyde, Robert, and Eugene—took turns driving the crash cars, playing the role of injured claimant, and negotiating settlements.[54] In Louisiana, Larry and Kenneth DeMary, working sometimes with their other brother Earl and sister Elda, may have been the most successful brother team of accident stagers of all time. The DeMary brothers staged hundreds of accidents that brought in hundreds of thousands of dollars over the course of several years. In scripting their collisions, the DeMarys used the vocabulary of "hitter" cars and "targets," "drivers" and "riders."[55] The DeMarys themselves often drove the hitter car, frequently a 1961 Corvair. They recruited riders at bars and nightclubs, body shops and barbecues— anywhere people might be found who were interested in making a few hundred dollars for a few minutes' work. When prospective claimants asked about the dangers of accident staging, Larry DeMary replied that he had taken his own wife for a ride while she was pregnant. "If you brace yourself," he assured a nervous father-to-be about his wife's safety, "it's no worse than hitting a big bump or something."[56]

Like all of the great brother teams of accident fakers, the DeMarys divided up the labor to maximize profits. Larry DeMary ran the operation in their hometown of Lake Charles in southwestern Louisiana, while Kenneth set up branch offices near Shreveport. In Lake Charles, Larry DeMary routinely called on a dozen or so riders, including his wife Joyce, and an assortment of hitters, among them a milk truck driver. A few recruiters helped him with the details of the crashes, and two or three lawyers and doctors were actively involved in the schemes, even occasionally suggesting variations on the style of collision when they felt that rear-enders were getting too predictable. Up north, Kenneth DeMary was doing the same, arranging collisions in cities in and around Shreveport, Bossier City, and Luckey, Louisiana. When riders had too many accidents in one region, they were sent to work with the other brother elsewhere in the state. And when a scenario got old in one place—the ring was ultimately caught for abusing the "dropped stogie ploy"—it was recycled in another.

With dozens of crashes under their belts in cities all around the state, the fake accident business became routine for the DeMarys. The brothers began to delegate increasing amounts of authority to recruiters, one of whom would later tell a federal court how a typical crash was set up: "Larry [DeMary] told me to get a car with four riders and a hitter and set up an accident to happen either in Alexandria or right around Lake Charles," Robert Deville explained.

> We were going to try to have it out of Lake Charles because we didn't want to have too many right in Lake Charles. . . . I got the car. Dennis LeJeune's wife had a car, and they were two of the passengers (Dennis wasn't, but the wife was one of the passengers). I got the rest of the passengers—Nolan Breaux and Iva Pitts, and her husband—I don't remember his name, and Mr. and Mrs. Pitts, to ride. And for this I was going to get $25 a piece for each rider and $50 for getting the car. . . . [57]

The DeMary brothers sold these set-up cases to attorneys who stood to make several thousand dollars per person. Over time, the attorneys gained control of a good deal of the ring's activities, accelerating the production of fake accidents to meet their needs. At one point Larry DeMary began to worry that he was working at too high a volume over too short a time and that he might be sending too many cases to one particular attorney. But the attorney assured him that insurers would never notice the repetition, instructing DeMary: "Don't stop bringing them until I holler."[58]

Prosecution of the DeMary brothers' ring dragged on through the 1970s, with one federal judge later pronouncing it a "Louisiana-wide get-rich-quick scheme" that turned into an "American tragedy" in which professional careers were ruined and "financially pressed expectant mothers" were exploited for gain. The most surprising and "saddening" aspect of the case, for the judge, was the fact that he was sure that it was happening elsewhere in the country and probably not so far away. The judge was right. While the DeMary ring members were still awaiting final sentencing, people throughout neighboring states—men and women, doctors and lawyers, teenagers and retirees—were getting into the fake accident business: Eddie Galloway of Memphis was stuffing friends, and friends' relatives, into his truck to be rammed by another friend driving a Hertz rental car.[59] Harold Lee Pless, Sr., of Concord, North Carolina, along with his wife Linda Jo and a number of friends, hit on the idea of finding women driving alone in new cars then stopping short in front of them.[60] Pless, described as the "kingpin" of the ring, drove a "big fancy car" and carried a thick roll of money to pay his riders; he was connected to several dozen of these accidents before being caught by ICPI agents working in conjunction with North Carolina state investigators. On the other side of the state, Roland Rhodes, his wife Patricia, and some friends were doing much the same thing, getting a lot of mileage out of a Mercury Cougar whose distinctive checkerboard vinyl roof ultimately gave them away to ICPI investigators.[61] Another North Carolinian, Orlando Hart, worked panic-stop claims up and down the road to Philadelphia for twenty years before he was finally arrested and jailed in 1981.[62]

The spread of accident schemes from one region of the country to another, from one decade to the next, has always been a curious study in folk knowledge: The genealogy of the idea of crashing a car for cash can be traced along many family trees; the recipe for various slip-and-fall schemes has somehow been handed down across generations. Whispers of self-injury for profit seem to accompany economic hard times as surely as high inflation—be it the 1890s, 1930s, or the late 1970s.

For a time, the ICPI and its new agents had to learn the basic plots— Ahern referred to a "learning curve" of two or three years for agents with no previous experience. The ICPI also needed a vocabulary: In training films, manuals, and seminars, agents were taught the distinction between "paper" accidents (where no collision really occurs); "staged" accidents (where damage is created in a controlled way, either by one car or by two in collusion); and "caused" accidents—the "most vicious of accident schemes"—in which "criminal claimants" load up an automobile, head out on the road looking for a new car driven by a well-dressed person (sure to be insured), then pull in front and slam on the brakes.[63] After agents understood the plots and terms, what remained was the hard work of puzzling through endless variations on themes: schemes that start in one place and pop up somewhere else; names that sound familiar from cases handled several years ago; dents on cars that don't match up with other cars. With the help of the regional Index Bureaus and, later, their own indexing system, ICPI agents spent their days hunting for connections, links, and ties between claimants in hitter and target cars which might indicate a staged collision where a traffic cop and an insurance adjuster may have seen only a suspicious accident. The rubber-stamp signature of the dead doctor, the telltale sign of the "dropped stogie ploy," the checkerboard vinyl roof of a car—ICPI agents turned these and similar details into prosecutions. In Kansas City, Missouri, for instance, the Nellie Young gang of accident fakers was caught simply because the name "Nellie Young" showed up as a claimant in almost all of the gang's stagings.[64]

Sometimes the links between cases were obvious, there to be seen by anyone who glanced over the claims files. Most times, however, teasing them out took some work. In Columbus, Ohio, an ICPI agent was aware of one stager who had "been a thorn in the side of the insurance companies since the 1960s," but who eluded prosecution through much of the 1970s until a beat-up Ford LTD finally made the case against him. "I knew about [him]," Agent Robert Herzog later said, "and I just got to digging into the case when I began to find those pictures of that LTD."[65] Working with Ohio law enforcement, Herzog charted all of the cases. He found that more than a dozen of the man's sixty or so crashes staged from 1974 through 1978 involved the LTD, and almost all occurred within a ten-block area where his crew liked to look for victims—women or taxi drivers, preferably, because of their reluctance to dispute liability. Another gang, this one operating around Fort Worth, Texas, in the mid-1970s, looked for women and cabbies to stop short in front of on freeway on-ramps.[66] And from 1972 through 1983, "Crazy Jack" Olderman's various rings staged the same types of drive-down collisions in Ohio, Phoenix, and San Diego, where Crazy Jack was finally caught.[67]

Inflicting crude injuries to support fake claims has always been a technique of professional accident fakers, and many of those who operated in the 1970s stuck to these ancient rites. John "Big Jack" Rodamaker, a 270-pound Iowa roofer, ran a ring that would later be termed "the grandest, most imaginative insurance rip-off in Iowa history," but in fact had been common to other regions since the Great Depression. Big Jack's accidents almost always were one-car stagings, where a lone ring member would drive to a remote area at night and steer his car into a ditch, as if forced from the road by a reckless driver headed in the other direction. The driver would collapse over the wheel, then wait to be discovered by another member playing the part of a passing motorist, who would call the police upon discovering the body. The real blood, broken noses, and cut faces on the pretend crash victims prevented the claims from being questioned. To inflict the injuries, Big Jack paid a short but powerful Mexican prizefighter named Leonard Chester Zappa to punch, bruise, lacerate, and generally "prepare" drivers for their accidents. Big Jack called the boxer's work a "zapping." A "first-class" zapping cost Big Jack $200 in cash to the little boxer, but it helped him get settlement money literally hand over fist. Leonard Zappa was generally happy with his job. After his arrest, however, he admitted that he once regretted having to zap a woman. "Zappa told me he really didn't like hitting girls," one investigator on the case reported. "He said he didn't want to take any money because the woman cried. But he did anyway because he figured she was going to make a lot of money."[68] Big Jack occasionally allowed himself to be zapped in order to collect on hundreds of his short-term accident and health policies, but the whole ugly business came to a halt in the late 1970s: Another ring member made a full confession to ICPI agents and state investigators. Big Jack and Leonard Zappa were each sentenced to four years in an Iowa prison. (After his release Big Jack moved to South Lake Tahoe, California. Early in 1994 he would be arrested there along with his wife and daughter for crashing cars into bridge railings and poles, or driving into ditches, then making personal injury claims on ninety-six hospitalization policies. A year later he was found guilty and sent back to prison.)[69]

At different times in the history of insurance crimes, the names of certain towns or regions have become synonymous with certain schemes: In the 1890s, many residents of Beaufort, North Carolina, and Lebanon County, Pennsylvania, had become totally consumed with the idea of insuring people's lives, then hastening their deaths; much later Detroit would come to be seen as a haven for arson. In the late 1960s and early 1970s, the idea of trading body parts for cash on accident policies had just one name among insurance investigators around the country: Vernon, Florida. A backwoods town in the Florida Panhandle, Vernon had a general store, a combination post office/barber shop, one police car, and a main street that stretched only a block and a half. Selling reptiles from a roadside stand was a good business in Vernon; hunting turkeys, an obsession for some. For a time, though, losing limbs, fingers, arms, or legs in freak accidents became the town fashion. More than fifty such cases came out of Vernon in just a few years, a number that becomes all the more unusual when it is understood that the town's total population was less than 500. Investigators refused to name the town at the time, telling newspaper reporters only that they referred to it as Nub City. Self-amputees from the city, investigators said, were casually referred to as members of the Nub Club. "Somehow they always shoot off the parts they seem to need least," one investigator remarked of the disproportionate number of left hands claimed lost as compared with right ones.[70] Another investigator, John J. Healy of New York, worked cases in Vernon for a number of major insurers and later wrote about it at some length. "The second biggest occupation [in Vernon] seems to be the observation of hound dogs mating in the town square," he noted back in 1975. "The biggest occupation was the deliberate maiming or severance of limbs to collect insurance money. . . . To sit in your car on a sweltering summer evening on the main street of Nub City, watching anywhere from eight to a dozen cripples walking along the street, gives the place a ghoulish, eerie atmosphere."[71]

Most of the limbs lost in Nub City were shot off at close range with hunting rifles. The contrived accidents were all similar: triggers pulled unexpectedly as victims climbed fences; guns misfiring in the middle of being cleaned or after being dropped. And all of the mishaps involved men. ("Women never do dismemberments," Healy later observed.) In the late 1950s, when the first claims came out of Nub City, a typical dismemberment was worth $1,500; by the early 1970s, the average claim was bringing tens of thousands of dollars. Over the years, Nub City got under the skin of investigator Healy, a nationally known expert in murder for insurance cases. "As inured as I am to all kinds of maimings and weird dismemberments, Nub City holds a morbid fascination for me," he wrote. "I keep asking myself: How did it all start? What drove these people to sacrifice their limbs for money?"[72] Healy tried to imagine the conversations that might have taken place between those who had already profited from losing a limb and those who were considering it. One man talks about the ten thousand dollars he got for his left hand and how he could use the money to buy a house or a car or a color television. "The other man looks at his own hand—the hand that probably has not earned him ten thousand dollars in five years," Healy writes.

> It is dirty, worn, the index finger crooked from a fracture that never was set straight. The fingers are tobacco-stained. He looks at it, turning it slowly, reflectively. Ten thousand dollars or more, he thinks. In one fell swoop. That's more money than he's ever seen in his life, probably more than he will ever see. He's fifty years old and has been doing odd jobs for twenty years. He's tired. His 1947 Plymouth may or may not start in the morning to get him to whatever job he may have.

In the end, the man completes a calculation that has been made by Americans at least since the depression of the 1890s, and probably earlier. "Does it hurt much?" he asks his friend, now talking more about strategy than principle. And with that, the deal is done, but for the bloody doing itself. A knowing look washes over the man's face as he weighs the relative merits of knives, axes, or shotguns, and debates with friends the relative anesthetic properties of different brands of whiskey. "I hope I never have to go into that town again and see the mangled stump of an arm or a leg and listen to the old familiar story," Healy concluded of Nub City. "But deep down inside me, I know that I will."

Slip-and-fallers always have had their distinctive styles, their calling-card flops, their signature scenarios—for some, their banana peels. And the slip-and-fallers first encountered by the ICPI during the 1970s continued tradition: Mrs. Shirley Hill, a forty-year-old widow from Dallas, liked to fake falls on pats of butter in restaurants. (Jailed once in 1965, Mrs. Hill got back into butter after her release, and stayed there until being caught again in 1974.)[73] Kenneth Arnold Parsley also worked the Dallas area in the early 1970s, specializing in falls in supermarkets on broken eggs and melted ice cream and in slips in office buildings on rainwater leaks.[74] William Leon Jones of nearby Oklahoma City used to place a tomato in the aisle of local supermarkets, then twist the heel of his shoe into it, fall to the ground, and cry out in pain for a store manager.[75]

Discerning a fake slip and fall from a bona fide one was an art for which there were few reliable guides for ICPI agents. The training literature warned that "since the success of these scams depends on the claimant's acting ability, the accidents are as varied as the claimants themselves." The literature then offered a rough list of slip-and-fall fraud indicators: "Claimant is a transient or out-of-towner on vacation." "Claimant is overly pushy and demanding for a quick settlement." "Typical defrauder will claim that as a result of his fall, he suffered personal injury, lost time from work, and broke his eyeglasses, dentures, or other expensive props, such as cameras or wristwatches." The trick was to apply these general rules to a man in Miami, a retired car salesman who actually carried a pair of broken eyeglasses to toss by his feet before throwing himself to the floor of discount stores, pharmacies, or in the concourse of the dog track.[76] Or to perceive the patterns in the claims scripted by a Philadelphian adjuster who worked on the side as manager of a number of slip-and-fallers who operated in banks and auto parts stores.[77] Or to suspect a minister like Roland Gray of Chicago of falling to his knees for any other reason than prayer.[78] Then there was the case of Richard Mark Swimm of Greensboro, North Carolina, whose troupe of slip-and-fallers and "food artists" went undetected for years. For the slip and falls, Swimm's ring members would enter supermarkets or convenience stores, open a soda, take a mouthful, secretly spit it on the floor, and slip on it. "The glass-swallowing schemes were more sophisticated," explained investigator Dan Stone.[79] A ring member would break off some glass from a beer bottle, then go to a different store, buy the same beer, insert a few shards in the drink and put another in his mouth before going to the manager to make a claim. No fraud indicator on any training checklist would have told a doctor working for insurers to ask one of Swimm's gang to save his stools so that they could be checked for glass. Nor was there any manual telling Swimm to prepare his ring members with the shards of glass to insert in their stools just in case the doctor asked. Intuition and experience were the only real guides.

After a few years on the job, ICPI director James Ahern told a magazine reporter about the "virtually endless" slip-and-fall schemes the ICPI had worked hard to uncover. "There was one man who only fell down in front of Catholic churches," Ahern began. "Another guy picked the wet linoleum in front of the ice-making machine of Holiday Inns." In subsequent years, the ICPI would also discover mothers working with sons, as did Marguerite and Brian Flynn of California;[80] slip-and-fall families, including the Dames of Albany, New York;[81] and husband-and-wife teams such as Bridget and Stanley DiDolce of Pittsburgh. (After his wife was jailed in the slip-and-fall scheme, Stanley DiDolce, a former prison guard and an ex-marine, entered a Pittsburgh-area hair salon with a .22 caliber rifle and held hostages until the FBI granted his request to tell his side of the story to a federal judge.) [82] Perhaps the most hotly pursued slip-and-faller from the early years of the ICPI was Robert Clark Ridge, a man of undetermined middle age who dressed in polyester leisure wear and wore his hair in a natty pompadour. Ridge's early history was unclear: He said that he had served time in Folsom Prison during the mid-1960s, but for what, he would not specify. After his release, however, the account becomes sharper. Ridge began to make a living faking falls in almost every city in the country, concentrating on small towns in Washington, Oregon, and Colorado. Ridge's claims were distinctive: The pretext for his falls usually involved jelly of the sort that is packaged in square-inch plastic containers and served with toast in restaurants. More specifically—and this, in the end, was his undoing—Ridge always used *mint* jelly in his accident stagings. In a typical case, Ridge would be found lying on the floor of a restaurant or hotel bathroom, covered in blood with deep cuts over his left eye and various gashes about wrists and arms. He would claim to have slipped on the mint jelly, left carelessly on the floor by the staff. Then he would let it be known that he was amenable to a quick, out-of-court settlement of his potential personal injury claim against the restaurant, but that he needed to do it immediately because he had business in another town or was just passing through on vacation or was late for a business convention in Hawaii.[83]

When his slip-and-fall scheme worked, "Mint Jelly" Ridge would make off with somewhere between $400 and $2,000 cash, in addition to free meals and lodging while the matter was being settled. Late in 1979, however, a team of ICPI agents and other law enforcement officials finally began to close in on

FIGURE 6.1. Robert Clark Ridge, a longtime slip-and-fall artist, being arrested in Morro Bay, California in 1979. Ridge, sometimes referred to as "Mint Jelly Ridge" for his habit of pretending to slip on mint jelly in restaurants, became the subject of an elaborate sting operation conducted by agents of the Insurance Crime Prevention Institute (ICPI) and local police after they tracked him to central California earlier in the year. (This photograph was printed as part of a lengthy account of Ridge's arrest in a 1979 issue of the ICPI Report.)

Ridge in a small town in central California. Early one afternoon they converged on Dorn's restaurant in Morro Bay, where it was learned that a man meeting Ridge's description had suffered a fall in the bathroom and was taken to a nearby hospital. The cause of the fall, doctors at a local hospital reported to investigators, was said to have been some mint jelly on the bathroom floor. The next day the investigative team set up a sting operation that led to the arrest of Ridge outside of the restaurant, where he had just accepted a $1,000 settlement check and was headed back to his hotel before leaving town. Ridge's arm was badly gangrenous because he had maintained self-inflicted wounds on it for years. Doctors initially feared they would have to amputate. (Weeks after his hospitalization, Mint Jelly Ridge pleaded guilty to the charges against him and was sentenced to four years in state prison.)

People have always been interested in the life stories of career slip-and-fallers or in the actions of a band of car crashers. It is intriguing to learn that some have been doing on a grand scale what may have once occurred to others to do themselves. Insurance ripoffs are so closely tied to the acts of everyday life that they seem imaginable by a wider range of people than might seriously consider a stick-up or a bank heist; and the personal injury underworld has become the most personal of them all. In the end, however, people want to know that the insurance criminal did not get away with it. Their sense of justice is offended not just by the fact that someone is profiting at everyone else's expense through rising premiums, but also by the prospect that someone might get away with something that they could have gotten away with had they tried.

For most of this century, news about accident frauds has reached the public primarily from the defrauded corporations themselves by way of newspapers and magazines. "The Business of 'Beating' Street Railways," a cover story in *Harper's Weekly* magazine in 1907, was illustrated with photographs and anecdotes "from the archives of street railway companies," to take one of the earliest examples. "Fake Accidents, Inc.," a center spread in the *Saturday Evening Post* in 1936, was derived primarily from information supplied by the Claims Bureau of the American Casualty and Surety Underwriters Association. The relation between news organizations that have to find stories to tell and industries that want their particular story told is complicated. One message often underlies the bizarre details of individual accident frauds; insurers, by way of reporters, want readers to understand the story in one particular frame: that insurance fraud is not a victimless crime so long as policyholders continue to pay for it with higher premiums. Equally voluminous, of course, have been the consumer advocate or trial lawyer protestations that insurers overstate the fraud problem in order to justify rate increases as something other than profit-taking.

For James Ahern and the ICPI, insurance fraud was not just a consumer issue about rising rates, it was an emerging crime problem to be taken seriously on its own. What critics might have called insurance industry propaganda, Ahern thought of as "deterrent publicity." The phrase was not new in personal injury fraud fighting circles. Back in 1909, at a meeting of railway claims men, one agent from Baltimore rose to support the idea of circulating news of convicted accident fakers beyond the pages of the railway claims *Bulletin* because doing so might have "a deterrent effect on others." But the ICPI did not just talk about deterrent publicity, it was central to the agency's mission. For an organization with a modest budget, the ICPI spent heavily on all sorts of public relations material, including a whole catalog of films with fairly high production values—stunts, dramatic reenactments, and a gritty true-crime narration. Some of these early 23-minute reels included such genre classics as *Accident by Appointment, Inside Insurance Crime,* and *Chasers.* (Described in promotional literature as a "dramatic detective narrative concerned with the crime of ambulance chasing," *Chasers* won a top honor at the U.S. Industrial Film Festival in 1977.) Ahern's group also circulated the ICPI *Report*, a quarterly newspaper with full-page, illustrated splashes on slip-and-fallers and accident rings. Headlines in the *Report* might be matter-of-fact—"Slip & Fall Cheat Slips Up in Miami Drugstore"—but many reached for punchier tags—"Nevada Human Fly Convicted" or "'Godfather Figure' Indicted." One insurance executive called the ICPI *Report* the tabloid newspaper of insurance crime; everyone who had access to it read it cover to cover, and few issues were thrown away. This was by design: Unlike the *Bulletin*, an important investigatory tool for railway claims men to be held close to the vest, the ICPI *Report* was aimed at a larger audience of journalists. *Report* editors hoped these journalists would be intrigued enough by what they read to pick up on their stories.

Many reporters did adapt ICPI stories for use in their own pages. But other newspapers, magazines, and TV stations were intrigued beyond what could be learned from a training video, news release, or industry newspaper. They stopped taking all of their cues on the subject from the insurance industry and began to send their own correspondents into America's personal injury underworld. The exposure of the Friends of the Friendless by reporters from the *Los Angeles Times* was an example of some of the best and earliest original reporting on personal injury frauds. Without these reports, the political pressure to shut down the ring might never have mounted, and the subsequent disclosures about accident faking might never have followed. Another series that ran in the *Miami Herald* a few years later found a chasing culture as well developed as any, complete with chasers nicknamed "Red" and "Alabama," cops on the take, and a number of "whippie mill" hospitals in the poorer neighborhoods around Miami. Several lawyers and doctors were arrested and, later, convicted for buying chased cases; among them was an attorney who did not disguise the origin of his quick riches, naming his speedboat *The Whiplash*.[84] One exposé bred another, as Mike Wallace and TV's *Sixty Minutes* followed up with their own investigation of Miami's "pain and suffering racket." The program featured some of the first hidden-camera footage of fraud, the airing of secretly made tape recordings ("If you go to a doctor a couple of times a week," one chaser told a prospective client, "then we can get you some bread"), and interviews with the actual participants in the schemes, not just investigators.[85] Two years after Wallace's report on whiplash in Miami, *60 Minutes* again returned to the personal injury underworld with Dan Rather's report on freeway swoop-and-squatters in Los Angeles.[86]

During the 1970s, reporters moved progressively closer to the personal injury underworld; late in the decade, one group in Chicago finally entered it themselves: Acting on tips that "accident brokers" were controlling an enormous trade in false and illegally solicited personal injury claims and that some area hospitals existed almost solely to help pad bills for fake claims, a joint investigative team from the *Chicago Sun-Times* and a local Chicago TV station decided to go undercover. Many months later they returned with thousands of pages of notes, stacks of still photographs, and rolls of hidden-camera film. All of it combined to form something completely unexpected, a chapter in Chicago's celebrated organized crime history that no one had seen before. Reporters found that many in the city's personal injury underworld often patterned themselves on Chicago's famed gangster tradition—from the sartorial stylings of the accident brokers (many wore silk suits and diamond rings and drove Cadillacs and Lincoln Continentals), right down to the subtle homage of some chaser nicknames: "Machinegun Kelly," "The Bull," "Big Cornelius," and "Freddie Dollar." Reporters met with accident brokers such as Fred Harvey, who bragged about how many lawyers he had bought and sold during his twenty-year career. Harvey also acknowledged having been found guilty of hiring a hit man to kill one attorney, then attempting to stab the hit man to death after the hit was botched.[87] Other Chicago chasers, the reporters learned, fought for clients with gunplay like neck brace–wielding Al Capone's: "It's the unwritten code," one chaser told them, "if someone tries to take your money, you blow their head off."[88]

Undercover reporters did not learn much that ICPI investigators in Chicago did not already have good reason to suspect was going on. In fact, ICPI agents provided reporters with some initial introductions to informants. The difference was in the texture of the reporters' account—the details of time and place, the mechanics of the different operations, the glimpses of the personalities involved. The reporters did not just tell about ambulance chasers counseling people to fake symptoms, they showed Wes McKinney in a powder-blue suit worried that his fake claimants will forget to tell the doctor that they had not slept for two nights. Not content just to name the fact that laymen bought professional licenses for their own use in faked claims, we are shown Archie Burton, an accident broker with a taste for antique cars, propo-sitioning an attorney while on prison work-release for mail fraud. ("That license of yours is a gold mine," Burton reportedly tells the lawyer. Another attorney is warned away from Burton by a friend who says that Burton has "one foot in jail and the other foot on a banana peel.") And then there is John Rusniak, once jailed for drug smuggling, who told reporters that personal injury is "just a business, all about money." When the reporters revealed their true identities, the white-haired man with stooped shoulders and bell-bottom pants runs up six flights of stairs and hides in a bathroom.[89]

The reporters' account of Chicago's personal injury underworld went beyond the relatively narrow purpose of deterrent publicity or prosecution, even though the series continued to have a demonstrable deterrent effect fifteen years after it first ran. More than just answering the question of why auto insurance rates were so high, the reporters found an entire criminal culture complete with its own language and institutions, leaders and lieutenants. Paul Skidmore, an aging chaser in a worn tweed coat who had been jailed for solicitation in the 1960s, was one of the first to initiate the reporters into the underworld's rituals and ceremonies: He put neck braces on them and snapped Polaroids to show insurance adjusters. Then he taught them the magic catchphrases that brought money: He told one to act "all shook up . . . like scrambled eggs." To the others he handed out sets of symptoms like a favorite uncle passing out gifts. "OK, you can take tingles," he said to one of them, "and you can take hips or your shoulder. But don't go saying the exact same things."[90]

Of all of the images to come out of the Chicago reporters' investigation, the most unexpected were those involving the hospitals. Insurance investigators had long talked about the existence of "whiplash hotels," or "whippie mills," where fake claimants went to build up a claim. But something about the whole phenomenon did not ring true until reporters went inside the Community Hospital of Evanston. There they found little functioning medical equipment, no doctors, nurses who talked freely about the fact that none of the patients were "real," and administrators who discouraged any "real" nurses from applying for work in the hospital. ("You're going to be so bored here," one applicant with experience in intensive care was told. "There is nothing to do.") A "courtesy van" brought fake claimants to the hospital from clinics around the city, and even the driver knew that none of his passengers was really in need of care: "No one is really hurt," he told reporters about why his job was so easy, "no one gets sick on me and I don't have to worry about people in wheelchairs or crutches." As incoming patients filed into the bus, the driver would assure them that there would be free color TV at the hospital and a generally laid-back atmosphere where they would be free to socialize and to have a good time. "It's more like a hotel," the bus driver liked to say. And he was more right than he knew: The pillow cases on the hospital's forty-seven beds had been purchased at a fire sale and were stamped Villa Motel. Patients often referred to one another as "sleepers."[91]

One study of Medicaid fraud during the 1970s, citing a Pulitzer Prize–winning exposé, described "a new class" of medical mill doctors on the Lower East Side of New York complete with "hawkers" who rounded up potential patients outside, all of which was created by incentives in the new state insurance program for the poor. The story of the abuse of Medicaid has a clear beginning—1968—and an even clearer message about the power of insurance incentives to corrupt systematically, to give rise to a "subculture of medical deviancy."[92] The personal injury whippie mills did not grow up in response to some specific state program, however. On the contrary, and in a way that is far more revealing of the general culture, whippie mills evolved in the non-system, the unregulated free market, which evolved "naturally" for Americans during the previous century to link accident victims with their just compensation. In the early 1970s the Friends of the Friendless had infiltrated a hospital to solicit legitimate cases; later in the decade a loosely affiliated group of Chicago accident brokers had completely taken over the Community Hospital of Evanston in order to build fake claims. It was the logical next step to the broker's owning law offices and medical clinics, and Abe Gatner probably would have called it progress. But progress had a pathetic look as it played itself out in the hospital, where boredom was the chief complaint of sleepers passing time and the self-prescribed cure was to use water bottles for basket-balls, to smoke pot in the bathrooms, and to run out to the store for whiskey and cigarettes if the need arose. Progress did not look much better in the clinics, where doctors readied patients for the hospital courtesy van even before examining them, then cupped their ears like children when the patients—in this case, the undercover reporters—said that they were not really injured. And the picture was the same in the law offices, where attorneys or their office managers made their own medical diagnoses on the spot, then called for the courtesy van to take sleepers to hospital beds. When asked persistently by an undercover reporter what reason he should give his wife for going to the hospital, one attorney finally voiced the rationale for most of the sad shenanigans that went on in the personal injury underworld: "To make money. That's the reason. To make money. Do you need it any simpler than that?" Inside the hospital, most people knew that this was exactly why they were there. "I'm here because I'm suing for $10,000," one patient told a nurse before describing his intention to buy his own taxi. "Now I'll sit back and wait for the money to come." Meanwhile, added the man who had obviously not been reached by deterrent publicity from the ICPI or anyone else, "I like to get high, make love, and party."

The ICPI had initially agreed to cooperate with the *Sun-Times* investigation on the condition that their agents, the state bar, and federal investigators would have a chance to take action on the various cases before the articles were published. The deal fell apart one afternoon, though, when an accident broker called the home of someone he thought was a fake claimant and spoke to a young child who said his mother was actually a reporter.

The investigation, which had begun so originally, ended predictably: Cases were pursued against more than 150 people, but only a few were indicted and even fewer stood trial. Law offices dropped fake claims as quickly as they had been initiated, and the trail to most of the major accident brokers, doctors, and lawyers quickly froze over.[93] The Community Hospital of Evanston lost its accreditation and closed. But courtesy vans simply began taking sleepers to a handful of other institutions whose status as whiplash hotels was not as complete but still would do in a pinch. Among policymakers and legal scholars, the *Sun-Times* series sparked new talk of the need for the reform of a tort system in which people with serious legitimate injuries were often undercompensated and smaller claims were paid off with such a regularity and disregard for merit that they could become a steady underworld trade. "The sad commentary on Chicago is that for widespread elements of society, liability law has become corrupt," concluded law professor and long-time no-fault insurance advocate Jeffrey O'Connell of the "well-documented and depressing" articles.[94] In fact, Chicago was not the only city to boast a highly-developed tort underworld, and there was nothing new about organized corruption in high-volume personal injury law.

A chasing culture such as that uncovered in Chicago in the late 1970s was usually the smoke that said the fire of outright accident faking was burning somewhere nearby. The chaser hearings of the 1920s in New York led to investigation of the Laulicht flopping ring, for instance, and the inquiry into the Friends of the Friendless turned into a lesson on the swoop-and-squat. In Chicago, the aftermath of the "Accident Swindlers" series in the *Sun-Times* brought news of cars stopping short in front of other cars on freeway on-ramps and exits, some with their brake lights purposely disabled beforehand. Sally Wirth, a thirty-one-year-old employee of a realty firm near Chicago, told reporters how terrifying it had been to be set up for a crash on the freeway. Two "big guys" in a "big old car," she said, had stopped suddenly in front of her for no apparent reason.[95] David Gronwick, the driver of a ten-ton flatbed truck hauling rubber products, later told police about his own experience as a target of a staged collision:

> I was driving eastbound on the Eisenhower Expressway when two cars began 'playing chicken,' starting and stopping in front of me. I didn't want to hurt anyone, so I slowed down. But one of the cars zoomed into the right lane and the other stayed right in front of me. Then at the same

> time both of them stopped dead in the middle of the expressway. I tried
> to stop, but I plowed into the car in front of me, smashed the trunk into
> the back seat, and knocked it into the Sacramento Avenue exit.[96]

Gronwick thought he had killed the passengers inside the one car. Before he
could get out to help them, however, another car pulled up and took away two
of the passengers—most likely one of whom was a "professional accident
causer" used by the ring. As the drivers would be needed in many more crashes,
they could not be risked by being named as a claimant in every accident.

Chicago's accident rings sometimes involved the same ambulance chasers and accident brokers whom reporters had gotten to know at the whippie
mills; other times they functioned as totally separate organizations. One ring
planned their crashes in a South Side bar, offering $150 and fake IDs to
passengers willing to sit in the cars for crashes. The leader of this loose group
of thirty-six was known to have staged dozens of accidents by stopping short
in front of old people, women, and suburbanites on the Dan Ryan and
Eisenhower freeways.[97] A different ring from this same time also operated on
the expressways, but supplemented the caused accidents with paper ones
where believable damage was created by ramming cars into walls.

"A few years ago I would have said the Mafia was behind it," ICPI director
James Ahern said when asked about the rise in accident faking in Chicago and
elsewhere in the country. "But now I think it's ordinary people with larceny in
their hearts."[98] The truth of the matter lay somewhere in between. Traditional
organized crime probably had never been involved in the personal injury
underworld as heavily as the former police chief had initially believed, and the
frauds of ordinary people did, in fact, account for a lot of the activity. One had
only to talk with "Big Jack" Rodamaker or to visit Nub City to see that this was
not La Cosa Nostra. The personal injury underworld always had been peopled
with a mix of gangster types and regular folks who worked with doctors and
lawyers on the fringes of professional practice to exploit an insurance bureaucracy. The result was a criminal hybrid of street operators and white-collar
types that is hard to classify. Reporters in earlier years tried to locate the
"accident racketeers" among the Bugsy Siegels and Dutch Schultzes of organized crime, and several later angles on the story gave a central role to the Black
Mafia. Yet by the late 1970s and early 1980s, the story changed. Investigators
and reporters seemed to stop casting about for comparisons and links to
traditional organized crime. They began to view ambulance chasers and
accident brokers, sleepers and stagers, doctors and lawyers as constituting a

criminal culture in their own right, with car accident staging becoming the center around which the rest of this odd underworld revolved.

Late in 1979, a *New York Times* reporter took note of the new proliferation of "criminal rings" involved in the "flourishing racket of staging automobile accidents." *Sixty Minutes* followed with its own inside looks at the "organized rings" staging crashes across the country. The ICPI, too, was taking a harder look at the problem, especially in light of the "Accident Swindlers" series and its aftermath. Bringing together information about rings from all parts of the country—from St. Louis to Springfield, Massachusetts, from Greensboro, North Carolina, to Portland, Oregon—the ICPI began referring to accident staging as "an increasingly pervasive American criminal institution." "Never before have so many prosecutions of major rings been in progress at the same time," one ICPI agent reported in the early 1980s, and this was largely because never before had there been so much activity to prosecute. In 1984 a two-page spread in the ICPI *Report* newspaper announced, "The Emerging National Anti–Staged Vehicular Accident Campaign."[99] It was not the kind of operation name that would ever catch on outside of a narrow audience of specialists, but the point was clear: Ambulance chasing had once again given way to accident staging and the accident stagers were more active than ever before.

In Los Angeles, the hearings on the Friends of the Friendless had started the first real public discussion about accident faking in the region. The conversation was still going strong five years later: Rings were found to be staging thousands of collisions a year, and dollar estimates of stagers' earnings were now in the hundreds of millions. By 1980 two new law enforcement groups had been established in California specifically to go after the stagers. Initially underfunded and undermanned, these groups could do little but chart the activities of the different rings, then stand back and watch as staged accidents became one of the region's leading products and, later, a top export to cities around the country. The Friends of the Friendless had been the first sign of the rise of Los Angeles as the new capital of America's personal injury underworld. Looking back, a few Friends in the county hospital and coyotes on the street were nothing compared with the spectacle that was soon to come: thousands of bulls and cows rushing toward the roads and freeways of Southern California to swoop-and-squat on a scale never before seen anywhere in the world.

CHAPTER 7

EL TORO Y LA VACA

In a city not only largely conceived as a series of real estate promotions, but largely supported by a series of confidence games, in a city afloat on motion pictures and junk bonds and the B-2 stealth bomber, the conviction that something can be made of nothing may be one of the few narratives in which everyone participates.

—Joan Didion, "LA Noir," 1989

THE TIERRA BLANCA CLUB BAR was a nondescript stucco building in East Los Angeles adorned with only a few neon signs and some cheap colored lights strung without care. In a dirt parking lot adjoining the bar, music from an AM radio station played Spanish-language rock through plastic speakers fixed atop a chain-link fence. The bar was owned by a young Guatemalan man named Gerardo, but much of the business that transpired there was conducted by his younger brother, Luis Alfredo Martinez, who liked to be called Freddy.[1]

Freddy was born and raised in a small town near Guatemala City where farming jobs were common. He moved to Los Angeles in his early twenties and worked for a time as a janitor, before helping to manage his brother's bar. Sometime in the late 1980s, Freddy began to make money as an accident capper in the city's booming personal injury underworld. He found cars, insurance policies, and people, then scripted crash situations for them all to come together profitably. He directed the collisions of cars, vans, and small trucks in back alleys, empty streets, and, often, in the parking lot of the Tierra

Blanca. Then he called the police to make a report. Freddy shopped his fake cases to a handful of law offices, which bought them for set dollar amounts in order to get back much higher set dollar amounts from insurance companies when the cases settled. Freddy also knew people at clinics who could be counted on to prepare the medical bills the lawyers needed to make the claims. Freddy was good at what he did. The secret to his success was no secret at all to cappers in Southern California's thriving trade in fake accidents: old cars, fresh policies, and a constant supply of new passengers for the stagings.

In Freddy's staged crashes, "bull" cars with insurance rammed "cows" stuffed with three-to-four passengers. *El toro y la vaca*—the bull and the cow—was how Freddy and the nation's newest group of accident cappers in Los Angeles referred to their set-ups. The phrase added a south-of-the-border twist to utilitarian talk of hammer cars banging nails (or the vaguely military jargon of weapons and targets) that had been popular for decades. For Freddy, rounding up cows was a matter of making phone calls, stopping by friends' apartments, asking around at the bar, and mining neighborhood contacts. Cows and bulls would become as important to Freddy in Los Angeles as they had been to farmers back in Guatemala. He kept the names and dates of their accidents in a red ledger that he never let out of his sight.

To glimpse Freddy at work is to see demonstrated again the curious transmission of folk knowledge on how to stage crashes for cash, played out from one generation to the next, one city to another, one ethnic group after another for more than a century. New to Los Angeles in its Latino lingo, its players, and its scale, the trade was almost antebellum in its purposes and design. One night in December 1990, for instance, a man named Juan Acosta would walk into the Tierra Blanca bar on advice from a friend who told him that Freddy could help him do an accident. Freddy was playing pool when Acosta arrived, but he quickly dropped the game for the opportunity to do business. A few minutes later the two men were out in the half-light of the parking lot examining Acosta's 1979 Oldsmobile for damage and surveying the details of his new insurance policy. When everything checked out, Freddy decided that the accident would happen the next night. Acosta agreed to the terms of the deal—he would get $500 up front and another $500 in a week or so when the law office could be sure that the bull's policy was good and that the claim would probably be paid. The next night Acosta returned to the Tierra Blanca, where he was met by a man in a big green hat. The man, Marvin Noguera, introduced himself as the owner of the cow car, an old Toyota, which Acosta was going to hit. Out in the parking lot, Noguera discussed the scenario with Freddy, then Freddy told Acosta what to do: drive out of the Tierra Blanca parking lot in time to hit the cow car coming the other way in traffic. Acosta was surprised that he would actually be doing the driving himself. He asked if it wasn't too dangerous for a novice, or if Freddy would be in the car to help. Freddy brushed off the question in favor of talking to someone else about the mechanics of the kind of crash he wanted. Then he headed back into the bar to help rustle up more passengers for the cow car. Ana Colindres worked as a waitress at the Tierra Blanca, but Freddy could use her in an accident on a night like this when it was hard to find people. Freddy asked Noguera to call his brother Henry to drive the cow car; then Marvin, acting on his own, found a friend to be a passenger in the cow car. Victor Donado, a bartender at the Tierra Blanca, was roped in at the last minute by Freddy to drive the bull car—Acosta seemed too nervous to do it himself.

The arrangements had taken longer than either Acosta had expected or Freddy had hoped. Then, when the crash was first attempted, it failed. Henry Noguera, in the cow car, was driving too fast, and Victor Donado, in the bull car, missed him. For the second try, Freddy and Marvin Noguera directed the action more closely from the side of the road and the cars came together in just the right way: Front quarter panel to rear quarter panel was the most believable combination of damage, Freddy thought. Victor hopped out of the driver's side of the bull car and told a startled Acosta to pretend he had driven the car himself. Freddy leaned his head in the window of the car just long enough to say that Acosta should tell the police that he and Ana were friends and that they were on their way to get something to eat when the crash occurred. Then Freddy went back inside the Tierra Blanca. Marvin Noguera crossed the street to the Astro Burger restaurant and called 911 to report the accident. Noguera watched as two police cars, the Highway Patrol, and a paramedic rescue unit arrived on the scene to tend to the injured; then he, too, went back to the bar. When Acosta returned later that night, Freddy greeted him with a smile and offered congratulations for the way he had handled the police. Freddy counted out $500 in odd bills from the pack he wore around his waist and, in handing them to Acosta, said, "Let's do it again."

Doing it again was exactly what Juan Acosta had in mind. Freddy said that he would pay for referrals of other bulls or cows, so, a week later, Acosta went back to the Tierra Blanca with a friend named Jesus Martinez. Freddy met the men in the parking lot and went through the usual drill: He checked the coverage on Martinez's policy, sized up the man's 1982 Buick, planned the crash, then set about rustling up some cows for the other car. He phoned a friend named José Gonzalez to tell him that the accident they had discussed earlier in the day was on and that Gonzalez should come down to the bar as soon as possible. Gonzalez brought his brother Nelson with him as well as a woman friend of his (all of whom knew one another other, and Freddy, from their hometown in Guatemala). Freddy got his cousin to drive the bull car; the two men had lived together and been close friends for most of the three or four years that they had been in the United States. Victor Donado, the driver of Acosta's car in the previous week's staging, helped execute this crash, also. After the first attempt failed to create as much damage as Freddy wanted, Victor got into his van and rammed the cow car a few times in a dark part of the Tierra Blanca parking lot. The cars were then driven to a nearby 7-Eleven store, where the debris from the initial crash was spread out as if the accident had occurred there. Then the police were called to write a report. Again Freddy was pleased with the results. Back at the Tierra Blanca, the men settled accounts, and Freddy asked Acosta if he would like to recruit some more friends. Acosta, excited about the prospect, replied that he "had a lot of friends" and that he would be back to the bar with more of them soon.

The next time Acosta met Freddy at the Tierra Blanca, he did indeed bring along some friends. But, like himself, they were all undercover officers working for the State of California in a special division—the Bureau of Fraudulent Claims (BFC)—formed ten years earlier to fight the accident fakers. "Juan Acosta" was really agent Danny Naranjo, and his friend "Jesus Martinez" was Henry Avina, one of the most experienced undercover men working staged accident cases anywhere in the country. The officers had learned of the Tierra Blanca stagings the previous month from another state agency. Narcotics detectives had staked out the Tierra Blanca to gather evidence of drug trafficking, but what they saw instead was the strange spectacle of men in the parking lot debating, then crashing cars. An informant for the narcotics officers learned that another accident was going to be staged in the parking lot of the Tierra Blanca the next night, so Danny Naranjo of the BFC led a surveillance team to film it. It was a typical Freddy crash: two cars smashed together intentionally followed by men collecting the broken glass and plastic in bags to be used later. A few weeks later Naranjo met with one of Freddy's gang at a Denny's restaurant and learned the extent of the faking activity. The informant provided Naranjo with his first introduction to Freddy, then Naranjo took it from there, "stiffing" in one undercover officer after the next in a style perfected by the BFC to build a case against accident rings.

In February 1991, Naranjo (as Acosta) met Freddy at the Tierra Blanca to do another accident. Among his friends this time were undercover officers Ron Carrillo and Tom Sarinana as well as hidden-cameramen for the ABC News magazine *PrimeTime Live*, who brought along some friends of their own:

several million viewers nationwide who, as the correspondent later stated, were going "to see for [themselves] how these staged accidents work." Freddy was late to his television debut. Naranjo had to call him at home from the bar then wait around for a half hour or so. And then it was show time: As the news cameras rolled, Naranjo and Sarinana stood in the parking lot of the Tierra Blanca chatting up a taciturn and businesslike Freddy about money he owed them for past accidents. Then they discussed the logistics of the present crash:

Sarinana:	Right here's where you want [the damage], huh, Freddy?
Freddy:	No, I was thinking in the back.
Sarinana:	Oh, in the back? Okay. Sure. A rear-ender?
Naranjo:	A rear-ender, yeah.
Sarinana:	That's more for the neck injuries, huh?
Freddy:	Yeah. We can get the money sooner.

With the plan set, everyone drove a few blocks from the bar to an empty parking lot in front of a mortuary. Naranjo and Sarinana lined up the cars, then everyone waited as Victor Donado crashed them. This night Victor was dressed in a white sweatsuit and clean white cap like a sinister Good Humor ice cream man on a drunk; Freddy called him Don Juan. Victor gave the cow car one shot from behind. But, this being television, and the damage not being serious enough, Victor was forced to do a second take, jolting the cow car into the mortuary wall unintentially. ("Is that good, or do we need one more?" Sarinana asked Freddy while evaluating the damage from the second hit. "You want to do one more?") A few minutes later Sarinana double-checked with Freddy on the story he should tell the police: "Okay, so it was eight-thirty. I was driving on Beverly, right past Atlantic, and I dropped something and when I looked up, he was there and I hit him?" Freddy nodded in agreement. Then there was the matter of the money, which the detectives discussed with Freddy in a way that the ABC producers could not have scripted better themselves, so neatly did it reduce the fake accident business to just a few simple ideas:

Sarinana:	And you'll go ahead and pay me a thousand on Friday then, right?
Freddy:	Yes.
Sarinana:	Okay. That sounds real good. Real good.
Freddy:	That's nice and easy money.
Sarinana:	Oh, yeah. It's a nice way to make some money.

For a few moments—maybe a minute and a half of air time—television had captured much of the street-level reality of L.A.'s personal injury underworld: strangers, mostly immigrants, recruited at the last minute to crash cars in parking lots, to feign injury for police or insurance adjusters, then to pocket some money. How much? They were probably not really sure until they got it. Afterward, they might go to a medical clinic to be "treated." This could mean sitting in a room with a hot pack, or lying on a therapeutic roller-bed, or maybe undergoing something more sophisticated, such as electrical muscle stimulation of various sorts, or traction. But more often it was just a matter of signing a name in a log book, then leaving, day after day for a few months; or else signing all at once in different colored ink and never coming back. "When you do this type of business," Freddy explained to the undercover officers at the outset, "you need to make time to go to the clinic." Later the officers refused to go to the clinic, and Freddy pleaded with them to change their minds: "Please, I ask you to go to the clinic. . . . You can get some money out of it, but you need to sacrifice and go to the clinic twenty or thirty times." You can lead a cow down the path to easy money, frustrated cappers like Freddy might have lamented, but you cannot make them go to a medical clinic four or five times a week for three months to submit to unnecessary physical rehabilitation.

At the time of the Tierra Blanca accidents, the amount of money floating around Southern California's personal injury underworld was estimated in the hundreds of millions each year. And if other "softer" personal injury frauds were added, the number was closer to a billion. The real money was not changing hands in the Tierra Blanca, of course; it was concentrated in the bank accounts of the lawyers and doctors who bought cases from cappers. The professionals, overwhelmingly Anglos, were central to the success of the schemes, but they were always elsewhere in the fake claims process. They were almost mythic in their ability to be on the minds of cappers and cows everywhere, yet to be nowhere at all when official investigations began: Most of the people who sat in Freddy's cow cars would never know the attorneys or the doctors as anything more than generic physical descriptions, having gone to the offices only once or twice and dealt with a clerk or assistant exclusively. At the Bureau of Fraudulent Claims, most investigators knew the names and addresses of the biggest fraud-mill attorneys and doctors, but could not get to them in any significant way until the early 1990s, when they finally collared Myron Toplitzky and Jorge Taracena (attorney partners who bought thousands of staged cases from a host of cappers throughout the 1980s) and Warren Finn and his partner Alan Shapiro, who reportedly tried to have his lead capper, Jorge Ventura Santamaria, killed to prevent Ventura's testifying against him. In the personal injury underworld, contact between the street-level actors and the white-collar professionals was not necessary or usual. When all went well, names of injured passengers rose up from the street to law offices and medical clinics like answered prayers. And, on the street, cappers like Freddy invoked the names of attorneys and doctors in a magical incantation whose only meaning was money. Manufacturing profits from the nothingness of claimed pains in the neck and back, to paraphrase Joan Didion's words on the enduring conviction of making something of nothing in Los Angeles, was the one narrative in which everyone in the personal injury underworld could participate.

The seemingly accidental rise of the staged auto accident industry in America was on purpose: not the result of the failure of a state plan to manage the enormous negative consequences of mass automobile travel, but precisely the result of a *lack* of such a plan altogether; not the singlehanded invention of individuals, more the unchecked handiwork of the invisible hand of free market forces—like the very forces that shaped the famous sprawl of the region in which the underworld grew to its greatest dimensions.

By the time Los Angeles became the nation's accident fraud capital, it had long been home to more cars per person than anywhere in the country— since the 1920s when the region had one car for every 1.6 people, a level which the rest of the nation did not reach until the 1950s. The city had long been home to more lawyers and chiropractors per square inch than anywhere in the world. Los Angeles also had the bodies to sit in the cars for the crashes. During World War II, the federal government bused in Mexican laborers under the "Bracero" (literally "arms") program; the migratory routes and patterns thus begun would be followed for decades by immigrants, legal and illegal. In the 1970s and 1980s, the city became the main destination of the new immigration from Latin America, Southeast Asia, and the nations of the Pacific Rim. Boosters hailed L.A. as America's first "world city" while others more skeptical swiped at the city as the "capital of the Third World." To the accident stagers, the new immigration was simply a boon to business.

Los Angeles was not only the ideal venue for large-scale accident frauds, but its very shape—the lack of a vital central downtown, the famed "metro-sea" of sixty suburbs in search of a city—seemed a perfect emblem for how the personal injury underworld had evolved in the second half of this century: The ungainly spread of the L.A. metropolitan region resulted from unmanaged urban growth just as the personal injury underworld in America grew from the lack of a decent social plan to deal adequately with the compensation of accident victims. At the heart of both lay the fact of the automobile: The irrational attachment to cars over most other mass transit options made L.A. the nation's greatest urban "autopia"; and the laissez-faire attitude toward the automobile's routinely destructive consequences created the conditions for an illegal market in faked claims. Urban planners, remarking on L.A.'s emphasis on freeways to the exclusion of other transit options, decried the "uncoordinated, unplanned, unreasoned, and uneconomic spreading out of the metropolitan area by a series of private decisions on the part of speculators and developers."[2] Legal scholars who looked at the sprawl of low-level personal injury law on the American landscape saw much the same thing: "What emerges . . . is the total absence of any rational scheme for compensating victims of accidental injury in the United States—no integration or coordination of existing mechanisms, and no underlying philosophy based on clearly defined social objectives. . . . It is a 'system' that has evolved more by accident than by design."[3] Just how accidental it was that Americans would look to the market—to private interests such as insurers and plaintiffs' attorneys—for the solution to the social problem of increasing death and injury from auto accidents is a matter of interpretation. Americans seem to put faith in the market to cure all ills. That an enormously profitable underworld in faked claims would grow out of this free market, however, seems less accidental than inevitable. And that the capital of this underworld would come to be Los Angeles seems almost natural.

The history of Los Angeles is shot through with grand-scale frauds and deceptions. The city itself was made habitable by a water diversion scam; populated by railroad and real estate insider dealings; made rich by petroleum speculators; and made famous by seventy-five years of make-believe on false-front soundstages. With the auto accident scams, the means of fraud became democratized. Where once only a handful of Hungtingtons, Mulhollands, and Otises were in a position to create value from dirt, now cappers and cows could manufacture dollars from dents in alleyways and parking lots. In contrast to the exclusivity of the Hollywood star system, here was a staging industry built on the performances of a cast of thousands willing to sit in cars for crashes, then to play bit parts in predictable medicolegal dramas.

Before large-scale auto accident faking helped make Los Angeles the capital of America's personal injury underworld, the city had passed through all of the different phases of the underworld's development. Back in the years just after World War I, floppers such as Ila May Boggs beat Los Angeles streetcar companies out of untold thousands of dollars from faked falls. ("I have never had a case which is such a plain open-and-shut bit of fakery as this," a judge was moved to say before sentencing the Boggs to a term in jail. "Never.")[4]

In the early 1930s, local bar associations campaigned against ambulance chasers as much as their counterparts in the East. In later decades an office of the insurance industry's Claims Bureau was set up in the region to fight "claim evils," and newspaper reporters uncovered whippie mills.[5] Various oddball self-mutilation schemes occurred in Los Angeles, also, as elsewhere. In 1958, for example, Jerome Alan Rader, an aircraft worker, had himself drugged unconscious, arranged for his limbs to be smashed with a baseball bat and a padded brick—then to have the same done to his wife and a fellow aircraft worker—before all three were to be placed at the site of a Buick that had been pushed over a cliff. (When asked by a coconspirator whether there was any chance of being caught, Rader was secretly tape-recorded as replying: "Hell, no. No one would ever believe that I was crazy enough to actually have my bones fractured to set up a phony accident.")[6]

Word about organized auto accident gangs in the city did not come until the early 1960s, when a newspaper published a series of articles that began with the claim that fake accident claims had become a "multimillion-dollar-a-year 'business' in the Los Angeles Area." Some ten years later, the city again got a glimpse of organized accident staging during the Friends of the Friendless hearings, and investigation into staged accident gangs in Los Angeles was beefed up steadily thereafter. At the L.A. County District Attorney's office, a group of investigators began to specialize in these cases. By the mid-1970s they developed a picture of what was happening. In addition to the usual runners and solicitors working for attorneys, they discovered rings of thirty to forty people who were engaged in several different types of "accidents through prearrangement." Some rings crashed cars intentionally in traffic, one complicit car into another; and others worked strictly paper accidents where damage was created to support a made-up collision.[7] The structure of the rings was similar to what state investigators would later find in the Freddy case: Cappers arranged the accidents and sold them to law firms through office managers. (Charles Kelson, a fraud investigator with the L.A. District Attorney's office, called them "super cappers.") Then the office managers arranged for the clients to build up their claims at a medical clinic. The dollar figures were different in the 1970s—cappers got $200 to $250 per person, compared to the several thousand dollars that Freddy would later get per cow. Some of these earlier cappers actually tried to solicit victims of genuine accidents before "resorting to prearrangement." But the bottom line was the same: "The variations contrived to defraud insurance companies are endless," Kelson wrote, "and [are] only limited by the imagination of the participants." And imaginations were quite active.

Some L.A. accident fakers from the 1970s were so brazen as to write their own "Scam" theme song, which began: "S is for the settlements we work for/ C is for the claims we love to fake/A is for the accidents we engineer/ M is for the money that we make."[8]

The investigative methods used by Kelson and the other D.A. investigators were basic: They charted all suspicious accidents, then looked for patterns. If a pattern was found, they used surveillance or undercover officers to develop the evidence necessary for prosecution. Agents at the insurance industry's ICPI also used charts. So did claims investigation specialists at individual insurance companies; on occasion, private detectives working on contract to insurers used charts, too. Sometimes one chart could evidence a pattern. In the case of the Hungarian ring, however, many charts needed to be combined. Laszlo Daroczi, an investigator with the D.A.'s office in the late 1970s, kept a chart for several years on the stagers who, like him, had come to America from Hungary after the failed 1956 uprising. Fred Stewart, a prosecutor with the district attorney's office, also kept charts on the Hungarians. His office was a checkerboard of file boxes labeled with Hungarian names. On one wall of his office hung a map of Los Angeles on which he marked suspected staged accidents with little circles—a different color for the stagings of the different "cells" of the Hungarian organization. ("One of them might drive along Sunset until he spotted an expensive car sure to be insured," Stewart explained the types of crashes he charted. "Then, he'd drive in front and, wham, hit the brakes. . . .")[9] Private investigator Richard Stenzel kept his own chart on the Hungarians. He and his partner wrote a handful of names in the centers of circles with dozens of lines radiating out in all directions to other names and great, arcing lines connecting the different circles to one another in a complicated geometry of conspiracy. Agents of the ICPI assembled similar charts on the Hungarians. When all of the charts were combined, a picture began to become clear of the first major, documented fake auto accident group to dominate Southern California's emerging personal injury underworld.

The Hungarian ring was enormous, even by later standards. At different times during the 1970s, the ring was believed to have involved several hundred people who helped stage thousands of faked claims worth many tens of millions of dollars. For two and a half years, beginning early in 1976, Investigator Daroczi, Prosecutor Stewart, and others made it their business to learn all that they could about the group. Occasionally the group would target unsuspecting drivers. Most of the crashes, however, were cases in which cappers arranged for two cars to lock bumpers in a carefully scripted way.

Everything a Hungarian capper needed to know about the business—executing the crashes, buying the right insurance coverage, and negotiating settlements—was consolidated into an instruction manual, *They've Got You Covered*, written under the patriotic pen name "Gary Hunn," which spelled the name of the author's homeland when the names were read in reverse. Xerox copies of the thin instructional volume were found stuffed in glove compartments and rolled up in back pockets all over Southern California. The book left the matter of whom to recruit for the crashes to individual cappers. Sometimes they asked family, friends, or neighbors; other times they might try to find people who would work for the least pay.

"Istvan," one of the Hungarian ring's cappers, apparently preferred people with drug problems willing to take almost any amount as long as they were paid up front in cash. Robert Sterling was typical of the drivers Istvan recruited for accidents. In 1975 Sterling was in his early thirties with dull blue eyes and a big mustache. His face bore the record of his hard living, and his several driver's licenses told the story of his westward drift over the years from New York to New Mexico to San Francisco before the trail ended in an apartment in Venice Beach. There Sterling met Istvan one afternoon, when Istvan came to explain how he could make $300 by renting a truck and running into a woman's car. Sterling took $50 in cash from Istvan right away, then went out and smashed a U-Haul into a 1968 Pontiac. Years later Sterling would confess to private investigators about what he had done. When pressed for information, he said that he did not know much about Istvan, only that he was "somewhere in the chain of command" of a much larger organization run by Hungarians. Sterling had heard Steve mention some of the other names, but he could only dimly remember one: "Simon."

To insurance investigators in Southern California and around the country, Simon was believed to be the leader of the Hungarian Ring. ("I can't prove he's the head of this Hungarian crowd," the head of ICPI's Western Regional office said. But "it would appear that he is.")[10] Simon operated from a plain office in a residential area of North Hollywood. He reportedly worked the phones, mostly, negotiating settlements with insurance adjusters whom he got to know on a first-name basis over the years. He also gave instructions to field lieutenants such as Istvan and at least a half dozen or so others. Cappers in the Hungarian ring were each the leaders of their little cells, but all were thought to be "tithing into the center," according to Stewart, meaning paying a percentage of their profits to Simon. The organization proved to be very efficient. "There are all kinds of insurance fraud rings, probably involving every ethnic group you can think of," Stewart explained back in 1978. "But there's nobody better at it than the Hungarians."[11] After just a few years in the business, Simon and a few of his cappers were doing exceedingly well: They were earning six-figure annual incomes, living in exclusive developments in the Hollywood hills, and driving the nicest cars. For many of them, it was an American success story. "Some of the Hungarians in this ring came here with nothing," Stewart observed. "Their skills wouldn't permit them to lead the kind of life they wanted. They found insurance and it has proved to be a bonanza."

The Hungarian ring stayed together so long primarily because everyone was making money and had no reason to quit; another reason was Simon's hold on his cappers, which was reported to be "tight." Prosecutors found it difficult to get any of the Hungarians to testify against one another. "They only talk to each other and they sure won't talk to authorities about each other," Stewart said in 1977. "It's very difficult to prove an accident was staged, unless someone sees it or one of the participants talks. And nobody sees them and nobody talks."[12] The few crashes that were ultimately prosecuted mostly involved non-Hungarians such as Robert Sterling; or the Guatemalan girlfriend of one of the core group members, who told all she knew about the ring after the two broke off their relationship; or Timothy John Gillespie, who had once been given $600 to crash a rented Ford Pinto into a 1963 Buick. When the rental car agency went after Gillespie for wrecking one of their cars, Gillespie went to the D.A.'s office and provided a confession that helped get a conviction and a multiyear jail term for one of the more successful Hungarian cappers. Prosecutor Stewart called the sentence a "blockbuster." Later, however, Stewart showed his frustration as he struggled to get the jail time he wanted in the case: "We have a situation here where it just cries out for a State Prison sentence," he pleaded at a sentencing hearing for one of the Hungarian cappers. "I'm quoting the probation officer: 'It would be ludicrous to consider this defendant suitable for probation.' . . . We've granted him asylum from a communist country, and what does he do? He turns around and rips off society to such an extent it becomes appalling."[13] Stewart got the sentence he wanted in this case, but, on the whole, his best efforts over several years amounted to nothing more than a few dents in the total Hungarian operation. No one ever got to Simon—not private investigators, the D.A.'s office, nor the anonymous gunmen who fired a round of shots into Simon's bedroom window in November 1984 during an apparent predawn assassination attempt.[14]

The Hungarian ring was an incredible case. Some in law enforcement circles called their fake accident activities the biggest species of organized crime of any sort in all of California.[15] But, in retrospect, it was just one of several cases from the late 1970s that indicated the accident racketeers were in Los Angeles to stay and that a formal response from the state was needed to slow their progress; stopping them dead was already an impossibility. One case investigated at the same time as the Hungarian ring was important mainly because it confirmed so much of what was known about the accident scams: Stagers used "battering rams" to crash cars in Long Beach, or else crafted strictly paper accidents, then made claims through the office of an attorney in West Hollywood. The attorney then either ordered fake medical reports when he needed them, or made up his own medical reports and sent them to an insurance adjuster who was working for him on the inside.[16]

Another of the major cases of the late 1970s was important for all that it suggested investigators did *not* know about the region's growing fake accident underworld and could not have guessed. The stagers in this case were based in California, crashing cars in remote areas late at night; but they also operated in Nevada, Michigan, and Minnesota. The group did not involve the usual players: cappers, attorneys, doctors. It consisted mainly of students—several hundred of whom were in the country on special visas from countries in the Middle East. The most sensational part of the story— reported on the front pages of the New York Times, L.A. Times, and Washington Post—was that they were believed to be Palestine Liberation Organization (PLO) sympathizers who were using the money to fund operations overseas.[17] The deputy chief of the California Highway Patrol (CHP) expressed his belief about the nature of the ring: "Members of the group live in low-rent apartments of poor quality, not the kind of place that people would ordinarily live in with the kind of money they were getting. It appears the money was going somewhere else." Another investigator was more forthright: "There's no question about it," the man told the New York Times. "These people essentially are just front people for the PLO. They told me their job is to raise money to support their soldiers in the Middle East. They've learned the vulnerabilities of our insurance companies and they exploit them to the point it has been paying off like a slot machine." The CHP, the FBI, and the ICPI could never conclusively trace the money, however, and only a few of the alleged ring members were ever arrested. Later claims about the PLO ring's activities were substantially scaled down. "We have no evidence that money from Arab insurance claimants in this country is going to the PLO," ICPI director James Ahern stated in May 1977. "But it certainly is a possibility."[18]

In the end, the story of the PLO ring may have been as much about American hysteria over Middle East terrorism as it was about accident frauds. The early television coverage of the story, in particular, did everything but suggest that Yassir Arafat was scripting swoop-and-squats from an underground bunker on the West Bank. Still, for the CHP, which first detected the ring's activities, the case was the biggest fake accident case it had ever handled, even if it never was able to solve the mystery of the money. Lieutenant Glenn Sewell of the CHP had been in charge of the case, and, when it was over, he began to see the need for more investigations into accident stagings in the state. For years Sewell and a handful of other CHP officers had become fairly experienced detecting patterns in styles of reported crashes, spotting similarities in names from one accident to the next, or noticing the same car turning up in several accidents within a short period of time. Stagers did not have to be as ingenious or as well organized as the Hungarians to succeed in a climate where few people were ever prosecuted and only a handful of investigators from the D.A.'s office or the CHP or the BFC were even working cases. If one or two attorneys managed to get caught in connection with accident faking, some seventy-five or a hundred were thought to be out there working with impunity and little fear of investigation. "It's so easy," admitted ICPI director Ahern in 1979. "It's pathetic."[19]

With attention focused on accident staging after the PLO case, Glenn Sewell of the CHP saw an opportunity to solidify a commitment from the state to pursue fake claims on a permanent basis. In 1979, due in large part to Sewell's hard sell of the idea in Sacramento, the state legislature recognized auto insurance frauds as "one of the biggest and fasting growing" crimes in California, and created the BFC to help slow the growth. California was not first to start an insurance fraud bureau—Florida held that distinction, and New York also had one before 1979. But California's bureau would be the biggest and the most focused on claims frauds. Fifteen years after its founding, the BFC, renamed the Fraud Division in 1992, would have more than 165 investigators, each fully empowered to do surveillance and undercover work (as they did in the Freddy case), and to serve search warrants, interrogate suspects, carry guns, and make arrests. In a given year, more than 10,000 suspected fraudulent auto accident claims would be reported to the Fraud Division by insurers, who were required to do so by law. Of these, hundreds would be assigned for investigation, and a few dozen would be developed for prosecution every few months. All claims would be entered into a massive statewide computer database that was for the state what the databases of the Index System and the National

Insurance Crime Bureau were to the rest of the nation. Beyond just collecting the claims, the Fraud Division submitted them to analysis by a "fraud intelligence specialist team" (FIST) which prepared "target packages" for bureau supervisors to study and evaluate.[20] The Fraud Division would even publish its own quarterly magazine. By the early 1990s, the division had become one of the premier law enforcement groups in California and perhaps the most experienced and successful body of criminal insurance investigators in the country, if not the world.[21]

Back in 1979, however, the Bureau of Fraudulent Claims was a big name for a very small operation. Glenn Sewell had taken a leave of absence from the Highway Patrol in order to run the BFC, but he was given few resources to work with. There was only funding enough for five investigators to cover the entire state, and initially none of these officers was allowed to carry a gun or exercise any more police powers than a claims adjuster. In the north, Clarke Walker worked a beat that covered eleven Bay Area counties, and he did it largely by himself.[22] In Southern California, the state's effort to fight the fakers boiled down to two men, Ron Warthen and Jerry Treadway, who alone were responsible for investigating all of the suspected frauds from Santa Barbara south to the Mexican border. In May 1979 Warthen and Treadway were set up in an anonymous office on Wilshire Boulevard and told to take it from there. "We showed up one day with desks and a secretary and we didn't know quite what to do," Treadway later remembered. "In those days, I probably saw more of Ron than my own family." Warthen was the senior of the two men, with years of insurance fraud–fighting experience. Over the next decade, Warthen (along with a tenacious and talented prosecutor named Albert MacKenzie) would become the personification of the fight on fraud in Southern California. Warthen and Treadway operated blind at first, without the benefit of fraud specialist teams providing neat packages of cases and charts on suspected rings. In their first few months on the job, they had to go door to door at local insurance companies for referrals, then to prosecutors to explain who they were and what they were trying to do. Then they had to hit the bricks to find the fakers. "If we could have had instant expertise," Treadway said in hindsight, "it would have been like shooting fish in a barrel." As it happened, though, the early catch was slow.

In these first few years of the BFC, Warthen and Treadway investigated cases "historically." This meant charting suspected fake accidents, like their forerunners in the D.A.'s office and their counterparts at the ICPI, then looking for patterns or queer details or the clichéd story that just didn't smell right. One of the earliest historical cases grew out of the curious discovery that the claimant's alleged addresses checked out as runways at Los Angeles International Airport and a golf course in El Segundo.[23] Historical work often got investigators in the door of a ring, but then some regular old police work was necessary to develop informants and to coax the confessions that made a case. For a time, in fact, many of the biggest and best cases worked by BFC investigators in Southern California derived in one way or another from the work of a single informant—a "professional snitch"—named Kay Mitchell. Mitchell was a creature of the streets—"a real down-and-outer with holes in his clothes and a beat-up Ford Grenada," one investigator recalled—who had found a way to make a decent living by providing information on drug dealers, prostitutes, loan sharks, or whomever else he thought would interest federal officials. When he happened to come across some information about the buying and selling of faked accident claims, Mitchell found his way to Ron Warthen and Jerry Treadway at the BFC. Mitchell was set up as an accident capper. Over five or six years, Treadway worked as Mitchell's case agent, following Mitchell through whatever situations he could get involved with. "He'd call me and say he was having a meeting with so and so and I'd go leave my family and sit out in the van on Sunset Boulevard and tape him having dinner with cappers. . . . I think one year he was responsible for 80 percent of our arrests."

At one point, Kay Mitchell managed to get Treadway stiffed into a group of stagers who were active in L.A. and San Diego but also had connections in Detroit. Treadway, born in Arkansas, schooled in Russian, and trained in Army Intelligence, was admittedly "without the look or the language" to make it in urban undercover work. Nevertheless, he played the part of the owner of an old Chevy Impala who heard from a friend that he could make a few dollars by having an accident. With BFC supervisors parked in a surveillance van down the street, Treadway met the stagers in a largely deserted residential neighborhood. He then stood by while they put one of their drivers into his car. "Leave it to the pros," one joked as another took the wheel. The man drove the car to the end of the street, then made a U-turn and came back to rear-end an old Camaro that was driving slowly in anticipation of the impact. The crash itself seemed almost anticlimactic—a momentary thud of one car into the other—and, in this case, it was not even sufficient to create substantial enough damage for the claim. After a brief caucus around the cars in the middle of the street, the stagers reset the scene. Ring members watched from the sidewalk as the cars neared one another again, then cheered on impact and exchanged celebratory slaps of hands and pats on backs. A cheer also rose up in the surveillance van down the street, where BFC agents were getting it all on tape. The evidence helped indict seventeen people two years later; several were convicted and sentenced to terms in federal prison. The footage of Treadway's staging became part of a BFC training video—the Body Slammers.

To an automobile-dependent city like Los Angeles, the staged accident in which ring members targeted innocent motorists for a rear-end collision was like a mugging in a walking city like New York: a brief, sometimes violent clash, usually between people of different social classes, for the purpose of transferring money from one to the other.

Of course, the people most closely involved rarely conceived of the accidents in this way. The fakers saw themselves more as con artists who were not really hurting anyone; and investigators generally accepted the white-collar tag for their work. But, as swoop-and-squats became more common, some reporters began to adopt a tone usually reserved for more traditional street crime. "If you're involved in an accident you believe to have been staged, remain calm," a reporter for *Los Angeles Magazine* advised his upscale readership. The passage began somewhat hysterically—"It's open season on the streets of L.A., and anybody driving a car is potentially fair game." The tone was reminiscent of a 1978 novel about a freeway sniper in which one investigating officer says to his partner: "Everyone on the freeway's afraid. Or crazy. Or pissed off. And they're all bait, Al. They're all bait."[24] The reporter went on to adapt the standard urban survival advice to fit the fakers. "Remember, they're not after you, they're after your insurance-policy number."[25] Another feature from the same time—"STAGED-WRECK FRAUD THRIVES IN AUTO-RICH L.A. SUBURBS"—related the stories of two successful career women being targeted by gangs for crashes, then passed along an investigator's warning that any "affluent consumers driving nice cars" were "a stager's dream come true."[26] In 1984 a Los Angeles-based insurance company launched an extensive "community education campaign"—Operation Anti-Scam—explaining steps for motorists to take to keep from being victims of the new criminal threat of accident stagers.[27]

As the menace of the swoop-and-squatters on highways and roads became more widely understood, the public was introduced to a few of them by name. In one article readers met "Derek," who "says he was recruited at a car wash with the promise of a quick $300" and "soon was part of a ring that deliberately crashed automobiles into cars of unsuspecting motorists."[28] Another piece told of "Bobby," the capper of swoop-and squat accidents who "recruits right off the street, almost always in depressed neighborhoods."[29]

"Jerry," a capper who appeared on a national news program in disguise, played up the Hollywood aspects of his profession. "I would call myself a director," he said, "and the place where I [stage accidents], the studio."[30] And then there was "Mustang," who talked about the roadways of Los Angeles as the scene of an almost Darwinian struggle between stagers and their potential victims. "Basically," he explained, "it's the hunter and the hunted."[31] Derek, Bobby, Jerry, and Mustang had each come to reporters by way of the Bureau of Fraudulent Claims, whose agents had developed the evidence to prosecute them. In just a few years, the BFC had not only grown in size—between 1979 and 1985, the number of agents statewide had more than tripled—but it had also developed a more detailed knowledge about the stagings than any group ever had done before. "We've found rings that involve up to 75, 100 people," Ron Warthen said, summarizing some of the bureau's new understanding of the almost "paramilitary" structure of some accident organizations. "They have professional training manuals, driving classes that teach the finer points of staging accidents. They work in shifts, with designated territories. They even have quotas to meet."[32]

In the early years of the BFC, when undercover infiltration of rings was rare, much of what was known about the organization of accident frauds came from the collected confessions of participants: the Dereks, Bobbys, and Mustangs, and, most extensively, from a capper who identified himself only as Dave. At one point in the early 1980s, Dave sat alone on one side of a large conference table, dressed in a striped short-sleeve leisure shirt, and answered questions about his life in the fake accident trade posed to him by Ron Warthen and Clarke Walker of the BFC. "Depending on the mood I was in, or on how well other stagings had gone that day, I might have to do three accidents a day," Dave said. "But otherwise I preferred one quick one in a matter of hours and that's it." Over the course of a lengthy interview, Dave walked the investigators through his operation.

> I bought most of my cars used from the newspaper. I preferred Cadillacs, models '70 to '76 because they could take more damage. We called them "buckets," and all of them together were my "fleet." I would be out in a bucket looking for someone making some kind of vehicle or traffic violation—U-turn, failing to yield, running a stop sign—and I would just hit him. That's what we call a "ride down." I would go out to Beverly Hills or Westwood at rush hour or lunchtime looking for people making violations, not really paying too much attention to me: We called 'em "vic's." Then I would hit 'em in the rear quarter panel area so as to make

it look like they was more at fault than they actually were. I just basically wanted a dent in the car to show there was an accident, then I would fake the injuries. If I had to bait them, I would. On several occasions, when I've been riding all day and just didn't get anything, I would fake stop, just tell the people to come on—pretend like I was looking for an address or something, or wave them on—then, once they're out there, I hit 'em. They'd get out all angry and say I told them to go. But I'd just deny it and ask for their insurance number, and they'd give it to me. Most people don't think there are people like me out there.

Dave continued.

Actually, there's hundreds of people like myself in Los Angeles. I couldn't put a definite number to it, but every section of the city has what we call a "crew." I, for one, had a crew of ten active working people under my direction. I also had people I called "ghosts" to sit in the cars just for the ride-downs, but they wouldn't get any of the real money. I would just tell them we're going to the beach or something, they were as unsuspecting as the "vics" we hit. I would be the head man in charge of the crew. I would set everything up—the driver's license, the attorneys, the doctors, everything you needed for an accident. It's common knowledge to know which attorneys to go to. At any one time, I had twenty to twenty-five attorneys, ten chiropractors and seventeen medical doctors. And you meet new ones each and every day. They'd pay me $400 to $450 as front money for each person from my ride-downs. If you have a good rapport with the attorneys or doctors, they will finance you, help you get a bigger fleet, maintain larger crews. I had associates who had this kind of backing. They were sophisticated, organized. They could turn a $20,000 investment from an attorney into $200,000 in just a few weeks of accidents, doing two to three a day, five days a week. I'd say there were about fifty stagers in L.A. doing it on this basis.[33]

In a city known for its extremes of poverty and wealth, there seemed no more stark clash of haves and have-nots than when a stager and his crew locked bumpers with a "vic's" Mercedes. Dave and his associates in the ride-down trade were an unwelcome nightmare reality behind the dream that many Southern Californians had about their roads and their cars. Many people saw their car as the ultimate instrument of freedom—*freedom to do* things (go where they wanted, when they wanted) and *freedom from* other things (mainly the crime and social problems of the "inner cities" from which many had fled). Powered by the endlessly moving wheels of America's cars, a popular Ford Motor advertisement from the 1950s projected, "the nation is steadily traveling beyond the troubles of this century, constantly heading toward finer tomorrows." And no one traveled faster or more often in this direction than the people of Southern California. But then trouble itself in the form of the swoop-and-squatters and drive-downers got a car of its own and headed out on that same road to materialize a different dream of the good life.

For everyone who believed in some way that his or her car was an extension of their house, and that both were safe from the crime of the old central cities, Dave in his buckets shattered peace of mind. For all those who felt themselves at the height of civilization behind the wheels of their cars— riding unimpeded from single-family homes to the places of their choosing, with music and temperature adjusted to comfort and taste—Mustang the crasher was there to reimpose a primitive order of the hunter and the hunted. The language of survival was appropriate: The auto accident gang was a perfect evolutionary adaptation of the street gang idea to the conditions of a city where few people actually congregated or mixed on the street. Only in America could a mugging at thirty miles an hour be imagined. But only in Los Angeles could it become so common that a regular notice in the local automobile club and in insurance magazines offered checklists of "staged accident warning signs" (car in front slams on brakes; older car; more than two passengers); and warnings on "who's likely to be a target" (women, older people, commercial vehicles); and a glove compartment guide for the driver who believes he or she has been set up for a crash.

By the mid-1980s, the BFC had learned whatever could be learned through informants like Kay Mitchell or confessions from cappers like Mustang or Dave. Historical investigations where investigators charted claims histories also had been useful in developing a number of good cases. But there was something decidedly secondhand about all of this. Recording a confession with a capper after the fact was different than meeting "Freddy" in a parking lot to discuss how to crash cars, and good prosecutions required the latter. At a certain point, the problem for the BFC shifted from needing to understand what frauds were being perpetrated to needing to find a way to take the rings down from the inside. Bureau supervisors would later call this "being proactive." Back in the mid-1980s, though, the phrase had only one practical translation: Get a wire on investigator Henry Avina, get him a car and an insurance ("pretext") policy, and send him into the field to meet the bad guys and stage accidents.

If the history of the Bureau of Fraudulent Claims were ever divided into eras, much of the first five or six years could accurately be described as Pre-Henry. Born in Guadalajara, Mexico, in the early 1950s and educated through college in Southern California, Henry Avina helped expand the bureau's vocabulary of accident frauds from buckets, ghosts, and hammers and nails, to bulls and cows. Avina understood the workings of the personal injury underworld as well as anyone. During the decade before he joined the BFC, he had done hundreds of undercover assignments for the State Medical Board and hundreds more for a different state agency that dealt mainly with faked disability claims. Just as important, though, Avina understood the culture of the accident stagers. He knew what they cared about, what they might be thinking while standing around waiting for cars to collide, how backing off from doing an accident on a given occasion might help win their confidence. Even after arrests were made, many subjects of Avina's undercover work made it a point to say that they were not angry at him, that he was just doing his job, and that they considered him a sort of friend whom they would cooperate with if asked.

The Henry Avina period at the BFC is not easy to date precisely. For several years before he actually joined the bureau, Avina was frequently on loan to the BFC from other state agencies in order to help work specific cases. Back in 1984, for example, Avina was brought in to help the BFC, the ICPI, and a large task force of federal agents crack what was then the biggest accident ring ever uncovered in Southern California: a group of stagers from Long Beach who initially came to the attention of the Secret Service for suspected counterfeiting of $20 bills, but who turned out to be minting more money through accidents involving professional "hitters" and "crackers."[34] One of the group's innovations was to cause crashes with cars driven by men who had just picked up prostitutes in order to embarrass them into admitting fault immediately. Avina, who was then an investigator for the State Medical Board, was sent to the ring's main chiropractor to document unnecessary treatments; the undercover work would later help put the man in jail.[35] At the time, the case was described as an "unprecedented blow" against Southern California's "highly organized" fake accident trade. And the head of a federal insurance fraud task force described the investigation itself as the biggest ever mounted, with thirty people working the case around the clock in shifts and postal inspectors brought in from five states to help make the arrests. But in the next few years, Avina would play an integral role in a number of investigations that knocked this case off the charts. "In those days, I grew my hair long, wore a scraggly goatee, an old baseball cap, cheap Levi's," Avina later recalled. "With my look and my accent, no one really questioned me too much. And if they did ask me, 'Are you a cop?' or 'Are you recording this?' I would go with it and say, 'Yeah, I'm LAPD, you're under arrest' or 'I'm with the FBI, who are you with?' And we would laugh and that would be the end of it."

When Henry Avina joined the BFC officially in 1987, the number of investigators in the Los Angeles office had increased by more than a dozen since 1979 but no one there was doing undercover work full time, and no one was able to consistently break into the bottom levels of the rings, which were mostly ethnically homogenous and nonwhite. "I might do my best to be down and dirty," recalled Mike "Bud" Ingram, a beefy Anglo supervisor with a thick Wild West style mustache and an even thicker law enforcement demeanor, "but the cappers would get hinky on me and wouldn't want me around for the stagings." The situation was much the same at the Highway Patrol's Staged Collision Unit, which had been started by the same man who pushed for the creation of the BFC and had been in existence for almost as long. CHP officers Dennis Ryan, Sue Mustaffa, and Theresa Clark were as knowledgeable and experienced about accident frauds as anyone at the BFC, but they were also limited in their ability to infiltrate rings. In later years, an officer named Marco Ruiz would give the CHP's Staged Collision Unit a solid undercover option, but, before he joined them, they called on outside help like Henry Avina. "Back then, I was working all the time, keeping spare clothes and I.D.'s in my car," Avina recalled. "I had to be available to leave the house at any time if a capper called to do an accident. For a while it felt like me against the underworld."

In one of his early cases with the CHP, Avina was able to get into an accident with a group of stagers tied to Los Diablos, a Filipino street gang. The ring was run by a capper named Dave Buzan who liked to damage cars near freeway on-ramps. Buzan would then pull onto the freeway and spread out some wreck debris, as if the accident had occurred on the road, before calling the police. His ring also staged real swoop-and-squats on the freeway, Avina learned one night as he stood among a number of cars getting ready to go out on the freeway to find a squat victim. As Buzan explained it, two "Guardian Angel" trucks driven by members of Los Diablos would box in the target car; then another Guardian Angel would swoop to allow the crash car to squat in front. As the car engines started, Avina realized he would have to shut down the ring right there before an accident with an innocent motorist was caused. Speaking into the wire he wore under his shirt, Avina signaled for fifteen CHP and BFC officers to descend to make arrests while an LAPD helicopter circled overhead. Buzan later confessed his guilt. "There was a time that we produced almost thirty-two cases in a month's period of time," he said. "This is organized crime. It's not Mickey Mouse hits somebody in the rear end anymore. This is truly organized."

Dave Buzan had hardly been read his rights before the CHP and BFC put Avina back on the streets staging accidents for a different capper somewhere else in the city. In the case of Vladimir Grishin, a middle-age Russian man from the valley, Avina arrived with a car and insurance; ring members crashed his car in the back of a hardware store, gave him some money, and sent him to a ring doctor to build up the claim.[36] In another of these early undercover cases, Avina got close to Jorge A., a man reputed to be a major capper, who liked to do business from a booth at a Winchell's Donut shop. At one meeting, the capper used a doughnut wrapper to diagram the accident scenario that he wanted Avina to use. Unlike the Russians who outlined scenarios on paper, but then made claimants recopy them in their own handwriting so as not to leave an incriminating paper trail, Jorge A. was not so careful. He gave Avina the wrapper to throw away, and Avina palmed it. Later Avina cleaned off the chocolate icing, then handed it over to prosecutors, who fashioned a criminal indictment from it.

During his first few years at the BFC, Avina worked constantly—he was in the field at least as much as he was in the office. He was "Jesus Martinez," (his favorite undercover identity), more than he was Henry Avina. Clearly, there was more work than he could do by himself. With a number of successful undercover cases behind him, and with increased state funds resulting from the heightened politics of auto insurance reform in California during the late 1980s, Avina started to assemble a team of undercover officers. First he called Danny Naranjo, a detective he knew from his days investigating unemployment and disability frauds. The next year he called on Gilbert Rosas, a former colleague from the State Medical Board. Working together, Avina, Naranjo, and Rosas— along with Marco Ruiz, from the CHP Staged Collision Unit and, later, Tom Sarinana, a former marine who learned the trade as Avina's apprentice at the BFC—formed the core of the state's drive against accident staging in Southern California. The team would be central to almost every major investigation in the region. By the early 1990s, Avina and Sarinana would be recognized nationwide as leading experts in their field, teaching a seminar in fake accident undercover work at the FBI Training Academy in Quantico, Virginia. Supervised by seasoned senior investigators at the BFC and the CHP, this group of Latino insurance detectives would uncover details about the workings of the city's personal injury underworld that had only been guessed at in the decade and a half since the city first learned of the Friends of the Friendless.

During the 1980s, immigrants to Southern California from Mexico and Latin America became as much the backbone of the underground economy in faked personal injuries as they had long been the secret, silent, shadow population behind the success of so much legitimate industry in the region. In L.A.'s personal injury underworld, Latinos were just one in a multitude of groups of all races, ethnicities, and social classes scrambling for quick cash at the bottom of the accident fraud food chain. But unlike most others, Latinos seemed unique in their ability to participate in and be welcomed by all stagers as bodies or names for claims. They were the workhorses of the industry, the universal currency in which any ring would ultimately deal if it grew big enough. It was economics as much as anything. Just as landscapers or restauranteurs or textile manufacturers relied on finding cheap Latino labor at the last minute, accident entrepreneurs of any color or ethnicity could always count on Latino claimants to show up in parking lots (if they weren't there already waiting for day labor) to make a few dollars. Avina and the other Latino undercover officers exploited this fact to get stiffed into almost any ring, almost every time out—be it Vladimir Grishin's group in the Valley, Freddy's gang in East L.A., or the crew of a plain old American capper like Dave Buzan, whose long hair and gravelly tone of voice lent him the slightly burned-out aspect of a heavy-metal groupie.

The continual hunt for passengers with fresh policies and even fresher faces filled the days of most cappers, whatever their background. So, when a Henry Avina came in as Jesus Martinez from Jalisco, Mexico—the Latino Everyman of Southern California's fake accident industry—it was like a gift, especially if his paperwork was in order and he had been referred by a good contact. The accident was almost always approved right away and the staging would occur shortly thereafter. It mattered little to Avina whether he were dealing with a capper like Keith Aaron Hayes in south central Los Angeles or Juan Pablo Vela based near downtown. In fact, at one point in the late 1980s, Avina was working with both at the same time. For Hayes, who was better known by his Muslim moniker Jamil Shabazz, Avina was a hammer or a nail; for Juan Pablo Vela, a twenty-eight-year-old born in Ecuador, Avina's name was recorded in a capping log with two long columns of names marked "Vaca" and "Toro." Shabazz worked out of the Crenshaw Café, whose blue canopy and full menu did not suggest that accident frauds were often the order of the day. Vela's office was the street, a restaurant, or, most often, a second-floor medical clinic on 8th Street in Koreatown. Differences aside, the two gangs ("Crenshaw Cafe" and "8th Street") operated in a remarkably similar manner. Accident gangs, be they Anglo, African

American, Latino, Hungarian, MiddleEastern, Korean,[37] or other, all had the same idea—to stage collisions and fake personal injury claims for money—and they began by mining their own resources in their own areas of the city before branching out.

Accident organizations like Crenshaw Café and 8th Street were not street gangs in the sense of wearing the same colors, bearing the same tattoos, using the same handshakes, or anything of the sort often discussed when L.A. gangs are mentioned. The vast majority of the rings did not even have a catchy name, or if they did, it was usually given to them by law enforcement or the newspapers. But neither were the accident gangs much like traditional organized crime groups with a hierarchical or family structure. At ground level, accident gangs were more like the crews that splintered off from street gangs in order to perform specific jobs, usually crimes. For many members of the Crenshaw Café ring, especially, the accident gang was a kind of transition from the street gang to some kind of legitimate business or career. The Crenshaw Café itself, nestled between a nail salon and a record store, featured a full menu of home-cooked favorites and was something of a community meetingplace: During the year following the L.A. "riots" of 1992, Ted Koppel broadcast several episodes of *Nightline* from the restaurant. Jamil Shabazz was identified as a restaurant owner and "community leader," and he had a lot to say about the economic conditions that led to the uprising and still needed addressing. A few years earlier Henry Avina and the other undercover officers at the BFC and CHP had come to know Shabazz as a leader of a different sort—the leader of one of the oldest accident rings ever known. And the Crenshaw Café was his headquarters.

The first break in the Crenshaw Café case came in July 1988 with a phone call from a confidential informant to Larry Stanford, an investigator who had worked several years at the ICPI before joining the BFC in 1985. The informant told Stanford of having been recruited by an acquaintance to stage an accident with a group that worked out of a restaurant on Crenshaw Boulevard near Inglewood. The informant said he had been given a wreck script to memorize, which included all of the facts of his alleged crash into a 1977 Buick Regal filled with three passengers at an intersection in Compton. The insurance company resisted the claim, however, after an inspection of the Regal revealed "several separate, distinct indentations in the rear of the vehicle" that "appeared to have been done by a large heavy object, such as a sledgehamer." Realizing that this might be an in to a potentially big operation, Stanford arranged for the informant to introduce an undercover officer to the ring members.

By early 1990, undercover officers had met a number of Shabazz's cappers. Many were women who worked out of their homes, reporting periodically to the café to talk over the details of cases and to talk money with Jamil. Shabazz himself often did business from his home, a handsome single-story building in a quiet, moderately upscale neighborhood. Here Investigators, led by Postal Inspector Bill Davis (a veteran of the regional wars against the accident fakers), would meet Shabazz, offer their insurance policies and their cars (which were rammed into telephone poles by ring members),then wait outside Shabazz's bedroom for their money. A number of black investigators infiltrated the ring, including George Robinson of the BFC. Robinson ultimately was able to introduce Shabazz to Henry Avina—or, in this case "Ernie Zapata," an undercover identity Avina came up with by altering the name of Emiliano Zapata, the Mexican agrarian revolutionary from the early 1900s. Avina thought of Zapata, a true folk hero, every time he heard cappers speak in vainglorious terms about how they were revolutionary or Robin Hood types battling an oppressor power (symbolized by the insurance industry) in order to benefit "their people." Avina also thought his mustache, curled at the edges, resembled Zapata's.

In the year or so that he worked with the Crenshaw Café ring, Postal Inspector Davis and a handful of black investigators gradually gained credibility and responsibility within the organization. BFC investigator Robinson, for one, was sent to the ring's medical clinic with other passengers to learn what to say to doctors about his aches and pains and how to sign a patient log book fifteen or twenty times in different colored ink during one visit. One afternoon, Robinson got an urgent call from the capper who had first brought him into the ring. She told Robinson that she needed twelve people without insurance and four cars "to do a situation." (Fearful of investigators who might be tapping the phone, the capper had told Robinson to refer to accidents as "situations.") Recruiting passengers for nail cars seemed like a step up from bringing in hammers—it would bring Robinson $75 or $100 per person up front. Shabazz downplayed the deal later when Robinson mentioned the money to him, however. Shabazz told him that he would pay $100 per carload and nothing more, while taking $200 per person for himself when the cases settled. Of the nail car passengers Shabazz told Robinson, "We need them, but you don't make no money." Shabazz then advised him to stick with bringing in hammers.

As Robinson grew closer with Shabazz and the Crenshaw Café ring, Avina (working this case as Jesus Martinez) was building his relationship with Juan Pablo Vela and Javier Francisco Luzerraga, the young leaders of the 8th Street gang, who had known one another since their youth in Ecuador.

Luzarraga learned the accident business as a capper for others, then, in 1989, he approached his friend Vela about starting a clinic of their own. Vela, who had a business degree from Cal State Northridge and worked in hospital administration, was able to find a doctor for their St. Joseph's Clinic, to whom they paid a monthly salary. "I approached it as a business, not as a scam," Vela later said, claiming to have known nothing about set-up accidents when he began. Vela kept the books and often wrote the medical reports. Luzarraga worked more with the street-level crashers and recruiters who kept the clinic steadily supplied with claimants (usually newly arrived immigrants from the same ethnic group of the capper). Vela later opened his own law firm on Wilshire Boulevard by purchasing the use of the license of a seventy-year-old-blind lawyer who rarely left his home/office in East L.A., where he maintained a small community legal clinic. Avina was brought into the 8th Street gang as a bull who had an insurance policy and a car to ram into one of Vela's cows. Unlike Shabazz's method of crashing the hammer cars into telephone poles or using a sledgehammer on the nails, Avina soon found out, Vela and Luzerraga liked to ram bulls and cows together. "After going out on a few crash runs with Vela and Luzerraga, I realized how smooth these guys were," Avina later said. "These crashes would always take place at midnight in a dark alley. One of these guys would position the car sideways and the other, going twenty to thirty miles per hour, would smack it a few times. They were such pros at this, they didn't even bother to inspect the damage. The first few times out I was scared, but once I knew what was coming, it was nothing."[38] With over 1,000 of these crashes staged since the mid-1980s, and between $15 and $20 million in unsettled claims at the time of their arrest, the 8th Street gang might have rivaled the older Crenshaw Café ring had it survived long enough to process its fake claims. Both rings would be brought down together.

On October 16, 1990, after a year and a half of the most extensive undercover infiltration of accident gangs ever (and, not uncoincidentally, just a few weeks before a state election for insurance commissioner), 100 officers from the BFC, CHP, and U.S. Postal Inspection Service met at five-thirty in the morning for a briefing. They were about to execute what would later be termed the "nation's biggest roundup of its kind in history."[39] Fanning out across Southern California, officers arrested twenty people connected to the Crenshaw Cafe, including Shabazz, some of his cappers, and a few of the ring's crash specialists. They also arrested Vela, Luzerraga, and sixteen other people from the 8th Street gang as well as some others in two different cases. Some were surprised in bed at home, others were led away from their offices in cuffs. The following day Ira Reiner, the L.A. District Attorney, held a press conference to announce the arrests of fifty-one people linked to one or another accident gang. Reiner took the occasion to speak out against the "multibillion-dollar underground industry" in faked accidents and injuries which was "dominated by cappers" and "supported by a cadre of unscrupulous attorneys [and] doctors." Reiner said that L.A. had come to be known as the "auto insurance fraud capital of the United States" over the last decade, due in large part to the unwillingness of insurers to investigate fraud, while passing along the cost to policyholders in the form of raised premiums.[40] In response, insurers claimed that they had been preparing criminal cases for years, but that most prosecutors were not interested in them. After the arrests, however, everyone seemed to agree that things were different now and that accident staging and personal injury frauds were going to be investigated and prosecuted. "ARMY OF SCAM ARTISTS MILKS MILLIONS FROM INSURERS" was the headline of a *Los Angeles Times* feature on the unchecked proliferation of accident gangs in Southern California that had appeared earlier in the year.[41] And now there was going to be a small corps of industry investigators, law enforcement officers, and prosecutors allied more closely than before in opposition.

A month after the arrests, John Garamendi, California's first elected insurance commissioner, picked up on the combat imagery when he declared his own war on the fake accident underworld. "By the end of my four-year term," pledged a man many believed was on his way to the governorship, "Los Angeles will no longer be called the insurance fraud capital of this nation." Translated into practical terms at the BFC, this meant: Get a wire on Henry, Danny, Marco, Gil, and Tom, and send them back into the streets.

In fact, Avina and the others at the BFC had already begun undercover infiltration of several different rings by the time the insurance commissioner declared war on the stagers—the Freddy case, and another, the Esther case. And then there was the Casino ring. In all three cases, investigators found massive numbers of paper accidents being staged *el toro y la vaca* style, with body damage created by crashing cars in a controlled way in back lots or alleys or deserted streets. Freddy's ring was based out of a bar in East L.A., and Esther's was run from a suburban home. The third, and perhaps the largest, was centered around the "card club" casinos located around L.A. County, and was run almost entirely by Armenians such as Hagop Semerdjian. A first-generation immigrant who had been a dentist in Yerevan during the late 1970s, Semerdjian stopped capping teeth and began capping car accidents after following his family and friends to North Hollywood in the mid-1980s.

When local residents and state legislators opposed the licensing of some of the newer, bigger card club casinos during the mid-1980s (smaller establishments offered the same low-stakes gambling on a few specified games) they said that they feared an increase in crime, especially white-collar crime involving payoffs to city officials or shady deals by casino operators. The kind of crime they actually got could not have been predicted. Patrolling the gaming floors, Armenian accident cappers watched for losers—the bigger the better—then propositioned them in the parking lot. For the temporary use of the person's name, insurance policy number, and car, cappers offered $1,000 cash, a welcome salve for the wounds inflicted on them by Pai Gow poker, "Texas Hold 'em," and the other oddball card games that were legal in the clubs.[42] The cities that had approved the card clubs, and quickly became dependent on them for as much as 40 percent of annual municipal revenues, were counting on much the same things that the cappers were: mainly, that people would feel lucky enough, or be financially strapped or greedy enough, to put down some money to make more back in a low-risk environment. And to do it fast.

The Casino ring initiated its own demise when one leader asked a guard at the Commerce Club casino if he wanted to make a quick $1,000 in a staged accident. The guard, a hulking man named Larry Elmore, expressed a willingness to do the accident. Then Elmore set up another meeting where he secretly recorded the conversation and allowed his 1981 Plymouth Champ to be "hammered" by the capper's 1976 Cadillac in a far corner of the club's parking lot. The next day Elmore took his audiotape, and the wreck script he was given (he was to say that he hit a Toyota filled with passengers in a supermarket parking lot), and went to Marco Ruiz at the CHP's Staged Collision Unit. Ruiz listened to Elmore's tape and looked at the documents: The capper, who went by the Italian-sounding Tony Baroni but who was really an Armenian named Antranik Terzian, told Elmore that he had done nothing but stage these kinds of accidents at card clubs for the previous six years. Dealers and card club regulars were Terzian's most frequent hammers. Passengers for the nail cars were mainly friends of a handful of the ring's cappers or else were drawn from acquaintances in the large Armenian populations in East Hollywood and Glendale. Many Armenian immigrants had arrived in L.A. by way of Lebanon and Iran in the mid-1970s, and some 13,000 others came from Soviet Armenia in the late 1980s, as a result of *glasnost* policies that eased restrictions on leaving the Soviet Union.[43]

For the next six months, Ruiz directed a dozen or so undercover stagings with various cappers of the Casino ring, each of whom worked different card clubs at different times—Terzian at the Commerce Club, one day, "Grachik" at the Bicycle Club in Bell Gardens on another, and "Setrak" at the Normandie Club, for instance. Each capper's stagings followed roughly the same pattern: up-front cash payments for insurance policies (usually in crisp $100 bills that investigators would photocopy in sheets for their files), the crashing of cars somewhere near the casino, the writing up of the wreck script (they liked accidents to occur in supermarket parking lots), and the requests for referrals of more people with fresh policies to be hammer cars. Initially Terzian and some of the other Armenian cappers wanted Elmore and the undercover officers to bring him black drivers. "We like to use blacks to hit whites," he explained, in order to keep the insurance companies from being suspicious of an ethnically or racially homogeneous gang. Later Ruiz asked another capper whether an Armenian could ever hit another Armenian and was told they could not because insurance companies know that Armenians "make accidents." From the Armenian standpoint, any non-Armenian would do—African American, Latino, Asian. By the end of the summer of 1989, Ruiz had no difficulty capping Henry Avina into one of Antranik Terzian's accidents at the Commerce Casino.

"Jesus Martinez" would ride once again. After being briefed on the facts of the accident, then reporting it to his insurance company, Avina found himself in his Olds Delta '88 with Terzian and another Armenian ring member, driving the car into a light pole in the parking lot of the Commerce Casino. He walked away with ten new $100 bills. The Armenians, like most of the others before and after them, befriended Avina and tried to involve him in as many accidents as they could. One capper couple, Alexan Kouyoumadjian and his wife, Ovsanna, hosted Avina at their apartment several times for small cups of potent Turkish tea and talk about accidents they had staged in the past. Alexan later arranged for Avina to graduate from the hammer car to the nail, and then got him in with a chiropractor who would let him sign in for multiple treatments at once on one condition: "If you say it's bullshit [to the doctor]," he warned, "you go to jail."

Hagop Semerdjian also liked Avina. Semerdjian liked to deal with Armenians, for the most part, but the Kouyoumadjians persuaded him that Avina was okay and Semerdjian agreed to meet him. After Avina explained that he was strapped for cash, Semerdjian responded by scripting a crash for him to take place in a parking lot near the L.A. River. At the end of the night, Semerdjian paid Avina $1,500 in bills he took from a white plastic bag he kept on the floor of his car. Six months later Avina arrested Alexan and his wife, Semerdjian, and dozens of others whom prosecutors claimed had staged some 3,000 accidents over the years and had filed as much as $50 million in fake personal injury claims.[44] In the summer of 1991, Avina and Tom Sarinana of the BFC returned to the casinos—this time the baccarat table at the Mirage in Las Vegas, where they found Antranik Terzian (aka Tony Baroni) after a tip-off from Vegas police. A fugitive since the arrests of the other Armenian cappers that April, Terzian was brought back to L.A. for a trial that ended in conviction and jail.

By 1990 the amount of money floating around in L.A.'s fake accident underworld was estimated as ranging from the hundreds of millions of dollars to well over $1 billion annually. At the level of the cappers, bulls, and cows, however, it was as unsexy a billion dollars as anyone could imagine, assembled a few thousand at a time in back-alley transactions. Less like the mounting box-office take of a Hollywood blockbuster, the dollars that changed hands from cappers to stagers was more like Monopoly money played with for a time, kept in hastily made rolls in pockets or in bags on car floors, then blown on the next roll of the dice. Some money concentrated in the hands of cappers, taking the form of nicer-than-usual homes or fancy cars, but this was not where the money was and everyone knew it, especially the BFC and L.A. County prosecutors. One newspaper report on the arrests of the Casino ring led with the fact that "one group was conspicuously absent from the roundup—lawyers."[45] Even Roberto Vallarino, an Ecuadoran-born, college-educated clinic owner and one-time stager arrested in the October 1990 sweep, would later comment that "they only got the donkeys, the mules, the Indians. . . . They called me a 'ringleader' but I barely knew any of the people they arrested as part of my ring."

Undercover officers were getting into the offices of the doctors and attorneys who dealt in fake accidents, but they were not getting to the professionals themselves. Many investigations stalled at the level of the "office administrators" or "claims managers" who sometimes really controlled the offices, paying the professionals a monthly salary for the use of their names; but just as often the professionals installed these administrators to keep themselves insulated from the dirty work of buying cases from street cappers. Even in the early days of the BFC, when cases were investigated historically, a handful of attorneys and doctors were successfully (if still painstakingly) prosecuted: In 1984 attorney Roger Ammann, a one-time deputy district attorney and candidate for Beverly Hills City Council, confessed to directing the staging of sixty-six panic-stop style crashes over a few years. "I knew the accidents were not genuine," Ammann said of the collisions, which mainly targeted unsuspecting female drivers in new cars.[46] A few years later an aging attorney, Michael T. Bota, was convicted for his connection to fifty-four staged accidents, most of them also panic stops targeting single drivers in new cars on busy streets at moderate speeds.[47] (Many of Bota's accidents were staged by a capper from Long Beach, who fled before being arrested and was never prosecuted.) Another lawyer, Kenneth Gottlieb, was first arrested in 1980 but was not finally prosecuted until the mid-1990s in what was perhaps the longest case in L.A. County history. Successful prosecutions of doctors dealing in capped cases through the 1980s were equally rare. Albert MacKenzie, the prosecutor who worked intently on many of these cases throughout the decade, was not hopeful about the deterrent effect of his work. Of the doctors and lawyers in Southern California buying staged accident cases, MacKenzie observed: "They're living in a $5 million house, driving luxury cars, I don't have the feeling these people go to bed at night shaking in their boots that they're going to get caught."[48] Indeed, the subtitle of a cover story on the subject published in California Lawyer in 1991 noted: "Southern California's multi-billion-dollar staged-accident business couldn't function without lawyers—and only the unlucky ones get caught."

The Insurance Commissioner's "war" on the accident fakers was begin-ning to look like a rigged fight. The powerful resources of a state agency lined up against random poor people recruited at the last minute to do a few relatively nonserious acts (standing around while cars were crashed, telling an insurance adjuster that they had been in a crash when they had not), which many of them did not even fully understand to be criminal. The commissioner had a snappy line for his announcement of the arrests of the Casino ring cappers—"You've rolled your last dice; you've crapped out"—but he did not have any attorneys and doctors. District Attorney Reiner acknowledged the shortcoming: "Proving that doctors and lawyers are in on the scheme is the hardest part of these cases," he said after the casino arrests. "They are always carefully insulated from the dirty work—like the big boys at the top of narcotics rings. . . . You can only get to them by working up through the ranks, one layer at a time—like peeling an onion." And this is exactly what was finally done successfully in the Esther case.

The "Esther" in the Esther case was Esther Diaz. A fifty-year-old mother of three who was born and raised in Buenos Aires, Argentina, Diaz emigrated to New York in the late 1950s, then moved to L.A. in 1964, where she ran a succcession of different import-export companies and sewing shops. Not getting into fake accidents until the mid-1980s, she originally worked in the law office of a legitimate attorney who helped low-income clients with routine civil matters: bankruptcy, landlord-tennant relations, taxes. One afternoon, Diaz says, she met a friend for lunch who told her that real money for an office administrator of a law firm was in doing what he did: buying capped personal injury cases in high volumes from a variety of street-level operatives. The man who she says gave her this advice, Enrique Otero, had been working at the law office of Toplitzky and Taracena for several years before recruiting Esther Diaz to join him. From her desk in Toplitky and Taracena's downtown office, Esther learned how to negotiate with the cappers who came in from the street with cases to sell; then learned how to script her own accidents to order. Diaz conducted her claims-faking more like a business than most fake accident entrepreneurs. When undercover officers first met one of her stagers to discuss an accident, they were handed three-page scripts that had been photocopied from an original (which Esther maintained in her files) and were stapled together. Esther called them her "bibles." Diaz reportedly ran a tight ship. Undercover officers who dealt with her underlings often were told that they would have to wait for her cappers to "speak to the lady" or "call the office." Esther claimed to have drawn the line at swoop-and-squat accidents targeting innocent drivers: At Toplitzky and Taracena's law office she used to watch as men—"Mexicans with big mustaches," she later said—came in to sell these kinds of accidents, but she claimed never to have knowingly bought or scripted one.

Although news accounts described Esther Diaz as having held seminars in accident staging in her living room, she never did business at home. At first, she worked out of Toplitzky and Taracena's office, dealing almost exclusively with Taracena. Later she rented an office in a minimall, where she told prospective ring members about what kind of insurance policies to get, or how to make believable damage to a car, or what to tell a doctor about your injuries. Just as often Esther would take to the road, like a Tupperware dealer or Avon representative, and meet "clients" at their own homes or at the apartments of her cappers. One night she held one of these sessions for a couple of undercover officers in an apartment near downtown L.A. Arriving like any traveling salesman in a newish Chevy Celebrity, Esther was accompanied by Otero, a fifty-year-old man who was married with three children of his own, and possessed an advanced degree in mechanical engineering from the University of La Paz in Bolivia, where he was born. Esther and Enrique handed out their literature—the stapled wreck scripts marked "T" for *toritos* (bulls) and "V" for *vacitos* (cows). After allowing a few minutes for questions from the officers, Otero quizzed them on the details of the made-up crashes, while Esther sat back in her chair correcting him if she thought he was saying anything wrong. While Otero rammed together toy cars on a coffee table to demonstrate how the collision would happen, two of Esther's crashers took the keys to the undercover vehicles and went out to create the damage. Then, thorough to the last, Esther had everyone drive to the site she had chosen for the accident, where she briefed the fake claimants on the details of the crash once more.

After a year and a half of investigation, all of the undercover officers had been through Esther's seminars—first Marco Ruiz of the CHP, then Danny, Gil, Henry, and Tom from the BFC. They had also been through her trash, and it was here that they found some documents that completed their trail of evidence into the law offices of Myron Toplitzky and Jorge Taracena. Back in April 1991, the picture that had accompanied the *L.A. Times* story of the first arrests in the Esther case showed Latino men and women seated around a room, every one of whom had their hands covering their faces. A heavyset man sat bare-chested at the end of the room, having been dragged out of bed early in the morning.[49] In February 1992, the picture was completely different: District Attorney Reiner stood at a podium of microphones, flanked by Ron Warthen and Clarke Walker, two of the original five BFC investigators from back in 1979. Beside them were two photographs of attorney Taracena displayed on an easle—one showing the attorney with his toupé, the other without.[50] A few weeks earlier Taracena had been a personal injury lawyer in good standing with the state bar and in possession of a thriving practice. Now, Reiner announced, Taracena was a fugitive from justice, having been connected to more than 200 accidents staged by Esther Diaz and her group. (Many suggested that he had returned to his home in Guatemala where allegedly he had been secreting all of his money for years; others said he was in Costa Rica.) His partner, Myron Toplitzky, was arrested on his way to the office a week earlier. In his briefcase, he carried a capping ledger that matched in large part the ledgers Diaz kept at her home, with *torito* and *vacito* columns.

Although Taracena had evaded arrest, the message from the fraud fighters in the city was clear. "Every lawyer and doctor dealing in staged accidents needs to be looking over their shoulders wondering if they are going to be our next target." A few weeks later, in Costa Mesa, the message was heard again as Thomas F. Mullen became one of the first personal injury attorneys in Orange County to be prosecuted on charges of conspiracy to commit insurance fraud. After a two-year undercover investigation led by Theresa Clark of the CHP Staged Collision Unit, Mullen was firmly linked to a capper named José Jesus Toribio, who staged crashes with mostly Latino cows for a 50/50 split with the attorney. Back in 1987, Toribio began sending his cows to a physical therapist whose practice was sagging, with instructions that she was to bill Thomas F. Mullen $3,500 for each patient. The therapist suspected the accidents were staged: "My common sense told me that [there were] too many accidents with four people," she later told investigators. And it was "very difficult to get people to come in and get their therapy."[51] The next year she married Toribio, then sold him her clinic a few months later. With funding from Mullen, Toribio bought a second clinic shortly thereafter. Working together, Mullen and Toribio, the workers in the clinics and the stagers in the street, had brought in more than $1 million over two years.

Capping offers the most opportunity for upward mobility in the fake accident underworld: Passengers almost always stay passengers and professionals stay professionals, but cappers can move from the grubbiness of the street to the relative refinement of a desk in the law office. José Toribio went through the complete cycle of upward mobility in the fake accident underworld in just a few years. First he made the successful transition from occasional stager to street capper; then he achieved the goal of most street cappers: to become the office administrator at a personal injury office, directing his own crew of street cappers and getting closer to the money. Some office administrators go one step further by moving out on their own, buying the use of an attorney's name and license from some aging practitioner, then essentially running the whole show themselves. When rings are infiltrated and arrests are made, street cappers and office administrators are usually the first ones fingered, and through the early 1990s, they were usually the ones left holding the bag. Only persistent undercover work and the painstaking piecing together of files changed things, turning the Esther case into the Toplitzky and Taracena case, and helping to push past José Toribio to Thomas Mullen. A few years later federal investigators would shut down the law office of an attorney known throughout Southern California for his aggressive television and print advertising; five of the attorney's cappers, led by thirty-year-old Tommy Choi, would later be indicted also.[52]

With investigators and prosecutors closing in on attorneys in the early 1990s, relations between attorneys and cappers got more tense. Late in the summer of 1992, the BFC arrested Alan Shapiro and Warren Finn, two personal injury attorneys who were among the biggest traffickers in staged accidents in the city. Within a week, the word on the street was that one of their main street cappers, Jorge Ventura Santamaria, was a marked man. The prosecutor in the case asked that Ventura's testimony be recorded immediately to give attorney Shapiro "less incentive to have Ventura killed."[53]

As a former member of the army during some of the bloodiest years of civil war in his native El Salvador, Jorge Ventura Santamaria was no stranger to killing and guns. He owned a number of weapons himself, including an AR-15 rifle that he may have carried carry across his lap as he cruised villages and city streets in an anonymous four-wheel-drive jeep for the army. Since moving to Los Angeles in the mid-1980s, however, Ventura had taken up a less violent position as an occasional member of a staged accident gang, then as a street capper. He now sought out fellow countrymen who also had emigrated to Los Angeles in order to play parts in his staged accidents. So it must have come as something of a blast from his own past to hear from friends, then from prosecutors who worried about the safety of their star witness, that attorney Alan Michael Shapiro, a personal injury attorney with whom he had been dealing closely for more than a year, may have taken out a contract on his life.

It is not clear whether the threat actually would have been carried out had it not been exposed. What is certain, though, is that Ventura knew a lot about the kind of office Shapiro and Finn operated that the attorneys did not want used against them at trial. Ventura had started setting up accidents in 1986, when he lived with several others in an apartment in South Pasadena. The next year, at a medical clinic, he met an office administrator named Simon "Goody" Basa, who was cruising for patient referrals. Ventura and Basa started talking, and, before long, Basa gave him his business card with an invitation to come work for him: The card was for the law offices of Shapiro & Finn, which is where Ventura went to see Basa a few days later. In a brief meeting, Basa set down the terms of their business arrangement: $1,000 for every passenger. Then Basa mentioned the medical clinics that he favored (any number of storefront offices in minimalls all across the region) and the insurers he liked to avoid (those whom attorney Finn felt were looking too closely at the claims). Occasionally Ventura would sell cases to office administrators at different law firms—he liked dealing with an Ethiopian administrator at a firm in the valley who took on the cases that Shapiro and Finn rejected—but the bulk of his work was with Goody Basa. In the beginning, Ventura would bring Goody one to four accidents a week; a few years later he was averaging between five and eight cases per week and was in line for a promotion to office manager himself.

Back in January 1990, Henry Avina got his first introduction to Ventura from someone who had done a few accidents with him but was disgruntled after being cheated out of some money. Once again assuming the identity of Jesus Martinez, and, of course, arriving purposely a half-hour or forty-five minutes late to keep from seeming too eager, Avina met Ventura one night at Ventura's home. Ventura now lived in his own ranch home in South Gate complete with a large front lawn and a pool in the back. Avina was taken first to the garage, where Avina saw a man seated at a makeshift desk filling out claims paperwork. Then Avina was led back through the house where he passed others filling out claims forms before reaching a den where a man sat behind a desk with an open briefcase on it. This was Jorge Ventura Santamaria, the former Salvadoran army member turned fake accident entrepreneur. Ventura asked Avina for his insurance information, which he recorded on his own preprinted claims forms, of which he kept more than a hundred in file cabinets in his office. Explaining to Avina that the cars would be crashed to create believable damage—a man named "Jaime" was one of the ring's favorite crash artists—Ventura worked the phones to find some other passengers for the accident. Failing to get the people he needed, Ventura called off the staging. He asked Avina to come back the next night and to bring some friends if he knew anyone who would be interested.

When he returned to Ventura's house the next night, Avina was Jesus Martinez just long enough for Ventura to give him a wreck script for the accident he had come to stage that night. Then Martinez once again became Avina, leading a team of officers on a raid of the house. Avina went right for the file drawers where Ventura kept his papers and came away with a carton full of wreck scripts, the majority of which, it would later be shown, resulted in claims processed through Shapiro and Finn's office. The names of the bulls and cows were indistinguishable from one another (mostly Spanish), and paperwork for Jesus Martinez's unconsummated claim was right in the midst of them. Other ring members in the house were also found with wreck scripts in their pockets. More important, though, investigators found ample evidence of Ventura's connection to the attorneys: there was stationery, envelopes, and claims forms from the office of Shapiro & Finn as well as business cards for the Shapiro & Finn law firm with George S. Ventura's name on them. All of Ventura's subordinates carried his card. (One of Ventura's brothers, Arturo, carried his own Shapiro & Finn business cards along with a capping ledger that he kept separate from Jorge's in an apparent attempt to establish himself as a capper in his own right; Rafael Ventura Santamaria, Arturo's cousin, carried a signed document from Shapiro & Finn that said he was a "legal assistant" at the firm.) Even more telling of Ventura's close relationship with the attorneys was a diagram that he carried in his briefcase showing the renovation plans for Shapiro & Finn's floor in a mid-Wilshire office building: On the new plan, Ventura would share an office with two Filipino street cappers who were also being tapped for promotions to office administrator status. A seat in the Shapiro & Finn office meant that Ventura would now manage his own stable of street cappers; it would mark the culmination of his successful rise through L.A.'s personal injury underworld. Ventura never made it into the office, however, and the diagram became just one more piece of evidence linking him to Shapiro and Finn.

More than anything, money formed the basis of the otherwise improbable partnership between the Salvadoran and the two Anglo attorneys from suburban L.A. And the seizure of extensive bank records bore this out in the most damning detail. On the night of the initial raid of Ventura's apartment, a year's worth of bank statements were found that showed some $630,000 in checks to Ventura from Shapiro and Finn, from which Ventura had paid out $460,000 to the bulls and cows who worked for him. The difference between deposits and withdrawals—$170,000—represented part of Ventura's cut for just one year; over a two-year period, there were more than $1.3 million in payments from Shapiro & Finn trust accounts to street cappers. One month later, in early March 1990, a search of the Shapiro & Finn office itself uncovered even more bank records showing payments to cappers, as well as an especially incriminating $10,000 withdrawal from a client trust account apparently used to bail Ventura out of jail in February. During the search, David Shin, Goody Basa's fellow office administrator, headed for the elevator with his briefcase. Shin was stopped by investigators and was asked to open the briefcase. Inside was a blue capping book that named more than 1,000 bulls and cows who had taken part in 664 different stagings. The "cases" were later listed alphabetically by the names of cows, filling twenty pages of single-spaced typing that read like a phone book of ethnic L.A.: Asian Changs, Chois, Chungs, and whole pages of Kims and Lees, who were brought in by Basa and Shin's extensive capping connections in Koreatown, as well as a mixture of Latino Lopezes, Martinezes, and Rodriguezes. In the far-right column of the listings, the settlement amounts awarded by insurers are listed: Ranging from $1,500 to $35,000 per case, the total settlement money reflecting in this one capping log, covering a period of a little more than a year, was more than $7.2 million. And Shapiro and Finn's total annual intake from staged accidents, pieced together from records of more than ninety checking accounts at fourteen different banks, was estimated at more than double this.

At 6:00 A.M. one day in August 1992, Alan Shapiro was arrested after finishing a workout at a YMCA, and his partner, Warren Finn, was taken into custody near his home in Marina Del Rey as he prepared for a jog.[54] The arrests could not have been a complete surprise to the attorneys: They knew that Ventura and a few of his stagers had been arrested a year and a half earlier, and they knew also that Ventura was cooperating with the investigation. After Ventura's arrest, Shapiro had even gone to investigators with his father, Haskell, who founded the law office in the 1950s. According to investigators, the younger Shapiro stated that Ventura was never paid for referrals and that

Shapiro–Finn Conspiracy

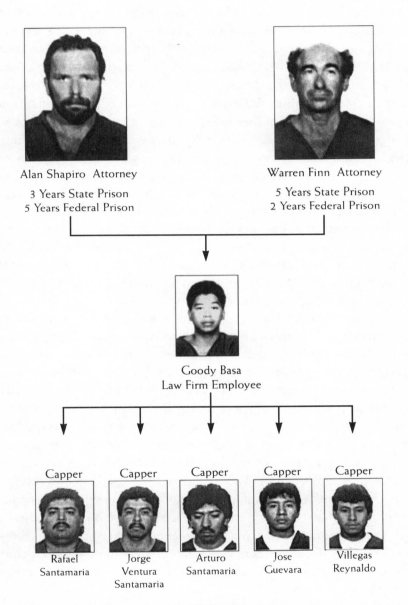

Alan Shapiro Attorney

3 Years State Prison
5 Years Federal Prison

Warren Finn Attorney

5 Years State Prison
2 Years Federal Prison

Goody Basa
Law Firm Employee

Capper

Rafael
Santamaria

Capper

Jorge
Ventura
Santamaria

Capper

Arturo
Santamaria

Capper

Jose
Guevara

Capper

Villegas
Reynaldo

Figure 7.1. This chart was prepared by Los Angeles County Prosecutors for the trial of lawyers Alan Michael Shapiro and Warren Finn, who were arrested in 1992 and, later, convicted of buying staged accidents from cappers, who arranged them in various ways. The chart shows graphically the different levels of present-day accident gangs.

he did not even know Ventura, a statement which was at least partially true, because Finn was shown to have dealt with Ventura almost exclusively.

The fact of two attorneys being arrested as kingpins of an accident ring was so rare a bird, and the pursuit of attorneys in general by the BFC and others had so long been largely fruitless, that it hardly seemed real. Some six months earlier, District Attorney Reiner had likened such attorneys to drug kingpins: powerful, insulated from their street-level contacts, maybe even willing to use violence to enforce their deals. Initially, it may have been hard to reconcile this image with the reality of the middle-age men in jogging outfits who were brought into a downtown court to face the charges against them. Working up from the back alleys where cars are crashed and the garages where claims forms are filled out in bulk, the attorneys seem like distant but benevolent gods who have the power to rain money down on people who knew how "to do an accident" or take part in "a situation." Their names are passed along from capper to cow like hot stock tips among the moneyed set; the directions to the law offices on Wilshire are followed like a yellow brick road to Oz. The arrests of Shapiro and Finn were like the pulling back of the curtain to see the wizards, short and balding in running shoes; later it would be demonstrated that they were not only mortal but arrestable, prosecutable, and convictable.

"The significance of this case is enormous," Insurance Commissioner Garamendi said of the arrests of Shapiro and Finn. "In the 13-year history of our Fraud Bureau, only a handful of attorneys have been arrested for auto fraud because they manage to insulate themselves so well. But this time we've nailed the true ringleaders." At a press conference District Attorney Reiner added somewhat vengefully: "These are the first really big-time lawyers, the first major operators we've gotten . . . [and] we want to take everything we can from them . . . to break them financially."[55] And this they did—first convicting them on insurance fraud conspiracy charges at the county level, then turning them over to the U.S. Attorney for prosecution on federal tax evasion charges relating to millions of dollars in unreported income. A three-year federal investigation showed that Shapiro and Finn were just one part of "a huge underground economy" in capped and staged personal injury cases with money being laundered "at a frantic pace" through check-cashing outlets, convenience stores, and front companies to avoid detection by the Internal Revenue Service.[56]

The arrests of Shapiro and Finn, resulting from their involvement with Jorge Ventura Santamaria, his brother Arturo, and the other stagers, had the same quieting effect on the regional market in faked accidents and personal injuries as the arrests sixty-five years earlier in New York of the attorneys linked to accident racketeers like Daniel Laulicht and his brother Ben. Claims dropped off in ways that BFC detectives could notice. Cappers looked for new scenarios, new attorneys or clinics, or new combinations of claimants of different ethnicities or races to keep investigators off their trail, while attorneys sent out "drop" letters on a lot of their capped cases. In the new Crenshaw Cafés or Tierra Blanca bars, or wherever men and women would show up looking to do an accident on the advice of a friend of a friend, suspicion had replaced the easy acceptance with which new bulls or cows might once have been greeted. After more than a decade of almost wholly unchecked growth in Southern California's personal injury underworld, things were quiet.

And then, as surely as the capital of the underworld had migrated west from New York to Los Angeles over the course of the preceding century, the L.A. rings were said to be radiating out in all directions. "It's getting a little too hot in L.A.," said a spokeswoman for the California Department of Insurance in late 1992.[57] BFC investigators, working in concert with the FBI, later confirmed the rumors. Some accident gangs first formed in Southern California were now reappearing in Phoenix and Houston, Denver and Seattle.

A *Time* magazine cover story on Los Angeles published in late 1991 spoke of California (and Los Angeles in particular) as "America's bright strange cultural outrider" where what was working or not working about the American Dream could be read off sooner, and in bigger letters, than anywhere else in the country.[58] The long history of the formation of gangs to stage accidents for money stretched back too many decades in too many cities to allow the idea that Los Angeles was exporting a totally new kind of crime to the rest of the country, however. If Henry Avina had been working undercover ten years earlier, he may have met the Hungarian cappers or the Middle Eastern students who were said to have been staging crashes for the good of the PLO. And if he had worked sixty or seventy years before that on the streets of New York, he probably would have been turned away from rings for his lack of Yiddish in the same way that many of his supervisors at the BFC failed undercover for their shortcomings in Spanish.

Specific cappers, lawyers, and doctors were relocating—this was true. And it was also true that some BFC investigators were being flown to other cities to track them down. But the real story was not about Los Angeles imposing another cultural trend on the rest of America, like so many theme parks, rollerblades, or attorney advertisements (which, while made legal in 1977 by a Supreme Court case originating in Phoenix, were first proliferated on a national basis by Southern California's Jacoby & Meyers).[59] Rather, the point was about the legal culture in the United States that has provided fertile ground for the personal injury underworld to grow throughout the past century, thriving more or less in different climates. Far from specific to California soil, this growth has always followed closely the in-and-out migrations of bulls and cows, whose movements across the country are not always predictable.

CHAPTER 8

MAPPING THE UNDERWORLD

We are aware of organized criminal groups which stage phony car accidents. . . . Many of the staged automobile accident cases involve highly structured groups which operate organizations throughout the United States.

—Louis Freeh, FBI director, 1995

D onna Willard, a thirty-four-year-old hairdresser from Philadelphia, began sleeping with a hammer, an ice pick, and two switchblades at her bedside after becoming convinced that someone was trying to kill her. One evening in early March 1990, Willard answered a knock at her door to see something that must have been even more frightening than her worst imaginings: a man in a hooded sweat shirt with dark shoe polish smeared on his face carrying a 9 mm pistol in his right hand. Just moments earlier the man had sat in a car parked down the street from Willard's tiny red-brick rowhouse and negotiated with another man on a price to kill the petite mother of three— $980 plus $20 worth of heroin. Now the small-time hit man was inside Willard's home, pushing her back toward a staircase where she ultimately fell. He pumped two shots into the back of Willard's head, execution style. Then he ran out the same way he had barged in, joined his associates in the car (to whom he announced "Job done" with a gangster's straight face), and sped away. The next day, all close to Willard were shocked by her sudden awful death, particularly her twelve-year-old son, who had witnessed the shooting from the top of the stairs. At the same time, Robert B. Burke, a Philadelphia personal injury attorney, read the news report of the death and was said to have sighed. "He went 'Pfeww!'" recalled a man who claimed to have been involved with the lawyer in planning and carrying out the murder. "[Burke] was relieved."[1]

Some three and a half years later, Robert Burke would be sentenced to life in prison for ordering the murder of Donna Willard. The motive: to keep Willard from testifying against him in a federal probe of accident claims he had faked over the years. Burke had staged several accidents himself: In 1987, for instance, Burke, his brother Keith, and Keith's girlfriend drove a rental car into a guard rail in Philadelphia's Fairmount Park. Then they gathered up the debris and cruised the city looking for a spot where they could steer the car into a ditch, spread out the debris, and make it look as if they had been run off the road by a hit-and-run driver (an act of simulation that involved Burke purposely banging his head against the steering wheel to cause bleeding and swelling).[2] Burke alone made some $65,000 on this accident from twenty-three different accident policies in his own name. Some six months later Burke scripted another accident—nicknamed Rolling Thunder—that involved the planned crash of a rental car with a van carrying eight passengers, most of whom Burke recruited from a suburban construction firm. Most likely Burke was involved in other accident stagings over the years. More frequently, however, he would create false medical documentation for claims (mostly legitimate) brought to him by others, at least a dozen of whom were members of the Philadelphia Police Force. Burke wrote the medical reports himself under the name of Dr. Robert Segin, a friend of Burke's father whom Burke befriended after the doctor fell on hard times in the early 1980s.[3] Burke's brother Keith handled most of the money from the accidents.

Buoyed by his fake claims, Robert Burke prospered throughout much of the 1980s. His legal practice reportedly provided an income great enough to make the payments on a Rolls-Royce, a Mercedes, and a Cadillac. In his free time he taught a business class at a local college; he pursued his hobbies as a movie buff and a gun collector; and he even worked part time on a suburban police force filling in for cops who called in sick. In May 1989, however, Burke learned that a federal grand jury had been empaneled to hear testimony about his insurance frauds. He immediately set on a course of cover-up. Over the next few months he arranged meetings with everyone who had been subpoenaed to testify before the grand jury in order to coach them to lie convincingly. Meeting sometimes at his home, his office, or, most preferably for the rotund attorney who later joked with a jury about his girth ("You may have noticed I'm just a couple pounds overweight"),[4] Burke held meetings at his favorite restaurants. At first, Burke met with Dr. Segin. In between bites of steak and after downing some ulcer pills, Burke wanted to make sure that the doctor was not cooperating with the federal investigation; he checked in with the doctor periodically to "keep any animosity from growing up between them." At later meetings Burke would introduce Segin to the people the doctor allegedly treated, so that they could coordinate their stories. The atmosphere at the meetings was often light-hearted. Introducing one of the fake claimants to Segin at a favorite seafood restaurant, Burke joked that the two must be well acquainted given the dozens of times the man supposedly treated with the doctor. ("Oh yeah, we've met a hundred times," the man added. "Forgot about that," the doctor said, going along with the gag also.)[5] Packing away shrimp and snapper this time, Burke coached everyone on how to lie to the federal grand jury and joked about how awful it would be if Frank Passerini, the postal inspector who was the lead investigator on the case, walked into the restaurant. Parked in a surveillance van across the street, and listening to all of these dinnertime strategy sessions through a microphone taped to the doctor's chest, Passerini would have the last laugh. The conversation helped convict Burke two years later. In early 1991, the attorney was sentenced to a five-year prison term for insurance fraud and obstruction of justice. At the time of his sentencing, the attorney still had not been officially named as a suspect in the murder of Donna Willard. But this did not keep Willard's family from voicing their suspicions: "He's a murderer," shouted Thomas "Turtle" Tyrell, Willard's fiancé, as Burke passed him in the courtroom.[6] Willard's sister seconded the sentiment: "It's got to be Burke."[7]

Donna Willard's involvement with Burke was limited—he had represented her in a claim resulting from a legitimate accident in Wildwood, New Jersey, in 1987. Willard seems to have gone along with the initial scheme to pad her claim with fake medical bills, but, when the federal investigation began, she let Burke know that she would not go along with the cover-up. Burke had tried on one occasion to coach her in how to respond to questions about her fake injuries, but Willard was nervous about it and told him she could not go through with it. As far as Burke knew at the time, Willard was the first of his claimants to threaten the cover-up. One day early in March 1990, just after Willard was subpoenaed to testify before the grand jury, Burke called her at the "So Hair It Is" salon, her workplace. According to later testimony from a friend who was in the salon that day, Willard said that if she didn't testify in Burke's favor, she "would wind up with two bullets in her head." The call left Willard so frightened that she had to lie down in the back of the salon the rest of the afternoon. Later that week Willard went to an attorney for advice, but the attorney discounted the death threats as improbable. "I got the impression that she was a very scared young lady," the attorney later said. "She told me several times that she believed she would come to physical harm because of Mr. Burke. . . . [But] I told her this was not an organized crime case, not a drug case, that this was nothing but an insurance fraud case . . . and that I didn't believe she would be murdered."[8] A few days later Willard was shot dead. All eyes turned almost immediately toward Burke, and they remained there—an embittered, accusatory glower from the victim's family. But no formal criminal action was taken against him for almost two years.

For all the speculation about Burke's role in Donna Willard's murder, no charges would have been brought against him if a man named John Foley had not walked into the FBI building in Philadelphia in December 1990 and provided a full account of the crime.[9] In his confession, Foley told how he had helped plan the killing after a friend named James David Louie, who knew Burke from the Rolling Thunder accident, came looking for a hit man to quiet someone who was going to "sing to the feds" about some insurance frauds. Foley introduced Louie to a twenty-three-year-old drug addict named Javier Lebron, who would do the job on the cheap. Foley, Louie, and Lebron drove past Willard's home a few times before the night when they finally parked, negotiated a price (Lebron wanted $2,000 initially but gladly accepted half from Louie), and carried out the hit. Foley did not name Burke as the originator of the murder plot, but later James Louie did. Once arrested and charged with the crime himself, Louie confessed to being "like a soldier to Bob"; by this he meant he had been willing to stage phony accidents and, later, to help Burke coach, bribe, and intimidate witnesses into lying before the grand jury.[10] Louie also firebombed the office of an attorney with whom Burke had once had a dispute over money—again on Burke's orders, Louie claimed (and there was little reason to think Louie would have done this on his own). Dale "Crusher" Thompson, a short, balding car thief who helped Louie with the firebombing, later testified about another plot involving Burke: Thompson claimed that Burke was going to pay him to find Dr. Segin and to kill him, after Burke realized that Segin had been the one cooperating with the government.[11]

In August 1993 Burke was called in from prison, where he was serving his insurance fraud sentence, in order to stand trial for murder. For two weeks a jury heard from the prosecution about how Burke's fear of having his accident schemes found out led him to increasingly desperate measures to eliminate the evidence against him. Burke's "massive campaign to obstruct justice," the prosecutor argued, culminated in the ordering of the death of Donna Willard, who threatened to expose everything Burke had tried so hard to conceal. By contrast, the defense presented Burke as someone who had his faults and who already had admitted to wrongdoing with respect to the accident frauds. "Robert Burke, unfortunately, fell into this easy money thing," his defense attorney told the jury on the first day of the trial, but he would not have resorted to murder to save himself. Rather, it was James Louie who had his own reasons for having Willard killed, the defense claimed. Then, after Foley sold him out to the FBI, it was James Louie who had incentive to pin it all on Burke to reduce his own sentence. ("It was in Bob's interest, as well as in my interest, that the girl died," Louie finally admitted under intense questioning by the defense.) It was also James Louie, not Burke, who caused John Foley to fear so much for his life that he went to the FBI in the first place, according to the defense. "Louie was very paranoid," Burke testified. "Myself and the other people involved just didn't take it that serious—it was sort of like a big joke to us." Burke's defense attorney picked up on this theme in his own remarks, claiming that "Robert Burke was on David Louie's hit list." But the jury did not seem to buy it. "It boiled down to whether we believed Louie or Burke," one juror said; in a "tale of two liars," as a newspaper headline summarized the trial, Louie won out.[12] Returning from deliberations after less than a day—much sooner than expected—the jury announced Burke's guilty verdict in front of a mostly empty courtroom. A few months later Burke was brought back to the courtroom from Holmsburg Prison to receive his life sentence. (Prosecutors were barred from seeking the death penalty.) Despite his appeals, Burke remains in prison.[13]

Since the late nineteenth century, the personal injury underworld had always been a relatively benign criminal subculture—more the home of banana-peelers and relatively small-time white-collar crooks than the turf of toughs and hit men. But in the early 1990s a number of cases of organized accident faking culminated in murder. A teenage girl in New Mexico was shot dead in her car by hit men believed to have been hired by leaders of a Vietnamese accident gang based in Orange County, California; a drifter in New Orleans was thought to have been killed by a group of crooked policemen looking to cover up their participation in a local accident ring; an elderly man in Massachusetts was killed when two accident fakers accelerated their truck into his car. And then there was Donna Willard in Philadelphia.

As fake accident operations went, Robert Burke's was nowhere near as big as rings in Los Angeles, and was not even among the largest in Philadelphia. In earlier years, the city had seen enough accident frauds to earn the distinction of Whiplash City,[14] the East Coast capital of America's present personal injury underworld. One South Philadelphia ring was proven to have staged dozens of accidents using elderly claimants (one of whom claimed she needed the money to fix her teeth);[15] countless individuals and loosely organized groups were found to have targeted the city's mass transit system for passenger "jump-ons" of the sort common to Philadelphia since a newspaper reported on the phenomenon in 1893;[16] and, in the largest case in the city's history, William Mele, a former numbers runner for the Philadelphia mob, became the office manager for a downtown law firm that dealt in hundreds of fake accidents staged by cappers working in every area of the city. Nicholas "Fat Nick" Romano recruited claimants for Mele at Johnny's Place Bar in Overbrook, for example, then usually drove somewhere nearby to crash the cars into telephone poles or brick walls; and, in the northeast, a woman known as "Big Mama" (named for her 300-pound weight and her eleven kids) scripted accidents in her neighborhood then took the claimants down to Mele to get paid.[17] Mele himself, a high school dropout, made more money in the fake accident business than Burke; and David Rosenfield, Mele's attorney partner who spent most of his days at the Philadelphia Athletic Club, got even richer, earning a few million dollars in just a few years. When the investigation began, Mele used his connections to reputed mob bosses Harry "the Hunchback" Riccobene and Nicodemo "Little Nicky" Scarfo to attempt to intimidate the hundreds of potential government witnesses. But murder of the sort later proven in the Burke case seemed out of the question. "The fact is that in your typical fraud case, you're not dealing with witness security and murder plots," said one federal investigator who worked on the Donna Willard case.[18] James Trovarello, the postal inspector who busted Bill Mele's ring and founded Philadelphia's Insurance Fraud Task Force, agreed that the Willard murder was an anomaly in the fake accident business. "It's very rare and hopefully it will continue to be rare," he said. "It's bizarre. It's no reason to kill anybody."[19]

If it was an unlikely idea to murder a potential informant in an accident fraud case, however, it may not have been one unique to James Louie and Robert Burke in Philadelphia. Less than a year before Javier Lebron murdered Willard, another young woman was shot twice in the head by a Latino hit man believed to have been hired by members of an accident gang who wanted the woman silenced. The death of Kaitlyn Arquette, an eighteen-year-old student killed while in her car one Sunday night in July 1989, was initially branded a random, drive-by shooting by the Albuquerque, New Mexico, police. In the weeks that followed, though, Arquette's family became aware of Kaitlyn's involvement with an accident gang operating in Orange County's Little Saigon.[20] Kaitlyn's boyfriend of more than a year and half, Dung Nguyen, had settled in Little

Saigon after coming to the United States from Vietnam and had maintained ties there after his move to New Mexico. When he was strapped for cash, Dung called on some friends in Little Saigon who were accident cappers for a Vietnamese attorney. The capper reportedly sent a car for Dung, brought him back to California, and had him drive the bull car in a rear-ender with other ring members.[21] Some months later, in March 1989, Dung brought Kaitlyn to Orange County in order to have her lend her name to another of the gang's stagings, an act for which she was paid the usual bull's fee: $1500 from Dung's alleged capper, Bao Tran.

Kaitlyn Arquette seems to have gotten involved with accident staging for many of the same reasons she had moved out of her parents' house and into an apartment with Dung just months before her death: She was fiercely independent and liked the chance to follow her curiosity wherever it led. "She was really into the excitement," one of her friends later explained to Kaitlyn's mother about the accident schemes. Her friend continued: "[Kaitlyn] wanted to know all about how the wrecks were set up. By the time they got back from L.A., she knew everything about them. She'd even met the Vietnamese lawyer who arranged them."[22] Kaitlyn's mother later put it this way:

> Our daughter was young and naive, and she fell in love with the wrong person. . . . The car wreck scam probably seemed to her to be just a mischievous, victimless prank that would permit her out-of-work boy-friend to get enough money to pay his share of the apartment rent. She had no way of knowing that this was the tip of the iceberg and that what lay underneath it was the stuff that horror stories are written about.[23]

Kaitlyn Arquette's excursion into the personal injury underworld seemed to have turned fatal around the time she initiated a breakup with Dung. Unlike Donna Willard, who told the people close to her that she feared harm would come to her, Kaitlyn kept her troubles with Dung mainly to herself. Only later did her mother recall Kaitlyn's mentioning any of the accident scams. "She said, 'Do you know what Dung's dumb friends do for fun? They bump cars into each other.' We both laughed at it. It sounded like kids playing 'chicken'; that's all we could think of."[24]

After Kaitlyn's death, Mrs. Arquette faced the same disbelief about the possibility of serious violence evolving from an accident scam that Donna Willard had met from her attorney just prior to her death. Mrs. Arquette, a nationally known author of teen novels published under the pen name Lois Duncan—and the author of her own nonfiction story, *Who Killed My*

Daughter?—refused to accept the police version of her daughter's death. She sought help from anyone she could: a newspaper reporter; private detectives; an attorney from Orange County who specialized in insurance fraud; and a half-dozen psychics whose readings she came to trust, even if others thought her reliance on them tainted her credibility. Within months Mrs. Arquette had developed a variety of different substantial leads, all seeming to point in the direction of a murder plot by a Vietnamese gang that wanted to cover its interstate operations in accident faking and possibly also drug trafficking. She went to the Albuquerque police with reports in hand showing the fake accidents that Kait and Dung had participated in. She also brought other facts, including a phone record showing two calls from Kait's apartment to the accident cappers in Little Saigon made *after* her death (the theory being that someone close to Dung made the calls to report the successful hit to those who had ordered it). But the Albuquerque police dismissed much of the information as the idle speculations of a mother who could not accept the randomness of her daughter's death. "Nothing in California needs to be investigated," one detective allegedly told her. "Nobody there had reason to want to harm your daughter."[25]

Local police decided to record an interview with Dung Nguyen only after an exposé ran in an Albuquerque paper which suggested the Vietnamese accident gang connection to Kaitlyn's death. Dung freely admitted to being driven out to Orange County to participate in Bao Tran's stagings. He also said that Tran knew that Kaitlyn was aware of the ring's illegal activities, but that Tran never mentioned it in the context of not trusting Kaitlyn or in fearing that she would squeal to the police. By the end of the interview, the Albuquerque police detective still seemed unconvinced that any of this added up to murder, however, and five years later this remained the extent of the official investigation.[26]

In October 1993, the family of Paul Langevin in Springfield, Massachusetts, joined the relatives of Donna Willard and Kaitlyn Arquette in having to confront the strange fact of serious violence and death evolving from an otherwise relatively benign accident scam. Langevin, a seventy-one-year-old retired insurance broker, had not involved himself with an accident gang as a claimant, even in passing. He was just a man driving his car near his suburban home when he became a victim of one of the hundreds of staged accidents that may occur on any given day in America.

On June 3, 1993, Langevin's car was broadsided by a U-Haul truck rented by two men acting on the idea that they could get some $10,000 each for personal injuries if they had an accident. Thirty-seven-year-old Stephen Wojcik rented the truck along with his twenty-three-year-old nephew Robert, then they persuaded a friend to drive it, allowing them to later make a claim against the insurance coverage they purchased with the rental.[27] On the day of the accident, Robert and Stephen Wojcik sat in the cab as passengers. The man they hired to drive the truck for them had no idea of the accident staging scheme until it happened: Robert Wojcik, seeing a good opportunity for a crash, reached his left foot over to the driver's side, where he placed it on top of the driver's foot and accelerated into Paul Langevin's car. To his stunned driver Robert Wojcik explained simply, "Don't worry, we're going to get paid."[28]

In the months after the crash, Langevin's family came to accept the fact that Paul had been in an accident in the grudging way that people ultimately make peace with things that are out of their control. Later they had to deal with a new kind of pain and anger when they learned from the Springfield D.A.'s office that the crash had been staged for insurance money. Langevin's daughter found it especially hard to believe that a few thousand dollars in insurance money could be worth the death of her father and that Robert Wojcik had shown the nerve to make a psychological stress claim on top of it (based on a concocted version of events in which he said he held the dying Langevin in his arms). "That was very hard to accept," she said, "that even after he knew that he caused the death that he continued with his little plan."[29] Some measure of justice for the family came with the Wojciks' prosecution in the summer of 1994. In the end, the Wojciks didn't get paid: They got matching life sentences for second degree murder, with the possibility of parole only after fifteen years.

The deaths of Donna Willard, Kaitlyn Arquette, and Paul Langevin each came suddenly and violently to ordinary people with little or no serious criminal involvement in personal injury frauds. The same might be said for the shooting death of Eugene Russell, a twenty-five-year-old drifter and low-level drug dealer, suspected to have been ordered killed by two New Orleans cops looking to cover up their role in an accident ring in which Russell was an occasional participant.[30] A similar fate was shared by an attorney in Southern California involved more deeply with an accident gang. He was found shot dead in the walk-in closet of his home, reportedly killed after he told his cappers and administrators that he no longer wanted to front for their accident mill.[31]

Taken separately, these deaths were exceptions to the general rule of nonviolence in the personal injury underworld. Minor players in larger accident frauds were not being silenced with a new regularity, as the Willard case might suggest; and innocent motorists targeted for ride-downs or swoop-and-squats did not frequently suffer serious injury or death in the manner of Paul Langevin, although such instances most definitely occurred in greater numbers than have been detected. If not the crest of a wave of a newly violent criminal culture, however, these cases did say something about a personal injury underworld in America that was spilling over its traditional boundaries. Lines now blurred that once had separated the purely "economic" or "white-collar" crime of stealing from a private insurer from the street-level reality of increasing numbers of gangs scouting public roads for innocent victims to crash into. And, at the street level itself, divisions now often dissolved between gangs that once had organized for personal injury frauds alone and those that also dealt in more traditional street crimes, such as narcotics. The historical separation between the "soft" opportunist type of personal injury frauds and the "hard" professional sort of organized faking still made sense conceptually, but the gap between the two had widened. The soft frauds continued to grow more widespread. One study completed by the RAND Corporation in 1995 showed in a systematic way what anecdotal evidence had long indicated—that more than a third of all medical costs claimed by auto accident victims nationwide were in some way excessive or exaggerated.[32] Another study, published that same year, established generally that Americans were making more claims for personal injury based on fewer accidents than ever before.[33] At the same time that the soft frauds continued their spread, the hard, criminal frauds got harder. Evidence from law enforcement groups around the country indicated that gangs were now crashing more cars for more money in more cities than this nation, or any nation in the world, had ever known.

Reliable numbers on the amount of money generated by accident fakers have always been hard to come by. Still, certain dollar figures have circulated at different times that suggest the total annual take of the professional fakers, the accident mills, and the clinics—the hard core of the personal injury underworld. These numbers reveal the underworld's broad, steady expansion. They were in the millions during the time when the Laulichts ran their ring in Lower Manhattan, the tens of millions when David Schiffer went to prison in 1948, and in the hundreds of millions as television reporters took their first undercover peeks at accident faking for money. During the first two decades of the operation of the ICPI (the insurance industry's fraud police founded in

1971), estimates of the total cost of hard and soft personal injury frauds crossed into the billion-dollar range. And, in 1992, when the ICPI merged with another industry group to form the National Insurance Crime Bureau (NICB), the estimated numbers for all personal injury frauds nationwide, again hard and soft together, were well into the double-digit billions. Of this, the organized hard-core accident rings and medical mills accounted for a relatively small amount of the total—maybe 5 percent, maybe 10 percent nationally—but still enough money to make the earliest banana-peelers and accident stagers flush with pride.[34]

Numbers were one way to talk about the growth of the nation's personal injury underworld over time, but there were other measures. Beginning in the late 1970s, several dozen states specifically recognized insurance claims frauds as crimes, often felonies. (California's insurance fraud legislation first included specific language about staged accidents in the mid-1980s, and other states have recently adopted similar language.) Roughly half of all fifty states have created special departments to investigate and develop cases of insurance claims fraud for prosecution.[35] The largest of these state units are full-blown insurance fraud detection agencies, ranging in size from one investigator in Montana and Nebraska (where swoop-and-squats were documented with links leading back to Southern California); to a dozen or so investigators in North Carolina, the busiest department in the region; to close to a hundred in Florida, New York, and New Jersey. (New Jersey's aggressive fight on fakers made a national splash in 1993 when bus accidents were staged in Camden as a sting operation to catch "ghost riders" recruited to jump on the buses to make claims.)[36] In many of these states, prosecutors, long resistant to spending too much of their scarce resources on insurance crimes, have grown increasingly aggressive. In the mid-1980s, some began making creative use of the Racketeer Influenced and Corrupt Organizations (RICO) statute, enacted in 1970 for use against traditional organized crime, in order to prosecute some of the larger rings. On the private side, individual insurers, too, have formalized some of their fight on fraud with the development of in-house Special Investigative Units (SIUs). Beginning slowly in the mid-1970s in Massachusetts, the idea of the SIU gradually took hold throughout the rest of the country.[37] In the early 1980s, there were still hardly enough SIU investigators in the Northeast to field a softball team, and meetings were held in the backs of diners; by the early 1990s, there were national and international associations of SIUs with membership in the many thousands and annual conferences at resort hotels.[38] Often lost in the alphabet soup of industry trade groups are the tens of thousands of private investigators working on contract to insurers. Private investigation firms—ranging in size from one-man outfits to Bill Kizorek's massive InPhoto Surveillance, which has more than 100 agents nationwide completely outfitted with custom vans, cameras, and, in some cases, camouflage jump-suits designed to look like shrubbery—constitute one of the fastest-growing segments of an insurance fraud–fighting community that itself is expanding rapidly enough to boast its own self-supporting national quarterly newspaper.

In January 1992 the insurance industry's new message about fraud took on a new air of seriousness and urgency when a former U.S. Army general stepped forward at a Washington, D.C., press conference to announce the formation of the National Insurance Crime Bureau, with himself as the first director. Arnold Schlossberg, Jr., had come to the NICB directly from the Pentagon, where he served as one of the higher-ups in the Bush administration's "war on drugs." So when he declared the latest in a century's worth of insurance industry "wars" on insurance fraud, people listened. At the press conference, General Schlossberg stood alongside his "friends," the deputy director of criminal investigations at the FBI, the chief of the Postal Inspection Service, and the director of the Customs Service Enforcement Division, and talked about insurance fraud as a criminal threat to the American way of life equal in many ways to drug trafficking in terms of its economic cost and its creeping erosion of moral values. "Now, I know we're here in the nation's capital and we have a lot of violent crime going on and a lot of drug crime that gets the attention and gets the headlines," he said. "But we need public help to try to stop and do something about this [insurance fraud] problem because it's affecting every single one of us."[39] The general promised that his agents operating nationwide would lead the fight against fraud, with their access to extensive claims databases and strong relationships with law enforcement groups at all levels. But he also asked citizens to do their part by phoning in suspicions of accident frauds to his group's new twenty-four-hour hotline—1-800-TEL-NICB—the private equivalent of the FBI's tip line. Near the end of the press conference, a reporter asked how long before all of these efforts would actually cut his own auto insurance premium, to which the general replied frankly, "You know, that's hard to know. But we hope it's quickly." And then the general set out to make it happen.

Under General Schlossberg, NICB agents were sent into the field armed with a new sense of purpose—this was a war and the general told them it was winnable. They also were assured a new commitment of cooperation from other law enforcement groups. The FBI even allowed the NICB access to its own crime database, a privilege not granted to any other private group. Field agents were now armed with new laptop computers connecting them with various NICB on-line services. At first the older agents did not know what to do with the new contraptions, but over time they came to appreciate them as a technological emancipation from the old wait for claims histories to arrive on index cards through the mail. Seventy-five years earlier, railway claims detectives passed along their most timely warnings about possible fakers through their monthly *Bulletin*. Now, when NICB agents turned on their computers, "Nationwide Alerts" told them about the movements of certain gangs or families of slip-and-fallers minute by minute.

The new war on insurance fraud would be led by the NICB and the SIUs, using the latest in information technology, with increasing support from local, state, and federal law enforcement groups, some of which were following specific legislative mandates to fight the fakers. Representatives from all of these varied public and private groups would also join together behind the shield of a new organization, The Coalition Against Insurance Fraud, formed in June 1993 "to combat a national, multi-billion dollar problem." The new fraud-fighting initiatives at the national level were appropriate to the nature of the frauds themselves; by the 1990s, they, too, had become increasingly multistate in scope.

Among accident rings that operated in more than one region, the first region usually was Southern California. Just as Abe Gatner spoke in 1927 of the spread of flopping rings out of New York to Cleveland, Detroit, and Chicago, the story some three-quarters of a century later was of accident rings radiating out of Los Angeles and Orange counties to all points north, east, and south. Again, the ties were often ethnic and the reasons, economic. The scenario involving Dung Nguyen being brought in to Orange County from Albuquerque for a staging was not unusual. The Vietnamese cappers of Little Saigon were some of the most ambitious recruiters of out-of-staters, frequently importing participants for fake claims from the large immigrant populations in New Orleans and Seattle's International District, or from communities in states as different as Arizona and Nebraska. ("[Southern California] was like the hub of a wheel," said one head of investigation for a major insurer who used his claims database to follow up on leads in the Kaitlyn Arquette case. "Spokes extend[ed] into New Mexico, Texas, Utah, Arizona, Kansas, Oklahoma, Oregon, Washington, and beyond.")[40] Many cappers, clinic owners, office administrators, and attorneys who had made money in the fake accident trade in Southern California during the 1980s began to sense a change in the early 1990s as they witnessed the success of the State Fraud Division in infiltrating rings. Some got out of the business, but others simply took their show on the road. In the new import/export trade in faked personal injury claims, cappers might travel out of the region to strike up business relationships with new attorneys and doctors to replace those whose names had grown stale with overuse. Out-of-state crash participants were also brought in to serve as fresh names and faces. The development of interstate networks of accident gangs leading out of Southern California, like the mounting instances of violence, was not yet the norm. But their very existence was a far cry from the work of isolated floppers 100 years earlier and was enough to catch the attention of the FBI. The Bureau's Operation Sudden Impact, which began with a push from the L.A. Regional Office and culminated in a "national take-down event" in 1995, would mark another stage, perhaps a final one, in the making of a personal injury underworld in America.

The need for the cappers of Little Saigon to go out of state for claimants grew partly from competition. By the early 1990s, dozens, and perhaps as many as fifty different law offices were paying cappers to solicit or stage fake claims within in an area of Orange County that had become to the Vietnamese in the 1970s and 1980s what the Lower East Side of New York had been to the Jews in the early part of this century. Not immigrants so much as refugees, though, many of the Vietnamese who arrived in Orange County beginning in the mid-1970s were professionals with no place in the Communist order of things, or peasants and fisherfolk fleeing poverty, or young men who did not want to fight in Vietnam's new wars against China and Cambodia. For many of them, the journey to Southern California was at least as perilous as a steerage passage to America from Europe at the turn of the century or coyote-assisted travel north across the Mexican border in the suffocating heat of a truck or boxcar. One account described the trip from Vietnam in this way:

> Escaping by sea, often aboard rickety, overcrowded craft, the boat people were lashed by savage storms or ran out of food and water, and many were robbed, raped, even murdered by pirates. Those who reached Thailand or Malaysia were frequently turned away or confined to refugee camps, sometimes for years. And those lucky enough to get to America arrived amid the severest inflation in a generation, followed by the worst recession in a half-century. [41]

Like earlier groups of newcomers to the United States, many went the route of hard work as merchants, entrepreneurs, teachers, and professionals, embracing some aspects of the new culture and holding on to parts of the old. Some of the young also wanted what America had to offer, but wanted it fast and fell into street gangs to get it. The Vietnamese gangs of Orange County and New York City were often cited among the new faces of organized crime in America. As the author of a book on the Born to Kill gang observed: "The underworld was now an ethnic polyglot with a new generation of gangsters taking over where the Irish, the Jews, and the Italians left off."[42] And somewhere on this continuum, in the gray area where those who adopted the ethic of hard work mingled with those motivated by the equally American idea of the get-rich-quick scheme, were the men (almost exclusively men) who found their way into Little Saigon's booming personal injury underworld.

Among the early refugees from Vietnam to settle in Orange County were men who had been lawyers in Vietnam before the war. Often these men worked to reestablish themselves in offices in Little Saigon during the late 1970s doing the sorts of legal work open to them: immigration, real estate, divorce, and, personal injury, which they soon came to understand to be the most lucrative of them all. By the late 1980s, however, many of these attorneys found it next to impossible to make a living in personal injury law without buying cases from cappers, just as an earlier generation of Jewish personal injury attorneys in New York gradually recognized the necessity of hiring ambulance chasers. Some of these attorneys decided to move out of Little Saigon or into other areas of legal practice. Others were driven out by enterprising Anglo attorneys who opened branch offices in Orange County. More often than not these attorneys had sold the use of their name to assorted Vietnamese cappers, office managers, legal negotiators, and businessmen for $2,000 to $4,000 a month or the short end of a 70-30 split in total profits. These predatory law offices caused price wars over contingent-fee rates on legitimate cases (newspaper ads in Vietnamese papers stated in large letters that the attorney would take only 12.99 percent or 13.99 percent instead of the customary 33 percent); these same offices bought up capped cases as fast as they could pay teenage clerks to type demand letters to insurance companies. "The capping's so open, it's outrageous," complained one attorney forced to move his practice out of the area. "You have 30 to 40 attorneys who have cappers showing up all the time . . . dripping with jewelry, driving fast cars, and thumbing their noses at the legal system."[43] One of the leaders of the

Vietnamese Bar Association of Orange County agreed. "The capping has gotten out of control," he said of the practices that he felt were corrupting his community. "I hope it will end."

Just as Sue Grafton's 1991 novel, *"H" Is for Homicide*, dramatized life in a fake accident gang in Los Angeles, Nina Vida's 1994 novel, *Goodbye Saigon*, described the capping culture of Little Saigon in rich detail, only thinly fictionalized from its sources. Vida, whose husband's experience as a lawyer in the region deeply informed the book, offered readers a heroine named Truong Anh who arrives in the United States in the early 1980s and ultimately settles in Little Saigon. At a local card casino, Anh meets a swashbuckling attorney named Dennis Morgan. (Anh supports her family by working as a "shoeshiner," advising high-rolling men like Morgan on the finer points of the Asian card games.) When Morgan disappears, Anh tries to find him at his law office on the second floor of a minimall, where hundreds of law offices began to appear in Little Saigon during the decade, very few of which were presided over by attorneys. With Morgan incapacitated by a drug problem, Anh proposes to run the law office herself with Morgan's assistant Jana. Jana protests that she's not a lawyer and does not want to go to jail, but Anh explains in broken English: "There law office on every corner in Little Saigon, but no lawyer in there. Smart people find some lawyer and use his name, and they settle case."[44] Jana agrees to go along with the plan only when Anh assures her that they will not deal in fake accidents. Anh agrees, but soon she is propositioned by the leader of a Vietnamese gang, Nep Lai, who comes to the law office to sell his fake accidents. "I heard you've been going around in Little Saigon asking people to send you cases for a commission," Lai says. "I've got business I can bring you too."[45] Anh puts off Lai, but later the gang leader is more insistent over drinks at a nightclub: "I got people arranging accidents . . . I've got four done already. I don't want to bring them to you till we figure out the percentage. I want forty for myself. The people will get something from me. Then I want expenses. We got to bust up the cars a little . . . maybe a few scratches on the people inside . . . [and] that costs money."[46] When Anh resists Lai's attempt to make her office into an accident mill, Lai trashes her office and kills her brother Thinh. Anh's revenge on the fake accident gangster provides the book's dramatic conclusion. But it is Vida's depiction of the everyday interactions of office administrators, absentee Anglo attorneys, and accident stagers that rings most true to life in Little Saigon's personal injury underworld.

In *Goodbye Saigon*, a deputy district attorney tries unsuccessfully to prosecute a woman who was "stuffed" into a fake accident set up by Lai's gang. In real life, the opportunity to get inside a Little Saigon accident mill did not arise until 1991; and, when it did, the case resulted in prosecutions of not just cappers and claimants, but also a doctor and an attorney. Detectives at the Fraud Division (formerly the BFC), knew that accident faking in Orange County had grown rapidly in the late 1980s and early 1990s. Rumors and suspicions intensified around the idea that a new breed of Asian cappers was dominating the scene there in much the same way that other groups had taken turns dominating Los Angeles County. Leads were often hard to pursue, however. The names themselves were hard to follow: Most investigators did not know how to make sense of the different compound names of Cambodians, Laotians, Thai, and, especially, Vietnamese, much less to be able to follow the activities of cappers, claimants, or office managers whose addresses, phones, or beeper numbers changed from month to month, all within a famously insular community. For a time, Vietnamese stagers crashed only with Vietnamese, Cambodians with Cambodians, Thai with Thai. When it became necessary to keep the claims believable, they mixed and matched among the different Asian groups. Early in 1991 word came to the Fraud Division that some Vietnamese cappers were looking for Latino claimants to cap into their accidents. What seemed to make good business sense for the cappers also finally provided the Fraud Division with a way into the fake accident trade in Little Saigon.

In April 1991, while the insurance commissioner was telling the members of the Casino ring that they had "just crapped out " and Esther Diaz and Jorge Ventura Santamaria were on their way down as cappers, Duc Minh Nguyen believed he was on his way up. Born in Vietnam, Duc Minh Nguyen came to America through California's Camp Pendleton in the mid-1970s and settled in Little Saigon. In Vietnam, Duc was an engineer; in Little Saigon, Duc found a new career buying, selling, and scripting accidents and personal injuries to a number of law offices that had come into being primarily to process fake claims. Duc Minh Nguyen, like cappers of any ethnicity, practiced his trade in the parking lots of convenience stores, in minimalls, and in the apartments of a "friend of a friend." His office was often a booth at a McDonald's in Santa Ana, where he could be generous in buying Big Macs for prospective claimants. Once he had his crash participants, his cars, and his insurance paperwork, Duc liked to create damage on the cars himself. He then drove around with his claimants looking for a place to pretend the collision by spreading broken glass and other debris (which he collected in a paper sack after creating the damage) on the ground before calling the police to report an accident. Duc paid the usual sums of money to the people who helped him with the stagings—anywhere from $1,000 to $1,500 for a hammer car and an insurance policy, a few hundred dollars for passengers in the nail car. And attorneys paid him for cases at rates standard within the fake accident industry, based on routine payouts for routine claims by insurance companies.[47]

Tom Sarinana of the Fraud Division first met Duc Minh Nguyen in a booth at a McDonald's. Over the next year and half Duc would lead Sarinana through a labyrinthine network of front law offices and sham medical clinics that had become as numerous as noodle shops in Little Saigon. Duc seemed pleased to be doing business with Sarinana, who called himself Tomas Dominguez. But Duc was also suspicious at this first meeting, and, it seemed, at every other meeting with undercover officers. Duc did not fear the Fraud Division; he only wanted to know if Sarinana was with the FBI and, on several occasions, felt the agent's chest and back for wires. (Later a different Vietnamese capper would make Sarinana swear that he was on the level. "Number one, are you a cop?" the man asked. "Number two, are you working for an insurance company?") Satisfied that Sarinana was who he represented himself to be, Duc explained the kind of accident he wanted, sprinkling the conversation with a lot of comments about making easy money and "doing much business together." During this first meeting it came out that Duc wanted Sarinana to stage an actual collision with another moving car full of Latinos whom Sarinana would recruit himself. "I give you $1,500 to pay [the other driver]," Duc explained, "but only after I get a police report and a claim number from the insurance company. If you want to keep $500 for yourself and only pay your friend $1,000, that is okay with me."

Perhaps assuming that Latinos would put themselves at risk in actual accidents that Asians would not get involved in, Duc planted the seed in Sarinana's mind that he wanted a serious collision. A few days after their initial meeting, Duc underlined this point by phone. "Tomas, I just called to tell you, the bigger the crash, the more money for everyone," he began. "You make sure it is a good accident and it happens on a busy street in the middle of the day. You must make sure the guy you get to hit you do a good job and do a lot of damage." Before hanging up, Duc could not resist one more plea. "Tomas, remember, I want a big, big crash, lots of damage."

After the crash Duc praised Sarinana for doing a good job, then directed him and his fellow accident victims to Dr. Danh Cong Truoung for "treatments" of a sort that would later earn the doctor a prison sentence.[48] In future meetings with Sarinana, Duc repeated his hopeful sales talk about this being just the beginning of a successful "new business venture." Duc dreamed of buying his own Anglo attorney to front for his own accident mill. Over time, he developed aspirations for Sarinana, also, assuring him often that he could rise from the street level to be a capper or an administrator himself. "Tomas, you and I will do much business together and we will make lots of money doing accidents," he said after another successful staging. "I will try to talk to the lawyer and get you more money for all your hard work." The lawyer, in this case, was James Michael MacPhee. A forty-one-year-old graduate of a local L.A. law school, MacPhee had been practicing personal injury law for more than a decade when he said he was approached by a Vietnamese legal administrator who wanted to use his name to open a law office in Little Saigon. MacPhee went along with the plan, which brought him a steady monthly income and allowed him to go into the office only when he felt like it. Unfortunately for MacPhee, however, one of these days in the office happened to be when Sarinana, Henry Avina, and Danny Naranjo of the BFC showed up as claimants in one of Duc's staged accidents.

While a Vietnamese office manager named Larry Lam conducted much of the real business of buying and selling cases in the office, MacPhee was free to sit down with the undercover officers. MacPhee seemed almost nostalgic for the Latino claimants whom he used to deal with often in his old practice but who were a rarity in his Little Saigon office. He spoke openly about his personal life, telling the investigators about a date he had that night with a woman who was "size 38 double D." He also talked openly about his dealings in fake claims—how he had done some in the past but how he was growing sick of the business. "When you get into this business, man, it is a fuckin' crock of bullshit," he told the investigators, who were astonished to be dealing this directly and this openly with the attorney. "I'll tell you," MacPhee continued, "I mean, after a while I'm just going, I'm quitting, I'm going . . . before I get arrested and sent to the big house."[49] Later MacPhee led the investigators out of earshot of Larry Lam and suggested that if they had friends who wanted to deal with him directly, he would be open to it. The entire experience shocked investigators, who rarely encountered attorneys in their work; even when they did, the attorneys usually were more circumspect, discussing fake accidents as "deals" or "situations," and were deeply angered by any straight talk about setups. ("Should I tell my friends about our little joke?" Sarinana asked a different attorney who Duc brought him to see at one point. The attorney had just spent fifteen minutes going through an elaborate charade of righteousness about not getting involved with fraud before agreeing to handle the setup case. "You tell your friends to keep their fucking mouths shut!" the attorney shot back. "As a matter of fact," he added, "don't even mention the fact about the accident being set up to any of my people who work here in the office, you just deal with me.")

As surprised as Sarinana, Avina, and Naranjo were to have had so much direct contact with MacPhee, Duc Minh Nguyen was just as shocked and disappointed to meet the investigators one cold morning in January 1993 when they came for his arrest. Duc shivered in his thin work shirt and joked nervously while he and a few dozen others were taken into custody and a number of different locations were searched in what was then the largest fake accident case in Orange County history. Duc would be the first of the major players in Little Saigon's accident underworld to be convicted and sent to prison, receiving a five-year sentence in August 1993.[50] The next summer MacPhee was convicted along with a few others who worked in his office. In June 1995, all received the same sentence—sixteen months in prison.[51] (MacPhee's law partner, Timothy Elliott, had also been arrested back in 1993 and had watched MacPhee's trial intently, but fled the country just after MacPhee's conviction. Elliott's office manager, Tony Nguyen, a former colonel in the Vietnamese army, was arrested, tried, and sentenced for capping.) That MacPhee would receive the same sentence as a clerk in his office who claimed to have just been following orders disappointed prosecutors. The sentence also left open the question of whether MacPhee was just an employee himself, hired by a Vietnamese office administrator who was not even indicted in the case, and who had since moved on to another law office in Little Saigon.

The breakup of the Vietnamese ring centered around James MacPhee was felt throughout Orange County, where a number of other law offices had also been buying cases from Duc Minh Nguyen. The arrests also reverberated in Seattle, where MacPhee had associated himself with Vietnamese cappers who ran a personal injury office under his name. MacPhee was also connected to a Seattle medical clinic managed by his Vietnamese girlfriend; he spent a lot of time in that city when not in Little Saigon. After MacPhee was arrested in Orange County, the attorney's office manager in Seattle, Viet "Dean" Dinh, got nervous and left the country for Vietnam. A few months later Dean Dinh returned to Seattle where he feuded with MacPhee's girlfriend at the clinic, at one point threatening to blow up the place.[52] Later Dinh would return to the clinic, where he tried to string together enough English to intimidate a claims adjuster who was resisting settling one of his fake accident claims: "Don't try to fooling around with us . . . the FBI and the police, you know, will [have to] protect you and escort you. You need protection . . . I am not threatening you. I tell you the truth, OK. Because you are worth nothing."[53] The shakeup at MacPhee's operation was just the beginning of a larger shakeout of Seattle's new but surprisingly well-developed personal injury underworld.

Seattle's International District was like Orange County's Little Saigon in miniature—a haven for immigrants from Southeast Asia since first-generation Chinese and Filipino men settled there in the 1920s; a city within a city, which offered an oasis of familiarity within a largely unknown American culture. Many of the residents of the International District had family ties to Little Saigon or L.A. County, or originally came from the same village or city as people there, or were linked to businesses based in Southern California. So it seemed natural that accident cappers and personal injury entrepreneurs would move freely between the two sites. And this is just what happened. During the early 1990s, cappers and office managers from Southern California—now billing themselves as "bilingual intermediaries"—went to Seattle to establish the complex and often overlapping networks of lawyers, doctors, and claimants necessary to operate organized accident mills. The Seattle mills quickly evolved along the same lines established in Little Saigon a decade earlier and on the Lower East Side of New York some seventy-five before that. Initially, runners chased legitimate cases, preying on less claims-savvy members of their own communities, counseling them to exaggerate injuries, and often cheating them out of their settlements; then fake claims were scripted, cars were crashed on purpose, and claims were manufactured with the help of complicit doctors and lawyers. In Southern California, a fake accident culture grew up over the course of several decades during the 1970's and 1980s. In Seattle and, to a lesser extent, Portland, Oregon, an organized personal injury underworld was planted there by Southern Californians and seemed to grow up overnight. For a time in the early 1990s, fake accident operations seemed to be coming into the Pacific Northwest as fast as Starbuck's coffee franchises were branching out.

Court proceedings never settled the question of whether James MacPhee was in control of his branch offices in Seattle, or if he was an employee of his administrators. What is clear, though, is that MacPhee and his handlers were not the only accident racketeers to open branch offices in Seattle during the early 1990s. At least a dozen or so doctors and lawyers licensed in California, most of whom had already sold the use of their names for accident mills in Little Saigon, had become involved with medical and legal clinics opened in their names up north. One Vietnamese office manager for an L.A. attorney later explained his move to Seattle from Little Saigon: "I came here and told [the attorney] that it looked pretty good." The attorney thought it looked good also, apparently, so he allowed the man to set up a law office and manage it for him. This same attorney also reportedly had similar arrangements in other states—all modeled on his practice in Little Saigon, as described at one point by Thinh Lee, his office manager in California: "I rent him," Thinh told an undercover officer just before the office was searched as part of the MacPhee investigation. "I pay for him. He is my employee. . . . We control him. He don't control you."[54] For a group of accident entrepreneurs eager to open offices in Seattle, it made little difference that the lawyers and doctors whose names they used for fronts were not licensed to practice in Washington State. According to one federal investigator, letterhead stationery was cut and pasted from the California offices to reflect Seattle addresses. Some homemade forms were photocopied so often and so poorly that dustmarks had become enlarged to the size of dimes, and boilerplate "diagnoses" in the reports were either too blurry or too nonsensical to be deciphered by claims adjusters. One doctor's name was routinely misspelled on his own reports.

Two of the earliest players on the Seattle scene were Frank and Visitacion Duat, a married couple from the Philippines who lived in Los Angeles before venturing north to establish an accident mill. In 1989 the Duats opened a legal clinic called Personal Injury of Washington (PIWI), an accident mill disguised as a legitimate law office, using the names of local attorneys without their consent (just as Milwaukee chaser Louis Saichek had done in the 1920s in establishing his bogus and non-ethnic-sounding National Claim and Adjustment Bureau). One insurance investigator called PIWI "the first of the organized California operations to come up [to Seattle]." Dick Clever, the Seattle reporter who first documented the story of the organized frauds in Seattle, called PIWI "the first ant at the picnic."[55] The Duats reportedly paid runners for cases, demanded kickbacks from some doctors for referrals, and owned other doctors outright, having purchased a medical clinic next door to a PIWI location. With the infrastructure in place to process the claims, the Duats began recruiting claimants from the large Filipino community in Seattle; they soon got involved with Vietnamese cappers and office managers in the International District. The Duats did not deal in swoop-and-squats, drive-downs, or other sorts of accidents staged with unsuspecting victims, for the most part, and neither did many of the other new accident entrepreneurs in the city. Cappers concentrated on paper setups; if necessary, damage was created on cars by running them into other cars or stationary objects. With the money generated through PIWI claims, the Duats were able to buy an expensive house in one of Seattle's most exclusive neighborhoods and to pay $42,000 cash for a new Mercedes. The couple was reported to have been smuggling most of their money back to the Philippines to build a "dream house" for their eventual return.

Following on the Duats' success was another Filipino couple from Los Angeles, Amihan and Gabriel "Gigi" Gonzales. Once in Seattle, the Gonzaleses reportedly did as they had done back in L.A. and bought a medical clinic, then started to network with cappers to bring in claimants at the low price of $600 a head. Gabriel Gonzales wrote most of the medical reports himself, bragging to an undercover officer about his standard twelve-page works, which never failed to read like the real thing.[56] The Gonzaleses paid a doctor with a history of alcohol abuse to front for them and to sign Gabriel's reports. (Perhaps not fully grasping what was going on, the doctor complained to the Gonzaleses that he had not treated "one legitimate patient nor seen anyone with a true illness" in several months at the clinic.)[57] The Gonzaleses also worked with a man named Roberto Salgado who owned a local restaurant but made a lot of his real money arranging accidents to generate patients for the couple's clinic as well as for other clinics and law offices. Salgado himself had moved to Seattle from Southern California two years earlier, so when he needed fresh names for his claims he might call on his old contacts. He once arranged for a man to fly in from L.A. in order to drive a hammer car into a nail filled with four people waiting stationary in the middle of a deserted street late at night. On other occasions, Salgado and other people he worked with paid drivers from Vancouver to come south to lend their names and cars for crashes in Seattle and L.A. in exchange for a few thousand dollars cash.[58] The claims were often processed through doctors and lawyers in L.A. or through a number of different mills owned by people in L.A.

As suddenly as the medical mills and legal clinics appeared in Seattle was as fast as many of them headed out of the country when it was learned they were being investigated by a federal task force led by the FBI. In February 1994, Amihan and Gabriel Gonzales were arrested in Los Angeles as they prepared to flee to Manila, where their main capper, Roberto Salgado, was believed to have already landed.[59] At around the same time, Frank Duat was stopped at the Seattle-Tacoma International Airport as customs officials questioned him about $10,000 in cash and $75,000 in cashier's checks that he carried with him. Duat was ultimately allowed to board a plane to the Philippines (where he remains a fugitive), but his wife Visitacion was not so lucky. She was arrested after trying to reclaim the $85,000 her husband lost at the airport; later she pled guilty to one charge against her and was sentenced to eighteen months in federal prison. Dean Dinh, one of James MacPhee's Seattle operators, had been lucky once in fleeing the country; but on his second attempt at flight he was caught at the airport with his wife about to board a plane bound for Ethiopia. In April 1995, another young capper was arrested in Los Angeles and brought back north to face federal charges, while his partner, also a young capping transplant to Seattle from L.A., successfully eluded arrest.[60] Before the end of the *Seattle-Post Intelligencer's* series on Seattle's new capping culture, the region's *News Tribune* published its own exposé of capping in Tacoma.[61]

In Portland, Oregon, just a few years earlier, a similar scene had been played out in the aftermath of a different FBI-led investigation known by the uncharacteristically colorful codename Operation Kung Pow. A network of law offices and clinics in Portland was linked to one another by ethnic ties from Southeast Asia, by way of Southern California.[62] Again Anglo attorneys allowed their offices to be all but taken over by Vietnamese cappers and administrators who had lived in Orange County before settling in Portland. In one case, capper Michael Lai was the one to find passengers for made-up accidents, then to coach them through the claims process. Lai also staged accidents to create pretexts for his claims, banging together two cars in a deserted area to create believable damage, then taking fake claimants to medical mills that knew how to churn the bills for him. Lai was caught, like many cappers, after he involved an undercover officer in one of his stagings. The agent was able to gather some of the evidence needed to arrest Lai and a number of his associates early in 1993 and later, to convict him.[63] Like many of his counterparts in Seattle, Lai fled the country before serving his sentence. Unlike many of the others, however, Lai would return of his own volition to face the charges against him. Claiming to have had a religious awakening in a monastery in Thailand—and also apparently wanting to rejoin his family, who had remained in Portland—Lai returned with his newly shaved head bowed in shame to begin serving jail time in 1995.

Of all of the cities in the country, San Francisco had the longest record of importing staged accident culture from Southern California. Evidence that some attorneys, cappers, or clinics operated fake accident mills in both regions of California was reported sporadically in the 1970s, then more frequently in the mid-1980s, when some of the first major prosecutions of accident fakers in the Los Angeles area was believed to have created the initial pressure to move north. By the late 1980s, the evidence was overwhelming. Beneath a front-page headline announcing "AUTO-CRASH SCAMS HIT THE BAY AREA," a 1988 feature in the *San Jose Mercury News* reported that "big league auto insurance fraud . . . is spreading from Southern California to the Bay Area." According to state investigators, "Lawyers from Los Angeles, the 'insurance fraud capital of the world' [were] opening branch offices here to recruit people to stage accidents and to pose as [accident] victims."[64] A few years later another front-page feature, this time in the *San Francisco Examiner*, reported the continued northward migration of accident gangs. "Once considered strictly a Southern California phenomenon, the scam is now moving to the Bay Area and the Sacramento Valley," the article stated. "Reasons for the move northward: the increased presence here of economically disadvantaged groups often implicated in fraud, a faltering economy, and a crackdown on Los Angeles–area auto insurance rings, forcing lawyers, doctors and chiropractors to look for new markets."[65] By the early 1990s, some industry experts were estimating that some twenty-five accident mills from L.A. had established a connection in the north. "It is a big problem," observed Joe Del'Marmol, a CHP officer who remembered the days when his biggest case involved a motorcyclist from San Jose who had his girlfriend chop off his foot with an ax to support a hit-and-run accident claim. "It is frightening how big it [has become]."[66]

Like Seattle and Portland, the San Francisco Bay Area was home to its own fledgling fakers before the transplants from L.A. ever arrived: families of slip-and-fallers;[67] stagers whose panic-stop accidents caused prosecutors to question whether a car could be considered a deadly weapon and staged accidents a form of assault;[68] a church pastor who persuaded two brothers to help him stage collisions with unsuspecting drivers.[69] But larger-scale frauds and an organized capping culture were not uncovered in any major way in the Bay Area before the early 1990s. One of the new big rings involved a capper recruiting claimants for attorneys through a phony legal referral service at San Francisco Memorial Hospital, like a Northern California version of the Friends of the Friendless scheme active two decades earlier down south.[70] Another major investigation that ultimately led to the arrests of a chiropractor and attorney began when managers at Bay Area McDonald's restaurants complained to state officials that cappers were borrowing their employees for fake accidents.[71] The largest of the Bay Area accident organizations to be uncovered in the early 1990s was known as the Vang gang. The case showed how accident faking had become as much a criminal specialty for the city's traditional street gang members as loan-sharking, selling crack cocaine, trading in automatic weapons, and dealing in stolen computer chips, all of which the Vang gang did in addition to its apparent mainstay: manufacturing fake personal injury claims from staged accidents.

First uncovered in the summer of 1992, the Vang gang was named for its leader, twenty-one-year-old Billy Dong Vang—short, slightly built, "with a shock of unruly black hair," according to one newspaper description, and probably "the last person you would take for a master criminal."[72] Vang, born in Vietnam and once a settler of Orange County, worked with more than a dozen others who shared his background and were also in their twenties. Vang innovated his own terminology for accident staging, calling hammer cars "quarterbacks" and nails "receivers." But otherwise his schemes followed predictable patterns: Vang offered anywhere from $1,000 to $1,500 to quarterbacks with insurance policies and a few hundred dollars to receivers to play the part of injured accident victims, sometimes supplementing cash with a few grams of cocaine to make up a shortfall. Vang had the run of a law office ostensibly run by an Anglo attorney but almost wholly dedicated to processing his fake claims; he also had the usual business relationships with a number of different medical mills.[73] Like many cappers, Vang often worked out of restaurant booths or from his car, a new green Mercedes. Here he stashed money or drugs for payoffs in paper bags on the floor, wrote accident scripts on the back of fast food wrappers, and frequently drove around the city looking for places to use as accident locations. In his dealings with undercover officers, Vang seemed unwilling to crash the cars himself, telling them that he knew someone who would "total" a car if it proved necessary or else suggesting that the quarterbacks do it themselves by smashing into a wall or lamp post. Although undercover officers never observed or documented any violence, members of the Vang gang talked openly of fears for the safety of themselves and their families as reasons why they might not cooperate with the state investigation. Ultimately, investigators came to suspect core members of the Vang gang of being part of a larger Vietnamese organized crime syndicate with connections in other cities around the country.

The Bay Area and the cities of the Pacific Northwest were among the more popular destinations for accident organizations looking to branch out from Southern California. At the same time, the cities of the Southwest— Phoenix and Houston, especially—were also proving to be attractive places for relocation. "New pastures" is how an FBI agent in Phoenix described the outlook of the Southern California gangs that set their sights on the Southwest in the early 1990s. "It's our speculation that it's simply part of the migration out of Los Angeles," the agent continued, likening the movement of fake accident gangs across state borders to the drug-dealing street gangs that had already moved from L.A. to take over the Phoenix crack cocaine market. "It's not a whole lot different than the Crips and Bloods," he concluded. "The heat there has caused them to branch out."[74] In Houston, an agent with the National Insurance Crime Bureau used the same phrase to explain why a handful of major staged accident rings from Southern California had moved into his part of the country: "There's too much heat in L.A."

Phoenix and Houston—and on a slightly smaller scale, Las Vegas, which also became a frequent destination of L.A. accident gangs looking for new markets—shared a lot of basic similarities with Southern California: a dependence on the automobile, a high concentration of professionals handling low-level accident claims, and a rapidly expanding population, swelled in large part by new immigration from Latin America. Onto this scene appeared cappers who knew how to combine all of these different elements—cars and bodies, doctors and lawyers—into a successful fake accident enterprise. Some of the new Vegas rings would simply drive claimants through the desert to stage crashes, then would process the claims back at mills in L.A. just to cross-up claims adjusters weary of the same scenarios.[75] But many of the Phoenix and Houston rings were true transplants, setting up branch offices a few hundred miles to the east of home base. In the early 1990s, a handful of cappers and clinic owners from Los Angeles approached lawyers and doctors in these cities about selling the use of their licenses for accident mills.[76] A number of L.A. attorneys opened branch offices in Houston and Dallas that reportedly made local arrangements for accident fakings.[77] Whatever indigenous fake accident operations had existed in these cities were quickly being overtaken, like mom-and-pop drugstores in the shadow of Wal-Mart.

If tapping into sources of water made many of the desert cities of the Southwest habitable, cultivating a rich supply of immigrants from Latin and Central America made the fake accident trade there profitable. Regardless of the ethnicity of those at the higher levels of the rings, Latino immigrants were usually the street-level cows of choice. Anglo cappers may have found them first, but, over time, they had also been discovered by African American rings, Armenians, Hungarians, Filipinos, Vietnamese, and now, it was becoming clear in several different FBI investigations conducted simultaneously around the country, by cappers from Bangladesh. Coming originally from one of the poorest nations in the world where subsistence farming of rice, tea, and jute was the mainstay of the economy, the Bangladeshi cappers learned how to harvest dollars from fake accidents. Having come from a country where chickens, ducks, and goats were among the most valuable commodities, the new Bangladeshi cappers soon discovered bulls and cows on the streets of American cities—from Phoenix and Houston, to Fairfax, Virginia, and New York.

As with so many stories of accident gangs operating in more than one state in the early 1990s, the story of the spread of the Bangladeshi-controlled rings began at the Fraud Division in Los Angeles. Late in 1993, a man came to the FBI claiming to have been flown to L.A. from Virginia to stage an accident for a Bangladeshi capper named Enamul Karim. Karim, who was born in Bangladesh but became an American citizen during the 1980s, originally worked in Southern California as an aerospace engineer. His drift into L.A.'s personal injury underworld began with a proposition from a fellow engineer, also originally from Bangladesh, to go into the personal injury business. Karim had just quit his aerospace work and was running an Indian restaurant on Wilshire Boulevard. By the end of 1990, Karim owned a medical clinic on Wilshire and had bought an attorney to front for a law office. When this attorney was disbarred, Karim and his partner put an ad in a legal newspaper worded in such a way that only those interested in lending their name to an accident mill needed to apply. Bruce Bright, a young lawyer who maintained a legitimate (but not sufficiently lucrative) practice elsewhere, answered the ad and soon became the attorney front man for Karim's law office at 3550 Wilshire. With their law office established, Karim and his partner soon made the necessary connections with the cappers who cruised the Wilshire high-rises with fake accidents to sell. José Oscar Coreas, a twenty-seven-year-old capper from El Salvador, was one of the most frequent visitors. Over a two-year period, he sold at least 167 freeway swoop-and-squats to the Bruce Bright law firm. All of Coreas's accidents were the same: Immigrants recruited from a downtown park were stuffed into old cars for sudden stops in front of nicer cars at high speeds. "These were horrifyingly dangerous acts," said Loren Naiman, the L.A. County prosecutor who ultimately jailed Coreas, Karim, and Bright. "They did this sometimes at 55 or 60 miles an hour."[78] For a time in the early 1990s, half of the files in the Bruce Bright office on Wilshire were José Coreas's swoop-and-squats.

In November 1993, Tom Sarinana of the Fraud Division, working in conjunction with FBI agents who developed intercity connections between Bangladeshi cappers, went undercover to learn more about Karim's operation. What he found was not much different from what he had seen in the "Freddy" case at the Tierra Blanca bar in East L.A. or in his dealings with Duc Minh Nguyen in Little Saigon. Early one evening, Sarinana was sent to one of Karim's cappers, a woman who did business from her apartment near downtown Los Angeles. Once inside, he met the usual suspects: a number of Latino men standing around with insurance paperwork passing time with routine chatter about "doing accidents" and getting money. After the capper verified the insurance coverage and scripted the claim, everyone set out for a place to crash the cars: This night, after some false starts, the crash would occur at a deserted intersection in the industrial wasteland north of the city. Then it was back in the cars to Karim's apartment to get paid. Arriving at around 9:00 P.M, Sarinana and the others found Karim at home relaxing with his wife. Karim asked about how the accident went, expressed his preference for making claims against some insurance companies rather than others (to be kept in mind for future stagings), then started peeling off the hundreds from a roll he kept in his pocket. Like Duc Minh Nguyen, Karim saw Sarinana as someone who could deliver him the Latino claimants he needed to run through his claim mills. Before letting Sarinana leave, Karim put his arm around the undercover officer and explained that he would be open to any cases Sarinana wanted to bring in. "Be careful," though, Karim warned. "You never know who you are talking to, this is a very dangerous thing we are doing. We could go to jail."

Karim should have heeded his own advice. Two months after his meeting with Sarinana he was arrested himself by federal agents. Not long thereafter, another Bangladeshi capper made the mistake of taking a Latino undercover officer into his ring—only this time it was in Phoenix, as part of an FBI-led investigation codenamed Operation Crash. When Operation Crash culminated in the arrests of a few dozen people in November 1994, a local newspaper reported in bold headlines that the "PROBE UNFOLDED LIKE A THRILLER NOVEL," and a member of the Phoenix police was quoted as saying that his department "couldn't quite believe the cast of characters involved and the amounts of money."[79]

Detective Johnny Vasquez was the first to follow a tip from an undercover informant into Phoenix's newly developing personal injury underworld. "I got involved with some people from Bangladesh who wanted help setting up wrecks," he later recalled his first meetings with cappers early in 1994. "I was told to go into the housing projects to hire people who would ostensibly be in wrecks." Over the next few months Vasquez and a handful of other Latino undercover officers worked the case. They staged wrecks, went through medical mills, met law office administrators in office towers on Central Avenue, and pocketed money from cappers. Then they would use one officer to bring in another to do it all over again. If the methods of investigation were similar to those used in Los Angeles, so were the findings: that some nine different law offices were paying cappers for staged accidents, many of them run by administrators who purchased the use of the attorney's license; and that a number of medical clinics had been opened or taken over by accident entrepreneurs to process the claims. During the 1980s Phoenix had seen a few small-time frauds: a middle-age man who staged thirty-eight car accidents to take advantage of his hospital indemnity policies;[80] a "Gypsy" family of fakers who specialized in accidents where they pretended to be run off the road;[81] a Nigerian gang from Denver that got caught staging freeway accidents while passing through the city.[82] (Houston also had its local fake accident enterprises, including one massive ring of many dozens of people staging hundreds of accidents since the mid-1980s.)[83] But the interlocking networks of rings— "cells," as the FBI called them—with out-of-state connections that Detective Vasquez was coming to know in Phoenix were much more evolved, more organized, than anything the city had ever known. Estimates of the numbers of crashes staged by the Phoenix groups—300—and the amount of money generated—$12 to $16 million over just a few years—merited respect even by California standards. "We knew a few accidents were being staged," one Phoenix police lieutenant said. "But we soon found that scores of accidents were being rigged each month. Innocent people were being hurt, and the fraud was in the millions of dollars."[84]

While the Phoenix detectives were working the rings from the ground up, the FBI was investigating the interstate connections. Aware of the activities of Bangladeshi cappers like Karim Enamul in Los Angeles, the FBI followed a trail that led into Phoenix and, later, to Houston, where a group of Bangladeshi cappers bought the law office of an Anglo lawyer to use as a base for their fake accident operations.[85] In February 1995, the trail led back to where it started—northern Virginia—where a handful of Bangladeshi cappers operated out of four clinics. They also owned law offices, which they bought from attorneys who answered classified ads in the *Washington Post*; they staffed the offices with their own people and converted them to accident mills.[86] Talk of criminal organizations having "tentacles" that reached across the country was usually reserved for more traditional criminal syndicates. But, in the case of the Bangladeshi accident cappers operating in the early 1990s, the phrase seemed to fit.

As Operation Crash developed, local detectives and federal agents confirmed their suspicions that several personal injury attorneys in Phoenix, most of them Anglos with small, solo practices, had sold the use of their names to cappers who had come into the city from L.A. to start accident mills. What they did not anticipate in any way was the larger framework in which the ring seemed to operate. In an odd ethnic division of labor, Iranians were believed to have controlled many of the medical clinics that processed the claims from the Bangladeshi cappers. And, at the top of the entire operation, it was believed, were the most unlikely kingpins: at least one Russian ex-KGB agent and possibly others with allegedly strong ties to Russian organized crime (the "Organizatsiya"). In similar cases, one accident stager and clinic owner from Los Angeles (who also set up accident mills in Dallas with an Iranian partner) was allegedly connected to Russian organized crime;[87] and members of a federal insurance fraud task force in Philadelphia noted an increase in Russian accident stagers who brought in claimants from Pittsburgh when they ran out of crash victims locally.[88] The Russian connections were probably truer than they may have seemed at first. Journalist Scott Anderson spent much of 1995 "looking for Mr. Yaponchik," the reputed boss of the new Russian emigré Mafia, as a way of finding the substance behind news reports about the Organizatsiya's control of everything from prostitution to the sale of nuclear material. Like much of the talk of the power of the Russian mobs, Mr. Yaponchik turned out to be more a creation of cops and journalists than a criminal master pulling strings around the nation from his headquarters in New York's Little Odessa. Disabused of preconceptions, Anderson went back to his collection of articles on the Russian Mafia, this time scrutinizing ones he had skimmed over the first time, the "insignificant items in the back pages of newspaper Metro sections."[89] And what he found "was a consistent and overwhelming pattern of fraud," often organized, with insurance fraud at the top of the list. Coming from a country where political corruption was the norm, Anderson reasoned, many of the Russian emigrés knew how to lie, cheat, and steal to survive. Once in America, some men "frantically [sought] to make their way in a strange new world where everything was a potential commodity"—car accidents and personal injuries, of course, being one of the strangest but most profitable of the new commodities to be mined for cash. To these men, this was America: "A bountiful land that offered endless opportunity for those with the gall to exploit it." Pioneer ambulance chaser Abe Gatner observed the exact same thing in his confession in the Brooklyn Eagle seventy years earlier—a fact that takes the emphasis off the immigrant's "gall" and refocuses it on the persistent opportunity to make money in America through fake accidents that has always been here to greet him.

In May 1995, ninety years after a coalition of private industry announced the formation of The Alliance Against Accident Fraud, the director of the FBI held a press conference in Washington, D.C., to announce "the most significant investigation of alleged criminal fraud schemes involving staged automobile accidents" in the nation's history. As he spoke, federal, state, and local agents in thirty-one states were making arrests, executing search warrants, and issuing indictments in a "national takedown event" designed to punctuate a year and a half of FBI investigation into the workings of America's personal injury underworld. Codenamed Operation Sudden Impact, the investigation resulted from the Bureau's recognition of organized personal frauds as a significant crime problem across the country, in large metropolitan areas as well as smaller towns.

A number of the arrests announced as part of Sudden Impact had come out of earlier FBI investigations: Operation Kung Pow in Portland, Operation Crash in Phoenix, and the work of the SEACLINIC task force in Seattle. Other arrests resulted from different federal and state probes. In northern Indiana, Operation Claim Chaser was a three-year undercover investigation involving a capper named "Big Gun," who crashed cars in isolated areas late at night, and a drug-addicted doctor who traded fake medical reports for crack. In Georgia, state investigators concluded Operation Slam Scam with the arrests of accident stagers from the central part of the state as well as the exposure of a deeply competitive chasing culture in Atlanta where several dozen medical mills competed fiercely for claimants. A claims investigator from the city spoke to a reporter about threats to her life: "I've had runners tell me, 'You better be careful because you're messing with people who have a lot of money here and they'll kill you.'"[90] One Atlanta runner, Michael Lawrence, was later sentenced to an unusually harsh sentence of fifteen years in prison for staging hundreds of collisions on city streets and highways.[91]

Sudden Impact was felt throughout America's personal injury underworld. Down in South Florida, agents from the FBI, IRS, and the Fraud Division of the State Department of Insurance combined for a joint investigation— codenamed Swamp Rats—which concentrated on medical mills in Miami. Just up the coast in the cities surrounding West Palm Beach, another multiagency task force was tracking "an elusive, loose knit group" of accident stagers who used Haitian immigrants in the same way that rings in California and the Southwest used immigrants from Latin and Central America: as bodies to sit in cars and names to process through accident mills.[92] Sudden Impact also involved two separate rings of college students from Minnesota and North Dakota who traveled to Southern California to stage crashes on the advice of a former student working as an accident capper in Los Angeles.[93] Sudden Impact was not without its freak cases, also. In Ohio, a plan was exposed in which a few backwoods brothers crashed a van into a Norfolk Southern freight train, then filed a $1 million worth of claims against the railroad. Most of the passengers in that van, investigation later revealed, had come from hundreds of miles away and had paid anywhere from $5,000 to $10,000 for the opportunity to be a part of the crash, which promised each a return of $150,000 in settlement money.[94] The van accident was going to be the group's "big lick"—unlike the countless smaller jobs over the previous decade—on which many of them could live comfortably (in their modest way) for years.

On most accounts, Operation Sudden Impact was a success, despite some predictable interagency squabbling about who deserved credit for many of the investigations consolidated under the codename.[95] Backed by the authority of the nation's top crimefighter and reported by every major media outlet in the country, Sudden Impact got across a few simple messages: that there was indeed a personal injury underworld in America; that accident staging and medical mills were operating in most areas of the country; that the economic costs of all of this activity were extraordinary; and that the potential danger to unsuspecting motorists was real. Almost every local newspaper and television station that reported on Sudden Impact was able to include a local angle, a fact that said something in its own right about the pervasiveness of accident faking in America. Each area of the country seemed to have at least one case of organized accident faking that brought home the story; and each of these local stories featured at least one authority saying that this was "only the tip of the iceberg." In Kansas City, a ring of fathers and their teenage sons was accused of staging car crashes and pretending falls from apartment house balconies.[96] In larger cities like Philadelphia, there were several stories to choose from: A young suburban attorney and his father-in-law kept a "rainy day" log, and pictures of potholes and bad sidewalks, to help plan slip-and-falls. (The father-in-law committed suicide under the strain of the FBI investigation).[97] Philly also hosted an accident group run by a struggling singer-song-writer and his friend: "They would ram cars together," the U.S. attorney explained. "They would crash into telephone poles. They would bump taxi cabs when the passenger in the taxi cab was part of the phony ring but the cab driver was not. They would rent cars with the intent of banging them up."[98] In Chicago, one ring of stagers was found to have been run by a city politician; another group, uncovered in Operation Crystal Ball, dealt as often in narcotics as it did in staged accidents (which it classified as either "road jobs" or "wall jobs" depending on whether the accident involved an unsuspecting motorist or not).[99] Meanwhile, a number of lawyers named fifteen years earlier in the Accident Swindlers series in the *Chicago Sun-Times* continued to operate accident mills, albeit from behind the scenes of new firms.

The Sudden Impact map of America furnished a rough guide to the nation's personal injury underworld. While perhaps new to the FBI, the geography of the underworld had been long familiar to those adjusters, ICPI/NICB people, state agents, and postal inspectors who first charted it over previous decades: The terrain stretched from the barrios and urban ghettos to the high-rise office towers and the suburban malls; this seemingly bizarre criminal culture was as common to Butts County, Georgia, and Portsmouth, Ohio, as it was to Miami and Los Angeles. Stories of the large ethnic rings—of attorney kingpins lording over their fake accident empires like mafia dons with 1-800 numbers and of massive medical mills—made up one reality of the personal injury underworld, to be sure. But in their shadow always have been the pint-size schemes hatched at dinner tables, around office water coolers, or in supermarket parking lots—the schemes that drive the dollar estimates of the annual cost of the frauds. The small-timers' pervasiveness reminds us that the personal injury underworld is not some distant netherland of sin peopled solely by immigrants and corrupt professionals too greedy or desperate to stop themselves from taking easy money. It is a world as near as the driveway or a strip of sidewalk or the aisle of a grocery store. And it is a crime that grows so naturally out of everyday circumstances—crashes, falls, household accidents—that the move from our world to the underworld is often imperceptible.

In the South, a region of the country that has remained relatively immune from the larger, California-style accident frauds targeted in Sudden Impact, the fake accident culture has always been close to home. Operation Peachscam, the sexy codename for an investigation into accident faking in South Carolina, actually focused on the decidedly mundane world of fraud within a trailer park on Peachtree Road area near Myrtle Beach. The scheme started in the early 1980s when an out-of-work carpenter named Louis Orlando staged a crash with a friend. Over time Orlando involved his wife and kids in the schemes as well as his brother and his brother's family; later he brought in others who lived near him in the Dogwood Mobile Home Park: husbands and wives, ex-husbands and ex-wives, brothers-in-law, uncles. Most of the accidents involved two cars full of Peachtree area residents agreeing on a place to crash into one another, or else having one car full of people drive off the highway and fake a crackup with a tree. Occasionally group members would stop short in front of an unsuspecting driver, usually an old person in a new car. According to a federal indictment of the Peachscammers: "The defendants would basically drive around until an opportunity arose to cause an accident with an unknown party . . . the defendants' vehicles would suddenly slow down or stop or pull out in front of an innocent party at a point where a collision could not be avoided." Although the Peachscammers were involved somewhat with a local chiropractor, they took care of most of the medical reports close to home, working up fake hospital bills on a personal computer and marking them with a "Paid" stamp bought at a stationery store. Members took turns pretending to be supervisors at a fake landscaping business to verify each others' employment status in order to collect lost wages. Many ring members began by wrecking cars with axes to avoid onerous monthly car payments, then were persuaded not to waste a good wreck without filing a personal injury claim, also.[100]

After he was caught, tried, and sentenced, Louis Orlando agreed to travel to Washington, D.C., to speak at the press conference called to announce the formation of the NICB. Sharing a stage with General Schlossberg, the new NICB chief, as well as with some higher-ups from major federal agencies, Orlando was put forward as the face of a multi-billion-dollar criminal underworld to be taken as seriously as drug trafficking. Reporters were intrigued by Orlando. They directed more questions at him than they did anyone else, but Orlando's answers disappointed those who were probing for true-crime grit. When reporters pressed him about the full range of his activities, Orlando demurred politely that he mostly "just wrecked automobiles." When they pressed him about the money he made, Orlando said frankly that his personal take from a staged auto accident was never much more than $1,000. Finally, when asked where he found people to do the accidents and whether they "were deeply involved in [other] criminal activity," Orlando answered: "Well, it was more like your neighbors. You know, it weren't people that were involved in other different crimes. It was just people that got involved in something because they needed some money."[101] Later one of his neighbors answered a reporter's question the same way. "It [was] easy money," the man said. "I looked the other way. I [knew] it weren't right and I'm sorry."[102]

The South was filled with homespun accident fakers like the Peachscammers, most of whom worked outside of the standard attorney/doctor/capper structure, sidestepping the high-volume mill model of success. Russell Ramsey, a sixty-one-year-old man who sometimes made jewelry for a living and other times staged accidents, lived and worked in Mt. Vernon, Kentucky, another southern city that didn't make the Sudden Impact map. The Russell Ramsey ring, as the group was later called, was another loose collection of family, friends, and neighbors operating from an economically depressed part of town. Unlike some of the bigger organizations elsewhere, the Ramsey ring did not specialize in any one kind of accident. Ramsey himself had faked diverse claims over the years: hit-and-run car accidents, a fall while carrying a television set, and at least one mishap involving the rollover of a tractor lawn mower. Ramsey and his group did not own a medical mill; they actually drove more than 150 miles across the Tennessee border to find a few doctors who would write the phony reports and admit them to local hospitals to collect on some 3,000 claims made on 1,400 hospitalization policies yielding over $3.2 million in five years.[103] Billy Ray Walker, the namesake of the Billy Ray Walker ring in Gastonia, North Carolina, staged many of his ring's crashes himself. From 1989 until he was caught in 1993, Walker spent many days of the week cruising a busy intersection near the on-ramp to Interstate 85 in pursuit of old people and mothers preoccupied with children, in order to stop short in front of them or to sideswipe their cars. ("Who would take advantage of other people that way?" asked a seventy-two-year-old woman after learning that Walker had forced her into a collision that she had believed was her fault. "My life was at stake.")[104] A Pine Bluff, Arkansas, man also concentrated almost exclusively on colliding with elderly drivers changing lanes. Known as the Ramblin' Man, he staged more than 150 collisions in Kentucky, Mississippi, and Tennessee, mostly to make property damage claims on his battered Ford, but occasionally for minor personal injuries. Like Russell Ramsey and Billy Ray Walker, the Ramblin' Man did better in the fake accident business than he had in his previous occupation—a police officer.[105] His success was contagious. A year or so after his arrest, a former sheriff from White County, Arkansas, was arrested for his part in a fake accident scheme called "the largest ever in state history," although it was still mom-and-pop stuff compared to much of the rest of the country. The ex-lawman's group (largely members of one family) traveled through Missouri and Texas, renting U-Hauls to crash into cars filled with people they paid to play the part of the injured passengers.[106]

Mixed into the usual southern blend of backyard schemes have also been a few larger cases: During the 1980s the town of Corinth, Mississippi, led by its mayor, became something of the small-town capital of insurance crimes in America, with people buying multiple hospitalization polices at a local hang-out named B.J.'s, then taking to the streets in crash helmets for drive-downs. ("The risk is real dangerous to talk about insurance fraud here," one unidentified Corinth man told a TV reporter in 1986. "The people that's involved would have you killed instantly, if they knew you was telling about it.")[107] At around the same time in Greensboro, North Carolina, state investigators launched Operation Collision against a ring of accident stagers whose numbers had swelled to more than seventy. And in the early 1990s, North Carolina's newly formed Fraud Division began infiltrating its own ethnic rings. Just a few months before the Sudden Impact takedowns in 1995, Arinze Nwandu, the leader of a gang of mostly Nigerian immigrants, pleaded guilty to organizing twenty-seven car accidents from his restaurant in Raleigh.[108] In the few years previous, a number of other Nigerian accident stagers had been prosecuted in North

Carolina and Fraud Division leader William C. "Billy" Creel said the investigation was potentially "never-ending."

The FBI's Sudden Impact map stopped at the U.S. border, but America's capping culture might be spreading northward to Canada, at least according to several accounts from the early 1990s documenting a "flourishing underground economy" in staged accidents and faked personal injuries.[109] The fraud in question was said to have been "imported" from the United States—not at all what Canadians had hoped from NAFTA, the new free trade agreement between the two countries. Initial reports noted an increase in "Whiplash Willies" out to cheat the province's no-fault insurance system following an increase in benefit limits.[110] News reports followed with descriptions of a more organized capping and staging culture in metro Toronto that had reached "epidemic" proportions.[111] Then, in September 1995 came the arrests of five cappers from an accident ring in Toronto that had generated more than a million dollars by staging at least fifty-seven accidents in just a few years using claimants plucked from unemployment lines.[112] The ring involved Vietnamese office administrators and claimants with possible connections to gangs based in Orange County's Little Saigon. In response to some of these disclosures, the Canadian insurance industry declared war on the "accident benefit fraud rings."[113] Canada's war was fought primarily by its own Insurance Crime Prevention Bureau (staffed by over 100 investigators, all ex-police officers working from twenty-seven branch offices); aided by its own Casualty Claims Index Bureau; and led in lobbying by its own Coalition Against Insurance Fraud. The total estimated dollar loss to faked claims in all of Canada was still less than the estimated annual loss in Southern California alone, however. And it was not likely to climb higher so long as criminal investigation continued apace and state benefit rates could be re-scheduled downward (as they were in late 1995) to reduce incentive.

In Ireland, the state Motor Insurance Bureau reported a growing illegal market in faked claims during the early 1990s. They pointed to several different cases: Edward O'Leary, a professional slip-and-faller, was shown to have worked in restaurants and hotels; a popular soap opera actor pleaded guilty to taking 500 pounds to run his car into a taxi, when he was out of work and behind on his mortgage payments; a teenager was arrested for jumping aboard a crashed Dublin bus to make a personal injury claim; and some thirty car accidents were believed to have been staged between drivers working together to generate personal injury claims during a four year period beginning in 1989. Some believed that elements of organized crime in Dublin crime were getting involved in the newly organized accident frauds.[114] Others in Irelands' insurance defense field believed that the explosion in faked claims was due to broader trends: namely to the Irish adoption of the contingent fee ("no foal, no fee") and the recent allowance of attorney advertisements on radio, in phone books, and on the backs of buses which created a new response to a Dublin street accident: "Will I gerra claim outa it?"

Ireland's personal injury fraud problem, as minor as it is relative to the U.S., is the only thing of its sort in Europe. Where accident gangs exist in England, West Germany, and France (an ex-police investigator occupies the position of "Monsieur Fraud"), they are of the sort where damage is created on cars in controlled ways in order to make property damage claims, not to generate personal injury claims.[115] As America's personal injury underworld has grown over the past century—now with an organized criminal core of rings (sometimes working interstate), and with serious public investigatory resources alloted to fight it at all levels of government—other industrialized nations have watched with amazement and disbelief, having long since addressed the underlying structural-legal questions. As early as the late 1920s, one British legal journal described "How the English Chased the Ambulance Chaser," announcing that the "English ambulance chaser is as extinct as the dodo" thanks to a program of state and bar reforms;[116] another British journal looked on the ambulance chasing and accident faking of Abe Gatner and the Laulicht Brothers in New York as "a crying scandal."[117] Later, the editors of this same publication pressed the point even more strongly in a statement that still holds in large part—not just for England, but for almost every other country in the world. "However serious and undesirable [ambulance chasing and accident faking] have been in England, it is a matter of congratulation that they have by no means reached the amazing development attained by ambulance chasers in the United States of America."[118]

No matter how organized accident frauds have become in the United States over this past century, the spirit of the original American slip-and-fall artists has never died. The ghost of Frank Smith, the greatest of the great banana-peelers from the early part of this century, still hovers high above supermarket aisles, public buses or trains, department stores, movie theaters, or anywhere else that a purposeful slip-and-fall might be contemplated or carried out for profit. In the early 1990s, some food and drugstore chains, supermarkets, and public transit systems resolved no longer to be victims of the frauds, installing closed circuit cameras and hanging warning signs that they would prosecute "false claims of unwarranted slip and fall to the fullest extent of the law."[119] Atlantic City casino operators also launched a "crackdown on gamblers who angle to make a quick buck via bogus slip-and-fall claims against New Jersey's fat-cat casinos."[120] But the great tide of 100 years of slip-and-fall history will not be so easily swept back with a new broom. And no camera could ever really capture the legend of Banana Anna Strula, even if prosecutors had finally managed to jail the woman back in the first decade of this century. The great majority of slip-and-fallers still live a marginal, hand-to-mouth existence, doing accidents as just one of a number of minor cons to survive. A few slip-and-fallers do better than merely survive from claim to claim, but their means of doing so still ranks them among the saddest outlaws ever in the annals of American crime.[121]

David Ballog was a story unto himself. Until he walked into an FBI office in Chicago in April 1993, Ballog—a short man, with a barrel chest swelling into a round, mostly bald head with scarcely any neck in between—was as much the king of the slip-and-fallers as anyone ever had been. He was so good at what he did, so much the product of a century of evolution in the slip-and-fall arts, so practically postmodern in his methods, that he did not need to actually slip and fall to make millions of dollars in faked claims over two decades. Ballog had a con man's talent for reading people and situations, not a flopper's penchant for pratfalls. He liked making money from claims, not taking dives—and his central insight was that one did not have to do the latter to have the former. Accident faking was not essentially about accidents, he understood; it was about faking: a potentially pure con. Where some in his line of work would see sherbet melting on the floor of a supermarket as an opportunity for a fall, for instance, Ballog thought differently. He would merely report to the store manager that he had seen someone fall on the sherbet, then later he would find someone to call the store pretending to have been that person, and the claim would proceed from there. If Ballog thought an actual fall necessary, he would have someone else do it, preferably someone in his family or a member of his "crew," a loose group of twenty or so people he could call at any time to do a claim. Then Ballog would play the part of the husband, the father, the brother, or the uncle in order to negotiate the claims with the insurance company. "I was the best on the phone," he later recalled. "It sounds crazy but adjusters would fall in love with my voice. I never chopped anybody up. I always let the adjuster know that I didn't want to get rich off the insurance company, that I only wanted what was fair. They sucked it up. In truth, my main concern was the money. I worked all the time. I'd come home at night and just fall apart, exhausted."[122]

The record of just a few years in David Ballog's claims-faking life fills more than 100 pages on file at the U.S. District Court in Chicago. The document covers some sixty variations on the theme of finding a potential hazard somewhere on the property of a commercial establishment (the bigger the better), then exploiting it for $5,000, $10,000, or $20,000 in settlement money. A puddle of coffee on the floor of McDonald's, soap spilled on the bathroom of an Olive Garden restaurant, oil in the parking lot of a Red Lobster franchise, a tottering soda display in a Publix supermarket, chili-ooze on the grounds of MGM Studios, hot sauce squirted inadvertently in the entryway of a Taco Bell, torn carpet on a cruise ship: All of these nuisances were opportunities for Ballog, operating in and around Chicago, or on one of his fraud-funded vacations to southern Florida. And all would be said to have resulted in injuries such as broken noses (smeared with fresh blood extracted from elsewhere on the body and daubed on for effect), or compression fractures of the spine, a specialty of Tony Ziga, one of Ballog's distant cousins with whom he partnered for dozens of claims. ("Ziga was the goose that laid the golden egg," Ballog later said. But "almost everyone had something you could use in a claim.") The government's accounting of Ballog's activities was a good place to begin to understand the broad outlines of his life on the personal injury grift. But only Ballog himself could really fill in the details.

One morning in the early fall of 1995, Ballog sat in a hotel lobby in a northern Chicago suburb and talked about his rise and fall in America's personal injury underworld. "I was a pro," Ballog began in a slightly rehearsed way. He sat back in his chair initially and did not at any time remove his coat—a faux-satin baseball jacket from a hotel near O'Hare airport where he worked for a time while awaiting the start of his twenty-month prison term. "I mean, it sounds like I'm bragging. But the bottom line is I made a ton of money, I lived very high, very fast, through abusing insurance companies: slip-and-falls, mainly, but also jewelry claims, other things. I didn't use fake lawyers. I didn't use fake doctors. I used my wits. I'm not embarrassed to say I was one of the best in the country." Ballog paused for a moment, then moved forward in his chair to make eye contact: "I saw the first part of your book where you talk about a man and his wife traveling around the country breaking bones, or 'floppers' diving in front of trolleys. Those people were clowns. They're like these guys today beating each other up for claims: I laugh at them. They're comedians. Dumb-dumbs. You take me back to the 1800s and I'd blow them all away."

Ballog spoke for several hours. In the time since he had first surfaced in 1993, he had become used to answering questions—first from the FBI, then, beginning in late 1994, from insurance adjusters around the country who attended the fraud prevention seminars he conducted in conjunction with the NICB. If asked, in the original talk show–style format of his fraud seminars,

Ballog might discuss the details of his scams—how to get a fake social security card, how to set up an address for mail or a phone number for messages, how to get a legitimate doctor to write a fake medical report for free. As the seminars developed, however, Ballog would play a stand-up, in-your-face Don Rickles: He berated adjusters for their credulity ("You all think there's no fraud going on in your world. You know zip"). And he taunted them with put-downs: "Anybody know what a tomato is? How 'bout chump? Dolly? Carrot? You know what we call you people? Carrots." After a little less than a year on the road with NICB agent Jerry Dolan, his amiable, even-tempered straight man, Ballog had come to refer to his fraud prevention seminars as "shows." The more shows he agreed to do, the longer his prison sentence would be delayed. Some adjusters who heard Ballog speak could not help but feel that the shows were just another rabbit Ballog had pulled out of his hat to benefit himself. Most likely, they felt, they would always be just carrots in the con man's eyes.

Going one-on-one in an interview, Ballog's low energy indicates that he is used to speaking for higher stakes: big crowds conferring star status on him, chumps giving him money, women. He is guarded with the details of his upbringing because he thinks that he will be able to turn them into cash at some later date with a book deal. He lets slip just enough information for a sketch of his early years: Born on the streets of Chicago, a Hungarian Gypsy, he says, Ballog quit school in eighth grade in part because he had a hearing problem that made learning difficult, but mainly because he could use the time to make money having adults lay down bets for him at the track. He married at seventeen, had three sons, then divorced in order to marry his sons' baby-sitter, a sixteen-year-old girl whose brother would later be largely responsible for Ballog's having to turn himself in to the FBI. Ballog's father, a violin player and lounge entertainer whom he occasionally joined for a song ("'San Francisco,' 'Because of You,' things like that") was pained right up until his death in 1991 that son David had not used his sharp mind or musical talent to lead an honest life. Ballog himself reports this fact as if pained himself. He says that he might have become a doctor or a lawyer or a senator if his energies had been aimed in a positive direction. (At the beginning of the century Abe Gatner had similar regrets; he had studied to become a lawyer himself before getting lost in the ambulance-chasing and accident-faking arts.) The conclusions Ballog ultimately arrives at about himself and his choices seem pulled from one of his talks. "The biggest con I ever pulled was the con I pulled on myself," he says at one point. Later: "As smart as I was about claims was as dumb as I was about my life."

To look across a table at David Ballog, to listen to him speak, to read about him in newspapers, court documents, or insurance industry publications, it is easy to lose sight of him in any number of different clichés common to personal injury fraud stories: the little guy taking on the system (albeit through fraud), the "Gypsy" leader of a family of thieves, the criminal mastermind. Ballog seems to try each of these on for size in speaking about himself. Sometimes he presents himself as a populist champion leading the fight against the monolithic insurance industry, rationalizing that it is "not like really hurting anyone" to steal from them. At other times, Ballog talks about first learning of doing fake claims from another Gypsy family, the Kallaos of Detroit. "I was twelve and Tommy Kallao was eighteen driving a Rolls-Royce with money he got from claims," he says. "That opened my eyes." (Far from anything he chose to do, then, Ballog sometimes paints fraud as just "a way of life" for his people. "At a wedding, when somebody shows up with a new car or a new suit the questions everybody asks are, 'How much did you collect?' and 'Who was the company?' And then they ask you, 'Know anybody who can come to my new house and fall on the steps?'") One moment Ballog presents himself as a con man, plain and simple. But then, in the next sentence, he might want you to know that he was more than this—that he lived high (when he traveled, he stayed in the best hotels; his home, he says, cost over $250,000); and that he was in trouble with some of the biggest players in Chicago organized crime on account of "juice" loans for his gambling, but that he got out of it by surreptitiously turning mob collectors to his side for use in fake claims. ("The mob thought I was working for them, but, in the end, they were working for me.") When a newspaper writer elevates Ballog to the status of "godfather of fraud," he likes this, too: "If that's what they want to call me, I'm okay with that," he says, perhaps thinking of possible angles for his autobiography. But then later he seems uncomfortable with this frame for his life: "They label me 'mastermind,' and that's fine. But you didn't have to be a mastermind to make big money off a company."

The problem of what to think of David Ballog is in many ways the question of how to understand the larger personal injury underworld. Ballog was a walking history of the personal injury underworld, an amalgam of its different inhabitants all in one. Ballog's three main criminal identities—the lone con man, the family ring member, the organized faking crewman—were the three main profiles of accident stagers throughout the past century. Ballog's story did not involve doctors or lawyers or cappers, some of the main players in the most important cases. But not being fully representative of the most pervasive or costly types of hard frauds did not keep him from somehow being symbolic of the larger fraud culture. Much of the ambiguity about the place of the accident fakers in American crime and culture could be read into two views of Ballog printed in a *Chicago Tribune Magazine* cover story: In staged color photographs showing Ballog helping a young girl (who happens to be his daughter) pretending to have been hit by a Lincoln Town Car, Ballog is pictured in the way he most wanted to be seen: an upscale con man who is to be admired for his ingenuity, his offbeat manner of crime, and his smart double-breasted suit. On a back page, though, Ballog is shown in a black-and-white mug shot stripped of his schtick with patchy beard growth and an intent predatory stare. In this picture Ballog seems every bit the man who may have once tried to move his legitimately injured son from a hospital room in order to use him in a faked fall down a set of steps, despite the risk of causing further injury. The problem of how to understand David Ballog, and accident insurance criminals in general, is also evident in two differing portrayals of him on television. One is framed with some cute footage of Buster Keaton pratfalls in silent movies; another is a tough interview with Ballog as "Mr. X" in which he is shown in shadowy silhouette to protect him from possibly violent reprisals from his enemies.

Ross Silverman, the former U.S. Attorney who prosecuted Ballog, was one of the few people who dealt head-on with these two visions of David Ballog and came down hard on one side. "Everyone sees [Ballog] as this short, fat, disarming, cute, inarticulate, sincere crook," Silverman observed. "But really he's a bad guy. He really is a bad guy." But a lot of the badness to which Silverman referred involved Ballog's noninsurance–related swindles, leaving open some of the real questions what to think of the accident fakers. Ballog stole from insurance companies, clearly, and this is bad in the sense of raising premiums, but it is not the same sort of moral badness that attaches more naturally to a mugger, rapist, or murderer. Perhaps, then, this just means that there is a difference between white-collar and street crimes. But then was someone like Ballog, who did some of his stealing from insurers with the help of fake vomit he mixed up from potatoes and Thousand Island dressing, a "white-collar" criminal? Arguing in the other direction, the fake accident enterprise—Ballog's faking crews, as well as the more differentiated rings of Southern California and elsewhere—can be thought of as analogous to the street gang or the mob syndicate. But then there is the picture of David Ballog standing next to Michael Anthony Spilotro, a real godfather later portrayed in a violent Hollywood gangster movie, which put the self-promoting godfather of fraud back in his place. "I was at the bottom of the totem pole, when you looked at what I did on the scale of crimes," Ballog said at one point,

FIGURE 8.1 A/B. Two views of David Ballog, Jr., who arranged slip-and-fall accident claims for almost two decades. The top photo is a booking print taken at the time of Ballog's arrest in the early 1990s. The bottom photo was staged for the cover of the *Chicago Tribune Sunday Magazine* in 1995. The problem of how to reconcile these two images—hard-core criminal and sideshow performer—is in many ways the problem of how to think of America's personal injury underworld in general. (*Chicago Tribune* photo by Bill Hogan.)

coming to terms with the kind of criminal he was. "But, on the other hand, I was making as much money as anyone in organized crime except for drug dealers." The point was not simply about the self-esteem of a thief questioning his status among thieves. It was about an underworld both silly and, at times, more seriously criminal, based on a crime that was less a violation of a commandment than an expression of American cultural confusion about the proper relationships among everyday accidents, insurance, and money.

Ballog is now in the parking lot, standing near his car. It is not a Rolls-Royce, if ever he drove one; it is a domestic sedan, slightly high-end but not new. He talks about what he expects prison to be like and resolves to not tell the other inmates his business. Ballog repeats his desire to write a book about his life upon his release, but also allows that he might use his strengths in negotiating to help legitimate personal injury victims get their due from insurers. Mainly, he hopes to continue doing "motivational speaking" and "education sessions" for insurance claims representatives—only this time for a fee. A few months earlier he told an interviewer how satisfied he was with his work for the insurance industry and how dramatically his life had changed since he had turned himself in to the FBI. He said he had grown closer with his kids from his second marriage, who did not know what he did for a living until their teens (they thought he was a trainer at the track) and, in fact, did not even know that their name was Ballog during much of this time. ("They thought it was Marshall, one of my aliases.") Ballog also reports enjoying a closer relationship with his wife, who, also for years, did not know how he made his money and had urged him to quit after she found out. "For the first time in as long as I can remember, I am proud of what I am doing," he says. "And when [claims adjusters] come up to me and shake my hand and wish me good luck, it feels good. I finally feel good about who I am and what I am doing."

As Ballog navigates the parking lot—the very venue in which he may have once thought to crash the car into a light pole in order to collect the debris for a faked claim—his parting words still hang in the air: "I didn't have the education, and I needed the quick money, so I took a shot and it lasted twenty-five years. Now it's over." His tone recalled David Schiffer, a slip-and-fall organizer on Ballog's scale, who reflected on his arrest in 1948 after some twenty years in the business: "The judge gave me four-to-eight in Sing Sing. This sentence was more than I anticipated but I am man enough to take it as all my life I lived with the adage that in playing with fire I will get burnt some day."

Ballog's words gave out for a moment. Then he began again, this time seeming to put aside his new role as insurance industry advisor. Ballog once again recalled the glory days of his twenty-five-year run in America's personal injury underworld—his apprenticeship under Tommy Kallao, his delight in mastering his craft, his high living. Listening to him, it is hard to imagine that he will be able to buck the long-term trend of career accident fakers and actually stay away from the easy money of faked claims after prison. The image of recidivist banana-peelers and swoop-and-squatters colored the scene as Ballog tried to shrug off his upcoming prison run for falls on fake vomit. "I'm fifty years old," he started one last attempt at summary. The beginnings of a smile took shape on his mouth, and the glimmer of countless thousands and millions of successfully faked claims over the past century seemed to flash through his small eyes. "If I die tomorrow"—his words lingered in the parking lot as his car receded from view—"I have lived a good life."

WHO KILLED JOSÉ LUIS LOPEZ PEREZ?

THE MAKING OF A PERSONAL INJURY UNDERWORLD IN AMERICA

The history of the city's gangs can be seen as running close parallel to the progress of commerce. From small, specialized establishments narrowly identified with particular neighborhoods, gangs branched out, diversified, and merged . . . demonstrating their mingled respect and derision for the world outside their turf through parody: parody of order, parody of law, parody of commerce, parody of progress.

—Luc Sante, *Low Life: The Lures and Snares of Old New York*

No one whom I encountered in Los Angeles in all the time I spent there ever wholly relinquished this conception of the city as the center of the California dream, the capital of America's America. The businessman in the California Club and the poorest Salvadoran immigrant alike wanted it so.

—David Rieff, *Los Angeles: Capital of the Third World*

WHO KILLED JOSÉ LUIS LOPEZ PEREZ? More than three years after the twenty-nine-year-old Salvadoran was crushed in the backseat of a Pontiac (a casualty of a failed swoop-and-squat accident on an L.A. freeway), the official answer is unsatisfying. None of the main defendants in the case has yet been tried: neither Gary P. Miller, the personal injury lawyer alleged to have been in line to buy the staged case; nor Phil Santiago, Miller's main capper; nor Elena Shamis, Miller's office manager, arrested at her expensive home in the valley in the summer of 1995; nor Juan Carlos Amaya, a suspected swoop-car driver in Santiago's crashes. Only some minor participants have pleaded guilty to insurance fraud charges and most received only sentences of probation.

In April 1994 Jorge Sanchez, the driver of the Pontiac, became the first to plead guilty to a greater charge—vehicular homicide—and to be sentenced to four years in state prison.[1] But what did this really mean? If Perez had not switched seats with Sanchez just before the accident, the question here might be, Who killed Jorge Sanchez? And if the accident with the Pontiac had gone wrong on the second of the earlier staging attempts, and not the third, the question may have been Who killed Ruben Garcia or Angel Hernandez (two crash participants from the previous day's failed staging)? In these cases, Perez himself, as the driver of the Pontiac, may have been part of the answer, not the subject of my question.

For a while, I hoped that the case's prosecutions would be completed before I finished this book. Over time, however, the legal outcome seemed less important to me. All of the players seemed interchangeable with any number of others who could just as easily have been brought together to do the crash, to process the resulting claim, or to face the criminal charges if things went wrong. And this crash was interchangeable in many ways with countless others, from Phoenix, Chicago, or Philadelphia whose outcomes were not as dramatic, or as well documented, but whose broad outlines were identical: crash cars bought cheap at auction; cappers finding bodies "to ride" at the last minute; doctors and attorneys off somewhere in the misty distance waiting for names to insert into boilerplate medical reports and settlement demand letters to insurers. In surveying the last century's reporting on accident fakers, what has often passed for the "real story" is the dollars-and-cents, bottom-line for consumers: The estimate of the annual costs of such frauds nationally is reported like the Dow for its periodic fluctuations, always upward, reinforcing the opinion of one writer from 1936, who observed: "There is nothing new about the [fake] claim racket except its size."[2] The comment proved only partially true. For me, the only thing truly "new" and unreported about organized accident faking in America was the fact of its long and enduring history.

After I left Los Angeles and quit the business of investigating fake claims, much of what I had learned about cappers, swoop-and-squats, and medical mills began to fade. But then I came back to the pictures of the crushed Pontiac in the paper and the coroner's photograph of the dead Perez, and it all came back to me as something real and important. If this fringe culture of accident stagers and personal injury fakers held any meaning beyond the framework of an insurance scam, then understanding the death of José Luis Lopez Perez was going to be my way into it. For me, the fatal staging was not primarily about the guilt of individuals or groups. Nor was I interested in defining the case as an example of the problem of personal injury frauds in order to polemicize about possible solutions. When I looked at the photograph of the dead Perez or the mug shot of banana-peeler Frank Smith, or tried to imagine the sad procession of people through Duke Gemellaro's House of Pain during the Great Depression, I never thought, for example, about the need for reforms such as no-fault auto insurance, as important as this issue may be. In this respect, perhaps, I had reached a point that A. C. Campbell had come to a century earlier. In his massive study of insurance crimes, Campbell had confronted the similar reality that "the abuse of insurance" had "bred a class of men ready to risk their lives for a comparatively small share of the money they 'earned' by casting away ships." To those who pressed him to go beyond his stated claims or the bounds of his self-styled authority, however, Campbell wrote: "My plain answer to the question as to what change should be made in the law is: I don't know."[3]

For years I have cast about for the right frame in which to put the pictures of the crushed Pontiac and the dead Perez. Thinking of it all as either bizarre or new, or as the innovation of desperate recent immigrants, just did not hold up for me in light of the history connecting the accident underworlds of old New York with present-day Los Angeles. And not thinking of the fatal accident at all was not easy, so emblematic had the case become of the larger story of the personal injury underworld. More than any other case of its kind, the staged crash that ended in death for a young Salvadoran and led to a murder rap for a middle-age Anglo attorney contin-ued to resonate long after it was first reported. The story has outlasted the

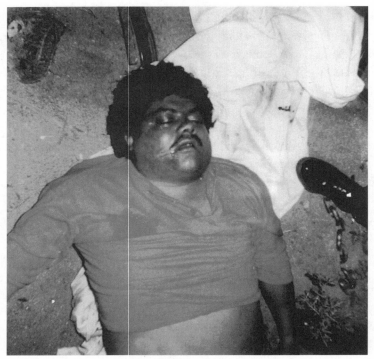

FIGURE E.1. This picture of Jose Luis Lopez Perez was taken by the Los Angeles County Coroner's Office just hours after his death in June 1992. A day-laborer originally from El Salvador, Perez was killed while staging an accident with a big-rig truck on a Los Angeles freeway.

notoriously poor shelf life of crash racket stories popular since the early years of this century. Accounts from the fake-accident underworld are usually shot up like signal flares, here and there, in newspaper back sections—first with the spark of arrests and talk of a crackdown, then with the fizzle of cases that do not develop fast enough to rivet readers. The story of twenty-seven people arrested for insurance fraud is usually something we only half hear while concentrating on other things. Such stories are often reported as news fillers or as an extension of public relations efforts by the insurance industry or law enforcement groups. Since leaving Los Angeles, however, the story of the fatal crash on the I-5 freeway has persisted in the institutional memory of newspaper writers and claims investigators. Now the standard tag line in crash racket stories, no matter where they occur, is to mention the man (sometimes "the immigrant") from Los Angeles who got killed staging a crash with a truck on a freeway. Investigators around the country might not know of many cases outside of their locality, but they are certainly aware of the

June 1992 fatal crash on the I-5 freeway and of the subsequent murder charge against Gary P. Miller. I myself had pursued the sexy idea of being a private investigator in Venice Beach, but found, in the end, that my real fascination lay in the story behind a relatively mundane back-page news account of a traffic accident and its aftermath.

Over the years, the mere mention of the Perez case has become a shorthand form of a larger argument, a story whose message is clear just from the telling of the bare facts: people in cars trying to get rear-ended for money; lawyers willing to exploit immigrants and insurers to get money; aggressive attorney advertisements subtly encouraging the poor to trade on their lives for "money in the pocket," a key phrase in (borderline illegal) aggressive ads targeting Spanish speakers in the city. All of it seemed to beg the question (asked since the days of "railway spine"): What is this country coming to? And to come locked with its own resigned conclusion: Only in America. Some of the initial news stories and features focused on the setting of the case, Los Angeles, lumping the dangerous accident scheme along with the "riots" that had occurred a few months earlier—all under the general rubric of Los Angeles as city-going-to-hell; or Los Angeles as an apocalyptic nightmare of riots, floods, fires, and, now, predatory drivers with no value for their own lives or those of others on the road. Another strand of thinking about the case began a year and a half after the accident on the I-5, when it was reported that Gary Miller had filed a disability claim on his own behalf for the stress of being accused of murder and had actually collected $85,000 for it. ("I get physically sick when I get near a courthouse," the attorney claimed. "I sleep a lot, procrastinate.")[4] For a time, the tragic story of Perez's fatal run had taken a backseat to the farce of the "attorney who says he's allergic to court," a perfect tale of outrageous lawyer exploits in a culture that loves to villainize lawyers—especially those who deal in personal injury and advertise on television—as the institutional stand-ins for its own legally sanctioned overreaching. For a while, the Miller story was more widely reported than the initial investigation. But then, with the announcement of prison terms for a few participants in the same staged accidents in 1994, the focus came back to the fatal crash on the I-5 freeway, the crushed Pontiac, and the dead Perez.

Who killed José Luis Lopez Perez? In March 1996, the question brought me back to Los Angeles. This time my goal was less to probe further into the story of his death, than simply to find someone who had known the man in life. Two factors combined to make this harder than I first thought: Many of those who were connected to Perez were in some way still involved in ongoing litigation (and so were not free to talk); and others, many of them illegal immigrants, were so thoroughly unconnected to any institution that would help me locate them that I soon despaired of trying.

At the end of my research I did what I had done five years earlier at the beginning of my career as an investigator in Venice: I canvassed my subject's last known address for a trace of him. Early in the afternoon on the type of sunny day in Southern California that never ceases to amaze me for its disregard of season, I found myself driving a rental car and looking for the apartment building that Perez had left for the last time on a Wednesday afternoon in June 1992. I arrived at a standard stucco cluster of dingbat units with a banner out front advertising rentals available. The building was located in the shadows of downtown L.A. where I had spent so much of my time as an investigator; the experience of ringing the building manager brought back memories of countless trips into the field for the insurance companies. I worried that my Spanish might not suffice to get me understood in even the most basic way, but was relieved to find an English speaker on the other end of the intercom. I tried to explain that I was interested in finding information about a former tenant named José Luis Lopez Perez. I stated the name deliberately, framed it with silence, like a secret password that would open doors for me if heard by those familiar with the history. If not, I thought, at least I would be able to get in on some other grounds and maybe look at his rental agreement to see if it contained personal information that would help me reach some kind of closure. After a pause, a woman's voice told me to come in.

For the next hour and a half, I stood (and, after an hour, sat) and spoke with the building manager, Milagro, through her English-speaking daughter Sylvia. I learned quickly that I had arrived only months too late to find José's wife: She recently had moved to Rapid City, South Dakota, where she was learning to butcher meat before moving to Minneapolis to live with her sister. In a sense, this was a disappointment, but just talking to someone who knew José and Martha—Milagro was friendly enough with Martha ("Martita") to have hosted her for a Christmas visit just months earlier—was greatly satisfying. Milagro had been in the United States from El Salvador for more than a decade and had been a tenant in the building before becoming the manager just a few years earlier. Most of her tenants were from El Salvador, she said. Some were legal; many were not. On the day of the crash, Milagro remembered, Isiais Aguilar, a surviving passenger from the failed staging with the Pontiac who still lived in the building, had to be persuaded by José Perez to leave the building, so scared was he of deportation. Jorge Sanchez, the driver, had lived across the street before the accident that sent him to state prison. Milagro said he was a "bad guy" who generally caused trouble in the building.

Milagro remembered José Perez; friends called him "Luis" Lopez, she said. Some two years before his death, he and Martita moved into the apartment already occupied by her father. Their two kids, a boy and a girl, were left back with Luis's parents in Cara Sucia, a small farming town near Chalatenango, El Salvador, close to the northern border with Honduras. Luis and Martita did not return for visits; they planned to stay for good and to bring their children north when they could afford it. For her part, Martita worked during the week as a live-in housekeeper, returning to her apartment mainly on weekends; Luis did odd construction jobs and day labor, mostly agricultural. Sometimes he did not work for weeks at a time, Milagro remembered, and he could often be loud with his friends late into the night.

After answering my questions for quite a while, Milagro told me about the days after the fatal accident. The police swarmed the building, searching everywhere—why, or for what, Milagro had no idea, and feared it had something to do with immigration. Martita was bereft; yet, even in her grief, she did not miss a day of work. She tried to get a lawyer to represent her in a case against the truck driver whose negligence she believed had led to the death of her husband, but every lawyer she approached told her that they could not represent her because the accident was staged on purpose by her husband and the others for insurance money. Martita did not believe it then and, to this day, refuses to believe that Luis had been involved in any kind of wrongdoing. Hers was not a posture of denial to justify a civil action against the trucker; she genuinely shared the disbelief of investigators, reporters, and others at the proposition of a staged freeway collision with a speeding big-rig truck for the prospect of any money, especially not for only a few hundred dollars. Before I left her apartment, Milagro gave me Martita's address in Rapid City, but she suggested that the address would not hold for long. Martita did not have a phone, but even if she did, what more did I really want to learn from her about the death of her husband?

Who killed José Luis Lopez Perez? At a certain point the question dissolves into others: Who killed Kaitlyn Arquette? Or Donna Willard? Or Paul Langevin? And, once the questions start, they are not easily stopped. Who planted the very idea of staging crashes for cash in the minds of people as diverse as Duc Minh Nguyen in Little Saigon, Billy Ray Walker in Gastonia, North Carolina, and William Mele in Philadelphia? And how did the scenarios persist so unchangingly from those first enacted by an entirely different cast of characters in Lower Manhattan close to a century earlier? Who plotted passenger jump-ons of public buses in New Jersey in the early 1990s and of street trolleys in South Philadelphia 100 years earlier? How were East L.A.'s

Friends of the Friendless different from Abe Gatner's all-star ambulance-chasing team on New York's Lower East Side? Who tossed the first fruit peel to the ground with thoughts of settlement money in mind? And how did such intentional slip-and-falls on trains, flops in front of streetcars, self-inflicted wounds, and sixty or seventy years of staged car accidents of varying riskiness grow from obscure cons to a multi-billion-dollar illegal market in America without hardly being noticed? How is it that America became the only country on the planet where pretending a fall on homemade fake vomit has rewards beyond a comic payoff?

Behind the swervings of a Pontiac on a Los Angeles freeway, I came to see in the end, there is an impulse to profit from accidents that runs deep through American life, even if we have bracketed it as bizarre and alien since the days of the early "wars" on the (mostly Jewish) chasers and shysters. The accident in which José Luis Lopez Perez was killed was on purpose—staged for a few hundred dollars in auto insurance money—like the original collisions nearly a century earlier in New York. When the American promise of progress through industrial capitalism went one way with the rise of the automobile at the turn of the century—"ever forward, always moving," in the words of one hopeful Ford Motor Company ad from 1951—the fake accident industry took the promise in another direction. Following this low road through the highest aspirations of the previous century, one finds the accident faker, holding up a distorted mirror to the traditionally American ideal of achieving economic freedom through starting your own business, and the self-mutilator, of 1890s rural Nebraska, 1930s houses of pain, and 1960s Nub City, offering a perversely literal interpretation of the idea of getting ahead in America through self-sacrifice. Who killed Jose Luis Lopez Perez? It is tempting to say that Adam Smith's "invisible hand" of free market forces, which created the conditions for an illegal market in personal injury claims in the first place (accidentally, on purpose), was as much at work as a specific capper or attorney. "It was worth coming here," Rubidia Lopez said of her decision to emigrate to America despite her involvement in the fatal crash and the subsequent criminal charges against her. "Here, there are opportunities for progress."[5]

José Luis Lopez Perez slipped into America's personal injury underworld in the same way that most people did: on the advice of a friend of a friend. And he stayed for the same reasons that most people did: because it was the easiest money he had ever made in his life, and because whatever risks there were in terms of safety or getting caught seemed minor in comparison. Who killed him? Some people would say he did it to himself and that he may have helped do it to the others in his car or to an innocent trucker. Others might be satisfied to see Gary P. Miller go to jail for the crime.[6] I am inclined to look elsewhere—back through a century of accident faking history from which Perez's bizarre actions could have been arrived at in logical increments; inward to a culture that encouraged him to cash in on his accidents (a representative of a law office going door-to-door soliticited his personal injury business with a frequent-claimers' "credit card") then seemed shocked when he went out of his way to create them.

Shortly after Lopez Perez's death, Milagro and a number of others who had known him took up a collection to pay for a brief ceremony in a funeral parlor in East L.A. and to cover the cost of flying the body back to his birthplace in Cara Sucia, El Salvador, for burial. I have often tried to imagine how I would have explained his death to his children.

NOTES

PROLOGUE

1. For the initial news account of the crash, see Julie Tamaki, "1 Killed, 3 Hurt as Truck Crushes Car on Freeway," *Los Angeles Times*, 18 June 1992, B4. For the rest of my understanding of this case, I have relied on articles, where cited, and on court documents and original interviews.
2. Hereafter, for clarity, I shall refer to him as José Perez.
3. Phil's letter is quoted in Amy Pyle, "Lawyer's Drive for Success Is Measured in Fraud Case," *Los Angeles Times*, 22 November 1992, B3.
4. Julie Tamaki, "Key Fraud Suspect Held in Texas," *Los Angeles Times*, 26 March 1994, B3.
5. For the initial reports of the murder charges, see: Amy Pyle, "Murder Charge Upheld in Insurance Scam Case," *Los Angeles Times*, 7 October 1992, B3; and Amy Pyle and Bob Pool, "Lawyer Held as Planner of Crash Frauds," *Los Angeles Times*, 31 October 1992, B1.
6. Quoted in Pyle, "Lawyer's Drive for Success Is Measured in Fraud Case."
7. Ibid.
8. James Quinn and Amy Pyle, "Accident Victim Is Linked to Insurance Fraud Ring," *Los Angeles Times*, 5 July 1992, B3.
9. Amy Pyle and James Quinn, "Scam Targets Truckers in Risky Crashes, Officials Say," *Los Angeles Times* 13 July 1992, 1.
10. Jim Herron Zamora, "Truckers Get Tips on How to Avoid Staged Accidents," *Los Angeles Times*, 26 July 1992, B3.
11. Quoted in Amy Pyle, "More Arrests Expected in Crash Probe," *Los Angeles Times*, 16 July 1992, B1.
12. Wendy Kaufman, "Auto Insurance Fraud Uncovered in California," National Public Radio (Morning Edition), 16 July 1992.
13. Quoted in Pyle and Quinn, "Scam Targets Truckers in Risky Crashes."
14. See Lewis Leader, "Scams People Play: 'Swoop and Squat' on Freeway," *San Francisco Examiner*, 21 September 1980, A24; and Baxter Ward, *Illegal Attorney Referral Activity in Los Angeles County: A Report on the Problem, Including an Analysis of the Handling of the Friends of the Friendless Ring by the County Department of Health Services* (Los Angeles: County Board of Supervisors, 1974), 73-74. Freeway swoop-and-squats were also mentioned by a capper identified only as "Dave" in an interview

conducted by investigators from the California Bureau of Fraudulent Claims in the early 1980s. When asked if he staged this type of accident, Dave replied: "Too dangerous, too dangerous. The purpose is to make money, not to create injuries. We never wanted to hurt anyone, just to submit a claim. To commit one on the freeway would be dangerous to everyone."

15. "Two Cleveland Men Indicted for $22G Caused Accident Fraud Scheme," *ICPI Report* 17 (2nd issue, 1990), 1.

16. NICB agent Lisa Polk was talking about the results of Operation Crystal Ball in Chicago. She is quoted in Ashley Craddock and Mordecai Lawrence, "Swoop-and-Squats," *Mother Jones* (September/October 1993), 20.

17. Charles Remsberg, "Accident Fraud is Highway Robbery, *Reader's Digest* (February 1964), 201.

18. E. D. Fales Jr., "Beware of Accident Fakers," *Popular Science Monthly* (May 1961), 198.

19. Ibid., 52.

20. One of the earliest "real-life" private eye accounts I have seen describes Irwin Blye's initiation into private investigation work through a job as an insurance investigator while in his early twenties. Even after establishing his own investigative practice, Blye continued to work "the whiplash trade." Writer Nicholas Pileggi observes of Blye: "In insurance fraud cases Blye has spent weeks trying to trick claimants out of their feigned ailments. He has put weights in their garbage cans or given them flat tires and then photographed them carrying out the garbage or fixing flats to prove that their multimillion-dollar incapacitation suits are fake." See Nicholas Pileggi, *Blye, Private Eye* (Chicago: Playboy Press, 1976), 16.

For a time, I was influenced by Josiah "Tink" Thompson's *Gumshoe: Reflections in a Private Eye* (New York: Fawcett Crest, 1988), written by a former philosophy professor who left the academy for surveillance work at $5 an hour. In deciding to write this book, I liked to think of myself as a Thompson type—especially when I read a profile of him by one of his college friends, Calvin Trillin, who observed: "As someone who often seemed uncomfortable in the sort of academic hierarchy that made some other professors feel secure, [Thompson] liked doing research in a field that recognized no credentials." (See "Tink," *New Yorker*, 27 November 1978, 129.) Over time, I came to realize that there were class distinctions among private investigators and, as an insurance specialist, I was not in the same league with Thompson and the other "Magnum Ph.D's" profiled in a cover story by *California Lawyer* (February, 1992). My suspicion was confirmed by a quote from Thompson in an earlier magazine profile in which he said, "As a general rule, the only type of cases I won't take involve personal injury." ("From Philosopher to Flatfoot," *U.S. News and World Report*, 11 July 1988, 51.)

For a selection of other accounts of "real-life" private eyes, see: Nicholas Pileggi, "Daylighting: Going Undercover with Gillian Farrell and the New Private Eyes," *New York Magazine*, 20 April 1987, 45; Steve Lohr, "A New Breed of Sam

Spade Trails Crooks' Hidden Assets," *New York Times*, 20 February 1992, 1; Matthew Rosenbaum, "Here's Looking at You, Kid: Private Detectives and Investigators," *Occupational Outlook Quarterly* (Summer 1994), 32-36; and Geoff Edgers, "Gen-X Private Eyes: Watching the Detectives," *Boston Phoenix*, 17 November 1995, Section 2, 1.

21. Thomas Meehan, "Case of the Insurance Detective," *New York Times Magazine*, 6 March 1960, 53.

22. Sue Grafton, "H" is for Homicide (New York: Fawcwtt Crest, 1991), 191.

INTRODUCTION

1. A sketch of the life of William Turtle is found in Elias Colbert, *Colbert's Chicago: Historical and Statistical Sketch of the Garden City from the Beginning until Now* (Chicago: P.T. Sherlock, 1868), 566-570.

2. A sketch of Dr. Lewis's life is found in the *Travelers Record* 33 (April 1897), 1.

3. Alexander Colin Campbell, *Insurance and Crime: A Consideration of the Effects Upon Society of the Abuses of Insurance Together With Certain Historical Instances of Such Abuses,* (New York: G.P. Putnam's Sons, 1902), 31.

4. *The Criminal Recorder; or Biographical Sketches of Notorious Public Characters*, Vol. 1 (London: James Cundee, Ivy-Lane, 1811), 68-71. Among the notorious criminal types advertised on the book's cover are: murderers, traitors, pirates, mutineers, incendiaries, defrauders, rioters, sharpers, highwaymen, footpads, pickpockets, swindlers, and housebreakers. Apparently ship scuttling was not yet referred to by name among crime-chroniclers, or insurance crime was not sexy enough for mention on a book cover. Lancey is indexed as an "incendiary."

5. Throckmorton is quoted in *Report from the Select Committee on Marine Insurance* (London: HMSO, 1810), 88.

6. Quoted in *The Trial of William Codling, Mariner, et al. for Willfully and Feloniously Destroying and Casting Away The Brig Adventure* (London: Martha Gurney, 1803), 210.

7. Raymond Flower and Michael Wynn Jones, *Lloyd's of London: An Illustrated History* (New York: Hastings House Publishers, 1974), 151.

8. Frederick Martin, *The History of Lloyd's and of Marine Insurance in Great Britain* (London: Macmillan and Co., 1876), 264.

9. Ibid., 267.

10. Quoted in *The Trials of Patrick Maxwell Stewart Wallace and Michael Shaw Stewart Wallace for Willfully Destroying The Brig Dryad, Off Cuba, With Intent to Defraud the Marine Insurance Companies and Underwriters* (London: Williams and Son, 1841), 21-22.

11. Campbell, *Insurance and Crime*, 66.

12. Ibid., 288.

13. See *The Queen v. Holdsworth, Berwick, Webb, and Dean for the Wilful Scuttling of the Ship Severn* (London: Association for the Protection of Commercial Interests, 1867).

14. Campbell, *Insurance and Crime*, 81.

15. Quoted in *A Full Report of the Trial of Captain William H. Tower, Charged with Feloniously Scuttling the Barque Brothers' Pride* (Saint John, New Brunswick: Telegraph Steam Job Print, 1880), 31.

16. Ibid., 44, 41.

17. Quoted in Flower and Jones, *Lloyd's of London*, 113.

18. Samuel Plimsoll, *Our Seamen: An Appeal* (London: Virtue & Co., 1873), 82.

19. Ibid., 14.

20. Ibid., 72.

21. One writer on the subject cast doubt on Plimsoll's contentions based on a combination of his personal experience, the seeming absurdity of risking life for insurance money, and an apparent concern that shipowners not be subject to unnecessary regulation on the basis of Plimsoll's campaign. Richard Lowndes writes:

> As for over-insuring as part of a deliberate scheme to cast away a ship, I have heard much talk of it, but seen so very little of it in the course of a good long life time spent among such matters, that I am convinced it is a rare and exceptional crime; the risk to life in the process, and the almost certainty of detection afterwards, in a matter which requires usually more than one accomplice, must always prevent its becoming a popular profession, like housebreaking. It is at all events not a matter common enough to deserve any widespread and harassing precautions . . . the question whether the saving of life is worth the restriction of trade cannot be evaded . . . how much life may you reasonably hope to save, and how much trade must you destroy for the purpose.

See Richard Lowndes, *Insurable Interest and Valuations* (London: Stevens and Sons, 1884), 105-106.

22. Justin McCarthy, *A History of Our Own Times, Volume II* (New York: Harper & Brothers, 1898), 568.

23. Plimsoll was not satisfied that widespread overloading and overinsuring were no longer being practiced. He took up the cause once more in print in a "second appeal for our seamen" published with "pressing urgency" in 1890. See Samuel Plimsoll, *Cattle Ships* (London: Kegan Paul, Trench, Trübner, & Co., 1890). Twentieth-century scuttlings seem to be carried out mainly as property frauds without routine danger to seamen. See the chapter entitled "Vanishing Vessels: Marine Insurance Fraud" in G. O. W. Mueller and Freda Adler, *Outlaws of the Ocean: The Complete Book of Contemporary Crime on the High Seas* (New York: Hearst Marine Books, 1985).

24. John Francis, *Annals, Anecdotes, and Legends: A Chronicle of Life Assurance* (London: Longman, Brown, Green, and Longmans, 1853), 100-101.

25. J. B. Lewis and C. C. Bombaugh, *Remarkable Stratagems and Conspiracies: An Authentic Record of Surprising Attempts to Defraud Life Insurance Companies* (New York: G.W. Carleton & Co., 1878), 11.

26. Francis, *Annals, Anecdotes, and Legends,* 141.

27. Quoted in Viviana A. Rotman Zelizer, *Morals and Markets: The Development of Life Insurance in the United States* (New Brunswick, NJ: Transaction Books, 1983), 69.

28. Quoted in Francis, *Annals, Anecdotes, and Legends,* 149.

29. Ibid., 142.

30. Campbell, *Insurance and Crime,* 221.

31. "Does a Man Shorten His Life by Insuring it?" *Hunt's Merchant's Magazine,* July 1856, 110.

32. "Fraud Upon Underwriters," *Hunt's Merchant's Magazine,* February 1840, 289.

33. Ibid., 298.

34. See *A Report of the Examination of Messrs. Amasa Chapin, et al., Charged With a Conspiracy to Burn the Steamboat Martha Washington* (Cincinnati: Cincinnati Gazette Company Print, 1853).

35. Lewis and Bombaugh, *Remarkable Stratagems and Conspiracies,* 50.

36. Ibid., 350.

37. Ibid., 342.

38. The Goss-Udderzook case was one of the most famous cases of its day (second perhaps only to the Maybrick or Hunter-Armstrong cases). For accounts of Goss-Udderzook, see: William G. Davies, "Mysterious Disappearances, and Presumptions of Death in Insurance Cases," a speech delivered before the New York Medico-Legal Society on March 1, 1876, published in *The Sanitarian,* Vol. 4 (1876), 170-177. The case is also summarized in a contemporary collection of murder for insurance cases under the title "The Man Who Would Not Stay Down" in Jad Adams, *Double Indemnity: Murder for Insurance* (London: Headline Books, 1994), 247-252.

39. Lewis and Bombaugh, *Remarkable Stratagems and Conspiracies,* 168.

40. Ibid., 259.

41. Harold Schecter, *Depraved: The Shocking True Story of America's First Serial Killer* (New York: Pocket Books, 1994), 278.

42. Ibid., 195, 282.

43. Ibid., 347.

44. Ibid., 352.

45. Ibid., 342.

46. For news accounts of Holmes's death and burial, see "Holmes Cool to the End," *New York Times,* 8 May 1896, 1 and "Holmes in a Ton of Cement" *New York Times,* 9 May 1896, 1.

47. John B. Lewis and Charles C. Bombaugh, *Stratagems and Conspiracies to Defraud Life Insurance Companies: An Authentic Record of Remarkable Cases* (Baltimore: James H. McClellan Publisher, 1896), 53. One early account of the graveyard cases is found in "Speculating in Human Life!," *The Insurance Monitor*, February 1881, 82.

48. Lewis and Bombaugh, *Stratagems and Conspiracies*, 53.

49. Ibid., 54.

50. Ibid., 56.

51. Ibid., 59.

52. Ibid., 58.

53. "Set Fires for Profit," *New York Times*, 1 June 1895, 2. The cases are summarized in The Insurance Society of New York's *The Fire Insurance Contract: Its History and Interpretation* (Indianapolis: Rough Notes Co., 1922), 590-593.

54. "Gang Leaders Captured," *New York Times*, 5 June 1895, 5.

55. "Mrs. Leddy Charged with Arson," *New York Times*, 14 August 1894, 1.

56. "Schoenholz's Many Fires," *New York Times*, 19 December 1896, 16.

57. "How Zuker's Fire Was Set," *New York Times*, 18 December 1896, 3. Zuker's name is sometimes spelled Zucker.

58. "Conversations of Zuker," *New York Times*, 22 December 1896, 9.

59. See the following articles in the *New York Times*: "Evidence for Zuker All In," 24 December 1896, 8; "Isaac Zuker Found Guilty," 29 December 1896, 2; and "Zuker Now in Sing Sing," 30 December 1896, 8. Zuker's appeal of the conviction was denied. (See *People v. Zucker*, 46 NY Supp 766 [1897].)

60. *New York Times*, 29 March 1893, 2.

61. *New York Times*, 23 June 1895, 1.

62. *New York Times*, 19 January 1891, 3.

63. *New York Times*, 7 August 1894, 6.

64. Jacob A. Riis, *How the Other Half Lives: Studies Among the Tenements of New York* (Cambridge, MA: Harvard University Press, 1970 [1890]), 76.

65. "Glueckman a Witness," *New York Times*, 7 July 1896, 9.

66. "The Gordon Arson Trial," *New York Times*, 29 December 1895, 15.

67. *New York Times*, 4 July 1896, 8.

68. "Herschkopf In a Web," *New York Times*, 9 July 1895, 9.

69. "Was Lured From Europe," *New York Times*, 27 June, 1895, 8.

70. "Our Foreign Criminals," *New York Times*, 16 July 1896, 9.

71. "Knew All the Firebugs," *New York Times*, 25 February 1895, 16.

72. "No Mercy for Firebugs," *New York Times*, 26 January 1895, 13.

73. See "Grauer Gets Thirty Years," *New York Times*, 22 February 1895, 16 and "Startling Scenes in Court; Mrs. Lieberman Shrieks Wildly When Convicted of Arson," *New York Times*, 17 February 1895, 1.

74. Quoted in A. C. Campbell, *Insurance and Crime*, 264.

75. Quoted in Viviana A. Rotman Zelizer, *Pricing the Priceless Child: The Changing Social Value of Children* (New York: Basic Books, 1985), 118.

76. Riis, *How the Other Half Lives*, 126-127.

77. Quoted in Zelizer, *Pricing the Priceless Child*, 120-121.

78. Quoted in Campbell, *Insurance and Crime*, 265-266.

79. Mr. Clarke Aspinall is quoted in *Fourth Report of the Commissioners Appointed to Inquire Into Friendly and Benefit Building Societies* (London: HMSO, 1874), 135.

80. Campbell, *Insurance and Crime*, 285.

81. *New York Times*, 16 July 1896, 4. Race seemed to be on the minds of Herschkopf's attorneys also, as they asked Mrs. Herschkopf for help in spotting the anti-Semites among prospective jurors. "He hates Jews," she would whisper to the attorneys of a particular juror. "We don't want him." (See "Herschkopf's Counsel Relied on a Woman's Intuition," *New York Times*, 4 July 1896, 8.)

82. *New York Times*, 8 February 1896, 4.

83. *New York Times*, 19 January 1897, 6.

84. "Life Bugs," *Insurance Monitor* (August 1895), 326.

85. Frank Moss, *The American Metropolis: From Knickerbocker Days to the Present Time* (New York: Peter Fenelon Collier, 1897), vol. 3, 191-192.

CHAPTER ONE

1. See the *Bulletin* of the American Railway Claims Association (May 1921), 241.

2. *Bulletin* (January 1923), 171.

3. For "Banana Anna," see F. Dalton O' Sullivan, *Crime Detection* (Chicago: O'Sullivan Publishing House, 1928), 95. Banana Anna was caught mainly due to the effective exchange of cards between the New York and Boston Index Bureaus following one of Strula's faked claims on the Boston Elevated Railway Company. (See J. J. Reynolds, "A Card Index and What It Means," *Proceedings of the American Railway Claim Agents' Association* [1915], 68.)

   Another highly successful female banana-peeler, Mrs. Sadie Esther Abramson, was active well into the 1930s. Ultimately admitting to getting settlement money from at least thirty-three faked cases, Mrs. Abramson operated in hotels, department stores, buses, subways, and streetcars. "In most cases," a newspaper account revealed, "she attributed her injuries to faulty stairways, torn carpets or the carelessness of the owners in not removing orange or banana peelings from dimly lit passages." (See "Woman Is Arrested in Insurance Frauds," *New York Times*, 19 February 1936, 5.) Abramson is also mentioned in Robert Monaghan, "The Liability Claim Racket," *Law and Contemporary Problems* (1936), 496. Monaghan explains that Abramson started with a legitimate claim that she handled through a lawyer whose brother ultimately initiated her into the arts of fakery, taking her in hand and coaching her "as to the technique of staging falls or 'flops,' as they are termed in the racket." Monaghan claims that Abramson confessed to having faked fifty claims in three years. He does not mention banana peels specifically as Sadie's specialty, however, only vault lights, defective steps, "and the like."

4. For the fullest accounts of the accident faking of the Freeman family, see: "Imposture as a Profession," *Railway Surgeon* 1 (1895), 528-533 and Dr. Pearce Bailey, "Simulation of Nervous Disorders Following Accidents," *Railway Surgeon* 3 (1897), 439-442. See also "Mother and Two Daughters Arrested," *New York Times*, 8 February 1895, 11.

5. "Imposture as a Profession," 529.

6. Ibid., 531.

7. See the *Bulletin* (May 1921), 241.

8. See Smith R. Brittingham, *The Claim Agent and His Work: Investigation and Settlement of Claims for Personal Injuries* (New York: Ronald Press, 1927), 218-219.

9. See the *Bulletin* (May 1921), 242.

10. *New York Times*, 26 January 1921, 15.

11. See "An Abrupt End to a Deadend Journey" in the *Bulletin* (February 1921), 178.

12. For an account of the Wheelrights' frauds, see the editorial entitled "Fragility," *New York Times*, 25 May 1881, 4. Husband-and-wife teams constituted something of a trend among the early accident fakers. Albert and Mae Woods of Manhattan worked the Third Avenue cable car for a few claims before going north to New England, then south to Baltimore, landing ultimately in state prison for three to five years. (For the Woods' frauds, see: "Accident Fakirs Run Down in New York," *Street Railway Journal*, 21 October 1905, 789 and "Accident Fakirs Convicted in New York," *Street Railway Journal*, 6 January 1906, 63.) Another married couple, Maurice and Rose Cocoran, worked the streetcars in Boston, with the wife hiding behind a pole or some shrubs before finding just the right moment to dive out near a passing streetcar, and the husband assisting her to safety and making a claim on her behalf. See "Exposure of Alleged Street Railway Swindlers," *Street Railway Journal*, 21 March 1903, 464.

13. See "The Railroad Accident Man," *New York Times*, 1 June 1872, 3. The editorial is almost surely satire: The claims man is depicted as a heartless front man for the cruel, pennypinching railroads; he cannot even say the word "accident." ("Accident, applied to a railroad, is a term I will not allow. Grant that word accident and you let in a whole flood of charges that would swamp us. Carelessness, recklessness on the part of passengers which ends fatally, I may concede.") The question remains, however, about the truth behind the satire as regards the professional fakers alluded to in the article.

14. Ambroise Paré, *On Monsters and Marvels* (Chicago: University of Chicago Press, 1982), 78.

15. The story of the "counterfeit crank," Nicholas Jennings, was first set down by Thomas Harman in his collection *A Caveat for Common Cursitors* (1566). It has been reprinted in many collections, including the one in which I found it: A. V. Judges, *The Elizabethan Underworld* (London: George Routledge & Sons, Ltd., 1930), 85-91.

16. Paré, *On Monsters and Marvels*, 84.

17. Ibid., 87. Among his other begging tricks, Jennings was also shown to have dressed up like a sailor, told a story that he had lost his ship at sea, and pleaded for donations.

18. See Kellow Chesney, *The Victorian Underworld* (London: Temple-Smith Publishers, 1970), 196.

19. See Luc Sante, *Low Life: Lures and Snares of Old New York* (New York: Vintage, 1991), 315. Panhandling in New York remains highly competitive, especially on subways. Writer Nicholas Dawidoff found a few panhandlers practicing the ancient arts of feigning blindness, lameness, and other disfigurements, but he found no Fagin schools for cripples or any larger organization or brotherhood of beggars. The latest innovation in the begging world, Dawidoff discovered in his three-week tour of the subways, was the "protracted tale of woe" pitched to a captive subway car audience. (See "The Business of Begging: To Give or Not to Give," *New York Times Magazine*, 24 April 1994, 36.)

20. Judges, *The Elizabethan Underworld*, 373-374.

21. Dr. Hector Gavin, *On Feigned and Factitious Diseases, Chiefly of Soldiers and Seamen, On the Means Used to Simulate or Produce Them, And on the Best Modes of Discovering Impostors* (London: John Churchill, 1843), 364. Gavin distinguishes among different types of feigned disease: "Pretended" disease is created just by the utterances of the malingerer; "simulated" disease involves pretending with the addition of real-seeming symptoms; "exaggerated" diseases arise naturally in the malingerer but are said to be much worse than they are; "aggravated diseases" arise naturally in the malingerer but are physically made to be much worse than they would have been if left alone; and "factitious" disease is completely manufactured by deed and utterance (10).

22. For all of these feigned conditions, see Ibid., 380-410.

23. See Sir John Collie, *Malingering and Feigned Sickness, With Notes on the Workmen's Compensation Act, 1906, and Compensation For Injury, Including the Leading Cases Thereon* (London: Edward Arnold, 1917), 1.

24. Ibid., 209.

25. Ibid., 231.

26. Ibid., 377.

27. Ibid.

28. Ibid., 92.

29. Ibid., 376-377.

30. Ibid., 421.

31. Ibid., 431.

32. Ibid., 478.

33. Ibid., 407.

34. See Sir John Collie, *Fraud in Medico-Legal Practice* (New York: Longmans, Green & Co., 1932), 172-173.

35. Collie, *Malingering and Feigned Sickness*, 51.

36. Ibid., 258.

37. Ibid., 9.

38. Ibid., 508-513.

39. Ibid., 50.

40. Ibid., 418.

41. F. Dalton O'Sullivan,*Crime Detection*, 95.

42. Dr. J. Adelphi Gottlieb, "Feigned Diseases—Their Importance, Purpose, and Recognition," *Medico-Legal Journal* 16 (1899), 134.

43. Dr. J. A. Ritchey, "The Malingerer,"*Medico-Legal Journal* 18 (1900), 399, 404.

44. John B. Lewis and Charles C. Bombaugh, *Stratagems and Conspiracies to Defraud Life Insurance Companies: An Authentic Record of Remarkable Cases* (Baltimore: James H. McClellan, Publisher, 1896), 667.

45. Ibid., 669.

46. Ibid., 669-670.

47. See Michael B. Katz, *In the Shadow of the Poorhouse: A Social History of Welfare in America* (New York: Basic Books, 1986), 147-150.

48. For all of these self-mutilation accident cases, see Lewis and Bombaugh, *Stratagems and Conspiracies*, 667-680.

49. Dr. Frederick L. Mosser, "Malingering," *Proceedings of the American Electric Railway Claim Agents' Association* (1924), 38.

50. See David W. Maurer, *The Big Con: The Story of the Confidence Man and the Confidence Game* (New York: Pocket Books, 1940), 8.

51. Ibid., 10.

52. See the *Bulletin* (July 1922), 36.

53. Ibid. (January 1923), 171.

54. See the *Proceedings of the American Street and Interurban Railway Claim Agents' Association* (1909), 159-163.

55. For information on the early organization and work of the index bureaus, see H. R. Goshorn, "The Practical Value of the Index Bureau With Some Statistics and Illustrations," *Proceedings of the American Electric Railway Claim Agents' Association* (1911), 62-72.

56. J. J. Reynolds, "A Card Index and What It Means," *Proceedings of the American Electric Railway Claim Agents' Association* (1915), 65-68, 79.

57. Cecil G. Rice, "The Practical Value of the Index Bureau with Some Statistics and Illustrations," *Proceedings of the American Electric Railway Claim Agents' Association* (1911), 75.

58. A. J. Graham, "The Claim Faker," *Proceedings of the American Electric Railway Claim Agents' Association* (1934), 88.

59. See the *Bulletin* (August 1923), 68.

60. *Bulletin* (June 1923), 15.

61. *Bulletin* (September 1924), 131. Hoffman is also the subject of an earlier *Bulletin* report (August 1924, 95-96) in which his three alleged falls from passenger trains are documented. In this report, Hoffman is described by claims man Parks C. Archer as being "light brown" in color, "medium height and build, 'Charlie Chaplin' mustache, speaks slowly, uses fairly good language and dwells a whole lot upon his religion and [his] desire to do what is right."

62. Ibid. (August, 1924), 95.

63. Ibid. (November 1923), 148. A man named C. J. Johnson was arrested along with Castle on suspicion of being an accomplice to Castle's fakery, but was later released for want of proof.

64. Ibid. (January 1925), 220.

65. Ibid. (December 1923), 172.

66. "A Woman Accident Fakir Run Down," *Street Railway Journal*, 16 July 1904, 114.

67. Ibid. (March 1924), 249-250. For the report of the capture and jailing of Betty Lewis, see the *Bulletin* (April 1924), 276.

68. *Bulletin* (October 1923), 115.

69. *Bulletin* (November 1923), 149.

70. *Bulletin* (April 1924), 277.

71. See Brittingham, *The Claim Agent and His Work,* 13-14. Brittingham had an ambitious program for the training of claim agents who, he believed, were fast establishing themselves as professionals of the stature of doctors and lawyers. "The ideal claim agent must be at once both practical and theoretical because life is made up of both practicalities and theories. He should be honest, keen-minded, logical, highly observant, industrious, mindful of details but capable of seeing beyond them, able in a moment to fit himself into any stratum of society, and he must be educationally inclined" (10). Brittingam believed that success as a claim agent required a broad familiarity with all of the "highways of the world's literature, including art, biography, business, drama, essays, fiction, government, history, nature, philosophy, religion, science, travel and even poetry" (14).

72. For examples of the writing on the proper relationship between railway surgeons and claims men, see the *Medico-Legal Journal* 14 (1896-97), 7-14; 401-413. For an example of the railway surgeon as claims-fighting crusader, see Dr. Willis P. King,

Perjury for Pay: An Exposé of the Methods and Criminal Cunning of the Modern Malingerer (Kansas City, MO: The Burton Company, 1906).

73. See the comments of J. A. Hinsey, Special Agent of the Chicago, Milwaukee and St. Paul Railway Company, *Minutes of the Association of Railway Claim Agents,* Twelfth Annual Meeting, Cleveland, Ohio, May 22-25, 1901, 58-59. Through the 1920s, the railroad police continued to help claims men investigate personal injury claims. "Police investigators have saved thousands of dollars over the years by showing that the person who claimed damages as a result of personal injury, suffering, and loss of time was not seriously injured, and in fact lost no time from work," one study concluded. "This is especially the case in wrecks and in cases for damages arising out of falls from cars in motion or trains that have stopped and suddenly started again." See J. P. Shalloo's *Private Police* (Philadelphia: The American Academy of Political and Social Science, 1933), 14. For more background on the railroad police, see Frank Morn, *The Eye That Never Sleeps: A History of the Pinkerton National Detective Agency* (Bloomington: Indiana University Press, 1982).

74. W. P. Christiansen, "The Investigation of Street Railway Accident Cases," *Proceedings of the American Electric Railway Claim Agents' Association* (1913), 53.

75. See F. Dalton O'Sullivan's *Crime Detection,* 93. For additional detail on the work of the railroad detectives, see his chapter entitled, "Railroad Detective Work Absorbing," 91-99. According to O'Sullivan, many railroad detectives started as claim agents who investigated freight thefts before graduating to personal injury work. The career of Special Agent J. A. Hinsey provides a perfect case in point: "I commenced service with the company I am now serving in the claim department on the 5th day of May, 1865, a little over 36 years ago," Hinsey told his colleagues at a claims convention. "At that time the company had 230 miles of railroad; now almost 7000. Then I was a claim agent, detective, looked up all of my own cases and assisted in trying those that went to litigation. Even got into lost baggage, lost freight. There is nothing pertaining to that department which I have not had personal experience with." (See the *Minutes of the Association of Railway Claim Agents* [1901], 56.)

76. "Cripple Who Successfully Fleeced Many City Lawyers," *New York Times,* 10 June 1899, 12. The working of this kind of con game against personal injury lawyers continued well past the turn of the century. In 1926, under the heading, "A Fake Client," the Chicago *Bar Record* (10, no. 3 [December 1926]) would report on "a man who has been imposing on various lawyers in Chicago. . . . Members of the Association are urged to be on the lookout for him with a view to causing his arrest and stopping his fraudulent practices." More recently, in 1983, some seventy lawyers in Los Angeles were hoodwinked out of anywhere between $100 and $1,100 by a few con men who portrayed themselves as victims of a collision caused by a drunk trucker: "The suspects allegedly went from office to office, posing as an investigator and one or more car-wreck victims who wore plaster casts, hobbled on crutches and even broke into sobs," one account stated. "They

would retain attorneys' services, then ask for expense money." (See "A 'Dream Case' That Backfired: Accident Scam Proves Costly to as Many as 70 Lawyers," *National Law Journal*, 28 November 1983, 3.)

77. *New York Times*, 14 December 1894, 1. Several weeks after Maurer was exposed, another report indicated that he had changed his scheme and was now portraying himself as a German immigrant from Perth Amboy, New Jersey, named Charles W. Muller. Maurer was still victimizing attorneys, but his new scheme involved pretending to have a rich heir whose safety deposit box needed opening upstate if only he could get some advance money from the attorney to get there. Maurer had worked ten attorneys in this way over the preceding week and was still at large. See "More Lawyers Swindled: John W. Maurer Has a New Scheme and a New Alias,"*New York Times*, 31 December 1894, 6.

78. The *Sun* story is from 6 October 1902 and is reprinted in Allan McLane Hamilton, *Railway and Other Accidents, With Relation to Injury and Disease of the Nervous System* (New York: William Wood and Company, 1904), 280-281.

79. For this account of Doran, see "Ex-Contortionist Swindles Philadelphia Streetcar Line," *New York Times*, 2 September 1902, 1.

80. Pape's story is included in "The Business of 'Beating' Street Railway Companies," *Harper's Weekly*, 14 September 1907, 1341. In another account, it was stated that Pape may not have worked alone, but rather had combined with two accomplices and a New York lawyer who took care of the gang's legal work. This account also stated that Pape got his strange physical deformity from an injury to his back that resulted from an unsuccessful dive from a height of forty feet into a vat containing six feet of water, a fact that might suggest Pape once had been a circus performer. See "Accident Fakir Run Down in Philadelphia," *Street Railway Journal*, 9 September 1905, 396.

81. The distinction between the two classes of accident faker was set out by one of the leaders of the alliance in the months following the meeting at Muskoka Lakes. See James R. Pratt, "Bogus Claims Against Street Railway Companies,"*Street Railway Journal*, 7 October 1905, 673. The alliance was formed to take action after years of taking it on the chin from the fakers. "The question . . . which most concerns us now is not so much the methods pursued by fakirs, malingerers and ambulance chasers to obtain money dishonestly," Pratt wrote, but rather "how to eliminate them."

82. See "Combine to Run Down Accident Swindlers," *New York Times*, 16 July 1905, 5. One speaker at the meeting seemed to allude directly to ex-contortionist William J. Doran when he spoke of an acrobat who

> held a position unique among accident fakers. . . . This man didn't mind letting street cars bump him all over the street. He would be picked up by a confederate and carried to a furnished room. Then the confederate would be bandaged up and the acrobat would go out again to get bumped. Again

a confederate would go to bed with the injuries the acrobat was supposed to have received. Getting of witnesses was easy. The gang had little trouble in collecting damages. Finally they were caught and punished.

83. *New York Times*, 26 October 1905, 7.

84. See the *Weekly Underwriter*, 20 January 1906, 43. See also "Alliance Against Accident Fraud," *Street Railway Journal*, 27 January 1906, 163.

85. Pratt, "Bogus Claims Against Street Railway Companies," 674.

86. See "Traps Man Who Faked 300 Minor Injuries," *New York Times*, 16 November 1928, 2.

87. This is an allusion to Roger A. Bruns' excellent book, *Knights of the Road: A Hobo History* (New York: Methuen, 1984).

88. For an excellent discussion of this, see Gary H. Lindberg, *The Confidence Man in American Literature* (New York: Oxford University Press, 1982). Lindberg writes:

> My hypothesis is in fact that the confidence man is a covert cultural hero for Americans. . . . When we denounce someone publicly and then privately laugh up our sleeves at his exploits, we celebrate the cult of the con man. It is not our official pieties he represents but our unofficial reward systems, the strategies that we have for over two centuries/ allowed to succeed. He clarifies the uneasy relations between our stated ethics and our tolerated practices (3-4).

89. See Alice Morse Earle, *Stage-Coach Days and Tavern Nights* (New York: Macmillan, 1915), 367.

90. Annie Platzer's story is told in Gordon Fellowes, *Insurance Racketeers* (London: George Allen & Unwin Ltd., 1935), 50-55.

CHAPTER TWO

1. *In the Matter of Samuel Kopleton, an Attorney* (1930), 229 App. Div. 112.

2. *In the Matter of Moses Cohen, an Attorney* (1930), 229 App. Div. 480, 485. Most of the details of Irving Fuhr's flopping career come from this case. For Fuhr's account of things, see "Fake Accident Ring is Bared by Convict," *New York Times*, 11 July 1928, 25. Other details of the connections among Fuhr, Cohen, and Daniel Laulicht are reported in "Disbars 2 Lawyers in Accident Frauds," *New York Times*, 30 May 1930, 21. Here the relationships between the three men is stated clearly: "Daniel Laulicht was head of this fraudulent claim group, the court said, and employed Irving Fuhr as one of his 'floppers.' Fuhr got to know Cohen, decided to go into business for himself, and employed Cohen as his attorney." For the frustration

that claims men felt in dealing with floppers like Fuhr, see "Liability Claim Fakers Put in Many Busy Hours,"*Weekly Underwriter*, 14 July 1928, 94.

3. *Matter of Cohen*, 485.

4. Ibid., 479.

5. Ibid., 480.

6. Ibid., 480-481.

7. Ibid., 482.

8. Ibid.

9. Ibid., 485.

10. Ibid., 486-487. Of Cohen's actions, the judges concluded: "The destruction of these records at a time when the Laulicht group operations were under investigation and when there was much agitation for an investigation of the whole ambulance chasing situation, leads to only one conclusion, that is, that [Moses Cohen] desired to rid himself of the incriminating evidence which his papers contained."

11. Ibid., 488.

12. This brief account of the history of mass transportation derives in general from Charles W. Cheape's *Moving the Masses: Urban Public Transit in New York, Boston, and Philadelphia, 1880-1912* (Cambridge, MA: Harvard University Press, 1980) and from the "Streets" section of Luc Sante's *Low Life: The Lures and Snares of Old New York* (New York: Vintage, 1991).

13. Barron Collier, *Stopping Street Accidents: A History of New York City's Bureau of Public Safety* (New York: Tabard Press, 1925), 31.

14. Fried, *The Rise and Fall of the Jewish Gangster in America*, 2-5.

15. Fried mentions major gangsters in all of these cities: Chicago's "Twentieth Ward Group" near Maxwell Street; Philadelphia's Max "Boo Boo" Hoff and Nig Rosen; the "Cleveland Four"; Charles "King" Solomon in Boston; the "Purples" of Detroit's "Little Jerusalem"; and Newark's Joseph Reinfeld and Abner "Longy" Zwillman (103-105). There is every reason to believe that equally significant, though substantially less well-known, accident racketeers existed in these same Jewish ghettoes.

16. Fried, *The Rise and Fall of the Jewish Gangster*, 43.

17. These figures are cited in "Nine Arrests Bare Insurance Swindle," *New York Times*, 4 May 1927, 1. In an article published less than a year earlier, writer Boyden Sparkes was more cautious in his estimate of the dimensions of auto insurance fraud nationwide. He writes: "In 1925, insurance companies paid out to claimants for injuries sustained as the result of ownership, operation, and maintenance of automobiles $50,897,144, but there is no statistician sufficiently gifted to indicate what part of that sum was paid to satisfy judgments gained by fraud or to buy releases from fakers." ("Highway Robbers," *Saturday Evening Post*, 2 October 1926, 62.)

18. *In the Matter of Charles D. Sprung, an Attorney* (1930), 229 App. Div. 502.

19. Ibid., 503.

20. Ibid.

21. For the connections between these claims, see the *Matter of Sprung*, 502-507. At trial, Sprung claimed that Laulicht had made up the story of his involvement in accident faking in order to extort money from him, although he did not deny having paid Laulicht to bring him legitimate referrals on a commission basis. See "Two Deny Dealing With Accident Ring," *New York Times,* 18 July 1928, 9. Of Sprung's claim not to have known that the Laulicht cases were fraudulent, a lower court judged said: "It is inconceivable to my mind to accept as true [Sprung's] contention that these three cases were accepted by him in good faith. The most simple-minded person, let alone an attorney of several years' practice, must have known that three such accidents of exactly the same kind, with the same number of men and women involved, did not happen within a span of a few weeks" (*Matter of Sprung,* 506-507). The judges of the Appeals Court agreed: "The records of the Laulichts is well known to this court. They were members of a group engaged in the business of prosecuting fraudulent claims. . . . When respondent came in contact with them he had been admitted to the bar and engaged in active practice for more than three years. His prior experience would indicate knowledge of the ways of the world. We cannot believe that respondent was unaware of the category to which the Laulicht's belonged" (Ibid., 510-511).

22. *Matter of Sprung,* 505.

23. *In the Matter of Morris H. Katz, an Attorney* (1930), 230 App. Div. 177-178.

24. Ibid., 175.

25. *In the Matter of Samuel Kopleton, an Attorney* (1930), 229 App. Div. 113.

26. "Ten Fraud 'Flops' Staged for $17.50," *New York Times,* 12 July 1928, 25.

27. *Matter of Kopleton,* 112.

28. Schlosser, *Lawyers Must Eat* (New York: Vanguard Press, 1933), 130-131.

29. "Forgets 26 Mishaps for Which He Sued," *New York Times,* 21 April 1928, 8. See also the chapter entitled "The Ambulance Chaser on the Run" in Schlosser, *Lawyers Must Eat,* 130-133. Plastik, an automobile rental agent, processed his claims through attorney Samuel Eichner, who lived near Plastik in Brooklyn. Plastik was jailed for his nonresponses to the prosecutor's questions, a performance that an incredulous Judge Isidor Wasservogel interpreted as a "willful" and "deliberate" concealment of the truth. ("I am willing [to tell the truth]," Plastik deadpanned, "but I just don't remember.") See "'Chasers' Witness Evasive, Is Jailed," *New York Times,* 25 April 1928, 29. For his part, attorney Eichner claimed to have had little knowledge of the daily operation of his office and that he had instructed his stenographer, Miss Katz, to file most suits using fill-in-the-blank legal forms. Although perhaps an accurate description of how many high-volume negligence attorneys ran their personal injury law offices, it was rejected as "beyond the realm

of possibility" that Eichner could have had no knowledge of the Plastik actions. Eichner was disbarred in 1930.

30. *Matter of Kopleton,* 113-114.

31. *Matter of Morris H. Katz,* 173. Katz denied using solicitors, and prosecutors did not attempt to prove that he did. In his defense, Katz added: "I want to say this, that the average settlements in the cases were nominal, so much so that they just barely paid a little over and above the actual disbursements and the time and the help and whatever I had in the office."

32. Ibid., 182. The judges concluded that Morris Katz "well knew the character of the Laulichts, knew what they were doing, conspired with them and played his part in the carrying out of their fraudulent schemes."

33. *Matter of Louis L. Katz,* 104.

34. Ibid. The Lobisch case was originally handled by attorney Joel Kirschner of 305 Broadway but was passed on to Katz. The sham medical exam was conducted in Katz's office, and Katz was there for part of the time, but attorney Kirschner was the one who was originally arrested, tried, and sentenced to three years in prison for his involvement in the case. See "Lawyer and 4 Aides Sentenced for Fraud," *New York Times,* 14 April 1928, 6 and "Charges Adjusters Aided Fraud Claims," *New York Times,* 13 July 1928, 18.

35. "Nine Arrests Bare Insurance Swindle," *New York Times,* 4 May 1927, 1.

36. "After Accident Fakers,"*Weekly Underwriter,* 17 May 1924, 1154. Gracchino Caruso, the forty-year-old head of the family and the ring, was described by the prosecutor as a "much injured man" who alone staged at least twelve of the ring's fifty known accidents.

37. "3 Indicted in Auto Insurance Frauds; Companies Hunt Band Accused of Obtaining $100,000 Through Fake Accidents," *New York Times,* 4 March 1922, 9.

38. "Highway Robbers,"*Saturday Evening Post,* 2 October 1926, 44.

39. Ibid.

40. Ibid., 42.

41. Ibid., 44.

42. Ibid., 62.

43. See "Indicted in Fraud Inquiry," *New York Times,* 10 August 1916, 15 and "Hold Doctor for Fraud" in the *Times,* 25 August 1916, p. 5:2. Dr. Loewthan was also documented as having instructed an auto mechanic named Thomas Hill to stage a fall in the pit of his Harlem garage in order to collect worker's compensation. "[Say] you've got a dislocated shoulder and a lot of other injuries," Loewthan instructed Hill after the fall. "I'll bandage you up and you can get a lot of money from your boss under the Employers' Liability act." Loewthan was arrested at his summer home on Long Island after an insurance company found out that Hill was working as a "furniture hoister" while collecting benefits and that he had none of the injuries the doctor had claimed.

44. "Fake Injury Claims Win $150,000 a Year; Woman Charged with Getting Herself Hurt by Autos, Trucks, Trolleys, and Coal Holes; Let Subway Drag Her," *New York Times*, 18 June 1916, I-14.

45. For Seymour's gang, see these articles in the *Street Railway Journal*: "Accident Fakirs Run Down in New Jersey and Philadelphia," 20 February 1904, 301, and "Disclosures Made at the Trial of the Philadelphia Accident Fakir," 5 March 1904, 387.

46. See Edward Hungerford, "The Business of 'Beating' Street Railway Companies: The Tricks of the Swindlers Who Claim Damages for Injuries They Have Never Received, and the Part that Detectives and Cameras Play in Exposing Them,"*Harper's Weekly*, 14 September 1907, 1340.

47. Ibid., 1341.

48. Ibid. After noting the existence of more sophisticated gangs of chasers, doctors, and lawyers who work together for the "wholesale mulcting of traction companies," Hungerford notes that "it has not yet been necessary for any railroad company to send a lawyer or a doctor to the penitentiary" (1357).

49. "Accident Fakirs Sentenced in Baltimore,"*Street Railway Journal*, 25 November 1905, 963. The gang was convicted partly on the basis of entries in Martha Bobson's diary, one of which referred to an accident staged in Brooklyn for a payoff of $2,000. A letter sent by Edward Reilly to Frank Bobson also was incriminating: Reilly asked for $11 to help him get a job as a motorman on a Cleveland rail line, which he told Bobson was best for "our business."

50. "Accident Fakirs Apprehended in Cleveland,"*Street Railway Journal*, 2 September 1905, 367.

51. *Philadelphia Press*, 7 March 1893, 10. Even earlier, a "gang of conspirators" was arrested in Philadelphia for beating a traction company there out of a small fortune (some $10,000). The gang consisted mainly of a husband and wife, and their fake claims involved alleging to have been thrown from streetcars, then paying witnesses falsely to swear on their behalf. See "Accused of Conspiracy; Trying to Obtain Money for Alleged Damages in Philadelphia," *New York Times*, 1 January 1890, 1.

52. Quoted from the annual report of the Philadelphia Rapid Transit Company in "Ambulance Chasing" reproduced in the *Green Bag* 20 (1908), 145.

53. "The Measure of Damages for Personal Injuries on Railways,"*Hunt's Merchant's Magazine* 63 (1870), 359. The phenomenon of ambulance chasing in which agents are hired to solicit claims and to create elaborate street-level networks for referrals was not really significant until the late 1890s. Legal historian Randolph Bergstrom dates the origin of ambulance chasing conservatively from 1900 to 1910. (See his *Courting Danger: Injury and Law in New York City, 1870-1910* [Ithaca, NY: Cornell University Press, 1992], 93.)

54. *Congressional Record*, Fifty-Sixth Congress, 24 July 1897, 2961.

55. "Report of Committee on Legal Education and Admission to the Bar" in American Bar Association *Reports* (1897), 378.

56. *Street Railway Journal*, 10 August 1896, 484.

57. L. G. Smith, "The Evolution of the Ambulance Chaser,"*Green Bag* 14 (1902), 263-264. At the heart of the author's rhymes is an analogy between the hard-shelled creatures ("luckless mites" and "trilobites") that roamed the earth "back in primeval times" and the ambulance chasers of modern times, a "swarming brood of creatures of most rapacious mien." The closing rhyme plays off the word "trilobite" from the previous stanza: "Who are these greedy objects who swarm the city street?" it is asked. "Oh those, sirs, are the lawyers who in accidents delight/ The chasers of the ambulance—the modern trolleybite."

58. "Report of Committee on Contingent Fees," *Report of the New York State Bar Association* 31 (1908), 123.

59. This language comes from a report by the State Bar Association of Minnesota quoted, along with an excerpt from a similar report from Birmingham Alabama, in Julius Henry Cohen, *The Law—Business or Profession?* (New York: Banks Law Publishing Co., 1916), 182-184, 238.

60. Ibid., 185.

61. See *McCloskey v. San Antonio Traction Co.* (1917), 192 S.W. 1116-17 and *McCloskey v. San Antonio Pub. Serv. Co.*, (1932) 51 S.W. 2d 1088, 1089.

62. Cohen, *The Law—Business or Profession?*, 124.

63. Joseph Lilly, "Eagle Bares Corrupt Acts of 'Ambulance Chasing' Lawyers Operating in City," *Brooklyn Eagle*, 13 September 1927, 1.

64. Arthur Train, *The Confessions of Artemas Quibble* (New York: Charles Scribner's Sons, 1911), 62-63. Although the book is fiction, Train, a former prosecutor in New York City, well knew the actual conditions he was writing about and only thinly embroidered upon them in his books. Train's fictional "Quibble," like many who found their way into the accident business early in the century, began by being paid a cash referral fee for bringing a legitimate case to an attorney, then proceeded to full-time ambulance chasing. "You don't have to be a lawyer to get clients," he is told by an attorney. "Hustle around among your friends and drum up some trade and you'll do almost as well as if you could try cases yourself" (45-46). In addition to New York, the early centers of ambulance chasing included all of the major cities in the Northeast as well as several cities in Alabama and Minnesota. (Cohen, *The Law—Business or Profession?*, 238.)

65. *In the Matter of Edward Gordon, an Attorney* (1930), 229 App. Div. 91.

66. Ibid.

67. These figures are quoted from the "Report of the Committee of Censors to the Law Association of Philadelphia,"*Massachusetts Law Quarterly* (1928), 7.

68. "Moses Again Refuses to Aid 'Chaser' Hunt," *New York Times*, 21 July 1928, 24. Gondelman was shown to have employed three chasers, each of whom were paid a weekly salary of $50 to $75; he also made deals with newspaper reporters, gave money and bought suits for Brooklyn police officers, and bought leads directly

from doctors. He was disbarred in 1929. (*In the Matter of Sidney Gondelman, an Attorney* [1929], 225 App. Div. 462.)

69. George W. Alger, "Cleaning the Courts,"*Atlantic Monthly*, March 1928, 407.

70. *In the Matter of Harry E. Kreindler, an Attorney* (1930), 228 App. Div. 493-496.

71. *In the matter of Henry Clay Littick, an Attorney* (1929), 225 App. Div. 247. See also "Says Lawyer Split Fee with Him," *New York Times*, 10 July 1928, 11.

72. "Admits Forgeries, Blames Law Clerk," *New York Times*, 4 April 1928, 31.

73. *In the Matter of Samuel Flatow, an Attorney* (1930), 228 App. Div 254.

74. Charles L. Aarons, "The Practice of Law by Non-Lawyers,"*Marquette Law Review* 14 (1929), 1.

75. Abraham Gatner, "Operating Room Invaded by Ambulance Chaser, Pressing Patient to Sue," *Brooklyn Eagle*, 16 September 1927, 1.

76. Abraham Gatner, "Ex-Ambulance Chaser Tells How Accident Suits Are Obtained by Lawyers," *Brooklyn Eagle*, 14 September 1927, 1. All of the articles in Gatner's confession were actually written by *Eagle* reporter Joseph Lilly "as told by Abraham Gatner." Other sources on Gatner include Murray T. Bloom, *The Trouble with Lawyers* (New York: Simon and Schuster, 1968); and Robert Monaghan's "The Liability Claim Racket," *Law and Contemporary Problems* 3 (1936), 491-504. Monaghan's account seems to have derived from Gatner's confession in the *Brooklyn Eagle*. Monaghan states cautiously enough that "ambulance chasing as a business" began around 1907 (an estimate that was nevertheless off by more than a decade); and Monaghan also notes that Gatner was one of three full-time chasers working at the time (493). Bloom embellishes this by saying that Gatner was "our first ambulance chaser" and that Gatner himself came up with the name "ambulance chasing." Bloom goes on to offer a tongue-in-cheek celebration of Gatner as the visionary pioneer of the "injury industry," which he describes as "one of the few enduring and continually profitable sub-industries of our time." Bloom then wants to recognize Gatner for his dubious achievements: "The founder of the still-growing American injury industry has been overlooked. The man who almost singlehandedly set the industry on its modern path and invented most of its illicit angles, the man who showed generations of American lawyers the road to its surest dollar, has never been honored. There are no laudatory biographies or films, no law school chairs named after him, no ABA prizes in his honor. Not even a footnote in any legal text." Although said in jest, the underlying idea that ambulance chasing was the invention of "a fresh-faced hustling lad of eighteen who had two years of high school," as Bloom describes Gatner, is misleading. Clearly false is Bloom's later assertion that Gatner "had a hand in the first actually faked accident case"(Bloom, 127). This may have been a misreading of Monaghan's statement that Gatner, in 1912, while working as a corporate claims man, found out about the idea that accidents could be faked (Monaghan, 494).

77. "Ambulance Chaser Offers to Bare Illegal System of Scores of Law Firms," *Brooklyn Eagle*, 6 September 1927, 1. For more of the anticipation of Gatner's "revelations,"

see "Ambulance Chasing Expose Starts in Eagle Tomorrow; To Show Far-Reaching Evils," *Brooklyn Eagle*, 13 September 1927, 1.

78. *In the Matter of Aaron M. Becker, an Attorney, In the Matter of Joseph Levy, an Attorney* (1930), 229 App. Div. 63.

79. Ibid., 63-64. Several of these same chasers—Irving Wolf, David Schaeffer, Tony Sagona—worked at different times for attorney Moses N. Schleider, according to attorney Schleider's own reluctant admissions (227 App. Div. 537).

80. *Matter of Becker and Levy*, 229 App. Div. 65.

81. Ibid., 69-72.

82. Abraham Gatner, "Ambulance-Chasers Find Police Headquarters Big Source of Accident News," *Brooklyn Eagle*, 15 September 1927, 1.

83. Abraham Gatner, "Police Precincts, Individual Cops Bribed, by Ambulance Chasers," *Brooklyn Eagle*, 19 September 1927, 1. On one occasion the source of the misinformation was not limited to individual cops but was more widespread, Gatner recounts. "Secret Conferences were held, and after much perspiration I was consulted by those who thought I should know. I prowled about and discovered that two 'chasers' were intercepting the slips in the Telegraph Bureau, to which they had purchased entry."

84. *American Bar Association Journal* 14 (November 1928), 562.

85. Abraham Gatner, "Police Precincts Invaded, Individual Cops Bribed, by Ambulance Chasers," *Brooklyn Eagle*, 19 September 1927, 1. Chasers from this time were also working upstate. Although they made less money, upstate chasers, such as Joseph Michels of Syracuse, were no less resourceful in buying contacts for accident leads. Michels, in fact, was shown to have gotten cases directly by telegraph from a clerk at the New York Central Railroad. (See *In the Matter of James E. Newell, an Attorney*, 174 App. Div. 95-96.)

86. *Weekly Underwriter*, 20 March 1909, 211.

87. Abraham Gatner, "Ambulance Chasers Lay 'Pipe Lines' in Hospitals; Sign Patients at Bedside," *Brooklyn Eagle*, 20 September 1927, 1.

88. Ibid.

89. Abraham Gatner, "Ambulance Chaser Gets Insurance Adjusting Job to Learn Tricks of Trade," *Brooklyn Eagle*, 17 September 1927, 1.

90. Smith R. Brittingham, *The Claim Agent and his Work: Investigation and Settlement of Claims for Personal Injuries* (New York: Ronald Press, 1927), 297. Brittingham recommends a number of attitudes and psychological strategies as being most conducive to success as a claim agent. Among them: "Flattery" ("there is no question but that all members of the human family are susceptible to flattery"); "Logic and Dialectic" ("the ignorant claimant may be made to feel the force of a logical presentation of the railroad's position just as well as the intellectual claimant"); "Sincerity" ("if a claim agent has no confidence in his position . . . he should work the case over in his mind, get a grasp of the railroad's position, convince himself of the righteous-

ness of his view and then proceed"); and "Sympathetic Visits" to the claimant's home, which serve the double purpose of showing concern while also beating out "anti-railroad influences" such as "shyster lawyers or other busybodies." Other tactics include: "Expediency of Ignoring Claimants," "Appeals to the Moral Sense," "The Display of Cash," and the "Resort to Diversions in Argument." (See the chapter entitled "Psychology and Claim Agency.")

91. Ibid., 313-314.

92. "The policy of railway companies is generally to discourage [personal injury] suits, and to make them as expensive and as unproductive as possible," it was written in 1870, "in order that other people, in a similar condition, may be deterred from prosecuting them. . . . The company is sure to find some dark question as to the character of the negligence of which they are accused, some doubtful instruction of the court, or some error of the jury, on which to found an 'appeal,' and to keep him paying costs and fees, perhaps for years longer, before—if ever—he receives his money." ("The Measure of Damages for Personal Injuries on Railways"*Hunt's Merchant's Magazine* [1870], 357.) In 1897 lawyer Eli Hammond noted the fact that the railroads, "almost without exception everywhere...adopt the policy of 'fighting' every claimant for damages, no matter how clear their liability, unless it may be they will 'compromise' when they can pay a nominal and wholly inadequate sum." In addition to hunting up whatever evidence they can find to evade payment on legal grounds, Hammond notes, the railroads also "send their runners,' in the shape of claim agents, local lawyers, doctors, surgeons, and nurses, to take 'statements' that are, to say the least, if not perverted to suit their interests [are] with great injustice made to speak most favorably for the company, and these are sometimes used as impeaching testimony under circumstances that shock the commonest sense of humanity." (See Eli Shelby Hammond, "Personal Injury Litigation,"*Yale Law Journal* [1897], 328.) In 1928 even the legal elites who were petitioning for hearings into ambulance chasing in New York also noted the chasing activities of the defense: "In many instances there are races between the solicitors for lawyers and representatives of prospective defendants who seek to obtain releases at the bedsides of the disabled persons" (quoted in *New York Times*, 9 January 1928, 16).

93. "Fighting Accident Suits," *New York Times*, 27 October 1905, 8.

94. Gatner, "Ambulance Chaser Gets Insurance Adjusting Job." Gatner writes: "At first, I reported the facts as I found them, but I soon was given instructions which I understood to mean that what was wanted were statements from witnesses who saw the accident from a perspective favorable to the company." Gatner also writes of his distaste in settling cases for a dollar with people who did not think they deserved money for their injuries, and mentions giving them $10 or $20 as a "present" from the company in exchange for their signed release forms.

95. *In the Matter of Henry A. Robinson, an Attorney* (1912), 151 App. Div. 589. Other defense attorneys, such as Frank Verner Johnson, were expert at using all legal means to

defeat personal injury claims. Among lawyers, in fact, the real personal injury "specialists" were said to have been the handful of defense experts who monopolized the practice, not the changing multitude of plaintiff's lawyers who fought and scraped for whatever actions they could. (See Bergstrom, *Courting Danger*, 97.) In Boston, where poor immigrant claimants and "shysters" were also closely associated with personal injury litigation, the defense lawyers were really the only constant presence over time and were the main professionals to profit from personal injury litigation. "If stereotypes were to be pointed out in personal injury suits," legal historian Robert A. Silverman writes, "then one should have pointed to the defense table, which was normally occupied by a well-bred Yankee barrister on behalf of a large business or the city government. . . . Defense attorneys were a homogenous group. Most were Yankees who had attended Harvard, clerked with a prominent lawyer, joined the Boston Bar Association, and practiced for ten years or more. This circle of specialists handled more than three-fourths of all negligence defenses presented in 1900" (*Law and Urban Growth: Civil Litigation in the Boston Trial Courts, 1880-1900* [Princeton, NJ: Princeton University Press, 1981], 116, 119.) When a New York judge denounced the "Accident Trust" in 1911, he meant both the plaintiffs and the defense specialists who, together, controlled so much of the accident litigation in the courts that they were rarely available to come to trial. The judge asserted his belief that both sides often conspired together to delay cases in court while they negotiated settlements. ("Justice Goff Raps Accident Lawyers," *New York Times*, 16 December 1911, 7.)

96. "Gatner Names 15 Lawyers," *New York Times*, 20 June 1916, 19.

97. Gatner named two of the slip boys, Matty Martin and James McManus, whom he paid $5 a week for typed lists of accidents and $10 a week for phone tips. Gatner also told the court about how two of his runners "controlled" two police stations; that is, they were known in the stations and were given leads exclusively. One of the runners worked on his own downtown, the other worked out of a tailor shop across from the station. (See "Charges Police Aid Ambulance Chasing," *New York Times*, 11 April 1928, 13.)

98. "Charges 'Runners' Get Hospitals' Aid," in the *New York Times*, 12 April 1928, 8.

99. "Ambulance Chaser Guilty," *New York Times*, 7 February 1928, 29. In this case, Gatner was found to have manufactured evidence in support of a claim. Earlier that year Gatner had unsuccessfully attempted to sue attorneys Levy and Becker for $40,000 in chasing commissions owed to him ("Loses Suit Against Lawyers," *New York Times*, 27 January 1928, 8). In the mid-1930s, Gatner was convicted of extortion, most likely resulting from an attempt by him to shame or scare attorneys into paying him the money he was owed for referrals (*People v. Gatner* [1937], 249 App. Div. 804).

100. Gatner, perhaps untruthfully, put it this way:

> My connection with the "ambulance chasing" industry, now happily finished, has been intimate, but it is nothing of which I wish to boast. I

> do not want to give the impression that I participated in such business of corruption as I have just described. I came to know the facts in this and other situations because I am a curious and inquiring fellow, and from the start I made it my affair to know every possible detail of the industry and the methods of every one connected with it.

See Gatner, "Police Precincts Invaded, Individual Cops Bribed."

101. Joseph Lilly, "Card Index Links Families, Lawyers and Doctors in Many Fake Damage Suits," *Brooklyn Eagle*, 7 September 1927, 3. One case investigated by the alliance involved an allegedly dead mouse in a milk bottle. "An autopsy was performed upon the mouse," however, "and it was found that far from having been drowned in the milk it had had its neck broken in a trap."

102. Joseph Lilly, "Card Index Links Families, Lawyers and Doctors in Many Fake Damage Suits," *Brooklyn Eagle*, 7 September 1927, 3.

103. "600 Theaters Out for Campaign on 'Chaser' Lawyers," *Brooklyn Eagle*, 22 September 1927, 30. See also Joseph Lilly, "Public Pays the Piper as Ambulance Chasers Mulct Movie Theaters," *Brooklyn Eagle*, 28 September 1927, 1.

104. Joseph Lilly, "Theater Men to Demand Action on Eagle Expose of Ambulance Chasing," *Brooklyn Eagle*, 26 September 1927, 1.

105. Joseph Lilly, "Another Group in Fight on Ambulance Chasing; Affidavits Are Offered," *Brooklyn Eagle*, 27 September 1927, 1.

106. Joseph Lilly, "City-Wide War Declared on 'Ambulance Chasers' at Distinguished Meeting," *Brooklyn Eagle*, 24 September 1927, 1.

107. "Mons. Belford Lauds Eagle Ambulance-Chasing Expose," *Brooklyn Eagle*, 22 September 1927, 30.

108. Abraham Gatner, "Big Corporations Aware of Fake Injuries But Pay Ambulance-Chasing Claims," *Brooklyn Eagle*, 22 September 1927, 1.

109. "Bar Association Will Act on Gatner Charges," *Brooklyn Eagle*, 29 September 1927, 1.

110. "Bar Assn. Dodges Gatner Charges," Brooklyn Eagle, 30 September 1927, 1.

111. See Frank Carstarphan, "Review of the Work of the Citizens Committee Against Fraudulent Claims and Other Public Agencies During the Past Year in Combating and Eradicating the Evils pertaining to Ambulance-Chasing Attorneys and Fellow Conspirators," *Proceedings of the American Electric Railway Claim Agents' Association* (1928), 33.

112. Ibid., 45.

113. Ibid., 41.

114. Oscar Handlin, *Adventure in Freedom: Three Hundred Years of Jewish Life in America* (New York: McGraw-Hill, 1954), 182.

115. Moss, *The American Metropolis*, vol. 3, 220.

CHAPTER THREE

1. Herbert Mitgang, *The Man Who Rode the Tiger: The Life and Times of Judge Samuel Seabury* (Philadelphia: J.B. Lippincott, 1963), 173.

2. "Kresel's Career One of Activity," *New York Times*, 17 January 1935, 9.

3. "Ambulance Chaser Faces Court Action," *New York Times*, 9 January 1928, 16. For the full text of the court's decision, see *In re Association of the Bar of the City of New York, et al.* (1928), 222 App. Div. 580. Three months later the court would approve a similar petition for chaser hearings filed by a Brooklyn bar group in order "that this nefarious business be brought to a speedy end" (*In re Brooklyn Bar Association et al.* [1928], 223 App. Div. 150).

4. *New York Times*, 9 February 1928, 24.

5. For this background on the start of the chaser hearings, see these articles in the *New York Times*: "Kresel to Unearth Ambulance Chasing," 12 February 1928, Sec. 2, 1; "Lawyers Chosen in 'Chaser' Inquiry," February 23, 1928, 23; "Ambulance Chaser Under Fire Today," 20 February 1928, 25; and "Maps Plan to Curb Ambulance Chaser," 21 February 1928, 24.

6. For Abraham Oberstein's encounter with Kresel, see "Admits Forgeries, Blames Law Clerk,"*New York Times*, 4 April 1928, 31.

7. "Charges Attorney Hiding in Jersey," *New York Times*, 29 May 1928, 14. See also *In the Matter of Samuel M. Goldberg* (1930), 227 App. Div. 502. Goldberg was ultimately censured for his use of solicitors.

8. Quoted in "'Chaser' Evils Held Proved by Evidence," *New York Times*, 25 July 1928, 9. Kresel expanded on these remarks at a speech he delivered before an overwhelmingly appreciative crowd at the annual meeting of the New York State Bar Association in 1929. For an audience of mostly upstate bar members who hung on his every word, Kresel described the chasers' system of soliciting cases on the streets, in hospitals, and at police stations. See Isidor J. Kresel, "Ambulance Chasing, Its Evils, and Remedies Therefor," *Proceedings of the Fifty-Second Annual Meeting of the New York State Bar Association* (Albany: Argus Company, 1929), 329.

9. In his speech before the New York State Bar Association in 1929, Kresel further described the way that corporate claims men "did a little ambulance chasing of their own." Justice Wasservogel of the State Supreme Court also noted the chasing practices of the corporate claims men. "The evils inherent in the practice of 'ambulance chasing' are by no means confined to the activities of lawyers for the claimants," Wasservogel wrote. "In many instances it is a race between solicitors for lawyers . . . and representatives of the prospective defendants . . . as to which of these would reach the bedside first." In his final report on the hearings, Justice Wasservogel found evidence to support this claim, reiterating that "frequently the insurance adjuster races with the 'ambulance chaser' to the bedside of the injured person to obtain a release from him while he is overwrought and in pressing need of money." Isidor Wasservogel,

In the Matter of the Investigation Ordered by the Appellate Division of the Supreme Court in and for the First Judicial Department, by Order Dated February 7, 1928, upon the Petition of the Association.of the Bar of the City of New York, New York County Lawyers Association and Bronx County Bar Association, for an Inquiry by the Court into Certain Abuses and Illegal and Improper Practices Alleged in the Petition (New York: M.B. Brown Printing, 1928), 11.

10. Wasservogel's findings are summarized in "74 Lawyers Cited in 'Chaser' Report," *New York Times,* 3 October 1928, 1.

11. Sidney Handler, *The Results of the Ambulance Chasing Disbarment Proceedings in the Appellate Division, First Department* (1931), 5 p.

12. The principal provisions of the antichaser bills voted on by the legislature called for: the total prohibition of employing runners, the regulation of contingent fees, and the approval of the court in the settlement of all personal injury cases, a bureaucratically unrealistic aim even then. Roosevelt sent a special message to the legislature urging the passage of these bills, saying that they were necessary to "eliminate this practice of ambulance chasing, which not only brings into disrepute a noble profession but threatens some of the fundamentals upon which respect for our law and our courts and their administration is founded" ("Roosevelt Message Hits 'Chaser' Evil," *New York Times,* 22 January 1929, 10). The sponsor of the bills and all those who supported them, including Isidor Kresel, were heckled when they spoke to the legislature. ("Is it true that you have just been made counsel for a big insurance company?" an assemblyman from Syracuse asked Kresel derisively.) The upstate Republicans objected to what they saw as the hypocrisy of the big-city corporate lawyers regulating the law practices of attorneys with lesser clienteles. ("Kills Bills to Stop Ambulance Chasing," *New York Times,* 6 March 1929, 32 and "Up-State Righteousness," *New York Times,* 7 March 1929, 24.) Roosevelt did not give up easily on the chaser bills, but the upstaters, led by Horace Stone of Syracuse, ultimately won out. ("Roosevelt Renews Fight on 'Chasers,'" *New York Times,* 9 March 1929, 10, and "Attack Roosevelt on 'Chaser Bills,'" *New York Times,* 22 March 1929, 10.)

13. "Quiz of Lawyers a Volunteer Job," *New York Times,* 15 April 1928, Sec. 10, 10.

14. Jerold S. Auerbach, *Unequal Justice: Lawyers and Social Change in Modern America* (New York: Oxford University Press, 1976), 315 n18.

15. Initially, counsel for the prosecution in the Bank of United States case said he would not call on Kresel to testify, but, weeks later, called him anyway in a move that many saw as motivated more by politics than by justice. See "Kresel to Testify," *New York Times,* 18 January 1931, 32; "Kresel Subpoenaed to Testify," *New York Times,* 31 January 1931, 19; and "Kresel Testifies," *New York Times,* 6 February 1931, 1.

16. George Martin, *Causes and Conflicts: The Centennial History of the Association of the Bar of the City of New York, 1870-1970* (New York: Houghton Mifflin, 1970), 231-232.

17. For the aftermath of the reversal of Kresel's conviction, see the following articles in the *New York Times:* "Kresel Conviction Reversed and Indictment Dismissed," 17

January 1935, 1; "Kresel Overjoyed at His Exoneration," 17 January 1935, 8; "Kresel's Career One of Activity," 17 January 1935, 9; "Kresel Prepares to Rebuild Career," 18 January 1935, 15; "Kresel Reinstated as Member of Bar," 5 February 1935, 21.

18. Erwin O. Smigel, *The Wall Street Lawyer: Professional Organization Man?* (London: Collier-Macmillan Limited, 1964), 166.

19. Auerbach, *Unequal Justice* , 41. Julius Henry Cohen was one bar elite of this era who saw the chasers and the Wall Streeters clearly as two sides to the same coin of commercialization and asked genuinely what the difference was between them. Both operated their practices more along business principles than along the old professional norms, Cohen shows, only the chasers modeled themselves after the low business world of tailors and dry-goods shops while the Wall Streeters took on the organization of the big, corporate clients they served. See generally Julius Henry Cohen, *The Law—Business or Profession?* (New York: Banks Law Publishing Co., 1916), 189, 211-212. In the book, Cohen seems not so much to be asking whether the law is a business but to have recognized that some areas of the law were already conducted like a business, then to question whether this was good for the profession.

20. Auerbach, *Unequal Justice*, 52.

21. Ibid., 49-50. For more on how legal elites set up restrictive barriers to entry into the profession specifically to keep out people they thought were undesirable, see the chapters entitled "Controlling the Production of Lawyers" and "The Consequences of Controlling Entry" in Richard L. Abel, *American Lawyers* (New York: Oxford University Press, 1989).

22. Kresel, "Ambulance Chasing, Its Evils and Remedies Therefor," 329, 337.

23. Ibid., 325.

24. See "Power to Compel Testimony in General Court Investigations,"*Harvard Law Review* 42 (1928), 107-108.

25. Quoted in the later appeal, *The People of the State of New York, Respondent, v. Isidor J. Kresel, Appellant* (1935), 243 App. Div. 143.

26. Oscar Handlin, *Adventure in Freedom: Three Hundred Years of Jewish Life in America* (New York: McGraw-Hill, 1954), 144.

27. Auerbach, *Unequal Justice*, 315 n18.

28. See generally the chapter entitled "Antilawyer Sentiment in the Early Republic" in Maxwell Bloomfield, *American Lawyers in a Changing Society, 1776-1876* (Cambridge, MA: Harvard University Press, 1976). Bloomfield writes that the exaggerated fears of the power of lawyers in the years following the Revolution filled "a void in the national mythology" for an enemy class on whom to blame the economic problems of the struggling republic. The legal profession, looking to shore-up a positive and vital place in American life (and to tighten a professional monopoly on legal services) in the early decades of the twentieth century, may have similarly scapegoated the ambulance chasers.

29. *American Bar Association Journal* 14(November 1928), 1.

30. *Milwaukee Sentinel*, 2 March 1927, 1. A week later Buer was expelled from the Milwaukee Socialist Party for conduct unbecoming a member. See "Buer Expelled from Socialist Party," *Milwaukee Sentinel*, 10 March 1927, 1.

31. "Milwaukee Ambulance Chasers Disciplined,"*Journal of the American Judicature Society* 11 (October 1927), 83-85. According to Lyman Wheeler of the Lawyer's Club, there was no plan to use Buer as the pretext for their petition. Attorney Ed Yockey of the club had been merely "fortunate" to have been involved with the case and was "alert" to have thought to cross-examine Buer so extensively once he learned that Buer was a chaser. The subhead attached to Wheeler's letter reinforce this explanation: "Recent clean-up of Bar follows accidental disclosure of ring of lawyers and lay agents."

32. "Prominent Lawyers Face 'Chasing' Inquiry," *Milwaukee Sentinel*, 1 May 1927, 1.

33. See "Court Orders Search for Two Missing Suit Chasers; Inquiry Is Adjourned Pending Hunt for Saichek, Hoffman," *Milwaukee Sentinel*, 15 June 1927, 1, and "'Key Witness to Give Chaser History Today; Hoffman Back from Chicago to Testify on Wife's Request," *Milwaukee Sentinel*, 21 June 1927, 3. When he returned, Hoffman told the court that he had worked as a chaser for attorneys Arthur, Sanger, Louis Metz, and Samuel Kops at a salary of $60 a week. Hoffman also spoke of a code of ethics that the chasers found "to their mutual advantage" to observe. "If I got to an injured person's home and found a car belonging to one of the other boys outside, I would wait until that solicitor came out," he said. "If he had failed to sign up the case, he would tell me so, and I would then go in and try my luck" (*Milwaukee Sentinel*, 22 January 1927, 1).

34. Benjamin McFagin's story is told in "Chaser Ready with Papers at Hospital Door; Crippled Man Says He Signed Contract as He Fought Pain," *Milwaukee Sentinel*, 14 June 1927, 1.

35. "Koenig's Fee for Service in Accident Case Probed,"*Milwaukee Sentinel*, 4 May 1927, 1.

36. Paul A. Holmes, "The Circuit Court Inquisition Into Legal Abuses," *Marquette Law Review* 11 (1927), 188.

37. Louis Swichkow, *A Dual Heritage: The Jewish Community of Milwaukee, 1900-1970* (Ann Arbor, MI: University Microfilms, 1973), 303.

38. Ibid., 211.

39. "Rubin Charges Conspiracy in 'Chaser' Quiz," *Milwaukee Sentinel*, 6 May 1927, 1.

40. "Rubin to Ask New Probe of Legal Abuses; 'I've Got the Goods on the Lily Whites,' Attorney Declares," *Milwaukee Sentinel*, 11 May 1927, 1.

41. See "Ready to Fight, Rubin Declares," *Milwaukee Sentinel*, 7 May 1927, 1 and "Rubin Returns to Prove 'Plot' Charges," *Milwaukee Sentinel*, 8 May 1927, 1. Two days before testifying at the chaser probe, Rubin spoke to an overflowing crowd of 600 supporters, mostly union men. First he hurled some vague charges at the directors of the Lawyer's Club, one of whom, he claimed, was "one of the worst ambulance

chasers in town," another of whom "has had ambulance chasers galore in his office." Rubin also claimed that Ed Buer, the king of Milwaukee ambulance chasers, would have detailed for the court his chasing relationships with Lawyer's Club members had he not been silenced on these points. Rubin closed by sounding some of the populist themes that would characterize his later run for governor: "I am and always have been in favor of cleaning up this rotten practice of ambulance chasing provided the claim adjusting business be cleaned up too," he said before going on to mention the abuses of corporate counsel, which he felt were even more reprehensible than chasing personal injury cases. "Let's investigate on all sides if we are going to investigate . . . let's investigate lawyers who have lobbied against the people." See "Rubin Accuses Chaser Quiz Heads," *Milwaukee Sentinel*, 14 May 1927, 1.

42. "Rubin Is Given 30 Day Term for Contempt," *Milwaukee Sentinel*, 16 May 1927, 1.

43. At the start of the public chaser hearings in New York, a personal injury lawyer named Alexander Karlin refused to testify and was promptly cited for contempt and thrown into the 37th Street jail. In arguing to uphold the contempt charge against Karlin, Isidor Kresel was able to cite, among other things, the successful case against William B. Rubin in Milwaukee. (See "Lawyer is Jailed in 'Chasers' Inquiry," *New York Times*, 21 March 1928, 29, and *People ex rel Karlin v. Culkin* [1928], 248 N.Y. 467.) In discussing the jailing of Karlin, one law review found little precedent in the common law for compelling lawyers to testify in a general court investigation of their practices and outlined the case against the hearings in much the same terms that Justice Crownhart of Wisconsin had done in his dissent to Rubin. (See the note entitled "Power to Compel Testimony in General Court Investigations,"*Harvard Law Review* 42 [1928], 104-108.)

44. *Rubin v. State*, 216 N.W. 514-515.

45. George W. Alger, "Cleaning the Courts," *Atlantic Monthly*, March 1928, 410. The next month the *Bulletin of the State Bar of Wisconsin* was proud to be able to report that the Atlantic Monthly had "approved" of their inquisition.

46. Quoted in the *Milwaukee Sentinel*, 5 May 1927, 1.

47. "Saichek Says He Posed as Lawyers' Aid; Names of Attorneys Used to Arrange Claims, Quiz Told," *Milwaukee Sentinel*, 28 June 1927, 1.

48. Ibid.

49. "Attorneys Assail Ambulance Chasers," *Philadelphia Inquirer*, 7 March 1928, 2. For newspaper articles on the Philadelphia chaser probes of the 1920s, 1930s, 1940s, and early 1970s, I have relied mainly on the clipping files at Temple University's Urban Archives in Philadelphia. Some citations are incomplete, others were not recorded correctly.

50. "Philadelphia Bar Investigates Contingent Fee Scandals,"*Journal of the American Judicature Society* 13 (1929), 144.

51. McGirr's words are recorded in the "Sanitation of the Bar," *Journal of the American Judicature Society* 4 (1920), 6. As early as 1898, a judge in a Philadelphia Common

Pleas Court commented on the chasing conditions in the city and urged action against them:

> There are lawyers who make it a business to hunt up litigation and take cases upon speculation. . . . Not even death can keep these ghouls of society at bay; their emissaries invade the house of mourning; they enter the hospitals; no place is sacred from their intrusion. If any more such exist it is hoped that the Board of Censors of the Law Association will continue their laudable efforts until the offenders shall be discovered and driven out of the profession.

Judge Arnold's words are reprinted in the *Evening Bulletin*, 6 October 1928, 1.

52. See "Law Censors Assail Accident Case Evils," *Philadelphia Inquirer*, 2 October 1928, 2, and "Ask Ambulance Chasing Probe,"*Evening Bulletin*, 6 March 1928, 3.

53. "Law Body Defers Actions on 'Runners,'"*Evening Bulletin*, 3 October 1928, 2.

54. See "Question Lawyers in Accident Suits,"*Evening Bulletin*, 19 May 1928, 6. The methods of the Philadelphia probe are detailed in a section entitled "The Procedure of the Committee" in "Philadelphia Bar Investigates Contingent Fee Scandals," 145-146, and a copy of the questionnaires sent to plaintiffs and defense lawyers is appended as "Exhibit A," 157-158.

55. Quoted in Auerbach, *Unequal Justice*, 127.

56. Ibid., 125.

57. *Philadelphia Inquirer*, 17 October 1928, 2. For the text of the rules that were finally adopted, see "Judges Pass Rules Curbing 'Runners,'"*Evening Bulletin*, 4 January 1929, 5. Commenting on the new antichaser rules adopted in Philadelphia and in New York in 1928, one lawyer's magazine later stated in too-hopeful terms that there was "no danger of a relapse to the outrageous conditions which led to last year's investigations." See the *Journal of the American Judicature Society* 12 (1929), 177.

58. "40 Lawyers Facing Inquiry Charges; Bar Submits Its Report to Judges on Results of Investigation,"*Evening Bulletin*, 5 May 1942, 1. The investigation was begun in November 1941 and was paid for jointly by the Philadelphia Bar Association and the city. In addition to the chasers, the probe also targeted "Divorce Rings" in which attorneys paid court clerks for information that would lead to clients, and attorneys' agents looked out for couples in trouble and counseled divorce in cases where legal action had not been contemplated previously.

59. "Who's Accused? Judges Know, But Won't Tell; Hush-Hush Policy on Racket Probe Embarrasses Honest Lawyers," *Philadelphia Record*, 7 May 1942, 1.

60. "2 Judges Attack Publicity Given to Bar Report," *Philadelphia Record*, 9 May 1942, 3, and "4 Judges Condemn Baring of Names in Bar 'Racket' Probe," *Philadelphia Inquirer*, 9 May 1942, 1.

61. "John R. K. Scott and 46 Others Accused by Bar," *Philadelphia Record*, 8 May 1942, 1.

62. Paul F. Levy and Harmon Y. Gordon, "Bar Association's Probe of 'Ambulance Chasing' Termed a Witch Hunt by Lawyer," *Evening Bulletin*, August, 1971.

63. Frank Moss, *The American Metropolis: From Knickerbocker Days to the Present Time* (New York: Peter Fenelon Collier, 1897), vol. 3, 182.

64. Ibid., 183.

65. Ibid., 191. It is not clear whether the Jewish shysters that Moss envisions were personal injury lawyers in addition to handling criminal cases. Just prior to the Scheuster story, Moss describes a personal injury lawyer—not a Jew, but an Irishman named Tommy Nolan who "is a great hand to try 'accident cases.'" Moss goes on to paraphrase one of Nolan's speeches about how "this sad accident happened to my unfortunate client" (180-181). Nolan is clearly intended to be seen as a clever, smooth-talking, unscrupulous plaintiff's advocate out to screw corporate defendants, but, in Moss's book, the rotund Irishman was no shyster.

66. Quoted in Gerald Leonard Cohen, "Origin of the Term 'Shyster,'" *Forum Anglicum* (Frankfurt: Verlag Peter Lang, 1982), Band 12, 7-8. Cohen spent some five or six years sorting through the twelve different theories of the origin of the word "shyster" which, prior to his effort, comprised one of the great etymological swamps and mysteries of all time. In addition to disproving Moss's Scheuster story, Moss argues through the following hypotheses: that shyster derived from the Gaelic "siostair" (barrator); that shyster was the result of the combination of "shy" (either from "Shylock" or from "shy," meaning disreputable) with "-ster," a one-size-fits-all derogatory suffix; or that shyster came from the Dutch, from Yiddish, or from Gypsies (ibid., 6-23).

67. Ibid., 47-48.

68. Ibid., 65.

69. Ibid., 2, 26-27, 32.

70. Ibid., 85-89.

71. Ashley Cockrill, "The Shyster Lawyer," *Yale Law Journal* 21 (1912), 385-386.

72. Richard H. Rovere, *Howe & Hummel: Their True and Scandalous History* (New York: Farrar, Straus, and Company, 1947), 34-35. See also Luc Sante, *Low Life: Lures and Snares of Old New York* (New York: Vintage, 1991), 211-214.

73. Rovere, *Howe & Hummel*, 106.

74. Ibid., 61.

75. Ibid., 107-108.

76. Ibid., 36-39.

77. Ibid., 109.

78. John Gross, *Shylock: A Legend & Its Legacy* (New York: Simon and Schuster, 1992), 314.

79. R. L. Harmon, "The Lawyer and the Shyster," *Reports of the Alabama State Bar Association* (1897) 41.

80. For background, see the chapter on the East European immigrants in Mark H. Elovitz, *A Century of Jewish Life in Dixie: The Birmingham Experience* (Birmingham: University of Alabama Press, 1974).

81. Harmon, "The Lawyer and the Shyster," 50. Earlier in his speech, Harmon may have been subtly situating the shyster within other popular stereotypes of the Jew when he warned: "The shyster, in his worst form in the legal profession, is a greater menace to society than the socialist. He is more dangerous to the peace and prosperity of the people, and the future stability and well-being of the government, than the anarchist."

82. *American Bar Association Journal* 2 (1916), 556. In an Alabama State Bar report from a few years earlier, chasing conditions in and around Birmingham were described: a vast array of tipsters demanded a "rake-off" in exchange for case referrals; runners and claim agents "use the negro preacher, the one to obtain the client and the other for the purpose of settling the case"; and often the biggest cases were skimmed off the top of the Birmingham market by major law firms in Georgia, where juries were known to award larger settlements. The report did not use the word "shyster" at all and was very clear about the unfair settlement practices of the corporate defendants that were "equally reprehensible." ("Report of the Committee Upon Certain Unethical and Improper Practices in Jefferson County," *Reports of the Alabama State Bar Association* [1912], 311-320.) Even earlier, another report from Alabama came down harder on the activities of the defense counsel than on the plaintiff's runners. To those same corporate attorneys who complain of the plaintiff's as "vultures," the report reminds them of their own methods of "sending out their hirelings, detectives, and claim agents, who, by threats, promises, persuasion and the necessities of the injured passengers or employees, obtain or force from them releases of damages . . . when they were unable to obtain counsel or too ignorant to understand their rights." ("Report of Central Council," ibid., 1904, 186.)

83. *Proceedings of the Alabama State Bar Association* 47 (1924), 107.

84. Ibid., 1927, 91.

85. Alabama State Bar Association, *Report of Proceedings of the Annual Meeting* 49 (1926), 40.

86. Ibid., 38-39.

87. Ibid., 1929, 13-14.

88. Ibid., 1926, 40.

89. Ibid., 41. Later in the meeting, a lawyer from Birmingham complained about defending personal injury actions against biased juries and shyster attorneys (53-54), and a judge from Selma delivered a diatribe on the biological threats to white racial superiority in America posed by Jews and others (93-104).

90. Elovitz, *A Century of Jewish Life in Dixie*, 84.

91. *Proceedings of the Alabama State Bar Association* 50 (1927), 9.

92. Kresel is quoted in "Buccaneer Lawyers of New York Routed," *Journal of the American Judicature Society* 12 (1928), 101.

93. Cockrill, "The Shyster Lawyer," 385. Cockrill blamed the "shyster" for popular prejudice about lawyers exhibited in jokes, press reports, and the theater. Seconding Webster's tracing of "shyster" to the German word "sheisse," Cockrill adds that "the shyster is indeed the excrement, the filthiness of the legal profession . . . who should be eliminated from the profession and banished from the bar."

94. See Max Radin, "Maintenance by Champerty," *California Law Review* 24 (1935), 48-78.

95. Law professor Jeffrey O'Connell puts this point a different way. He looks at traffic accidents as a very valuable asset that people are often coming into by chance, but which can be taken away or augmented by experts—insurers, on the one side, who are trying to buy this asset at the cheapest price, and chasers, on the other side, who are trying to swell its value. "As long as this explosive situation exists," he writes,

> the countless and interminable suggestions and campaigns for 'cracking down' on ambulance chasing and for regulating contingent fees are going to be about as effective as enforcing Prohibition. Human nature being what it is, you cannot prevent, by ethical exhortation or otherwise, the few people qualified to turn very valuable assets into economic reality from having access to the otherwise helpless owners of those assets.

See Jeffrey O'Connell, *The Injury Industry and the Remedy of No-Fault Insurance* (Urbana: University of Illinois Press, 1971), 67.

CHAPTER FOUR

1. *New York Times*, 19 January 1932, 14.

2. Ibid., 20 January 1932, 4.

3. Frank Wagenaar had died as a result of skull fractures suffered in a fall down some tenement, according to Lustberg's autopsy report, but prosecutors believed that Lustberg himself had had a hand in Wagenaar's death. After exhuming Wagenaar's body, prosecutors became even more convinced of foul play in the case, but Wagenaar's widow, the beneficiary of her husband's life insurance policy, successfully impeded the reopening of the case. (See "Body Exhumed in Connection with False Accident Reports,"*New York Times*, 26 March 1932, 14, and "Widow Seeks to Bar Exhumation of Body as Evidence in Inquiry," *New York Times*, 8 April 1932, 16.)

4. For the additional arrests in the Lustberg case, see "Lay High Insurance Plots in Jersey," *New York Times*, 21 January 1932, 2, and "Jersey Lawyers Held in Insurance Frauds," *New York Times*, 23 January 1932, 34.

5. "Passaic Doctor Convicted," *New York Times*, 20 February 1932, 22.

6. "7 in Passaic Indicted in an Accident Ring," New York Times, 27 April 1934, 3. Around this same time in nearby Paterson, New Jersey, another doctor was found guilty of involvement in faking car accidents. Dr. Charles F. Baxter, the head of the Electro-Medical Institute, faked his own injuries in order to collect on a few thousand dollar claim, then was sentenced to one and a half to three years in state prison. See "Doctor Accused of Fraud," *New York Times*, 10 June 1934, 22, and "3 Jailed in Insurance Fraud," *New York Times*, 30 June 1934, 30.

7. Quoted in Studs Terkel, *Hard Times: An Oral History of the Great Depression* (New York: Pantheon Books, 1986), 303.

8. John Steinbeck, *The Grapes of Wrath* (New York: Penguin Books, 1980 [1939]), 256.

9. William Cavanaugh, "Fraudulent Claims and Their Cost," *Proceedings of the Twenty-Fourth Annual Convention of the International Claim Association* (1933), 83, 85, 90-91.

10. Dr. Kauffman's story is mentioned in a number of different articles, but I have relied primarily on William Inglis, "$14,000,000 for Fake Accidents," *New York Herald Tribune*, 16 April 1933, 5.

11. A doctor in Dallas was later arrested for advertising for fake claimants in much the same way by placing ads for secretarial jobs which were usually answered by middle-age, married women looking to supplement family income. "End Activities of Fake Accident Ring in South," *Weekly Underwriter*, 3 February 1940, 289.

12. Robert Monaghan, "The Liability Claim Racket,"*Law and Contemporary Problems* 3 (1936), 492. One "food artist" from the time, William Brodsky from New York, pled guilty to having framed at least one case by dropping glass into the orangeade being drunk by a friend's wife, then settling the claim against the restaurant on her behalf for $75. ("3 More Lawyers Quit in Fraud Inquiry," *New York Times*, 16 April 1937, 8.) The case originated a year earlier, when Brodsky was arrested for felonious assault after having put slivers of glass into Mrs. Louis Goodman's drink, a stunt that Mr. Goodman had declined to get involved in when Brodsky propositioned him with it moments earlier. (The original arrest is described in "Hospital Owner Indicted in Fraud," *New York Times*, 21 August 1936, 16.)

13. Kearney, "Fake Accidents Inc.," 18. The article was illustrated with cartoon representations of all of the denizens of the 1930s accident underworld: the "crooked lawyer" with his briefcase; the "crooked doctor" with a top hat and a sinister expression; the "crooked victim" carrying a crutch; the "crooked witness" with a devious grin. More than forty of these cartoon figures were depicted dancing like jackals around a nice family that evidently has been set up for a staged car crash. Over the heads of the shocked, victimized passengers, a cartoon dialogue bubble reads: "Gosh! We are framed!"

14. Ibid.

15. John C. R. MacDonald, *"Crime Is a Business:" Buncos, Rackets, Confidence Schemes* (Stanford, CA: Stanford University Press, 1939), 253-254.

16. William Corbin, "What We Pay for the Crash Racket,"*American Magazine*, March 1936, 110-111. See also Cavanaugh, "Fraudulent Claims and Their Cost," 87.

17. For the Cleveland accident frauds, see the following articles from the *Plain Dealer*: "Insurance Fraud Probe Demanded; Ohio Supreme Court Asked to Investigate Gigantic Fake Claims Racket," 28 March 1936, 6; "Fake Claim Quiz Put Up to Davey," 29 March 1936, 9; "Indict 33, Arrest 13 in Mahoning Probe of Insurance Fraud," 4 April 1936, 6; and "Cleaning Up a Bad Situation," 8 May 1936, 10. Years before this probe, a writer for the same Cleveland paper noted the increase in fraudulent fire, theft, and auto insurance claims that had developed since the crash of the stock market in 1929. "The Byproduct," 27 October 1931.

18. See the "Study of the Fake Claim Racket in Kansas City, Missouri" prepared by the Special Committee of the Chamber of Commerce of Kansas City, Missouri, 1935.

19. The work of the postal inspectors, aided by agents of the Claims Bureau, in uncovering the Kirksville Ring is described in N. Morgan Woods, "'The Evil That Men Do Comes Back to Them,'"*Casualty and Surety Journal* 4 (January 1943), 14.

20. See "Ten Are Arraigned in Fake Accidents; Brooklyn Group Accused of Getting $40,000 Payments on Pretended Bone Fractures," *New York Times*, 17 August 1934, 16 and "Lawyer Indicted in Accident Ring," *New York Times*, 9 June 1934, 32.

21. For social conditions in Pittsburgh during the Great Depression, I have relied solely on Chapters 7 and 8 of John Bodnar, Roger Simon, and Michael P. Weber, *Lives of Their Own: Blacks, Italians, and Poles in Pittsburgh, 1900-1960* (Urbana: University of Illinois Press, 1982).

22. Elliott, "Faking Car Accidents," 601. For another account of Duke Gemellaro's House of Pain, see Monaghan, "The Liability Claim Racket," 499. Gemellaro may be the Pittsburgh accident ringleader referred to in another account of a man who had once been an insurance broker in Brooklyn but later posed as a lawyer in Pittsburgh to broker his faked claims. The man often traveled by automobile to cities throughout Ohio, Pennsylvania, and upstate New York to "set up the accidents which never happened, after supplying the insured car." See Cavanaugh, "Fraudulent Claims and Their Cost," 87-88.

23. Burt A. Richardson, *Questionable Life and Accident Claims* (Atlanta: Foote and Davies Co., 1937), 208.

24. Ibid., 207.

25. Ibid., 204.

26. Ibid., 206.

27. Ibid., 208-209.

28. Ibid., 213-214.

29. Ibid., 215.

30. Ibid., 216.

31. Paul W. Kearney, "Burn Your Own Home!" *Reader's Digest*, October 1933, 64.

32. Thomas Meehan, "Case of the Insurance Detective," *New York Times Magazine*, 6 March 1960, 53.

33. For reports on George Mondello's arson service, see "Arson Service Data to Go to Grand Jury," *New York Times*, 1 January 1937, 29; "Arson Ring Suspects Jailed Without Bail,"*New York Times*, 3 January 1937, 17; and "3 Indicted for Arson in Westchester Fires," *New York Times*, 9 January 1937, 4.

34. Quoted in Richardson, *Questionable Life and Accident Claims*, 171.

35. For accounts of the ring that sought to profit from Fred Bottger's death, see the following articles from the *New York Times*: "Six Are Arrested in Insurance Fraud," 8 January 1936, 5; "9 Indicted in Kings For Insurance Fraud," 22 January 1936, 2; "31 Indicted as Ring in Insurance Fraud," 20 February 1936, 1; "9 More Arrested in Insurance Plot," 31 March 1936, 46; "38 Plead Guilty in Insurance Plot," 22 January 1937, 12; "Two Jailed in Insurance Fraud," 28 April 1937, 19). The Bottger case is also discussed in Richardson, *Questionable Life and Accident Claims*, 157-161.

36. "Sand-Buried Body is Linked to Plot; Philadelphia Butcher Digs Up Body of Man Believed Slain in Insurance Scheme," *New York Times*, 8 January 1936, 13.

37. "Insurance Slayer a Suicide in Jail," *New York Times*, 12 January 1936, 15.

38. "Charges a Murder Racket; New Yorker Says Indian Gang Here Kills Tribesmen for Insurance" *New York Times*, 26 April 1933, 19. According to an informant, an "organized gang of fake Indians" from New York would collect relief money for poorer Indians elsewhere in the country then would keep the money for themselves, and when a "real" American Indian came to the city, that Indian would be robbed of his property, then insured and murdered "in such a clever way that every death has been pronounced a suicide."

39. "Father Drowns Girl to Obtain Insurance," *New York Times*, 25 July 1934, 36.

40. "Two Women Held in Auto Slaying," *New York Times*, 21 June 1934, 48. Eva Coo was executed by electric chair on June 28, 1935.

41. For accounts of the Murder Trust see "Insurance Murder Charged to Five," *New York Times*, 13 May 1933, 28, and "3 Die at Sing Sing for Bronx Murder," *New York Times*, 8 June 1934, 44. The case is also discussed in Meehan, "The Case of the Insurance Detective," 56, and in the section entitled "Malloy the Mighty" in Edmund Pearson, *More Studies in Murder* (New York: Harrison Smith & Robert Haas, 1936), 132-140.

42. Kael is quoted in Studs Terkel, *Hard Times: An Oral History of the Great Depression* (New York: Pantheon Books, 1986), 346. In another example of insurance-mindedness during the Depression, Terkel interviews a man who recalls how he cooperated with the members of bootlegging "syndicates." One day the bootleggers came to his home and kidded about bumping someone off, but the

man's mother shot back that they couldn't do it until she took out life insurance on the person (36).

43. Dr. Muhlberg is quoted in Richardson, *Questionable Life and Accident Claims*, 57-58.

44. Ibid., 73-74.

45. Ibid., 74. Some forty years later, another insurance detective would explain the formula to one of his colleagues in simple terms. "Any object falling from a height tends to drift outward from the base of the height," John J. Healy states. "Somebody falling out of a window will land relatively close to the bottom of the building; but a person who jumps will land farther away from the base. There's an equation—which I don't happen to have with me—that computes the height, plus the weight of the object, the rate of the fall, and roughly how far out it should land from the base of the height." See John J. Healy, *A Game of Wits* (New York: David McKay Co., 1975), 35.

46. Ibid., 78-79.

47. "Claim Evils Draw Fire," *Casualty and Surety Monthly Bulletin* 2 (1927), 1-2.

48. Descriptions of the earliest claims investigation efforts of the National Bureau of Casualty and Surety Underwriters are derived primarily from two sources: Monaghan, "The Liability Claim Racket," 499-503, and Kearney, "Fake Accidents Inc.," 50-51.

49. Barent Ten Eyck, "The Claims Bureau," *Casualty and Surety Journal* 1 (1940), 17. For other information about the Claims Bureau, see R.G. McCallum, "The Index System—History," *Casualty and Surety Journal*, 1(1940), 34-38; Barent Ten Eyck, "Who Are the Men of the Claims Bureau?" *Casualty and Surety Journal* 1 (1940), 42-46; Wayne Merrick, "Service and Policies of the Claims Bureau," *Casualty and Surety Journal* 1 (1940), 21-23.

50. Some of these cases are mentioned in "Fraudulent Casualty Claims," *Bulletin of the Association of Casualty and Surety Executives*, no. 36 (February 1934), 4. In this report, a "new wrinkle" in accident racket is also reported from Jacksonville, Florida, where a chaser outfitted his car with a shortwave radio so as to be the first on the scene of a collision.

51. Of the situation in Massachusetts, editorialists at the *New York Times* commented that "the filing of swollen and dishonest claims has become a habit. That ingenious professional specialism which we know so well in New York flourishes [in Boston]" (see "Motor Insurance Frauds," 20 November 1931, 22). The governor of Massachusetts also commented on the situation, saying that "the number of unscrupulous doctors or lawyers who today thrive on false accident claims is a reproach to our administration of justice." Governor Allen blamed the situation as much on the crooks as on the insurance companies, bar associations, medical societies, and public prosecutors who had never made any serious effort to combat the fraud. (The governor is quoted in the *Bar Bulletin* of the Association of the Bar of the City of Boston, no. 51 [1931], 9.)

52. Wayne Merrick, "A Guy Who Never Had a Chance," *Casualty and Surety Journal* 10 (1949), 1.

53. For Schiffer's confession, see David Schiffer, "I Stole a Million, *Collier's* 123 (5 February 1949), 13, 42-43, and 123 (12 February 1949), 34-35, 72-73. In the quoted passages, I have consolidated Schiffer's words without showing breaks.

54. For a news account of the arrest, see "Fake 'Mishap' Ring Reported Blasted," *New York Times*, 16 April 1948, 48. Following the arrests, an assistant district attorney was quoted as saying that a number of potential prosecution witnesses were threatened with death by "professional men" [doctors and lawyers] if they testified for the state. (See "Seized as Leader in Accident Fraud," *New York Times*, 20 May 1948, 58.) At the sentencing, Judge John Mullen handed out tough sentences to everyone but Meyer Siegal, the boxer hired by Schiffer to take the medical exams. "You are just a stupid person," the judge said to Siegal in court. "I believe the punching around you've taken in the ring affected your judgment." (See "4 Get Prison Terms in Insurance Fraud," *New York Times*, 9 December 1948, 43.)

55. Monaghan, "The Liability Claim Racket," 492.

56. For Louis A. Stone's remarks on the 1928 chaser probe, see his letter to the editor of the *New York Times*, 4 June 1936, 22.

57. C. J. S. Thompson, *The Quacks of Old London* (1929; reprint, Detroit: Singing Tree Press, 1971), 28. Most quacks of the sixteenth century were tradesmen who tried to make some money on the side by performing their own brand of medical treatment. Thomas Lufkin, for instance, was a blacksmith who advertised his blood-letting services by asking:

> If any man, woman or child be sick or would be let blood or be diseased with any manner of inward or outward griefs, as all manner of agues or fevers, pleurisies, colic, stone, strangulation, imposthumes, pustules, kanker, gout, bone-ache and pain of the joints which cometh for lack of blood letting, let them resort to the 'Saracen's Head' in the East Lane and they shall have remedy by me, Thomas Lufkin. (26)

58. For a history of American quackery, see, generally, David Armstrong and Elizabeth Metzger Armstrong, *The Great American Medicine Show: Being an Illustrated History of Hucksters, Healers, Health Evangelists, and Heroes From Plymouth Rock to the Present* (New York: Prentice-Hall, 1991).

59. "Doctors to Fight Medical Rackets," *New York Times*, 21 December 1937, 47. Also see: "Crooked Doctors Face Swift Curb," *New York Times*, 14 April 1937, 11, and "Doctors Facing Loss of Licenses in Frauds," *New York Times*, 16 April 1937, 2.

60. For the creation of the Accident Frauds Bureau, see the following articles in the *New York Times*: "New Unit to Fight Accident Frauds," 26 February 1936, 6; "Dodge Pushes Inquiry into Fake Accidents," 14 April 1936, 14; "New Drive Begun on Shady Lawyers," 26 May 1936, 19; "Funds Voted to Sift Fake Accident Cases," 6

June 1936, 15; "Accident Ring Drive Prepared by Dodge," 8 June 1936, 8; and "'Chaser' Inquiry Gets 15 Free Attorneys," 19 June 1936, 10.

61. For Nicholas Ferranti's arrest, see "Two More Arrested in Fake Claims Cases," *New York Times*, 13 August 1936, 7, and for his later acquittal see "Acquitted of 'Chasing," *New York Times*, 20 January 1937, 6. For Max Korbin's arrest, see "Accident Lawyer Held," *New York Times*, 4 September 1936, 7. For the case against Irving B. Linden, see "2 More Surrender in Chasing Inquiry," *The New York Times*, October 1936, 52:3.

62. Elliott Arnold, "The Ambulance-Chasing Game", *Nation*, 28 November, 1936, 630.

63. For the arrests and later guilty pleas of Chester W. McNally and F. Chester Steup, see these articles in the *New York Times*: "Two More Seized in Accident Ring," 22 July 1936, 7; "3 Testify for State in Fake Claim Case," 18 August 1936, 35; "2 Insurance Men Guilty of Fraud," 1 September 1936, 11; and "Jailed in Indemnity Case," 15 September 1936, 3.

64. See these articles in the *New York Times*: "5 Police Demoted in Chaser Inquiry," 7 August 1937, 30; "8 Policemen Heard at Chaser Inquiry," 19 August 1937, 40; "Ambulance Chasing Is Laid to 19 Police," 8 October 1937, 11; and "More Patrolmen Out," 7 November 1937, 25.

65. Botein is quoted in Murray Teigh Bloom, *The Trouble with Lawyers* (New York: Simon and Schuster, 1968), 132.

66. See the section entitled "The Runner: The Root of the Evil" in Bernard Botein, *Accident Fraud Investigation: Report to the Appellate Division of the Supreme Court, 1st Judicial Department, The Association of the Bar of the City of New York, The New York County Lawyers Association, and Hon. William Copeland Dodge, District Attorney of New York County*, 1937.

67. Ibid., 18.

68. Ibid., 22.

69. "New Arrest Made in Chasing Inquiry; Brooklyn Man Is Trapped in Phone Booth as Member of Bogus Accident Ring," *New York Times*, 1 December 1936, 10.

70. "Prison for Chief of Accident Ring; Bornstein Confessed His Fake Claims Defrauded Insurance Concerns of Huge Sum," *New York Times*, 7 April 1937, 52.

71. For reports on the Hurwitz gang, see these articles in the *New York Times*: "Insurance Broker Seized," 13 June 1936, 13; "11 In Accident Ring Admit Fraud Guilt," 6 August 1936, 10; "Fake Claims Scout Gets Prison Term," 27 August 1936, 13; and "Tells of Car Fraud Plot," 18 May 1937, 14.

72. "2 Men Plead Guilty in Insurance Plots," *New York Times*, 15 December 1936, 17.

73. For the relationship between Dr. Benjamin and Edward Hausman, see "Bar Inquiry Asked on Huge Fraud Ring," *New York Times*, 7 February 1936, 1; "Bogus Lawyer Sentenced," *New York Times*, 1 February 1936, 3; and "Man and Wife Seized in Accident Racket," *New York Times*, 12 February 1936, 2.

74. Quoted in Melvin M. Fagen, "The Status of Jewish Lawyers in New York City," *Jewish Social Studies* 1 (1939), 74.

75. "Doctor Gets 15 Months," *New York Times*, 28 July 1936, 11.

76. For Dodge, see "Dodge Pushes War on Fake Accidents," *New York Times*, 25 January 1937, 9, and "New Fraud Bureau to Be Permanent," *New York Times*, 25 April 1937, 7. For Geoghan, see "District Attorney Geoghan Plans Ambulance Chasing Inquiry in Brooklyn," *New York Times*, 3 February 1937, 24.

77. For most of this story of the politics of racket-busting in New York City in the 1930's, I have relied on the chapter entitled "The Special Prosecutor" in Alan Block, *East Side—West Side: Organizing Crime in New York, 1930-1950* (Cardiff, Wales: University College Cardiff Press, 1980).

78. *New York Times*, 19 May 1937, 1. See also, "15 Indicted by U.S. in Insurance Plot; 10 Doctors Named," *New York Times*, 31 July 1937, 1.

79. "Insurance Fraud Traps Ten More," *New York Times*, 3 June 1937, 1.

80. Ibid.

81. "39 Indicted Here in Fake Disability," *New York Times*, 7 July 1938, 1.

82. "Suspects Guarded from Gang Threat in Insurance Case," *New York Times*, 21 May 1937, 1.

83. *Reader's Digest* (February 1939), 93-96.

84. Don Eddy, "Racketeers by Accident," *American Magazine* (December 1940), 42.

85. Monaghan, "The Liability Claim Racket," 493.

86. Gordon Fellowes, a British transplant to America whose father was a railroad detective, worked initially as an undercover investigator for the California State Insurance Fund. In this position, Fellowes mainly did surveillance on people who fraudulently collected the standard $20 a week disability payments from the state. Fellowes also writes at length about his investigations of murder for insurance, bootlegging, and the key role he played in finding Aimee Semple McPherson, the enormously popular evangelist from Los Angeles who staged her own death/disappearance at Venice Beach in 1926. Sometime in the late 1920s, Fellowes moved to St. Louis, where he again investigated accident and worker's compensation claims. Fellowes described the "shyster lawyers" who employed runners for $100 a week to "go round waiting for people to be knocked down in the street." Fellowes does not mention accident faking, but he does write of the "highly organized" chasing racket in the city that involved doctors, lawyers, and judges on the take. Fellowes, who says he had to flee back to England because he learned too much about racketeers like Al Capone and Bugs Moran, tries to place the accident racketeers into perspective. "[They] were not really gangsters," he writes, "but on the edge of crime." For Fellowes's experiences with the chasers of St. Louis see his first book, *They Took Me for a Ride* (London: George Allen & Unwin, 1934), 78-81. For his work at the California State Insurance Fund, see Fellowes's *Insurance Racketeers* (London: George Allen & Unwin, 1935). Both books, Fellowes states, were written while he was a fugitive from members of the American mob who wanted to see him dead.

87. Corbin, "What We Pay for the Crash Racket," 59.

88. "Hastings Pledges Fight on Crime; Asserts He Has Saved Millions for Taxpayers by Drive on Fake Accidents," New York Times, 6 October 1937, 12.

89. Frances Fox Piven and Richard A. Cloward, Regulating the Poor: The Functions of Public Welfare (New York: Vintage Books, 1993), 22-23.

90. Quoted in Goldstein et al. v. United States (1942), 62 S. Ct. 1005.

91. "'Invalid' Describes Faking of Disease; Bronx Dairyman Tells How Heart Trouble Was Simulated to Get Compensation," New York Times, 8 January 1938, 17.

92. See "Two Found Guilty in Insurance Plot," New York Times, 4 March 1938, 3 and "2 Doctors Guilty in Insurance Plot," New York Times, 5 March 1938, 3. Joe Weiss and one of his chasers was originally sentenced to three years in prison; Dr. Goldstein got a year and a day. ("4 Get Prison Terms in Insurance Fraud" [8 March 1938, 5].)

93. See "Nine Admit Guilt in Fake Disability; Ring Accused of $3,000,000-a-Year Swindle Now Broken, Prosecutor Says," New York Times, 15 July 1938, 38, and "5 More Admit Guilt in Insurance Fraud," New York Times, 19 July 1938, 37.

94. For reports of the Supreme Court's two reversals on the legality of the wiretaps in the fake disability cases, see "High Court Widens Wiretapping Ban; Bars Indirect Use," New York Times, 12 December 1939, 1, and "Tapping of Wires Upheld by Court," New York Times, 28 April 1942, 23.

95. "Facing 640 Years, Resents 20 Months; Garrow, Insurance Racketeer, Who Helped Government, Is Bitter Over Sentence," New York Times, 17 May 1939, 6.

96. For Dewey's accident probe, see these stories in the New York Times: "24 in 'Chasing' Ring Accused by Dewey," 11 March 1939, 1; "Charges Name 8 Lawyers," 4 April 1939, 26; "3 Admit 'Chasing' Clients," 8 August 1939, 38; "Plot to Send Away Witness Charged," 14 January 1940, 13; "Four on Trial Admit Ambulance Chasing," 16 January 1940, 24; "14 Receive Terms as Ambulance Ring," 29 February 1940, 20.

CHAPTER FIVE

1. George Malcolm-Smith, The Travelers: One Hundred Years (Hartford, CT: Travelers Insurance Company, 1964), 49.

2. Ibid., 120.

3. Appleby's story is told in James P. Gannon, "Fake Accident Claims Rise, Prompting Auto Insurers to Crack Down," Wall Street Journal, 28 August 1964, 1.

4. "The Crash Artists," Newsweek, 22 August 1966, 80. Chicago detectives first learned of the Anderson-Radford gang in 1961 when one of its members confessed. By August 1964, more than seventy people associated with the group had been

convicted. Big Red Anderson himself got five years in the Illinois State Penitentiary.

5. Wayne Merrick, "New Picture in an Old Frame," *Casualty and Surety Journal* 6 (1945), 26.

6. The Tumbling Womacks are mentioned in a number of articles from the late 1940s and early 1950s, including Frank Rasky, "Insurance Racket Busters and How They Work," *New York Star*, 22 August 1948.

7. On at least one faked fall in a Greyhound Bus Station in Reno, Annie went too far with her falls, losing consciousness and undergoing an actual head operation to remove some bone. For a few of the accounts of Rimrock Annie, see: "The Tumbler,"*Time* 57 (1951), 68-70; Thomas M. Meehan, "Case of the Insurance Detective," *New York Times Magazine*, 6 March 1960, 51; and Frank Gibney, *The Operators* (New York: Harper and Brothers, 1960), 137.

8. Charles Remsberg, "Accident Fraud Is Highway Robbery," *Reader's Digest* (February 1964), 201.

9. Henry La Cossitt, "It's Easier When You're Honest," *Nation's Business* 41 (1953), 40.

10. For background on Woods, see N. Morgan Woods, "Fraudulent Automobile Insurance Claims," *Police* (September-October 1961), 15.

11. For this sampling of features, see: Vance Packard, "Why Your Auto Insurance Costs So Much," *American Magazine* (May 1953), 28; "Why Cost of Auto Insurance Goes Up and Up," *U.S. News & World Report*, 20 February 1959, 56; and "Crisis in Auto Insurance—What Can Be Done About It?" *U.S. News & World Report*, 14 June 1965, 112.

12. Rust is quoted in "Moral Breakdown Seen in Auto Claims," *New York Times*, 16 July 1958, 43.

13. N. Morgan Woods, "Combating the Fraudulent Claims Menace," *Federation of Insurance Counsel Quarterly* 10 (1960), 72

14. Woods is quoted in "Car Claim Frauds Laid to Amateurs," *New York Times*, 6 July 1965, 67.

15. Quoted in Andrew Tobias, *The Invisible Bankers: Everything the Insurance Industry Never Wanted You to Know* (New York: Simon & Schuster, 1982), 101-102. Elsewhere Tobias observes:

> As a practical matter, it is of little import "who started" this escalating fracas between insurers and insureds. In the earlier years of this century, the companies were doubtless guilty of the lowest blows. The citizenry then were burdened with an old-fashioned morality, coupled with a greater fear of the wrath of large institutions. But even as insurers have tended to mend their ways, policyholders seem to have moved in the opposite direction, increasingly prone to exploit a vulnerable system. (99)

16. For a review of the literature on whiplash injury, see the section entitled "Mechanism of Injury" in William deGravelles, Jr. and John H. Kelly, *Injuries Following Rear-End Automobile Collisions* (Springfield, IL: Charles C. Thomas Publishers, 1969), 12-25.

17. "Whiplash Gets Put to the Test," *Business Week*, 20 July 1968, 96-97.

18. E. A. Cowie, "The Economics of Whiplash,"*The Continuing Revolt Against "Whiplash"*(Milwaukee: Defense Research Institute, 1964), 35.

19. Quoted in deGravelles and Kelly, *Injuries Following Rear-End Automobile Collisions*, viii.

20. Ibid.

21. Ibid., ix.

22. Sanford H. Eisenberg, "'Whiplash Injuries' of the Spine,"*The Revolt Against "Whiplash"*(Milwaukee: Defense Research Institute, 1960), 13.

23. Ibid., 2.

24. Harold E. Crowe, "A New Diagnostic Sign in Neck Injuries,"*The Continuing Revolt Against "Whiplash,"* 21.

25. Dr. Henry Miller, "Accident Neurosis: Lecture II," *British Medical Journal*, 8 April 1961, 997-998.

26. For a criticism of the research procedures of several studies of whiplash patients purporting to show the predominance of psychosocial factors in the formation of the symptoms, see Bogdan P. Radanov et al., "Role of Psychosocial Stress in Recovery from Common Whiplash," *The Lancet* 338 (1991), 712. For a criticism of Gotten's study specifically, see Ian Macnab, "The Whiplash Syndrome," *Clinical Neurosurgery* 20 (1974), 235. For a general repudiation of a number of follow-up studies that claim to show that whiplash patients are cured by insurance money and not medicine, see George Mendelson, "Follow-up Studies of Personal Injury Litigants," *International Journal of Law and Psychiatry* 7 (1984), 179-188.

27. *Revolt Against "Whiplash,"* 4.

28. Harvey J. McNeal, "'Whiplash'—An Unrealistic Psychological Word,"*The Continuing Revolt Against "Whiplash,"* 45.

29. J. E. M. Thomson, "The Counterfeit Phrase of Neck Lash Injuries" in *The Revolt Against "Whiplash,"* 16.

30. Macnab, "The Whiplash Syndrome," 232.

31. Stanley C. Morris is quoted in *The Revolt Against "Whiplash,"'* 20.

32. Harlan Dodson, "A Defendant's Point of View of 'Whiplash,'" *Defense Law Journal* 13 (1964), 528.

33. Bert E. Strubinger, "Unmasking of Fraudulent Claimants and Malingerers," *Insurance Law Journal* 12 (1951), 695.

34. Alvin R. Cristovich, "Some Comments on the Defense of 'Whiplash' Claims and Suits,"*The Revolt Against "Whiplash,"'* 23.

35. Ray C. Simmons, "Whiplash: Big Business & Serious Problem," *For the Defense*, 24 (1992), 14.

36. Simon Carette, "Whiplash Injury and Chronic Neck Pain," *New England Journal of Medicine* 330 (1994), 1083-1084.

37. Dr. Atha Thomas, "Whiplash—A Misnomer: Controversy in Medico-Legal Fields," *Trial* 2 (1965), 27-30.

38. *New York Times,* 3 February 1879, 4.

39. Dr. H. G. Brainerd, "Railway Spine," *Street Railway Journal* (May 1891), 248.

40. Dr. George Chafee, "Expert Examination of the Plaintiff in Damage Cases When Ordered by the Court," *Medico-Legal Journal* 13 (1896), 11-12.

41. Clark Bell, "Railway Spine," *Medico-Legal Journal* 12 (1894), 133.

42. Ibid., 135.

43. "The 'Railway Spine'—A New Disease," *New York Times,* 15 October 1866, 2.

44. Dickens's letter is quoted in Michael R. Trimble, *Post-Traumatic Neurosis: From Railway Spine to the Whiplash* (New York: John Wiley & Sons, 1981), 27-28.

45. John Eric Erichsen, *Railway and Other Injuries of the Nervous System* (London: Walton and Maberly, 1866), 95-96.

46. Ibid., 9.

47. Ibid., 3.

48. Quoted in Wolfgang Schivelbusch, *The Railway Journey: Trains and Travel in the 19th Century* (New York: Urizen Books, 1979), 120.

49. *The Lancet,* 10 March 1866, 262. One such person claimed to have been in a rail accident and to have suffered symptoms like "weakness, giddiness, stars before the eyes, and bleeding from the nose," the *Lancet* editors noted. This man was ordered by a doctor to get some rest, but, instead of doing so, he went to a music hall to "indulge in dissipation," at least according to the report of two railroad detectives.

50. Dr. Thomas Buzzard, "Shock to the Nervous System," *The Lancet,* 6 January 1866, 23.

51. A. M. Hamilton, *Railway and Other Accidents* (New York: William Wood and Company, 1904), 2.

52. Page is quoted in Trimble, *Post-Traumatic Neurosis,* 27. Page's revision of Erichsen is also discussed in Schivelbusch, *The Railway Journey,* 142-143.

53. Freud is quoted in Trimble, *Post-Traumatic Neurosis,* 49.

54. Ibid., 30.

55. Dr. Mayberry of Enid, Oklahoma, is quoted in *Minutes of the Association of Railway Claim Agents* (1901), 51.

56. Ibid., 61.

57. Willis P. King, *Perjury for Pay: An Exposé of the Methods and Criminal Cunning of the Modern Malingerer* (Kansas City, MO: The Burton Company, 1906), 26.

58. Ibid., 19.

59. Ibid., 8.

60. Ibid., 27-28.

61. "John Eric Erichsen Dead," *New York Times*, 24 September 1896, 5.

62. Quoted in Jeffrey O'Connell and Rita James Simon, *Payment for Pain and Suffering* (Urbana: University of Illinois Press, 1972), 93.

63. King, *Perjury for Pay*, 20.

64. Quoted in *Minutes of the Association of Railway Claim Agents* (1901), 10.

65. Blewett Lee, "Anti-Railroad Personal Injury Litigation in Mississippi," in *The Damage Suit Disease: A Compilation of Editorials, Letters and Addresses Upon Personal Injury Litigation Against Railroads in Mississippi* (Chicago: Chicago Legal News Press, 1913), 32-33.

66. Ann Fabian, *Card Sharps, Dream Books & Bucket Shops: Gambling in 19th-Century America* (Ithaca, NY: Cornell University Press, 1990), 153-154.

67. Ibid., 162.

68. *The Damage Suit Disease*, 30.

69. This is a paraphrase of the ideas set down more carefully and elegantly in David M. Engel, "The Oven Bird's Song: Insiders, Outsiders, and Personal Injuries in an American Community," *Law & Society Review* 18 (1984), 551-581. Engel's study of attitudes toward personal injury claimants in "Sander County" Illinois in the 1980s reads like a story in the small about the historical evolution of the railway spine/whiplash stigma to personal injury litigation. The county, once a tightly knit farming community, was now changing, with industrial manufacturing (a local canning plant) bringing outside wage laborers who were seen as the ones more likely to press a personal injury claim. Engle concludes:

> Local residents who denounced the assertion of personal injury claims and somewhat irrationally lamented the rise in "litigiousness" of personal injury plaintiffs, were . . . participating in a more broadly based ceremony of regret that the realities of contemporary American society could no longer be averted from their community if it were to survive . . . The denunciation of personal injury litigation in Sander County was significant mainly as one aspect of a symbolic effort by members of the community to preserve a sense of meaning and coherence in the face of social changes that they found threatening and confusing. It was in this sense a solution—albeit a partial and unsatisfying one—to a problem basic to the human condition, the problem of living in a world that has lost the simplicity and innocence it is thought once to have had. (570)

For a related explanation of the origin and meaning of perceived "eruptions of pathological litigiousness," see: Marc Galanter, "Reading the Landscape of Disputes: What We Know And Don't Know (And Think We Know) About Our Allegedly Contentious and Litigious Society," *U.C.L.A. Law Review* 31 (1983), 4-71.

70. Ibid., 21.

71. Robert B. Shaw, *A History of Railroad Accidents, Safety Precautions, and Operating Practices* (N.p.: Vail-Ballou Press, 1978), 42-43.

72. Quoted in Robert C. Reed, *Train Wrecks: A Pictorial History of Accidents on the Main Line* (New York: Crown Publishers, 1978), 25.

73. Much of this account of famous rail disasters relies on the chapter entitled "The Horrors of Travel" in ibid.

74. Ernest Bloch is quoted in Schivelbusch, *The Railway Journey*, 132. A similar point is made in Ralph Harrington, "The Neuroses of the Railway: 19th Century Anti-Railroad Sentiment," *History Today* 44 (July 1994), 15.

75. Seymour Dunbar, *A History of Travel in America, Volume IV* (Indianapolis: The Bobbs-Merrill Company, 1915), 766-767.

76. Reed, *Train Wrecks*, 18.

77. Quoted in Dunbar, *A History of Travel in America*, 1056-1057.

78. Walter Licht, *Working for the Railroad: The Organization of Work in the Nineteenth Century* (Princeton, NJ: Princeton University Press, 1983), 197.

79. Ibid., 205.

80. Michael B. Katz, *In the Shadow of the Poorhouse: A Social History of Welfare in America* (New York: Basic Books, 1986), 85.

81. Licht, *Working for the Railroad*, 199.

82. Randolph E. Bertstrom, *Courting Danger: Injury and Law in New York City, 1870-1910* (Ithaca, NY: Cornell University Press, 1992).

83. Lawrence Friedman, A History of American Law, 2nd ed. (New York: Touchstone, 1995), 470.

84. Johnson is quoted in Malcolm-Smith, *The Travelers*, 44. Johnson also claimed to have erected some of the first billboards in New York and originated "car cards" on the sides of public busses. On one occasion, Johnson set up an enormous screen on top of a downtown building where he projected "pictures of stage beauties, pretty landscapes and other subjects, interspersed with Travelers advertisements. Great crowds gathered to see the show" (43).

85. Harry Porter, "Advertising as a Factor in the Selling of Accident Insurance" in H. P. Dunham and J. E. Rhodes, eds., *Accident and Health Insurance: A Series of Lectures Delivered Before The Insurance Institute of Hartford* (Hartford, CT: The Insurance Institute of Hartford, 1915), 95.

86. Preston is quoted in Malcolm-Smith, *The Travelers*, 32.

87. Batterson is quoted in ibid., 19.

88. Law professor Margaret Jane Radin considers monetary compensation for pain and suffering along with the buying and selling of babies, sexual services, and human organs as "contested commodities" that test the limits of what can properly be the subject of a market transaction. Commodification itself is not a bad thing, on Radin's view, but, in the matter of matching body parts with commensurable dollar values, she recognizes that there might be some negative cultural conse-

quences: "a degradation of personhood, an inferior conception of human flour-ishing." Nevertheless, Radin holds out the possibility that compensation can be taken "symbolically," and not literally as a buying and selling of body parts or lost emotional attachments, thus maintaining an essentially noncommodified concep-tion of compensation while applying the money as so much salve to otherwise irreversible wounds. See Radin's *Contested Commodities* (Cambridge, MA: Harvard University Press, 1996), 203-204. One version of what an openly free market in personal injury claims would look like (unlike the shadowy underworld of tort) envisions victims selling their claims to third parties up front, reducing delay and uncertainty in payment, while third parties negotiate the details among them-selves. See Marc J. Shukaitis, "A Market in Personal Injury Tort Claims," *Journal of Legal Studies* 16 (June 1987), 329-349. The main obstacles Shukaitis sees are a "long common-law tradition" barring an open market in claims, and conventional morality which "might find the very act of selling personal injury tort claims offensive." (330)

89. J. A. Ritchey, "The Malingerer," *Medico-Legal Journal* 18 (1901), 402.

90. Quoted in Vivianna A. Rotman Zelizer, *Morals and Markets: The Development of Life Insurance in the United States* (New Brunswick, NJ: Transaction Books, 1983), 73.

91. Ibid., 136.

92. Ibid., 30.

93. Ibid., 57.

94. Ibid., 132.

95. *Statement of Claims and Compensation Awarded by the Railway Passengers Assurance Company and Testimonies of the Press as to its Utility* (London: Railway Passengers Assurance Company, 1851), 6.

96. "Underestimating the Benefit," *Travelers Record* 15 (November 1879), 4.

97. *New York Times*, 1 July 1906, Sec. 3, 6.

98. "A Growing Evil," *The Travelers Record* 33 (April 1897), 4

99. Eli Hammond, "Personal Injury Litigation," *Yale Law Review* 6 (1896-97), 329.

100. Quoted in Alfred Julien, "President's Column," *NACCA Newsletter* 2 (December 1958), 1.

101. Jacob D. Fuchsberg, "A Letter to an Editor," *Plaintiff's Advocate* 3 (April 1959), 4. See also Alfred Julien, "President's Column," *NACCA Newsletter* 2 (March 1959), 1. "We have no way of knowing whether the program now under discussion was inspired or not," Julien wrote of the charges of an insurance industry influence on the content of network television programming. "As to that, inquiry may well be worthwhile."

102. See "President's Column," *NACCA Newsletter* 5 (November 1962), 1, and "President's Column," *NACCA Newsletter* 5 (December 1962), 1.

103. Herman Glaser, "The President's Message," *Plaintiff's Advocate* 8 (April 1964), 3.

104. James D. Ghiardi, "The Defense Research Institute," *Federation of Insurance Counsel Quarterly* 14 (1964), 64.

105. "A Call to Arms," *For the Defense* 3 (October 1962), 57-58.

106. Ibid., 61.

107. William E. Knepper, "Our Common Interests," *Federation of Insurance Counsel Quarterly* 13 (1963), 45.

108. E. Wayne Covert, "Termites in the Temple of Justice or Fortunes From Misfortune," *Federation of Insurance Counsel Quarterly* 15 (1965), 55.

109. Quoted in Martin Mayer, *The Lawyers* (New York: Harper & Row, 1966), 267.

110. H. Laurence Ross, *Settled Out of Court: The Social Process of Insurance Claims Adjustment* (New York: Aldine Publishing Company, 1980 [1970]), 75.

111. Jerome E. Carlin, *Lawyers on Their Own: A Study of Individual Practitioners in Chicago* (New Brunswick, NJ: Rutgers University Press, 1962), 74.

112. One such new chaser is profiled in Robert M. Yoder, "How an Ambulance Chaser Works," *Saturday Evening Post*, 23 March 1957, 19.

113. Ibid., 84-85.

114. Roger Bryant Hunting and Gloria S. Neuwirth, *Who Sues in New York City? A Study of Automobile Accident Claims* (New York: Columbia University Press, 1962), 109.

115. Melvin M. Belli, *Ready for the Plaintiff* (New York: Popular Library, 1965 [1956]), 200.

116. Stuart Speiser, *Lawsuit* (New York: Horizon Press, 1980), 267. For Belli's extralegal exploits see Robert Wallace, *Life and Limb: An Account of the Career of Melvin M. Belli, Personal-Injury Trial Lawyer* (Garden City, NY: Doubleday & Company, 1955) and Melvin M. Belli (with Robert Blair Kaiser), *Melvin Belli: My Life on Trial* (New York: William Morrow and Company, Inc., 1976).

117. Belli, *My Life on Trial*, 134.

118. Ibid., 88.

119. Ibid., 128.

120. See Hunting and Neuwirth, *Who Sues in New York City?* 107-109.

121. F. B. MacKinnon, *Contingent Fees for Legal Services: A Study of Professional Economics and Responsibilities* (Chicago: Aldine Publishing Company, 1964) 14-15.

CHAPTER SIX

1. George Reasons and David Rosenzweig, "Ring Used Hospital Charity to Mask Illegal Activities," *Los Angeles Times*, 19 March 1974, 3. This article is the first of a series on which I have relied for most of my account of the Friends of the Friendless.

2. Abraham Gatner, "Ambulance Chasers Lay 'Pipe Lines' in Hospitals; Sign Patients at Bedside," *Brooklyn Daily Eagle*, 20 September 1927, 1.

3. Ibid.

4. Reasons and Rosenzweig, "Ring Used Hospital Charity to Mask Illegal Activities."

5. Ibid.

6. Ibid.

7. John Gregory Dunne, *True Confessions: A Novel* (New York: E.P. Dutton, 1977), 218.

8. Ibid., 213.

9. Luis Alberto Urrea, *Across the Wire: Life and Hard Times on the Mexican Border* (New York: Anchor Books, 1993), 12.

10. Ibid., 15-16.

11. Ronald L. Soble, "Swindle Squad Helps Latin Community," *Los Angeles Times*, 12 August 1979, Sec. 2, 1.

12. See the section entitled "'Friends of the Friendless' Scandal (1971-1974)" in Helen Eastman Martin, *The History of the Los Angeles County Hospital (1878-1968) and the Los Angeles County-University of Southern California Medical Center (1968-1978)* (Los Angeles: University of Southern California Press, 1979), 257-258.

13. George Reasons and David Rosenzweig, "Ring Preyed on Accident Victims in Barrios," *Los Angeles Times*, 20 March 1974, 1.

14. George Reasons and David Rosenzweig, "Ring Wrote Medical Reports to Back Claims," *Los Angeles Times*, 21 March 1974, 1.

15. *In the Matter of Silas B. Axtell, an Attorney* (1930), 229 App. Div. 325, 329-330.

16. George Reasons and David Rosenzweig, "Aliens Steered to Ring by Mexican Consulate," *Los Angeles Times*, 22 March 1974, 1.

17. Reasons and Rosenzweig, "Ring Preyed on Accident Victims in Barrios."

18. William Farr, "Hatcher Indicted on Bad Check Charges," *Los Angeles Times*, 29 May 1974, Sec. 2, 1.

19. George Reasons, "Ambulance-Chasing Figure's Ledgers Seized as Evidence," *Los Angeles Times*, 15 May 1974, Sec. 2, 1.

20. William Farr, "Hatcher, Mexico Aide, 11 Others Indicted in L.A. Ambulance Ring," *Los Angeles Times*, 30 August 1974, 1.

21. George Reasons and David Rosenzweig, "2 Mexican Officials Shifted; One Linked to Ambulance Ring," *Los Angeles Times*, 8 June 1974, Sec. 2, 1. The legal officer initially claimed diplomatic immunity from prosecution for his role in the Friends scandal, then waived it for fear of being "deprived the right to clear his name with the people of the community and his government." (William Farr, "Diplomat Drops Plea for Immunity Hearing," *Los Angeles Times*, 21 September 1974, 22.) Silva was never convicted.

22. William Farr, "Leader of Ambulance Chasers Gets 2 Years," *Los Angeles Times*, 30 June 1976, Sec. 2, 1. Hatcher was sent to county jail and not prison partly because

the judge considered the "underground rumor'" that Hatcher was a "marked man" and that the "Mexican Mafia want[ed] to do him in."

23. George Reasons and David Rosenzweig, "Ambulance Chasers: Moving In on Bus Crash," *Los Angeles Times*, 4 November 1974, 3.

24. See "Probe of Ambulance Chasing at Hospital Ordered by Supervisors," *Los Angeles Times*, 20 March 1974, 1, and "Probe of Hospital Ring Launched by Busch," *Los Angeles Times*, 23 March 1974, 23.

25. George Reasons and David Rosenzweig, "Laxity on Hospital Crackdown Told," *Los Angeles Times*, 26 March 1974, 1. A number of county hospital administrators were demoted and reprimanded for not taking action against the Friends during the eighteen months they had known about the group prior to the publication of the newspaper exposé that finally led them to action. ("6 Disciplined Over Ambulance-Chasing Ring at Medical Unit," *Los Angeles Times*, 3 May 1974, 3.)

26. George Reasons and David Rosenzweig, "State Bar President Denies Hahn Charge," *Los Angeles Times*, 27 March 1974, 1.

27. "Sen. Song Comments on Hatcher Articles," *Los Angeles Times*, 29 March 1974, Sec. 2, 6. The Ethics Committee of the California State Legislature found that there was not enough evidence of violations of conflict of interest to justify an investigation. ("Ethics Panel Won't Probe Sen. Song's Links to Hatcher," *Los Angeles Times*, 29 March 1974, 3.)

28. "Coyotes in the Legal Wasteland" (ed), *Los Angeles Times*, 25 March 1974, Sec. 2, 4.

29. George Reasons, "Legal Referral for Hospital Patients Slated," *Los Angeles Times*, 21 September, 1974, 18.

30. Baxter Ward, *Illegal Attorney Referral Activity in Los Angeles County: A Report on the Problem, Including an Analysis of the Handling of the Friends of the Friendless Ring by the County Department of Health Services* (Los Angeles: County Board of Supervisors, 1974), 3. See also George Reasons and David Rosenzweig, "New Testimony Given on Hospital 'Pressure'" *Los Angeles Times*, 20 July 1974, 25.

31. Ward, "Illegal Attorney Referral Activity in Los Angeles County, 9-10. See also George Reasons, "Study Finds Ambulance Rings Common Practice," *Los Angeles Times*, 30 August 1974, Sec. 2, 1.

32. Ward, "Illegal Attorney Referral Activity in Los Angeles County," 73-74.

33. Ibid., 77.

34. "It's No Accident," *Sixty Minutes*, CBS News Transcript, 9 December 1979, 5.

35. Roxton's case was discussed by McMullen in Ward, "Illegal Attorney Referral Activity in Los Angeles County," 79-83. A fully detailed chart of all of the staged collisions investigated by McMullen follows the narrative.

36. George Reasons and David Rosenzweig, "Officials Failed to Act Against Lawyers, Hospital Probe Told," *Los Angeles Times*, 18 July 1974, 3. See "18 Indicted for Alleged Part in Fake Accident Insurance Fraud," *Los Angeles Times*, 16 May 1974, Sec. 2, 1.

37. See "18 Indicted for Alleged Part in Fake Accident Insurance Fraud," *Los Angeles Times*, 16 May 1974, Sec. 2, 1. A few years earlier a different ring was indicted and, again, chiropractors were the only professionals named. See "10 Named in Indictments on Auto Insurance Fraud Counts," *Los Angeles Times*, 20 May 1972, Sec. 2, 1.

38. "The Insurance Swindlers," *Newsweek*, 7 April 1975, 49.

39 Quoted in Jay Kobler, "A New Attack on Insurance Fraud," *Best's Review* (Property/Casualty), September 1971, 68.

40. Frank A. Muscolina, "Exposing the Fake Claim Racket," *Journal of Criminal Law and Criminology* 41 (1950), 217.

41. Kobler, "A New Attack on Insurance Fraud," 18. For the announcement of the initial formation of the group, see "Casualty Insurers Form Association to Crack Down on Fraudulent Claims," *National Underwriter* (Property/Casualty), 21 July 1970, 1.

42. Joseph B. Treaster, "Referee for a Rally: James Francis Ahern," *New York Times*, 2 May 1970, 14.

43. Linda Greenhouse, "New Haven Police Chief Gives Reasons for Retiring," *New York Times*, 28 December 1970, 62.

44. "New Haven Ex-Chief Heads Antifraud Drive," *New York Times*, 6 January 1971, 25.

45. "The $1.7 Billion Insurance Ripoff, and the Ex-Police Chief Who Is Out to Stop It," *People*, 30 June 1975, 20.

46. James F. Ahern, "The Insurance Crime Prevention Institute and White Collar Crime in the Insurance Industry," *Insurance Counsel Journal* 38 (October 1972), 438.

47. Ibid.

48. Ronald Koziol, "Widen Investigation to 21 Cities in Accident Insurance Racket," *Chicago Tribune*, 17 January 1972, 4.

49. John O'Brien, "Federal Grand Jury Probing Phony Auto Accident Claim Operation Here," *Chicago Tribune*, 2 December 1973, 22.

50. The case involved a body shop owner who damaged cars then created medical bills for fake passengers. His story was featured in an ICPI film *Accident by Appointment*. Another related case from Providence involved Samuel Donato, a hairdresser, who scripted collisions, then steered fake claimants to a local law office. See *State v. Samuel A. Donato* (1980), 414 A. 2d 797-799.

51. John O'Brien, "51 Nigerians Accused in Insurance Scheme," *Chicago Tribune*, 11 February 1974, 2. Also active around this same time in Chicago was the team of Kevin Foley and Leonard "Big Dutch" Macek, who targeted a seventy-year-old man for one crash and staged another collision "to get Christmas money." See Pamela Zekman, "5 Indicted in Phony Accidents," *Chicago Tribune*, 21 May 1974, 8.

52. W. James Van Vliet and Richard M. Peery, "16 Indicted in Insurance Fraud Here," *Cleveland Plain-Dealer*, 4 June 1976, 1.

53. Details on the Barnard brothers case are found in *George James Barnard and Philip Weinstein, et al. v. United States* (1965), 342 F.2d 309.

54. *United States v. Clyde Reynolds, Robert Reynolds, Eugene Reynolds* (1979), 601 F. 2d 591.

55. *United States v. Mayo Perez et al.* (1974), 489 F. 2d 51. Most of the details on the DeMary brothers' ring derives from information in this court record. For more on the DeMarys, see the chapter entitled "A Big Bump" in E. J. Kahn Jr., *Fraud: The United States Postal Inspection Service and Some of the Fools and Knaves It Has Known* (New York: Harper & Row, 1973), 273-277.

56. Kahn , *Fraud*, 274.

57. *United States v. Mayo Perez et al.*

58. Kahn, *Fraud*, 275.

59. *United States v. Dr. Odis Strong et al.* (1983), 702 F. 2d 98-99.

60. "ICPI Agent's Long Memory Brings Auto Fraud Ring to Light," *ICPI Report* 6 (August, 1978), 5.

61. "North Carolina Staged Auto Accident Ring Smashed: Checkerboard Vinyl Roof Caper," *ICPI Report* 10 (January/February/March 1982), 7.

62. United Press International (Nexis), 18 January 1982.

63. See *Insurance Fraud: ICPI Handbook for Insurance Personnel* (Westport, CT: ICPI, 1978), 8-10.

64. "Indicted Pair Named One-Time Members of 'Nellie Young Gang,'" *ICPI Report* 7 (October/ November/December 1979), 6. The actual Nellie Young was unaware of the use of her name in the scheme.

65. "Beat-Up LTD Used in 15 Staged Accidents," *ICPI Report* 7 (October/November/December 1979), 7.

66. "Alleged Caused/Staged Accident Ring Indicted in Texas," *ICPI Report* 10 (September/December 1982), 1.

67. "Man Who 'Wrote Book on Insurance Fraud' Sentenced to Seven Years in Arizona, Indicted for Auto Fraud in Ohio," *ICPI Report* 11 (First Quarter, 1984), 1.

68. "'Big Jack' Draws Four Years for 'Grandest' Fraud Scheme," *ICPI Report* 6 (August 1978), 1.

69. Jack Hovelson, "4 Charged in $1 Million Insurance Fraud Scheme," Gannett News Service (nexis), 25 March 1994. Big Jack was convicted in June of 1995. See *United States v. John J. Rodamaker* (Westlaw).

70. Hal Lancaster, "Faked Out: Insurance Companies Cheated for Centuries Are Still Being Taken," *Wall Street Journal*, 23 December 1974, 1.

71. Healy, *A Game of Wits*, 246. Most of the details on Nub City derive from Healy's excellent account.

72. Ibid.

73. Carl Freund, "Fake Claims Charged," *Dallas News*, 10 June 1975.

74. "Fraud Suspect Takes 3-Year Fall," *Dallas Herald*, 1 July 1976.

75. "Oklahoma Slip & Faller Sentenced," *ICPI Report* 8 (August/September/October, 1981), 1.

76. "Slip & Fall Cheat Slips Up in Miami Drugstore," *ICPI Report* 7 (August/September, 1979), 1.

77. "Agent Charged as Arranger of Phony Flops in Stores, Banks," *ICPI Report* 7 (October/November/December 1979), 1.

78. "Minister Musters for Jail Term," *ICPI Report* 7 (May/July 1979), 1. See also Jane Fritsch, "Clergyman Gets 2 Years in Welfare Fraud Case," *Chicago Tribune*, 19 May 1979, 4.

79. "Slip-and-Fall Ring Sentenced in North Carolina," *ICPI Report*, 10 (April/June 1983), 3.

80. "Mother & Son Fraud Team Sentenced," *ICPI Report* 12 (Fourth Issue, 1985), 2.

81. "The Family That Slips Together Falls Together," *ICPI Report* 7 (January/February/March, 1980), 7.

82. "Phony Soap Products Distributor's Slip & Fall Scheme Comes Out in the Wash," *ICPI Report* 7 (July/August, 1980), 10. For the subsequent standoff with the FBI, see Mark Stultz, United Press International (Nexis), 9 June 1982 and United Press International (Nexis), 4 November 1982.

83. For most of the details on Mint Jelly Ridge, I have relied on "Ten-Year Career Ends For Dedicated, Determined Slip-and-Fall Artist," *ICPI Report* 7 (October/November/December, 1979), 5.

84. William Amlong and Al Messerschmidt, "Everybody Talks of Claims Fraud, Few Do Anything," *Miami Herald*, 15 May 1977, 1. See also William R. Amlong, "Whiplash—'People Paid to Suffer,'" *Miami Herald*, 11 May 1977, 1. The *Herald* series began the investigation of a personal injury mill run by Anthony Capodilupo, who was ultimately jailed. For the details on Capodilupo's relations with runners and doctors, see "Lawyer, MD's Accused in Fraud Setup," *Miami Herald*, 15 October 1977, B-1; "11 Indicted in Insurance Fraud Case," *Miami Herald*, 1 December 1977, 1; and "Insurance-Swindle Probe Target Gets Year in Jail," *Miami Herald*, 9 July 1981, C-1.

85. "Pain & Suffering," *Sixty Minutes*, CBS News Transcript, 18 September 1977, 5.

86. The story "It's No Accident" was followed by charges that CBS had "staged" some news of its own. Correspondent Dan Rather was shown to have chased a man around a parking lot trying to get him to admit he was the administrator of a medical mill (when he was not) and to have wrongly stated that a certain doctor signed a phony medical report. Although *Sixty Minutes* and Dan Rather were ultimately absolved of any liability, one reporter observed at the time that, more than just a slander trial, the case was a test of the credibility not only of Rather and *Sixty Minutes* but of the methods of exposé-style reporting and television news in general. See Peter J. Boyer, "'60 Minutes' Finds Itself in Hot Seat," *Los Angeles Times*, 24 May 1983, 1.

87. Pamela Zekman and Gene Mustain, "Accidents too Good to Leave to Lawyers," *Chicago Sun-Times*, 14 February 1980, 1. For a condensed version of the investigation, see "The Great Insurance Scam," 20/20, ABC News Transcript, 26 June 1980, 9-18.

88. Zekman and Mustain, "Chasers Converge on Accident Scene . . . and It Becomes the Scene of a Crime," *Chicago Sun-Times*, 15 February 1980, 6.

89. Zekman and Mustain, "How Superswindling Pays: Just a Little Nets a Lot If Accident Case Is 'Perfect,'" *Chicago Sun-Times*, 12 February 1980, 1.

90. Zekman and Mustain, "The Accident Swindlers: They're Getting Away with $3 Billion a Year—and All You Drivers Pay," *Chicago Sun-Times*, 10 February 1980, 1.

91. Zekman and Mustain, "A Hospital for Greedy," *Chicago Sun-Times*, 17 February 1980, 1.

92. Paul Jesilow, Henry N. Pontell, and Gilbert Geis, *Prescription for Profit: How Doctors Defraud Medicaid* (Berkeley: University of California Press, 1993), 34, 188. For a summary of William Sherman's 1973 exposé on medical mills, see 36, 50-51.

93. Attorney Harold Kriv pled guilty to mail fraud charges and was sentenced to a year in prison; three other attorneys were suspended from practice; one chiropractor and one accident broker—Wes McKinney—were found guilty of mail fraud and sentenced to sixteen months in prison.

94. Jeffrey O'Connell and C. Brian Kelly, *The Blame Game: Injuries, Insurance, and Injustice* (Lexington, MA: Lexington Books, 1987), 58. For a previous discussion of these same issues and similar cases, see the chapter entitled "The Underworld of Tort" in Jeffrey O'Connell, *The Lawsuit Lottery: Only the Lawyers Win* (New York: Free Press, 1979).

95. Zekman and Mustain, "Smashup Cheats—How They Get YOU," *Chicago Sun-Times*, 6 April 1980, 8. Wirth suffered a deep cut on her lip that left a permanent scar. The men she hit seemed fine at the time, but one of them, a singer with a band, claimed that his teeth had started to fall out as a result of the crash. ("You wouldn't want me up there singing with no front teeth," he argued at trial.)

96. Lynn Emmerman, "Jury Investigates Accident-causing Ring," *Chicago Tribune*, 12 January 1983, B-1.

97. Linnet Myers, "County Grand Jury Indicts 37 in Auto Insurance Fraud Scheme," *Chicago Tribune*, 6 March 1986, C-3.

98. Ahern is quoted in Ralph Blumenthal, "Auto Fraud Rings Cause Heavy Losses for Insurers," *New York Times*, 21 November 1979, Sec. 4, 8. Earlier that year Ahern spoke to the ICPI Board of Governors about his change in thinking about the nature of insurance frauds. He said: "[It is] no longer confined to large cities—it is in the suburbs, on the farms and ranches of rural America. Nor does it respect any class or occupational boundaries. Street criminals and respectable citizens are equally prone to using their insurance policies for fraud." See *ICPI Report* 7 (May/June/July 1979), 11.

99. *ICPI Report* 12 (First Quarter, 1984), 6-7.

CHAPTER SEVEN

1. Details of the Tierra Blanca case derive from reports of the initial investigation, follow-up interviews with some of the crash participants, original interviews with some of the investigating officers, and a report by ABC News' *Prime Time Live,* "It's No Accident," 23 May 1991, 2-8.

2. Urban planner Richard Graves, writing in 1953, is quoted in Richard Davies, *Age of Asphalt: The Automobile, the Freeway, and the Condition of Metropolitan America* (Philadelphia: Lippincott, 1975), 49.

3. Eli P. Bernzweig, *By Accident, Not Design: The Case for Comprehensive Injury Reparations* (New York: Praeger, 1980), 150.

4. Quoted in *The Bulletin* (December 1923), 172.

5. See the following articles by James P. Bennett in the *Los Angeles Herald-Examiner:* "Insurance—Target for Larceny," 3 November 1963, B1; "'Whiplash' Becomes Target for Insurance Larceny," 4 November 1963, B1; and "The Insurance Swindle and the 'Padding,'" 8 November 1963, B1.

6. Rader's story is told in James P. Bennett, "False Claims Increase Insurance Rates," *Los Angeles Herald-Examiner,* 7 November 1963, D1. The case was also described as "the grimmest case of accident faking in Claims Bureau files" in E. D. Fales, Jr., "Beware of Accident Fakers," *Popular Science Monthly* (May 1961), 52-53.

7. Charles Kelson, "Insurance Fraud Investigations," *The Police Chief* (May 1975), 60.

8. The song was written in 1978 by a man named Allan Michael Katz who, along with two others, was later found guilty of accident staging. See "Scam Song Hits Sour Note," *ICPI Report* 7 (January/February/March, 1980), 1. The song is reprinted in full in "Scammer's Theme Song," *John Cooke Fraud Report* 1 (July/August, 1994), 31.

9. Stewart is quoted in Richard Baker, "The Claim Game: Hit Me, I'm Insured," *New West Magazine,* 11 September 1978, 96. Other details on the case derive from the following sources: "Hungarian Ring of Southern California," *ICPI Report* 7 (May/June/July, 1979), 3-4; documents from the Superior Court of California; and original interviews.

10. Baker, "The Claim Game," 98.

11. Ibid., 96.

12. Stewart is quoted in "Hungarian Ring: One Staged Accident Results in $174,000 Payoff, Complaint Says," *Insurance Adjuster* (November 1977). 8

13. From *People v. Choka* (L.A. Superior Court).

14. "Three Attacks in Posh Hillside Homes May Be Connected," United Press International (Nexis), 27 November 1984. Within a one-hour period, the gunmen fired on Simon's home as well as the nearby homes of two of Simon's business partners.

15. Baker, "The Claim Game," 94. Laurence Rooker, an investigator with the Los Angeles District Attorney's office, said that he and his colleagues referred to the

group as the Hungarian Mafia. See William Farr, "Phony Accident Ring Investigated," *Los Angeles Times*, 12 August 1976, 3.

16. Dorothy Townsend, "U.S. Jury Indicts 14 in Auto Insurance Swindle," *Los Angeles Times*, 3 November 1978, II-2. A year later the attorney was interviewed about the fraud by Dan Rather of *60 Minutes*. The attorney claimed that the scheme was the idea of the adjuster. He said of of the adjuster: "He was the chief claims adjuster for the company. He said, 'Send me some staged claims. Don't worry about the facts too much. Nobody's going to check them. I—I've got absolute control. I can settle anything I want.' I said, 'Well, what about the medical bills?' He said, 'Well, just prepare them in your office.'" ("It's No Accident," *60 Minutes*, CBS News Transcript, 9 December 1979, 3.)

17. For different accounts of the P.L.O. Ring, see: Ron Roach, "Arab Students in U.S. Held in Insurance Plot," *Los Angeles Times*, 15 February 1977, 3; Robert Lindsey, "Insurance Frauds by Arab Students Said to Aid P.L.O," *New York Times*, 20 February 1977, 1; Bill Richards, "Auto Insurance Fraud Laid to P.L.O. in U.S.," *Washington Post*, 21 February 1977, 1; and "CHP Probing Reports of P.L.O. Link to Insurance Plot," *Los Angeles Times*, 21 February 1977, 3.

18. "P.L.O. Swindle?" *New York Times*, 8 May 1977, 25.

19. Ahern is quoted in "Auto Fraud Rings Cause Heavy Losses for Insurers," *New York Times*, 21 November 1979, Sec. 4, 8.

20. The "fraud intelligence process" at the California Department of Insurance is described in their magazine, *The Investigator* 1 (Winter 1995), 17-24.

21. Gary A. Hernandez, "Fighting Insurance Claims Fraud in California," unpublished manuscript, 1995, A-3.

22. For Walker's "beat" and other details about the early days of the Bureau of Fraudulent Claims, see Lewis Leader, "Big Business of Car Fraud," *San Francisco Examiner*, 21 September 1980, 1.

23. See Eric Malnic, "8 Named as Suspects in Phony Auto Accident Scheme," *Los Angeles Times*, 14 November 1980, Sec. 2, 8.

24. Deanne Barkley, *Freeway: A Novel* (New York: MacMillan, 1978), 138.

25. Russell Reid, "Accident My Foot!," *Los Angeles Magazine* (December 1984), 180.

26. Patricia Manisco, "Staged-Wreck Fraud Thrives in Auto-Rich L.A. Suburbs," *Los Angeles Times*, 15 July 1985, Sec. 2, 1.

27. "Operation Anti-Scam," a public education program produced by 20th Century Insurance, was described in Alfred G. Haggerty, "Insurer Gears Up to Brake Phony Auto Accident Scams," *National Underwriter*, 27 July 1984, 2.

28. For "Derek," see "Fraudulent Auto Accidents Viewed as a Thriving Racket," *New York Times*, 29 November 1985, Sec. 2, 25.

29. "Bobby" is quoted in Reid, "Accident My Foot!" 76.

30. "Jerry" is interviewed in "It's No Accident," *Prime Time Live* (May 1991), 5.

31. Mustang's words were incorporated into a fifteen-minute public relations videotape produced by the Western Insurance Information Service: *The Hunter and the Hunted: Don't Be a Victim*, 1991.

32. Warthen is quoted in Manisco, "Staged-Wreck Fraud Thrives in Auto-Rich L.A. Suburbs."

33. Dave's words are condensed from a forty-five-minute videotape, *Accident Fraud Investigation*, produced during the mid-1980s by the California Bureau of Fraudulent Claims.

34. William Overend, "Staged Accidents Cited in Probe of Insurance Fraud," *Los Angeles Times*, 17 July 1984, 1. The ring, reportedly run by a man named Julian Johnson, was said to have made more than $2 million over two years by putting damage on cars in a controlled way, then churning the medical bills of the alleged passengers through a number of different medical clinics owned by the Johnsons and a partner named Ronald Burton. The investigation was conducted by a joint agency task force led by Tom Dugan of the Postal Inspection service. See also "Fifteen, Including Attorney and Doctor, Indicted in Multi-Million Dollar Staged Accident and Personal Injury Ring," *ICPI Report* 11 (Second Quarter, 1984), 1.

35. Chiropractor Jesus N. Dominguez pleaded guilty to fraud and was sentenced to a year in prison. Fourteen other members of the ring, including Gregory Benson, the main driver of crash cars, were successfully prosecuted. See Dorothy Townsend, "Car Crash Ring Prosecutions Near End," *Los Angeles Times*, 10 August 1985, Sec. 2, 6.

36. The principals in the ring were Vladimir Grishin and Dr. Stefan Snyder; the claimants were a mix of Latinos and Armenians. See Kim Murphy, "12 Indicted in Accident Fraud Case," *Los Angeles Times*, 28 September 1988, Sec.2, 3.

37. For an accident ring run by Ed Ok, see George Ramos, "7 Held in Alleged Claims Scam," *Los Angeles Times*, 1 September 1988, Sec. 2, 3.

38. Avina is quoted in Virginia Rivers, "Fraud: L.A. Is the Capital of Auto Insurance Fakery," *Los Angeles Reader*, 30 August 1991, 8-9.

39. See Lois Timnick, "51 to Face Charges in Auto Insurance Fraud Roundup," *Los Angeles Times*, 18 October 1990, Sec.2, 1.

40. Reiner is quoted in David Tobenkin, "Insurance Companies at Long Last Assume a Role in Detecting Fraud," *Los Angeles Business Journal*, 29 October 1990, 14.

41. Dan Weikel and Sonni Efron, "Army of Scam Artists Milks Millions from Insurers, Officials Say," *Los Angeles Times*, 1 March 1990, 30. Later in the year an insurance industry study would show that California led every state in the nation in the number of bodily injury claims it filed relative to the number of property damage claims. Fraud was cited as one factor, as was a higher attorney involvement in claims in California than elsewhere. See Kenneth Reich, "State Leads Nation in

Filing Injury Claims for Auto Accidents," *Los Angeles Times*, 19 December 1990, 1. The results of a similar study for Southern California alone was reported in Frederick M. Muir, "Inflated Claims Seen as Fast Lane to Easy Money," *Los Angeles Times*, 23 January 1989, 1.

42. For background on the Southern California card casinos, see Sandra Sutphen, "The Painless Tax: Card Clubs Mean Money For Cities. Do They Also Mean Trouble?" *California Journal* (January 1993), 29-33.

43. See the entry on Armenia in Zena Pearlstone, *Ethnic LA* (Beverly Hills: Hillcrest Press, 1990), 110-112.

44. Eric Malnic, "Auto Insurance Fraud Ring Broken Up, Authorities Say," *Los Angeles Times*, 12 April 1991, Sec. 2, 1.

45. David Newdorf, "PI Counsel Escape Insurance Scam Bust; 15 Firms Are Searched, But 'Big Boys' Insulated So Far," *The Recorder*, 24 April 1991, 1.

46. Bill Farr, "Attorney Admits Staging 66 Crashes for Insurance," *Los Angeles Times*, 22 December 1984, Sec. 2, 12. Ammann was sentenced to five years in federal prison. (See William Overend, "Staging Auto Accidents Earns Lawyer 5 Years in Prison," *Los Angeles Times*, 2 April 1985, 20.) Ammann died shortly after his release.

47. Kim Murphy, "Tip to Anaheim Police Helps Break Up Insurance Fraud Ring," *Los Angeles Times*, 13 March 1986, Sec. 2, 4. Bota was later sentenced to three years and four months in the Men's Correctional Institution in Chino, California. See "Lawyer Sentenced for Auto-Insurance Fraud," *Los Angeles Times*, 2 March 1988, Sec. 2, 9.

48. MacKenzie is quoted in Mark Thompson, "Highway Robbery," *California Lawyer*, May, 1991, 32.

49. Kenneth Reich, "18 Arrested in 4th Large Insurance Fraud Ring," *Los Angeles Times*, 31 July 1991, Sec. 2, 1.

50. Kenneth Reich, "Estimate of Insurance Fraud Hiked," *Los Angeles Times*, 7 February 1992, Sec. 2, 1.

51. The therapist is quoted in Lily Dizon, "Fraud Trial of Costa Mesa Attorney to Begin Today," *Los Angeles Times* (Orange County Edition), 18 February 1992, Sec. 2, 1. For the original arrests in this case, see James M. Gomez, "Lawyer Held in $1-Million Auto Insurance Scam," *Los Angeles Times* (Orange County Edition), 5 January 1991, Sec. 2, 1.

52. For the case against Choi, see "'Capper' Case Brought by IRS Goes to Jury," *Los Angeles Daily Journal*, 28 July 1994, 1.

53. Deputy District Attorney Richard Rosenthal is quoted in Josh Meyer, "Lawyer Suspected of Trying to Have Key Witness Slain," *Los Angeles Times*, 11 August 1992, Sec. 2, 3. No charges arose from this allegation.

54. For an account of the arrests, see Josh Meyer, "2 Attorneys Held in $14-Million Insurance Fraud," *Los Angeles Times* (Valley Edition), 6 August 1992, Sec. 2, 1.

55. Garamendi is quoted in "Fraud Bureau Arrests Two Suspected Attorneys," *Business Wire* (Nexis), 5 August 1992.

56. "Rampant Tax Fraud in Personal-Injury Industry," *Business Wire* (Nexis), 20 June 1994.

57. Quoted in Peggy Y. Lee, "Insurers Say Crash Scams Are Increasing," *Los Angeles Times* (Ventura County Edition), 27 November 1992, Sec. 2, 1.

58. "California: The Endangered Dream," *Time*, 18 November 1991, 38.

59. The "war against the ambulance chasers," fought initially in the 1920s over the idea that some personal injury lawyers practiced law as if it were a business, was revisited again in the form of the debate over attorney advertising: After a 1977 U.S. Supreme Court decision (*Bates v. Arizona State Bar* 97 S. Ct 2691) held that legal advertisements were commercially protected speech, the ads first began to appear—first as relatively tame entries in phone books, then, within a few years, as full page spreads with crashed cars, dollar signs, and slogans like "Will Fight For Top Dollar" or "We Will Get You Money for Your Accident." In the early 1980's, the TV attorney came to be widely known for his insistence on fighting for your rights and getting you the money you deserved before those chiseling insurers cheated you out of your just desserts. As in the earlier "wars" on ambulance chasers, the subsequent debates over attorney ads often broke down along class lines between corporate lawyers and solo practitioners. (See, for example, Gail Diane Cox, "Battle on Legal Ads Comes Down to Class," *National Law Journal*, 25 May 1987, 19.) Though the imagined function of lawyer ads, like that of the contingent fee itself, was put forward by a legal clinic that envisioned universal access to lawyers, the social purpose was not often evident in the brash appeals, the dramatic reenactments of terrible accidents, sirens, jingles, and the testimonials from people about how much money a certain lawyer had won for them. "The cardinal rule of lawyer advertising is to never forget that the successful commercial is a sales pitch . . . not a lesson in the law," one of the nation's leading attorney ad-men wrote in an article on "Do's and Don'ts for Television Commercials." That such a point could be made in the pages of the *National Law Journal's* special issue on lawyer ads (25 May 1987) was just one indication that the old nationwide war on ambulance chasers had been lost, at least in the sense that one area of legal practice had developed more as a business than a profession. The general public derision and, often, mockery of the TV attorney and the internecine bar-battles over what aspects of the ads were proper and ethical is one indication of how much at war Americans remain with themselves about the connections linking money, accidents, insurers, and plaintiffs' attorneys. The connection between the proliferation of legal ads since *Bates* (especially personal injury ads) and increases in fraudulent claims is no doubt real although hard to prove; but that accidents were faked for money by organized professionals and freelancing amateurs long before the Supreme Court decision is equally clear.

CHAPTER EIGHT

1. Emilie Lounsberry, "Key Witness: Burke Wanted Willard Killed," *Philadelphia Inquirer*, 27 April 1991, B1. Most of the details of this account of the murder, and of the subsequent case against attorney Robert Burke, derive from extensive reporting by the *Philadelphia Inquirer* over several years, especially by Emilie Lounsberry and Susan Caba. Some information also derives from original interviews.

2. Henry Goldman, "Philadelphia Lawyer Faces More Charges of Fraud," *Philadelphia Inquirer*, 3 August 1990, B7. See also Emilie Lounsberry, "2 More Admit Guilt in Insurance Scam," *Philadelphia Inquirer*, 16 October 1990, B4.

3. Susan Caba, "Witness: Probe Worried Burke; Their Dinner Chat was Tape-Recorded," *Philadelphia Inquirer*, 14 August 1993, B1.

4. Susan Caba, "Burke Denies Ordering Killing: He Rebuts Testimony by a Former Associate That He Paid $1,0000 to Have Donna Willard Slain and Guarantee Her Silence," *Philadelphia Inquirer*, 24 August 1993, B1.

5. Emilie Lounsberry, "Dinner—With a Side of Fraud," *Philadelphia Inquirer*, 22 March 1991, A1.

6. Emilie Lounsberry, "Lawyer Burke Gets Prison in Insurance Scam," *Philadelphia Inquirer*, 11 January 1991, B1.

7. Emilie Lounsberry, "Heat Is on Lawyer in Willard Case," *Philadelphia Inquirer*, 7 January 1991, B1.

8. Willard's attorney is quoted in "Burke Trial Hears Details of Slaying," *Philadelphia Inquirer*, 17 August 1993, B1.

9. Emilie Lounsberry, "Two Arrested in Killing of Witness in Insurance Probe," *Philadelphia Inquirer*, 29 December 1990, A1.

10. Susan Caba, "Burke Trial Hears of Hit Man in Action," *Philadelphia Inquirer*, 18 August 1993, B1.

11. Susan Caba, "Witness Says He Was Hired to Kill," *Philadelphia Inquirer*, 13 August 1993, B1.

12. For this juror's statement, see Susan Caba, "Burke Guilty in the Slaying of Willard," *Philadelphia Inquirer*, 27 August 1993, A1. It is important to note that the testimony which proved crucial for this one juror, and possibly for others, came from a man who shared a prison cell with Burke for just a few hours. In that time, the man claimed, Burke had acknowledged to having "offed" Donna Willard.

13. Susan Caba, "Burke Gets Life for Ordering Murder," *Philadelphia Inquirer*, 2 December 1993, B1. Initially prosecutors sought the death penalty in the case because it involved the murder of a federal witness. But a federal district court disallowed the sentencing option as unconstitutional. See Gary Cohn, "Death Penalty Barred in Slaying of Witness," *Philadelphia Inquirer*, 7 November 1992, B1.

14. See the following editorials in the *Philadelphia Inquirer*: "Scam City," 25 October 1989, A14, and "Whiplash City," 17 April 1993, A18. See also, Larry Fish and Gary Cohn, "Why Phila. Car Insurance Is Nation's Highest," *Philadelphia Inquirer*,

22 October 1989, A1, and Ronnie Polaneczky, "Scam City: How Philadelphia Became America's Personal-Injury Capital, And How Much It Costs Us Every Day," *Philadelphia Magazine* (March 1993), 48. Postal Inspector James Trovarello, perhaps the most experienced fraud investigator in the city, put it this way: "No doubt about it, Philadelphia is the hub of insurance fraud for the East Coast. South Philly, North Philly, West Philly, Kensington—there are neighborhoods where there are rings that do this." See Larry Fish, "An Insurance 'Fraud Squad' Targets Phila.," *Philadelphia Inquirer*, 17 October 1989, B4.

15. For the story of the accident ring run by James Giannattasio and Maurice Pisano, see Gary Cohn and Larry Fish, "Fraud Is a Principal Contributor to City's High Car-Insurance Rates," *Philadelphia Inquirer*, 13 December 1989, A1.

16. Michael deCourcy Hinds, "Philadelphia Transit Wincing Over Faked Injuries," *New York Times*, 28 April 1990, 1. One woman was later sentenced to jail for claiming to have been injured on an elevated train on a day when she saw what she believed was a legitimate train crash but was really a mock evacuation drill conducted for safety. See Rita Giordano, "Woman Gets Jail in SEPTA Fraud," *Philadelphia Inquirer*, 29 November 1995, B3.

17. For a few accounts of the ring run by William Mele and attorney David Rosenfield, see Tim Weiner, "How a $1 Million Insurance Caper Came Undone," *Philadelphia Inquirer*, 13 February 1984, A1; Joseph Busler, "Collapse of an Empire," *Courier-Post*, 20 January 1985, A1; "Fall of a Fraud Empire," *ICPI Report* 12 (Second Issue, 1985), 6-7; and Jeff Shear, "The Philadelphia Story," *Insurance Review* (April, 1986), 63-65.

18. Emilie Lounsberry, "In Common Fraud Case, A Rare Turn to Violence: Did Burke's Souring Scam Lead to Murder?" *Philadelphia Inquirer*, 18 May 1992, B1.

19. Ibid.

20. The story of Kaitlyn Arquette's involvement with accident stagers in California is told by her mother in Lois Duncan, *Who Killed My Daughter?* (New York: Bantam Doubleday, 1992). For the factual outlines of the case as well as findings that occurred after the publication of Duncan's book, I have relied primarily on unpublished materials prepared by a team of lawyers and investigators working on the Arquettes' behalf.

21. Duncan, *Who Killed My Daughter?* 181-182.

22. Ibid., 105.

23. Lois Arquette's words are quoted from a talk she gave before an audience of insurance investigators in March, 1994, as reproduced in Leslie Kim, "Who Killed Kaitlyn Arquette?" *The John Cooke Fraud Report* 2 (May/June, 1995), 37.

24. Ibid., 1.

25. Duncan, *Who Killed My Daughter?*, 194.

26. The John Cooke Fraud Report has published a number of stories on the case, each followed by calls for investigators to send any relevant information. The family and people assisting them hope that the case will be retried at the federal level.

27. For brief accounts of the case, see "Fraud Investigators See Rise in Staged Accidents," *Journal of Commerce*, 21 June 1994, 7A, and Jeff Donn, "2 Men Sentenced to Life in Prison for Murder During Insurance Scam," *Dallas Morning News*, 26 June 1994, 12A. A remarkably similar scheme, which did not end in death, occurred in San Diego County at around the same time. Two gas station attendants, also an uncle-and-nephew team, rented a U-Haul and looked for cars (albeit empty ones) to crash into. See *NICB Spotlight* 3 (Spring 1994), 5.

28. Wojcik is quoted in a subsequent CNBC television report on the case: "Profile: Insurance Fraud Takes Life of Accident Victim," *Steals & Deals*, 25 August 1995.

29. Ibid.

30. See Matt Scanlan, "Insurance Scam Tied to Killing," *New Orleans Times-Picayune*, 4 January 1996, B1, and Walt Philbin, "N.O. Cop Suspended, Booked Again in Scam," *New Orleans Times-Picayune*, 11 January 1996, B2.

31. Mention of this case is made by L.A. private detective Tom Grant in John Sweeney, "California Vignette: In L.A. the Bad Guy Is Only Nailed in Detective Stories," *Ottawa Citizen*, 17 September 1994, B1.

32. Stephen Carroll, Allan Abrahamse, and Mary Vaiana, *The Costs of Excess Medical Claims for Automobile Personal Injuries* (Santa Monica, CA: RAND Institute for Civil Justice, 1995). The authors make reference to the frauds of criminal rings uncovered through law enforcement sting operations and investigative reports. But, for the purposes of their analysis, they do not distinguish these from the everyday buildup frauds of ordinary citizens. The authors relied on statistics from two of the toughest no-fault insurance states, New York and Michigan, as a base-line against which to judge excessiveness and exaggeration, so perhaps it comes as no surprise that they recommend no-fault laws with a tough verbal threshold as the chief policy solution to the problem.

33. *Trends in Auto Injury Claims* (Oak Brook, IL: Insurance Research Council, 1995).

34. The Quality Planning Corporation of Oakland, California, estimates the dollar value of organized personal injury frauds at slightly less than the longtime industry rule of thumb of 10 percent when they state that $3 of every $100 in auto accident claims money goes to staged accidents and just over $8 goes to pay for the work of the medical mills (some of which is overlap).

35. See Robert W. Emerson, "Insurance Claim Fraud Problems and Remedies," *University of Miami Law Review* 46 (March 1992), 934-938. This information is updated monthly in insurance fraud reports issued by the Insurance Information Institute.

36. See Peter Kerr, "'Ghost Riders' Are Target of an Insurance Sting," *New York Times*, 18 August 1993, 1. Despite the early indictments of ten doctors, four lawyers, two police officers, a number of cappers and fake claimants, Dr. Henry Miles Sherman, a Morristown doctor who admitted to padding bills in the ghost rider cases, was the only major figure prosecuted. See Robert Rudolph, "Doctor Admits Crash Course in Insurance Fraud; Staged Collision of Bus and Jeep Snared MD Who Treated 'Riders,'" *Newark Star-Ledger*, 1 December 1995, 1. The New Jersey Insur-

ance Fraud Division, once hailed as the "largest, busiest, and most aggressive agency of its kind in the country" (Jay Romano, "A State Crackdown on Insurance Fraud," *New York Times*, 27 December 1992, 13), was criticized in 1996 by a group of doctors who felt they were being "shaken down" by threats of prosecution for unnamed frauds if they did not pay monetary restitution preemptively. See "Fraud Patrol: New Jersey Insurance Fraud Division Goes Too Far and Doctors Fight Back," *Dateline NBC* Transcript, 13 March 1996.

37. The early history of SIUs is told in Susan Guarino Ghezzi, "A Private Network of Social Control: Insurance Investigation Units," *Social Problems* 30 (June 1983), 521-531. Ghezzi worries about the SIUs as the latest in a long line of private police schemes by big industry that exist outside of judicial control and ultimately infringe on the rights of consumers.

38. SIU veteran Frank R. Vespe is quoted in Bill Thorness, "The New SIU Team: A Claims Specialty Grows for Investigators of Suspicious Claims,"*Claims* (September 1994), 53.

39. A transcript of the news conference is published by the Federal News Service, 7 January 1992 (Nexis). General Schlossberg is quoted at greater length on his view of the similarity between the war on drugs and the war on insurance fraud in an interview with writer Loretta Worters, *Insurance Review* (August 1991), 12.

40. Reported in Kim, "Who Killed Kaitlyn Arquette?," 36.

41. Stanley Karnow, "In Orange County's Little Saigon, Vietnamese Try to Bridge Two Worlds," *Smithsonian* 23 (August 1992), 34.

42. T. J. English, *Born to Kill: America's Most Notorious Vietnamese Gang, and the Changing Face of Organized Crime* (New York: William Morrow, 1995), 8.

43. Jeffrey Brody, "Little Saigon Seen as Hotbed of Scams," *Orange County Register*, 14 January 1993, 1.

44. Nina Vida, *Goodbye Saigon* (New York: Ballantine Books, 1994), 119-120.

45. Ibid., 142.

46. Ibid., 158.

47. Except where specifically cited, most of this account of accident faking in Little Saigon derives from court documents and original interviews.

48. "Doctor Convicted of Insurance Fraud," *Los Angeles Times*, 21 January 1996, B7.

49. This exchange between MacPhee and the undercover officers is reported in William Vogeler, "Big Trouble in Little Saigon,"*California Lawyer* (May 1995), 49.

50. Rene Lynch, "Fake Accident Scam Gets Man 5-Year Term," *Los Angeles Times*, 18 August 1993, B7.

51. For MacPhee's conviction, see Rene Lynch, "Lawyer Guilty of Insurance Scam Felonies," *Los Angeles Times*, 12 August 1994, B1. For the sentences of MacPhee and his office staff, see Lee Romney and Rene Lynch, "Woman Ordered to Prison in Insurance Fraud," *Los Angeles Times*, 8 October 1994, B3, and Ken Ellingwood and

Sarah Klein, "Lawyer Gets Prison in Fraud Case," *Los Angeles Times*, 3 June 1995, B1.

52. Dinh's confrontation with MacPhee's girlfriend is described in Dick Clever, "Clinics Dispense More Paper Than Medicine," *Seattle Post-Intelligencer*, 9 February 1994, A1.

53. Dick Clever, "Charges Filed in Fraud Probe," *Seattle Post-Intelligencer*, 14 May 1994, B1.

54. Quoted in Dick Clever, "Lack of Control Can Lead to Trouble in Lawyers' Offices," *Seattle Post-Intelligencer*, 8 February 1994, A1.

55. Quoted in Dick Clever, "Questioning the Profit in Pain," *Seattle Post-Intelligencer*, 8 February 1994, A1.

56. The Gonzaleses' clinic is described in Dick Clever, "Clinics Dispense More Paper Than Medicine," *Seattle Post-Intelligencer*, 9 February 1994, A1.

57. Quoted in Dick Clever, "4 Arrested in Insurance Fraud Investigation," *Seattle Post-Intelligencer*, 7 February 1994, A1.

58. See Jes Odam, "Seattle Police Charge 4 in Staged Car-Accident Scam Involving ICBC," *Vancouver Sun*, 10 February 1994, B6.

59. Dick Clever, "Crash-Fraud Case Suspect Disappears," *Seattle Post-Intelligencer*, 16 February 1994, B2.

60. For the indictments of cappers Romeli Dejesus Alfaro and Marvin Danis Gonzalez see "2 Men Indicted in Staged-Accident Scam,"*News Tribune*, 14 April 1995, B2.

61. Debby Abe, "Lawyers: 'Cappers' Prey on Injured Asians," *News Tribune*, 13 February 1994, B1.

62. In Portland, as in Seattle, the ethnic rings operated alongside local rings that had operated in the area for many years. One of these local rings, operating at around the same time as that of Michael Lai, was run by a capper named Steven Terry Hill, who staged a number of major accidents, complete with major damage to cars, self-mutilation to simulate crash injuries, and, later, major settlements. For Hill's arrest, see Dave Hogan, "10 Charged With Fraud," *Portland Oregonian*, 13 May 1992, C1.

63. For some of the results of Operation Kung Pow, see Dave Hogan, "FBI Investigates Offices of Doctors, Lawyer in Alleged Insurance Scheme," *Portland Oregonian*, 13 March 1993, D8, and Dave Hogan, "4 Plead Guilty in Insurance Fraud Case," *Portland Oregonian*, 29 May 1993, D3. Following the successful prosecution of Lai and the others, Allstate insurance company filed a civil suit against them to recover whatever lost monies they could. See Fiona M. Ortiz, "Allstate Files $4.3 Million Suit in Insurance Fraud Scheme," *Portland Oregonian*, 22 September 1995, B2. This was also a practice popularized in L.A. during the early 1980s.

64. Elias Castillo, "Auto-Crash Scams Hit the Bay Area," *San Jose Mercury News*, 8 August 1988, 1A.

65. Scott Winokur, "Auto Insurance Fraud Explodes," *San Francisco Examiner*, 26 January 1992, 1A.

66. Officer Joe Del'Marmol is quoted in Molly Kinetz, "Cruising for Fraud: CHP Does More than Issue Tickets," *Sacramento Bee*, 9 February 1992, N3. The case involving the motorcyclist Robert Yarrington who had his girlfriend hack off his left foot with an ax in the Santa Cruz mountains in November 1979 was reported by Reuters (Nexis), 16 September 1982.

67. See United Press International (Nexis), 11 April 1984.

68. "Staged Car Crash a Violent Crime?" in *ICPI Report* 7 (January/February 1979), 1.

69. The story of the Reverend Leotis Smith is reported in Clarence Johnson, "Pastor, 3 Others Arrested for Fraud," *San Francisco Chronicle*, 21 June 1986, 3.

70. See Jim Herron Zamora, "Lawyer Accused of Insurance Fraud," *San Francisco Examiner*, 23 September 1995, A6.

71. David Sylvester, "State Probers Arrest 5 in Car Insurance Scam," *San Francisco Chronicle*, 24 November 1993, A17.

72. Bill Wallace, "Government Records Portray Vang as an All-Purpose Criminal," *San Francisco Chronicle*, 11 August 1994, A17.

73. One of Vang's medical mills was allegedly run by a Russian chiropratcor, whose office supplied medical bills for treatments, never administered, resulting from accidents that were staged by undercover officers and Billy Vang. See Bill Wallace, "S.F. Chiropractor to Be Charged in Probe of Insurance Fraud Ring," 13 March 1996, *San Francisco Chronicle*, A18.

74. Jim Walsh and William Hermann, "Experts: Phoenix Is Ripe for Scams," *Arizona Republic*, 17 November 1994, A1.

75. "Bets Are Off on Vegas Ring," *NICB Insurance Crime Alert* 2 (1994) 3. Many cappers in Las Vegas work the casinos, especially the sports books, looking for people who seem to be down on their luck. They will offer cash for the use of an insurance policy or rental car in a staged accident.

76. See, for example, Bill Lodge, "An Accident Waiting to Happen; Investigators Say 2 Men Linked to Ring Making Millions on Staged Car Crashes," *Dallas Morning News*, 8 March 1996, 35A.

77. Hugh Aynesworth, "Texas Probe Finds Insurance Fraud, Staged Auto Crashes," *Washington Times*, 15 January 1996, A3.

78. Quoted in "Insurance Fraud," *City News Service* (Nexis), 9 January 1996.

79. William Hermann, "Probe Unfolded Like a Thriller Novel," *Arizona Republic*, 17 November 1994, A1. For the details of the investigation, see also Dennis Wagner, "Lawyers Escape Scam; None Yet Indicted in Huge Car-Wreck Fraud," *Phoenix Gazette*, 5 December 1994, A1, and Susan E. Clarke, "Phoenix Auto Scams Come to a Screeching Halt," *John Cooke Fraud Report* 2 (January/February 1995), 7.

80. "Driver Gets Term, Fine in Schemes," *Arizona Republic*, 20 September 1986, B1.

81. J. W. Brown, "Gypsy Family Admits Fraud, Pays $135,000," *Phoenix Gazette*, 20 March 1990, B1.

82. John Winters, "Nigerian Ring Suspected of Defrauding Insurers," *Arizona Republic*, 28 April, 1989, B7.

83. Joe Stinebaker, "Two Doctors Among 100 Charged in Fraud Ring," *Houston Chronicle*, 20 January 1995, A1. On this case, see also Marty Graham, "California Officials Not Surprised About Car Insurance Scam Here," *Houston Post*, 20 January 1995, A17, and "15 People Sentenced for Roles," *Houston Post*, 31 March 1995, A28.

84. William Hermann and Jim Walsh, "Car-Wreck Bared $16 Million Believed Lost in False Insurance Claims," *Arizona Republic*, 17 November 1994, A1.

85. Jerry Urban, "Grand Jury Indicts Lawyer, 10 Others," *Houston Chronicle*, 20 May 1994, A27.

86. Bill Miller, "Investigators Allege Elaborate Scheme to Defraud Car Insurers," *Washington Post*, 25 February 1995, B3. One month later, two of the accused accident stagers pled guilty. See "Two Men Convicted of Staging Accidents," *Washington Times*, 25 March 1995, A11.

87. For the allegations about Soviet-born Michael Rapapport and his Iranian partner, Amir Zamyad, see Bill Lodge, "An Accident Waiting to Happen."

88. A number of other, separate cases of organized accident staging and faking of personal injury claims by Russians in Philadelphia were explicitly *not connected* to any larger crime syndicate. For the details on the ring run by doctor Arie Oren, Boris Zolatarev, his wife Anna, Victor Tsan, and Alexander Zaverukha, see the following accounts by Joseph A. Slobodzian in the *Philadelphia Inquirer*: "Doctor Faces Charges of Fraud Again," 17 December 1994, B2, and "Three From Northeast Convicted in Insurance Scam," 26 July 1995, B2.

89. Scott Anderson, "Looking For Mr. Yaponchik: The Rise and Fall of a Russian Mobster in America," *Harper's* (December 1995), 47.

90. For accident staging in Atlanta, see the following articles in the *Atlanta Journal and Constitution*: Shelley Emling, "4 Accused of Fraud in Alleged Bilking of Insurance Firms," 22 September 1995, 2C, and Pamela Monastra, "Seven Face Charges in Insurance Fraud Plot; Police Say the Arrests Are 'Tip of the Iceberg,'" 9 March 1994, J1. For the long-standing, competitive chasing culture in the city, see: Kathy Scruggs, "Car Insurance Scams an $8.2 Million 'Industry'; Fraud Feeds on Payoffs for Victims' Names," 13 June, 1994, B1; and Connie Green, "Accident Chasers Preying on Victims in Scam to Bilk Insurance Companies," 7 June 1987, B1.

91. "Man Admits Insurance Fraud Scheme," *Atlanta Journal-Constitution*, 10 December 1995, G12.

92. Douglas T. Cohen and Scott Montgomery, "Ring Faking Wrecks, Injuries for Profit," *Palm Beach Post*, 4 April 1993, 1A.

93. See Maura Lerner, "11 Minnesota Students Facing Fraud Charges," *Star Tribune*, 4 April 1995, 1B, and David Shaffer, "Minnesota Figures in Fraud Ring," *St. Paul Pioneer Press*, 4 April 1995, 1B. The students were all Pakistanis whose visas precluded them from holding jobs in the United States, an issue of legitimate concern to students' organizations and academics in the state.

94. Ben L. Kaufman, "Insurance Scam Netted Millions; Portsmouth Group Succeeded for Years Before Plot Uncovered," *Cincinnati Enquirer*, 5 June 1995, A1. The group, led by a legendary accident fraudster, was believed to have staged many dozens of accidents, arsons, and other insurance crimes over the past fifteen or twenty years. See "31 Are Accused of $2 Million Insurance Fraud," *Cleveland Plain Dealer*, 13 January 1995, 12B. For later indictments coming out of this investigation, see "Hilliard Man Among Accused," *Columbus Dispatch*, 26 January 1996, 6B.

95. Marcia Myers, "FBI Overstates Role in Fraud Arrests Stemming from Staged Car Accidents," *Baltimore Sun*, 27 May 1995, 2B.

96. "Seven Persons Accused of Staging Auto Collisions for Profit," *Kansas City Star*, 16 September 1995, C8. In an earlier, unrelated case from Kansas City, George W. Turley was convicted of having staged car accidents for a living, then getting himself admitted to hospitals to run up his bills. Turley was sentenced to three years in Leavenworth Penitentiary. See "Prison for 3 in Scam," *Kansas City Star*, 1 October 1994, C1.

97. For the case involving lawyer Thomas S. Conroy and his father-in-law J. Robert Wall, see Julia C. Martinez, "A Lawyer Admits Role in Fraud," *Philadelphia Inquirer*, 14 March 1995, B1.

98. For the ring run by songwriter Edmond F. Daniels and Billy Barriner, see Emilie Lounsberry, "Insurance Fraud Task Force Brings Charges Against 31," *Philadelphia Inquirer*, 12 July 1991, B1; and Gary Cohn, "Two Phila. Men Given 3-Year Prison Terms for Insurance Fraud," *Philadelphia Inquirer*, 7 October 1992, B3.

99. For the case against Alderman Perry Hutchinson, see "Alderman, 19 Others Indicted," *Chicago Tribune*, 14 April 1987, C3; William B. Crawford Jr., "U.S. Outlines Its Case Against Ex-Alderman," *Chicago Tribune*, 15 March 1988, C8; and Linnet Myers, "Former Alderman Convicted of Fraud," *Chicago Tribune*, 20 May 1988, C1. For the results of Operation Crystal Ball, see Linnet Myers, "'Stunt Drivers' Among 146 Charged in Insurance Scam," *Chicago Tribune*, 8 August 1986, C1, and "'Operation Crystal Ball' Indicts 43 For $228G Caused and Staged Auto Accident Scheme," *ICPI Report* 16 (Second Issue, 1989), 1. For stager Donald Brown and Cordell Cherry's distinction between "road jobs" and "wall jobs," see "Accomplice Describes Auto Insurance Scam," *Chicago Tribune*, 8 December 1987, C3, and "Ex-Ambulance Chaser Tells Court About Snafus," *Chicago Tribune*, 11 December 1987, C3.

100. See Bob Kudelka, "10 Charged in Fake Crashes For Money," *The Sun News*, 13 December 1990, 1A; Bruce Smith, "Operation Peachscam Claims 30 More Indictments for Fraud," *Florence Morning News*, 14 May 1991, 1; and "'Operation Peachscam' Bears Fruit with 15 Convictions," *ICPI Report* 18 (Spring, 1991), 1.

101. "News Conference Concerning the New War on Insurance Crime," Federal News Service Transcript (Nexis), 7 January 1992, 14.

102. Quoted in Bob Kudelka, "4 Sent to Prison for Scam," *The Sun News*, 22 April 1991, 1C.

103. For the Russell Ramsey Ring see: Gail Gibson and Robert H. Campbell, "Six Indicted in Insurance Fraud," *Lexington Herald-Leader*, 20 November 1993, A1; Gail Gibson, "Investigators Spent 2 Years Tracking Insurance Claims," *Lexington Herald-Leader*, 23 November 1993, B1.

104. Chip Wilson, "Fraud Ring's Wrecks Were Setups," *Charlotte Observer*, 28 October 1993, 1A.

105. "Arkansas 'Ramblin' Man' Charged in Interstate Car Crashes," *ICPI Report* 18 (Spring, 1991), 8.

106. Julieanne Miller, "Ex-sheriff 1 of 13 Indicted in Scheme to Bilk Insurers," *Arkansas Democrat-Gazette*, 3 February 1993, 1B.

107. Quoted in "Money For Nothing," 20/20, ABC News Transcript, 31 July 1986, 11. See also "Mississippi Mayor, Seven Other Professionals Indicted for Staged Vehicular Accident Ring," *ICPI Report* 16 (Third Issue, 1989), 1.

108. Craig Jarvis, "Accident Scam Ring Runs On, Police Say, Despite Conviction," *News & Observer*, 13 March 1995, A1. See also Madhuri V. Bhat, "Billy Creel: North Carolina's Insurance Sleuth," *Triangle Business Journal*, 12 May 1995, 22.

109. Bob Meyer, "Robbing Premium-Paying Public Blind," *The Edmonton Journal*, 6 March 1995, B5.

110. Lisa Wright, "Whiplash Willies Failing to Deceive," *Calgary Herald*, 24 April 1994, A8.

111. Paul Beneditti, "Insurance Fraud Costs 'Millions'; Phony Accidents Becoming 'Epidemic,' Investigator Says," *Ottawa Citizen*, 24 October 1993, A1.

112. Barry Brown, "Cost of Insurance Scam Might Exceed $7 Million,"*Buffalo News*, 17 September 1995, 5A. See also Paul Vierira, "Auto Insurance: Ontario System Too Easily Bilked, Industry Says," *Ottawa Citizen*, 15 September 1995, B7.

113. Johanna Powell, "Industry Wants Crackdown on Insurance Fraud,"*Financial Post*, 7 May 1994, S17. See also Erik Heinrich, "Canada: Ex-Police Join War on Insurance Fraud," *Financial Post*, 15 May 1993. In order to deal with "the escalating problem of staged auto accidents" and benefit fraud rings in Ontario, this latter article reports, several state insurers began to hire additional investigators and specially trained claims adjusters.

114. Alan Murdoch, "Hoping to Gerra Lucky Break; Dubious Accident 'Victims' Find the Streets of Dublin Paved with Gold," *Independent*, 30 August 1993, 17. See also "'Fair City' Actor Admits Part in Insurance Fraud," *Irish Times*, 13 January 1996, 8.

115. For a survey of insurance crimes in major Western industrialized nations, I have primarily relied on Michael Clarke, "Insurance Fraud," *British Journal of Criminology* 29 (Winter 1989), 1-20 and Michael Clarke, "The Control of Insurance Fraud: A Comparative View," *British Journal of Criminology* 30 (Winter 1990), 1-22. One British (property damage) accident gang staged accidents with a horse-drawn carriage in order to claim the loss of the horse (whom they killed themselves) during the first decade of this century: "Their *modus operandi* was simple. In certain areas where the cobblestone road-bed had sunk, one could find stretches of tram

track so defective that it was pretended cats could crawl under the metals. The gang, choosing such a section in a quiet neighbourhood, would wait until the coast was clear and then stage their show." See William Charles Crocker, *Far From Humdrum: A Lawyer's Life* (New York: World Publishing, 1967), 65-66.

116. "How the English Chased the Ambulance Chaser," *Central Law Journal* 93 (1921), 165-167.

117. "Ambulance Chasing in the United States," *Solicitors' Journal* 73, (20 April 1929), 242.

118. Ibid., 247.

119. Laura Brooks, "Smith's Joins Stores Cracking Down on Slip, Fall Scam," *Arizona Daily Star*, 15 May 1995, 1A. For a similar response by supermarket chains in western Pennsylvania, see Earl Bohn, "Stores' Downfall: Retailers Easy Prey for 'Slip-and-Fall' Lawsuits," *Pittsburgh Press*, 21 August 1991, B1. See also "Buses to Get Video Cameras," *Indianapolis News*, 5 September 1994, D10.

120. Dan Heneghan, "As Casino Patrons 'Slip,' Their Bogus Claims 'Fall' Apart," *New Jersey Lawyer*, 19 June 1995, 1.

121. David Lee Heath, for example, a man described as having "no permanent address," landed in a federal prison in Minnesota in 1994 for his slips on liquid found around urinals in Chi-Chi's Mexican Restaurants. See "Man Who Faked Falls to Gain Insurance Money Gets 2 1/2 Years," *Minneapolis Star-Tribune*, 25 March 1994, 3B. A few years earlier Patricia Latham, a fifty-nine-year-old woman who represented herself falsely as a kindergarten teacher named Jacqueline Johnson, used rubber bands tightened around her wrist to cause swelling for claims against fast food restaurants across the country. Latham also nearly got away with a $1 million faked fall on torn carpet at Don Carter's All-Star Bowling Lanes in Boca Raton, before an undercover videotape showing her able to use her wrist at Disney World got her a three-year prison sentence instead. For Latham, see Jodi Mallander, "'Professional Plaintiff' Slips Up Lawyers: Public 'Falls' Were Hoaxes," *Palm Beach Post*, 15 March 1991, 1A; Christine Stapleton, "Slip-Fall Con Artist Gets 3 Years in Prison: Swollen-Wrist Mystery Solved in Plea Bargain," *Palm Beach Post*, 27 September 1991, 1B. (Melvin Belli, the aging "King of Torts" who served as Latham's lawyer in one case, claimed shock when the woman was unmasked in court. "I've been practicing over 60 years, and this is the first time this has ever happened to me," he said. "She was the nicest, most honest, most believable woman that I've ever seen." Belli is quoted in Bill Callahan, "Plaintiffs Become Defendants: Belli Clients' Suit Spurs Plot Charges," *San Diego Union-Tribune*, 10 April 1993, B1.) In the early 1990s, Garen Cooke was documented by the NICB as having staged seventy-one slip-and-falls in sixteen states over eleven years using twenty-four aliases, and later claimed to have faked hundreds more since first learning the craft from relatives at age fifteen. If he had been in circulation seventy-five years earlier, he would have kept railway claims men busy writing to their *Bulletin* for years. As it happened, Cooke gained his national reputation

through appearances as slip-and-fall expert Jake Stone on tabloid TV shows, including *Geraldo* and *A Current Affair*. In 1994 Cooke also served as an on-air adviser to ABC News' *Prime Time Live*, where he explained how a professional slip-and-faller viewed a supermarket: "It's not water on the floor, it's not a stack of soda pop, it's a stack of money, or a pile of money on the floor. That's what you see. And you know what it's worth." Later in the broadcast, when Cooke was asked how often he might fake a fall for money, he recited the American slip-and-fallers' creedo: "You can do it every couple weeks," he said, "And you can do it forever." For Cooke, see Marlys Duran, "Chatty Con Man Leaves Cold Trial: Accident-Prone Pedestrian Suspected of Filing at Least 70 Fraudulent Insurance Claims," *Rocky Mountain News*, 22 November 1993, 22A, and "Slip & Fall," *Prime Time Live*, ABC News Transcript, 26 May 1994. Cooke was sentenced to a sixteen-year term for his accident faking, two years of which he was expected to spend in prison, the rest of which he will likely spend in a halfway house working to repay the money he stole from insurers. See Marlys Duran, "Slip-and-Fall 'Victim' Gets 16-Year Term," *Rocky Mountain News*, 21 January 1995, 24A.

122. This account of David Ballog's life in the personal injury underworld is derived largely from court records, original interviews, and additional information provided by the NICB. I have also made extensive use of excellent reporting on Ballog by writer Matt O'Connor of the *Chicago Tribune*, principally his thorough magazine profile, "A Fraudulent Life: For Chicago's King of Slip-and-Fall the Con Was Everything," *Chicago Tribune Magazine*, 17 December 1995, 15, but also the following news accounts: "15 Years of Insurance Fraud End," *Chicago Tribune*, 8 November 1994, 1, and "Godfather of Fraud Takes a Fall," *Chicago Tribune*, 28 June 1995, 1. Additional quotes from Ballog derived from Leslie Kim, "A Chat with David," *The John Cooke Fraud Report* 2 (July/August, 1995), 1.

EPILOGUE

1. Julie Tamaki, "Driver Sentenced to Prison in Fatal Car Crash, Insurance Scam," *Los Angeles Times*, 27 April 1994, B4. Less than a month later, in a related case, two men involved with staging forty big-rig accidents around the same time as Jose Lopez were convicted and sentenced to three years in prison. In sentencing Jorge Ibarra and Marco De La Garza, a Superior Court judge said: "They were just small cogs in the wheel, but without the cogs, the wheel doesn't turn." See "Pair Sentenced for Auto Insurance Fraud," United Press International (Nexis), 13 May 1994.

2. Robert Monaghan, "The Liability Claim Racket," *Law and Contemporary Problems* 3 (1936), 491.

3. Ibid., 385.

4. Julie Tamaki, "Insurance Firm Sues Lawyer to Recover $85,000 Liability," *Los Angeles Times*, 20 December 1993, B3.

5. Quoted in Ashley Craddock and Mordecai Lawrence, "Swoop-and-Squats," *Mother Jones* (September/October 1993), 20.

6 As this book went to press, Gary P. Miller was convicted of seven counts of insurance fraud and two counts of conspiracy, but the jury deadlocked on the issue of whether Miller was also guilty of second-degree murder in Perez's death. Miller did not testify in his own defense. Off the stand, Miller made light of the charges: "They're calling me the mastermind of a ring. Some *don* I am." But the prosecution hammered away at its theory that responsibility in the crash conspiracy went "right up the line through all [the] co-conspirators to Gary Miller. It doesn't matter he didn't know Perez." Prosecutors had not decided whether they would retry Miller on the murder count. (Miller and prosecutor Leonard J. Shaffer are quoted in Gail Diane Cox, "Lawyer's Role in Accidents Called Murder," *National Law Journal*, 26 August 1996, A10.)

Filemon Santiago pled guilty to charges of insurance fraud and manslaughter; he faces six years in prison. Rubidia Lopez and Isiais Aguilar Martinez, passengers in the Pontiac on the night of the failed staging, were acquitted of all charges against them. Juan Carlos Amaya, the suspected swoop-car driver, and Elena Shamis, Gary Miller's office manager, are set to be tried later this year.

INDEX